# THE ILIAD
# OF
# HOMER

# THE ILIAD
# OF
# HOMER

TRANSLATED BY RICHMOND LATTIMORE

INTRODUCTION AND NOTES BY RICHARD MARTIN

THE UNIVERSITY OF CHICAGO PRESS

CHICAGO AND LONDON

RICHMOND LATTIMORE
was professor emeritus of
Greek at Bryn Mawr College at
the time of his death in 1984.
He was coeditor (with
David Grene) of *The Complete
Greek Tragedies*, translator of
*Greek Lyrics*, and author
of *Poems from Three Decades*, all
published by the University
of Chicago Press.

RICHARD MARTIN
is the Antony and Isabelle
Raubitschek Professor of
Classics at Stanford University.

The University of Chicago Press, Chicago 60637
The University of Chicago Press, Ltd., London
© 1951, 2011 by The University of Chicago
All rights reserved. Published 2011.
Printed in the United States of America

20  19  18  17  16  15  14  13          3  4  5

ISBN-13: 978-0-226-47048-1 (cloth)
ISBN-13: 978-0-226-47049-8 (paper)
ISBN-10: 0-226-47048-2 (cloth)
ISBN-10: 0-226-47049-0 (paper)

Homer.
[Iliad. English. 2011]
The Iliad of Homer / translated by Richmond Lattimore ;
introduction and notes by Richard Martin.
p.   cm.
Includes bibliographical references.
ISBN-13: 978-0-226-47048-1 (cloth : alk. paper)
ISBN-10: 0-226-47048-2 (cloth : alk. paper)
ISBN-13: 978-0-226-47049-8 (pbk. : alk. paper)
ISBN-10: 0-226-47049-0 (pbk. : alk. paper)
I. Lattimore, Richmond Alexander, 1906–1984.
II. Martin, Richard P.   III. Title.   IV. Title: Iliad.
PA4025.A2L38 2011
883'.01—dc22
2011007970

♾ This paper meets the requirements of
ANSI/NISO Z39.48–1992 (Permanence of Paper).

# Contents

# Introduction to
# Richmond Lattimore's *Iliad*

RICHARD P. MARTIN

STANFORD UNIVERSITY

## THE TROJAN WAR IN TIME AND PLACE

The literature that has come to be called "Western" begins with a long poem about the siege of a great city on the coast of what is now Turkey by heroic warriors from Greece. Yet, in the early twelfth century BC—the time period in which this story is set—there were no identifiable concepts of "Western" and "Eastern" cultures (much less "Greece" or "Turkey" as nation-states). Even when the *Iliad* was composed, somewhere in the "archaic" period of Greek history between 750 and 550 BC, there seems to have been little concern among cultures bordering the Mediterranean to differentiate East from West: from Sicily to Sardis and beyond, trade goods, musical modes, stories, artistic styles, and people circulated and interacted in creative profusion.

It was early in the fifth century BC that attitudes changed. In 490 and again 480–79 BC, invasions by the massive forces of the expanding Persian empire (centered in modern-day Iran) were turned back by a ragtag coalition of Greek city-states, on Greek soil. This spectacular, unexpected victory was celebrated by Greeks of the ensuing "Classical" age through temple sculpture, murals, vase painting, oratory, and dramatic literature that proudly made verbal and visual analogies between the Persian wars of recent times and the heroic successes of the Trojan War. The Greek historian Herodotus, writing in the middle of the fifth century, attributes to Persian intellectuals (*logioi*: *Histories* 1.1) the view that the ancient expedition to bring home Helen of Sparta was the beginning of antagonism between Asia and Europe. But it is clear that Greeks of the historian's own time were thinking the same way.

The singular beauty and importance of our *Iliad* stand out starkly in contrast to such later, politicized interpretations of the story of Troy and to an insidious Orientalism that has its roots in Greek antiquity. It is not about a clash of civilizations, much less so a contest between evil and good. Unlike many a later epic (including Virgil's *Aeneid*), this poem does not deal with ethnic, national, religious, or ideological conflicts and aspirations. In fact, it is difficult to determine the poem's real protagonist: the Greek Achilleus and his victim, the Trojan Hektor, are attractive and repellent in equal degrees. Some would say Hektor is actually the more sympathetic character. The *Iliad* is about heroes as humans, and what constitutes humanity. Its enduring value lies in the poem's recognition that even the worst enemies are deeply, fundamentally the same—desirous of glory and immortality, while subject to pain and death. Its power—like that of so much Greek literature—comes from the realistic depiction of mortals as they gradually learn that they can never be gods. In this existential recognition, it transcends the anxieties of tribe or state.

The story of a war to take Troy, in other words, is primarily a backdrop for human concerns that fascinate audiences in any age. The *Iliad* would be just as compelling a piece of art even if Troy existed only in the imagination of poets. Nevertheless, through the centuries, the attractive power of the epic has been compounded for many readers by the dark mysteries that surround it. Did a Trojan War really take place? How did the poet Homer know of it? Did a man named Homer even exist? When, where, and how was the epic composed? How did it achieve such perfection and influence? In what follows, we shall explore briefly the answers that have been offered for these questions—though never totally agreed upon—while placing the *Iliad* in a series of relevant historical and cultural contexts.

First of all, it is important to realize that the *Iliad* is an Iron Age poem about an event supposed to have taken place in the Bronze Age. Historians in ancient Greece, working with family memories and temple records, came up with a range of dates for the Trojan War from 1184 BC (Eratosthenes), to around 1250 BC (Herodotus) to 1334 BC (Douris). More than four centuries thus elapsed between the latest traditional date given by the ancient Greeks themselves for the destruction of Troy and the earliest possible recording of the epic in written form—a longer gap than that which separates us from the time of Shakespeare's maturity. Therefore, the *Iliad* as we have it cannot be based directly on an eyewitness account, or even a reliable reminiscence from the poet's great-grandfather. It is not impossible that it ultimately derives from poems and stories originating with actual survivor tales, but the form in which we have it cannot possibly itself date to the twelfth or thirteenth century BC. To begin with, most of the linguistic forms in the *Iliad* come from a later period. By extension, the concerns of the poem are most likely not those of the original fighters at Troy but of a society—or multiple societies—generations later that looked back to the Trojan War as an important symbolic event, perhaps for the very foundation of their own communities. Even if the kernel of the *Iliad* was put into poetic form nearer to the time of the fall of Troy, in the intervening centuries before it achieved its final status the story was certainly subjected to all sorts of changes in length, expansiveness, and detail, through stylization, shifts of emphasis, and innovations in characterization and plot. Above all—as literary critics since Aristotle have acknowledged—the epic makes no attempt to narrate the whole story of a war against Troy, focusing instead on only a few days in the tenth and final year of the Greek siege against the city, and on a personal dispute (albeit one with vast consequences) within the ranks of the assembled Greek warriors. The poem's concentrated force relies on an audience that *already* knows most of the basic details about the struggle, an audience that has probably encountered many other versions of the tale of Troy, from tellers whose names we will never discover.

Greeks and Romans in ancient times had little doubt that there once existed a mighty city of Troy a few miles from the sea near the Hellespont, the narrow entrance to the Propontis, which leads in turn to the Black Sea and its resource-rich hinterlands. By the seventh century BC, a town was established by settlers of Greek ancestry on the ruins of an earlier site. It was called Ilion—a name used already in the epic for Troy, and the word from which the *Iliad* gets its name. In later ages, celebrities like Xerxes the king of Persia, Alexander the Great, and Julius Caesar visited the place, confident that they were gazing on the very soil where Hektor and Achilleus clashed and the towers of Troy were toppled. On his way to punish the mainland Greeks, in the spring of 480 BC, Xerxes dedicated a sacrifice of one thousand oxen to Athene of Ilion, while his sage-priests, the magi, poured offerings to "the heroes." The historian Herodotus (7.43) does not speculate on the royal motives, or whether the dead warriors thus honored were Greek or Trojans. What counts is that generations of military leaders associated their own deeds with those from the gloried past through their ostentatious tourism at the spot. The Romans had further reasons for venerating Troy, since it was claimed that they were direct descendants of the Trojan hero Aeneas, who escaped the city's destruction and traveled with his kin to Italy to start afresh. Augustus, the first Roman emperor, visited Troy in 20 BC. Both Julius Caesar, before him, and the emperor Constantine, three centuries later, contemplated building a new Roman capital on the site.

Ilion survived after the Roman empire in the West had fallen to barbarian tribes in the fifth century AD. But after 1200 AD, when the site seems finally to have been abandoned, Troy evaporated into the mists of myth. Even as the *Iliad* itself was being preserved through the efforts of scholars and scribes in Byzantium (the inheritor of the eastern Roman empire), the landscape associated with it was gradually forgotten. The eighteenth century, which saw an increase in travel to the eastern Mediterranean, brought aristocratic memoirists like Lady Mary Wortley Montagu and amateur antiquarians like her compatriot Robert Wood (1716–1771) to the broader region of the Troad. They found—or imagined they found—topographical details that matched those in the texts of the *Iliad*. Lady Montagu remarks on the pleasure she took "in seeing the valley where I imagined the famous duel of Menelaos and Paris had been fought, and where the greatest city in the world was situated." She professes admiration for "the exact geography of Homer, whom I had in my hand. Almost every epithet he gives to a mountain or plain is still just for it."[1] Wood's tour resulted in the posthumously published, widely read *Essay upon the Original Genius and Writings of Homer: With a Comparative View of the Ancient and Present State of the Troade* (1775). Insisting on the exactness of Homeric descriptions, whether of wind directions or landscape, Wood concluded that "stript of all poetical embellishments" the *Iliad* contained "in general a consistent narrative of military events, connected and supported by that due coincidence of the circumstances of time and place which History requires."[2]

Despite such on-site observations, most scholars in the early nineteenth century remained skeptical about whether real historical events lay behind the stories of the Greek heroic age. The British historian George Grote (1794–1871) in his influential twelve-volume *History of Greece* chose 776 BC—the traditional date for the founding of the Olympic games—as the beginning of reliably recorded history. Within thirty years of the publication of his first two volumes (1846), Grote was proved mistaken: the Homeric epics, which he had spurned as evidence, emerged as more trustworthy guides to the past than had been imagined. Civilizations with features described by Homeric poetry, going back to seven centuries before Grote's starting date for Greek history, were now laid bare.

It was the labor of amateurs, rather than academics, that paved the way to a new understanding of the *Iliad*'s historicity. The first, Frank Calvert (1828–1908), worked as a businessman and representative of British and American interests in Ottoman-ruled Asia Minor during the middle decades of the nineteenth century. A passionate, self-taught antiquarian, he had concluded from intimate acquaintance with the landscape that the mound (*tell*) of Hisarlik, a few miles from the sea, was the most likely location of Homer's Troy. He managed to buy a portion of the area, but officials of the British Museum turned down his requests for the necessary further funding, and Calvert abandoned the project after a few trial digs in 1865. Always at the service of interested travelers, Calvert in August 1868 explained his theories to a visiting German explorer, Heinrich Schliemann (1822–1890). Another self-educated amateur, Schliemann was a visionary and wealthy entrepreneur who had forged his own way, starting out as a poor office boy (among his other profitable endeavors, he had sold provisions to miners during the California gold rush and war supplies to armies in the Crimea). He was also a tireless, if not downright mendacious, self-promoter, prone to manipulate facts to his own advantage. Whatever the truth or fantasy in Schliemann's autobiographical "recollections"—that he had been inspired to rediscover Troy as a boy, upon seeing a picture book of the saga, or hearing a drunken miller recite Homeric verses in Greek—there is no doubt that it was his resources and persistence that finally uncovered the remains of a great city at Hisarlik.

Starting in October 1871 and for the next two years, Schliemann excavated the mound of Hisarlik, digging relentlessly to the lowest level. As he was more or less inventing archaeological practice—an art still in its infancy—he did not take care to record the layout of higher strata on the site, destroying valuable clues in the process. Calvert correctly deduced from the presence of stone rather than bronze artifacts that Schliemann's widely heralded discovery of the "city of Priam" in fact revealed a much older phase of habitation. Subsequent investigations by Schliemann, up to his death in 1890, then for a season (1893–1894) by his successor Wilhelm Dörpfeld, and from 1932 to 1938 by the American archaeologist Carl Blegen, exposed a total of nine layers and nearly fifty sublayers. The earliest layer, "Troy I," was occupied in the Early Bronze Age, around 3000 BC. "Troy II," which Schliemann had thought to be contemporaneous with the *Iliad*'s events, is in fact a thousand years older than the estimated period of the Trojan War. If the city underwent siege and destruction, as described by Homeric poetry, the likeliest stages for it are the levels designated "Troy VI" (1800–1275 BC) and "Troy VII" (1275–1100 BC). Archaeologists believe that during the latter period, in particular, many more people took refuge inside the defensive walls of the upper town, having for some reason abandoned the lower. There are no inscriptions to pinpoint this site as the place that the Greeks destroyed. But the era would match ancient calculations for the period of the war, and the physical remains are suggestively reminiscent of details in the *Iliad*. Moreover, excavations led by Manfred Korfmann of Tübingen University from 1995 until his death in 2005, have now shown that the upper city on the site (which critics had long dismissed as being too small for the Homeric Troy) was merely a fraction of a much more extensive settlement, capable of sustaining a population of nearly ten thousand.

If the mound at Hisarlik can now be recognized as having concealed a series of fortified citadels that resemble those known from the ancient Near East, complete with surrounding lower town, there is also further evidence that might explain why a war could have been fought over this place. The major political force in Anatolia (present-day Turkey) in the second millennium BC was the Hittite empire, centered on Hattusa (now Bögasköy, near modern Ankara). Continuing archaeological work, combined with increasing knowledge of the ancient Hittite language (from texts first deciphered in the early twentieth century) have produced a picture of a wide-reaching, highly organized imperial power with connections extending as far as the Levant and Egypt.

Troy, it appears, was a vassal state. Hittite official documents mention *Taruwisa* and *Wilusa*, which closely match the Greek words used, apparently as synonyms, for the besieged city in the *Iliad*: *Troiê* and (*w*)*Ilios* (traces of an original initial "w" sound can be detected in the *Iliad*'s verses). Even more intriguing, a royal treaty of King Muwattalli II (circa 1290–1272 BC) pledges support for one *Alaksandu* of *Wilusa*—possibly a Hittite form of the Greek name Alexander (another name for the Trojan warrior Paris), although the document was written a century before the putative date of the war that this son of Priam caused by abducting the Greek queen Helen. The Hittite texts also refer to *Ahhiyawa*. This term was probably borrowed from one of the words early Greeks used to describe themselves: *Achaioi*. Unfortunately, it remains unclear where the Hittites located the people thus named, whether further down the coast of Asia Minor (near ancient Miletus), on offshore islands like Lesbos, or on the other side of the Aegean (mainland Greece). Nor is the precise relationship of *Ahhiyawa* to Trojans specified: were they considered enemies, neighbors, or a distant power?

Troy must have been an important ally, given its strategic location in ancient times on the seacoast, before accumulated silt pushed the shoreline farther from the city. An attack could well have provoked a defensive response from a number of cities in the Hittite sphere of influence throughout western Asia Minor. The *Iliad*, in fact, represents the number of far-flung Trojan allies as far outnumbering fighters from the city itself and, since they speak many languages, harder to control than the unified Greek forces (2.803–4).

Several scenarios have been suggested to explain why and by whom Troy might have been destroyed in the twelfth century BC. At this time, a general disruption and movement of populations occurred around the Aegean, with numbers of settlements falling into disuse. Natural disasters, crop failures, or pressure from groups in the hinterland may have been the root causes. Egyptian inscriptions of the era refer to problems with marauding "Sea Peoples," possibly coming from the east. Perhaps these mysterious bands carried out attacks that were later attributed to Greeks who ended up settling the coast near Troy. On the other hand, it is not unlikely that Greek warriors themselves were involved in widespread raids during this time of general collapse. What has become clear only in the last century is the extent to which Greek civilization, in the form of a highly bureaucratized, palace-centered culture, had already spread its influence by the era of Troy's fall. Once again, Schliemann can be credited with a major role in bringing this early Greek culture to light. Temporarily blocked by Ottoman authorities after his first season at Hisarlik, he turned to other sites. In August 1876, Schliemann began excavations at the ancient citadel of Mykenai, discovering in a short time shaft graves rich in ancient artifacts, including gold burial masks. His dating of the tombs, which he believed were the resting places of Agamemnon and Klytaimestra, was again too early by several centuries. But this find, together with subsequent discoveries, proved that a network of palace centers existed from around 1600 BC until around 1100 BC, when the Bronze Age in the Mediterranean came to an end. The civilization shared by these sites was given the name "Mykenaian."

Scholars soon recognized that the centers of this newly emerging archaic culture matched, to a remarkable extent, the fabled sites celebrated in Greek myths, some of which had no longer been inhabited in historical times. Thebes, Athens, Orchomenos, Tiryns, Sparta, and Pylos arose as Mykenaian powers; they also were the subject of rich storytelling traditions about the age of heroes from a generation or two before the Trojan War. The circumstantial evidence that the Mykenaians were, in fact, Greeks, took longer to verify. Arthur Evans, a British archaeologist, in 1900 uncovered a vast palace complex at Knossos, Crete, predating Mykenaian remains on the mainland, and characterized by signs of high civilization—masterpieces of wall painting, elaborately carved gemstones, precious vessels, imports from Egypt, statuettes, and ritual artifacts. He dubbed this newly found culture "Minoan," after the mythical King Minos, who was said to have ruled the vicinity at the time of the hero Theseus. Evans also found thousands of clay tablets bearing inscriptions in an unknown, picture-based writing system. Carl Blegen, who had moved on from Troy to excavate the western Greek site of Pylos in 1939, discovered a similar trove of six hundred tablets there—at a Mykenaian palace site. Yet more emerged from Thebes and western Crete. Whether by sudden invasion or gradual infiltration (perhaps after the weakening effects of earthquakes and tsunamis), Mykenaians, it became clear, had taken over former Minoan palaces in Crete. In 1952, their so-called Linear B tablets, dating from 1300 to 1200 BC, were deciphered by the English architect and self-taught cryptologist Michael Ventris (1922–1956). The language proved to be Greek; the texts were official accounts concerning personnel and supplies in the palace economy.

In short, the discoveries of a few generations showed that something like the war depicted in the *Iliad* could well have taken place, at the site of Hisarlik, with allies of the Hittite empire unsuccessfully sustaining a siege by Mykenaian Greeks. The relative time frame remains unclear, especially when it comes to causes and effects. Were the conquerors of Troy refugees from a catastrophic collapse of the Mykenaian palace system in mainland Greece, desperate to get the riches of the city that guarded the route to the Black Sea? Or did an extended siege like that in the epic *bring about* the downfall of major Mykenaian centers by draining resources and sapping manpower? Further enigmas await the discovery of new evidence. Were a series of small-scale attacks over decades compressed by later popular imagination into a "Trojan War"? What is the relation between the attacks on the coast of Asia Minor and later Greek colonization of the area? And how does the fall of the Hittite empire based at Hattusa—also around the pivotal year 1200 BC—fit into the entire puzzle? It is possible that the next several decades will bring clarification of at least some of these mysteries.

Whatever its connections to actual historical events, the *Iliad* as we have it is far from containing the whole story of the Trojan War. The poem sometimes alludes to episodes from the beginning of the conflict, but in a brief and indirect fashion, often within the speeches by individual characters, like the recollections of Odysseus in 2.299–332. There are no extended flashbacks in the poet's own voice. In order to reconstruct the entire series of relevant events, we must go back to the origins of the world, according to Greek myth. We can piece together the story from such sources as the *Theogony* of Hesiod (roughly contemporary with the rise of Homeric poetry in the eighth century BC) and the so-called Cyclic epics of the seventh and sixth centuries BC (filling out the Trojan War narrative "cycle") of which only random citations and a few plot summaries from later sources now survive. As an audience for Homeric epic most likely had these details in mind, it is worthwhile reviewing them.

Gaia, the Earth, was one of the first creatures. She saw to it that her abusive husband, Ouranos ("sky") was overthrown by their son Kronos, who was in turn displaced by her favorite grandson, Zeus. With the aid and advice of his grandmother, the young god Zeus gained the kingship, overcoming the older divinities in pitched battles, and by swallowing a dangerous wife, Mêtis ("cunning intelligence"), came to ensure that his own reign would never be overthrown. Instead of producing a son stronger than her spouse, as had been predicted, Mêtis (now inside her husband) bore Athene, who sprang full-grown from the Zeus' head. Since Zeus owed Gaia a debt for her support, when she eventually complained of the increasingly heavy burden of human life on her land surface, he allowed a massive war to decrease world population. Thus the conditions for the Trojan War were put in place by political maneuverings early in cosmic history.

The more immediate cause arose from another unusual marriage involving divinity. The ever-amorous Zeus desired a sea nymph Thetis, but the same fear—that the offspring of a powerful goddess might oust him from his rule—led him instead to marry her off to an unsuspecting mortal, Peleus, allegedly to reward the hero's pious behavior in resisting the adulterous advances of a mortal queen. It was at the wedding of Peleus and Thetis that Discord (Eris), who had not been invited, tossed the famous apple inscribed *kallistêi*—"to the fairest." Three goddesses—Hera, Athene, and Aphrodite—each claimed to match that description. Zeus chose a Trojan youth named Paris to decide the contest. He favored Aphrodite's promise of pleasure (after rejecting the lure of wisdom or power offered by the others) and received, as his reward, the ability to seduce the world's fairest woman, Helen—inconveniently married at that time to Menelaos, a powerful king in Greece. The *Iliad* refers to this scenario only once (24.25–30). As with so many other background details, this tale was undoubtedly known already to the hearers of the epic. It was told in one of the many poems or sagas now lost.

Helen's unusual birth foretold a remarkable career. Her father was Zeus, who visited her mother Leda (already married) in the form of a swan, the result of their union taking the form of two eggs. From one came Helen and her sister Klytaimestra, from the other her brothers Castor and Pollux (the "sons of Zeus" or Dioscuri whom she seeks in vain to catch sight of at 3.236–44). By the time Helen was of marriageable age, she had suitors from every part of Greece. Menelaos, the son of Atreus, was chosen to be her husband. His brother Agamemnon married Klytaimestra. As if foreseeing eventual trouble, the unsuccessful suitors of Helen swore an oath to retrieve her if the need ever arose. Odysseus, the suitor who had suggested this harmonious solution, was in return rewarded by Helen's (nominal) father, the mortal Tyndareus, king of Sparta, who persuaded his niece Penelope to marry the Ithacan hero. It is not unlikely that we are meant to recall this family bond when, in the *Iliad*, Odysseus repeatedly takes the side of the sons of Atreus and does their will.

From the *Iliad*, we get glimpses of a world in which the elite members of different cultures around the Mediterranean maintain friendly relations, exchanging gifts and visits. Hosted by Menelaos in Sparta as a guest-friend, Paris first caught sight of the woman promised for his judgment. Armed with Aphrodite's seductive wiles, he persuaded Helen to elope with him to Troy, taking with her much of her husband's wealth and leaving behind a nine-year-old daughter, Hermione. The oath of the suitors thus was put into effect and, after a failed diplomatic mission to Troy, Greek troops mustered to take vengeance and recover the errant wife. Complications immediately arose. Before leaving for Troy, the Greeks convened at Aulis, the main port for the city of Thebes in eastern Boeotia. An ominous sign occurs at their communal sacrifice: a snake emerges near the altar and devours eight sparrows along with their mother. Kalchas, the official seer of the expedition, interprets this to mean that it will take nine years of siege at Troy before the city can be taken in the tenth.

(The seer's prophecy is recalled by Odysseus at 2.299–332 as he tries to rally the weary Greeks.)

The attempt as described above ends in confusion and failure. The Greeks cross the Aegean but mistakenly land at Mysia, a region south of Troy, and sack the chief city there, thinking it to be their goal. Telephos, a Greek-born son of Herakles, while defending his adopted Mysian city is wounded by Achilleus. The Greeks retreat, yet still fail to reach Troy because a storm scatters their ships. Some versions have Achilleus land on the island of Skyros at this stage, where he weds the royal princess Deidameia, later to bear him a son, Neoptolemos. Others place the meeting earlier, saying that Thetis, his mother, hid the young hero, disguised as a girl, in the royal court on Skyros so that he would not have to go to war. In this latter version, it is Odysseus on a recruiting mission who tricks Achilleus into giving himself away. Pretending the island is under attack, he sounds a trumpet and the young man, eager for martial glory, leaps to arms. Ironically, Odysseus himself had been tricked into going to the war from his home island: an earlier recruiting party had placed his infant son Telemachos in front of the plow driven erratically by Odysseus while he feigned madness. It was clear he was sane when he swerved aside. Odysseus later took his revenge by framing Palamedes, the Greek recruiter who detected his charade, prompting the warrior's execution for treason.

With the troops gathered again in Aulis to ready their second attempt on Troy, Telephos visits Achilleus to be cured (which can be done only using the weapon that earlier wounded him) and stays in order to guide the Greek ships back to the right location. Another ominous sacrifice takes place. Artemis sends contrary winds against the fleet in punishment for Agamemnon's killing of a sacred stag. Kalchas reveals that Agamemnon must offer up his own daughter, Iphigeneia, to enable the expedition to depart. On the pretense that she is to be engaged to Achilleus, the girl is lured to Troy and killed (or, in some versions, miraculously spirited off by Artemis at the moment of the sacrifice, with a stag left in her place). The *Iliad* refrains from ever mentioning this episode—perhaps to characterize Agamemnon more sympathetically—but versions of the sacrificial scene became famous in the fifth-century dramas of Aeschylus (*Agamemnon*) and Euripides (*Iphigeneia at Aulis*).

Even before establishing a beachhead, the Greeks lose two important leaders: Philoktetes, abandoned with a festering snakebite on Lemnos (cf. 2.716–25), and Protesilaos, struck down by Hektor as the Greek troops storm ashore (cf. 2.698–702). Once landed, they first aim for a peaceful solution, sending another diplomatic embassy to the city to ask for Helen's return, but it comes back to camp empty-handed. The Greeks settle in for a long siege. The failure to take Troy for nine years, as the *Iliad* depicts it, stems less from poor strategy than from the natural advantage of the defenders: the citadel is well fortified and allied cities from all over the Troad and beyond have sent troops to swell the number of fighters. Luring the Trojan heroes from their stronghold is the only way to gain the upper hand. Meanwhile, the Greeks engage in attacks on smaller cities along the coast in an effort to cut off Troy's lines of supply. Achilleus himself boasts of leading twenty-three such raids (9.328–29). Chryseis, the priest's daughter whose ransoming sparks the *Iliad*'s central quarrel, was acquired as a captive in one of these forays (1.366–69), the same one that killed the father and brothers of Andromache, Hektor's wife, in Thebes (6.414–28), while Achilleus gained his own war bride Briseis in yet another, at Lyrnessos (2.688–93).

As noted already, the events narrated in the *Iliad* occupy only a few weeks in the tenth and final year of the siege of Troy. Part of the remarkable artistry of the poem is the way in which it manages to allude to many previous and subsequent events in the war, while keeping a sharp dramatic focus on the main storyline, which is as much about an internal struggle in the Greek ranks as it is about the external enemy. We need only mention the major plot elements here, noting the tight handling of the time frame, as each reader will best experience the power of the *Iliad* by plunging directly into Lattimore's rendition and reading, as far as possible, straight through the poem. A more detailed analysis of the craft of the narrative is in the "Style" section below.

The *Iliad* derives much of its force from a simple, lucid structure—cause, effect, solution—with each of these three narrative movements generated by crucial human decisions. The epic opens dramatically when Achilleus, on the tenth day of a ruinous plague sent by Apollo, publicly asks Kalchas to name its cause. The seer blames Agamemnon's impious rejection of the aged priest Chryses, who had ventured to the Greek camp to plead for the return of his captive daughter (Chryseis). Agamemnon reluctantly gives back the girl, but is provoked by Achilleus' criticism into taking in turn for himself Briseis, that hero's concubine. Insulted at this loss of status, Achilleus withdraws from the battle. Meanwhile, he begs his divine mother

Thetis to pressure Zeus to favor the Trojans temporarily, thus punishing the Greeks who he thinks dishonor him.

Destruction ensues. In the absence of their best fighter, the Greeks agree to a truce, long enough to stage a duel between the aggrieved parties, Menelaos and Paris (also called Alexandros), the Trojan who eloped with Helen. The duel is inconclusive (Paris having been spirited off the field), the truce is broken, and battle rages, with the gods taking an increasingly interventionist role. Another duel, between Aias and Hektor, ends in a draw, and a daylong cessation of conflict allows both sides to bury their dead. The Greeks use the time to construct a defensive wall. In view of mounting losses, Agamemnon is forced to send an embassy, promising Achilleus extensive gifts if only he will return to the fight. He refuses. In the worsening situation, the main leaders of the Greeks are wounded and Hektor leads his Trojans to breach the Greek wall. Meddling by various gods turns the fight into a tug-of-war. Patroklos, the closest companion of Achilleus, enters the battle in his younger friend's armor, kills Sarpedon, a son of Zeus, and is in turn felled by Hektor (with the assistance of Apollo). Only this catastrophe rouses Achilleus, who rejoins the battle with new, divinely made armor. After a climactic battle in which the gods take sides in the general destruction, Achilleus (with aid from Athene) slays Hektor. But rather than giving back the corpse to the Trojans, in his continuing rage over the loss of Patroklos he drags it each day around the city, bound by the feet to his chariot. The poem concludes with a mirror image of its beginning: an old man (Priam) ventures to the camp of his enemy in order to ransom his child, but—unlike the priest Chryses—is pitied and given what he wants: the body of Hektor for burial. The *Iliad* ends with Hektor's funeral back in Troy.

The solution of the conflict between Agamemnon and Achilleus, with Achilleus' final acknowledgment of his foe's humanity, leads to the conclusion of the *Iliad* but not the war. The poem foreshadows the imminent death of Achilleus in several passages. The hero is aware that he is destined to die young if he fights at Troy (9.410–16). One of his horses, temporarily given voice, warns that Achilleus' doom is near (19.407–10). And Hektor, on the point of dying, foretells that his slayer will be slain by Paris and Apollo at the gates of the city (22.358–60). Alongside these explicit testimonies, the demise of Achilleus' stand-in, Patroklos, provides an extended foreshadowing of the grief to come. It is not accidental that the name *Akhilleus* is most plausibly etymologized as "grief [*akhos*] for the fighters [*laos*]."

A few episodes of the overall saga intervene between the death of Hektor, narrated in the *Iliad*, and that of Achilleus (not told in the poem). The Amazon Penthesileia, the daughter of the war god Ares, newly arrived to help the Trojans, is slain by Achilleus. Another ally from the east, Memnon the son of the goddess Dawn, meets the same fate (but is immortalized, thanks to his mother's entreaties). Achilleus is killed on the point of entering Troy, and Aias carries his body back to the Greek camp for burning, but Thetis snatches the body from the pyre and takes her son to a place called the White Island—whether he, too, is immortalized in the post-*Iliad* tradition is unclear. The reminiscence of Achilleus' funeral in the *Odyssey* (24.35–94) presents a different story: Achilleus is cremated, his bones are placed in a golden urn with those of Patroklos, and the vessel is entombed under a prominent mound.

Odysseus, in competition with Aias to inherit the arms of the fallen hero, manages to pervert justice, and Aias, insane with anger, kills the herds of the Greeks and then himself. Learning that only the bow of Philoktetes can take Troy, Odysseus (or in some versions his friend Diomedes) brings the long-abandoned hero back from Lemnos: it is he who kills Paris. Odysseus also brings Neoptolemos, the son of Achilleus, from Skyros to Troy. The stage is set for the final conquest. By Athene's instruction (or a plan of Odysseus), the Greeks build a towering, hollow wooden horse and fill it with their chosen warriors, while the rest of the troops pretend to sail away in defeat. Brought into the city as a dedication to the gods amid joyous revels, the horse enables the Greeks to infiltrate the citadel of Troy. While the fleet returns from its offshore hiding place, the leading fighters eliminate the Trojan elite. Neoptolemos kills Priam at the very altar of Zeus; Menelaos retrieves Helen; the "lesser" Aias (son of Oïleus) rapes Cassandra, the Trojan priestess, tearing her away from Athene's altar while she clutches a talismanic statue of the goddess. The Greeks burn the city and sacrifice Polyxena, a daughter of Priam, at the tomb of Achilleus, as if in compensation for all his grief. The family of Hektor is treated brutally: Odysseus (or Neoptolemos) flings the young Astyanax to death from the city walls, and Neoptolemos claims as his war prize the boy's mother, Andromache. Knowing about this ending deepens the emotional experience of the *Iliad*'s depiction of Hektor's last moments with his wife and child (6.390–502).

Athene's wrath at the desecration of her altar hounds the Greeks—including Odysseus—on their journey home. The *Odyssey* details his incredible ten years of wandering until being reunited with the long-suffering Penelope. As a contrast to this main plot, the *Odyssey* prominently mentions the successful homecoming of Nestor to Pylos; how the lesser Aias lost his life at sea; the delayed trip of Menelaos; and the fatal return of his brother Agamemnon. The cautionary tale of Agamemnon—slain by his wife and her lover Aigisthos soon after his triumphant return—is given as a warning for Odysseus by none other than the victim himself in the underworld (*Odyssey*, book 11).

These individual heroic fates were more fully narrated, it seems, in the *Nostoi* (Returns). As with the other non-Iliadic episodes just mentioned, our main source for this lost epic comes from late antiquity in the form of a condensed plot summary of the so-called Cyclic epics. These poems of the archaic period (seventh–sixth century BC) are attributed to a number of obscure poets thought to have lived later than Homer. They include the *Cypria*, which told of events from the wedding of Peleus through the first nine years of the Trojan War; the *Aithiopis*, which picks up where the *Iliad* ends and continues the story to the dispute over Achilleus' armor; and the *Little Iliad* and *Sack of Ilium*, which together narrate the last days of the city and the departure of the Greeks. Although the Cyclic epics might have been designed after the composition of the Homeric poems, to fill in the gaps and provide details not narrated in them, it is also likely that earlier versions of their material existed even during the era in which the *Iliad* was shaped. Parallel motifs abound, for which it is difficult to assign priority. It has been suggested that the death of Patroklos and the fight over his body (*Iliad* books 16 and 17) are modeled on a more familiar story of the death of Antilochos, a son of Nestor, known to the Cyclic poets as well as later tradition. What is more important is the strong possibility that the early audiences for the *Iliad* had in their minds the entire Trojan saga as it came to be written down later in the Cyclic poems, including the origins of the conflict and the ultimate fates of the Greek veterans. Every *Iliad* character and theme would have taken on greater resonance and depth for such listeners. That a body of such lore, perhaps even in poetic form, already existed when the *Iliad* was composed can explain why the Homeric poet is at liberty to begin the poem in the midst of the war, without a long exposition, filling out the picture with fleeting references as the narrative progresses.

Having seen where that narrative fits in the broader scheme of the saga, one can speculate briefly about the deeper roots for the entire Trojan story. In a traditional culture of oral storytelling—such as that of archaic Greece—tales are constantly remodeled but their elements are often centuries old. The *Iliad* comes at the end of a tradition that may reach back for a millennium in the region of the Aegean, even—paradoxically—to a time before any historical Trojan War of the twelfth century BC. Starting about 1700 BC, paintings that show the siege of a city and attacking ships adorned the walls of Minoan houses. The Town Mosaic, a series of terracotta plaques from the palace at Knossos on Crete, depicts house facades, soldiers, and a ship (although the underlying narrative, if any, is unclear). A somewhat later series of fresco scenes in the West House at Akrotiri, on the island of Santorini (Thera), features a flotilla of ships, and warriors marching with body-length shields near a town, while women watch from the walls. Perhaps epics about famous sieges were already in circulation a thousand years before Homeric poetry was put into definite form, centuries before Greek culture came to replace that of the Minoans.

Further afield, Near Eastern parallels to early Greek literature have captured the attention of scholars in recent decades. Achilleus' relationship with Patroklos looks remarkably like the bond between Enkidu and Gilgamesh, the protagonist of an epic tradition reaching back to 2000 BC and widespread for 1,500 years in the region of the Tigris and Euphrates rivers (modern Iraq). Recorded on cuneiform tablets, in various versions in Sumerian, Akkadian, Hurrian, and Hittite, the earlier epic tells of the gods' creation of Enkidu, a man of the wild, to be a match for the city hero Gilgamesh. Together they win fame as slayers of the monstrous forest guardian Humbaba, yet this and the slaughter of the Bull of Heaven eventually entail Enkidu's death. The Near Eastern story then shifts into an *Odyssey*-like journey to a mythical land where Gilgamesh seeks from Utnapishtim the secret of immortality. But episodes such as the hero's encounter with his companion's ghost (tablet 12; cf. *Il.* 23), his conversation with his goddess mother, and the discomforting of a love goddess who subsequently complains to her divine parents (Ishtar in *Gilgamesh*, Aphrodite in 5.348–80), remind one of the *Iliad*. Unlike the Homeric poem, *Gilgamesh* depicts a primeval struggle between forces of nature and culture. An overall tragic tone, however, and similar attitudes toward the ephemeral nature of fame and mortality, pervade both compositions.

At the furthest remove, some plot elements of the *Iliad* might go back to the period when Greek was not yet fully differentiated from the dialects that would evolve into Latin, Persian, Sanskrit, and early forms of the western European languages (the Celtic, Germanic, and Slavic groups). On the basis of detailed grammatical resemblances among the historically attested tongues, an unrecorded parent language, dubbed "Indo-European," has been reconstructed. It was probably spoken by tribes living in what is now southern Russia around 3000 BC. The hypothesis of a shared Indo-European linguistic origin accounts for resemblances among individual words: thus Greek *patêr*, Sanskrit *pitar*, and Latin *pater*—all meaning "father"—derive from one older stem. Similarly, names for some divinities—*Zeus* (Greek), *Dyaus* (Sanskrit) and *Ju-piter* (an archaic Latin compound, meaning "sky father")—can be traced to a common original. Shared elements in legal procedure and religious ritual are also convincingly explained by assuming that Indo-European speakers carried their culture with them as they moved out from their common homeland toward the Balkans and the Mediterranean, on the one hand, and on the other to central Asia and the Indian subcontinent. Furthermore, pieces of poetic diction, metrical patterns, and narrative motifs appear to show a common Indo-European heritage. The *Iliad*'s backstory of an abducted bride who is won back by warrior brothers appears in the Sanskrit epic *Ramayana* (circa fourth century BC), while aspects of Hittite law and ritual have been detected in Homeric language, and the Homeric concept "unwithering fame" (Homeric *kleos aphthiton*) is paralleled exactly in the archaic literature of India and Ireland.

More work remains to be done on all the sources that may have contributed to the masterwork of the *Iliad*. It is clear that the poem will always be much more than the sum of such parts, a new and distinctively Greek vision, albeit it with very ancient origins.[3]

### THE VISION OF THE *ILIAD*: THE LIMITS OF MORTALITY

The *Iliad* depicts the events of a few weeks in the last year of the siege of Troy. Within this concentrated space, the poem gives a sense of greater magnitude by alluding to all of the most important episodes in the ten-year saga, going back to the abduction of Helen. At the same time, while recounting in detail fierce attacks and pitched battles, it also manages to impart an indelible vision about the nature of human existence.

In the universe painted by the *Iliad*, humans are at the blazing center. Their motivations and concerns generate the action in the poem, while the gods are often reduced to the role of enablers or spectators. The passionate decisions of heroes like Achilleus and Hektor—to avenge a companion's death, to take a stand outside the Trojan walls—are what determine the arc of the *Iliad*'s plot. The style of the poem collaborates with this vision: the spaciousness of the epic means that every thought and gesture, spear cast and threat, intimate conversation and lament can be recorded. The poetic consciousness behind the *Iliad* demands that these *must* be recorded: the meticulous attention to living detail is another way of expressing the centrality and worth of human experience, whether Greek or Trojan.

Because men and women, human psychology and social institutions, are at the heart of the *Iliad*, it is inevitably a poem about death, the chief element that distinguishes mortals from gods. The opening lines highlight the destructive wrath of Achilleus, which to the harm of his enemies as well as his own companions, "hurled in their multitudes to the house of Hades strong souls of heroes, but gave their bodies to be the delicate feasting of dogs, of all birds." The last scenes of the poem center on the funeral for Hektor, victim of Achilleus' anger. All through the intervening books, death shadows every action. We hear of the slaying of scores of warriors—240 named, many others anonymous—and view the sometimes spectacular demise of several at excruciatingly close range: Deukalion decapitated (20.481), Erymas, his skull smashed, his mouth spewing blood (16.345), Mydon trampled by his own horses (5.588). Constantly at the edge of our vision is the specter of mass destruction, either of the Trojans defending their doomed city or of the attackers, beset by plague and slowly wasting away (1.49–52). Death is neither abhorred nor celebrated in this world, however. Instead, just as the *Iliad* distills the Trojan saga into a few days of intense fighting, it crystallizes by means of this one theme—death in battle—the essence of what it means to be human. Life is a struggle each person will ultimately always lose; the question is how one acts with that knowledge.

Homeric heroes respond to this fate with a mixture of resignation and resistance. "As is the generation of leaves," says Glaukos to Diomedes, "so is that of humanity" (6.146), as he tries to defuse his opponent's attempt to compare heroic genealogies. A similar broad view of the cycle of human existence marks the words of Apollo to Poseidon (21.464), except the god makes a different point: that he and fellow divinities should therefore not waste their effort on mankind. Achilleus at the end of the poem, with his new, hard-won clarity about the working of the world, tells the old Trojan king Priam of the stewardship of Zeus, who mixes disproportionately from "an urn of evils, an urn of blessings" (24.528). Unlike the *Odyssey*, the *Iliad* contains no extended depiction of the underworld, Hades' realm, a grim holding area where strengthless ghosts maintain little more than their names. It is simply a place where (as Achilleus exclaims on seeing his companion's ghost) "there is left something, a soul and an image, but there is no real heart of life in it" (23.103). Whereas modern readers assume that one's inner spirit is somehow the "real" self, the *Iliad* describes the opposite: the *psykhai* (souls, spirits) of dying heroes fly off to Hades while their "selves" (*autous*) are left behind (in the form of their dead bodies). In line with this view of the afterlife, it is well understood that a life on earth of striving, even of pain, is preferable to an eternity of gloom.

Counterbalancing the darkness of death and loss is the brilliance of glory, which ensures that a person's name, a marker for his or her self, lives on forever. The most detailed description of the ideology underlying the heroic quest for glory comes in the words of Sarpedon of Lycia to his companion, Glaukos (12.315–28):

> ... It is our duty in the forefront of the Lykians
> to take our stand, and bear our part of the blazing of battle
> so that a man of the close-armored Lykians may say of us:
> "Indeed these are no ignoble men who are lords of Lykia,
> these kings of ours, who feed upon the fat sheep appointed
> and drink the exquisite sweet wine, since indeed there is strength
> of valor in them, since they fight in the forefront of the Lykians."
> Man, supposing you and I, escaping this battle
> would be able to live on forever, ageless, immortal,
> so neither would I myself go on fighting in the foremost
> nor would I urge you into the fighting where men win glory.
> But now, seeing that the spirits of death stand close about us
> in their thousands, no man can turn aside nor escape them,
> let us go on and win glory for ourselves, or yield it to others.

Several points are worth noting: first, if mortals could live forever—that is, could be like gods—glory would be useless. Only death gives value to renown. Second, glory is a commodity to be exchanged: one wins it by the effort to kill an opponent, and the vanquished give it, like a gift, to the conqueror. In this zero-sum game, there is only so much glory to go around. Third, glory has both an economic and symbolic reality. Warriors are honored by the community with special privileges, grants of land, and feasts because on its behalf they risk death. This in turn gives them a wide reputation, spreading the fame of their people, which gives grounds for the community's expenditure and ensures that their lives will not be forgotten. At the same time, the rewards of their fighting, whether cattle, weapons, or women, are visible marks of the honor they hold in the community, and a means of maintaining status among fellow warriors. For this reason, the quarrel between Achilleus and Agamemnon is deadly serious. Forced to return the young woman Chryseis, his prize of honor (*geras*), to end a divinely sent plague, Agamemnon in turn takes Achilleus' war prize, Briseis, prompting the hero's boycott in protest at his consequent loss of honor. In Achilleus' view, status alone motivates Agamemnon's greater *geras*, despite his own equal efforts (1.161–68). Their clash over entitlement emphasizes the disequilibrium between authority and ability, a mismatch familiar still today between those with power and those with talent.

Ideally, the short-term glory by which a warrior is recognized while alive, comprising material marks of honor, is a foretaste of long-term fame, one's reputation after death. The reputation desired by Iliadic heroes is that represented by the very medium itself of Homeric poetry, which bestows *kleos*—"fame," "report," or "glory bestowed by poetry." *Kleos* is literally "that which is heard" (cf. the verb *kluô*, "hear," cognate with English "loud"). The *Iliad* describes several warriors as having chosen to go to Troy "for glory" (*meta kleos*: for example, Iphidamas 11.227). Other characters express awareness of their eventual commemoration. Helen believes that she and Paris will be "subjects of song" (*aoidimoi*) for future generations (*Il.* 6.358). Hektor imagines something akin to poetic epitaphs mentioning him (7.89–91).

Achilleus is seen performing stories of fame (9.186–89), while accompanying himself on a lyre. The hero of the *Iliad* apparently sings about past figures, such men as Meleagros, whose unfortunate tale, an example of the "glories of heroes" (*klea andrôn hêrôôn*), is recounted to him later in the same episode by the aged Phoinix (9.524–25). The *Iliad* itself, meanwhile, is explicitly characterized by the poet as what has been heard from the Muses, in contrast to and relying on what the goddesses, with timeless knowledge, once observed when events were unfolding (2.484–86). For

Achilleus, however, "unwithering fame" (*kleos aphthiton*) must come at the price of death at Troy, in contrast to a return home without glory (9.413). He was never fated to enjoy the short-term rewards of war, over which he has quarreled. Instead, his desire to punish his fellow Greeks because they do not honor him enough only hastens his own death. Hard-pressed because Zeus has been persuaded by Achilleus' mother to turn the tide against them, the Greeks beg Achilleus to return. But, in his magnificent reply to their embassy in book 9, the hero rejects the entire system of honor as material payment, tainted by injustice as it now appears to him. He seems to believe, as well, that the choice his mother Thetis once told to him—that he can leave Troy for a life of anonymity—is a real option. He declares to Odysseus that he will take ship the very next morning. After the speeches of his old guardian Phoinix and his fellow fighter Aias (9.432–642), he hedges, softening his attitude until he finally concedes the possibility of returning to battle if the Trojans manage to push all the way to the beached Greek ships. Meanwhile, an audience familiar with the character of Achilleus knows that he will never sail back home, abandoning long-term glory. The only suspense comes from not knowing exactly how and when he will return to the war that will eventually spell his death.

Here, another aspect of the *Iliad* vision becomes crucial: the importance of companionship. For this theme the poem seems to draw most deeply on actual experiences, ancient but instantly identifiable to moderns, as shown by the work of the psychiatrist Jonathan Shay with veterans of the Vietnam and Iraq conflicts. It is a universal theme in war stories, glimpsed in documents like a Japanese kamikaze pilot's letter to his parents a week before his death: "My co-pilot is Uno Shigeru, a handsome boy, aged nineteen, a naval petty officer second class. His home is in Hyogo Prefecture. He thinks of me as his elder brother, and I think of him as my younger brother. Working as one heart, we will plunge into an enemy vessel."[4]

In the battle scenes of the *Iliad*, the closeness of male friends, with the consequent desire to take revenge for a companion's death, is regularly the prime motivation for one warrior to attack another. The core of the poem is shaped out of one such episode, writ large. Patroklos, an older fighter who has been sent to guide and advise Achilleus, begs out of pity for the devastated Greeks to be sent into the fray dressed in Achilleus' own armor, to terrify the Trojans at least long enough for the troops to get a brief pause to recover. Still nursing his wounded pride, Achilleus accedes to this request by his nearest and dearest companion. Patroklos succeeds in mowing down scores of the enemy but is killed by Apollo, Euphorbos, and Hektor, acting in sequence. Grief and rage over Patroklos' death induce Achilleus to abandon his boycott, enter the battle, and slay Hektor, even though he knows this means imminent death for himself. The poet never makes moral judgments, but leaves it to Achilleus to voice in self-reproach one of the deepest conclusions of the *Iliad*—that personal honor, no matter how precious, cannot take precedence over the life of a friend (18.97–105).

Pity turns out to be a key component in the total vision of this surprising epic. Achilleus' rage persists even after he kills his friend's slayer, leading him to mistreat Hektor's corpse, dragging it behind his chariot as he races around the ramparts each day, a taunt to the Trojans and a horrific continuation of revenge. Pity becomes the concluding note of the poem. In what are among the most humane lines of the *Iliad*, Achilleus after a tense conversation, seeing the aged Priam sitting before him, thinks back to his own father and weeps (24.509–12). This moment of shared grief brings him to surrender the corpse of his enemy. It is appropriate that the poem concludes with the funeral of Achilleus' victim, for Hektor of all warriors evokes the most pity. The audience has listened, in book 6, to the tender scene of his parting from his wife Andromache, as he goes off to certain death; they have heard of his proud delight in their infant son (knowing, despite the poet's reticence, that the child will not survive the fall of Troy). And from the concluding lament by Helen—ironically, the woman who unwittingly caused the whole war—we finally learn of Hektor's gentleness of manner in his role as her only friend in the city.

Even the gods feel pity. Poseidon, emerging from the sea to view the ongoing battle on the plain of Troy, empathizes with the Greeks whom he sees being overcome by their enemies (13.15). Moved by pity, the gods as a group discuss how they might steal away Hektor's corpse when they see Achilleus mistreat it (24.23). While the *Iliad* yields center stage to humans, much of the power of its vision in fact comes from its depiction of the gods as beings that feel, and act, like humans. As the ancient literary critic Longinus (first century AD) remarked: "Homer seems to me, in recording the wounds of the gods, their conflicts, deeds of vengeance, tears, and bindings, all sorts of mixed passions, to have as much as possible made the men of the *Iliad* gods, and the gods men" (*On the Sublime* 9.7).

Through the poet's attention to the working of the divine in human lives, the *Iliad* gains depth and resonance in two major ways. First of all, the divine dimension sheds glory on the humans at Troy. That the gods are so intensely concerned with warriors and their fates elevates the mortals to a special plane. At a deeper emotional level, we hear throughout the *Iliad* of humans actually descended from Zeus or Ares or Poseidon. Achilleus himself is a grandson of Aiakos, who in turn was a son of Zeus. His elemental opponent, the river god Xanthos (also called Skamandros) is also a son of Zeus, making their encounter in book 21 something like a family fight. Although the Greek gods father many children, the *Iliad* persuades its audience that Zeus and his kin feel concern and anxiety for their individual offspring. When his son Sarpedon, a Trojan ally, is about to be killed by Patroklos, Zeus actually ponders whether he might save him (but abandons the idea when Hera objects: 16.433). In sum, mortals are separated from gods by only a few facts—chiefly, that they will grow old and eventually die. Ageless and immortal, fed on nectar and ambrosia, with clear *ikhôr* in their veins instead of blood, the gods live at ease in cloudless calm on the snowy height of Mount Olympos. They are more massive—when Athene mounts Diomedes' chariot in book 5, the axle groans with her weight— and they can choose to appear in whatever guise they like. But they are not alien: when they do communicate with humans in the *Iliad*, it is in human form (even if they may depart in the form of birds, like Poseidon at 13.62, or perch in trees, like Athene and Apollo at 7.59).

The second poetic consequence of the Homeric understanding of the gods stems from this closeness. The symbiotic bond of gods and mortals is always teetering between adoration and antagonism. Like the high-strung heroes of the poem, hypersensitive to their honor, the gods need humans to worship and acknowledge them (e.g., Poseidon, at 7.446). Because the gods are inquisitive, meddlesome, proud of their favorite humans, and dangerously quick to anger, mortals must offer sacrifice, making sure to fill heavenly nostrils with the savor of roasting meat or pouring out wine and prayers. At the same time, humans who get too close to the gods risk being struck down. The career of Achilleus is a prime illustration. Young, well-made, a warrior but also a singer (he is the only hero seen doing this), Achilleus looks and acts like Apollo. It is no accident that Apollo, as Hektor predicts in his own death speech (22.359) will ultimately be the god who slays Achilleus, just as he did his companion Patroklos. The epic through its formulaic style (see also the "Style" section below) draws attention to the dangers of heroes antagonizing gods. Patroklos rushes at Apollo on the field of battle four times "like a divinity" (*daimoni isos*)—and pays with his life. Zeus and his siblings have overthrown their own Titan parents, according to Greek myth; they themselves take care never to be subverted by mortals, even by half-divine heroes.

It would be a mistake, however, to depict the gods' world in the *Iliad* as a swirling chaos of divine powers. Most of the gods (Hades excepted) dwell together in an organized household on the peaks of Olympos (conceived as being simultaneously a real mountain and an unreachable ethereal space). Ruling from on high is the father-god Zeus, who backs up his commands with a white-hot thunderbolt. Hades and Poseidon, his brothers, have their realms of underworld and sea. Others fall into line as sons or daughters of Zeus. There is a nice economy in such a polytheistic system— one god balances another, and humans cover their bets by praying to many. The Trojan War intrudes on divine harmony, however, as gods take sides, some with the Trojans, others the Greeks. Aphrodite, goddess of sex and desire, is the distant cause of the conflict, inasmuch as it was she who gifted Paris with the ability to seduce Helen (in return for his naming her fairest among goddesses). She is also the mother of the Trojan ally Aeneas (the ultimate ancestor of the Romans), and therefore is devoted to the Trojan cause. Apollo, god of divination and harmony, the initiator of young men, is also connected with Troy, for reasons more obscure, perhaps related to the historical existence of important Apollo shrines in Asia Minor. His twin sister Artemis joins him, even egging him on to fight, until she has her ears boxed and is driven off by Hera (21.481). Finally supporting Troy is Ares, the god of all-out war and battle madness.

Allied with the Greeks are the powerful goddesses Hera and Athene, the wife and daughter of Zeus, respectively. Athene is goddess of crafts, including warcraft (as opposed to mere murderous strength), and Hera is connected with marriage and sovereignty. The two are naturally opposed to Troy, since Paris passed them over in favor of Aphrodite in the divine beauty contest. Poseidon's enmity seems to originate a generation earlier, when he helped build Troy's wall for the king Laomedon, who then failed to pay as promised. Another elemental god, the divine blacksmith Hephaistos, forges new armor for Achilleus at the request of Thetis, and later scorches the river Xanthos in order to rescue the hero from its flood.

The Greeks worshiped multiple gods, as can be seen in the excavated remains of ancient temples, cult sites, and altars, with their great number of dedicated votive objects, from humble figurines to precious gold-clad statues. The vividness and variety of the divine depictions, however, were seen by at least some in antiquity not as an age-old tradition but rather as the invention of specific poets. The fifth-century BC historian Herodotus attributed to Homer and his contemporary Hesiod such basic information as the genesis and forms of the gods, as well as the titles, honors, and skills by which they were known (*Histories* 2.53). This is to say, poetry supplemented or even guided the Greek religious imagination, much more than did the activity of priests. In the absence of dogma or a sacred book, ancient Greek religious thought was more open to innovation and creative reshaping, giving it a flexibility that seems strange to modern monotheists in highly organized, global faiths. The closeness of gods and humans within the *Iliad* and *Odyssey* can have occurred precisely because the composers of epic were always free to elaborate their own thoughts concerning both the divine and mortal worlds, and drew them alike.

Of course, the poems do not celebrate just *any* mortals: the major epic characters are heroes. Both poet and audience know that men of their own time cannot compare with those of the heroic age of the Trojan War, who were mighty in war, and physically stronger. Heroes were celebrated for *aretê*, "excellence," or "virtue." Relying on this, they strove to be "best" (*aristos*—root of "aristocracy"), and their bids for martial success, as stylized in the *Iliad* (e.g., Diomedes' extended killing spree in book 5), are called *aristeiai*, "displays of excellence." Various members of the audiences for epic would have traced their own ancestry back to heroes—either those associated with the Trojan War, or some of the nearly nine hundred other mortal figures who were locally important and celebrated in antiquity for heroic skills ranging from wrestling prowess to skill at sacrifice. More surprising for the modern audience, ancient Greeks worshiped these figures, bringing them offerings of animals and food, in something resembling ancestor cult or the medieval devotion to saints. The tombs of heroes were considered sites of power, and heroes could be invoked to favor the worshiper, protect his family and city-state, and even heal illnesses. While almost any warrior in the *Iliad* can be designated *hêrôs*, the ideology of heroism extended far beyond the fictional inventions of poets.

The idea of the *hêrôs* who has a status between man and god appears to be a uniquely Greek invention. Herakles, whose exploits took him over the known world, conspicuously combined a warrior's courage with aberrant, even berserk, behavior (sometimes excused as "madness" sent by his nemesis Hera). He died, but paradoxically lived forever after he was taken up onto Mount Olympos following his self-willed incineration on Mount Oita. His story may be taken as a paradigm for others—the hero fights, rules, often sins, dies, and then gains postmortem fame (a form of immortality) along with semidivine power. Even the parricide Oedipus was associated with heroic honors in several places; the tragedy *Oedipus at Colonus* by Sophocles (produced posthumously in 401 BC) tells of the struggle between Athens and Thebes over claims to the Theban hero's prized burial site. Most striking to modern sensibilities is the idea that heroes are not necessarily morally upright. An Achilleus or Odysseus can bring about the deaths of many, intentionally, without remorse, and still be considered a model of toughness, skill, or endurance.

With consummate artistry, the epic composer differentiates the heroic mortals in the *Iliad* by noting their different ways of speaking, of doing battle, and of interacting with other warriors, women, and the gods. A conspicuous and sophisticated set piece, the conversation on the walls of Troy (book 3), enables the poet to mention the variety of major male characters, while tacitly contrasting the views of them that we get from persons of different gender, age, and ethnicity (Helen and her interlocutor Priam): there is the kingly Agamemnon (or so he appears to Priam), Helen's former brother-in-law; Odysseus, broad and sturdy in appearance like a ram among ewes, whom Helen remembers for his cunning; the huge battle tower Aias; and godlike Idomeneus, leader of the Cretans. We do not glimpse Menelaos in this scene, although his laconic speaking style is recalled by one of the attendant Trojans, in contrast to Odysseus' rhetorical brilliance. A series of episodes introduces the audience to other main figures. Characterization through likeness and contrast subtly operates over the course of the poem. Achilleus, short-tempered and ardent, is unlike the more temperate, family-oriented Hektor, but bears a resemblance to the brash Diomedes. Agamemnon comes across as harsher and unfeeling, especially in contrast to the brother whom he overshadows, the milder Menelaos. Odysseus comes close to him in status, but is clearly far more strategically intelligent. In another pairing of brothers, Paris invites comparison with Hektor, emerging as a less important, even frivolous, figure, although more directly responsible for the war. The pair of Trojan allies Glaukos and Sarpedon evokes the dynamic relation between Patroklos and Achilleus, as also that between Hektor and his more cautious brother Poulydamas. Nestor, the aged adviser on the Greek side, finds a parallel in Priam among the Trojans. In short, the technique is kaleidoscopic, offering intriguing patterns and family resemblances that shift and deepen the further one works into the poem.

On a slightly smaller scale, the same approach produces a vivid, varied set of female characters. At first, the male focus seems to slight women: Chryseis, the captive girl about whom the initial quarrel erupts in the Greek camp, never speaks for herself. In this she resembles the anonymous women of Lesbos—famous only for skills at craft—whom Agamemnon promises to Achilleus in his later attempt to woo him back to war (9.270). But in the unfolding of the poem, women are far from being mute objects of exchange. Another captive, Briseis, whom we first hear about as a counterpart to Chryseis, turns out to make one of the most impassioned laments at the death of Patroklos (19.282), giving voice to a social category that another poet might have treated as marginal or forgettable. The acknowledged existence of strong, independent goddess figures makes an interesting background for the poem's depiction of mortal equivalents. Hekabē, the mother of Hektor, echoes something of Hera's nagging tone when she chastises her husband Priam (24.201). On the other hand, Andromache, wife of Hektor, is shown possessing a combination of strength and tender vulnerability that is never on view among divine females. She is clearly the summit of feminine virtue in the poem.

As such, she makes for a final, fascinating contrast with Helen. The woman whose elopement or abduction began the conflict at Troy, Helen remains the most intriguing female figure in the *Iliad*. The story with which she is connected is an old one paralleled in many cultures, as catalogued by Stith Thompson in *The Motif-Index of Folk-Literature*[5] (R151.1: "Husband rescues stolen wife"). Helen's mother was commonly said to be the Spartan woman queen Leda, impregnated by Zeus in the form of a swan, or—less commonly and more grimly—to be Nemesis, the goddess of divine retribution (cf. the mostly lost epic poem *Cypria*). We see Helen as the wife of Paris, but know she has been the consort of Menelaos: the doubleness tied to her character is persistent. Her earlier experiences before reaching Troy are rarely alluded to—for example, her flight from Sparta with Paris (3.444) and visit to Sidon (6.292)—thereby allowing the audience to judge her mostly by her own words, rather than pigeonholing her either as a wanton or a victim. Deftly sketched interactions over books 3 and 6 with the disguised Aphrodite, Priam, Paris, and Hektor show Helen, by turns, sarcastic, defiant, regretful, complaisant, ashamed, wistful, and resigned. She is a shimmering figure, impossible to pin down. It is appropriate that another tale, possibly as old as Hesiod (fr. 358 MW), elaborated by the choral poet Stesichorus in the sixth century BC and later exploited by

Euripides in his *Helen*, said that Helen never went to Troy: that was only a phantom image of her, an *eidôlon*, fought over by multitudes while the real woman stayed safe in Egypt.

Other evidence from the lore of mainland Greece connects Helen to the yearly worship of a fertility power, associated especially with trees. Again it is appropriate if, in the deep past, Helen had been a goddess. She retains the aura of being unattainable. And this quality is not just a feature of the folktale kernel behind the entire Trojan saga. Instead, in the stylized form of the Homeric vision, it becomes a statement for the human condition. You can't always (or ever) entirely get what you want. Helen, essence of desire, cannot be had without disastrous consequences. Or in the more succinct version of the poet Alcman, in a song made for girls' choruses in Sparta (Helen's own city) in the seventh century BC: "Let no man fly to heaven, or attempt to marry Aphrodite."

### THE WORLDS OF THE *ILIAD*

The vision that the *Iliad* offers need not be directly related to the historical circumstances in which the epic was composed. Its most pervasive message—that the all-important pursuit of glory is a hotly contested, zero-sum game—could have arisen in any culture with limited resources and an aristocratic warrior class. But what precise world—or amalgamation of worlds—does the *Iliad* depict? And when is it likely the poem was composed? Even if we had the answer to the second question, we could not readily assume that the society and institutions depicted in the epic mirrored those of the composer's era. It is well known that other epic poems, for which we have independent historical testimony, stylize, distort, or change completely the events and conditions they supposedly represent. The Old French *Song of Roland*, for example, accurately records that Charlemagne, king of the Franks, made an expedition into Spain in 778, some three hundred years before the poem was composed, but it completely changes the facts when it comes to the major episode: the king's retreating troops were massacred not by pagan Saracens but by a renegade Basque contingent (as Christian as the Franks). Similar distortions crop up in many other epic traditions, including Serbo-Croatian, Spanish, African, and Germanic.

We can try to winnow out actual historical elements of the *Iliad*, in contrast to how the poem envisions the heroic world (which may or may not have had a real basis) by observing continuities with later institutions and attested cultural practices in Greece, especially Athens of the Classical period. If features of the poem seem to have a plausible relationship with later, independently attested phenomena, there is a chance they are grounded in reality, even though we still cannot date them to a particular era before recorded Greek history.

Since 1952 (the year after Lattimore's *Iliad* translation was published), historians also have possessed another source for studying the actual basis of Homer's world: the earliest writing in Greek, from a period before the Trojan War. That year saw the decipherment of the mysterious Linear B script, a form of writing using eighty-nine different signs, incised on thousands of clay tablets that had been found at Knossos in Crete starting in 1900, and later at Pylos, Mykenai, and other palace sites on the Greek mainland. The tablets, which date to the end of the thirteenth century, had been preserved only because they were baked by the fires that destroyed their palatial surroundings. Michael Ventris, a young British architect and amateur linguist, made the remarkable discovery, thereby recovering voices from a civilization that had been known since Schliemann's excavations. Thanks to Ventris, it could be shown that the Mykenaians spoke an early dialect of Greek. Equally surprising was the content of the newly readable texts: meticulous tabulations of supplies and personnel, from grain and sheep to chariots and fighters, all tied into a complicated bureaucracy that most closely resembled the palace-centered economies of larger Near Eastern kingdoms. Unlike the archives of those kingdoms, however, the Mykenaian storerooms (at least those found so far) do not also contain personal or literary texts such as prayers, hymns, letters, or epics. Nevertheless, the Linear B tablets still offer precious insights into the daily life of a civilization that ended around the time of Troy's destruction.

The society revealed had several layers of authority. A king figure (*wanax*) ruled from a central palace, supported by "knights" with whom he apparently had feudal relations requiring them to furnish supplies and men. Local administration officials included several called *basileus*—the later Greek word for "king." Slaves were plentiful, and the gods had priests and priestesses dedicated to the functioning of shrines. Beyond this, we lack signs of social institutions, but that could just reflect the limitations of archival lists.

The Linear B picture offers a clear contrast with Homeric usage. In the *Iliad*, all the heroes are technically *basileis* (plural of *basileus*), although there does seem to be an executive council of eight or nine more important leaders (Nestor, Odysseus, Menelaos, et al.) who make decisions that the broader assembly of troops will then hear and ratify. Homeric Greek generally reserves the old word *wanax* to designate the "lord" of a house, master of a horse, or a divinity. It is not impossible, however, that the relationship between Agamemnon—often called *wanax andrôn* ("lord of men") and Achilleus recalls a Mykenaian feudal arrangement. In the Linear B tablets, there is no sign of a political function for the general populace (although this body, already called the *damos*, has common-land allotments). But in the assemblies of the *Iliad*, we can catch a faint glimmer of the future city-state with its politically involved, vocal citizen body, the *dêmos* that eventually will be enshrined in *dêmokratia* "rule by the people." It is difficult to say whether or not the audience for Homeric poetry already is aware of functioning predemocratic city-states, while the poet suppresses details in order to recreate what he imagines was a simpler, earlier era.

The Mykenaian tablets show that palace culture depended on long-distance networks and made extensive use of writing, although perhaps the skill was restricted to the palace scribes who tracked invoices. By contrast, in the *Iliad* and *Odyssey*, even kings live in what seem to be modest houses with a single large room at the center and a few servants. The form of the Mykenaian great hall is continued, surprisingly, by Greek temple architecture of the eighth century BC and later—not by royal homes. The *basileis* are still depicted as having control of extensive territories (Agamemnon promises Achilleus seven citadels at 9.291). But this is most likely an exaggerated, semi-imaginary portrayal. In reality, after the fall of the Mykenaian palace culture around 1200 BC (close to the time Troy underwent major destruction), a "Dark Age" of Greek culture set in, lasting nearly four hundred years. Large stone buildings were no longer constructed; the arts of pottery and implement making declined; populations shrank, and there were large-scale migrations. The darkness was not uniform: Athens, in particular, seems to have retained traces of the older high culture longer into the eleventh century; Euboea, Crete, and Cyprus offer further traces of continuity between the Mykenaian period and what archaeologists identify as a "renaissance" of Greek culture in the eighth century BC.

The discovery that at least some Greek speakers in the thirteenth century, before the decline, had access to a writing system presented the starkest contrast with Homeric epic, because nowhere in the poems is writing clearly mentioned. No one reads; messages are reproduced orally by heralds; there are no book scrolls, inscriptions, or clay tablets. Only once does awareness of something like writing seem to surface, at 6.168, which refers rather uneasily to the "mysterious symbols" scratched on a tablet and meant to order secretly the death of the bearer. This seems to represent the incomprehension and suspicion of people at a time when the old sign-based writing was no longer understood, and the new system (with a sign for each sound, rather than for every syllable, as in the rebus-like Linear B) had not yet been carried to Greece from its place of origin further east. Or perhaps the epic poet himself knows about writing but wants to paint an archaizing portrait of a period when heroes were ignorant of the skill. Scholars still debate the exact century when a form of the west-Semitic alphabet used by Phoenicians was first used to record Greek; the earliest surviving inscriptions date from the second part of the eighth century BC (and oddly enough, are used to scratch onto vases a few poetic lines not unlike Homeric verses). If Greek speakers used the art of writing before that, the evidence for that skill remains hidden. Most likely, when the palace economies of the Mykenaian period collapsed, the highly specialized scribal art was no longer practiced; a population with very simple needs could get along without elaborate recording systems.

Yet, because knowledge of writing seems to have vanished in the Dark Age (1200–800 BC), it is all the more striking that some real features of the earlier, Mykenaian culture do survive intact within the *Iliad*. These must have been remembered and passed down for generations, by word of mouth (see "Homeric Questions and Some Modern Answers" below). The heroes of the *Iliad* fight with bronze weapons, whereas iron was the most commonly employed metal in the post-Mykenaian period. The head-to-foot body shield used by Aias (7.219), though visible in Mykenaian art, was later replaced by smaller, round shields (more frequently used in the *Iliad*). The cup of Nestor (11.632–35) resembles elaborately decorated vessels from the early Mykenaian period. Like the cup, the boar's-tusk helmet worn by Odysseus (10.261–65), granted a long genealogy by the poet, may have been an heirloom piece that survived the Dark Ages into a later era.

Some of the places named in the Catalogue of Ships (book 2) as supplying troops and ships were abandoned after the twelfth century, so a Dark Age poet or one composing later could not have known firsthand of their importance. Eleon (2.500) was otherwise unfamiliar until the discovery in the mid-1990s of tablets at Thebes with the place-name *e-re-o-ni* (Ft 140.5) on a list of grain supplies. Other citadels—Pylos, Mykenai, Thebes—

survived as settlements after the Bronze Age, but with none of the prestige they possess in the epics.

Alongside these reminiscences of a distant past that probably coincided with the period of Troy's greatness, there are other equally clear markers of a later date. Although chariots occur frequently in the *Iliad*, the poet seems unclear about their proper use. In Bronze Age cultures of the east, warriors clashed in ranks of opposed chariots, but in Homeric poetry the heroes ride them into the fray, then step down to engage in battle with swords and spears. The style of fighting that the *Iliad* chooses to depict is largely man-to-man combat on foot, across a broad front. Scant attention is paid to the rank-and-file movement of troops toward one another, except when it sets the stage for single combat. Nestor's advice (2.362–63) that the troops should fight in formation by "phratry" ("brotherhood") is approved by Agamemnon but then ignored in the subsequent fighting. This formation foreshadows the vocabulary and style of heavy-armed fighting techniques adopted by the Greek city-states in the eighth or seventh century; it is likely to afford a glimpse of the latest stages of the poem's composition. Carrying two javelins, wearing crested helmets, and using shields with a central Gorgon head ornament, among other martial customs (5.741, 11.36), are among the signals (like the reference to the wealth of Egyptian Thebes at 9.382) that date the world of the *Iliad* to the mid-seventh century, in the view of many scholars.

Two other periods were important in shaping the poem. A key phase was the eighth century BC, when, after the years of Dark Age isolation that followed the collapse of Bronze Age palace complexes, various Greek communities began to share new institutions. This century saw the beginnings of the *polis* ("city-state"), a central urban space with associated rural territories. In time more than seven hundred such *poleis* developed. Dedication of votive objects at Apollo's shrine in Delphi also dates to this century; the *Iliad* knows of the temple's wealth (9.404). Delphi had a major role in organizing colonies sent by Greek cities, starting in the 700s, to the further reaches of the Black Sea, North Africa, and what is now southern France. The *Odyssey* especially seems aware of this phenomenon and the information thereby gained about regions even beyond the Mediterranean. The story of the *Iliad*, about an expedition from all parts of Greece to the coast of Asia Minor, may well have been elaborated in the context of broader "Panhellenic" movements of the eighth century. An eighth-century beginning to the process of composition would fit with the estimate of Herodotus (2.53) concerning the lifetime of Homer.

Finally, we cannot ignore the evidence for a quite late phase in the crystallization of the *Iliad*, at Athens in the sixth century BC when Peisistratus was the unelected, nonhereditary ruler ("tyrant" or *turannos*). A fairly plausible tradition holds that even a generation before the time of Peisistratus, the famous Athenian magistrate Solon inserted line 2.558 to support the claims that Athens made to sovereignty over the nearby island Salamis. An ineradicable Athenian dialect coloration seems to support the notion that the poems were ultimately written down in, or at least transmitted by way of, Athens.

The world of the *Iliad* extends beyond bronze weapons and fighting formations, into the realms of thought and behavior. The Linear B tablets, being so narrowly focused, reveal nothing about the morals or manners of Greeks in the Mykenaian period. On the other hand, the *Iliad* and *Odyssey* contain enough material to enable reconstruction of a number of customs, beliefs, and institutions. At least, one can glimpse the imaginary social world that must have been accepted as reasonable to generations of Greek audiences, since the poems continued to attract attention and be transmitted, even when writing was not an option.

First, its inhabitants live without formal, written rules established and enforced by legal authorities. But justice does not require law. In fact, the Greek word *dikê*, most often translated as "justice," is closer to the ideas of custom, habit, and propriety. The way things normally are, when family, community, and world are in order, is the way things should be. The running of society is subject to unwritten traditions of proper order (encapsulated in the Greek word *themis*—both common noun and name of a goddess). *Dikê*, in this archaic Greek sense, can even describe the working of nature; humans and animals sometimes go beyond the boundaries of this natural "justice." They do so when they disturb the order of things, either by refusing to give others their rightful due, or by trying to take somebody else's goods or honor. Such actions—the opposite of *dikê*—are called in Greek *hubris*.

Overstepping the limits eventually brings reprisal. In the *Odyssey*, the depredations of the suitors in his house brings down the wrath of

Odysseus, as the agent of such divine justice. The *Iliad* complicates the question of justice, since its protagonist seems to reject the whole system of compensation accepted by his community. Some interpreters try to make this rejection a sign of a hubristic overstepping on Achilleus' part, but it is impossible to disentangle the act from the natural character of the hero. Similarly, the revenge of Achilleus for his companion's death has the feel of completion, a "just" readjustment of the balance of forces; his subsequent maltreatment of Hektor's corpse, however, once more throws the system into disorder. Like the *Odyssey* (and so many dramas in later Greek literature), the *Iliad* concludes with the intervention of the gods to restore social stability, however temporary.

If there is an ideological excuse for the presence of thousands of Greeks besieging Troy to recover one man's wife, it is given in the name of *dikê*. On the level of human ethics, Paris violated the sacredness of the relations between host and guest (the institution called *xenia*) when he ran away from the palace of his host Menelaos with the host's wife, Helen—even though Aphrodite, we are led to believe, instigated the episode. The father of gods, Zeus, had a special title, *Xenios*, to denote his role as protector of this institution. Any infraction was thus an offense against the chief god. So Agamemnon and his fellow chieftains can claim that their mission to punish Troy has the blessing of Zeus. The further notion that a criminal brings pollution (*miasma*) on his entire community underlies the assumption that all of Troy must suffer for the delict of Paris.

*Xenia* represents one aspect of a larger cultural requirement for reciprocity. This greater principle can be seen at work in a number of other areas alluded to by the *Iliad*. Animal sacrifice, prayer, and warfare were based on the idea that equilibrium must be maintained by giving or paying back either favors or hostility, either among humans or between humans and gods. The reciprocal expectations underlying *xenia* can explain the semantics of the term. Just as any "stranger" was a potential "guest"—and had to be so treated—any "guest" was by implication a potential "host," as he was expected to pay back whatever treatment was received. By honoring his "guest-friend" with expensive gifts, an aristocrat could display his wealth and honor (the two were virtually synonymous). In book 6 of the *Iliad*, Diomedes and Glaukos agree not to fight one another because their ancestors had once entered into a guest-friend relationship.

Alongside this legal-ethical-religious current, and constantly intersecting it, runs the rich stream of actual Greek practices regarding the gods.

The vision of how the divine operates, in the world of epic, accords in one central way with what is known of Greek ritual: reciprocity predominates. But in other domains, the archaeological and historical record does not offer immediate help to interpret the poems. Major differences between the two fields occur in terms of emphasis. Thus, in the historical context of Homer, the major temple sites of Zeus, Athene, and Hera played a role in organizing the community. Apollo's oracles in Delphi and Asia Minor had a significant presence starting in the eighth century BC, but we hear little of these. Chryses is his priest, but oracles are not mentioned in this connection; Achilleus alludes to Delphi at 9.405 without commenting on the function of the shrine. In the *Iliad*, we see that Athene's shrine is at the center of Troy (disconcertingly, since she is opposed to the Trojans). Dionysos, worshiped as early as the Mykenaian period and extremely popular, does not appear and is hardly mentioned in the poem, except for a mythic reminiscence in book 6 (132–40). The same goes for Demeter, whose mystery cults and women's rituals at Eleusis, Athens, and many other sites argue for a much greater role in real Greek life than one would imagine for her, given only the *Iliad*. Hermes and Hephaistos do get cameo roles in the *Iliad*, but their presence, especially in Athenian worship, was much greater.

Of course, war conditions prevail, meaning that the Greeks are removed from their own territory: consequently, we do not see "normal" religious behavior, or get only a stylized, brief look at it. The sacrifices to gods that occur in the poem (at oath-taking, for example) in actual Greek practice would have been a regular part of starting military campaigns and seeking success while in progress. From later sources, we know that seers (like Kalchas) did interpret omens; that feasts and drinking parties accompanied sacrifices (as in the Greek camp); and that prayer, with vows to dedicate and with liquid libations, were deeply embedded in the rituals of Greek life.

Overall, the delicate stirring of reality into fiction within Homeric poetry means that it is almost impossible to separate out ingredients, much less date them. Although the institution of hero cult had been recognized as having some relation to the imagined heroes of the *Iliad*, for centuries it was thought that such heroic burials in the poem as that of Patroklos were mostly fantasy. In 1980, archaeologists working at Lefkandi on the island of Euboea found within a large mound the grave of a man and woman, along with signs that they had been buried inside a monumental building, resembling a later Greek temple. The tomb complex has been dated to around 950 BC, the Dark Age between the end of the Mykenaian kingdoms and

the eighth-century "renaissance" in Greece, or between the fall of Troy and
the rise of Homeric poetry. The man's ashes, wrapped in a cloth, were kept
in a bronze amphora imported from Cyprus; a sword and other weapons
lay nearby. The uncremated remains of the woman (a hero's consort? Or
was he hers?) were accompanied by expensive jewelry, again imported, and
including a Babylonian gorget, apparently a centuries-old heirloom at the
time it was buried. Bones of four horses that had apparently been sacri-
ficed were also in the tomb. The whole scene strikingly resembles that of
23.164–77. Does this mean that the *Iliad* poet knew somehow of extraor-
dinary burial customs at least two centuries before his time? That would be
the most positivist sort of answer, taking poetry as a secondary receptor of
historical events. Conversely, could the elite residents of Lefkandi already
have been listening to heroic poetry, not unlike our *Iliad*, that inspired
them to copy what they believed had been the habits of Mykenaian-era
royalty? This approach would incorporate "mentalities" into our view of
the Greek past. Most likely, the truth lies in the constant interplay of fact
and fiction, "real" practices and imagined, "history" always being not just
material (urns, burials, buildings) but "spiritual," too—the poetry and song
through which people live. In this sense the *Iliad* itself was a historical
phenomenon with its own power to make things happen.

## HOMERIC QUESTIONS AND SOME MODERN ANSWERS

There exists a Homeric "question" (more accurately *questions*) because no
reliable information about a historical Homer exists. It is not known who
composed the *Iliad* or *Odyssey*, when, where, for what audience, and how.

Guesses abound. For many readers in antiquity, Homer was a revered,
albeit shadowy, figure whose works included not only the two major ep-
ics about Troy and its aftermath, but also a picaresque tale (*Margites*—a
few scraps of which survive), shorter heroic poems concerning Troy and
Thebes, a mock epic called *Batrachomyomachia* ("Battle of the Frogs and
Mice"), brief epigrams, longer hymns to the gods, prayers, and curses. A
handful of *Lives* of Homer, probably dating to the second century AD (but
embedding earlier materials) attempted to fill in the missing details. Ac-
cording to these amusing compilations of folktale and legend, Homer was
the illegitimate son of a woman from Aeolis, the Greek-speaking region
of Asia Minor near Troy. After journeys as far as Ithaca (during which he
loses his sight), Homer returns to Ionia, the region of the central coast of

what is now western Turkey, and wanders from city to city, performing in civic centers and cobblers' shops, bargaining with his hosts for food and employment, several times even trading his precious poems, before setting out for Athens but on his way expiring on the island of Ios.

The *Lives* are obviously aimed at explaining the dialect mix of Homeric poetry (Aeolic and Ionic), finding "real" models for characters in the poems, and giving a nod to local lore. Seven main contenders vied for the honor of being his birthplace, their names (with suspect neatness) fitting a hexameter verse: "Smyrna, Chios, Colophon, Salamis, Rhodos, Argos, Athenai." As for his dates, ancient opinion ranged from a century after the Trojan War itself (according to Eratosthenes) to around 1000 BC (the Homeric critic Aristarchus) through a rather hazy period around 850 BC (Thucydides and Herodotus) all the way down to the seventh century: the historian Theopompus thought Homer was contemporary with the lyric poet Archilochus, flourishing around 650 BC. The last-mentioned deserves attention since Theopompus, coming from Chios, might have had privileged sources. Chios looms above the other proposed birth spots for several reasons. At least two poets from the archaic period apparently refer to Homer as the "man from Chios" (Simonides, and the author of the *Hymn to Apollo*, who identifies himself as the "blind man" from that rocky isle). And the Homeridai ("descendants of Homer"), a widely known guild of "rhapsodes," or traveling performers of Homeric poetry, made the island their base. Furthermore, a sense of the past ran deep on Chios: an inscription from the fifth century BC, honoring the Chian official Heropythos, tallies his ancestors going back fourteen generations.

A small group of critics named "Separators" (*Khôrizontes*) thought Homer had written only the *Iliad*, while the *Odyssey* was another man's work. But most readers in antiquity, including professional scholars, were satisfied with whatever patchy or fantastic information they possessed concerning the author. Not even the most hardened cynic doubted that Homer the master poet once existed. Then again, we should remember, the Greeks with unerring instinct managed to find a single master figure, person or god, for every one of their cultural achievements, ranging from meat sacrifice to the horse bit. If Homeric poetry existed, that must mean there had been a Homer.

The rational approaches of the Enlightenment (including the new "scientific" study of sacred texts) and burgeoning Romantic notions about "primitive" poetry led in the eighteenth century to a crisis of belief in the productions of an individual genius named Homer. The new skepticism about whether one person had composed the epics as we have them relied on bits of ancient evidence. The Hellenistic Jewish historian Josephus (circa 37–100 AD), seeking to show how recently Greek literature had arisen compared to Hebrew, asserted that Homer was illiterate and his works were preserved as songs and put together much later (*Against Apion* 1.12). A few other ancient sources reported that this assembling of the *Iliad* and *Odyssey* happened during the rule of Peisistratos and his sons in Athens (560–510 BC), when rhapsodic contests in Homeric recitation were established at the great Panathenaic games, and rules were put in place to ensure the correct sequence of episodes (apparently so no one rhapsode could get a competitive edge by grabbing the most gripping parts first).

Aware of such anecdotes, several scholars even in the Renaissance denigrated the style and overall design of the epics, noting their roughness and repetitiveness as compared with the elegant Latin epic of Virgil (considered the apogee of poetic style at the time). Later, the Abbé d'Aubignac (1604–1676), tutor of Richelieu's nephew, held Homer to the standard of French classicism and found him sadly lacking in politeness and good taste. His *Conjectures académiques ou Dissertation sur l'Iliade* (written in the 1660s, but not published until 1715) took the side of the moderns in what would soon become a "quarrel" with the tyranny of ancient literature. "Homer" had never existed; the poetry attributed to him represented simply a disorderly mass of separate compositions compiled sometime in the fourth century BC.

On the other side of the Channel, the depiction of humble things, and plain speaking, were virtues of Homer, as imagined by the Scottish scholar Thomas Blackwell (1701–1757). His book, *An Inquiry into the Life and Writings of Homer* (1735), sought to elevate the poor poet of Asia Minor above all who had written afterward. Blackwell treated Homer as a largely improvising singer, called him "bard," and noted his resemblance to the medieval Provençal troubadours, as a wandering minstrel with a good knowledge of men, lands, and manners. Such a view is understandable, coming in the same decades that saw a renewed appreciation of Chaucer's importance and Thomas Percy's recovery of fifteenth-century English verses (*Reliques of Ancient Poetry*, 1765). Blackwell also paved the way for readier appreciation of James Macpherson's hugely influential *Fingal* (1761) and *Temora* (1763), alleged translations of ancient Gaelic heroic ballads attributed to "Ossian" that he claimed (falsely) to have collected in the Highlands. To make the Classical analogy clearer, Macpherson himself translated the *Iliad* (1773) into a rhythmic prose even more primitive than the epic songs of his fictional ancient Scot.

Thus destabilized by both modernists and primitivists, the image of a magisterial literate poet Homer was toppled by two publications of the century's end. In 1788, J. B. C. d'Ansse de Villoison published the earliest full manuscript of the *Iliad*, Venetus Marcianus Graecus 454.[6] This precious codex preserved a great mass of marginal commentary compiled from ancient monographs on Homer. For the first time, scholars could see that thousands of lines from the texts that had been accepted as Homeric had as early as the third century BC been called into question by one or another learned critic—Zenodotus, Aristophanes of Byzantium, and the greatest of all, Aristarchus. They were either not in the right linguistic form, not in the right place in the poem, or not appropriate in tone or style for the august Homer. Then, in 1795, *Prolegomena ad Homerum*, a small book by the brilliant German classicist Friedrich August Wolf (1759–1824) drew logical conclusions from the newly available notes: an illiterate Homer may have composed heroic songs at an early period that were then passed down orally for generations, but the additions and distortions of countless rhapsodes and editors meant that he probably wasn't the person who left us the *Iliad* and *Odyssey* in the form we have them.

Wolf's careful study started a deconstructive craze that consumed the energy of a century of Homerists. Scores of scholars spent careers sorting out "real" from false Homer, authentic verses from interpolations, padded episodes from the kernel elements of the epics (sometimes reckoned at just a few thousand lines). Finding Homer became so difficult that it was much easier to invent your own, as J. V. Cunningham summarized the resulting effusion:[7]

> Homer was poor. His scholars live at ease
> Making as many Homers as you please.
> And every Homer furnishes a book.
> Though guests be parasitic on the cook
> The moral is: *It is the guest who dines.*
> I'll write a book to prove I wrote these lines.

By the early twentieth century, the French Homerist Victor Bérard (known as one of James Joyce's main informants about the *Odyssey*) could characterize the "Homeric question" in religious terms. Describing the state of scholarship after a century of destructive Analyst criticism, Bérard said: "In 1890 the infallible church of the critics demanded that each catechumen renounce Homer, his existence and his works, the fraternity of the two poems and the unity of each one." By contrast, noted Bérard, at the time of his own writing, after another aesthetic revolution, the "Unitarians" were in the ascendant. Homer had been resuscitated; it was he who had composed both *Iliad* and *Odyssey* according to rules of art, with their admirable style. It could be that very little in the poems was *originally* his, but without him we would not have the poems. Faith and love, says Bérard, are apparently the only ways that can lead us back to Him.[8]

Bérard published these words in 1924. The same year, a twenty-two-year-old Californian, Milman Parry, fresh out of Berkeley, arrived in Paris with his wife and small child to work with Victor Bérard on a doctorate focused on Homeric style. With the completion of Parry's dissertation four years later, the real revolution in Homeric studies began.

Parry was interested in the style of Homer, on which he had completed a master's thesis. He approached this the way one investigates the style of Jane Austen or John Milton—as a phenomenon with consistent tendencies and conventions, idiosyncrasies and predictabilities. Parry found precisely these things, but also discovered that Homer's could not be a style invented or developed by any *one* poet. By 1924, several philologists had already demonstrated that Homeric Greek contains a mixture of dialect forms, innovations, and archaisms governed by *metrical convenience*. That is why, for example, there exist five different forms for "of me" (the genitive of the personal pronoun *ego*) in Homeric diction, each with a different metrical shape. They are useful depending on what the poet needed to fit into the dactylic hexameter verse at a given point (something like the way nineteenth-century poets use English *o'er* and *e'er* versus the two-syllable *over* and *ever*). Duplicates in meaning existed only when their metrics were distinct. Parry found the same "economy" at work when he meticulously investigated the well-known system of adjectives applied to the important personages of the poems. "Achilleus of the swift feet" and "crafty" or "brilliant" Odysseus are at other lines described in the poetry as "shining Achilleus" or "Odysseus of many designs." When this happens, there is no perceptible shift in the narrative's emphasis, but the phrases involved match a different metrical shape (*podas ōkus Akhilleus*, for example, is two syllables longer than *dios Akhilleus*). Parry proved that for each and every major heroic and divine figure in Homer there existed one (and almost always only one) epithet per grammatical case. Therefore, Homeric poetry represents a multigenerational art form: no one poet would have devised a system so large, tight, and pervasive. It was most likely created for the rapid composition of verse and passed down as part of a popular art form, from older to younger poets. In a word, it was traditional, not individual.

It was only in a second phase of his research that Parry and his collaborator Albert Lord found through fieldwork in the former Yugoslavia, in the early 1930s, that similar extensive and convenient phraseological systems were employed by demonstrably illiterate performers of traditional heroic poetry. Lord, after the tragic early death of Parry in 1935, continued to visit the Balkans, eventually publishing the landmark presentation of their work in *The Singer of Tales* (1960). That volume makes the first sustained case for the proposition that Homeric poetry was indeed oral poetry, that is to say that it was the product of "composition-in-performance"—the poet putting together the epic on the fly each time it was sung to an audience, from a well-stocked storehouse of traditional words and narrative templates.

Since the first edition of Lord's study, more than five thousand books and articles relating to oral-traditional poetics in at least ninety languages, from the Native American West to the White Mountains of Crete to rural Japan, have emerged. From the behavior of the Homeric simile to the poetics of speeches and embedded genres such as lament and proverb, from associations with myth and hero cult to studies of type-scenes and cognitive scripts, the investigations prompted by Parry and Lord's groundbreaking work have clarified more of Homeric epic than any other scholarly advance since antiquity. What answers has this body of work provided to the Homeric question? Many aspects of it are now no longer either/or dilemmas. In a long and multiplex oral tradition, we can no longer expect to pinpoint the inventor of any given phrase, scene, or plot—and yet it is not only possible but in many places expected for individual poets to repurpose, reinvent, and add constantly to the tradition. Social contexts and competition are also crucial. As Minna Skafte Jensen has put it, compositions of the scale and beauty of our epics "must have sprung from an environment where many Homers were singing and where other long beautiful poems were produced besides the *Iliad* and the *Odyssey*."[9]

Despite such awareness, however, there is still some resistance to the notion that the tradition of the Homeric poems was, until quite late, open-ended, constantly subject to recomposition depending on performance contexts. Eight decades of oralist work have not managed to dislodge one major objection to the evidence that would closely connect the *Iliad* and *Odyssey* to the dynamics of oral tradition. This objection holds that the Homeric poems are *different* from other works with which they have been compared, because they are better; and they are *better* because they were the singular masterwork of a master poet—Homer—who may have employed the conventions of oral tradition but *transcended* them in making monumentally big epics. Proponents of a "big bang" theory of Homeric textualization believe that a one-time event, either the activity of an oral poet who learned to write, or a compressed series of dictations, produced the epics. The motive and opportunity for such an event are still difficult to imagine.[10]

By contrast, a multiple-event model seems more realistic. Gregory Nagy's present-day approach to the development of the Homeric epics offers the most plausible one. Nagy's theory, as formulated in the 1996 book *Homeric Questions* and expanded in *Homer the Classic* (2009), posits five stages in an evolutionary development from earliest beginnings near the time of the Trojan War: a fluid stage lasting from the second millennium through the mid-eighth century, in which there are a large variety of heroic poems and no written texts; a Panhellenic stage from mid-eighth century to mid-sixth century BC, during which time, with no written texts, a crystallization process has set in concerning what is accepted as Homeric by communities throughout the Greek world. The spread of rhapsodes out of the Greek east and the rise of regional festivals probably assisted this. After the hinge Peisistratean period (mid to late sixth century), there comes a definitive period centered on Athens, with potential texts arising from transcripts that aided rhapsodes and judges in what had become the major Homer-centered event, the Panathenaic contests. From an eventually established Athenian text, successive standardizations in the late fourth century at Athens and at Alexandria in the third and second centuries took place, with the continuing influence of rhapsodes, still performing their sometimes idiosyncratic versions, in evidence. Nagy's views of the *longue durée* of Homeric poetry never deny the possibility that one or more "genius" composers could have shaped the tradition at some point. But the individual genius is not required. Put another way, the genius of Homeric poetry is the powerful and flexible imaginative conception that keeps renewing itself through generations of performers and audiences.

The generations now alive may be in the optimal position to appreciate the style of the *Iliad*. Those familiar with the Westerns of John Ford, the samurai sagas of Akira Kurosawa, or American battle films from *Apocalypse Now* to *The Hurt Locker* understand how a sweeping scope and close-up cinematic realism can memorably portray the stories of individual soldiers. That is to say, Homeric epic already has developed the major tropes and techniques of the modern war movie. Thinking of the *Iliad* in visual terms, as the original blockbuster, can bring us closer to its greatness as verbal art.

First, its size must be taken into account. Experimental readings have shown that a full performance of the poem would take twenty-four hours. (The closest film equivalent might be Fassbinder's *Berlin Alexanderplatz* of 1983, running fifteen hours.) Plausible break points occur at the ends of book 8 and book 16, giving the whole composition a neat triadic structure of the type that every contemporary scriptwriter's manual recommends. Perhaps it was sung or recited in the course of three-day festivals, known from the archaic period onward. The most immediate consequence of the *Iliad*'s monumental proportions is its characteristic fullness, the sense that a world of experience has been packed into its 15,693 lines. And this, in turn, is achieved through several identifiable stylistic strategies. That the invention of a large epic automatically entailed such techniques cannot be proven, since smaller heroic poems from the period do not survive. That the Homeric poems are distinctive, however, was already seen in the fourth century BC by Aristotle (who had many shorter Cyclic epics for comparison). In the *Poetics*, his analysis of literary history and theory, he noted that Homer "takes only one portion of the story and makes use of many episodes, such as the Catalogue of Ships and others by means of which he diversifies his poetry. But the others make their poems about one person, one time, one action having many parts, as the composer of the *Kupria* and the *Little Iliad* did" (1459a35–1459b5). Homeric epic was unified but did not attempt to tell all, while the Cyclic epics comprised strung-together events, attempting a much longer expanse.

As Aristotle recognized, Homeric technique is that of the dramatist. This is what makes the highly concentrated *Iliad*, in which four days of fighting and two days of truce occupy all of books 2 through 22, so powerful. And yet a drama would have been only one-tenth as long. What makes the epic monumental is a further basic principle of *retardation*. The plots of both the *Iliad* and the *Odyssey* involve suspense. Will Odysseus make it home to Ithaca? Will Achilleus rejoin the battle in time? (One might wonder, in fact, whether it was the demand for long compositions that created such plots in the first place.) There are several ways of achieving the necessary delay. Given the plot of the *Iliad* (Zeus' promise to honor Achilleus by letting the Trojans succeed until the need for the hero's aid is desperate), a recurrent trick is to have the Greeks actually succeed, either through the valor of other warriors (Diomedes and the chieftains in book 11) or by the machinations of meddling gods (Poseidon and Hera in books 13 and 14). Another strategy is to repeat scenarios: the duel between Menelaos and Paris in book 3 is echoed by that between Aias and Hektor in book 7. Battle descriptions operate with an elaborate set of conventions, which produce gripping close-ups while actually delaying the major plot events in the story of Achilleus' wrath. The heroic *aristeia* (performance of prowess) is a primary poetic device. Five such displays support the middle arc of the poem: those of Diomedes (book 5), Agamemnon (11), Hektor (15), Patroklos (16), and Achilleus (19 through 22). The catalogic technique—listing the named victims of a warrior, with kaleidoscopic variations on their deaths—is closely related (e.g., the lists starting at 5.35 and 5.703).

The most obvious example of diversifying the narrative, noted already by Aristotle, is the Catalogue of Ships (2.494–759), which even some critics thought to be separable from the main composition. Nearly four hundred lines long (including the Trojan catalogue), it fulfilled many functions by presenting a vivid sense of the sheer numbers of fighters, recording for posterity the Greek city-states involved (and thus no doubt propping up local pride), increasing suspense before the long-awaited meeting of Paris and Menelaos, and displaying the powers of the poet and his Muse. Helen's miniature Catalogue of Greeks (in the "wall-viewing" or *teikhoskopia* scene of book 3) has a similar role, while characterizing her and her father-in-law Priam. Just as the Catalogue of book 2 comes one book in from the start of the poem, the funeral games of book 23 hold a symmetrical place in terms of the overarching poetic structure, one from the end. This episode too, though sometimes seen as a digression, can better be understood as a vital part of the compositional dynamic, a cooling-down diversion that in turn prepares an audience for Achilleus' quiet, tearful meeting with Priam in the final book. The finale, meanwhile, mirrors the opening of the poem: an aged father, in each, comes at great risk to the Greek camp to ransom a child (Chryseis/Hektor) and is met by a chieftain—though with opposite results. Such large-scale patterning suggests that the *Iliad* has been planned and plotted as an organic and rounded whole. This holds true even for the apparent digressions—a better word would be "elaborations"—in the epic. Foreshadowing (as in Zeus' predictions at 8.470 and 15.62, and the dying words of Hektor and Patroklos) reinforces the tightness of the composition.

Sixty percent of the *Iliad* is character speech. Here, too, one can see how a retarding, elaboration strategy becomes multifunctional, providing characterization and interest, color, exposition, and variation in voice and tone. Such matters must have been particularly entertaining to an audience listening to a rhapsode do all the voices. Like everything in the *Iliad*, speeches follow some basic templates, but no two patterns are ever exactly the same. Unless one appreciates Greek culture's powerful and persistent assertion that artful language deeply matters—that one must become, as Achilleus was, a "speaker of words and one accomplished in action" (9.443)—the obsession of Homeric poetry with the representation of every speech may remain puzzling. (Plato, on the other hand, pinpointed this mimetic technique as the central danger emanating from Homeric epic when he banned it from the ideal city-state of *The Republic*.)

Homeric poetry calls its most powerful utterances *muthoi* (the word which gives us, after several semantic shifts, "myth"). Such speeches have their own internal poetics in Homer. Moreover, comparative work shows that the types of speeches designated *muthoi* in Homer are in other living oral cultures social, nonpoetic yet formal genres of self-presentation: insults, commands, and memorializations of the past. When Agamemnon makes his powerful speech against Chryses (1.26) and Achilleus his splendid speech of rejection (9.307), they employ this "genre" of speaking, which always asserts the authority of the speaker. Nestor is best known for mastery of the art. He specializes in idiosyncratic renditions of martial glories in which he participated but that are almost mythical to his younger audiences (e.g., 11.669). Other subgenres of speech in the poem include prayers, laments, supplications, boasts, rebukes, public addresses to assemblies, advice-giving, and monologues addressed to one's own heart (e.g., 11.404, 17.91, 21.553, 22.99). The varied ways in which individual figures deploy these rhetorical resources tell us—without the narrator having to be explicit—much about their characters.

An essential aspect of the style of Homeric speeches—their pointed-ness—emerges from the way they are paired and linked. In this the *Iliad* displays a fine consciousness that speech events do not take place in isolation but confront unpredictable hearers, with the concurrent complications of switched addressees, failures to respond, and interruptions. The buildup of drama in book 1, for example, has much to do with the poet's artful blocking out of a five-person speech exchange, a turbulent stream of talk flowing from lines 59 through 305, but divided into five distinct and symmetrical smaller movements, that can be graphed like this:

Achilleus-Kalchas-Achilleus-Kalchas;
Agamemnon-Achilleus-Agamemnon-Achilleus;
Achilleus-Athene-Achilleus;
Achilleus to Agamemnon (no response)
Nestor-Agamemnon-Achilleus

The effect is operatic, creating emotional intensity through impassioned response but within a measured, circular structure that returns continually to the voice of the protagonist. Similar structures can be found in every book of the poem.

If the voices of Homeric characters are so prominent, that of the narrator, by contrast, is barely heard. The poet rarely intervenes to comment on the action, a restraint that makes such moments as his observation about Achilleus' summoning Patroklos (11.603: "the beginning of his evil") all the more ominous, like the voice of omniscient Zeus. A few times, he expresses dismay at witless behavior, as when Glaukos makes a bad exchange of armor (6.234) or the Trojans fail to heed the good advice of Poulydamas (18.311). To a few characters, at some times, the narrator speaks directly, as to Patroklos nearing his death (16.787). But there is another well-known device whereby an audience does hear, implicitly but more frequently, a narrator's individual voice and whereby, furthermore, the plotline gets elaborated and delayed: the simile.

Approximately 180 developed similes (that is, more than a phrase "like a lion" or "like fire") punctuate the *Iliad*. The technique is, again, multifunctional. Like movie theme music, it has a rhythmic as well as an emotional role. Increasing the frequency of similes enables the poet to emphasize the most dramatic portions of the action. Thus, as the troops of Greeks advance in the first mass-movement scene of the poem, an upswell of no fewer than six similes marks the moment (2.459). In battle scenes, the simile acts like a freeze-frame or a cutaway shot, allowing us to achieve a species of double vision. A dying warrior's head becomes, briefly, a garden poppy bowed down by rain (8.305). A god's healing wound switches, for an instant, to a dish of curdling milk (5.901). Similes are both musical and visual in their ability to counterpoint. Most often, the agony of battle is momentarily transmuted by them into familiar or affecting domestic scenes—a poor widow weighing wool (12.433), flies around a milk pail (16.641), a boy building sandcastles (15.362). Through detailed comparisons, the poet introduces worlds apart from the hot field at Troy, whether wild nature (forest fires, roaming carnivorous beasts) or humans at peace (harvesters and woodsmen, women washing clothes). Through creating the sense of alternative side-spaces, the poem concentrates attention on what is distinctive about the main action on which it dwells.

The art of the simile, with vivid immediacy, makes tangible the most difficult of ideas—the action of gods. Imagine the way Iris, the divine messenger, drops to earth (like the weight on a fishing line: 24.80), and the swift movement of Hera (like the thoughts of a traveler: 15.82). A simile can evoke terrified flight from approaching death by recalling a much more common experience, the way in which, in a bad dream, one cannot run fast enough to catch up (22.199). In short, similes work like miniature lyric poems enabling a narrator to express a range of attitudes toward the story being told. They are the link to the consciousness of the poet; through them an audience, almost unconsciously, takes on his panoramic view.

For all their stupendous variety (rarely being repeated exactly), similes are still remarkably formulaic. The work of Carroll Moulton and William Scott on their "oral" nature shows how a small number of elements can be almost infinitely combined to produce remarkable images. Compare, for example, the similes that occur near the start of two adjacent sections, books 9 and 10. Both revolve around a single phrase "in the breast" (en[i] stêthessin: 9.8, 10.9), and describe, respectively, the turbulent emotions of the Greek troops in general and of their leader, Agamemnon. The shared simile template is a description of weather effects seen from above in relation to a flat surface beneath. In the first instance, it is winds that suddenly clash on the sea, causing waves to crest and "far across the salt water scatters the seaweed." In the second vignette, the tense beating of the commander's heart is compared to unrelenting rain, hail, or a blizzard "when the snowfall scatters on ploughlands." Uniting these images are the juxtapositions of internal human emotional states with wide-screen meteorological views, a painterly contrast of darkness with white flecks (wave crests, snowflakes) and finally, shared diction.

Such simile-generated associations also play a larger role, structuring the poem. In the case just mentioned, upon hearing of Agamemnon's emotional condition as book 10 opens, the audience is prompted through imagery to recall the disturbed state of his troops seven hundred lines earlier: their leader feels as they do (but the poet shows this rather than says it). An exact repetition of similes, at a much greater distance from one another, constructs another striking analogy of character and situation. Agamemnon, in distress at Greek losses, stands up to address the assembled fighters "shedding tears like a spring dark-running" (9.14). The only other occurrence of this image, in very similar wording, comes when Patroklos beseeches Achilleus to take pity on the losing Greek forces (16.3). The dark spring simile thus precisely pinpoints two structurally cognate moments in the narrative, the embassy that will fail to sway the withdrawn hero (book 9) and the companion's plea that will inevitably trigger his return. Furthermore, it contrasts the ethos and rhetoric of Agamemnon and Patroklos: one helpless in the face of the crushing Trojan advance, the other hopeful that he himself can help; the commander proposing that the Greeks leave (9.27), and the subordinate warrior urging intervention in battle (16.38).

Even when similes are not themselves repeated, the poet of the *Iliad* manages to insinuate within the narrative itself their distinctive language, creating further rich resonances between the "real" plot and imaginary, peripheral views. This occurs particularly in the last half of the poem, when image-dense descriptive passages follow upon, or foreshadow, the formal similes with increasing frequency. A number of imagistic strands can be traced. For example, Achilleus' return to the field of battle, clad in divine armor, is celebrated with an elaborate simile comparing him to the moon, to a star, and to the gleam of fire, blazing on a distant mountain, as seen from the sea by sailors whom winds are bearing away from land-bound friends (19.374–81). When he speeds in his gleaming bronze and gold toward Troy, Achilleus is first espied by Priam, to whom he seems like a star— specifically, like Orion's Dog (Sirius), most prominent in autumn and a sign of distress and fever. Focalization through the eyes of the father of Hektor, whom Achilleus will soon slay, invests the shining description of the hero with darker meaning, while picking up on the minor note of loss in the earlier simile (sailors leaving friends). Wind, fire, and loss are subsequently all combined in the actual narrative of book 23, when Achilleus bids Boreas and Zephyros (the same winds as in the simile at 9.5) to blow aflame the pyre of his dead friend (23.194–218). All night Achilleus makes continual libations, calling on his lost companion (23.218–21). The poet switches to a simile (23.222–25) comparing Achilleus to a father who mourns while burning his son's bones—but this combination of act and image in turn echoes the actual prayer and libation of "shining wine" to "Zeus father" made by Achilleus at the moment Patroklos set out to imitate him and turn the battle (16.229–48). The entire, tightly arranged crescendo of evocative representations concludes with another star, the one that heralds Dawn's light about to spread over the sea (23.226–28).

The formulas permeating Homeric poetry may not be immediately obvious precisely because, as with similes, the master poets of this tradition learned so well how to vary and redeploy familiar phrases and runs of lines. The general principle of repetition with variation is most visible in two further techniques, type-scenes and epithets. But these are only individual points along a spectrum of adjacent poetic patterns that includes repeated single words in one metrical slot, whole lines, speech-framing devices, and stereotyped descriptions of motions and gestures. Once recognized by readers, these strategies can lead to fruitful comparisons of scenes and characters, providing a key to deeper meaning.

"Type-scenes" are repeated sequences of actions, employing similar language each time. Arming, supplication, assembling, and hospitality are prominent among the ready-made sequences. Unlike the similes, the variation in type-scenes comes through expansion or contraction. Thus, an ideally full sacrifice scene contains twenty-one elements, but reduced versions may have only half this many features. Within the first two books of the *Iliad*, one finds typically varied scenarios. When the Greeks return Chryseis to her father they offer an animal sacrifice. After washing of hands and scattering of barley, there is a prayer (adapted to the circumstances); the victims are slaughtered and skinned; thigh meat is cut and wrapped in fat, with shreds of flesh placed on the lumps. These are burnt, vitals are tasted, and better cuts of meat are then grilled and consumed (1.447–66). By contrast, at 2.402–429 a single ox is slain; no altar or handwashing is mentioned; the prayer is not fulfilled; wine is not poured on the offerings; and there is no mention of men standing around prepared for a meal. There are minor additions, however: the skewers of wood are leafless, the fire is that of Hephaistos. Such small variations cannot in themselves signify large differences. But what does emerge from the juxtaposition is the brusque, war-hastened quality of Agamemnon's camp sacrifice, as opposed to the leisurely homecoming celebration conducted by Chryses.

Other close comparisons of type-scenes yield similar suggestive differences. While with similes it was frequency that signaled dramatic spikes in the plot, the poet uses expansion to indicate important moments in type-scenes. The typical arming process, for instance, can be accomplished in nine lines (e.g., 3.330): greaves, corselet, sword, shield, helmet. But the entry of the great king Agamemnon into battle calls for a type-scene three times as long. The history and splendor of each piece is highlighted (the corselet a gift from Kinyras, the shield a tenfold construction of bronze). It is precisely because the audience knows the simplex form of the scene that they can appreciate and marvel all the more at the elaborated complex form. The same goes for brief battle clashes versus the baroque, extended runs that characterize the *aristeia* of each champion.

As with similes, repetition supports larger narrative structures. The type-scene of supplication is bound up with a net of associations in the poem. There are two subtypes. First, in the midst of battle a fighter caught in a precarious situation may entreat his potential killer, grasping his knees, calling out for pity, and promising a share of the precious goods owned by his father, in return for being spared. Adrestos begs Menelaos for his life in this way (6.45), but Agamemnon's arrival on the scene cuts short any hope he had of being kept alive for ransom: the fiercer of the Atreid brothers kills the Trojan on the spot. An enemy spy, Dolon, uses similar language and tactics, asking to be taken alive by Odysseus and his companion Diomedes rather than slain outright on their night raid (10.378), and promising abundant ransom. Here, the poet creates tension by prolonging the typical scenario: after Odysseus interrogates Dolon for another eighty lines, and the spy finally reaches out to touch the Greek's chin in supplication, Diomedes decapitates the trembling Trojan. A third variation is even more elaborate: Achilleus marvels to find that Lykaon, whom he has already taken alive once and sold for ransom, has returned to the battle and fallen within his clutches again (21.65). Significant small changes make the scene resonate all the more: Lykaon reaches out to immobilize not only his would-be killer's knees but also his spear; he recites twenty lines of autobiographical detail, explaining how he has arrived a second time in dire straits; and then it is Achilleus who first brings up the mention of rich ransom (*apoina*), only to deny that he will ever pay it, in a ringing speech asserting that all mortals—including himself—must die.

Type-scenes spring from the routines of life, and consequently are marked with all the minor variations and major significance life holds. The second subtype is thematically connected with the first, but even more importantly it frames the entire *Iliad*. Rather than begging for life on the field and alluding to the wealth of fathers, the suppliants in the first and last books of the poem *are* fathers, asking for their children back. Chryses (1.12) offers *apoina* for his daughter Chryseis, the war prize of Agamemnon, who turns the priest away with wrathful words. Plague, death, and quarrel ensue, leading to the withdrawal of Achilleus. After the slaying of Hektor, Priam offers *apoina* to Achilleus (24.502) in order to retrieve his son's corpse. This time, the supplicated warrior, prompted by the gods and stirred by memory of his own father, accedes to the request.

The fundamental basis of this art of repetition and elaboration is the use of epithets. To any reader of Homer, such recurrent phrases stand out in the memory: "Achilleus of the swift feet," "strong-greaved Achaians," "Menelaos of the great warcry." As discussed above, the study of such elements led Milman Parry to speak of the traditional, and ultimately oral-performance, origins of Homeric verse making. But identifying a practical function for the formula (defined as any group of repeated words used under the same metrical conditions to express one idea) is one thing; they undoubtedly enabled performing poets to compose in the very act of performance (just as the best freestyling rap artists do today). Finding how the formula can aid literary interpretation is another. For all its predictability—with Achilleus being "brilliant" (*dios*) when two syllables are called for, "of the swift feet" (*podas ôkus*) when the hexameter line requires four—the formulaic phrase still contains meaning. Achilleus is never "of many machinations" (that is for Odysseus) even though the epithet can be made to fit the meter.

The formulaic system is neither mechanical nor empty. It simply embodies an unfamiliar aesthetic: rather than the exquisite, right word, specially selected for each passage (a Romantic poetic requirement), epic style creates audience expectations by consistent depiction—and then, for maximum effect, at key moments, violates the norm. Agamemnon, to take one instance, is addressed eight times in the *Iliad* and twice in the *Odyssey* with a full-line formula: "son of Atreus, most lordly, and king of men Agamemnon" (*Atreïdê kudiste, anax andrôn Agamemnon*). Yet at the very start of the poem (1.122) Achilleus calls him "son of Atreus, most lordly, *greediest for gain of all men.*" To a tradition-aware audience familiar with the formulaic system, this is shocking, more than it can ever be for the modern reader. For the line's meaning depends not just on what is said (a pretty straight insult), but on what is obviously not said and known to be omitted. Achilleus has artfully and boldly replaced the title *anax andrôn*, referring to his foe's acknowledged kingship, with a phrase implying that the king is without ethics. Such a pointed rhetorical usage implies a compositional method dependent on a connoisseur audience, an audience that must have developed a hypersensitivity to formulaic variation based on repeated hearings of many poems in this style. Comparative work in modern performance traditions, from Bosnia to Egypt, shows that this is the way oral-traditional art operates.

The final effect of such repetitions, from the shortest formula up to large-scale structural elements that recur in the *Iliad*, remains difficult to summarize. It can best be experienced from repeated reading. It makes for familiarity and certainty—sometimes comforting, sometimes bleak, since human brevities are seen for what they are. Sky, earth, houses, and above all, the sea and ships (which even in this, the landed epic, are still crucial)—these will typically be starry, black, close-built, swift (even when beached). We can depend on these archetypes, as if divine, in a world full of gods, to endure.

This rough sketch of stylistic devices cannot do justice to their complex and varied uses within the poem, for comment on which the reader is referred to the extensive line-by-line notes in this volume. Nor can discussion of style, however expansive, answer such questions as what the poem "means," taken as a whole. For that, each generation must make up its own mind; as the next section will show, readers and writers in every era see the poem in different ways. While each generation can seek to learn from the previous, its own view will necessarily vary depending on historical, social, and cultural circumstances. It has been taken as a story of one man's hubris, an arrogance bred from a sense of entitlement and power. Yet sometimes the hubris is pinned on Agamemnon, sometimes on Achilleus. Another interpretive bent would concentrate on the character of a heroic fighter faithful to an ideal and ready to die in its defense. But are we then talking about Hektor, loyal to Troy to the end? Or Achilleus, defender of the very notion of the reciprocal privileges of heroism, as represented by marks of honor? Is the *Iliad* a celebration of heroism or an interrogation of its basic—potentially flawed—assumptions? Whom should we emulate, if anyone, in this somber depiction of men and women under extreme conditions? Is it an elegy for a lost golden age, when people lived more outsized and exciting lives? Or is it a warning about the catastrophes such lives engender? Is it a poem meant to shore up the ideological underpinnings of a fading aristocracy of self-centered warlords? Or does it capture the first glimmerings of a communal consciousness of the type that emerged in increasingly democratic (or at least nonelite) institutions within the city-state? The experience of the *Iliad* inevitably becomes one of self-exploration and self-definition in the face of such open-ended interpretive options.

### RECEPTION AND TRANSLATION

Every modern reader of the *Iliad* stands in the shadow of those scores of previous readers who preserved and interpreted the poem. The text itself survived transitions of medium from oral poem to papyrus scroll to handwritten codex, then (in 1488, in the Florentine edition of Demetrius Chalcondyles) made the leap to the new technology of the printed book, and finally has become available, with the rest of Greek literature, in digital form. Alongside this remarkable transmission runs a rich history of reception. Painters and poets, composers and dramatists, choreographers, comic book artists, film directors, and makers of video games have made use of Homeric materials, in astonishing variations—too many even to be mentioned, let alone to be treated in detail here.

At the same time, it could be argued that no single successor has been able to match the power of the original. The movie *Troy* (2004), directed by Wolfgang Petersen, proved how daunting is the prospect. While thousands of works allude to or represent Achilleus, Hektor, Helen, and Paris, it is difficult to pinpoint a single artistic effort that takes on the task of reproducing the *Iliad* whole—freshly imagined but with equal epic scope. By contrast, the *Odyssey* has seen a number of artful full-scale recastings just in the past century, from James Joyce's *Ulysses* to Derek Walcott's *Omeros*. What makes the reception of the *Iliad* different?

A straightforward answer might point to the relative challenges of plot-driven versus character-driven stories. The *Odyssey* provides a satisfying ending: spouses reunited, a family reintegrated, a community revived. Indeed, the poem has been viewed as the template for subsequent comedy and romance. The *Iliad* is not such a happy tale; its strength lies elsewhere. Achilleus is as interesting and complex a character as Odysseus, but the latter cannot master his fate on a homecoming buffeted by Athene and Poseidon, whereas the former, with god-like rage, initiates and controls almost all the events in his tragic story. The *Iliad* is about the individual wrath of Achilleus; the *Odyssey*, about a man who, despite divine wrath, made it home.

Achilleus' character has grounded the post-Homeric treatments of the *Iliad* story. Successive generations turned him into an embodiment of manhood, of plain-spoken courage (opposed to the cunning, smooth rhetoric of Odysseus), an icon of valor, and sometimes a warning against uncontrollable feeling. His figure is ripe for contesting. The tragedian Aeschylus produced, sometime in the early fifth century BC, a trilogy about several episodes of the Trojan War, of which a few fragments remain. In the opening drama (*Myrmidons*), his Achilleus sat silent and unmovable as the embassy of Greeks begged for his return. A generation later, Aristophanes in the *Frogs* (lines 911–15) mocked Aeschylus (and by extension his Achilleus) by depicting the playwright as massive and mute in the face of the clever talker Euripides. In the *Iphigeneia at Aulis* of Euripides (produced 405 BC), Achilleus is somewhat naive, upright, and blunt, though less laconic. His fame has been exploited in a plot to lure Agamemnon's daughter into being sacrificed, under the false promise of marriage to the great hero. Achilleus, on discovering the ruse, characteristically reacts with a pledge to rescue her even though the entire army threatens him with stoning. Iphigeneia's would-be protector is saved only by the girl's acceptance of her fate.

That the relative merits and characters of Odysseus and Achilleus were a hot topic among Greek intellectuals in the early fourth century is clear from Plato's dialogue *Hippias Minor*. In another Platonic work, the *Apology*, the philosopher's teacher Socrates is portrayed as consciously following the example of Achilleus by refusing to avoid his own death penalty (28b–d). At yet another point, however, Plato makes his old teacher demonstrate that the epics are inappropriate for teaching the guardians of the ideal state, since Homer depicts the gods as angry, lustful, and deceptive, and heroes as overpowered by their emotions (*Republic* 377–91e).

Roman treatments were more one-sided. Cicero (106–43 BC) shared Plato's distrust of passion (as did the Stoics, Cicero's philosophical masters). In the *Tusculan Disputations*, Achilleus becomes the antitype of the *sapiens*, the wise man in charge of his feelings. The Homeric hero's anger (*ira*) verges on madness (*insania*) (*Tusc.* 3.9.18). Virgil, who alludes to Achilleus twenty-six times in the *Aeneid* (19 BC) insists on his role as the killer who once threatened the Trojans—the ancestors of Rome. Turnus, the final nemesis of the champion Aeneas, is predicted to be a sort of reincarnation of the Greek, *alius Achilles*: "in Latium another Achilleus is brought forth, the offspring of a goddess, as well," says the prophetic Sybil (*Aen.* 6.89–90). The *Achilleid* by the later Roman poet Statius (45–96 AD) remained unfinished (a fate that would befall identically named compositions by Goethe in 1797 and Richard Wagner in 1850). But even in the extant 1,127 lines covering his early years, Achilleus emerges as violent or dangerous, a menace to young animals and girls. The Greeks consider him *belligerum numen*, "a divinity of war" (*Achilleid* 1.504). This image of the warrior would predominate in the centuries to come.

The twenty-five-year-old Edward Gibbon, future author of *The History of the Decline and Fall of the Roman Empire* (1776–1789) noted the hero's contradictory appeal, recording in his diary for July 2, 1762:

> I reviewed the whole eighteenth book of the *Iliad*. Homer is never more thoroughly awake: the first part of it shews him to be a perfect master of the tender passions. Achilleus receives the news of the death of Patroklos, with a mixture of fury and tenderness suitable to his character. We begin to love him; and the very excess of his rage, though terrible, pleases us, because it is directed only against the murderer of his friend.[11]

The nineteenth century saw monumental expression of varied aspects of this powerful character. Overwhelming grief—that which beset him and which he later aroused—made the hero an apt reference point for the "Achilleion," a summer palace built in 1890 on Corfu by Empress Elizabeth of Austria, in memory of her son Rudolf, dead at thirty. Triumph in war is commemorated by the statue of Achilleus dedicated in 1822 at Hyde Park Corner, London, to the Duke of Wellington, and cast from cannons taken at Waterloo. French painters of the period, in particular, sought to capture the complex moods of Achilleus as we know them from the *Iliad*: resignation (Lefebvre's *Thetis Consoles Achilleus*, 1858), fear (Schopin's *Achilleus Pursued by Scamander*, 1831), and pity (*Priam at the Feet of Achilleus*—depicted by Langlois in 1809 and Wencker in 1876) stand out among dozens of large-scale realistic representations.

The sufferings of the first World War, however, damped enthusiasm for the heroic embodiment of violent passion and revenge. In the Gallipoli campaign of 1915 more than 130,000 soldiers died on both sides of the conflict over the Dardanelles—a few dozen kilometers from the site of ruined Troy. The English poet Laurence Binyon noted the irony that this far-away place was for many young men already deeply familiar:

Isles of the Aegean, Troy, and waters of Hellespont
You we have known from of old
Since boyhood stammering glorious Greek was entranced
In the tale that Homer told.
There scornful Achilles towered and flamed through the battle
Defying the gods; and there
Hektor armed and Andromache proudly held
Up his boy to him, knowing not yet despair.[12]

As in his earlier ode *For the Fallen* (1914), Binyon looked more to the modern winning of Homeric fame—"pale legendary glories by our own youth outdone"—than to the grimness of death. The mood is similar in the verses of another Englishman, Rupert Brooke, who died in April 1915 from septicemia contracted at Gallipoli and is buried on Skyros—the island where Achilleus, before the war, hid among the daughters of Lyko-medes. The young soldier Patrick Shaw-Stewart (1888–1917), who survived Gallipoli, is more realistic. Overlooking the ruins at Hisarlik, he invoked the ancient hero as a companion and protector (or was it rather to be his substitute, like Patroklos?):

Was it so hard, Achilleus,
So very hard to die?
Thou knewest and I know not—
So much the happier I.

I will go back this morning
From Imbros over the sea;
Stand in the trench, Achilleus,
Flame-capped, and shout for me.[13]

For the rest of the blood-soaked century, the tale of Achilleus mostly symbolizes pain. W. H. Auden subverts the shining world of the shield fashioned by Hephaistos in book 18, making it depict instead the horrors of total war, which Thetis cannot comprehend:

She looked over his shoulder
   For vines and olive trees,
Marble well-governed cities
   And ships upon untamed seas,
But there on the shining metal
   His hands had put instead
An artificial wilderness
   And a sky like lead.

A plain without a feature, bare and brown,
   No blade of grass, no sign of neighborhood,
Nothing to eat and nowhere to sit down,
   Yet, congregated on its blankness, stood
An unintelligible multitude,
   A million eyes, a million boots in line,
Without expression, waiting for a sign.[14]

Execution and rape, casual knifings and mindless obedience: the human reality makes a goddess blanch.

It must be noted that a different Achilleus coexisted in the imagination of the West: the lover. His relationship with Patroklos in the *Iliad* is one of close companionship, but already by the fifth century BC, Aeschylus explicitly made it homoerotic, with Achilleus recalling the thighs and kisses of his friend.[15] Plato in the *Symposium* (180a) has a member of the drinking party, Phaedrus, declare that the gods rewarded Achilleus with afterlife in the Isles of the Blest because he had stood by his older lover. The Middle Ages celebrated Achilleus' love for women: Briseis (a natural extrapolation from Homer); Deidameia, by whom he fathered Neoptolemos (not mentioned in the *Iliad*, but said in the *Cypria* to be his wife); and, most spectacularly, Polyxena, daughter of Priam. In the *Hecuba* of Euripides (circa 425 BC), the ghost of Achilleus is said to have appeared above his tumulus at the shore, commanding the Greeks to sacrifice Polyxena for his honor. His son Neoptolemos carries out the command. By the time of Seneca's *Trojan Women* (circa 53 AD), the sacrifice had been transformed into a wedding-to-death, with Achilleus demanding a bride to consort with him in Elysium. Some centuries later, *The History of the Fall of Troy* (fifth century AD?) attributed to one Dares of Phrygia purports to be the eyewitness account of the Trojan War by a soldier on the losing side. In this late antique Latin text, a full-blown romance has developed. Achilleus falls for Polyxena at first sight and even agrees to abandon his warring against her family's city if he is allowed to marry her. Lured by Hecuba, supposedly for this purpose, to the Trojan shrine of Apollo, he is ambushed by Paris and slain. The romantic version, with yet more flourishes (and moralizing) became highly influential in the Middle Ages, through a hexameter epic on the fall of Troy by the crusader-poet, Joseph of Exeter (circa 1184) and Benoît de Sainte-Maure's twelfth-century *Roman de Troie*. It is this theme that finds its way to Dante's *Inferno* (circa 1310–1320) where the poet is commanded by his guide Virgil to observe the spirits of the lustful sinners (canto 5, lines 6–66):

> Elena vedi, per cui tanto reo
> tempo si volse, e vedi 'l grande Achille
> che con amore al fine combatteo

In Laurence Binyon's translation (1933):

> See Helen, for whose sake the long years drew
> Ill after ill; see great Achilles there
> Who fought with love in the end and whom love slew.

Paradoxically, the two strands of ancient traditions intertwine, as killer and lover merge.

One could spend years following up such ramifications of the Homeric tale. The invaluable *Oxford Guide to Classical Mythology in the Arts, 1300–1900s* allots fourteen close-printed pages to the afterlife of Achilleus; similar statistics can be found for Hektor, Helen, and Paris. The *Iliad* is the ultimate reference point for such disparate works as Ingres' painting of Hektor bidding farewell to Andromache (1801); Schubert's *Lied* on the same theme (1815); *Helen at the Scaean Gate* by the Symbolist artist Gustave Moreau (circa 1880), Offenbach's comic opera *La belle Hélène*, and Edgar Allan Poe's poem *To Helen* (1823); Milton's *Paradise Lost* and Shakespeare's *Troilus and Cressida*; dances by Martha Graham; series of illustrations by Rubens, de Chirico, Flaxman, and D. G. Rossetti; watercolors by Romare Bearden; and choral works by Gustav Holst. In brief, when traced through its offshoots the poem offers entry to an entire education in Western culture.

Lattimore's work of 1951 comes at the end of one long tradition, Homeric translation as it had been practiced from the seventeenth through nineteenth centuries, and near the start of another, the contemporary rendition of Homeric verse. Like any such work, it is also a work of interpretation. His style treats the events and characters of the poem as not quite of our day: their sentences are longer, their diction a bit higher, the very slightest patina of antiquity marks the whole. But at the same time, Lattimore achieves a clarity, vigor, and strength of poetic line such as few had reached. To conclude this brief survey, it will be worthwhile to consider three translators coming before Lattimore, and three afterward, by way of one small target passage, Achilleus' refusal of the embassy, a rhetorical apogee (9.319–27):

### Richmond Lattimore (1951)

We are all held in a single honour the brave with the weaklings.
A man dies still if he has done nothing, as one who has done much.
Nothing is won for me, now that my heart has gone through its afflictions
in forever setting my life on the hazard of battle.
For as to her unwinged young ones the mother bird brings back
morsels, wherever she can find them, but as for herself it is suffering,
such was I, as I lay through all the many nights unsleeping,
such as I wore through the bloody days of the fighting,
striving with warriors for the sake of these men's women.[16]

### George Chapman (1611)

With equal honour cowards die and men most valiant,
The much performer and the man that can of nothing vant.
No overplus I ever found when, with my mind's most strife
To do them good, to dangerous fight, I have exposed my life.
But even as to unfeathered birds the carefull dam brings meate,
Which when she hath bestow'd, her selfe hath nothing left to eat:
So when my broken sleepes have drawn the nights t'extremest length
And ended many bloody daies with still-employed strength.
To guard their weakness and preserve their wives' contents infract,
I have been robd before their eyes . . .

This version, the first full *Iliad* ever in English, probably known to Shakespeare and made famous by the poem of Keats (*On First Looking into Chapman's Homer*), uses rhymes; ancient Greek poetry is never rhymed. The effect, reinforced by the ballad meter of the "fourteener," borders on singsong. Diction strikes us as archaic (*meate* for "food," *dam* for "mother"), or unexpected (native English *overplus*, instead of the more common French-derived *surplus*). These were not antiques at the time, however. As with Shakespeare, vigorous Anglo-Saxon words (*wives'*) ring up against Latinate (*infract*—meaning "unbroken"), and hard monosyllable endings mark off nearly every line. (Contrast Lattimore's run of three trailing-off end-words: *suffering/unsleeping/fighting*.) Surprisingly, three hundred years after, a few Chapman phrases can work unvaried or nearly (e.g., *bloody days; single honour/equall honour*). On the other hand, Chapman goes off track frequently: "preserve the wives' contents infract" is almost satirical, something not in Achilleus' tone here, or in the Homeric narrator's ever.

*Alexander Pope (1720)*

Fight or not fight, a like reward we claim,
The wretch and hero find their prize the same.
Alike regretted in the dust he lies
Who yields ignobly or who bravely dies.
Of all my dangers, all my glorious pains,
A life of labours, lo! What fruit remains?
As the bold bird her helpless young attends,
From danger guards them and from want defends;
In search of prey, she wings the spacious air,
And with the untasted food supplies her care;
For thankless Greece such hardships have I braved,
Her wives, her infants by my labours saved;
Long sleepless nights in heavy arms I stood,
And sweat laborious days in dust and blood.

Lattimore (and the Greek text that he follows exactly in terms of line-numeration) accomplish in nine verses what Pope does in a leisurely fourteen. His elaboration is the essence of Augustan-era "wit"—finding a clever point at each turn, making a punchy contrast where none was implied, inverting adverbs to give a pleasing chiastic shape to the line (*yields ignobly/ bravely dies*). It is far from Homer in a different way than Chapman—farther in tone and worldview, as far as chatter of the drawing room is from laconic talk on the battlefield (a thing known better to Elizabethans, as to Greeks). The underlining above marks the padding not found in the original. Some of the most ringing lines (e.g., *Who yields ignobly or who bravely dies*) are the least supported by the Greek (which in this case reads simply "there dies the man who does not work and one who has worked much").

### F. W. Newman (1856)

Like portion hath the stay-at-home     as though he bravely battled
And equal honour is assign'd     to cowards and to heroes.
Dieth alike the lazy man     and he who much hath laboured
Nor aught of vantage do I win     that hardiment I suffer
And alway jeopardize my life     in perilous encounter
But as the parent bird doth bear     unto her unfledg'd nestlings
Morsels of meat, whate'er she seize     and her own welfare slighteth
So likewise many a sleepless night     and bloody day of combat
Your consorts to regain have I     in war of men accomplished.

This is the translation that prompted the critic Matthew Arnold to issue his penetrating lectures "On Translating Homer." Newman lacked the literary gifts of his more famous brother, John Henry Newman (writer, Catholic convert, and eventual cardinal). His influences are obvious: Anglo-Saxon verse, with its strong central caesura; "heroic" poetry of the Icelandic sagas (then finding wide circulation in England); Tennyson; and the King James Version of the Bible. The aura is exactly that of the Pre-Raphaelites, at this period busy making "medieval" art out of ancient Greek myth. The Arthurian diction (*vantage, hardiment*) and the inverted verbal structures (*have I accomplished*) are meant to feel archaic, but end up muddying Homer's clear syntax. (To be fair, Newman did provide a glossary to his translation.) His defense was that he had tried to make an *Iliad* as it would have sounded to Greeks of the Classical age, centuries after Homer (something like Shakespeare, or in spots Robert Burns, would sound to the nineteenth-century Oxford ear).

Arnold, in response, denied that one could recover such effects. Rather than making the text strange, he urged that it be made clear, especially as the audience of the present day (not to mention to come) were Greekless, unable to test a translation for accuracy on their own. Four qualities should guide the translator, wrote Arnold: Homer is rapid, plain in diction, direct in matter and ideas, and noble. His lectures of 1861–1862 remain a touchstone for the exact criticism of poetic style.

Finally, we can compare Lattimore's with three outstanding versions produced after his. (In the interest of full disclosure, I must say that Fitzgerald taught me; Fagles was my long-time Princeton colleague; I know Lombardo. In each case, therefore, I recall the translator's mien and voice, which helps.)

### *Robert Fitzgerald (1974)*

> The portion's equal
> Whether a man hangs back or fights his best;
> The same respect, or lack of it, is given,
> brave man and coward. One who's active dies
> like the do-nothing. What least thing have I
> To show for it, for harsh days undergone
> and my life gambled, all these years of war?
> A bird will give her fledglings every scrap
> she comes by, and go hungry, foraging.
> That is the case with me.
> Many a sleepless night I've spent afield
> And many a day in bloodshed hand to hand
> In battle for the wives of other men.

Fitzgerald, as do the next two translators, opts for a shorter line more familiar to readers of English poetry in iambic meter (especially Shakespeare). Lattimore, on the other hand, explicitly sought a free six-beat line, "a speed and rhythm analogous to the speed and rhythm I find in the original."[17] By avoiding dramatic touches (exclamations, broken sentences), Fitzgerald gives the impression of a speaker who is quiet, resigned, in control. "Donothing" is closer to the Greek (*a-ergos*, literally "without work") than the more colorful and moralistic "lazy" (Newman). Sticking to the plainness of the original, he produces a version most like Lattimore's, although more lyrical than epic in its shorter lines.

## Robert Fagles (1990)

One and the same lot for the man who hangs back
and the man who battles hard. The same honor waits
For the coward and the brave. They both go down to Death,
the fighter who shirks and the one who works to exhaustion.
And what's laid up for me, what pittance? Nothing—
and after suffering hardships, year in, year out,
Staking my life on the mortal risks of war.

Like a mother bird hurrying morsels back
To her wingless young ones—whatever she can catch—
but it's all starvation wages for herself.
                                                    So for me.
Many a sleepless night I've bivouacked in harness,
day after bloody day I've hacked my passage through,
Fighting other soldiers to win their wives as prizes.

This represents a compromise between the long line of Lattimore and the
shorter Fitzgerald, but at the risk of sounding unmetered and weak. In
terms of diction, however, Fagles has chosen to have Achilleus sound as he
imagines a modern veteran might. "Bivouacked" is soldier-talk; "all starva-
tion wages" is far beyond the Greek's plain "there is no surplus for me," but it
personalizes the speaker, just as the un-Homeric sequence "what pittance?
Nothing" tries to capture a mode of speech familiar from natural talk.
"Day after bloody day" makes the original (*êmata haimatoenta*—literally
"bloodied days") into a British-inflected soldier's swear, and "hacked my
passage" notches up the original's "made way through" (*dieprêsson*). In
sum, Fagles raises the verbal temperature by consistent overdramatizing.
He thus sharply distinguishes the narrator's verses from character-speech.
Yet in the original, speakers sound much more like the Homeric poet: there
is stylistic consistency.

## Stanley Lombardo (1997)

It doesn't matter if you stay in camp or fight—
In the end, everybody comes out the same,
Coward and hero get the same reward:

You die whether you slack off or work.
And what do I have for all my suffering,
Constantly putting my life on the line?
Like a bird who feeds her chicks
Whatever she finds, and goes without herself,
That's what I've been like, lying awake
Through sleepless nights in battle for days
Soaked in blood, fighting men for their wives.

The logical conclusion of the search for natural speech makes the lines highly speakable (and Lombardo's translation, like Fagles', is marketed in an audio version). At times, it thereby hews closer to the Greek (note "goes without herself," which resembles the original's literal "and she has ills" much more than do other attempts above). This can, however, mean foregoing strong verbs and nouns, while watering down the English until it risks cliché ("everybody comes out the same" for the original "with equal honor"; "putting my life on the line"). Lombardo's observation that his version "reflects the oral performance nature of the original poems" might blur the lines separating natural talk, unscripted improvised poems, and highly artificial, formulaic oral-traditional poetry made in a complex meter. But the resulting gain in vigor can often be worth the overstepping.

Of course only through a longer acquaintance with the entire poem, and by rereading it in variety of versions, will the reader be able to judge. Ultimately the choice among translations is a matter of taste. For many, Lattimore's will remain the most lucid and yet elevated—"noble"—of recent attempts.[18]

NOTES

1   From Mary Wortley Montagu, *The Letters and Works of Lady Mary Wortley Montagu*, edited by J. A. Stuart-Wortley-Mackenzie Wharncliffe, vol. 2 (N.p., 1837).

2   Robert Wood, *An Essay on the Original Genius and Writings of Homer*, rev. ed. (London, 1775), 4–5.

3   Potential parallels are accumulated by Martin West in two volumes: Martin West, *The East Face of Helicon: West Asiatic Elements in Greek Poetry and Myth* (Oxford, 1997); and *Indo-European Poetry and Myth* (Oxford, 2007). More analytical treatments of the poetic heritage on which Homeric poetry draws can be found in Calvert Watkins, *How to Kill a Dragon: Aspects of Indo-European Poetics* (New York, 1995); and Bruce Lincoln, *Myth, Cosmos and Society: Indo-European Themes of Cre-*

*ation and Destruction* (Cambridge, MA, 1986). On the highly debated questions of Greek cultural inheritance from Egypt and the Near East, see the three volumes by Martin Bernal, *Black Athena: The Afroasiatic Roots of Classical Civilization* (New Brunswick, NJ, 1987–2006). On the enduring ideologies that underlie studies of ancient myth, see Bruce Lincoln, *Theorizing Myth: Narrative, Ideology, and Scholarship* (Chicago, 1999).

4  From a letter of Nakao Takanori, in *Kamikaze Diaries: Reflections of Japanese Student Soldiers*, ed. Emiko Ohnuki-Tierney (Chicago, 2006), 208.

5  *Motif-Index of Folk Literature: A Classification of Narrative Elements in Folktales, Ballads, Myths, Fables, Mediaeval Romances, Exempla, Fabliaux, Jest-Books and Local Legends*, rev. & enl. ed., 6 vols. (Bloomington, IN, 1955–58).

6  Page images of the entire manuscript, from the original held in Venice, are viewable online courtesy of the Center for Hellenic Studies and Biblioteca Marciana: http://chs75.chs.harvard.edu/manuscripts/.

7  J. V. Cunningham, *The Exclusions of a Rhyme: Poems and Epigrams* (Denver, 1960).

8  V. Bérard, *Introduction à l'Odyssée*, vol. 1 (Paris, 1924). He thus allied himself with such earlier French defenders of Homer as Boileau and Dacier.

9  Skafte Jensen, *The Homeric Question and the Oral-Formulaic Theory* (Copenhagen, 1980), 112.

10  The main proponents of the early archaic, single-recording origin theory are Barry Powell, in *Homer and the Origin of the Greek Alphabet* (Cambridge, 1991); and Richard Janko, in "The Homeric Poems as Oral Dictated Texts," *Classical Quarterly* 48 (1998): 1–13.

11  *Miscellaneous Works of Edward Gibbon, Esquire: With Memoirs of His Life and Writings, Composed by Himself: Illustrated from His Letters with Occasional Notes and Narrative, by John Lord Sheffield in Three Volumes* (Dublin, 1796), 2:300.

12  "Gallipoli," in *The Cause: Poems of the War* (Boston, 1917), 68.

13  Quoted in *Patrick Shaw-Stewart*, by Ronald Knox (London, 1920), 160.

14  "The Shield of Achilles," in *The Shield of Achilles* (New York, 1955), 35.

15  Aeschylus, *Myrmidons*, fragments 135–37 in *Aeschylus: Fragments*, edited by A. Sommerstein (Cambridge, MA, 2008), 145–47.

16  In this edition of Lattimore's translation, spelling and punctuation have been altered to follow American usage rather than the British conventions employed in the 1951 edition. Thus, in the main body of the poem, *honour* will be spelled *honor*, etc. Otherwise, Lattimore's text of the poem appears here virtually unaltered, with the exception of half a dozen or so slight adjustments for the sake of grammar or clarity.

17  *The Iliad of Homer*, trans. and ed. Richmond Lattimore (Chicago, 1951), 55.

18  For many further examples, with a fine introduction, see *Homer in English*, edited by G. Steiner (Harmondsworth, 1996).

must concede that Homer has these qualities. I have tried as hard as I could to reproduce the first three. I do not think *nobility* is a quality to directly strive for; you must write as well as you can, and then see, or let others see, whether or not the result is noble. I have used the plainest language I could find which might be adequate, and mostly this is the language of contemporary prose. This usage is not "Homeric." Arnold points out that Homer used a poetic dialect, but I do not draw from this the conclusion, which Arnold draws, that we should translate him into a poetical dialect of English. In 1951, we do not have a poetic dialect, and if I used the language of Spenser or the King James Version of the Bible, I should feel as if I were working in Apollonius of Rhodes, or at best Arktinos, rather than Homer. I must try to avoid mistranslation, which would be caused by rating the word of my own choice ahead of the word which translates the Greek. Subject to such qualification, I must render Homer into the best English verse I can write; and this will be in my own "poetical language," which is mostly the plain English of today.

I wish to thank the editors and the staff of the University of Chicago Press for their sympathy and their belief in this project from its very beginnings; David Grene and Mabel Lang for reading the translation and offering valuable advice and criticism; Rhys Carpenter for very helpful criticism of the introduction; Alice Lattimore for her help in preparing the manuscript; and finally, all those friends who have sustained me in the belief that this work was worth doing, and refrained from asking "Why do another translation of Homer?"—a question which has no answer for those who do not know the answer already.

NOTE

1    *On the Study of Celtic Literature*; and *On Translating Homer*, Macmillan edition, 149.

# Maps

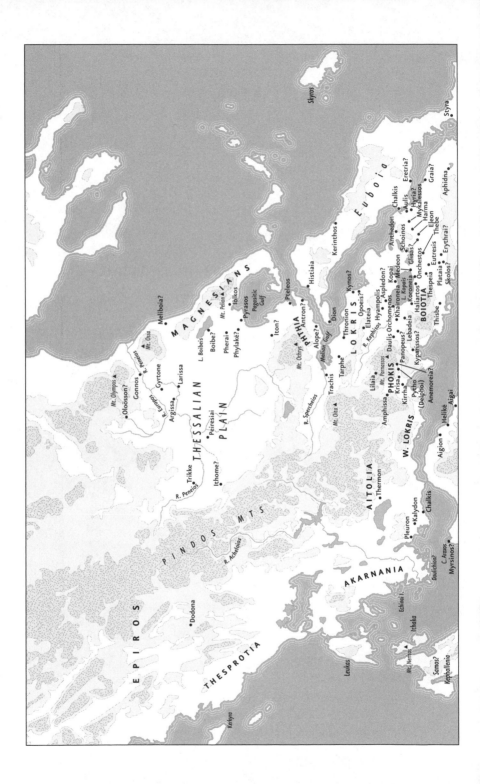

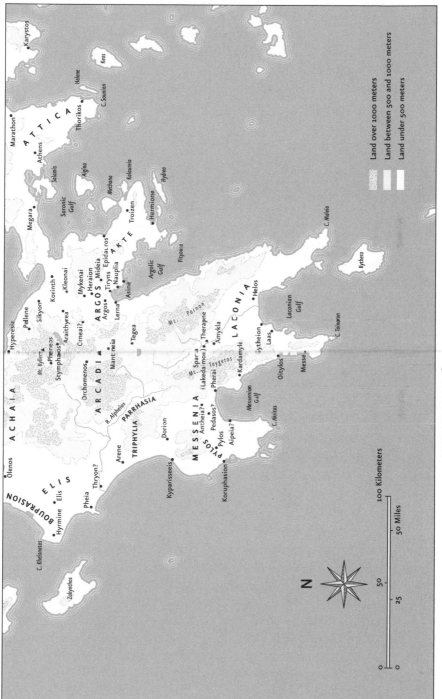

MAINLAND GREECE. © INTERNATIONAL MAPPING.

Land over 1000 meters
Land between 500 and 1000 meters
Land under 500 meters

N

100 Kilometers
50 Miles
0    25    50
0

Karystos
Keos
Helene
C. Sounion
Thorikos
Marathon
Athens
ATTICA
Aigina
Salamis
Methana
Kaloureia
Hydrea
Megara
Saronic Gulf
Hermione
Troizen
AKTE
Epidauros
Mideia
Mykenai
Heraion
Kleonai
Tiryns
Nauplia
Argolic Gulf
Asine
Pityoussa
Korinth
Argos
ARGOS
Lerna
Pellene
Sikyon
Hyperesia
Araithyrea
Pheneos
Crneai?
Tegea
Mt. Parnon
Mt. Kyllene
Symphalos?
Orchomenos
Mantineia
ARCADIA
Therapne
PARRHASIA
R. Alpheios
Sparta
(Lakedaimon)
Pherai
Mt. Taygetos
LACONIA
Amykla
Gytheion
Laas
Helos
Laconian Gulf
C. Malea
Kythera
C. Tainaron
ACHAIA
Mt. Kyllene
Kardamyle
Oityloa
Messe
Olenos
Kyparisseeis
Dorion
MESSENIA
Antheia?
Pedasos?
Aipeia?
Messenian Gulf
C. Akritas
PYLOS
Pylos
Koruphasion
TRIPHYLIA
Arene
Thryon?
ELIS
Hyrmine
Pheia
Elis
BOUPRASION
C. Khelonatas
Zakynthos

Ismaros?

Ainos

R. Hebros

Thasos

Samothrace

Propontis

Parion   Priapos   Kyzikos

Lampsakos
Perkote?
Sestos   Arisbe?
Abydos
Imbros   Dardanos

Zeleia

R. Grenikos

R. Aisepos

Hellespont
Sigeion   Dardania

Lemnos   Ilion
(Troy)

M Y S I A

Tenedos   R. Skamandros

▲Mt. Ida

Larissa   Lyrnessos?
Chryse?   Thebe
Hamaxitos   Hypoplakie
C. Lekton   Adramuttion

Lesbos

R. Kaikos

A e g e a n

S e a

L Y D I A

R. Hermos   L. Gyge?

Skyros

Mt. Sipylos ▲   Sardis

Smyrna   Mt. Timolos ▲

Chios

R. Kaÿstros

Euboia

Ephesos

R. Maiandros

Andros

Samos

Ikaria   ▲ Mt. Mykale

Miletos   ▲ Mt. Latmos

K A R I A

Delos

Paros
Naxos   Kalydnai I.

Kos

N

Nisyros   Syme

Ialysos

Kameiros

Rhodes

Lindos

Land over 1000 meters

Land between 500 and 1000 meters

Land under 500 meters

0          50          100 Kilometers

0     25      50 Miles

THE EAST AEGEAN COAST. © INTERNATIONAL MAPPING.

# THE ILIAD
# OF
# HOMER

# BOOK ONE

Sing, goddess, the anger of Peleus' son Achilleus
and its devastation, which put pains thousandfold upon the Achaians,
hurled in their multitudes to the house of Hades strong souls
of heroes, but gave their bodies to be the delicate feasting
of dogs, of all birds, and the will of Zeus was accomplished                    5
since that time when first there stood in division of conflict
Atreus' son the lord of men and brilliant Achilleus.

What god was it then set them together in bitter collision?
Zeus' son and Leto's, Apollo, who in anger at the king drove
the foul pestilence along the host, and the people perished,            10
since Atreus' son had dishonored Chryses, priest of Apollo,
when he came beside the fast ships of the Achaians to ransom
back his daughter, carrying gifts beyond count and holding
in his hands wound on a staff of gold the ribbons of Apollo
who strikes from afar, and supplicated all the Achaians,                15
but above all Atreus' two sons, the marshals of the people:
"Sons of Atreus and you other strong-greaved Achaians,
to you may the gods grant who have their homes on Olympos
Priam's city to be plundered and a fair homecoming thereafter,
but may you give me back my own daughter and take the ransom,          20
giving honor to Zeus' son who strikes from afar, Apollo."
Then all the rest of the Achaians cried out in favor
that the priest be respected and the shining ransom be taken;
yet this pleased not the heart of Atreus' son Agamemnon,
but harshly he drove him away with a strong order upon him:           25

"Never let me find you again, old sir, near our hollow
ships, neither lingering now nor coming again hereafter,
for fear your staff and the god's ribbons help you no longer.
The girl I will not give back; sooner will old age come upon her
30  in my own house, in Argos, far from her own land, going
up and down by the loom and being in my bed as my companion.
So go now, do not make me angry; so you will be safer."
    So he spoke, and the old man in terror obeyed him
and went silently away beside the murmuring sea beach.
35  Over and over the old man prayed as he walked in solitude
to King Apollo, whom Leto of the lovely hair bore: "Hear me,
lord of the silver bow who set your power about Chryse
and Killa the sacrosanct, who are lord in strength over Tenedos,
Smintheus, if ever it pleased your heart that I built your temple,
40  if ever it pleased you that I burned all the rich thigh pieces
of bulls, of goats, then bring to pass this wish I pray for:
let your arrows make the Danaäns pay for my tears shed."
    So he spoke in prayer, and Phoibos Apollo heard him,
and strode down along the pinnacles of Olympos, angered
45  in his heart, carrying across his shoulders the bow and the hooded
quiver; and the shafts clashed on the shoulders of the god walking
angrily. He came as night comes down and knelt then
apart and opposite the ships and let go an arrow.
Terrible was the clash that rose from the bow of silver.
50  First he went after the mules and the circling hounds, then let go
a tearing arrow against the men themselves and struck them.
The corpse fires burned everywhere and did not stop burning.

    Nine days up and down the host ranged the god's arrows,
but on the tenth Achilleus called the people to assembly;
55  a thing put into his mind by the goddess of the white arms, Hera,
who had pity upon the Danaäns when she saw them dying.
Now when they were all assembled in one place together,
Achilleus of the swift feet stood up among them and spoke forth:
"Son of Atreus, I believe now that straggling backward
60  we must make our way home if we can even escape death,
if fighting now must crush the Achaians and the plague likewise.
No, come, let us ask some holy man, some prophet,

even an interpreter of dreams, since a dream also
comes from Zeus, who can tell why Phoibos Apollo is so angry,
if for the sake of some vow, some hecatomb he blames us,                    65
if given the fragrant smoke of lambs, of he goats, somehow
he can be made willing to beat the bane aside from us."
    He spoke thus and sat down again, and among them stood up
Kalchas, Thestor's son, far the best of the bird interpreters,
who knew all things that were, the things to come and the things past,    70
who guided into the land of Ilion the ships of the Achaians
through that seercraft of his own that Phoibos Apollo gave him.
He in kind intention toward all stood forth and addressed them:
"You have bidden me, Achilleus beloved of Zeus, to explain to
you this anger of Apollo the lord who strikes from afar. Then             75
I will speak; yet make me a promise and swear before me
readily by word and work of your hands to defend me,
since I believe I shall make a man angry who holds great kingship
over the men of Argos, and all the Achaians obey him.
For a king when he is angry with a man beneath him is too strong,         80
and suppose even for the day itself he swallow down his anger,
he still keeps bitterness that remains until its fulfillment
deep in his chest. Speak forth then, tell me if you will protect me."
    Then in answer again spoke Achilleus of the swift feet:
"Speak, interpreting whatever you know, and fear nothing.                 85
In the name of Apollo beloved of Zeus to whom you, Kalchas,
make your prayers when you interpret the gods' will to the Danaäns,
no man so long as I am alive above earth and see daylight
shall lay the weight of his hands on you beside the hollow ships,
not one of all the Danaäns, even if you mean Agamemnon,                   90
who now claims to be far the greatest of all the Achaians."
    At this the blameless seer took courage again and spoke forth:
"No, it is not for the sake of some vow or hecatomb he blames us,
but for the sake of his priest whom Agamemnon dishonored
and would not give him back his daughter nor accept the ransom.          95
Therefore the archer sent griefs against us and will send them
still, nor sooner thrust back the shameful plague from the Danaäns
until we give the glancing-eyed girl back to her father
without price, without ransom, and lead also a blessed hecatomb
to Chryse; thus we might propitiate and persuade him."                   100

He spoke thus and sat down again, and among them stood up
Atreus' son the hero wide-ruling Agamemnon
raging, the heart within filled black to the brim with anger
from beneath, but his two eyes showed like fire in their blazing.
105 First of all he eyed Kalchas bitterly and spoke to him:
"Seer of evil: never yet have you told me a good thing.
Always the evil things are dear to your heart to prophesy,
but nothing excellent have you said nor ever accomplished.
Now once more you make divination to the Danaäns, argue
110 forth your reason why he who strikes from afar afflicts them,
because I for the sake of the girl Chryseis would not take
the shining ransom; and indeed I wish greatly to have her
in my own house; since I like her better than Klytaimestra
my own wife, for in truth she is no way inferior,
115 neither in build nor stature nor wit, not in accomplishment.
Still I am willing to give her back, if such is the best way.
I myself desire that my people be safe, not perish.
Find me then some prize that shall be my own, lest I only
among the Argives go without, since that were unfitting;
120 you are all witnesses to this thing, that my prize goes elsewhere."
   Then in answer again spoke brilliant swift-footed Achilleus:
"Son of Atreus, most lordly, greediest for gain of all men,
how shall the great-hearted Achaians give you a prize now?
There is no great store of things lying about I know of.
125 But what we took from the cities by storm has been distributed;
it is unbecoming for the people to call back things once given.
No, for the present give the girl back to the god; we Achaians
thrice and four times over will repay you, if ever Zeus gives
into our hands the strong-walled citadel of Troy to be plundered."
130    Then in answer again spoke powerful Agamemnon:
"Not that way, good fighter though you be, godlike Achilleus,
strive to cheat, for you will not deceive, you will not persuade me.
What do you want? To keep your own prize and have me sit here
lacking one? Are you ordering me to give this girl back?
135 Either the great-hearted Achaians shall give me a new prize
chosen according to my desire to atone for the girl lost,
or else if they will not give me one I myself shall take her,
your own prize, or that of Aias, or that of Odysseus,

going myself in person; and he whom I visit will be bitter.
Still, these are things we shall deliberate again hereafter.                    140
Come, now, we must haul a black ship down to the bright sea,
and assemble rowers enough for it, and put on board it
the hecatomb, and the girl herself, Chryseis of the fair cheeks,
and let there be one responsible man in charge of her,
either Aias or Idomeneus or brilliant Odysseus,                                 145
or you yourself, son of Peleus, most terrifying of all men,
to reconcile by accomplishing sacrifice the archer."
    Then looking darkly at him Achilleus of the swift feet spoke:
"O wrapped in shamelessness, with your mind forever on profit,
how shall any one of the Achaians readily obey you                             150
either to go on a journey or to fight men strongly in battle?
I for my part did not come here for the sake of the Trojan
spearmen to fight against them, since to me they have done nothing.
Never yet have they driven away my cattle or my horses,
never in Phthia where the soil is rich and men grow great did they             155
spoil my harvest, since indeed there is much that lies between us,
the shadowy mountains and the echoing sea; but for your sake,
O great shamelessness, we followed, to do you favor,
you with the dog's eyes, to win your honor and Menelaos'
from the Trojans. You forget all this or else you care nothing.                160
And now my prize you threaten in person to strip from me,
for whom I labored much, the gift of the sons of the Achaians.
Never, when the Achaians sack some well-founded citadel
of the Trojans, do I have a prize that is equal to your prize.
Always the greater part of the painful fighting is the work of                 165
my hands; but when the time comes to distribute the booty
yours is far the greater reward, and I with some small thing
yet dear to me go back to my ships when I am weary with fighting.
Now I am returning to Phthia, since it is much better
to go home again with my curved ships, and I am minded no longer              170
to stay here dishonored and pile up your wealth and your luxury."
    Then answered him in turn the lord of men Agamemnon:
"Run away by all means if your heart drives you. I will not
entreat you to stay here for my sake. There are others with me
who will do me honor, and above all Zeus of the counsels.                     175
To me you are the most hateful of all the kings whom the gods love.

Forever quarreling is dear to your heart, and wars and battles;
and if you are very strong indeed, that is a god's gift.
Go home then with your own ships and your own companions,
180   be king over the Myrmidons. I care nothing about you.
I take no account of your anger. But here is my threat to you.
Even as Phoibos Apollo is taking away my Chryseis.
I shall convey her back in my own ship, with my own
followers; but I shall take the fair-cheeked Briseis,
185   your prize, I myself going to your shelter, that you may learn well
how much greater I am than you, and another man may shrink back
from likening himself to me and contending against me."

      So he spoke. And the anger came on Peleus' son, and within
his shaggy breast the heart was divided two ways, pondering
190   whether to draw from beside his thigh the sharp sword, driving
away all those who stood between and kill the son of Atreus,
or else to check the spleen within and keep down his anger.
Now as he weighed in mind and spirit these two courses
and was drawing from its scabbard the great sword, Athene descended
195   from the sky. For Hera the goddess of the white arms sent her,
who loved both men equally in her heart and cared for them.
The goddess standing behind Peleus' son caught him by the fair hair,
appearing to him only, for no man of the others saw her.
Achilleus in amazement turned about, and straightway
200   knew Pallas Athene and the terrible eyes shining.
He uttered winged words and addressed her: "Why have you come now,
O child of Zeus of the aegis, once more? Is it that you may see
the outrageousness of the son of Atreus Agamemnon?
Yet will I tell you this thing, and I think it shall be accomplished.
205   By such acts of arrogance he may even lose his own life."
      Then in answer the goddess gray-eyed Athene spoke to him:
"I have come down to stay your anger—but will you obey me?—from the sky;
and the goddess of the white arms Hera sent me,
who loves both of you equally in her heart and cares for you.
210   Come then, do not take your sword in your hand, keep clear of fighting,
though indeed with words you may abuse him, and it will be that way.
And this also will I tell you and it will be a thing accomplished.
Some day three times over such shining gifts shall be given you

by reason of this outrage. Hold your hand then, and obey us."
Then in answer again spoke Achilleus of the swift feet: 215
"Goddess, it is necessary that I obey the word of you two,
angry though I am in my heart. So it will be better.
If any man obeys the gods, they listen to him also."
He spoke, and laid his heavy hand on the silver sword hilt
and thrust the great blade back into the scabbard nor disobeyed 220
the word of Athene. And she went back again to Olympos
to the house of Zeus of the aegis with the other divinities.

But Peleus' son once again in words of derision
spoke to Atreides, and did not yet let go of his anger:
"You wine sack, with a dog's eyes, with a deer's heart. Never 225
once have you taken courage in your heart to arm with your people
for battle, or go into ambuscade with the best of the Achaians.
No, for in such things you see death. Far better to your mind
is it, all along the widespread host of the Achaians
to take away the gifts of any man who speaks up against you. 230
King who feed on your people, since you rule nonentities;
otherwise, son of Atreus, this were your last outrage.
But I will tell you this and swear a great oath upon it:
in the name of this scepter, which never again will bear leaf nor
branch, now that it has left behind the cut stump in the mountains, 235
nor shall it ever blossom again, since the bronze blade stripped
bark and leafage, and now at last the sons of the Achaians
carry it in their hands in state when they administer
the justice of Zeus. And this shall be a great oath before you:
some day longing for Achilleus will come to the sons of the Achaians, 240
all of them. Then stricken at heart though you be, you will be able
to do nothing, when in their numbers before man-slaughtering Hektor
they drop and die. And then you will eat out the heart within you
in sorrow, that you did no honor to the best of the Achaians."
Thus spoke Peleus' son and dashed to the ground the scepter 245
studded with golden nails, and sat down again. But Atreides
raged still on the other side, and between them Nestor
the fair-spoken rose up, the lucid speaker of Pylos,
from whose lips the streams of words ran sweeter than honey.
In his time two generations of mortal men had perished, 250

those who had grown up with him and they who had been born to
these in sacred Pylos, and he was king in the third age.
He in kind intention toward both stood forth and addressed them:
"Oh, for shame. Great sorrow comes on the land of Achaia.
255   Now might Priam and the sons of Priam in truth be happy,
and all the rest of the Trojans be visited in their hearts with gladness,
were they to hear all this wherein you two are quarreling,
you, who surpass all Danaäns in council, in fighting.
Yet be persuaded. Both of you are younger than I am.
260   Yes, and in my time I have dealt with better men than
you are, and never once did they disregard me. Never
yet have I seen nor shall see again such men as these were,
men like Peirithoös, and Dryas, shepherd of the people,
Kaineus and Exadios, godlike Polyphemos,
265   or Theseus, Aigeus' son, in the likeness of the immortals.
These were the strongest generation of earth-born mortals,
the strongest, and they fought against the strongest, the beast men
living within the mountains, and terribly they destroyed them.
I was of the company of these men, coming from Pylos,
270   a long way from a distant land, since they had summoned me.
And I fought single-handed, yet against such men no one
of the mortals now alive upon earth could do battle. And also
these listened to the counsels I gave and heeded my bidding.
Do you also obey, since to be persuaded is better.
275   You, great man that you are, yet do not take the girl away
but let her be, a prize as the sons of the Achaians gave her
first. Nor, son of Peleus, think to match your strength with
the king, since never equal with the rest is the portion of honor
of the scattered king to whom Zeus gives magnificence. Even
280   though you are the stronger man, and the mother who bore you was
            immortal,
yet is this man greater who is lord over more than you rule.
Son of Atreus, give up your anger; even I entreat you
to give over your bitterness against Achilleus, he who
stands as a great bulwark of battle over all the Achaians."
285       Then in answer again spoke powerful Agamemnon:
"Yes, old sir, all this you have said is fair and orderly.
Yet here is a man who wishes to be above all others,

who wishes to hold power over all, and to be lord of
all, and give them their orders, yet I think one will not obey him.
And if the everlasting gods have made him a spearman,                    290
yet they have not given him the right to speak abusively."
    Then looking at him darkly brilliant Achilleus answered him:
"So must I be called of no account and a coward
if I must carry out every order you may happen to give me.
Tell other men to do these things, but give me no more               295
commands, since I for my part have no intention to obey you.
And put away in your thoughts this other thing I tell you.
With my hands I will not fight for the girl's sake, neither
with you nor any other man, since you take her away who gave her.
But of all the other things that are mine beside my fast black          300
ship, you shall take nothing away against my pleasure.
Come, then, only try it, that these others may see also;
instantly your own black blood will stain my spearpoint."

    So these two after battling in words of contention
stood up, and broke the assembly beside the ships of the Achaians.    305
Peleus' son went back to his balanced ships and his shelter
with Patroklos, Menoitios' son, and his own companions.
But the son of Atreus drew a fast ship down to the water
and allotted into it twenty rowers and put on board it
the hecatomb for the god and Chryseis of the fair cheeks             310
leading her by the hand. And in charge went crafty Odysseus.
    These then putting out went over the ways of the water
while Atreus' son told his people to wash off their defilement.
And they washed it away and threw the washings into the salt sea.
Then they accomplished perfect hecatombs to Apollo,                   315
of bulls and goats along the beach of the barren salt sea.
The savor of the burning swept in circles up to the bright sky.

    Thus these were busy about the army. But Agamemnon
did not give up his anger and the first threat he made to Achilleus,
but to Talthybios he gave his orders and Eurybates                    320
who were heralds and hard-working henchmen to him: "Go now
to the shelter of Peleus' son Achilleus, to bring back
Briseis of the fair cheeks leading her by the hand. And if he

will not give her, I must come in person to take her
325 with many men behind me, and it will be the worse for him."
He spoke and sent them forth with this strong order upon them.
They went against their will beside the beach of the barren
salt sea, and came to the shelters and the ships of the Myrmidons.
The man himself they found beside his shelter and his black ship
330 sitting. And Achilleus took no joy at all when he saw them.
These two terrified and in awe of the king stood waiting
quietly, and did not speak a word at all nor question him.
But he knew the whole matter in his own heart, and spoke first:
"Welcome, heralds, messengers of Zeus and of mortals.
335 Draw near. You are not to blame in my sight, but Agamemnon
who sent the two of you here for the sake of the girl Briseis.
Go then, illustrious Patroklos, and bring the girl forth
and give her to these to be taken away. Yet let them be witnesses
in the sight of the blessed gods, in the sight of mortal
340 men, and of this cruel king, if ever hereafter
there shall be need of me to beat back the shameful destruction
from the rest. For surely in ruinous heart he makes sacrifice
and has not wit enough to look behind and before him
that the Achaians fighting beside their ships shall not perish."
345 So he spoke, and Patroklos obeyed his beloved companion.
He led forth from the hut Briseis of the fair cheeks and gave her
to be taken away; and they walked back beside the ships of the Achaians,
and the woman all unwilling went with them still. But Achilleus
weeping went and sat in sorrow apart from his companions
350 beside the beach of the gray sea looking out on the infinite water.
Many times stretching forth his hands he called on his mother:
"Since, my mother, you bore me to be a man with a short life,
therefore Zeus of the loud thunder on Olympos should grant me
honor at least. But now he has given me not even a little.
355 Now the son of Atreus, powerful Agamemnon,
has dishonored me, since he has taken away my prize and keeps it."
So he spoke in tears and the lady his mother heard him
as she sat in the depths of the sea at the side of her aged father,
and lightly she emerged like a mist from the gray water.
360 She came and sat beside him as he wept, and stroked him
with her hand and called him by name and spoke to him: "Why then,

child, do you lament? What sorrow has come to your heart now?
Tell me, do not hide it in your mind, and thus we shall both know."
      Sighing heavily Achilleus of the swift feet answered her:
"You know; since you know why must I tell you all this?                365
We went against Thebe, the sacred city of Eëtion,
and the city we sacked, and carried everything back to this place,
and the sons of the Achaians made a fair distribution
and for Atreus' son they chose out Chryseis of the fair cheeks.
Then Chryses, priest of him who strikes from afar, Apollo,                370
came beside the fast ships of the bronze-armored Achaians to ransom
back his daughter, carrying gifts beyond count and holding
in his hands wound on a staff of gold the ribbons of Apollo
who strikes from afar, and supplicated all the Achaians,
but above all Atreus' two sons, the marshals of the people.               375
Then all the rest of the Achaians cried out in favor
that the priest be respected and the shining ransom be taken;
yet this pleased not the heart of Atreus' son Agamemnon,
but harshly he sent him away with a strong order upon him.
The old man went back again in anger, but Apollo                         380
listened to his prayer, since he was very dear to him, and let go
the wicked arrow against the Argives. And now the people
were dying one after another while the god's shafts ranged
everywhere along the wide host of the Achaians, till the seer
knowing well the truth interpreted the designs of the archer.             385
It was I first of all urged then the god's appeasement;
and the anger took hold of Atreus' son, and in speed standing
he uttered his threat against me, and now it is a thing accomplished.
For the girl the glancing-eyed Achaians are taking to Chryse
in a fast ship, also carrying to the king presents. But even             390
now the heralds went away from my shelter leading
Briseus' daughter, whom the sons of the Achaians gave me.
You then, if you have power to, protect your own son, going
to Olympos and supplicating Zeus, if ever before now
either by word you comforted Zeus' heart or by action.                   395
Since it is many times in my father's halls I have heard you
making claims, when you said you only among the immortals
beat aside shameful destruction from Kronos' son the dark-misted,
that time when all the other Olympians sought to bind him,

400 Hera and Poseidon and Pallas Athene. Then you,
goddess, went and set him free from his shackles, summoning
in speed the creature of the hundred hands to tall Olympos,
that creature the gods name Briareus, but all men
Aigaios' son, but he is far greater in strength than his father.
405 He rejoicing in the glory of it sat down by Kronion,
and the rest of the blessed gods were frightened and gave up binding him.
Sit beside him and take his knees and remind him of these things
now, if perhaps he might be willing to help the Trojans,
and pin the Achaians back against the ships and the water,
410 dying, so that thus they may all have profit of their own king,
that Atreus' son wide-ruling Agamemnon may recognize
his madness, that he did no honor to the best of the Achaians."
    Thetis answered him then letting the tears fall: "Ah me,
my child. Your birth was bitterness. Why did I raise you?
415 If only you could sit by your ships untroubled, not weeping,
since indeed your lifetime is to be short, of no length.
Now it has befallen that your life must be brief and bitter
beyond all men's. To a bad destiny I bore you in my chambers.
But I will go to cloud-dark Olympos and ask this
420 thing of Zeus who delights in the thunder. Perhaps he will do it.
Do you therefore continuing to sit by your swift ships
be angry at the Achaians and stay away from all fighting.
For Zeus went to the blameless Aithiopians at the Ocean
yesterday to feast, and the rest of the gods went with him.
425 On the twelfth day he will be coming back to Olympos,
and then I will go for your sake to the house of Zeus, bronze-founded,
and take him by the knees and I think I can persuade him."

    So speaking she went away from that place and left him
sorrowing in his heart for the sake of the fair-girdled woman
430 whom they were taking by force against his will. But Odysseus
meanwhile drew near to Chryse conveying the sacred hecatomb.
These when they were inside the many-hollowed harbor
took down and gathered together the sails and stowed them in the black
    ship,
let down mast by the forestays, and settled it into the mast crutch
435 easily, and rowed her in with oars to the mooring.

They threw over the anchor stones and made fast the stern cables
and themselves stepped out onto the break of the sea beach,
and led forth the hecatomb to the archer Apollo,
and Chryseis herself stepped forth from the sea-going vessel.
Odysseus of the many designs guided her to the altar                        440
and left her in her father's arms and spoke a word to him:
"Chryses, I was sent here by the lord of men Agamemnon
to lead back your daughter and accomplish a sacred hecatomb
to Apollo on behalf of the Danaäns, that we may propitiate
the lord who has heaped unhappiness and tears on the Argives."            445
    He spoke, and left her in his arms. And he received gladly
his beloved child. And the men arranged the sacred hecatomb
for the god in orderly fashion around the strong-founded altar.
Next they washed their hands and took up the scattering barley.
Standing among them with lifted arms Chryses prayed in a great voice:     450
"Hear me, lord of the silver bow, who set your power about
Chryse and Killa the sacrosanct, who are lord in strength over
Tenedos; if once before you listened to my prayers
and did me honor and smote strongly the host of the Achaians,
so one more time bring to pass the wish that I pray for.                   455
Beat aside at last the shameful plague from the Danaäns."
    So he spoke in prayer, and Phoibos Apollo heard him.
And when all had made prayer and flung down the scattering barley
first they drew back the victims' heads and slaughtered them and skinned
        them,
and cut away the meat from the thighs and wrapped them in fat,            460
making a double fold, and laid shreds of flesh upon them.
The old man burned these on a cleft stick and poured the gleaming
wine over, while the young men with forks in their hands stood about him.
But when they had burned the thigh pieces and tasted the vitals,
they cut all the remainder into pieces and spitted them                    465
and roasted all carefully and took off the pieces.
Then after they had finished the work and got the feast ready
they feasted, nor was any man's hunger denied a fair portion.
But when they had put away their desire for eating and drinking,
the young men filled the mixing bowls with pure wine, passing             470
a portion to all, when they had offered drink in the goblets.
All day long they propitiated the god with singing,

chanting a splendid hymn to Apollo, these young Achaians,
singing to the one who works from afar, who listened in gladness.
475 Afterward when the sun went down and darkness came onward
they lay down and slept beside the ship's stern cables.
But when the young Dawn showed again with her rosy fingers,
they put forth to sea toward the wide camp of the Achaians.
And Apollo who works from afar sent them a favoring stern wind.
480 They set up the mast again and spread on it the white sails,
and the wind blew into the middle of the sail, and at the cutwater
a blue wave rose and sang strongly as the ship went onward.
She ran swiftly cutting across the swell her pathway.
But when they had come back to the wide camp of the Achaians
485 they hauled the black ship up on the mainland, high up
on the sand, and underneath her they fixed the long props.
Afterward they scattered to their own ships and their shelters.

But that other still sat in anger beside his swift ships,
Peleus' son divinely born, Achilleus of the swift feet.
490 Never now would he go to assemblies where men win glory,
never more into battle, but continued to waste his heart out
sitting there, though he longed always for the clamor and fighting.
But when the twelfth dawn after this day appeared, the gods who
live forever came back to Olympos all in a body
495 and Zeus led them; nor did Thetis forget the entreaties
of her son, but she emerged from the sea's waves early
in the morning and went up to the tall sky and Olympos.
She found Kronos' broad-browed son apart from the others
sitting upon the highest peak of rugged Olympos.
500 She came and sat beside him with her left hand embracing
his knees, but took him underneath the chin with her right hand
and spoke in supplication to lord Zeus son of Kronos:
"Father Zeus, if ever before in word or action
I did you favor among the immortals, now grant what I ask for.
505 Now give honor to my son short-lived beyond all other
mortals. Since even now the lord of men Agamemnon
dishonors him, who has taken away his prize and keeps it.
Zeus of the counsels, lord of Olympos, now do him honor.

So long put strength into the Trojans, until the Achaians
give my son his rights, and his honor is increased among them."          510
    She spoke thus. But Zeus who gathers the clouds made no answer
but sat in silence a long time. And Thetis, as she had taken
his knees, clung fast to them and urged once more her question:
"Bend your head and promise me to accomplish this thing,
or else refuse it; you have nothing to fear, that I may know          515
by how much I am the most dishonored of all gods."
    Deeply disturbed Zeus who gathers the clouds answered her:
"This is a disastrous matter when you set me in conflict
with Hera, and she troubles me with recriminations.
Since even as things are, forever among the immortals          520
she is at me and speaks of how I help the Trojans in battle.
Even so, go back again now, go away, for fear she
see us. I will look to these things that they be accomplished.
See then, I will bend my head that you may believe me.
For this among the immortal gods is the mightiest witness          525
I can give, and nothing I do shall be vain nor revocable
nor a thing unfulfilled when I bend my head in assent to it."
    He spoke, the son of Kronos, and nodded his head with the dark brows,
and the immortally anointed hair of the great god
swept from his divine head, and all Olympos was shaken.          530
    So these two who had made their plans separated, and Thetis
leapt down again from shining Olympos into the sea's depth,
but Zeus went back to his own house, and all the gods rose up
from their chairs to greet the coming of their father; not one had courage
to keep his place as the father advanced, but stood up to greet him.          535
Thus he took his place on the throne; yet Hera was not
ignorant, having seen how he had been plotting counsels
with Thetis the silver-footed, the daughter of the sea's ancient,
and at once she spoke revilingly to Zeus son of Kronos:
"Treacherous one, what god has been plotting counsels with you?          540
Always it is dear to your heart in my absence to think of
secret things and decide upon them. Never have you patience
frankly to speak forth to me the thing that you purpose."
    Then to her the father of gods and men made answer:
"Hera, do not go on hoping that you will hear all my          545

thoughts, since these will be too hard for you, though you are my wife.
Any thought that it is right for you to listen to, no one
neither man nor any immortal shall hear it before you.
But anything that apart from the rest of the gods I wish to
550    plan, do not always question each detail nor probe me."
       Then the goddess the ox-eyed lady Hera answered:
"Majesty, son of Kronos, what sort of thing have you spoken?
Truly too much in time past I have not questioned nor probed you,
but you are entirely free to think out whatever pleases you.
555    Now, though, I am terribly afraid you were won over
by Thetis the silver-footed, the daughter of the sea's ancient.
For early in the morning she sat beside you and took your
knees, and I think you bowed your head in assent to do honor
to Achilleus, and to destroy many beside the ships of the Achaians."
560    Then in return Zeus who gathers the clouds made answer:
"Dear lady, I never escape you; you are always full of suspicion.
Yet thus you can accomplish nothing surely, but be more
distant from my heart than ever, and it will be the worse for you.
If what you say is true, then that is the way I wish it.
565    But go then, sit down in silence, and do as I tell you,
for fear all the gods, as many as are on Olympos, can do nothing
if I come close and lay my unconquerable hands upon you."

       He spoke, and the goddess the ox-eyed lady Hera was frightened
and went and sat down in silence wrenching her heart to obedience,
570    and all the Uranian gods in the house of Zeus were troubled.
Hephaistos the renowned smith rose up to speak among them,
to bring comfort to his beloved mother, Hera of the white arms:
"This will be a disastrous matter and not endurable
if you two are to quarrel thus for the sake of mortals
575    and bring brawling among the gods. There will be no pleasure
in the stately feast at all, since vile things will be uppermost.
And I entreat my mother, though she herself understands it,
to be ingratiating toward our father Zeus, that no longer
our father may scold her and break up the quiet of our feasting.
580    For if the Olympian who handles the lightning should be minded
to hurl us out of our places, he is far too strong for any.
Do you therefore approach him again with words made gentle,

and at once the Olympian will be gracious again to us."
    He spoke, and springing to his feet put a two-handled goblet
into his mother's hands and spoke again to her once more:                                    585
"Have patience, my mother, and endure it, though you be saddened,
for fear that, dear as you are, I see you before my own eyes
struck down, and then sorry though I be I shall not be able
to do anything. It is too hard to fight against the Olympian.
There was a time once before now I was minded to help you,                                   590
and he caught me by the foot and threw me from the magic threshold,
and all day long I dropped helpless, and about sunset
I landed in Lemnos, and there was not much life left in me.
After that fall it was the Sintian men who took care of me."
    He spoke, and the goddess of the white arms Hera smiled at him,                           595
and smiling she accepted the goblet out of her son's hand.
Thereafter beginning from the left he poured drinks for the other
gods, dipping up from the mixing bowl the sweet nectar.
But among the blessed immortals uncontrollable laughter
went up as they saw Hephaistos bustling about the palace.                                     600
    Thus thereafter the whole day long until the sun went under
they feasted, nor was anyone's hunger denied a fair portion,
nor denied the beautifully wrought lyre in the hands of Apollo
nor the antiphonal sweet sound of the Muses singing.
    Afterward when the light of the flaming sun went under                                    605
they went away each one to sleep in his home where
for each one the far-renowned strong-handed Hephaistos
had built a house by means of his craftsmanship and cunning.
Zeus the Olympian and lord of the lightning went to
his own bed, where always he lay when sweet sleep came on him.                               610
Going up to the bed he slept and Hera of the gold throne beside him.

# BOOK TWO

Now the rest of the gods, and men who were lords of chariots,
slept night long, but the ease of sleep came not upon Zeus
who was pondering in his heart how he might bring honor
to Achilleus, and destroy many beside the ships of the Achaians.
5    Now to his mind this thing appeared to be the best counsel,
to send evil Dream to Atreus' son Agamemnon.
He cried out to the dream and addressed him in winged words:
"Go forth, evil Dream, beside the swift ships of the Achaians.
Make your way to the shelter of Atreus' son Agamemnon;
10   speak to him in words exactly as I command you.
Bid him arm the flowing-haired Achaians for battle
in all haste; since now he might take the wide-wayed city
of the Trojans. For no longer are the gods who live on Olympos
arguing the matter, since Hera forced them all over
15   by her supplication, and evils are in store for the Trojans."
So he spoke, and Dream listened to his word and descended.
Lightly he came down beside the swift ships of the Achaians
and came to Agamemnon the son of Atreus. He found him
sleeping within his shelter in a cloud of immortal slumber.
20   Dream stood then beside his head in the likeness of Nestor,
Neleus' son, whom Agamemnon honored beyond all
elders beside. In Nestor's likeness the divine Dream spoke to him:
"Son of wise Atreus breaker of horses, are you sleeping?
He should not sleep night long who is a man burdened with counsels
25   and responsibility for a people and cares so numerous.
Listen quickly to what I say, since I am a messenger

of Zeus, who far away cares much for you and is pitiful.
Zeus bids you arm the flowing-haired Achaians for battle
in all haste; since now you might take the wide-wayed city
of the Trojans. For no longer are the gods who live on Olympos          30
arguing the matter, since Hera forced them all over
by her supplication, and evils are in store for the Trojans
from Zeus. Keep this thought in your heart then, let not forgetfulness
take you, after you are released from the kindly sweet slumber."

    So he spoke and went away, and left Agamemnon                        35
there, believing things in his heart that were not to be accomplished.
For he thought that on that very day he would take Priam's city;
fool, who knew nothing of all the things Zeus planned to accomplish,
Zeus, who yet was minded to visit tears and sufferings
on Trojans and Danaäns alike in the strong encounters.                  40
Agamemnon awoke from sleep, the divine voice drifting
around him. He sat upright and put on his tunic,
beautiful, fresh woven, and threw the great mantle over it.
Underneath his shining feet he bound the fair sandals
and across his shoulders slung the sword with the nails of silver,      45
and took up the scepter of his fathers, immortal forever.
Thus he went beside the ships of the bronze-armored Achaians.
    Now the goddess Dawn drew close to tall Olympos
with her message of light to Zeus and the other immortals.
But Agamemnon commanded his clear-voiced heralds to summon             50
by proclamation to assembly the flowing-haired Achaians,
and the heralds made their cry and the men were assembled swiftly.
    First he held a council session of the high-hearted princes
beside the ship of Nestor, the king of the race of Pylos.
Summoning these he compacted before them his close counsel:             55
"Hear me, friends: in my sleep a Dream divine came to me
through the immortal night, and in appearance and stature
and figure it most closely resembled splendid Nestor.
It came and stood above my head and spoke a word to me:
'Son of wise Atreus breaker of horses, are you sleeping?                60
He should not sleep night long who is a man burdened with counsels
and responsibility for a people and cares so numerous.
Now listen quickly to what I say, since I am a messenger

from Zeus, who far away cares much for you and is pitiful.
65 Zeus bids you arm the flowing-haired Achaians for battle
in all haste; since now you might take the wide-wayed city
of the Trojans. For no longer are the gods who live on Olympos
arguing the matter, since Hera has forced them all over
by her supplication, and evils are in store for the Trojans
70 by Zeus' will. Keep this within your heart.' So speaking
the Dream went away on wings, and sweet sleep released me.
Come then, let us see if we can arm the sons of the Achaians.
Yet first, since it is the right way, I will make trial of them
by words, and tell them even to flee in their benched vessels.
75 Do you take stations here and there, to check them with orders."
    He spoke thus, and sat down again, and among them rose up
Nestor, he who ruled as a king in sandy Pylos.
He in kind intention toward all stood forth and addressed them:
"Friends, who are leaders of the Argives and keep their counsel,
80 had it been any other Achaian who told of this dream
we should have called it a lie and we might rather have turned from it.
Now he who claims to be the best of the Achaians has seen it.
Come then, let us see if we can arm the sons of the Achaians."

    So he spoke and led the way departing from the council,
85 and the rest rose to their feet, the scattered kings, obeying
the shepherd of the people, and the army thronged behind them.
Like the swarms of clustering bees that issue forever
in fresh bursts from the hollow in the stone, and hang like
bunched grapes as they hover beneath the flowers in springtime
90 fluttering in swarms together this way and that way,
so the many nations of men from the ships and the shelters
along the front of the deep sea beach marched in order
by companies to the assembly, and Rumor walked blazing among them,
Zeus' messenger, to hasten them along. Thus they were assembled
95 and the place of their assembly was shaken, and the earth groaned
as the people took their positions and there was tumult. Nine heralds
shouting set about putting them in order, to make them cease their
clamor and listen to the kings beloved of Zeus. The people
took their seats in sober fashion and were marshaled in their places

and gave over their clamoring. Powerful Agamemnon 100
stood up holding the scepter Hephaistos had wrought him carefully.
Hephaistos gave it to Zeus the king, the son of Kronos,
and Zeus in turn gave it to the courier Argeïphontes,
and lord Hermes gave it to Pelops, driver of horses,
and Pelops again gave it to Atreus, the shepherd of the people. 105
Atreus dying left it to Thyestes of the rich flocks,
and Thyestes left it in turn to Agamemnon to carry
and to be lord of many islands and over all Argos.
Leaning upon this scepter he spoke and addressed the Argives:
"Fighting men and friends, O Danaäns, henchmen of Ares: 110
Zeus son of Kronos has caught me fast in bitter futility.
He is hard; who before this time promised me and consented
that I might sack strong-walled Ilion and sail homeward.
Now he has devised a vile deception, and bids me go back
to Argos in dishonor having lost many of my people. 115
Such is the way it will be pleasing to Zeus, who is too strong,
who before now has broken the crests of many cities
and will break them again, since his power is beyond all others.
And this shall be a thing of shame for the men hereafter
to be told, that so strong, so great a host of Achaians 120
carried on and fought in vain a war that was useless
against men fewer than they, with no accomplishment shown for it;
since if both sides were to be willing, Achaians and Trojans,
to cut faithful oaths of truce, and both to be numbered,
and the Trojans were to be counted by those with homes in the city, 125
while we were to be allotted in tens, we Achaians,
and each one of our tens chose a man of Troy to pour wine for it,
still there would be many tens left without a wine steward.
By so much I claim we sons of the Achaians outnumber
the Trojans—those who live in the city; but there are companions 130
from other cities in their numbers, wielders of the spear, to help them,
who drive me hard back again and will not allow me,
despite my will, to sack the well-founded stronghold of Ilion.
And now nine years of mighty Zeus have gone by, and the timbers
of our ships have rotted away and the cables are broken 135
and far away our own wives and our young children

are sitting within our halls and wait for us, while still our work here
stays forever unfinished as it is, for whose sake we came hither.
Come then, do as I say, let us all be won over; let us
140   run away with our ships to the beloved land of our fathers
since no longer now shall we capture Troy of the wide ways."

So he spoke, and stirred up the passion in the breast of all those
who were within that multitude and listened to his counsel.
And the assembly was shaken as on the sea the big waves
145   in the main by Ikaria, when the south and south-east winds
driving down from the clouds of Zeus the father whip them.
As when the west wind moves across the grain deep standing,
boisterously, and shakes and sweeps it till the tassels lean, so
all of that assembly was shaken, and the men in tumult
150   swept to the ships, and underneath their feet the dust lifted
and rose high, and the men were all shouting to one another
to lay hold on the ships and drag them down to the bright sea.
They cleaned out the keel channels and their cries hit skyward
as they made for home and snatched the props from under the vessels.

155      Then for the Argives a homecoming beyond fate might have
been accomplished, had not Hera spoken a word to Athene:
"For shame, now, Atrytone, daughter of Zeus of the aegis.
As things are, the Argives will take flight homeward over
the wide ridges of the sea to the land of their fathers,
160   and thus they would leave to Priam and to the Trojans Helen
of Argos, to glory over, for whose sake many Achaians
lost their lives in Troy far from their own native country.
But go now along the host of the bronze-armored Achaians.
Speak to each man in words of gentleness and draw him backward
165   nor let them drag down to the salt sea their oarswept vessels."
So she spoke, nor did the goddess gray-eyed Athene
disobey her, but went in speed down the peaks of Olympos,
and lightly she arrived beside the fast ships of the Achaians.
There she came on Odysseus, the equal of Zeus in counsel,
170   standing still; he had laid no hand upon his black, strong-benched
vessel, since disappointment touched his heart and his spirit.

Athene of the gray eyes stood beside him and spoke to him:
"Son of Laërtes and seed of Zeus, resourceful Odysseus:
will it be this way? Will you all hurl yourselves into your benched ships
and take flight homeward to the beloved land of your fathers,              175
and would you thus leave to Priam and to the Trojans Helen
of Argos, to glory over, for whose sake many Achaians
lost their lives in Troy far from their own native country?
Go now along the host of the Achaians, give way no longer,
speak to each man in words of gentleness and draw them backward,          180
nor let them drag down to the salt sea their oarswept vessels."

    So she spoke, and he knew the voice of the goddess speaking
and went on the run, throwing aside his cloak, which was caught up
by Eurybates the herald of Ithaka who followed him.
He came face to face with Agamemnon, son of Atreus,                       185
and took from him the scepter of his fathers, immortal forever.
With this he went beside the ships of the bronze-armored Achaians.
    Whenever he encountered some king, or man of influence,
he would stand beside him and with soft words try to restrain him:
"Excellency! It does not become you to be frightened like any             190
coward. Rather hold fast and check the rest of the people.
You do not yet clearly understand the purpose of Atreides.
Now he makes trial, but soon will bear hard on the sons of the Achaians.
Did we not all hear what he was saying in council?
May he not in anger do some harm to the sons of the Achaians!            195
For the anger of god-supported kings is a big matter,
to whom honor and love are given from Zeus of the counsels."
    When he saw some man of the people who was shouting,
he would strike at him with his staff, and reprove him also:
"Excellency! Sit still and listen to what others tell you,               200
to those who are better men than you, you skulker and coward
and thing of no account whatever in battle or council.
Surely not all of us Achaians can be as kings here.
Lordship for many is no good thing. Let there be one ruler,
one king, to whom the son of devious-devising Kronos                     205
gives the scepter and right of judgment, to watch over his people."
    So he went through the army marshaling it, until once more

they swept back into the assembly place from the ships and the shelters
clamorously, as when from the thunderous sea the surf-beat
210   crashes upon the great beach, and the whole sea is in tumult.

Now the rest had sat down, and were orderly in their places,
but one man, Thersites of the endless speech, still scolded,
who knew within his head many words, but disorderly;
vain, and without decency, to quarrel with the princes
215   with any word he thought might be amusing to the Argives.
This was the ugliest man who came beneath Ilion. He was
bandy-legged and went lame of one foot, with shoulders
stooped and drawn together over his chest, and above this
his skull went up to a point with the wool grown sparsely upon it.
220   Beyond all others Achilleus hated him, and Odysseus.
These two he was forever abusing, but now at brilliant
Agamemnon he clashed the shrill noise of his abuse. The Achaians
were furiously angry with him, their minds resentful.
But he, crying the words aloud, scolded Agamemnon:
225   "Son of Atreus, what thing further do you want, or find fault with
now? Your shelters are filled with bronze; there are plenty of the choicest
women for you within your shelter, whom we Achaians
give to you first of all whenever we capture some stronghold.
Or is it still more gold you will be wanting, that some son
230   of the Trojans, breakers of horses, brings as ransom out of Ilion,
one that I, or some other Achaian, capture and bring in?
Is it some young woman to lie with in love and keep her
all to yourself apart from the others? It is not right for
you, their leader, to lead in sorrow the sons of the Achaians.
235   My good fools, poor abuses, you women, not men, of Achaia,
let us go back home in our ships, and leave this man here
by himself in Troy to mull his prizes of honor
that he may find out whether or not we others are helping him.
And now he has dishonored Achilleus, a man much better
240   than he is. He has taken his prize by force and keeps her.
But there is no gall in Achilleus' heart, and he is forgiving.
Otherwise, son of Atreus, this were your last outrage."
So he spoke, Thersites, abusing Agamemnon
the shepherd of the people. But brilliant Odysseus swiftly

came beside him scowling and laid a harsh word upon him:                                245
"Fluent orator though you be, Thersites, your words are
ill-considered. Stop, nor stand up alone against princes.
Out of all those who came beneath Ilion with Atreides
I assert there is no worse man than you are. Therefore
you shall not lift up your mouth to argue with princes,                                 250
cast reproaches into their teeth, nor sustain the homegoing.
We do not even know clearly how these things will be accomplished,
whether we sons of the Achaians shall win home well or badly;
yet you sit here throwing abuse at Agamemnon,
Atreus' son, the shepherd of the people, because the Danaän                             255
fighters give him much. You argue nothing but scandal.
And this also will I tell you, and it will be a thing accomplished.
If once more I find you playing the fool, as you are now,
nevermore let the head of Odysseus sit on his shoulders,
let me nevermore be called Telemachos' father,                                          260
if I do not take you and strip away your personal clothing,
your mantle and your tunic that cover over your nakedness,
and send you thus bare and howling back to the fast ships,
whipping you out of the assembly place with the strokes of indignity."

So he spoke and dashed the scepter against his back and                                 265
shoulders, and he doubled over, and a round tear dropped from him,
and a bloody welt stood up between his shoulders under
the golden scepter's stroke, and he sat down again, frightened,
in pain, and looking helplessly about wiped off the tear-drops.
Sorry though the men were they laughed over him happily,                                270
and thus they would speak to each other, each looking at the man next him:
"Come now: Odysseus has done excellent things by thousands,
bringing forward good counsels and ordering armed encounters;
but now this is far the best thing he ever has accomplished
among the Argives, to keep this thrower of words, this braggart                         275
out of assembly. Never again will his proud heart stir him
up, to wrangle with the princes in words of revilement."

So the multitude spoke, but Odysseus, sacker of cities,
stood up holding the staff, and beside him gray-eyed Athene
in the likeness of a herald enjoined the people to silence,                             280
that at once the foremost and the utmost sons of the Achaians

might listen to him speaking and deliberate his counsel.
He in kind intention toward all stood forth and addressed them:
"Son of Atreus: now, my lord, the Achaians are trying
285 to make you into a thing of reproach in the sight of all mortal
men, and not fulfilling the promise they undertook once
as they set forth to come here from horse-pasturing Argos,
to go home only after you had sacked strong-walled Ilion.
For as if they were young children or widowed women
290 they cry out and complain to each other about going homeward.
In truth, it is a hard thing, to be grieved with desire for going.
Any man who stays away one month from his own wife
with his intricate ship is impatient, one whom the storm winds
of winter and the sea rising keep back. And for us now
295 this is the ninth of the circling years that we wait here. Therefore
I cannot find fault with the Achaians for their impatience
beside the curved ships; yet always it is disgraceful
to wait long and at the end go home empty-handed.
No, but be patient, friends, and stay yet a little longer
300 until we know whether Kalchas' prophecy is true or is not true.
For I remember this thing well in my heart, and you all are
witnesses, whom the spirits of death have not carried away from us;
yesterday and before, at Aulis, when the ships of the Achaians
were gathered bringing disaster to the Trojans and Priam,
305 and we beside a spring and upon the sacred altars
were accomplishing complete hecatombs to the immortals
under a fair plane tree whence ran the shining of water.
There appeared a great sign; a snake, his back blood-mottled,
a thing of horror, cast into the light by the very Olympian,
310 wound its way from under the altar and made toward the plane tree.
Thereupon were innocent children, the young of the sparrow,
cowering underneath the leaves at the uttermost branch tip,
eight of them, and the mother was the ninth, who bore these children.
The snake ate them all after their pitiful screaming,
315 and the mother, crying aloud for her young ones, fluttered about him,
and as she shrilled he caught her by the wing and coiled around her.
After he had eaten the sparrow herself with her children
the god who had shown the snake forth made him a monument,
striking him stone, the son of devious-devising Kronos,

and we standing about marveled at the thing that had been done.    320
So as the terror and the god's monsters came into the hecatomb
Kalchas straightway spoke before us interpreting the gods' will:
'Why are you turned voiceless, you flowing-haired Achaians?
Zeus of the counsels has shown us this great portent: a thing late,
late to be accomplished, whose glory shall perish never.    325
As this snake has eaten the sparrow herself with her children,
eight of them, and the mother was the ninth, who bore them,
so for years as many as this shall we fight in this place
and in the tenth year we shall take the city of the wide ways.'
So he spoke to us then; now all this is being accomplished.    330
Come then, you strong-greaved Achaians, let every man stay
here, until we have taken the great citadel of Priam."

So he spoke, and the Argives shouted aloud, and about them
the ships echoed terribly to the roaring Achaians
as they cried out applause to the word of godlike Odysseus.    335
Now among them spoke the Gerenian horseman, Nestor:
"Oh, for shame! You are like children when you hold assembly,
infant children, to whom the works of war mean nothing.
Where then shall our covenants go, and the oaths we have taken?
Let counsels and the meditations of men be given to the flames then,    340
with the unmixed wine poured and the right hands we trusted.
We do our fighting with words only, and can discover
no remedy, though we have stayed here a long time. Son of Atreus,
do you still as before hold fast to your counsel unshaken
and be the leader of the Argives through the strong encounters;    345
let them go perish, these one or two, who think apart from
the rest of the Achaians, since there will be no use in them
until they get back again to Argos without ever learning
whether Zeus of the aegis promises false or truly.
For I say to you, the son of all-powerful Kronos    350
promised, on that day when we went in our fast-running vessels,
we of Argos, carrying blood and death to the Trojans.
He flashed lightning on our right, showing signs of favor.
Therefore let no man be urgent to take the way homeward
until after he has lain in bed with the wife of a Trojan    355
to avenge Helen's longing to escape and her lamentations.

But if any man is terribly desirous to go home,
let him only lay his hands on his well-benched black ship,
that before all others he may win death and destruction.
360 Come, my lord: yourself be careful, and listen to another.
This shall not be a word to be cast away that I tell you.
Set your men in order by tribes, by clans, Agamemnon,
and let clan go in support of clan, let tribe support tribe.
If you do it this way, and the Achaians obey you,
365 you will see which of your leaders is bad, and which of your people,
and which also is brave, since they will fight in divisions,
and might learn also whether by magic you fail to take this
city, or by men's cowardice and ignorance of warfare."
       Then in answer again spoke powerful Agamemnon:
370 "Once again, old sir, you surpass the sons of the Achaians
in debate. O father Zeus, Athene, Apollo:
would that among the Achaians I had ten such counselors.
Then perhaps the city of lord Priam would be bent
underneath our hands, captured and sacked. But instead
375 Zeus of the aegis, son of Kronos, has given me bitterness,
who drives me into unprofitable abuse and quarrels.
For I and Achilleus fought together for a girl's sake
in words' violent encounter, and I was the first to be angry.
If ever we can take one single counsel, then no longer
380 shall the Trojans' evil be put aside, not even for a small time.
Now go back, take your dinner, and let us gather our warcraft.
Let a man put a good edge to his spear, and his shield in order,
let each put good fodder before his swift-footed horses,
and each man look well over his chariot, careful of his fighting,
385 that all day long we may be in the division of hateful Ares.
There will not even for a small time be any respite
unless darkness come down to separate the strength of the fighters.
There will be a man's sweat on the shield-strap binding the breast to
the shield hiding the man's shape, and the hand on the spear grow weary.
390 There will be sweat on a man's horse straining at the smoothed chariot.
But any man whom I find trying, apart from the battle,
to hang back by the curved ships, for him no longer
will there be any means to escape the dogs and the vultures."

So he spoke, and the Argives shouted aloud, as surf crashing
against a sheer ness, driven by the south wind descending,                          395
some cliff out-jutting, left never alone by the waves from
all the winds that blow, as they rise one place and another.
They stood up scattering and made for the ships; they kindled
the fires' smoke along the shelters, and took their dinner,
each man making a sacrifice to some one of the immortal                              400
gods, in prayer to escape death and the grind of Ares.
But Agamemnon the lord of men dedicated a fat ox
five years old to Zeus, all-powerful son of Kronos,
and summoned the nobles and the great men of all the Achaians,
Nestor before all others, and next the lord Idomeneus,                              405
next the two Aiantes and Tydeus' son Diomedes,
and sixth Odysseus, a man like Zeus himself for counsel.
Of his own accord came Menelaos of the great war cry
who knew well in his own mind the cares of his brother.
They stood in a circle about the ox and took up the scattering                      410
barley; and among them powerful Agamemnon spoke in prayer:
"Zeus, exalted and mightiest, sky-dwelling in the dark mist:
let not the sun go down and disappear into darkness
until I have hurled headlong the castle of Priam
blazing, and lit the castle gates with the flames' destruction;                     415
not till I have broken at the chest the tunic of Hektor
torn with the bronze blade, and let many companions about him
go down headlong into the dust, teeth gripping the ground soil."
He spoke, but none of this would the son of Kronos accomplish,
who accepted the victims, but piled up the unwished-for hardship.                   420

Now when all had made prayer and flung down the scattering barley,
first they drew back the victim's head, cut his throat and skinned him,
and cut away the meat from the thighs and wrapped them in fat,
making a double fold, and laid shreds of flesh above them.
Placing these on sticks cleft and peeled they burned them,                          425
and spitted the vitals and held them over the flame of Hephaistos.
But when they had burned the thigh pieces and tasted the vitals
they cut all the remainder into pieces and spitted them
and roasted all carefully and took off the pieces.

430 Then after they had finished the work and got the feast ready
they feasted, nor was any man's hunger denied a fair portion.
But when they had put away their desire for eating and drinking
the Gerenian horseman Nestor began speaking among them:
"Son of Atreus, most lordly and king of men, Agamemnon,
435 let us talk no more of these things, nor for a long time
set aside the action which the god puts into our hands now.
Come then, let the heralds of the bronze-armored Achaians
make proclamation to the people and assemble them by the vessels,
and let us together as we are go down the wide host
440 of the Achaians, to stir more quickly the fierce war god."
    He spoke, nor did the lord of men Agamemnon neglect him,
but straightway commanded the clear-voiced heralds to summon
by proclamation to battle the flowing-haired Achaians;
and the heralds made their cry and the men were assembled swiftly.
445 And they, the god-supported kings, about Agamemnon
ran marshaling the men, and among them gray-eyed Athene
holding the dear treasured aegis, ageless, immortal,
from whose edges float a hundred all-golden tassels,
each one carefully woven, and each worth a hundred oxen.
450 With this fluttering she swept through the host of the Achaians
urging them to go forward. She kindled the strength in each man's
heart to take the battle without respite and keep on fighting.
And now battle became sweeter to them than to go back
in their hollow ships to the beloved land of their fathers.

455     As obliterating fire lights up a vast forest
along the crests of a mountain, and the flare shows far off,
so as they marched, from the magnificent bronze the gleam went
dazzling all about through the upper air to the heaven.
    These, as the multitudinous nations of birds winged,
460 of geese, and of cranes, and of swans long-throated
in the Asian meadow beside the Kaÿstrian waters
this way and that way make their flights in the pride of their wings, then
settle in clashing swarms and the whole meadow echoes with them,
so of these the multitudinous tribes from the ships and
465 shelters poured to the plain of Skamandros, and the earth beneath their
feet and under the feet of their horses thundered horribly.

They took position in the blossoming meadow of Skamandros,
thousands of them, as leaves and flowers appear in their season.
  Like the multitudinous nations of swarming insects
who drive hither and thither about the stalls of the sheepfold          470
in the season of spring when the milk splashes in the milk pails:
in such numbers the flowing-haired Achaians stood up
through the plain against the Trojans, hearts burning to break them.
  These, as men who are goatherds among the wide goatflocks
easily separate them in order as they take to the pasture,               475
thus the leaders separated them this way and that way
toward the encounter, and among them powerful Agamemnon,
with eyes and head like Zeus who delights in thunder,
like Ares for girth, and with the chest of Poseidon;
like some ox of the herd pre-eminent among the others,                   480
a bull, who stands conspicuous in the huddling cattle;
such was the son of Atreus as Zeus made him that day,
conspicuous among men, and foremost among the fighters.

  Tell me now, you Muses who have your homes on Olympos.
For you, who are goddesses, are there, and you know all things,          485
and we have heard only the rumor of it and know nothing.
Who then of those were the chief men and the lords of the Danaäns?
I could not tell over the multitude of them nor name them,
not if I had ten tongues and ten mouths, not if I had
a voice never to be broken and a heart of bronze within me,              490
not unless the Muses of Olympia, daughters
of Zeus of the aegis, remembered all those who came beneath Ilion.
I will tell the lords of the ships, and the ships numbers.

  Leïtos and Peneleos were leaders of the Boiotians,
with Arkesilaos and Prothoënor and Klonios;                              495
they who lived in Hyria and in rocky Aulis,
in the hill-bends of Eteonos, and Schoinos, and Skolos,
Thespeia and Graia, and in spacious Mykalessos;
they who dwelt about Harma and Eilesion and Erythrai,
they who held Eleon and Hyle and Peteon,                                 500
with Okalea and Medeon, the strong-founded citadel,
Kopai, and Eutresis, and Thisbe of the dove-cotes;

they who held Koroneia, and the meadows of Haliartos,
they who held Plataia, and they who dwelt about Glisa,
505   they who held the lower Thebes, the strong-founded citadel,
and Onchestos the sacred, the shining grove of Poseidon;
they who held Arne of the great vineyards, and Mideia,
with Nisa the sacrosanct and uttermost Anthedon.
Of these there were fifty ships in all, and on board
510   each of these a hundred and twenty sons of the Boiotians.

But they who lived in Aspledon and Orchomenos of the Minyai,
Askalaphos led these, and Ialmenos, children of Ares,
whom Astyochē bore to him in the house of Aktor
Azeus' son, a modest maiden; she went into the chamber
515   with strong Ares, who was laid in bed with her secretly.
With these two there were marshaled thirty hollow vessels.
    Schedios and Epistrophos led the men of Phokis,
children of Iphitos, who was son of great-hearted Naubolos.
These held Kyparissos, and rocky Pytho, and Krisa
520   the sacrosanct together with Daulis and Panopeus;
they who lived about Hyampolis and Anamoreia,
they who dwelt about Kephisos, the river immortal,
they who held Lilaia beside the well springs of Kephisos.
Following along with these were forty black ships,
525   and the leaders marshaling the ranks of the Phokians set them
in arms on the left wing of the host beside the Boiotians.

Swift Aias son of Oïleus led the men of Lokris,
the lesser Aias, not great in size like the son of Telamon,
but far slighter. He was a small man armored in linen,
530   yet with the throwing spear surpassed all Achaians and Hellenes.
These were the dwellers in Kynos and Opoeis and Kalliaros,
and in Bessa, and Skarphe, and lovely Augeiai,
in Thronion and Tarphe and beside the waters of Boagrios.
Following along with him were forty black ships
535   of the Lokrians, who dwell across from sacred Euboia.
    They who held Euboia, the Abantes, whose wind was fury,
Chalkis, and Eretria, the great vineyards of Histiaia,
and seaborne Kerinthos and the steep stronghold of Dion,

they who held Karystos and they who dwelt about Styra,
of these the leader was Elephenor, scion of Ares,                                540
son of Chalkodon and lord of the great-hearted Abantes.
And the running Abantes followed with him, their hair grown
long at the back, spearmen furious with the out-reached ash spear
to rip the corselets girt about the chests of their enemies.
Following along with him were forty black ships.                                 545

But the men who held Athens, the strong-founded citadel,
the deme of great-hearted Erechtheus, whom once Athene
Zeus' daughter tended after the grain-giving fields had borne him,
and established him to be in Athens in her own rich temple;
there as the circling years go by the sons of the Athenians               550
make propitiation with rams and bulls sacrificed;
of these men the leader was Peteos' son Menestheus.
Never on earth before had there been a man born like him
for the arrangement in order of horses and shielded fighters.
Nestor alone could challenge him, since he was far older.                    555
Following along with him were fifty black ships.
    Out of Salamis Aias brought twelve ships and placed them
next to where the Athenian battalions were drawn up.

They who held Argos and Tiryns of the huge walls,
Hermionē and Asinē lying down the deep gulf,                               560
Troizen and Eïonai, and Epidauros of the vineyards,
they who held Aigina and Mases, sons of the Achaians,
of these the leader was Diomedes of the great war cry
with Sthenelos, own son to the high-renowned Kapaneus,
and with them as a third went Euryalos, a man godlike,                    565
son of Mekisteus the king, and scion of Talaos;
but the leader of all was Diomedes of the great war cry.
Following along with these were eighty black ships.
    But the men who held Mykenai, the strong-founded citadel,
Korinth the luxurious, and strong-founded Kleonai;                          570
they who dwelt in Orneai and lovely Araithyrea,
and Sikyon, where of old Adrestos had held the kingship;
they who held Hyperesia and steep Gonoëssa,
they who held Pellene and they who dwelt about Aigion,

575 all about the seashore and about the wide headland of Helikē,
of their hundred ships the leader was powerful Agamemnon,
Atreus' son, with whom followed far the best and bravest
people; and among them he himself stood armored in shining
bronze, glorying, conspicuous among the great fighters,
580 since he was greatest among them all, and led the most people.

They who held the swarming hollow of Lakedaimon,
Pharis, and Sparta, and Messe of the dove-cotes,
they who dwelt in Bryseiai and lovely Augeiai,
they who held Amyklai and the seaward city of Helos,
585 they who held Laas, and they who dwelt about Oitylos,
of these his brother Menelaos of the great war cry
was leader, with sixty ships marshaled apart from the others.
He himself went among them in the confidence of his valor,
driving them battleward, since above all his heart was eager
590 to avenge Helen's longing to escape and her lamentations.
They who dwelt about Pylos and lovely Arene,
and Thryon, the Alpheios crossing, and strong-built Aipy;
they who lived in Kyparisseeis and Amphigeneia,
Pteleos and Helos and Dorion, where the Muses
595 encountering Thamyris the Thracian stopped him from singing
as he came from Oichalia and Oichalian Eurytos;
for he boasted that he would prevail, if the very Muses,
daughters of Zeus who holds the aegis, were singing against him,
and these in their anger struck him maimed, and the voice of wonder
600 they took away, and made him a singer without memory;
of these the leader was the Gerenian horseman, Nestor,
in whose command were marshaled ninety hollow vessels.

They who held Arkadia under the sheer peak, Kyllene,
beside the tomb of Aipytos, where men fight at close quarters,
605 they who dwelt in Orchomenos of the flocks, and Pheneos,
about Rhipe and Stratia and windy Enispe;
they who held Tegea and Mantineia the lovely,
they who held Stymphalos, and dwelt about Parrhasia,
their leader was Angkaios' son, powerful Agapenor.
610 Sixty was the number of their ships, and in each ship

went many men of Arkadia, well skilled in battle.
Agamemnon the lord of men himself had given
these for the crossing of the wine-blue sea their strong-benched vessels,
Atreus' son, since the work of the sea was nothing to these men.
They who lived in Bouprasion and brilliant Elis,                           615
all as much as Hyrmine and Myrsinos the uttermost
and the Olenian rock and Alesion close between them,
of these there were four chieftains, and with each man ten swift
vessels followed, with many Epeian men on board them.
Of two tens Thalpios and Amphimachos were leaders,                         620
of Aktor's seed, sons one of Kteatos, one of Eurytos.
Ten more were led by Amaryngkeus' son, strong Diores,
and of the fourth ten godlike Polyxeinos was leader,
son of lord Agasthenes, of the race of Augeias.

They who came from Doulichion and the sacred Echinai,                      625
islands, where men live across the water from Elis,
Meges was the leader of these, a man like Ares,
Phyleus' son, whom the rider dear to Zeus had begotten,
Phyleus, who angered with his father had settled Doulichion
Following along with him were forty black ships.                           630

But Odysseus led the high-hearted men of Kephallenia,
those who held Ithaka and leaf-trembling Neriton,
those who dwelt about Krokyleia and rugged Aigilips,
those who held Zakynthos and those who dwelt about Samos,
those who held the mainland and the places next to the crossing.          635
All these men were led by Odysseus, like Zeus in counsel.
Following with him were twelve ships with bows red painted.

Thoas son of Andraimon was leader of the Aitolians,
those who dwelt in Pleuron and Olenos and Pylene,
Kalydon of the rocks and Chalkis beside the seashore,                     640
since no longer were the sons of high-hearted Oineus living,
nor Oineus himself, and fair-haired Meleagros had perished.
So all the lordship of the Aitolians was given to Thoas.
Following along with him were forty black ships.
Idomeneus the spear-famed was leader of the Kretans,                      645

those who held Knosos and Gortyna of the great walls,
Lyktos and Miletos and silver-shining Lykastos,
and Phaistos and Rhytion, all towns well established,
and others who dwelt beside them in Krete of the hundred cities.
650 Of all these Idomeneus the spear-famed was leader,
with Meriones, a match for the murderous Lord of Battles.
Following along with these were eighty black ships.

Herakles' son Tlepolemos the huge and mighty
led from Rhodes nine ships with the proud men of Rhodes aboard them,
655 those who dwelt about Rhodes and were ordered in triple division,
Ialysos and Lindos and silver-shining Kameiros.
Of all these Tlepolemos the spear-famed was leader,
he whom Astyocheia bore to the strength of Herakles.
Herakles brought her from Ephyra and the river Selleëis
660 after he sacked many cities of strong, god-supported fighters.
Now when Tlepolemos was grown in the strong-built mansion,
he struck to death his own father's beloved uncle,
Likymnios, scion of Ares, a man already ageing.
At once he put ships together and assembled a host of people
665 and went fugitive over the sea, since the others threatened,
the rest of the sons and the grandsons of the strength of Herakles.
And he came to Rhodes a wanderer, a man of misfortune,
and they settled there in triple division by tribes, beloved
of Zeus himself, who is lord over all gods and all men,
670 Kronos' son, who showered the wonder of wealth upon them.
Nireus from Syme led three balanced vessels,
Nireus son of Aglaia and the king Charopos,
Nireus, the most beautiful man who came beneath Ilion
beyond the rest of the Danaäns next after perfect Achilleus.
675 But he was a man of poor strength and few people with him.

They who held Nisyros and Krapathos and Kasos,
and Kos, Eurypylos' city, and the islands called Kalydnai,
of these again Pheidippos and Antiphos were the leaders,
sons both of Thessalos who was born to the lord Herakles.
680 In their command were marshaled thirty hollow vessels.
Now all those who dwelt about Pelasgian Argos,

those who lived by Alos and Alope and at Trachis,
those who held Phthia and Hellas the land of fair women,
who were called Myrmidons and Hellenes and Achaians,
of all these and their fifty ships the lord was Achilleus.                685
But these took no thought now for the grim clamor of battle
since there was no one who could guide them into close order,
since he, swift-footed brilliant Achilleus, lay where the ships were,
angered over the girl of the lovely hair, Briseis,
whom after much hard work he had taken away from Lyrnessos       690
after he had sacked Lyrnessos and the walls of Thebe
and struck down Epistrophos and Mynes the furious spearmen,
children of Euenos, king, and son of Selepios.
For her sake he lay grieving now, but was soon to rise up.

     They who held Phylakē and Pyrasos of the flowers,               695
the precinct of Demeter, and Iton, mother of sheepflocks,
Antron by the seashore, and Pteleos deep in the meadows,
of these in turn fighting Protesilaos was leader
while he lived; but now the black earth had closed him under,
whose wife, cheeks torn for grief, was left behind in Phylakē       700
and a marriage half completed; a Dardanian man had killed him
as he leapt from his ship, far the first of all the Achaians.
Yet these, longing as they did for their leader, did not go leaderless,
but Podarkes, scion of Ares, set them in order,
child of Iphikles, who in turn was son to Phylakos                 705
rich in flocks, full brother of high-hearted Protesilaos,
younger born; but the elder man was braver also,
Protesilaos, a man of battle; yet still the people
lacked not a leader, though they longed for him and his valor.
Following along with Podarkes were forty black ships.              710

     They who lived by Pherai beside the lake Boibeis,
by Boibe and Glaphyrai and strong-founded Iolkos,
of their eleven ships the dear son of Admetos was leader,
Eumelos, born to Admetos by the beauty among women
Alkestis, loveliest of all the daughters of Pelias.              715
     They who lived about Thaumakia and Methone,
they who held Meliboia and rugged Olizon,

of their seven ships the leader was Philoktetes
skilled in the bow's work, and aboard each vessel were fifty
720    oarsmen, each well skilled in the strength of the bow in battle.
Yet he himself lay apart in the island, suffering strong pains,
in Lemnos the sacrosanct, where the sons of the Achaians had left him
in agony from the sore bite of the wicked water snake.
There he lay apart in his pain; yet soon the Argives
725    beside their ships were to remember lord Philoktetes.
Yet these, longing as they did for their leader, did not go leaderless,
but Medon, the bastard son of Oïleus, set them in order,
whom Rhene bore to Oïleus the sacker of cities.

They who held Trikke and the terraced place of Ithome,
730    and Oichalia, the city of Oichalian Eurytos,
of these in turn the leaders were two sons of Asklepios,
good healers both themselves, Podaleirios and Machaon.
In their command were marshaled thirty hollow vessels.
They who held Ormenios and the spring Hypereia,
735    they who held Asterion and the pale peaks of Titanos,
Eurypylos led these, the shining son of Euaimon.
Following along with him were forty black ships.
They who held Argissa and dwelt about Gyrtone,
Orthe and Elone and the white city Oloösson,
740    of these the leader was Polypoites, stubborn in battle,
son of Peirithoös whose father was Zeus immortal,
he whom glorious Hippodameia bore to Peirithoös
on that day when he wreaked vengeance on the hairy beast men
and drove them from Pelion and hurled them against the Aithikes;
745    not by himself, for Leonteus was with him, scion of Ares,
Leonteus, son of high-hearted Koronos the son of Kaineus.
Following in the guidance of these were forty black ships.
Gouneus from Kyphos led two and twenty vessels,
and the Enienes and the Perrhaibians stubborn in battle
750    followed him, they who made their homes by wintry Dodona,
and they who by lovely Titaressos held the tilled acres,
Titaressos, who into Peneios casts his bright current:
yet he is not mixed with the silver whirls of Peneios,
but like oil is floated along the surface above him:

since he is broken from the water of Styx, the fearful oath-river.     755
Prothoös son of Tenthredon was leader of the Magnesians,
those who dwelt about Peneios and leaf-trembling
Pelion. Of these Prothoös the swift-footed was leader.
Following along with him were forty black ships.

These then were the leaders and the princes among the Danaäns.     760
Tell me then, Muse, who of them all was the best and bravest
of the men, and the men's horses, who went with the sons of Atreus.

Best by far among the horses were the mares of Eumelos
Pheres' son, that he drove, swift-moving like birds, alike in
texture of coat, in age, both backs drawn level like a plumb-line.     765
These Apollo of the silver bow had bred in Pereia,
mares alike, who went with the terror of the god of battle.
Among the men far the best was Telamonian Aias
while Achilleus stayed angry, since he was far best of all of them,
and the horses also, who carried the blameless son of Peleus.     770
But Achilleus lay apart among his curved sea-wandering
vessels, raging at Agamemnon, the shepherd of the people,
Atreus' son; and his men beside the break of the sea-beach
amused themselves with discs and with light spears for throwing
and bows; and the horses, standing each beside his chariot,     775
champed their clover and the parsley that grows in wet places,
resting, while the chariots of their lords stood covered
in the shelters, and the men forlorn of their warlike leader
wandered here and there in the camp, and did no fighting.

But the rest went forward, as if all the earth with flame were eaten,     780
and the ground echoed under them, as if Zeus who delights in thunder
were angry, as when he batters the earth about Typhoeus,
in the land of the Arimoi, where they say Typhoeus lies prostrate.
Thus beneath their feet the ground re-echoed loudly
to men marching, who made their way through the plain in great speed.     785

Now to the Trojans came as messenger wind-footed Iris,
in her speed, with the dark message from Zeus of the aegis.
These were holding assembly in front of the doors of Priam

gathered together in one place, the elders and the young men.
790 Standing close at hand swift-running Iris spoke to them,
and likened her voice to that of the son of Priam, Polites,
who confident in the speed of his feet kept watch for the Trojans
aloft the ancient burial mound of ancient Aisyetes,
waiting for the time when the Achaians should move from their vessels.
795 In this man's likeness Iris the swift-running spoke to them:
"Old sir, dear to you forever are words beyond number
as once, when there was peace; but stintless war has arisen.
In my time I have gone into many battles among men,
yet never have I seen a host like this, not one so numerous.
800 These look terribly like leaves, or the sands of the seashore,
as they advance across the plain to fight by the city.
Hektor, on you beyond all I urge this, to do as I tell you:
all about the great city of Priam are many companions,
but multitudinous is the speech of the scattered nations:
805 let each man who is their leader give orders to these men,
and let each set his citizens in order, and lead them."
    She spoke, nor did Hektor fail to mark the word of the goddess.
Instantly he broke up the assembly; they ran to their weapons.
All the gates were opened and the people swept through them
810 on foot, and with horses, and a clamor of shouting rose up.

    Near the city but apart from it there is a steep hill
in the plain by itself, so you pass one side or the other.
This men call the Hill of the Thicket, but the immortal
gods have named it the burial mound of dancing Myrina.
815 There the Trojans and their companions were marshaled in order.
    Tall Hektor of the shining helm was leader of the Trojans,
Priam's son; and with him far the best and the bravest
fighting men were armed and eager to fight with the spear's edge.
    The strong son of Anchises was leader of the Dardanians,
820 Aineias, whom divine Aphrodite bore to Anchises
in the folds of Ida, a goddess lying in love with a mortal:
not Aineias alone, but with him were two sons of Antenor,
Archelochos and Akamas, both skilled in all fighting.
    They who lived in Zeleia below the foot of Mount Ida,
825 men of wealth, who drank the dark water of Aisepos,

Trojans: of these the leader was the shining son of Lykaon,
Pandaros, with the bow that was actual gift of Apollo.

They who held Adresteia and the countryside of Apaisos,
they who held Pityeia and the sheer hill of Tereia,
these were led by Adrestos and Amphios armored in linen,                    830
sons both of Merops of Perkote, who beyond all men
knew the art of prophecy, and tried to prevent his two sons
from going into the battle where men die. Yet these would not
listen, for the spirits of dark death were driving them onward.

They who dwelt in the places about Perkote and Praktion,                   835
who held Sestos and Abydos and brilliant Arisbe,
their leader was Asios, Hyrtakos' son, a prince of the people,
Asios, son of Hyrtakos, whom huge and shining
horses carried from Arisbe and the river Selleëis.

Hippothoös led the tribes of spear-fighting Pelasgians,                    840
they who dwelt where the soil is rich about Larissa;
Hippothoös and Pylaios, scion of Ares, led these,
sons alike of Pelasgian Lethos, son of Teutamos.

Akamas led the men of Thrace with the fighter Peiroös,
all the Thracians held within the hard stream of the Hellespont.          845

Euphemos was leader of the Kikonian spearmen,
son of Troizenos, Keas' son, the king whom the gods loved.

Pyraichmes in turn led the Paionians with their curved bows,
from Amydon far away and the broad stream of Axios,
Axios, whose stream on all earth is the loveliest water.                  850

Pylaimones the wild heart was leader of the Paphlagonēs,
from the land of the Enetoi where the wild mules are engendered,
those who held Kytoros and those who dwelt about Sesamos,
those whose renowned homes were about Parthenios river,
and Kromna and Aigialos and high Erythinoi.                               855

Odios and Epistrophos led the Halizones
from Alybē far away, where silver was first begotten.

Chromis, with Ennomos the augur, was lord of the Mysians;
yet his reading of birds could not keep off dark destruction
but he went down under the hands of swift-running Aiakides              860
in the river, as he slew other Trojans beside him.

Phorkys and godlike Askanios were lords of the Phrygians
from Askania far away, eager to fight in the onfall.
Mesthles and Antiphos were leaders of the Maionians,
865  sons of Talaimenes, who was born of the lake Gygaian:
these led the Maionian men whose home was beneath Mount Tmolos.
The Karians of the outland speech were led by Nastes,
they who held Miletos and the leaf-deep mountain of Phthiron,
the waters of Maiandros and the headlong peaks of Mykalē;
870  of these the two leaders were Amphimachos and Nastes,
Nastes and Amphimachos, the shining sons of Nomion.
Nastes came like a girl to the fighting in golden raiment,
poor fool, nor did this avail to keep dismal death back;
but he went down under the hands of swift-running Aiakides
875  in the river, and fiery Achilleus stripped the gold from him.
Sarpedon with unfaulted Glaukos was lord of the Lykians
from Lykia far away, and the whirling waters of Xanthos.

# BOOK THREE

Now when the men of both sides were set in order by their leaders,
the Trojans came on with clamor and shouting, like wildfowl,
as when the clamor of cranes goes high to the heavens,
when the cranes escape the winter time and the rains unceasing
and clamorously wing their way to the streaming Ocean,                    5
bringing to the Pygmaian men bloodshed and destruction:
at daybreak they bring on the baleful battle against them.
But the Achaian men went silently, breathing valor,
stubbornly minded each in his heart to stand by the others.
    As on the peaks of a mountain the south wind scatters the thick mist,    10
no friend to the shepherd, but better than night for the robber,
and a man can see before him only so far as a stone cast,
so beneath their feet the dust drove up in a stormcloud
of men marching, who made their way through the plain in great speed.

    Now as these in their advance had come close together,              15
Alexandros the godlike leapt from the ranks of the Trojans,
as challenger wearing across his shoulders the hide of a leopard,
curved bow and sword; while in his hands shaking two javelins
pointed with bronze, he challenged all the best of the Argives
to fight man to man against him in bitter combat.                       20
    Now as soon as Menelaos the warlike caught sight of him
making his way with long strides out in front of the army,
he was glad, like a lion who comes on a mighty carcass,
in his hunger chancing upon the body of a horned stag
or wild goat; who eats it eagerly, although against him               25

are hastening the hounds in their speed and the stalwart young men:
thus Menelaos was happy finding godlike Alexandros
there in front of his eyes, and thinking to punish the robber,
straightway in all his armor he sprang to the ground from his chariot.

30      But Alexandros the godlike when he saw Menelaos
showing among the champions, the heart was shaken within him;
to avoid death he shrank into the host of his own companions.
As a man who has come on a snake in the mountain valley
suddenly steps back, and the shivers come over his body,

35      and he draws back and away, cheeks seized with a green pallor;
so in terror of Atreus' son godlike Alexandros
lost himself again in the host of the haughty Trojans.
But Hektor saw him and in words of shame rebuked him:
"Evil Paris, beautiful, woman-crazy, cajoling,

40      better had you never been born, or killed unwedded.
Truly I could have wished it so; it would be far better
than to have you with us to our shame, for others to sneer at.
Surely now the flowing-haired Achaians laugh at us,
thinking you are our bravest champion, only because your

45      looks are handsome, but there is no strength in your heart, no courage.
Were you like this that time when in sea-wandering vessels
assembling oarsmen to help you you sailed over the water,
and mixed with the outlanders, and carried away a fair woman
from a remote land, whose lord's kin were spearmen and fighters,

50      to your father a big sorrow, and your city, and all your people,
to yourself a thing shameful but bringing joy to the enemy?
And now you would not stand up against warlike Menelaos?
Thus you would learn of the man whose blossoming wife you have taken.
The lyre would not help you then, nor the favors of Aphrodite,

55      nor your locks, when you rolled in the dust, nor all your beauty.
No, but the Trojans are cowards in truth, else long before this
you had worn a mantle of flying stones for the wrong you did us."
Then in answer Alexandros the godlike spoke to him:
"Hektor, seeing you have scolded me rightly, not beyond measure—

60      still, your heart forever is weariless, like an axe-blade
driven by a man's strength through the timber, one who, well skilled,
hews a piece for a ship, driven on by the force of a man's strength:
such is the heart in your breast, unshakable: yet do not

bring up against me the sweet favors of golden Aphrodite.
Never to be cast away are the gifts of the gods, magnificent,                          65
which they give of their own will; no man could have them for wanting them.
Now though, if you wish me to fight it out and do battle,
make the rest of the Trojans sit down, and all the Achaians,
and set me in the middle with Menelaos the warlike
to fight together for the sake of Helen and all her possessions.                       70
That one of us who wins and is proved stronger, let him
take the possessions fairly and the woman, and lead her homeward.
But the rest of you, having cut your oaths of faith and friendship,
dwell, you in Troy where the soil is rich, while those others return home
to horse-pasturing Argos, and Achaia the land of fair women."                          75
    So he spoke, and Hektor hearing his word was happy
and went into the space between and forced back the Trojan battalions
holding his spear by the middle until they were all seated.
But the flowing-haired Achaians kept pointing their bows at him
with arrows and with flung stones striving ever to strike him                          80
until Agamemnon lord of men cried out in a great voice:
"Argives, hold: cast at him no longer, O sons of the Achaians.
Hektor of the shining helm is trying to tell us something."
    So he spoke, and they stopped fighting and suddenly all fell
silent; but Hektor between them spoke now to both sides:                               85
"Hear from me, Trojans and strong-greaved Achaians, the word
of Alexandros, for whose sake this strife has arisen.
He would have all the rest of the Trojans and all the Achaians
lay aside on the bountiful earth their splendid armor
while he himself in the middle and warlike Menelaos                                    90
fight alone for the sake of Helen and all her possessions.
That one of them who wins and is proved stronger, let him
take the possessions fairly and the woman, and lead her homeward
while the rest of us cut our oaths of faith and friendship."

    So he spoke, and all of them stayed stricken to silence;                          95
but among them spoke out Menelaos of the great war cry:
"Listen now to me also; since beyond all others this sorrow
comes closest to my heart, and I think the Argives and Trojans
can go free of each other at last. You have suffered much evil
for the sake of this my quarrel since Alexandros began it.                            100

As for that one of us two to whom death and doom are given,
let him die: the rest of you be made friends with each other.
Bring two lambs: let one be white and the other black for
Earth and the Sun God, and for Zeus we will bring yet another.
105   Bring, that he may seal the pledges, the strength of Priam:
Priam himself, for his sons are outrageous, not to be trusted;
lest some man overstep Zeus' oaths, and make them be nothing.
Always it is, that the hearts in the younger men are frivolous,
but when an elder man is among them, he looks behind him
110   and in front, so that all comes out far better for both sides."
      So he spoke, and the Trojans and Achaians were joyful,
hoping now to be rid of all the sorrow of warfare.
They pulled their chariots into line, and themselves dismounted
and stripped off their armor which was laid on the ground beside them,
115   close together, so there was little ground left between them.
Hektor sent away to the citadel two heralds
lightly to bring down the lambs, and to summon Priam;
and powerful Agamemnon in turn sent Talthybios
to go down to the hollow ships, with orders to bring two
120   lambs: he did not disobey the order of great Agamemnon.

      Now to Helen of the white arms came a messenger, Iris,
in the likeness of her sister-in-law, the wife of Antenor's
son, whom strong Helikaon wed, the son of Antenor,
Laodikē, loveliest looking of all the daughters of Priam.
125   She came on Helen in the chamber; she was weaving a great web,
a red folding robe, and working into it the numerous struggles
of Trojans, breakers of horses, and bronze-armored Achaians,
struggles that they endured for her sake at the hands of the war god.
Iris of the swift feet stood beside her and spoke to her:
130   "Come with me, dear girl, to behold the marvelous things done
by Trojans, breakers of horses, and bronze-armored Achaians,
who just now carried sorrowful war against each other,
in the plain, and all their desire was for deadly fighting;
now they are all seated in silence, the fighting has ended;
135   they lean on their shields, the tall spears stuck in the ground beside them.
But Menelaos the warlike and Alexandros will fight
with long spears against each other for your possession.

You shall be called beloved wife of the man who wins you."
Speaking so the goddess left in her heart sweet longing
after her husband of time before, and her city and parents.                    140
And at once, wrapping herself about in shimmering garments,
she went forth from the chamber, letting fall a light tear;
not by herself, since two handmaidens went to attend her,
Aithre, Pittheus' daughter, and Klymenē of the ox eyes.
Rapidly they came to the place where the Skaian gates stood.                   145

Now those who sat with Priam: Panthoös and Thymoites,
Lampos and Klytios, Hiketaon, scion of Ares,
with Antenor and Oukalegon, both men of good counsel:
these were seated by the Skaian gates, elders of the people.
Now through old age these fought no longer, yet were they excellent            150
speakers still, and clear, as cicadas who through the forest
settle on trees, to issue their delicate voice of singing.
Such were they who sat on the tower, chief men of the Trojans.
And these, as they saw Helen along the tower approaching,
murmuring softly to each other uttered their winged words:                     155
"Surely there is no blame on Trojans and strong-greaved Achaians
if for long time they suffer hardship for a woman like this one.
Terrible is the likeness of her face to immortal goddesses.
Still, though she be such, let her go away in the ships, lest
she be left behind, a grief to us and our children."                          160
So they spoke: but Priam aloud called out to Helen:
"Come over where I am, dear child, and sit down beside me,
to look at your husband of time past, your friends and your people.
I am not blaming you: to me the gods are blameworthy
who drove upon me this sorrowful war against the Achaians.                    165
So you could tell me the name of this man who is so tremendous;
who is this Achaian man of power and stature?
Though in truth there are others taller by a head than he is,
yet these eyes have never yet looked on a man so splendid
nor so lordly as this: such a man might well be royal."                        170
Helen, the shining among women, answered and spoke to him:
"Always to me, beloved father, you are feared and respected;
and I wish bitter death had been what I wanted, when I came hither
following your son, forsaking my chamber, my kinsmen,

175 my grown child, and the loveliness of girls my own age.
It did not happen that way: and now I am worn with weeping.
This now I will tell you in answer to the question you asked me.
That man is Atreus' son Agamemnon, widely powerful,
at the same time a good king and a strong spearfighter,
180 once my kinsman, slut that I am. Did this ever happen?"
This she said, and the old man spoke again, wondering at him:
"O son of Atreus, blessed, child of fortune and favor,
many are these beneath your sway, these sons of the Achaians.
Once before this time I visited Phrygia of the vineyards.
185 There I looked on the Phrygian men with their swarming horses,
so many of them, the people of Otreus and godlike Mygdon,
whose camp was spread at that time along the banks of Sangarios:
and I myself, a helper in war, was marshaled among them
on that day when the Amazon women came, men's equals.
190 Yet even they were not so many as these glancing-eyed Achaians."

Next again the old man asked her, seeing Odysseus:
"Tell me of this one also, dear child; what man can he be,
shorter in truth by a head than Atreus' son Agamemnon,
but broader, it would seem, in the chest and across the shoulders.
195 Now as his armor lies piled on the prospering earth, still he
ranges, like some ram, through the marshaled ranks of the fighters.
Truly, to some deep-fleeced ram would I liken him
who makes his way through the great mass of the shining sheep-flocks."
Helen, the daughter descended of Zeus, spoke then in answer:
200 "This one is Laërtes' son, resourceful Odysseus,
who grew up in the country, rough though it be, of Ithaka,
to know every manner of shiftiness and crafty counsels."
In his turn Antenor of the good counsel answered her:
"Surely this word you have spoken, my lady, can be no falsehood.
205 Once in the days before now brilliant Odysseus came here
with warlike Menelaos, and their embassy was for your sake.
To both of these I gave in my halls kind entertainment
and I learned the natural way of both, and their close counsels.
Now when these were set before the Trojans assembled
210 and stood up, Menelaos was bigger by his broad shoulders
but Odysseus was the more lordly when both were seated.

Now before all when both of them spun their speech and their counsels,
Menelaos indeed spoke rapidly, in few words
but exceedingly lucid, since he was no long speaker
nor one who wasted his words though he was only a young man.          215
But when that other drove to his feet, resourceful Odysseus,
he would just stand and stare down, eyes fixed on the ground beneath him,
nor would he gesture with the staff backward and forward, but hold it
clutched hard in front of him, like any man who knows nothing.
Yes, you would call him a sullen man, and a fool likewise.          220
But when he let the great voice go from his chest, and the words came
drifting down like the winter snows, then no other mortal
man beside could stand up against Odysseus. Then we
wondered less beholding Odysseus' outward appearance."

     Third in order, looking at Aias, the old man asked her:          225
"Who then is this other Achaian of power and stature
towering above the Argives by head and broad shoulders?"
     Helen with the light robes and shining among women answered him:
"That one is gigantic Aias, wall of the Achaians,
and beyond him there is Idomeneus like a god standing          230
among the Kretans, and the lords of Krete are gathered about him.
Many a time warlike Menelaos would entertain him
in our own house when he came over from Krete. And I see them
all now, all the rest of the glancing-eyed Achaians,
all whom I would know well by sight, whose names I could tell you,          235
yet nowhere can I see those two, the marshals of the people,
Kastor, breaker of horses, and the strong boxer, Polydeukes,
my own brothers, born with me of a single mother.
Perhaps these came not with the rest from Lakedaimon the lovely,
or else they did come here in their sea-wandering ships, yet          240
now they are reluctant to go with the men into battle
dreading the words of shame and all the reproach that is on me."
     So she spoke, but the teeming earth lay already upon them
away in Lakedaimon, the beloved land of their fathers.

     Now through the town the heralds brought the symbols of oaths pledged,          245
two young rams, and cheerful wine, the yield of the tilled land
in a goatskin wine sack, while another carried the shining

mixing bowl (the herald Idaios) and the golden wine cups.
Standing beside the aged man he spoke words to arouse him:
250 "Son of Laomedon, rise up: you are called by the chief men
of Trojans, breakers of horses, and bronze-armored Achaians
to come down into the plain that you may seal the oaths pledged.
For warlike Menelaos and Alexandros are to fight
with long spears against each other for the sake of the woman.
255 Let the woman go to the winner, and all the possessions.
Let the rest of them, cutting their oaths of faith and friendship,
dwell, we in Troy where the soil is rich, while those others return home
to horse-pasturing Argos and Achaia the land of fair women."
So he spoke, and the old man shuddered, but called his companions
260 to yoke the horses to the car, and they promptly obeyed him.
And Priam mounted into the car and gathered the reins back
as Antenor beside him stepped into the fair-wrought chariot.
Through the Skaian gates to the plain they steered the swift horses.
Now when these had come among the Trojans and Achaians,
265 they stepped down on the prospering earth from their car with horses
and made their way striding among the Achaians and Trojans.
On the other side rose up the lord of men, Agamemnon,
and the resourceful Odysseus rose up. Meanwhile the proud heralds
led up the victims for the gods' oaths, and in a great wine-bowl
270 mixed the wine, and poured water over the hands of the princes.
Atreus' son laid hands upon his work-knife, and drew it
from where it hung ever beside the mighty sheath of his war sword
and cut off hairs from the heads of the lambs; and the heralds thereafter
passed these about to all the princes of the Trojans and Achaians.
275 Atreus' son uplifting his hands then prayed in a great voice:
"Father Zeus, watching over us from Ida, most high, most honored,
and Helios, you who see all things, who listen to all things,
earth, and rivers, and you who under the earth take vengeance
on dead men, whoever among them has sworn to falsehood,
280 you shall be witnesses, to guard the oaths of fidelity.
If it should be that Alexandros slays Menelaos,
let him keep Helen for himself, and all her possessions,
and we in our seafaring ships shall take our way homeward.
But if the fair-haired Menelaos kills Alexandros,
285 then let the Trojans give back Helen and all her possessions,

and pay also a price to the Argives which will be fitting,
which among people yet to come shall be as a standard.
Then if Priam and the sons of Priam are yet unwilling
after Alexandros has fallen to pay me the penalty,
I myself shall fight hereafter for the sake of the ransom,                290
here remaining, until I have won to the end of my quarrel."
    So he spoke, and with pitiless bronze he cut the lambs' throats,
letting them fall gasping again to the ground, the life breath
going away, since the strength of the bronze had taken it from them.
Drawing the wine from the mixing bowls in the cups, they poured it       295
forth, and made their prayer to the gods who live everlasting.
And thus would murmur any man, Achaian or Trojan:
"Zeus, exalted and mightiest, and you other immortals,
let those, whichever side they may be, who do wrong to the oaths sworn
first, let their brains be spilled on the ground as this wine is spilled now,   300
theirs and their sons', and let their wives be the spoil of others."

    They spoke, but none of this would the son of Kronos accomplish.
Now among them spoke Priam descended of Dardanos also:
"Listen to me, you Trojans and you strong-greaved Achaians
Now I am going away to windy Ilion, homeward,                           305
since I cannot look with these eyes on the sight of my dear son
fighting against warlike Menelaos in single combat.
Zeus knows—maybe he knows—and the rest of the gods immortal
for which of the two death is appointed to end this matter."
    He spoke, a godlike man, and laid the lambs in the chariot,         310
and mounted into it himself, and pulled the reins backward.
Antenor beside him stepped up into the fair-wrought chariot.
These two took their way backward and made for Ilion.
Hektor now, the son of Priam, and brilliant Odysseus
measured out the distance first, and thereafter picked up              315
two lots, and put them in a brazen helmet, and shook them,
to see which one of the two should be first to cast with his bronze spear,
and the people on each side held up their hands to the gods, and prayed
to them. Thus would murmur any man, Achaian or Trojan:
"Father Zeus, watching over us from Ida, most high, most honored,       320
whichever man has made what has happened happen to both sides,
grant that he be killed and go down to the house of Hades.

Let the friendship and the sworn faith be true for the rest of us."
So they spoke, and tall Hektor of the shining helm shook
325   the lots, looking backward, and at once Paris' lot was outshaken.
All the rest sat down in their ranks on the ground, at the place where
the glittering armor of each was piled by his light-footed horses,
while one of them put about his shoulders his splendid armor,
brilliant Alexandros, the lord of lovely-haired Helen.
330   First he placed along his legs the fair greaves linked with
silver fastenings to hold the greaves at the ankles.
Afterward he girt on about his chest the corselet
of Lykaon his brother since this fitted him also.
Across his shoulders he slung the sword with the nails of silver,
335   a bronze sword, and above it the great shield, huge and heavy.
Over his powerful head he set the well-fashioned helmet
with the horse-hair crest, and the plumes nodded terribly above it.
He took up a strong-shafted spear that fitted his hand's grip.
In the same way warlike Menelaos put on his armor.

340     Now when these two were armed on either side of the battle,
they strode into the space between the Achaians and Trojans,
looking terror at each other; and amazement seized the beholders,
Trojans, breakers of horses, and strong-greaved Achaians.
They took their stand in the measured space not far from each other
345   raging each at the other man and shaking their spearshafts.
First of the two Alexandros let go his spear far-shadowing
and struck the shield of Atreus' son on its perfect circle
nor did the bronze point break its way through, but the spearhead bent back
in the strong shield. And after him Atreus' son, Menelaos,
350   was ready to let go the bronze spear, with a prayer to Zeus father:
"Zeus, lord, grant me to punish the man who first did me injury,
brilliant Alexandros, and beat him down under my hands' strength
that any one of the men to come may shudder to think of
doing evil to a kindly host, who has given him friendship."
355    So he spoke, and balanced the spear far-shadowed, and threw it
and struck the shield of Priam's son on its perfect circle.
All the way through the glittering shield went the heavy spearhead
and smashed its way through the intricately worked corselet;
straight ahead by the flank the spearhead shore through his tunic,

yet he bent away to one side and avoided the dark death.                                    360
Drawing his sword with the silver nails, the son of Atreus
heaving backward struck at the horn of his helmet; the sword-blade
three times broken and four times broken fell from his hand's grip.
Groaning, the son of Atreus lifted his eyes to the wide sky:
"Father Zeus, no God beside is more baleful than you are.                                    365
Here I thought to punish Alexandros for his wickedness;
and now my sword is broken in my hands, and the spear flew vainly
out of my hands on the throw before, and I have not hit him."
    He spoke, and flashing forward laid hold of the horse-haired helmet
and spun him about, and dragged him away toward the strong-greaved                           370
        Achaians,
for the broidered strap under the softness of his throat strangled Paris,
fastened under his chin to hold on the horned helmet.
Now he would have dragged him away and won glory forever
had not Aphrodite daughter of Zeus watched sharply.
She broke the chinstrap, made from the hide of a slaughtered bullock,                        375
and the helmet came away empty in the heavy hand of Atreides.
The hero whirled the helmet about and sent it flying
among the strong-greaved Achaians, and his staunch companions
        retrieved it.
He turned and made again for his man, determined to kill him
with the bronze spear. But Aphrodite caught up Paris                                         380
easily, since she was divine, and wrapped him in a thick mist
and set him down again in his own perfumed bedchamber.

    She then went away to summon Helen, and found her
on the high tower, with a cluster of Trojan women about her.
She laid her hand upon the robe immortal, and shook it,                                      385
and spoke to her, likening herself to an aged woman,
a wool-dresser who when she was living in Lakedaimon
made beautiful things out of wool, and loved her beyond all others.
Likening herself to this woman Aphrodite spoke to her:
    "Come with me: Alexandros sends for you to come home to him.                             390
He is in his chamber now, in the bed with its circled pattern,
shining in his raiment and his own beauty; you would not think
that he came from fighting against a man; you would think he was going
rather to a dance, or rested and had been dancing lately."

395    So she spoke, and troubled the spirit in Helen's bosom.
       She, as she recognized the round, sweet throat of the goddess
       and her desirable breasts and her eyes that were full of shining,
       she wondered, and spoke a word and called her by name, thus:
       "Strange divinity! Why are you still so stubborn to beguile me?
400    Will you carry me further yet somewhere among cities
       fairly settled? In Phrygia or in lovely Maionia?
       Is there some mortal man there also who is dear to you?
       Is it because Menelaos has beaten great Alexandros
       and wishes, hateful even as I am, to carry me homeward,
405    is it for this that you stand in your treachery now beside me?
       Go yourself and sit beside him, abandon the gods' way,
       turn your feet back never again to the path of Olympos
       but stay with him forever, and suffer for him, and look after him
       until he makes you his wedded wife, or makes you his slave girl.
410    Not I. I am not going to him. It would be too shameful.
       I will not serve his bed, since the Trojan women hereafter
       would laugh at me, all, and my heart even now is confused with sorrows."
       Then in anger Aphrodite the shining spoke to her:
       "Wretched girl, do not tease me lest in anger I forsake you
415    and grow to hate you as much as now I terribly love you,
       lest I encompass you in hard hate, caught between both sides,
       Danaäns and Trojans alike, and you wretchedly perish."
       So she spoke, and Helen daughter of Zeus was frightened
       and went, shrouding herself about in the luminous spun robe,
420    silent, unseen by the Trojan women, and led by the goddess.

       When they had come to Alexandros' splendidly wrought house,
       the rest of them, the handmaidens went speedily to their own work,
       but she, shining among women, went to the high-vaulted bedchamber.
       Aphrodite the sweetly laughing drew up an armchair,
425    carrying it, she, a goddess, and set it before Alexandros,
       and Helen, daughter of Zeus of the aegis, took her place there
       turning her eyes away, and spoke to her lord in derision:
       "So you came back from fighting. Oh, how I wish you had died there
       beaten down by the stronger man, who was once my husband.
430    There was a time before now you boasted that you were better
       than warlike Menelaos, in spear and hand and your own strength.

Go forth now and challenge warlike Menelaos
once again to fight you in combat. But no: I advise you
rather to let it be, and fight no longer with fair-haired
Menelaos, strength against strength in single combat                              435
recklessly. You might very well go down before his spear."
    Paris then in turn spoke to her thus and answered her:
"Lady, censure my heart no more in bitter reprovals.
This time Menelaos with Athene's help has beaten me;
another time I shall beat him. We have gods on our side also.            440
Come, then, rather let us go to bed and turn to lovemaking.
Never before as now has passion enmeshed my senses,
not when I took you the first time from Lakedaimon the lovely
and caught you up and carried you away in seafaring vessels,
and lay with you in the bed of love on the island Kranaë,                         445
not even then, as now, did I love you and sweet desire seize me."

    Speaking, he led the way to the bed; and his wife went with him.
So these two were laid in the carven bed. But Atreides
ranged like a wild beast up and down the host, to discover
whether he could find anywhere godlike Alexandros.                               450
Yet could none of the Trojans nor any renowned companion
show Alexandros then to warlike Menelaos.
These would not have hidden him for love, if any had seen him,
since he was hated among them all as dark death is hated.
    Now among them spoke forth the lord of men Agamemnon:            455
"Listen to me, O Trojans, Dardanians and companions:
clearly the victory is with warlike Menelaos.
Do you therefore give back, with all her possessions, Helen
of Argos, and pay a price that shall be befitting,
which among people yet to come shall be as a standard."                          460
    So spoke Atreus' son, and the other Achaians applauded him.

# BOOK FOUR

Now the gods at the side of Zeus were sitting in council
over the golden floor, and among them the goddess Hebe
poured them nectar as wine, while they in the golden drinking-cups
drank to each other, gazing down on the city of the Trojans.
5  Presently the son of Kronos was minded to anger
Hera, if he could, with words offensive, speaking to cross her:
"Two among the goddesses stand by Menelaos,
Hera of Argos, and Athene who stands by her people.
Yet see, here they are sitting apart, looking on at the fighting,
10  and take their pleasure. Meanwhile laughing Aphrodite forever
stands by her man and drives the spirits of death away from him.
Even now she has rescued him when he thought he would perish.
So, the victory now is with warlike Menelaos.
Let us consider then how these things shall be accomplished,
15  whether again to stir up grim warfare and the terrible
fighting, or cast down love and make them friends with each other.
If somehow this way could be sweet and pleasing to all of us,
the city of lord Priam might still be a place men dwell in,
and Menelaos could take away with him Helen of Argos."

20  So he spoke; and Athene and Hera muttered, since they were
sitting close to each other, devising evil for the Trojans.
Still Athene stayed silent and said nothing, but only
sulked at Zeus her father, and savage anger took hold of her.
But the heart of Hera could not contain her anger, and she spoke forth:
25  "Majesty, son of Kronos, what sort of thing have you spoken?
How can you wish to make wasted and fruitless all this endeavor,

the sweat that I have sweated in toil, and my horses worn out
gathering my people, and bringing evil to Priam and his children.
Do it then; but not all the rest of us gods will approve you."

Deeply troubled, Zeus who gathers the clouds answered her:          30
"Dear lady, what can be all the great evils done to you
by Priam and the sons of Priam, that you are thus furious
forever to bring down the strong-founded city of Ilion?
If you could walk through the gates and through the towering ramparts
and eat Priam and the children of Priam raw, and the other          35
Trojans, then, then only might you glut at last your anger.
Do as you please then. Never let this quarrel hereafter
be between you and me a bitterness for both of us.
And put away in your thoughts this other thing that I tell you:
whenever I in turn am eager to lay waste some city,                  40
as I please, one in which are dwelling men who are dear to you,
you shall not stand in the way of my anger, but let me do it,
since I was willing to grant you this with my heart unwilling.
For of all the cities beneath the sun and the starry heaven
dwelt in by men who live upon earth, there has never been one       45
honored nearer to my heart than sacred Ilion
and Priam, and the people of Priam of the strong ash spear.
Never yet has my altar gone without fair sacrifice,
the libation and the savor, since this is our portion of honor."

Then the goddess the ox-eyed lady Hera answered:                    50
"Of all cities there are three that are dearest to my own heart:
Argos and Sparta and Mykenai of the wide ways. All these,
whenever they become hateful to your heart, sack utterly.
I will not stand up for these against you, nor yet begrudge you.
Yet if even so I bear malice and would not have you destroy them,   55
in malice I will accomplish nothing, since you are far stronger.
Yet my labor also should not be let go unaccomplished;
I am likewise a god, and my race is even what yours is,
and I am first of the daughters of devious-devising Kronos,
both ways, since I am eldest born and am called your consort,       60
yours, and you in turn are lord over all the immortals.
Come then, in this thing let us both give way to each other,
I to you, you to me, and so the rest of the immortal
gods will follow. Now in speed give orders to Athene

65   to visit horrible war again on Achaians and Trojans,
     and try to make it so that the Trojans are first offenders
     to do injury against the oaths to the far-famed Achaians."

     She spoke, nor did the father of gods and men disobey her,
     but immediately he spoke in winged words to Athene:
70   "Go now swiftly to the host of the Achaians and Trojans
     and try to make it so that the Trojans are first offenders
     to do injury against the oaths to the far-famed Achaians."
     Speaking so he stirred up Athene, who was eager before this,
     and she went in a flash of speed down the pinnacles of Olympos.
75   As when the son of devious-devising Kronos casts down
     a star, portent to sailors or to widespread armies of peoples
     glittering, and thickly the sparks of fire break from it,
     in such likeness Pallas Athene swept flashing earthward
     and plunged between the two hosts; and amazement seized the beholders,
80   Trojans, breakers of horses, and strong-greaved Achaians.
     And thus they would speak to each other, each looking at the man next him:
     "Surely again there will be evil war and terrible
     fighting, or else now friendship is being set between both sides
     by Zeus, who is appointed lord of the wars of mortals."
85      Thus would murmur any man, Achaian or Trojan.
     She in the likeness of a man merged among the Trojans assembled,
     Laodokos, Antenor's son, a powerful spearman,
     searching for godlike Pandaros, if she might somewhere come on him.
     She found the son of Lykaon, a man blameless and powerful,
90   standing still, and about him were the ranks of strong, shield-armored
     people, who had followed him from the streams of Aisepos.
     Speaking in winged words she stood beside him and spoke to him:
     "Wise son of Lykaon, would you now let me persuade you?
     So you might dare send a flying arrow against Menelaos
95   and win you glory and gratitude in the sight of all Trojans,
     particularly beyond all else with prince Alexandros.
     Beyond all beside you would carry away glorious gifts from him,
     were he to see warlike Menelaos, the son of Atreus,
     struck down by your arrow, and laid on the sorrowful corpse-fire.
100  Come then, let go an arrow against haughty Menelaos,
     but make your prayer to Apollo the light-born, the glorious archer,

that you will accomplish a grand sacrifice of lambs first born
when you come home again to the city of sacred Zeleia."

   So spoke Athene, and persuaded the fool's heart in him.
Straightway he unwrapped his bow, of the polished horn from            105
a running wild goat he himself had shot in the chest once,
lying in wait for the goat in a covert as it stepped down
from the rock, and hit it in the chest so it sprawled on the boulders.
The horns that grew from the goat's head were sixteen palms' length.
A bowyer working on the horn then bound them together,                  110
smoothing them to a fair surface, and put on a golden string hook.
Pandaros strung his bow and put it in position, bracing it
against the ground, and his brave friends held their shields in front of him
for fear the warlike sons of the Achaians might rise up and rush him
before he had struck warlike Menelaos, the son of Atreus.              115
He stripped away the lid of the quiver, and took out an arrow
feathered, and never shot before, transmitter of dark pain.
Swiftly he arranged the bitter arrow along the bowstring,
and made his prayer to Apollo the light-born, the glorious archer,
that he would accomplish a grand sacrifice of lambs first born         120
when he came home again to the city of sacred Zeleia.
He drew, holding at once the grooves and the ox-hide bowstring
and brought the string against his nipple, iron to the bowstave.
But when he had pulled the great weapon till it made a circle,
the bow groaned, and the string sang high, and the arrow, sharp-pointed,  125
leapt away, furious, to fly through the throng before it.
Still the blessed gods immortal did not forget you,
Menelaos, and first among them Zeus' daughter, the spoiler,
who standing in front of you fended aside the tearing arrow.
She brushed it away from his skin as lightly as when a mother          130
brushes a fly away from her child who is lying in sweet sleep,
steering herself the arrow's course straight to where the golden
belt buckles joined and the halves of his corselet were fitted together.
The bitter arrow was driven against the joining of the war belt
and passed clean through the war belt elaborately woven;               135
into the elaborately wrought corselet the shaft was driven
and the guard which he wore to protect his skin and keep the spears off,
which guarded him best, yet the arrow plunged even through this also

and with the very tip of its point it grazed the man's skin
140  and straightway from the cut there gushed a cloud of dark blood.

As when some Maionian woman or Karian with purple
colors ivory, to make it a cheek piece for horses;
it lies away in an inner room, and many a rider
longs to have it, but it is laid up to be a king's treasure,
145  two things, to be the beauty of the horse, the pride of the horseman:
so, Menelaos, your shapely thighs were stained with the color
of blood, and your legs also and the ankles beneath them.
Agamemnon the lord of men was taken with shuddering
fear as he saw how from the cut the dark blood trickled downward,
150  and Menelaos the warlike himself shuddered in terror;
but when he saw the binding strings and the hooked barbs outside
the wound, his spirit was gathered again back into him. Agamemnon
the powerful spoke to them, groaning heavily, and by the hand held
Menelaos, while their companions were mourning beside them:
155  "Dear brother, it was your death I sealed in the oaths of friendship,
setting you alone before the Achaians to fight with the Trojans.
So, the Trojans have struck you down and trampled on the oaths sworn.
Still the oaths and the blood of the lambs shall not be called vain,
the unmixed wine poured and the right hands we trusted.
160  If the Olympian at once has not finished this matter,
late will he bring it to pass, and they must pay a great penalty,
with their own heads, and with their women, and with their children.
For I know this thing well in my heart, and my mind knows it.
There will come a day when sacred Ilion shall perish,
165  and Priam, and the people of Priam of the strong ash spear,
and Zeus son of Kronos who sits on high, the sky-dwelling,
himself shall shake the gloom of his aegis over all of them
in anger for this deception. All this shall not go unaccomplished.
But I shall suffer a terrible grief for you, Menelaos,
170  if you die and fill out the destiny of your lifetime.
And I must return a thing of reproach to Argos the thirsty,
for now at once the Achaians will remember the land of their fathers;
and thus we would leave to Priam and to the Trojans Helen
of Argos, to glory over, while the bones of you rot in the ploughland
175  as you lie dead in Troy, on a venture that went unaccomplished.

And thus shall some Trojan speak in the proud show of his manhood,
leaping lightly as he speaks on the tomb of great Menelaos:
'Might Agamemnon accomplish his anger thus against all his
enemies, as now he led here in vain a host of Achaians
and has gone home again to the beloved land of his fathers                    180
with ships empty, and leaving behind him brave Menelaos.'
Thus shall a man speak: then let the wide earth open to take me."

    Then in encouragement fair-haired Menelaos spoke to him:
"Do not fear, nor yet make afraid the Achaian people.
The sharp arrow is not stuck in a mortal place, but the shining           185
war belt turned it aside from its course, and the flap beneath it
with my guard of armor that bronze-smiths wrought carefully for me."
    Then in answer again spoke powerful Agamemnon:
"May it only be as you say, O Menelaos, dear brother!
But the physician will handle the wound and apply over it                  190
healing salves, by which he can put an end to the black pains."
    He spoke, and addressed Talthybios, his sacred herald:
"Talthybios, with all speed go call hither Machaon,
a man who is son of Asklepios and a blameless physician,
so that he may look at Menelaos, the warlike son of                        195
Atreus, whom someone skilled in the bow's use shot with an arrow,
Trojan or Lykian: glory to him, but to us a sorrow."
    He spoke, and the herald heard and did not disobey him,
but went on his way among the host of bronze-armored Achaians
looking about for the warrior Machaon; and saw him                         200
standing still, and about him the strong ranks of shield-bearing
people, who had come with him from horse-pasturing Trikka.
He came and stood close beside him and addressed him in winged words:
"Rise up, son of Asklepios; powerful Agamemnon calls you,
so that you may look at warlike Menelaos, the Achaians'                    205
leader, whom someone skilled in the bow's use shot with an arrow,
Trojan or Lykian: glory to him, but to us a sorrow."
    So he spoke, and stirred up the spirit within Machaon.
They went through the crowd along the widespread host of the Achaians.
But when they had come to the place where fair-haired Menelaos             210
had been hit, where all the great men were gathered about him
in a circle, and he stood in the midst of them, a man godlike,

straightway he pulled the arrow forth from the joining of the war belt,
and as it was pulled out the sharp barbs were broken backward.
215 He slipped open the war belt then and the flap beneath it
with the guard of armor that bronze-smiths wrought carefully for him.
But when he saw the wound where the bitter arrow was driven,
he sucked the blood and in skill laid healing medicines on it
that Cheiron in friendship long ago had given his father.

220    While they were working over Menelaos of the great war cry
all this time came on the ranks of the armored Trojans.
The Achaians again put on their armor, and remembered their warcraft.
    Then you would not have seen brilliant Agamemnon asleep nor
skulking aside, nor in any way a reluctant fighter,
225 but driving eagerly toward the fighting where men win glory.
He left aside his chariot gleaming with bronze, and his horses,
and these, breathing hard, were held aside by a henchman,
Eurymedon, born to Ptolemaios, the son of Peiraios.
Agamemnon told him to keep them well in hand, till the time came
230 when weariness might take hold of his limbs, through marshaling so many.
Then he, on foot as he was, ranged through the ranks of his fighters.
Those of the fast-mounted Danaäns he found eager, he would
stand beside these and urge them harder on with words spoken:
"Argives, do not let go now of this furious valor.
235 Zeus the father shall not be one to give aid to liars,
but these, who were the first to do violence over the oaths sworn,
vultures shall feed upon the delicate skin of their bodies,
while we lead away their beloved wives and innocent
children, in our ships, after we have stormed their citadel."
240    Any he might see hanging back from the hateful conflict
these in words of anger he would reproach very bitterly:
"Argives, you arrow-fighters, have you no shame, you disgraces?
Why are you simply standing there bewildered, like young deer
who after they are tired from running through a great meadow
245 stand there still, and there is no heart of courage within them?
Thus are you standing still bewildered and are not fighting.
Or are you waiting for the Trojans to come close, where the strong-sterned
ships have been hauled up along the strand of the gray sea,
so you may know if Kronos' son will hold his hand over you?"

Thus he ranged through the ranks of his men and set them in order.      250
On his way through the thronging men he came to the Kretans
who about valiant Idomeneus were arming for battle.
Idomeneus, like a boar in his strength, stood among the champions
while Meriones still urged along the last battalions.
Agamemnon the lord of men was glad as he looked at them      255
and in words of graciousness at once spoke to Idomeneus:
"I honor you, Idomeneus, beyond the fast-mounted
Danaäns whether in battle, or in any action whatever,
whether it be at the feast, when the great men of the Argives
blend in the mixing bowl the gleaming wine of the princes.      260
Even though all the rest of the flowing-haired Achaians
drink out their portion, still your cup stands filled forever
even as mine, for you to drink when the pleasure takes you.
Rise up then to battle, be such as you claimed in time past."
Then in turn Idomeneus lord of the Kretans answered him:      265
"Son of Atreus, I will in truth be a staunch companion
in arms, as first I promised you and bent my head to it.
Rouse up rather the rest of the flowing-haired Achaians
so that we may fight in all speed, since the Trojans have broken
their oaths: a thing that shall be death and sorrow hereafter      270
to them, since they were the first to do violence over the oaths sworn."

So he spoke, and Atreides, cheerful at heart, went onward.
On his way through the thronging men he came to the Aiantes.
These were armed, and about them went a cloud of foot-soldiers.
As from his watching place a goatherd watches a cloud move      275
on its way over the sea before the drive of the west wind;
far away though he be he watches it, blacker than pitch is,
moving across the sea and piling the storm before it,
and as he sees it he shivers and drives his flocks to a cavern;
so about the two Aiantes moved the battalions,      280
close-compacted of strong and god-supported young fighters,
black, and jagged with spear and shield, to the terror of battle.
Agamemnon the lord of men was glad when he looked at them,
and he spoke aloud to them and addressed them in winged words:
"Aiantes, O leaders of the bronze-armored Argives,      285
to you two I give no orders; it would not become me

to speed you, now that yourselves drive your people on to fight strongly.
Father Zeus, and Athene, and Apollo, if only
such a spirit were in the hearts of all of my people.
290 Then perhaps the city of lord Priam would be bent
underneath our hands, captured and utterly taken."

So he spoke, and left them there, and went among others.
There he came upon Nestor, the lucid speaker of Pylos,
setting in order his own companions and urging them to battle,
295 tall Pelagon with those about him, Alastor and Chromios,
Haimon the powerful, and Bias, shepherd of the people.
In front he ranged the mounted men with their horses and chariots,
and stationed the brave and numerous foot-soldiers behind them
to be the bastion of battle, and drove the cowards to the center
300 so that a man might be forced to fight even though unwilling.
First he gave orders to the drivers of horses, and warned them
to hold their horses in check and not be fouled in the multitude:
"Let no man in the pride of his horsemanship and his manhood
dare to fight alone with the Trojans in front of the rest of us,
305 neither let him give ground, since that way you will be weaker.
When a man from his own car encounters the enemy chariots
let him stab with his spear, since this is the stronger fighting.
So the men before your time sacked tower and city,
keeping a spirit like this in their hearts, and like this their purpose."
310 Thus the old man wise in fighting from of old encouraged them.
Agamemnon the lord of men was glad when he looked at him
and he spoke aloud to him and addressed him in winged words:
"Aged sir, if only, as the spirit is in your bosom,
so might your knees be also and the strength stay steady within you;
315 but age weakens you which comes to all; if only some other
of the fighters had your age and you were one of the young men!"
Nestor the Gerenian horseman spoke and answered him:
"Son of Atreus, so would I also wish to be that
man I was, when I cut down brilliant Ereuthalion.
320 But the gods give to mortals not everything at the same time;
if I was a young man then, now in turn old age is upon me.
Yet even so I shall be among the riders, and command them
with word and counsel; such is the privilege of the old men.

The young spearmen shall do the spear-fighting, those who are born
of a generation later than mine, who trust in their own strength."          325

So he spoke, and Atreides, cheerful at heart, went onward.
He came on the son of Peteos, Menestheus, driver of horses,
standing still, and about him the Athenians, urgent for battle.
Next to these resourceful Odysseus had taken position,
and beside him the Kephallenian ranks, no weak ones,                        330
were standing, since the men had not heard the clamor of battle
but even now fresh set in motion the battalions moved
of Achaians and Trojans, breakers of horses; so these standing
waited, until some other mass of Achaians advancing
might crash against the Trojans, and the battle be opened.                  335
Seeing these the lord of men Agamemnon scolded them
and spoke aloud to them and addressed them in winged words, saying:
"Son of Peteos, the king supported by God: and you, too,
you with your mind forever on profit and your ways of treachery,
why do you stand here skulking aside, and wait for the others?             340
For you two it is becoming to stand among the foremost
fighters, and endure your share of the blaze of battle,
since indeed you two are first to hear of the feasting
whenever we Achaians make ready a feast of the princes.
There it is your pleasure to eat the roast flesh, to drink                  345
as much as you please the cups of the wine that is sweet as honey.
Now, though, you would be pleased to look on though ten battalions
of Achaians were to fight with the pitiless bronze before you."
Then looking at him darkly resourceful Odysseus spoke to him:
"What is this word that broke through the fence of your teeth, Atreides?    350
How can you say that, when we Achaians waken the bitter
war god on Trojans, breakers of horses, I hang back from
fighting? Only watch, if you care to and if it concerns you,
the very father of Telemachos locked with the champion
Trojans, breakers of horses. Your talk is wind, and no meaning."           355
Powerful Agamemnon in turn answered him, laughing,
seeing that he was angered and taking back the word spoken:
"Son of Laërtes and seed of Zeus, resourceful Odysseus:
I must not be niggling with you, nor yet give you orders,
since I know how the spirit in your secret heart knows                     360

ideas of kindness only; for what you think is what I think.
Come now, I will make it good hereafter, if anything evil
has been said; let the gods make all this come to nothing."

So he spoke, and left him there, and went among others.
365 He came on the son of Tydeus, high-spirited Diomedes,
standing among the compacted chariots and by the horses,
and Kapaneus' son, Sthenelos, was standing beside him. At sight
of Diomedes the lord of men Agamemnon scolded him
and spoke aloud to him and addressed him in winged words, saying:
370 "Ah me, son of Tydeus, that daring breaker of horses,
why are you skulking and spying out the outworks of battle?
Such was never Tydeus' way, to lurk in the background,
but to fight the enemy far ahead of his own companions.
So they say who had seen him at work, since I never saw nor
375 encountered him ever; but they say he surpassed all others.
Once on a time he came, but not in war, to Mykenai
with godlike Polyneikes, a guest and a friend, assembling
people, since these were attacking the sacred bastions of Thebe,
and much they entreated us to grant him renowned companions.
380 And our men wished to give them and were assenting to what they asked for
but Zeus turned them back, showing forth portents that crossed them.
Now as these went forward and were well on their way, and came
to the river Asopos, and the meadows of grass and the deep rushes,
from there the Achaians sent Tydeus ahead with a message.
385 He went then and came on the Kadmeians in their numbers
feasting all about the house of mighty Eteokles.
There, stranger though he was, the driver of horses, Tydeus,
was not frightened, alone among so many Kadmeians,
but dared them to try their strength with him, and bested all of them
390 easily, such might did Pallas Athene give him.
The Kadmeians who lash their horses, in anger compacted
an ambuscade of guile on his way home, assembling together
fifty fighting men, and for these there were two leaders,
Maion, Haimon's son, in the likeness of the immortals,
395 with the son of Autophonos, Polyphontes stubborn in battle.
On these men Tydeus let loose a fate that was shameful.

He killed them all, except that he let one man get home again,
letting Maion go in obedience to the god's signs.
This was Tydeus, the Aitolian; yet he was father
to a son worse than himself at fighting, better in conclave." 400
So he spoke, and strong Diomedes gave no answer
in awe before the majesty of the king's rebuking;
but the son of Kapaneus the glorious answered him, saying:
"Son of Atreus, do not lie when you know the plain truth.
We two claim we are better men by far than our fathers. 405
We did storm the seven-gated foundation of Thebe
though we led fewer people beneath a wall that was stronger.
We obeyed the signs of the gods and the help Zeus gave us,
while those others died of their own headlong stupidity.
Therefore, never liken our fathers to us in honor." 410
Then looking at him darkly strong Diomedes spoke to him:
"Friend, stay quiet rather and do as I tell you; I will
find no fault with Agamemnon, shepherd of the people,
for stirring thus into battle the strong-greaved Achaians;
this will be his glory to come, if ever the Achaians 415
cut down the men of Troy and capture sacred Ilion.
If the Achaians are slain, then his will be the great sorrow.
Come, let you and me remember our fighting courage."

He spoke and leapt in all his gear to the ground from the chariot,
and the bronze armor girt to the chest of the king clashed terribly 420
as he sprang. Fear would have gripped even a man stout-hearted.
As when along the thundering beach the surf of the sea strikes
beat upon beat as the west wind drives it onward; far out
cresting first on the open water, it drives thereafter
to smash roaring along the dry land, and against the rock jut 425
bending breaks itself into crests spewing back the salt wash;
so thronged beat upon beat the Danaäns' close battalions
steadily into battle, with each of the lords commanding
his own men; and these went silently, you would not think
all these people with voices kept in their chests were marching, 430
silently, in fear of their commanders; and upon all
glittered as they marched the shining armor they carried.

But the Trojans, as sheep in a man of possessions' steading
stand in their myriads waiting to be drained of their white milk
435  and bleat interminably as they hear the voice of their lambs, so
the crying of the Trojans went up through the wide army.
Since there was no speech nor language common to all of them
but their talk was mixed, who were called there from many far places.
Ares drove these on, and the Achaians gray-eyed Athene,
440  and Terror drove them, and Fear, and Hate whose wrath is relentless,
she the sister and companion of murderous Ares,
she who is only a little thing at the first, but thereafter
grows until she strides on the earth with her head striking heaven.
She then hurled down bitterness equally between both sides
445  as she walked through the onslaught making men's pain heavier.

Now as these advancing came to one place and encountered,
they dashed their shields together and their spears, and the strength
of armored men in bronze, and the shields massive in the middle
clashed against each other, and the sound grew huge of the fighting.
450  There the screaming and the shouts of triumph rose up together
of men killing and men killed, and the ground ran blood.
As when rivers in winter spate running down from the mountains
throw together at the meeting of streams the weight of their water
out of the great springs behind in the hollow stream-bed,
455  and far away in the mountains the shepherd hears their thunder;
such, from the coming together of men, was the shock and the shouting.

Antilochos was first to kill a chief man of the Trojans,
valiant among the champions, Thalysias' son, Echepolos.
Throwing first, he struck the horn of the horse-haired helmet,
460  and the bronze spearpoint fixed in his forehead and drove inward
through the bone; and a mist of darkness clouded both eyes
and he fell as a tower falls in the strong encounter.
As he dropped, Elephenor the powerful caught him by the feet,
Chalkodon's son, and lord of the great-hearted Abantes,
465  and dragged him away from under the missiles, striving in all speed
to strip the armor from him, yet his outrush went short-lived.
For as he hauled the corpse high-hearted Agenor, marking

the ribs that showed bare under the shield as he bent over,
stabbed with the bronze-pointed spear and unstrung his sinews.
So the spirit left him and over his body was fought out 470
weary work by Trojans and Achaians, who like wolves
sprang upon one another, with man against man in the onfall.

There Telamonian Aias struck down the son of Anthemion
Simoeisios in his stripling's beauty, whom once his mother
descending from Ida bore beside the banks of Simoeis 475
when she had followed her father and mother to tend the sheepflocks.
Therefore they called him Simoeisios; but he could not
render again the care of his dear parents; he was short-lived,
beaten down beneath the spear of high-hearted Aias,
who struck him as he first came forward beside the nipple 480
of the right breast, and the bronze spearhead drove clean through the
    shoulder.
He dropped then to the ground in the dust, like some black poplar,
which in the land low-lying about a great marsh grows
smooth trimmed yet with branches growing at the uttermost tree-top:
one whom a man, a maker of chariots, fells with the shining 485
iron, to bend it into a wheel for a fine-wrought chariot,
and the tree lies hardening by the banks of a river.
Such was Anthemion's son Simoeisios, whom illustrious
Aias killed. Now Antiphos of the shining corselet,
Priam's son, made a cast at him in the crowd with the sharp spear 490
but missed Aias and struck Leukos, a brave companion
of Odysseus, in the groin, as he dragged a corpse off,
so that the body dropped from his hand as he fell above it.
For his killing Odysseus was stirred to terrible anger
and he strode out among the champions, helmed in bright bronze, 495
and stood close to the enemy hefting the shining javelin,
glaring round about him; and the Trojans gave way in the face
of the man throwing with the spear. And he made no vain cast,
but struck down Demokoön, a son of Priam, a bastard,
who came over from Abydos, and left his fast-running horses. 500
Odysseus struck him with the spear, in anger for his companion,
in the temple, and the bronze spearhead drove through the other

temple also, so that a mist of darkness clouded both eyes.
He fell, thunderously, and his armor clattered upon him.
505 The champions of Troy gave back then, and glorious Hektor,
and the Argives gave a great cry, and dragged back the bodies,
and drove their way far forward, but now Apollo watching
from high Pergamos was angered, and called aloud to the Trojans:
"Rise up, Trojans, breakers of horses, bend not from battle
510 with these Argives. Surely their skin is not stone, not iron
to stand up under the tearing edge of the bronze as it strikes them.
No, nor is Achilleus the child of lovely-haired Thetis
fighting, but beside the ship mulls his heartsore anger."
    So called the fearful god from the citadel, while Zeus' daughter
515 Tritogeneia, goddess most high, drove on the Achaians,
any of them she saw hanging back as she strode through the battle.

    Now his doom caught fast Amaryngkeus' son Diores,
who with a jagged boulder was smitten beside the ankle
in the right shin, and a lord of the Thracian warriors threw it,
520 Peiros, son of Imbrasos, who had journeyed from Ainos.
The pitiless stone smashed utterly the tendons on both sides
with the bones, and he was hurled into the dust backward
reaching out both hands to his own beloved companions,
gasping life out; the stone's thrower ran up beside him,
525 Peiros, and stabbed with his spear next the navel, and all his guts poured
out on the ground, and a mist of darkness closed over both eyes.
    Thoas the Aitolian hit Peiros as he ran backward
with the spear in the chest above the nipple, and the bronze point fixed
in the lung, and Thoas standing close dragged out the heavy
530 spear from his chest, and drawing his sharp sword struck him
in the middle of the belly, and so took the life from him,
yet did not strip his armor, for his companions about him
stood, Thracians with hair grown at the top, gripping their long spears,
and though he was a mighty man and a strong and proud one
535 thrust him from them so that he gave ground backward, staggering.
So in the dust these two lay sprawled beside one another,
lords, the one of the Thracians, the other of the bronze-armored
Epeians; and many others beside were killed all about them.

There no more could a man who was in that work make light of it,
one who still unhit and still unstabbed by the sharp bronze          540
spun in the midst of that fighting, with Pallas Athene's hold on
his hand guiding him, driving back the volleying spears thrown.
For on that day many men of the Achaians and Trojans
lay sprawled in the dust face downward beside one another.

# BOOK FIVE

There to Tydeus' son Diomedes Pallas Athene
granted strength and daring, that he might be conspicuous
among all the Argives and win the glory of valor.
She made weariless fire blaze from his shield and helmet
5   like that star of the waning summer who beyond all stars
rises bathed in the ocean stream to glitter in brilliance.
Such was the fire she made blaze from his head and his shoulders
and urged him into the middle fighting, where most were struggling.

There was a man of the Trojans, Dares, blameless and bountiful,
10   a priest consecrated to Hephaistos, and he had two sons,
Phegeus and Idaios, well skilled both in all fighting.
These two breaking from the ranks of the others charged against him
riding their chariot as Diomedes came on, dismounted.
Now as in their advance these had come close to each other
15   first of the two Phegeus let go his spear far-shadowing.
Over the left shoulder of Tydeus' son passed the pointed
spear, nor struck his body, and Diomedes thereafter
threw with the bronze, and the weapon cast from his hand flew not vain
but struck the chest between the nipples and hurled him from behind
20   his horses. And Idaios leaping left the fair-wrought chariot
nor had he the courage to stand over his stricken brother.
Even so he could not have escaped the black death-spirit
but Hephaistos caught him away and rescued him, shrouded in darkness,
that the aged man might not be left altogether desolate.
25   But the son of high-hearted Tydeus drove off the horses

and gave them to his company to lead back to the hollow vessels.
Now as the high-hearted Trojans watched the two sons of Dares,
one running away, and one cut down by the side of his chariot,
the anger in all of them was stirred. But gray-eyed Athene
took violent Ares by the hand, and in words she spoke to him:                    30
"Ares, Ares, manslaughtering, blood-stained, stormer of strong walls,
shall we not leave the Trojans and Achaians to struggle
after whatever way Zeus father grants glory to either,
while we two give ground together and avoid Zeus' anger?"

So she spoke, and led violent Ares out of the fighting                           35
and afterward caused him to sit down by the sands of Skamandros
while the Danaäns bent the Trojans back, and each of the princes
killed his man. And first the lord of men Agamemnon
hurled tall Odios, lord of the Halizones, from his chariot.
For in his back even as he was turning the spear fixed                           40
between the shoulders and was driven on through the chest beyond it.
He fell, thunderously, and his armor clattered upon him.
    Idomeneus killed Phaistos the son of Maionian Boros,
who had come out of Tarne with the deep soil. Idomeneus
the spear-renowned stabbed this man just as he was mounting                      45
behind his horses, with the long spear driven in the right shoulder.
He dropped from the chariot, and the hateful darkness took hold of him.
    The henchmen of Idomeneus stripped the armor from Phaistos,
while Menelaos son of Atreus killed with the sharp spear
Strophios' son, a man of wisdom in the chase, Skamandrios,                       50
the fine huntsman of beasts. Artemis herself had taught him
to strike down every wild thing that grows in the mountain forest.
Yet Artemis of the showering arrows could not now help him,
no, nor the long spearcasts in which he had been pre-eminent,
but Menelaos the spear-famed, son of Atreus, stabbed him,                        55
as he fled away before him, in the back with a spear thrust
between the shoulders and driven through to the chest beyond it.
He dropped forward on his face and his armor clattered upon him.
    Meriones in turn killed Phereklos, son of Harmonides,
the smith, who understood how to make with his hand all intricate               60
things, since above all others Pallas Athene had loved him.
He it was who had built for Alexandros the balanced

ships, the beginning of the evil, fatal to the other
Trojans, and to him, since he knew nothing of the gods' plans.
65 This man Meriones pursued and overtaking him
struck in the right buttock, and the spearhead drove straight
on and passing under the bone went into the bladder.
He dropped, screaming, to his knees, and death was a mist about him.
    Meges in turn killed Pedaios, the son of Antenor,
70 who, bastard though he was, was nursed by lovely Theano
with close care, as for her own children, to pleasure her husband.
Now the son of Phyleus, the spear-famed, closing upon him
struck him with the sharp spear behind the head at the tendon,
and straight on through the teeth and under the tongue cut the bronze blade,
75 and he dropped in the dust gripping in his teeth the cold bronze.
    Eurypylos, Euaimon's son, killed brilliant Hypsenor,
son of high-hearted Dolopion, he who was made Skamandros'
priest, and was honored about the countryside as a god is.
This man Eurypylos, the shining son of Euaimon,
80 running in chase as he fled before him struck in the shoulder
with a blow swept from the sword and cut the arm's weight from him,
so that the arm dropped bleeding to the ground, and the red death
and destiny the powerful took hold of both eyes.

    So they went at their work all about the strong encounter;
85 but you could not have told on which side Tydeus' son was fighting,
whether he were one with the Trojans or with the Achaians,
since he went storming up the plain like a winter-swollen
river in spate that scatters the dikes in its running current,
one that the strong-compacted dikes can contain no longer,
90 nor do the mounded banks of the blossoming vineyards hold it
rising suddenly as Zeus' rain makes heavy the water
and many lovely works of the young men crumble beneath it.
Like these the massed battalions of the Trojans were scattered
by Tydeus' son, and many as they were could not stand against him.
95     Now as the shining son of Lykaon, Pandaros, watched him
storming up the plain scattering the battalions before him,
at once he strained the bent bow against the son of Tydeus,
and shot, and hit him as he charged forward, in the right shoulder
at the hollow of the corselet; and the bitter arrow went straight through

holding clean to its way, and the corselet was all blood-spattered.          100
And the shining son of Lykaon cried aloud in a great voice:
"Rise up, Trojans, O high-hearted, lashers of horses.
Now the best of the Achaians is hit, and I think that he will not
long hold up under the strong arrow, if truly Apollo
lord and son of Zeus stirred me to come forth from Lykia."          105
        So he spoke, vaunting, but the swift arrow had not broken him,
only he drew back again to his chariot and horses,
and stood there, speaking to Sthenelos, son of Kapaneus:
        "Come, dear friend, son of Kapaneus, step down from the chariot,
so that you may pull out from my shoulder this bitter arrow."          110
        So he spoke, and Sthenelos sprang to the ground from his chariot
and standing beside him pulled the sharp arrow clean through his shoulder
and the blood shot up spurting through the delicate tunic.
Now Diomedes of the great war cry spoke aloud, praying:
"Hear me now, Atrytone, daughter of Zeus of the aegis:          115
if ever before in kindliness you stood by my father
through the terror of fighting, be my friend now also, Athene;
grant me that I may kill this man and come within spearcast,
who shot me before I could see him, and now boasts over me, saying
I cannot live to look much longer on the shining sunlight."          120
        So he spoke in prayer, and Pallas Athene heard him.
She made his limbs light again, and his feet, and his hands above them,
and standing close beside him she spoke and addressed him in winged words:
"Be of good courage now, Diomedes, to fight with the Trojans,
since I have put inside your chest the strength of your father          125
untremulous, such as the horseman Tydeus of the great shield
had; I have taken away the mist from your eyes, that before now
was there, so that you may well recognize the god and the mortal.
Therefore now, if a god making trial of you comes hither
do you not do battle head-on with the gods immortal,          130
not with the rest; but only if Aphrodite, Zeus' daughter,
comes to the fighting, her at least you may stab with the sharp bronze."

        She spoke thus, gray-eyed Athene, and went, while Tydeus'
son closed once again with the champions, taking his place there;
raging as he had been before to fight with the Trojans,          135
now the strong rage tripled took hold of him, as of a lion

whom the shepherd among his fleecy flocks in the wild lands
grazed as he leapt the fence of the fold, but has not killed him,
but only stirred up the lion's strength, and can no more fight him
140  off, but hides in the steading, and the frightened sheep are forsaken,
and these are piled pell-mell on each other in heaps, while the lion
raging still leaps out again over the fence of the deep yard;
such was the rage of strong Diomedes as he closed with the Trojans.
    Next he killed Astynoös and Hypeiron, shepherd of the people,
145  striking one with the bronze-heeled spear above the nipple,
and cutting the other beside the shoulder through the collar-bone
with the great sword, so that neck and back were hewn free of the shoulder.
He left these men, and went on after Polyidos and Abas,
sons of the aged dream-interpreter, Eurydamas;
150  yet for these two as they went forth the old man did not answer
their dreams, but Diomedes the powerful slew them. Now he
went after the two sons of Phainops, Xanthos and Thoön,
full grown both, but Phainops was stricken in sorrowful old age
nor could breed another son to leave among his possessions.
155  There he killed these two and took away the dear life from them
both, leaving to their father lamentation and sorrowful
affliction, since he was not to welcome them home from the fighting
alive still; and remoter kinsmen shared his possessions.
    Next he killed two children of Dardanian Priam
160  who were in a single chariot, Echemmon and Chromios.
As among cattle a lion leaps on the neck of an ox or
heifer, that grazes among the wooded places, and breaks it,
so the son of Tydeus hurled both from their horses
hatefully, in spite of their struggles, then stripped their armor
165  and gave the horses to his company to drive to their vessels.

    Now as Aineias saw him wrecking the ranks of warriors
he went on his way through the fighting and the spears' confusion
looking to see if he could find Pandaros the godlike;
and he came upon the strong and blameless son of Lykaon.
170  He stood before him face to face and spoke a word to him:
"Pandaros, where now are your bow and your feathered arrows;
where your fame, in which no man here dare contend with you
nor can any man in Lykia claim he is better?

Come then, hold up your hands to Zeus, and let go an arrow
at this strong man, whoever he be, who does so much evil                              175
to the Trojans, since many and great are those whose knees he has broken.
Unless this be some god who in wrath with the Trojans for offerings
failed afflicts them. The wrath of a god is hard to deal with."
　　Then in answer the shining son of Lykaon spoke to him:
"Aineias, charged with the counsels of the bronze-armored Trojans,                    180
I liken him in all ways to the valiant son of Tydeus,
going by his shield and the hollow eyes of his helmet
and by the look of his horses; but it may be a god, I am not sure;
and if this is a man, as I think, and the valiant son
of Tydeus, yet not without god does he rage so, but some one                          185
of the immortals, mantling in mist his shoulders, stands close beside him
who turned my flying arrow as it struck, elsewhere, away from him.
For I have shot my shaft already, and hit him in the shoulder,
the right one, hard driven through the hollow of his corselet,
and I said to myself I had hurled him down to meet Aïdoneus,                          190
yet still I have not beaten him; now this is some god who is angered.
But I have no horses nor chariot I could mount in, and yet
somewhere in the great house of Lykaon are eleven chariots,
beauties, all new made, just finished, and over them blankets
lie spread, and beside each chariot one brace of horses                              195
stand there, champing their white barley and oats. But Lykaon
the aged spearman spoke to me over and over, as I was
on my way from the house well compacted, advising me;
he told me to take my horses and chariots, and riding
there to be lord among the Trojans in the strong encounters.                         200
I did not let him persuade me, and that would have been far better,
sparing my horses, who had grown accustomed to eating all
they wished, from going hungry where the men were penned in a small
　　place.
So I left them and made my way on foot to Ilion
trusting my bow, a thing that was to profit me nothing.                              205
For now I have drawn it against two of their best men, Tydeus'
son, and the son of Atreus, and both of these I hit
and drew visible blood, yet only wakened their anger.
So it was in bad luck that I took from its peg the curved bow
on that day when I carried it to lovely Ilion                                         210

at the head of my Trojans, bringing delight to brilliant Hektor.
Now if ever I win home again and lay eyes once more
on my country, and my wife, and the great house with the high roof,
let some stranger straightway cut my head from my shoulders
215 if I do not break this bow in my hands and throw it in the shining
fire, since as a wind and nothing I have taken it with me."
   Then in turn Aineias, lord of the Trojans, answered him:
"Speak no more this way; there will be no time for changing
before you and I must face this man with horses and chariot
220 and strength against strength fight it out with our weapons. Therefore
mount rather into my chariot, so that you may see
what the Trojan horses are like, how they understand their
plain, and how to traverse it in rapid pursuit and withdrawal.
These two will bring us safe to the city again, if once more
225 Zeus grants glory to Diomedes the son of Tydeus.
Come then, taking into your hands the goad and the glittering
reins, while I dismount from my chariot and carry the fighting;
or else yourself encounter this man, while I handle the horses."
   Then in answer the shining son of Lykaon spoke to him:
230 "Keep yourself, Aineias, the reins and your horses. These will
carry better the curved chariot under the driver
they know best, if we must give way before the son of Tydeus;
for fear they might go wild with terror and not be willing
to carry us out of the fighting, as they listen and long for your voice,
235 for fear the son of high-hearted Tydeus charging upon us
might kill us both and drive away the single-foot horses.
Rather drive yourself your own horses and your own chariot
while with my sharp spear I encounter this man as he comes on."

   They spoke so, and mounting the wrought chariot held
240 their fast-running horses against the son of Tydeus, in fury.
And Sthenelos the shining son of Kapaneus seeing them
swiftly uttered his winged words to the son of Tydeus:
"Son of Tydeus, you who delight my heart, Diomedes,
look, I see two mighty men furious to fight with you.
245 Their strength is enormous, one of them well skilled in the bow's work,
Pandaros, who claims his right as son of Lykaon,
and the other Aineias, who claims he was born as son to

Anchises the blameless, but his mother was Aphrodite.
Come then, let us give way with our horses; no longer storm on
so far among the champions, for fear you destroy your heart's life."     250
    Then looking at him darkly strong Diomedes spoke to him:
"Argue me not toward flight, since I have no thought of obeying you.
No, for it would be ignoble for me to shrink back in the fighting
or to lurk aside, since my fighting strength stays steady forever.
I shrink indeed from mounting behind the horses, but as I am     255
now, I will face these. Pallas Athene will not let me run from them.
These two men, their fast-running horses shall never carry them
both back away from us, even though one man may escape us.
And put away in your thoughts this other thing I tell you.
If Athene of the many counsels should grant me the glory     260
to kill both, then do you check here these fast-running horses,
ours, tethering them with the reins tied to the chariot's rail and thereafter
remember to make a dash against the horses of Aineias,
and drive them away from the Trojans among the strong-greaved Achaians.
These are of that strain which Zeus of the wide brows granted     265
once to Tros, recompense for his son Ganymedes, and therefore
are the finest of all horses beneath the sun and the daybreak;
and the lord of men Anchises stole horses from this breed,
without the knowledge of Laomedon putting mares under them.
From these there was bred for him a string of six in his great house.     270
Four of these, keeping them himself, he raised at his mangers,
but these two he gave to Aineias, two horses urgent of terror.
If we might only take these we should win ourselves excellent glory."

    Now as these were speaking things like this to each other,
the two came fast upon them driving their swift-running horses.     275
First to Diomedes called out the shining son of Lykaon:
"Valiant and strong-spirited, O son of proud Tydeus,
you were not beaten then by the bitter arrow, my swift shot.
Now I will try with the throwing-spear to see if I can hit you."
    So he spoke, and balanced the spear far-shadowed, and threw it,     280
and struck the son of Tydeus in the shield, and the flying
bronze spearhead was driven clean through and into the corselet,
and the shining son of Lykaon cried aloud in a great voice:
"Now are you struck clean through the middle, and I think that you will not

285    hold up for much longer; you have given me great claim to glory."
           Then strong Diomedes answered, not frightened before him:
       "You did not hit me, you missed, but I do not think that you two
       will go free until one or the other of you has fallen
       to glut with his blood Ares the god who fights under the shield's guard."
290    He spoke, and threw; and Pallas Athene guided the weapon
       to the nose next to the eye, and it cut on through the white teeth
       and the bronze weariless shore all the way through the tongue's base
       so that the spearhead came out underneath the jawbone.
       He dropped then from the chariot and his armor clattered upon him,
295    dazzling armor and shining, while those fast-running horses
       shied away, and there his life and his strength were scattered.
           But Aineias sprang to the ground with shield and with long spear,
       for fear that somehow the Achaians might haul off the body,
       and like a lion in the pride of his strength stood over him
300    holding before him the perfect circle of his shield and the spear
       and raging to cut down any man who might come to face him,
       crying a terrible cry. But Tydeus' son in his hand caught
       up a stone, a huge thing which no two men could carry
       such as men are now, but by himself he lightly hefted it.
305    He threw, and caught Aineias in the hip, in the place where the hip-bone
       turns inside the thigh, the place men call the cup-socket.
       It smashed the cup-socket and broke the tendons both sides of it,
       and the rugged stone tore the skin backward, so that the fighter
       dropping to one knee stayed leaning on the ground with his heavy
310    hand, and a covering of black night came over both eyes.

           Now in this place Aineias lord of men might have perished
       had not Aphrodite, Zeus' daughter, been quick to perceive him,
       his mother, who had borne him to Anchises the ox-herd;
       and about her beloved son came streaming her white arms,
315    and with her white robe thrown in a fold in front she shielded him,
       this keeping off the thrown weapons lest some fast-mounted Danaän
       strike the bronze spear through his chest and strip the life from him.
           She then carried her beloved son out of the fighting.
           Nor did Sthenelos son of Kapaneus forget the commandments
320    that Diomedes of the great war cry had laid upon him,

but he held where they were their own single-foot horses
with their reins tied to the chariot rail, apart from the confusion,
and making a dash for the fluttering-maned horses of Aineias
drove them away from the Trojans among the strong-greaved Achaians,
and gave them to Deïpylos, his close friend, whom beyond all          325
others of his own age he prized, for their hearts were intimate,
to drive away to the hollow ships; meanwhile the warrior
mounted behind his own horses and caught up the shining
reins, and held the strong-footed team toward the son of Tydeus
headlong; and he swung the pitiless bronze at the lady of Kypros,     330
knowing her for a god without warcraft, not of those who,
goddesses, range in order the ranks of men in the fighting,
not Athene and not Enyo, sacker of cities.
Now as, following her through the thick crowd, he caught her,
lunging in his charge far forward the son of high-hearted             335
Tydeus made a thrust against the soft hand with the bronze spear,
and the spear tore the skin driven clean on through the immortal
robe that the very Graces had woven for her carefully,
over the palm's base; and blood immortal flowed from the goddess,
ichor, that which runs in the veins of the blessed divinities;        340
since these eat no food, nor do they drink of the shining
wine, and therefore they have no blood and are called immortal.
She gave a great shriek and let fall her son she was carrying,
but Phoibos Apollo caught him up and away in his own hands,
in a dark mist, for fear that some fast-mounted Danaän                345
might strike the bronze spear through his chest and strip the life from him.
But Diomedes of the great war cry shouted after her:
"Give way, daughter of Zeus, from the fighting and the terror. It is
not then enough that you lead astray women without warcraft?
Yet, if still you must haunt the fighting, I think that now you        350
will shiver even when you hear some other talking of battles."

So he spoke, and the goddess departed in pain, hurt badly,
and Iris wind-footed took her by the hand and led her away
from the battle, her lovely skin blood-darkened, wounded and suffering.
There to the left of the fighting she found Ares the violent           355
sitting, his spear leaned into the mist, and his swift horses.

Dropping on one knee before her beloved brother
in deep supplication she asked for his gold-bridled horses:
"Beloved brother, rescue me and give me your horses
360 so I may come to Olympos where is the place of the immortals.
I am in too much pain from the wound of a mortal's spear-stroke,
Tydeus' son's, who would fight now even against Zeus father."
  So she spoke, and Ares gave her the gold-bridled horses,
and, still grieved in the inward heart, she mounted the chariot
365 and beside her entering Iris gathered the reins up
and whipped them into a run, and they winged their way unreluctant.
Now as they came to sheer Olympos, the place of the immortals,
there swift Iris the wind-footed reined in her horses
and slipped them from the yoke and threw fodder immortal before them,
370 and now bright Aphrodite fell at the knees of her mother,
Dione, who gathered her daughter into the arms' fold
and stroked her with her hand and called her by name and spoke to her:
"Who now of the Uranian gods, dear child, has done such
things to you, rashly, as if you were caught doing something wicked?"
375   Aphrodite the sweetly laughing spoke then and answered her:
"Tydeus' son Diomedes, the too high-hearted, stabbed me
as I was carrying my own beloved son out of the fighting,
Aineias, who beyond all else in the world is dear to me;
so now this is no horrible war of Achaians and Trojans,
380 but the Danaäns are beginning to fight even with the immortals."
  Then Dione the shining among divinities answered her:
"Have patience, my child, and endure it, though you be saddened.
For many of us who have our homes on Olympos endure things
from men, when ourselves we inflict hard pain on each other.
385 Ares had to endure it when strong Ephialtes and Otos,
sons of Aloeus, chained him in bonds that were too strong for him,
and three months and ten he lay chained in the brazen cauldron;
and now might Ares, insatiable of fighting, have perished,
had not Eëriboia, their stepmother, the surpassingly lovely,
390 brought word to Hermes, who stole Ares away out of it
as he was growing faint and the hard bondage was breaking him.
Hera had to endure it when the strong son of Amphitryon
struck her beside the right breast with a tri-barbed arrow,

so that the pain he gave her could not be quieted. Hades
the gigantic had to endure with the rest the flying arrow                    395
when this self-same man, the son of Zeus of the aegis,
struck him among the dead men at Pylos, and gave him to agony;
but he went up to the house of Zeus and to tall Olympos
heavy at heart, stabbed through and through with pain, for the arrow
was driven into his heavy shoulder, and his spirit was suffering.           400
But Paiëon, scattering medicines that still pain,
healed him, since he was not made to be one of the mortals.
Brute, heavy-handed, who thought nothing of the bad he was doing,
who with his archery hurt the gods that dwell on Olympos!
It was the goddess gray-eyed Athene who drove on this man                    405
against you; poor fool, the heart of Tydeus' son knows nothing
of how that man who fights the immortals lives for no long time,
his children do not gather to his knees to welcome their father
when he returns home after the fighting and the bitter warfare.
Then, though he be very strong indeed, let the son of Tydeus                 410
take care lest someone even better than he might fight with him,
lest for a long time Aigialeia, wise child of Adrastos,
mourning wake out of sleep her household's beloved companions,
longing for the best of the Achaians, her lord by marriage,
she, the strong wife of Diomedes, breaker of horses."                       415
     She spoke, and with both hands stroked away from her arm the ichor,
so that the arm was made whole again and the strong pains rested.
But Hera and Athene glancing aside at her began
to tease the son of Kronos, Zeus, in words of mockery:
and the goddess gray-eyed Athene began the talk among them:                  420
"Father Zeus, would you be angry with me if I said
something? It must be the lady of Kypros, moving some woman
of Achaia to follow after those Trojans she loves so hopelessly,
laying hold on the fair dresses of the Achaian women,
tore the tenderness of her hand on a golden pin's point."                    425
     So she spoke, and the father of gods and men smiled on her
and spoke to Aphrodite the golden, calling her to him:
"No, my child, not for you are the works of warfare. Rather
concern yourself only with the lovely secrets of marriage,
while all this shall be left to Athene and sudden Ares."                     430

Now as these were talking in this way with each other
Diomedes of the great war cry made for Aineias.
Though he saw how Apollo himself held his hands over him
he did not shrink even from the great god, but forever forward
435  drove, to kill Aineias and strip his glorious armor.
Three times, furious to cut him down, he drove forward,
and three times Apollo battered aside the bright shield,
but as a fourth time, like more than man, he charged, Apollo
who strikes from afar cried out to him in the voice of terror:
440  "Take care, give back, son of Tydeus, and strive no longer
to make yourself like the gods in mind, since never the same is
the breed of gods, who are immortal, and men who walk groundling."
He spoke, and Tydeus' son gave backward, only a little,
avoiding the anger of him who strikes from afar, Apollo,
445  who caught Aineias now away from the onslaught, and set him
in the sacred keep of Pergamos where was built his own temple.
There Artemis of the showering arrows and Leto within
the great and secret chamber healed his wound and cared for him.
But he of the silver bow, Apollo, fashioned an image
450  in the likeness of Aineias himself and in armor like him,
and all about this image brilliant Achaians and Trojans
hewed at each other, and at the ox-hide shields strong circled
guarding men's chests, and at the fluttering straps of the guard-skins.
But Phoibos Apollo spoke now to violent Ares:
455  "Ares, Ares, manslaughtering, blood-stained, stormer of strong walls,
is there no way you can go and hold back this man from the fighting,
Tydeus' son, who would now do battle against Zeus father?
Even now he stabbed in her hand by the wrist the lady
of Kypros, and again, like more than a man, charged even against me."
460  So he spoke, and himself alighted on the peak of Pergamos
while stark Ares went down to stir the ranks of the Trojans,
in the likeness of the lord of the Thracians, swift-footed Akamas,
and urged onward the god-supported children of Priam:
"O you children of Priam, the king whom the gods love, how long
465  will you allow the Achaians to go on killing your people?
Until they fight beside the strong-builded gates? A man lies
fallen whom we honored as we honor Hektor the brilliant,

Aineias, who is son of great-hearted Anchises.
Come then, let us rescue our good companion from the carnage."

So he spoke, and stirred the spirit and the strength in each man.     470
Then Sarpedon spoke in abuse to brilliant Hektor:
"Where now, Hektor, has gone that strength that was yours? You said once
that without companions and without people you could hold this city
alone, with only your brothers and the lords of your sisters.
I can see not one of these men now, I know not where they are;     475
no, but they slink away like hounds who circle the lion,
while we, who are here as your companions, carry the fighting.
I have come, a companion to help you, from a very far place;
Lykia lies far away, by the whirling waters of Xanthos;
there I left behind my own wife and my baby son, there     480
I left my many possessions which the needy man eyes longingly.
Yet even so I drive on my Lykians, and myself have courage
to fight my man in battle, though there is nothing of mine here
that the Achaians can carry away as spoil or drive off.
But you: you stand here, not even giving the word to the rest     485
of your people to stand fast and fight in defense of their own wives.
Let not yourselves, caught as in the sweeping toils of the spun net,
be taken as war-spoil and plunder by the men who hate you,
men who presently will storm your strong-founded citadel.
All these things should lie night and day on your mind, forever,     490
supplication to the lords of your far-renowned companions,
to fight unwearying and hold off the strength of an insult."
Sarpedon spoke, and his word bit into the heart of Hektor.
Straightway in all his armor he sprang to the ground from his chariot
and shaking two sharp spears ranged everywhere through the army     495
stirring men up to fight and waking the hateful warfare;
and these pulled themselves about and stood to face the Achaians,
while the Argives held in their close order and would not be broken.
As when along the hallowed threshing floors the wind scatters
chaff, among men winnowing, and fair-haired Demeter     500
in the leaning wind discriminates the chaff and the true grain
and the piling chaff whitens beneath it, so now the Achaians
turned white underneath the dust the feet of the horses

drove far into the brazen sky across their faces
505 as they rapidly closed and the charioteers wheeled back again.
They drove the strength of their hands straight on, as violent Ares
defending the Trojans mantled in dark night the battle
and passed everywhere, since he was carrying out the commandments
of Phoibos Apollo, him of the golden sword, who had bidden him
510 wake the heart in the Trojans as he saw that Pallas Athene
was gone away now, she who stood to defend the Danaäns.
And out of the rich secret chamber Apollo sent forth
Aineias, and dropped strength in the heart of the people's shepherd.
So Aineias stood among his friends, who were happy
515 as they saw him coming back, still alive, and unwounded
and full of brave spirit; yet they asked him no question,
for the rest of their fighting work would not let them, that the silver-bow god
woke, and manslaughtering Ares, and Hate, whose wrath is relentless.

Now the two Aiantes and Odysseus and Diomedes
520 stirred the Danaäns to fight these; since themselves they did not
fear the force of the men of Troy nor their charges onward,
but stayed where they were, like clouds, which the son of Kronos
stops in the windless weather on the heights of the towering mountains,
motionless, when the strength of the north wind sleeps, and the other
525 tearing winds, those winds that when they blow into tempests
high screaming descend upon the darkening clouds and scatter them.
So the Danaäns stood steady against the Trojans, nor gave way.
And Atreus' son ranged through the masses with his many orders:
"Be men now, dear friends, and take up the heart of courage,
530 and have consideration for each other in the strong encounters,
since more come through alive when men consider each other,
and there is no glory when they give way, nor warcraft either."
He spoke, and made a swift cast with his spear, and struck down a great
man
Deïkoön, companion of high-hearted Aineias,
535 Pergasos' son, whom the Trojans honored as they honored Priam's
children, since he was a swift man to fight in the foremost.
Powerful Agamemnon struck his shield with spear, nor
could the shield hold off the spear, but the bronze smashed clean through

and was driven on through the belt to the deep of the belly.
He fell, thunderously, and his armor clattered upon him. 540
    Now Aineias killed two great men of the Danaäns,
the sons of Diokles, Orsilochos and Krethon,
men whose father dwelt in Phere the strong-founded,
rich in substance, and his generation was of the river
Alpheios, who flows wide through the country of the Pylians, 545
and who got a son, Ortilochos, to be lord over many
men, but the son of Ortilochos was high-hearted Diokles;
and to Diokles in his turn were two twin sons born,
Orsilochos and Krethon, both well skilled in all fighting.
These two as they were grown to young manhood followed along with 550
the Argives in their black ships to Ilion, land of good horses,
winning honor for the sons of Atreus, Agamemnon
and Menelaos; now fulfillment of death was a darkness upon them.
These, as two young lions in the high places of the mountains,
had been raised by their mother in the dark of the deep forest, 555
lions which as they prey upon the cattle and the fat sheep
lay waste the steadings where there are men, until they also
fall and are killed under the cutting bronze in the men's hands;
such were these two who beaten under the hands of Aineias
crashed now to the ground as if they were two tall pine trees. 560
    As these fell warlike Menelaos took pity on them
and he strode out among the champions, helmed in bright bronze,
shaking his spear, and the fury of Ares drove him onward,
minded that he might go down under the hands of Aineias.
But Antilochos, son of high-hearted Nestor, watched him, 565
and he strode among the champions in fear for the shepherd of the people,
lest he be hurt, and all their labor slip away into nothing.
So as Aineias and Menelaos raised hand and sharp spear
standing to face each other and furious to do battle,
Antilochos took his stand close beside the shepherd of the people. 570
Nor did Aineias hold his ground, though yet a swift fighter,
as he saw two men staying with each other against him.
These, when they had dragged back the bodies among the Achaian
people, dropped the poor youths into the hands of their company,
and themselves wheeled about once more to fight among the foremost. 575

There these killed Pylaimenes the equal of Ares,
lord of the Paphlagonian men in armor, high-hearted.
Menelaos the spear-famed, son of Atreus, stabbed him
with the spear as he stood his ground, and struck the collar-bone,
580 while Antilochos struck down Mydon, his charioteer and
henchman, Atymnios' brave son, as he wheeled the single-foot
horses about, with a stone striking mid-elbow, and from his
hands the reins pale with ivory dropped in the dust groundling.
Antilochos charging drove the sword into his temple,
585 so that gasping he dropped from the carefully wrought chariot
headlong, driven deep in the dust his neck and shoulders;
and there, since he chanced to light in a depth of sand, he stuck fast
while his horses trampled him into the dust with their feet. These
Antilochos lashed and drove back into the host of the Achaians.
590 Hektor saw them across the ranks, and drove on against them
crying aloud, and with him followed the Trojan battalions
in their strength; and Ares led them with the goddess Enyo,
she carrying with her the turmoil of shameless hatred
while Ares made play in his hands with the spear gigantic
595 and ranged now in front of Hektor and now behind him.
Diomedes of the great war cry shivered as he saw him,
and like a man in his helplessness who, crossing a great plain,
stands at the edge of a fast-running river that dashes seaward,
and watches it thundering into white water, and leaps a pace backward,
600 so now Tydeus' son gave back, and spoke to his people:
"Friends, although we know the wonder of glorious Hektor
to be a fighter with the spear and a bold man of battle,
yet there goes ever some god beside him, who beats off destruction,
and now, in the likeness of a man mortal, Ares goes with him.
605 Come then, keeping your faces turned to the Trojans, give ground
backward, nor be we eager to fight in strength with divinities."

He spoke, and now the Trojans had come very close upon them.
There Hektor cut down two men, well skilled in warcraft,
Anchialos and Menesthes both in a single chariot.
610 As these fell great Telamonian Aias pitied them
and stood close in and made a cast with the shining javelin,
and struck Amphios, Selagos' son, who rich in possessions

and rich in cornland had lived in Paisos, but his own destiny
brought him companion in arms to Priam and the children of Priam.
Now Telamonian Aias struck him beneath the war belt                              615
and the far-shadowing spear was fixed in the lower belly,
and he fell, thunderously, and shining Aias ran forward
to strip his armor, but the Trojans showered spears upon him,
sharp spears and glittering, and the great shield caught many.
Setting his heel on the chest of the corpse he pulled out the brazen             620
spear, yet could no longer strip the rest of the glorious
armor from his shoulders, since he was battered with spears thrown,
and he dreaded the strong circle made by the haughty Trojans,
who many and valiant stood over him, gripping their great spears,
and though he was a mighty man and a strong and a proud one                      625
thrust him away from them so that he gave ground backward staggering.

    So they went at their work all about the strong encounter.
But Herakles' son Tlepolemos the huge and mighty
was driven by his strong destiny against godlike Sarpedon.
Now as these in their advance had come close together,                           630
the own son, and the son's son of Zeus cloud-gathering,
it was Tlepolemos of the two who spoke the first word:
"Man of counsel of the Lykians, Sarpedon, why must you
be skulking here, you who are a man unskilled in the fighting?
They are liars who call you issue of Zeus, the holder                            635
of the aegis, since you fall far short in truth of the others
who were begotten of Zeus in the generations before us:
such men as, they say, was the great strength of Herakles,
my own father, of the daring spirit, the heart of a lion:
he came here on a time for the sake of Laomedon's horses,                        640
with six vessels only and the few men needed to man them,
and widowed the streets of Ilion and sacked the city;
but yours is the heart of a coward and your people are dying.
And I think that now, though you are come from Lykia, you will
bring no help to the Trojans even though you be a strong man,                     645
but beaten down by my hands will pass through the gates of Hades."
    In turn the lord of the Lykians, Sarpedon, answered him:
"In truth, Tlepolemos, he did destroy Ilion the sacred
through the senselessness of one man, the haughty Laomedon,

650 who gave Herakles an evil word in return for good treatment
and would not give up the horses for whose sake he had come from far off.
But I tell you, what you will win from me here will be death
and black destruction; and broken under my spear you will give me
glory, and give your soul to Hades of the famed horses."
655 So spoke Sarpedon, while the other lifted his ash spear,
Tlepolemos; and in a single moment the long shafts
shot from their hands, Sarpedon striking him in the middle
of the throat, and the agonizing spear drove clean through
and over his eyes was mantled the covering mist of darkness.
660 But Tlepolemos in turn had struck Sarpedon with the long spear
in the left thigh, and the spear smashed on through in fury
scraping the bone, but his father fended destruction away from him.
But his brilliant companions carried godlike Sarpedon
out of the fighting, weighted down as he was by the long spear
665 which dragged, yet not one of them noticed nor took thought,
in their urgency, to pull out of his thigh the ash spear
so he might stand, such hard work did they have attending him.

On the other side the strong-greaved Achaians carried Tlepolemos
out of the fighting; but brilliant Odysseus, who held a hardy
670 spirit, saw what had happened, and his heart within was stirred up,
but now he pondered two ways within, in mind and in spirit,
whether first to go after the son of Zeus the loud-thundering
or whether he should strip the life from more of the Lykians.
Yet, as it was not the destiny of great-hearted Odysseus
675 to kill with sharp bronze the strong son of Zeus, therefore
Athene steered his anger against the host of the Lykians.
And there he killed Koiranos, and Chromios, and Alastor,
Halios and Alkandros, and Prytanis and Noëmon.
And now might brilliant Odysseus have killed yet more of the Lykians
680 had not tall Hektor of the shining helmet sharply perceived him,
who strode out among the champions helmed in the bright bronze
bringing terror to the Danaäns; but Zeus' son, Sarpedon,
was glad as he saw him come up, and piteously bespoke him:
"Son of Priam, do not leave me lying for the Danaäns
685 to prey upon, but protect me, since otherwise in your city
my life must come to an end, since I could return no longer

back to my own house and the land of my fathers, bringing
joy to my own beloved wife and my son, still a baby."
  He spoke, but Hektor of the shining helm did not answer
but swept on past him in his eagerness with all speed                          690
to push back the Argives and strip the life out of many.
Meanwhile his brilliant companions laid godlike Sarpedon
under a lovely spreading oak of Zeus of the aegis,
and strong Pelagon, one of his beloved companions,
pushed perforce through and out of his thigh the shaft of the ash spear.       695
And the mist mantled over his eyes, and the life left him,
but he got his breath back again, and the blast of the north wind
blowing brought back to life the spirit gasped out in agony.
  But the Argives under the strength of Ares and bronze-armored Hektor
did not ever turn their backs and make for their black ships                   700
nor yet stand up to them in fighting, but always backward
gave way, as they saw how Ares went with the Trojans.

  Who then was the first and who the last that they slaughtered,
Hektor, Priam's son, and Ares the brazen? Godlike
Teuthras first, and next Orestes, driver of horses,                            705
Trechos the spearman of Aitolia and Oinomaos,
Helenos son of Oinops and Oresbios of the shining
guard, who had lived in Hyle much concerned with his property
in a place hard on the Kephisian mere, and beside him other
men of Boiotia lived and held the fine fertile country.                        710

  Now as the goddess Hera of the white arms perceived how
the Argives were perishing in the strong encounter,
immediately she spoke to Pallas Athene her winged words:
"For shame, now, Atrytone, daughter of Zeus of the aegis:
nothing then meant the word we promised to Menelaos,                           715
to go home after sacking the strong-walled city of Ilion,
if we are to let cursed Ares be so furious.
Come then, let us rather think of our own stark courage."
  So she spoke, nor did the goddess gray-eyed Athene
disobey her. But Hera, high goddess, daughter of Kronos                        720
the mighty, went away to harness the gold-bridled horses.
Then Hebe in speed set about the chariot the curved wheels

eight-spoked and brazen, with an axle of iron both ways.
Golden is the wheel's felly imperishable, and outside it
725   is joined, a wonder to look upon, the brazen running-rim,
and the silver naves revolve on either side of the chariot,
whereas the car itself is lashed fast with plaiting of gold
and silver, with double chariot rails that circle about it,
and the pole of the chariot is of silver, to whose extremity
730   Hebe made fast the golden and splendid yoke, and fastened
the harness, golden and splendid, and underneath the yoke Hera,
furious for hate and battle, led the swift-running horses.
     Now in turn Athene, daughter of Zeus of the aegis,
beside the threshold of her father slipped off her elaborate
735   dress which she herself had wrought with her hands' patience,
and now assuming the war tunic of Zeus who gathers
the clouds, she armed in her gear for the dismal fighting.
And across her shoulders she threw the betasseled, terrible
aegis, all about which Terror hangs like a garland,
740   and Hatred is there, and Battle Strength, and heart-freezing Onslaught
and thereon is set the head of the grim gigantic Gorgon,
a thing of fear and horror, portent of Zeus of the aegis.
Upon her head she set the golden helm with its four sheets
and two horns, wrought with the fighting men of a hundred cities.
745   She set her feet in the blazing chariot and took up a spear
heavy, huge, thick, wherewith she beats down the battalions of fighting
men, against whom she of mighty father is angered.
Hera laid the lash swiftly on the horses; and moving
of themselves groaned the gates of the sky that the Hours guarded,
750   those Hours to whose charge is given the huge sky and Olympos,
to open up the dense darkness or again to close it.
Through the way between they held the speed of their goaded horses.
They found the son of Kronos sitting apart from the other
gods, upon the highest peak of rugged Olympos.
755   There the goddess of the white arms, Hera, stopping her horses,
spoke to Zeus, high son of Kronos, and asked him a question:
"Father Zeus, are you not angry with Ares for his violent
acts, for killing so many and such good Achaian warriors
for no reason, and out of due order, to grieve me? And meanwhile
760   Kypris and Apollo of the silver bow take their ease and their pleasure

having let loose this maniac who knows nothing of justice.
Father Zeus, would you be angry with me if I were
to smite Ares with painful strokes and drive him out of the fighting?"
    Then in turn the father of gods and men made answer:
"Go to it then, and set against him the spoiler Athene,                765
who beyond all others is the one to visit harsh pains upon him."
    So he spoke, nor did the goddess of the white arms, Hera,
disobey, but lashed on the horses, and they winged their way unreluctant
through the space between the earth and the starry heaven.
As far as into the hazing distance a man can see with                 770
his eyes, who sits in his aerie gazing on the wine-blue water,
as far as this is the stride of the gods' proud neighing horses.
Now as they came to Troy land and the two running rivers
where Simoeis and Skamandros dash their waters together,
there the goddess of the white arms, Hera, stayed her horses,         775
slipping them from the chariot, and drifting close mist about them,
and Simoeis grew as grass ambrosia for them to graze on.

    Now these two walked forward in little steps like shivering
doves, in their eagerness to stand by the men of Argos,
after they had come to the place where the most and the bravest       780
stood close huddled about the great strength of the breaker of horses,
Diomedes; in the likeness of lions who rend their meat raw,
or wild pigs, boars, in whom the strength diminishes never,
there standing the goddess of the white arms, Hera, shouted,
likening herself to high-hearted, bronze-voiced Stentor,              785
who could cry out in as great a voice as fifty other men:
"Shame, you Argives, poor nonentities splendid to look on.
In those days when brilliant Achilleus came into the fighting,
never would the Trojans venture beyond the Dardanian
gates, so much did they dread the heavy spear of that man.            790
Now they fight by the hollow ships and far from the city."
    So she spoke, and stirred the spirit and strength in each man.
But the goddess gray-eyed Athene made straight for Tydeus'
son, and found the king standing by his horses and chariot,
cooling the wound that Pandaros made with the cast of his arrow.      795
For the sweat made him sore underneath the broad strap of the circled
shield; this made him sore, and his arm was tired. He held up

the shield-strap, and wiped the dark blot of blood away from it.
The goddess laid hold of the harnessed horses and spoke to him:
800 "Tydeus got him a son who is little enough like him,
since Tydeus was a small man for stature, but he was a fighter.
Even on that time when I would not consent to his fighting
nor drawing men's eyes, when he went by himself without the Achaians
as a messenger to Thebe among all the Kadmeians,
805 then I invited him to feast at his ease in their great halls;
even so, keeping that heart of strength that was always within him
he challenged the young men of the Kadmeians, and defeated all of them
easily; such a helper was I who stood then beside him.
Now beside you also I stand and ever watch over you,
810 and urge you to fight confidently with the Trojans. And yet
the weariness has entered your limbs from many encounters,
or else it is some poor-spirited fear that holds you. If so,
you are no issue then of the son of wise Oineus, Tydeus."
    Then in answer powerful Diomedes spoke to her:
815 "Daughter of Zeus who holds the aegis, goddess, I know you,
and therefore will speak confidently to you, and hide nothing.
It is no poor-spirited fear nor shrinking that holds me.
Rather I remember the orders you yourself gave me
when you would not let me fight in the face of the blessed immortals—
820 the rest of them, except only if Aphrodite, Zeus' daughter,
went into the fighting, I might stab at her with the sharp bronze.
Therefore now have I myself given way, and I ordered
the rest of the Argives all to be gathered in this place beside me,
since I see that this who is lord of the fighting is Ares."
825     Then in turn the goddess gray-eyed Athene answered him:
"Son of Tydeus, you who delight my heart, Diomedes,
no longer be thus afraid of Ares, nor of any other
immortal; such a helper shall I be standing beside you.
Come then, first against Ares steer your single-foot horses,
830 and strike him from close. Be not afraid of violent Ares,
that thing of fury, evil-wrought, that double-faced liar
who even now protested to Hera and me, promising
that he would fight against the Trojans and stand by the Argives.
Now, all promises forgotten, he stands by the Trojans."

So speaking she pushed Sthenelos to the ground from the chariot,    835
driving him back with her hand, and he leapt away from it lightly,
and she herself, a goddess in her anger, stepped into the chariot
beside brilliant Diomedes, and the oaken axle groaned aloud
under the weight, carrying a dread goddess and a great man.
Pallas Athene then took up the whip and the reins, steering    840
first of all straight on against Ares the single-foot horses.
Ares was in the act of stripping gigantic Periphas,
shining son of Ochesios, far the best of the men of Aitolia.
Blood-stained Ares was in the act of stripping him. But Athene
put on the helm of Death, that stark Ares might not discern her.    845
     Now as manslaughtering Ares caught sight of Diomedes
the brilliant, he let gigantic Periphas lie in the place where
he had first cut him down and taken the life away from him,
and made straight against Diomedes, breaker of horses.
Now as they in their advance had come close together,    850
Ares lunged first over the yoke and the reins of his horses
with the bronze spear, furious to take the life from him.
But the goddess gray-eyed Athene in her hand catching
the spear pushed it away from the car, so he missed and stabbed vainly.
After him Diomedes of the great war cry drove forward    855
with the bronze spear; and Pallas Athene, leaning in on it,
drove it into the depth of the belly where the war belt girt him.
Picking this place she stabbed and driving it deep in the fair flesh
wrenched the spear out again. Then Ares the brazen bellowed
with a sound as great as nine thousand men make, or ten thousand,    860
when they cry as they carry into the fighting the fury of the war god.
And a shivering seized hold alike on Achaians and Trojans
in their fear at the bellowing of battle-insatiate Ares.
     As when out of the thunderhead the air shows darkening
after a day's heat when the stormy wind uprises,    865
thus to Tydeus' son Diomedes Ares the brazen
showed as he went up with the clouds into the wide heaven.
Lightly he came to the gods' citadel, headlong Olympos,
and sat down beside Kronian Zeus, grieving in his spirit,
and showed him the immortal blood dripping from the spear cut.    870
So in sorrow for himself he addressed him in winged words:
"Father Zeus, are you not angry looking on these acts of violence?

We who are gods forever have to endure the most horrible
hurts, by each other's hatred, as we try to give favor to mortals.
875 It is your fault we fight, since you brought forth this maniac daughter
accursed, whose mind is fixed forever on unjust action.
For all the rest, as many as are gods on Olympos,
are obedient to you, and we all have rendered ourselves submissive.
Yet you say nothing and you do nothing to check this girl, letting
880 her go free, since yourself you begot this child of perdition.
See now, the son of Tydeus, Diomedes the haughty,
she has egged on to lash out in fury against the immortal
gods. First he stabbed the Kyprian in the arm by the wrist. Then
like something more than human he swept on even against me.
885 But my swift feet took me out of the way. Otherwise I should
long be lying there in pain among the stark dead men,
or go living without strength because of the strokes of the bronze spear."
    Then looking at him darkly Zeus who gathers the clouds spoke to him:
"Do not sit beside me and whine, you double-faced liar.
890 To me you are most hateful of all gods who hold Olympos.
Forever quarreling is dear to your heart, wars and battles.
Truly the anger of Hera your mother is grown out of all hand
nor gives ground; and try as I may I am broken by her arguments,
and it is by her impulse, I think, you are suffering all this.
895 And yet I will not long endure to see you in pain, since
you are my child, and it was to me that your mother bore you.
But were you born of some other god and proved so ruinous
long since you would have been dropped beneath the gods of the bright sky."
    So he spoke, and told Paiëon to heal him; and scattering
900 medicines to still pain upon him Paiëon rendered him
well again, since he was not made to be one of the mortals.
As when the juice of the fig in white milk rapidly fixes
that which was fluid before and curdles quickly for one who
stirs it; in such speed as this he healed violent Ares;
905 and Hebe washed him clean and put delicate clothing upon him.
And rejoicing in the glory of his strength he sat down beside Kronion.
    Meanwhile, the two went back again to the house of great Zeus,
Hera of Argos, with Athene who stands by her people,
after they stopped the murderous work of manslaughtering Ares.

# BOOK SIX

So the grim encounter of Achaians and Trojans was left
to itself, and the battle veered greatly now one way, now in another,
over the plain as they guided their bronze spears at each other
in the space between the waters of Xanthos and Simoeis.
First Telamonian Aias, that bastion of the Achaians,                    5
broke the Trojan battalions and brought light to his own company,
striking down the man who was far the best of the Thracians,
Akamas, the huge and mighty, the son of Eussoros.
Throwing first, he struck the horn of the horse-haired helmet
and the bronze spear-point fixed in his forehead and drove inward      10
through the bone; and a mist of darkness clouded both eyes.
Diomedes of the great war cry cut down Axylos,
Teuthras' son, who had been a dweller in strong-founded Arisbe,
a man rich in substance and a friend to all humanity
since in his house by the wayside he entertained all comers.           15
Yet there was none of these now to stand before him and keep off
the sad destruction, and Diomedes stripped life from both of them,
Axylos and his henchman Kalesios, who was the driver
guiding his horses; so down to the underworld went both men.
Now Euryalos slaughtered Opheltios and Dresos,                         20
and went in pursuit of Aisepos and Pedasos, those whom the naiad
nymph Abarbare had borne to blameless Boukolion.
Boukolion himself was the son of haughty Laomedon,
eldest born, but his mother conceived him in darkness and secrecy.
While shepherding his flocks he lay with the nymph and loved her,      25
and she conceiving bore him twin boys. But now Mekistios'

son unstrung the strength of these and the limbs in their glory,
Euryalos, and stripped the armor away from their shoulders.
Polypoites the stubborn in battle cut down Astyalos,
while Odysseus slaughtered one from Perkote, Pidytes,
with the bronze spear, and great Aretaon was killed by Teukros.
Nestor's son Antilochos with the shining shaft killed
Ableros; the lord of men, Agamemnon, brought death to Elatos,
whose home had been on the shores of Satnioeis' lovely waters,
sheer Pedasos. And Leïtos the fighter caught Phylakos
as he ran away; and Eurypylos made an end of Melanthios.

Now Menelaos of the great war cry captured Adrestos
alive; for his two horses bolting over the level land
got entangled in a tamarisk growth, and shattered the curving
chariot at the tip of the pole; so they broken free went
on toward the city, where many beside stampeded in terror.
So Adrestos was whirled beside the wheel from the chariot
headlong into the dust on his face; and the son of Atreus,
Menelaos, with the far-shadowed spear in his hand, stood over him.
But Adrestos, catching him by the knees, supplicated:
"Take me alive, son of Atreus, and take appropriate ransom.
In my rich father's house the treasures lie piled in abundance;
bronze is there, and gold, and difficultly wrought iron,
and my father would make you glad with abundant repayment
were he to hear that I am alive by the ships of the Achaians."
So he spoke, and moved the spirit inside Menelaos.
And now he was on the point of handing him to a henchman
to lead back to the fast Achaian ships; but Agamemnon
came on the run to join him and spoke his word of argument:
"Dear brother, O Menelaos, are you concerned so tenderly
with these people? Did you in your house get the best of treatment
from the Trojans? No, let not one of them go free of sudden
death and our hands; not the young man child that the mother carries
still in her body, not even he, but let all of Ilion's
people perish, utterly blotted out and unmourned for."
The hero spoke like this, and bent the heart of his brother
since he urged justice. Menelaos shoved with his hand Adrestos
the warrior back from him, and powerful Agamemnon

stabbed him in the side and, as he writhed over, Atreides,
setting his heel upon the midriff, wrenched out the ash spear.                    65

     Nestor in a great voice cried out to the men of Argos:
"O beloved Danaän fighters, henchmen of Ares,
let no man anymore hang back with his eye on the plunder
designing to take all the spoil he can gather back to the vessels;
let us kill the men now, and afterward at your leisure                            70
all along the plain you can plunder the perished corpses."
     So he spoke, and stirred the spirit and strength in each man.
Then once more would the Trojans have climbed back into Ilion's
wall, subdued by terror before the warlike Achaians,
had not Priam's son, Helenos, best by far of the augurs,                          75
stood beside Aineias and Hektor and spoken a word to them:
"Hektor and Aineias, on you beyond others is leaning
the battle-work of Trojans and Lykians, since you are our greatest
in every course we take, whether it be in thought or in fighting:
stand your ground here; visit your people everywhere; hold them                   80
fast by the gates, before they tumble into their women's
arms, and become to our enemies a thing to take joy in.
Afterward, when you have set all the battalions in motion,
the rest of us will stand fast here and fight with the Danaäns
though we are very hard hit indeed; necessity forces us;                          85
but you, Hektor, go back again to the city, and there tell
your mother and mine to assemble all the ladies of honor
at the temple of gray-eyed Athene high on the citadel;
there opening with a key the door to the sacred chamber
let her take a robe, which seems to her the largest and loveliest                 90
in the great house, and that which is far her dearest possession,
and lay it along the knees of Athene the lovely haired. Let her
promise to dedicate within the shrine twelve heifers,
yearlings, never broken, if only she will have pity
on the town of Troy, and the Trojan wives, and their innocent children.          95
So she might hold back from sacred Ilion the son of Tydeus,
that wild spear-fighter, the strong one who drives men to thoughts of terror,
who I say now is become the strongest of all the Achaians.
For never did we so fear Achilleus even, that leader
of men, who they say was born of a goddess. This man has gone clean              100

berserk, so that no one can match his warcraft against him."
So he spoke, and Hektor did not disobey his brother,
but at once in all his armor leapt to the ground from his chariot
and shaking two sharp spears in his hands ranged over the whole host
105    stirring them up to fight and waking the ghastly warfare.
So they whirled about and stood their ground against the Achaians,
and the Argives gave way backward and stopped their slaughtering,
and thought some one of the immortals must have descended
from the starry sky to stand by the Trojans, the way they rallied.
110    But Hektor lifted his voice and cried aloud to the Trojans:
"You high-hearted Trojans and far-renowned companions,
be men now, dear friends, and remember your furious valor
until I can go back again to Ilion, and there tell
the elder men who sit as counselors, and our own wives,
115    to make their prayer to the immortals and promise them hecatombs."
So spoke Hektor of the shining helm, and departed;
and against his ankles as against his neck clashed the dark ox-hide,
the rim running round the edge of the great shield massive in the middle.

Now Glaukos, sprung of Hippolochos, and the son of Tydeus
120    came together in the space between the two armies, battle-bent.
Now as these advancing came to one place and encountered,
first to speak was Diomedes of the great war cry:
"Who among mortal men are you, good friend? Since never
before have I seen you in the fighting where men win glory,
125    yet now you have come striding far out in front of all others
in your great heart, who have dared stand up to my spear far-shadowing.
Yet unhappy are those whose sons match warcraft against me.
But if you are some one of the immortals come down from the bright sky,
know that I will not fight against any god of the heaven,
130    since even the son of Dryas, Lykourgos the powerful, did not
live long; he who tried to fight with the gods of the bright sky,
who once drove the fosterers of rapturous Dionysos
headlong down the sacred Nyseian hill, and all of them
shed and scattered their wands on the ground, stricken with an ox-goad
135    by murderous Lykourgos, while Dionysos in terror
dived into the salt surf, and Thetis took him to her bosom,
frightened, with the strong shivers upon him at the man's blustering.

But the gods who live at their ease were angered with Lykourgos,
and the son of Kronos struck him to blindness, nor did he live long
afterward, since he was hated by all the immortals.                              140
Therefore neither would I be willing to fight with the blessed
gods; but if you are one of those mortals who eat what the soil yields,
come nearer, so that sooner you may reach your appointed destruction."
    Then in turn the shining son of Hippolochos answered:
"High-hearted son of Tydeus, why ask of my generation?                           145
As is the generation of leaves, so is that of humanity.
The wind scatters the leaves on the ground, but the live timber
burgeons with leaves again in the season of spring returning.
So one generation of men will grow while another
dies. Yet if you wish to learn all this and be certain                           150
of my genealogy: there are plenty of men who know it.
There is a city, Ephyrē, in the corner of horse-pasturing
Argos; there lived Sisyphos, that sharpest of all men,
Sisyphos, Aiolos' son, and he had a son named Glaukos,
and Glaukos in turn sired Bellerophontes the blameless.                          155
To Bellerophontes the gods granted beauty and desirable
manhood; but Proitos in anger devised evil things against him,
and drove him out of his own domain, since he was far greater,
from the Argive country Zeus had broken to the sway of his scepter.
Beautiful Anteia the wife of Proitos was stricken                                160
with passion to lie in love with him, and yet she could not
beguile valiant Bellerophontes, whose will was virtuous.
So she went to Proitos the king and uttered her falsehood:
'Would you be killed, O Proitos? Then murder Bellerophontes
who tried to lie with me in love, though I was unwilling.'                        165
So she spoke, and anger took hold of the king at her story.
He shrank from killing him, since his heart was awed by such action,
but sent him away to Lykia, and handed him murderous symbols,
which he inscribed in a folding tablet, enough to destroy life,
and told him to show it to his wife's father, that he might perish.              170
Bellerophontes went to Lykia in the blameless convoy
of the gods; when he came to the running stream of Xanthos, and Lykia,
the lord of wide Lykia tendered him full-hearted honor.
Nine days he entertained him with sacrifice of nine oxen,
but afterward when the rose fingers of the tenth dawn showed, then               175

he began to question him, and asked to be shown the symbols,
whatever he might be carrying from his son-in-law, Proitos.
Then after he had been given his son-in-law's wicked symbols
first he sent him away with orders to kill the Chimaira
180    none might approach; a thing of immortal make, not human,
lion-fronted and snake behind, a goat in the middle,
and snorting out the breath of the terrible flame of bright fire.
He killed the Chimaira, obeying the portents of the immortals.
Next after this he fought against the glorious Solymoi,
185    and this he thought was the strongest battle with men that he entered;
but third he slaughtered the Amazons, who fight men in battle.
Now as he came back the king spun another entangling
treachery; for choosing the bravest men in wide Lykia
he laid a trap, but these men never came home thereafter
190    since all of them were killed by blameless Bellerophontes.
Then when the king knew him for the powerful stock of the god,
he detained him there, and offered him the hand of his daughter,
and gave him half of all the kingly privilege. Thereto
the men of Lykia cut out a piece of land, surpassing
195    all others, fine ploughland and orchard for him to administer.
His bride bore three children to valiant Bellerophontes,
Isandros and Hippolochos and Laodameia.
Laodameia lay in love beside Zeus of the counsels
and bore him godlike Sarpedon of the brazen helmet.
200    But after Bellerophontes was hated by all the immortals,
he wandered alone about the plain of Aleios, eating
his heart out, skulking aside from the trodden track of humanity.
As for Isandros his son, Ares the insatiate of fighting
killed him in close battle against the glorious Solymoi,
205    while Artemis of the golden reins killed the daughter in anger.
But Hippolochos begot me, and I claim that he is my father;
he sent me to Troy, and urged upon me repeated injunctions,
to be always among the bravest, and hold my head above others,
not shaming the generation of my fathers, who were
210    the greatest men in Ephyrē and again in wide Lykia.
Such is my generation and the blood I claim to be born from."
        He spoke, and Diomedes of the great war cry was gladdened.
He drove his spear deep into the prospering earth, and in winning

words of friendliness he spoke to the shepherd of the people:
"See now, you are my guest friend from far in the time of our fathers.      215
Brilliant Oineus once was host to Bellerophontes
the blameless, in his halls, and twenty days he detained him,
and these two gave to each other fine gifts in token of friendship.
Oineus gave his guest a war belt bright with the red dye,
Bellerophontes a golden and double-handled drinking-cup,      220
a thing I left behind in my house when I came on my journey.
Tydeus, though, I cannot remember, since I was little
when he left me, that time the people of the Achaians perished
in Thebe. Therefore I am your friend and host in the heart of Argos;
you are mine in Lykia, when I come to your country.      225
Let us avoid each other's spears, even in the close fighting.
There are plenty of Trojans and famed companions in battle for me
to kill, whom the god sends me, or those I run down with my swift feet,
many Achaians for you to slaughter, if you can do it.
But let us exchange our armor, so that these others may know      230
how we claim to be guests and friends from the days of our fathers."
     So they spoke, and both springing down from behind their horses
gripped each other's hands and exchanged the promise of friendship;
but Zeus the son of Kronos stole away the wits of Glaukos
who exchanged with Diomedes the son of Tydeus armor      235
of gold for bronze, for nine oxen's worth the worth of a hundred.

     Now as Hektor had come to the Skaian gates and the oak tree,
all the wives of the Trojans and their daughters came running about him
to ask after their sons, after their brothers and neighbors,
their husbands; and he told them to pray to the immortals,      240
all, in turn; but there were sorrows in store for many.
     Now he entered the wonderfully built palace of Priam.
This was fashioned with smooth-stone cloister walks, and within it
were embodied fifty sleeping chambers of smoothed stone
built so as to connect with each other; and within these slept      245
each beside his own wedded wife, the sons of Priam.
In the same inner court on the opposite side, to face these,
lay the twelve close smooth-stone sleeping chambers of his daughters
built so as to connect with each other; and within these slept,
each by his own modest wife, the lords of the daughters of Priam.      250

There, there came to meet Hektor his bountiful mother
with Laodikē, the loveliest looking of all her daughters.
She clung to his hand and called him by name and spoke to him: "Why then,
child, have you come here and left behind the bold battle?
255 Surely it is these accursed sons of the Achaians who wear you
out, as they fight close to the city, and the spirit stirred you
to return, and from the peak of the citadel lift your hands, praying
to Zeus. But stay while I bring you honey-sweet wine, to pour out
a libation to father Zeus and the other immortals
260 first, and afterward if you will drink yourself, be strengthened.
In a tired man, wine will bring back his strength to its bigness,
in a man tired as you are tired, defending your neighbors."

Tall Hektor of the shining helm spoke to her answering:
"My honored mother, lift not to me the kindly sweet wine,
265 for fear you stagger my strength and make me forget my courage;
and with hands unwashed I would take shame to pour the glittering
wine to Zeus; there is no means for a man to pray to the dark-misted
son of Kronos, with blood and muck all spattered upon him.
But go yourself to the temple of the spoiler Athene,
270 assembling the ladies of honor, and with things to be sacrificed,
and take a robe, which seems to you the largest and loveliest
in the great house, and that which is far your dearest possession.
Lay this along the knees of Athene the lovely haired. Also
promise to dedicate within the shrine twelve heifers,
275 yearlings, never broken, if only she will have pity
on the town of Troy, and the Trojan wives, and their innocent children,
if she will hold back from sacred Ilion the son of Tydeus,
that wild spear-fighter, the strong one who drives men to thoughts of terror.
So go yourself to the temple of the spoiler Athene,
280 while I go in search of Paris, to call him, if he will listen
to anything I tell him. How I wish at this moment the earth might
open beneath him. The Olympian let him live, a great sorrow
to the Trojans, and high-hearted Priam, and all of his children.
If only I could see him gone down to the house of the death god,
285 then I could say my heart had forgotten its joyless affliction."

So he spoke, and she going into the great house called out
to her handmaidens, who assembled throughout the city the highborn

women; while she descended into the fragrant store-chamber.
There lay the elaborately wrought robes, the work of Sidonian
women, whom Alexandros himself, the godlike, had brought home          290
from the land of Sidon, crossing the wide sea, on that journey
when he brought back also gloriously descended Helen.
Hekabē lifted out one and took it as gift to Athene,
that which was the loveliest in design and the largest,
and shone like a star. It lay beneath the others. She went on          295
her way, and a throng of noble women hastened about her.
    When these had come to Athene's temple on the peak of the citadel,
Theano of the fair cheeks opened the door for them, daughter
of Kisseus, and wife of Antenor, breaker of horses,
she whom the Trojans had established to be Athene's priestess.         300
With a wailing cry all lifted up their hands to Athene,
and Theano of the fair cheeks taking up the robe laid it
along the knees of Athene the lovely haired, and praying
she supplicated the daughter of powerful Zeus: "O lady,
Athene, our city's defender, shining among goddesses:                  305
break the spear of Diomedes, and grant that the man be
hurled on his face in front of the Skaian gates; so may we
instantly dedicate within your shrine twelve heifers,
yearlings, never broken, if only you will have pity
on the town of Troy, and the Trojan wives, and their innocent children."  310
    She spoke in prayer, but Pallas Athene turned her head from her.

    So they made their prayer to the daughter of Zeus the powerful.
But Hektor went away to the house of Alexandros,
a splendid place he had built himself, with the men who at that time
were the best men for craftsmanship in the generous Troad,            315
who had made him a sleeping room and a hall and a courtyard
near the houses of Hektor and Priam, on the peak of the citadel.
There entered Hektor beloved of Zeus, in his hand holding
the eleven-cubit-long spear, whose shaft was tipped with a shining
bronze spearhead, and a ring of gold was hooped to hold it.          320
He found the man in his chamber busy with his splendid armor,
the corselet and the shield, and turning in his hands the curved bow,
while Helen of Argos was sitting among her attendant women
directing the magnificent work done by her handmaidens.

325     But Hektor saw him, and in words of shame he rebuked him:
        "Strange man! It is not fair to keep in your heart this coldness.
        The people are dying around the city and around the steep wall
        as they fight hard; and it is for you that this war with its clamor
        has flared up about our city. You yourself would fight with another
330     whom you saw anywhere hanging back from the hateful encounter.
        Up then, to keep our town from burning at once in the hot fire."
            Then in answer the godlike Alexandros spoke to him:
        "Hektor, seeing you have scolded me rightly, not beyond measure,
        therefore I will tell, and you in turn understand and listen.
335     It was not so much in coldness and bitter will toward the Trojans
        that I sat in my room, but I wished to give myself over to sorrow.
        But just now with soft words my wife was winning me over
        and urging me into the fight, and that way seems to me also
        the better one. Victory passes back and forth between men.
340     Come then, wait for me now while I put on my armor of battle,
        or go, and I will follow, and I think I can overtake you."
            He spoke, but Hektor of the shining helm gave him no answer,
        but Helen spoke to him in words of endearment: "Brother
        by marriage to me, who am a nasty bitch evil-intriguing,
345     how I wish that on that day when my mother first bore me
        the foul whirlwind of the storm had caught me away and swept me
        to the mountain, or into the wash of the sea deep-thundering
        where the waves would have swept me away before all these things had
                happened.
        Yet since the gods had brought it about that these vile things must be,
350     I wish I had been the wife of a better man than this is,
        one who knew modesty and all things of shame that men say.
        But this man's heart is no steadfast thing, nor yet will it be so
        ever hereafter; for that I think he shall take the consequence.
        But come now, come in and rest on this chair, my brother,
355     since it is on your heart beyond all that the hard work has fallen
        for the sake of dishonored me and the blind act of Alexandros,
        us two, on whom Zeus set a vile destiny, so that hereafter
        we shall be made into things of song for the men of the future."
            Then tall Hektor of the shining helm answered her: "Do not, Helen,
360     make me sit with you, though you love me. You will not persuade me.
        Already my heart within is hastening me to defend

the Trojans, who when I am away long greatly to have me.
Rather rouse this man, and let himself also be swift to action
so he may overtake me while I am still in the city.
For I am going first to my own house, so I can visit                       365
my own people, my beloved wife and my son, who is little,
since I do not know if ever again I shall come back this way,
or whether the gods will strike me down at the hands of the Achaians."

    So speaking Hektor of the shining helm departed
and in speed made his way to his own well-established dwelling,         370
but failed to find in the house Andromachē of the white arms;
for she, with the child, and followed by one fair-robed attendant,
had taken her place on the tower in lamentation, and tearful.
When he saw no sign of his perfect wife within the house, Hektor
stopped in his way on the threshold and spoke among the handmaidens:   375
"Come then, tell me truthfully as you may, handmaidens:
where has Andromachē of the white arms gone? Is she
with any of the sisters of her lord or the wives of his brothers?
Or has she gone to the house of Athene, where all the other
lovely-haired women of Troy propitiate the grim goddess?"             380
    Then in turn the hard-working housekeeper gave him an answer:
"Hektor, since you have urged me to tell you the truth, she is not
with any of the sisters of her lord or the wives of his brothers,
nor has she gone to the house of Athene, where all the other
lovely-haired women of Troy propitiate the grim goddess,              385
but she has gone to the great bastion of Ilion, because she heard that
the Trojans were losing, and great grew the strength of the Achaians.
Therefore she has gone in speed to the wall, like a woman
gone mad, and a nurse attending her carries the baby."
    So the housekeeper spoke, and Hektor hastened from his home        390
backward by the way he had come through the well-laid streets. So
as he had come to the gates on his way through the great city,
the Skaian gates, whereby he would issue into the plain, there
at last his own generous wife came running to meet him,
Andromachē, the daughter of high-hearted Eëtion;                      395
Eëtion, who had dwelt underneath wooded Plakos,
in Thebe below Plakos, lord over the Kilikian people.
It was his daughter who was given to Hektor of the bronze helm.

She came to him there, and beside her went an attendant carrying
the boy in the fold of her bosom, a little child, only a baby,
Hektor's son, the admired, beautiful as a star shining,
whom Hektor called Skamandrios, but all of the others
Astyanax—lord of the city; since Hektor alone saved Ilion.
Hektor smiled in silence as he looked on his son, but she,
Andromachē, stood close beside him, letting her tears fall,
and clung to his hand and called him by name and spoke to him: "Dearest,
your own great strength will be your death, and you have no pity
on your little son, nor on me, ill-starred, who soon must be your widow;
for presently the Achaians, gathering together,
will set upon you and kill you; and for me it would be far better
to sink into the earth when I have lost you, for there is no other
consolation for me after you have gone to your destiny—
only grief; since I have no father, no honored mother.
It was brilliant Achilleus who slew my father, Eëtion,
when he stormed the strong-founded citadel of the Kilikians,
Thebe of the towering gates. He killed Eëtion
but did not strip his armor, for his heart respected the dead man,
but burned the body in all its elaborate war-gear
and piled a grave mound over it, and the nymphs of the mountains,
daughters of Zeus of the aegis, planted elm trees about it.
And they who were my seven brothers in the great house all went
upon a single day down into the house of the death god,
for swift-footed brilliant Achilleus slaughtered all of them
as they were tending their white sheep and their lumbering oxen;
and when he had led my mother, who was queen under wooded Plakos,
here, along with all his other possessions, Achilleus
released her again, accepting ransom beyond count, but Artemis
of the showering arrows struck her down in the halls of her father.
Hektor, thus you are father to me, and my honored mother,
you are my brother, and you it is who are my young husband.
Please take pity upon me then, stay here on the rampart,
that you may not leave your child an orphan, your wife a widow,
but draw your people up by the fig tree, there where the city
is openest to attack, and where the wall may be mounted.
Three times their bravest came that way, and fought there to storm it
about the two Aiantes and renowned Idomeneus,

400

405

410

415

420

425

430

435

about the two Atreidai and the fighting son of Tydeus.
Either some man well skilled in prophetic arts had spoken,
or the very spirit within themselves had stirred them to the onslaught."
    Then tall Hektor of the shining helm answered her: "All these        440
things are in my mind also, lady; yet I would feel deep shame
before the Trojans, and the Trojan women with trailing garments,
if like a coward I were to shrink aside from the fighting;
and the spirit will not let me, since I have learned to be valiant
and to fight always among the foremost ranks of the Trojans,        445
winning for my own self great glory, and for my father.
For I know this thing well in my heart, and my mind knows it:
there will come a day when sacred Ilion shall perish,
and Priam, and the people of Priam of the strong ash spear.
But it is not so much the pain to come of the Trojans        450
that troubles me, not even of Priam the king nor Hekabē,
not the thought of my brothers who in their numbers and valor
shall drop in the dust under the hands of men who hate them,
as troubles me the thought of you, when some bronze-armored
Achaian leads you off, taking away your day of liberty,        455
in tears; and in Argos you must work at the loom of another,
and carry water from the spring Messeis or Hypereia,
all unwilling, but strong will be the necessity upon you;
and some day seeing you shedding tears a man will say of you:
'This is the wife of Hektor, who was ever the bravest fighter        460
of the Trojans, breakers of horses, in the days when they fought about Ilion.'
So will one speak of you; and for you it will be yet a fresh grief,
to be widowed of such a man who could fight off the day of your slavery.
But may I be dead and the piled earth hide me under before I
hear you crying and know by this that they drag you captive."        465

    So speaking glorious Hektor held out his arms to his baby,
who shrank back to his fair-girdled nurse's bosom
screaming, and frightened at the aspect of his own father,
terrified as he saw the bronze and the crest with its horse-hair,
nodding dreadfully, as he thought, from the peak of the helmet.        470
Then his beloved father laughed out, and his honored mother,
and at once glorious Hektor lifted from his head the helmet
and laid it in all its shining upon the ground. Then taking

up his dear son he tossed him about in his arms, and kissed him,
475 and lifted his voice in prayer to Zeus and the other immortals:
"Zeus, and you other immortals, grant that this boy, who is my son,
may be as I am, pre-eminent among the Trojans,
great in strength, as am I, and rule strongly over Ilion;
and some day let them say of him: 'He is better by far than his father,'
480 as he comes in from the fighting; and let him kill his enemy
and bring home the blooded spoils, and delight the heart of his mother."
So speaking he set his child again in the arms of his beloved
wife, who took him back again to her fragrant bosom
smiling in her tears; and her husband saw, and took pity upon her,
485 and stroked her with his hand, and called her by name and spoke to her:
"Poor Andromachē! Why does your heart sorrow so much for me?
No man is going to hurl me to Hades, unless it is fated,
but as for fate, I think that no man yet has escaped it
once it has taken its first form, neither brave man nor coward.
490 Go therefore back to our house, and take up your own work,
the loom and the distaff, and see to it that your handmaidens
ply their work also; but the men must see to the fighting,
all men who are the people of Ilion, but I beyond others."
So glorious Hektor spoke and again took up the helmet
495 with its crest of horse-hair, while his beloved wife went homeward,
turning to look back on the way, letting the live tears fall.
And as she came in speed into the well-settled household
of Hektor the slayer of men, she found numbers of handmaidens
within, and her coming stirred all of them into lamentation.
500 So they mourned in his house over Hektor while he was living
still, for they thought he would never again come back from the fighting
alive, escaping the Achaian hands and their violence.

But Paris in turn did not linger long in his high house,
but when he had put on his glorious armor with bronze elaborate
505 he ran in the confidence of his quick feet through the city.
As when some stalled horse who has been corn-fed at the manger
breaking free of his rope gallops over the plain in thunder
to his accustomed bathing place in a sweet-running river
and in the pride of his strength holds high his head, and the mane floats
510 over his shoulders; sure of his glorious strength, the quick knees

carry him to the loved places and the pasture of horses;
so from uttermost Pergamos came Paris, the son of
Priam, shining in all his armor of war as the sun shines,
laughing aloud, and his quick feet carried him; suddenly thereafter
he came on brilliant Hektor, his brother, where he yet lingered          515
before turning away from the place where he had talked with his lady.
It was Alexandros the godlike who first spoke to him:
"Brother, I fear that I have held back your haste, by being
slow on the way, not coming in time, as you commanded me."
    Then tall Hektor of the shining helm spoke to him in answer:          520
"Strange man! There is no way that one, giving judgment in fairness,
could dishonor your work in battle, since you are a strong man.
But of your own accord you hang back, unwilling. And my heart
is grieved in its thought, when I hear shameful things spoken about you
by the Trojans, who undergo hard fighting for your sake.                 525
Let us go now; some day hereafter we will make all right
with the immortal gods in the sky, if Zeus ever grant it,
setting up to them in our houses the wine-bowl of liberty
after we have driven out of Troy the strong-greaved Achaians."

# BOOK SEVEN

So speaking Hektor the glorious swept on through the gates,
and with him went Alexandros his brother, both of them minded
in their hearts to do battle and take their part in the fighting.
And as to men of the sea in their supplication the god sends
5  a fair wind, when they are breaking their strength at the smoothed
      oar-sweeps,
driving over the sea, and their arms are weak with weariness,
so these two appeared to the Trojans, who had longed for them.
     Each killed his man: Paris, the son of lord Areïthoös,
Menesthios, who lived in Arne, born to him of the war club
10  Areïthoös, and to ox-eyed Phylomedousa;
while Hektor with the sharp spear struck Eïoneus, under
the circle of the bronze helm, in the neck, and broke his limbs' strength.
And Glaukos, lord of the Lykian men, the son of Hippolochos,
struck down with the spear Iphinoös in the strong encounter,
15  Dexias' son, as he leapt up behind his fast horses, striking him
in the shoulder. He dropped from car to ground, and his limbs' strength
      was broken.

     Now as the goddess gray-eyed Athene was aware of these two
destroying the men of Argos in the strong encounter,
she went down in a flash of speed from the peaks of Olympos
20  to sacred Ilion, where Apollo stirred forth to meet her
from his seat on Pergamos, where he planned that the Trojans should
      conquer.
These two then encountered each other beside the oak tree,

and speaking first the son of Zeus, lord Apollo, addressed her:
"What can be your desire this time, O daughter of great Zeus,
that you came down from Olympos at the urge of your mighty spirit?     25
To give the Danaäns victory in the battle, turning it
back? Since you have no pity at all for the Trojans who are dying.
But if you might only do as I say, it would be far better.
For this day let us put an end to the hatred and the fighting
now; they shall fight again hereafter, till we witness the finish     30
they make of Ilion, since it is dear to the heart of you, who
are goddesses immortal, that this city shall be made desolate."
    Then in answer the goddess gray-eyed Athene spoke to him:
"Worker from afar, thus let it be. These were my thoughts also
as I came down from Olympos among the Achaians and Trojans.          35
Tell me then, how are you minded to stop these men in their fighting?"
    Now in turn the son of Zeus, lord Apollo, addressed her:
"Let us rouse up the strong heart in Hektor, breaker of horses,
if he might call forth some Danaän to do battle against him,
single man against single man, in bitter combat;                     40
and let the strong-greaved Achaians, stirred into admiration,
send forth a single man to do battle with brilliant Hektor."
    He spoke, nor failed to persuade the goddess gray-eyed Athene.
Now Helenos, Priam's beloved son, gathered into his heart their
deliberation, and all that pleased the musing divinities.            45
He went on his way and stood beside Hektor and spoke a word to him:
"Hektor, O son of Priam and equal of Zeus in counsel,
would you now be persuaded by me, for I am your brother?
Make the rest of the Trojans sit down, and all the Achaians,
and yourself call forth one of the Achaians, their bravest,          50
to fight man to man against you in bitter combat.
Since it is not your destiny yet to die and encounter
fate. For thus I heard it in the speech of the gods everlasting."

    So he spoke, and Hektor hearing his word was happy,
and went into the space between and forced back the Trojan battalions,  55
holding his spear by the middle, until they were all seated,
while Agamemnon in turn seated the strong-greaved Achaians,
and Athene and the lord of the silver bow, Apollo,
assuming the likenesses of birds, of vultures, settled

60     aloft the great oak tree of their father, Zeus of the aegis,
taking their ease and watching these men whose ranks, dense-settled,
shuddered into a bristle of spears, of shields and of helmets.
As when the shudder of the west wind suddenly rising
scatters across the water, and the water darkens beneath it,
65     so darkening were settled the ranks of Achaians and Trojans
in the plain. And now Hektor spoke forth between them:
"Listen to me, you Trojans and strong-greaved Achaians,
while I speak forth what the heart within my breast urges.
Zeus, son of Kronos, who sits on high, would not bring to fulfillment
70     our oaths, but is found to be of evil intention toward both sides
until that day when you storm Troy of the strong towers, or that day
when you yourselves are broken beside your seafaring vessels.
Seeing now that among you are the bravest of all the Achaians,
let one of you, whose heart stirs him to combat against me,
75     stand forth before all to fight by himself against brilliant Hektor.
Behold the terms that I make, let Zeus be witness upon them.
If with the thin edge of the bronze he takes my life, then
let him strip my armor and carry it back to the hollow ships,
but give my body to be taken home again, so that the Trojans
80     and the wives of the Trojans may give me in death my rite of burning.
But if I take his life, and Apollo grants me the glory,
I will strip his armor and carry it to sacred Ilion
and hang it in front of the temple of far-striking Apollo,
but his corpse I will give back among the strong-benched vessels
85     so that the flowing-haired Achaians may give him due burial
and heap up a mound upon him beside the broad passage of Helle.
And some day one of the men to come will say, as he sees it,
one who in his benched ship sails on the wine-blue water:
'This is the mound of a man who died long ago in battle,
90     who was one of the bravest, and glorious Hektor killed him.'
So will he speak some day, and my glory will not be forgotten."

     So he spoke, and all of them stayed stricken to silence
in shame of refusing him, and in fear to take up his challenge.
But now at long last Menelaos stood forth and addressed them
95     in scorn and reproach, and stirred within the heart to great sorrow:
"Ah me! You brave in words, you women, not men, of Achaia!

This will be a defilement upon us, shame upon shame piled,
if no one of the Danaäns goes out to face Hektor.
No, may all of you turn to water and earth, all of you
who sit by yourselves with no life in you, utterly dishonored.          100
I myself will arm against this man. While above us
the threads of victory are held in the hands of the immortals."
    So he spoke, and began to put on his splendid armor.
And there, O Menelaos, would have shown forth the end of your life
under the hands of Hektor, since he was far stronger than you were,          105
had not the kings of the Achaians leapt up and caught you;
and the son of Atreus himself, powerful Agamemnon,
caught you by the right hand, and called you by name, and spoke to you:
"Menelaos, beloved of God, you are mad; you have no need
to take leave of your senses thus. Hold fast, though it hurts you,          110
nor long in your pride to fight with a man who is better than you are,
with Hektor, Priam's son. There are others who shudder before him.
Even Achilleus, in the fighting where men win glory,
trembles to meet this man, and he is far better than you are.
Go back now and sit down in the throng of your own companions;          115
the Achaians will set up another to fight against this man,
and even though he is without fear, and can never be glutted
with rough work, I think he will be glad to leave off, even
if he comes off whole from the hateful fighting and bitter combat."

    The hero spoke like this and bent the heart of his brother          120
since he urged wisely. And Menelaos obeyed him; his henchmen
joyfully thereupon took off the armor from his shoulders.
Nestor among the Argives now stood forth and addressed them:
"Oh, for shame. Great sorrow settles on the land of Achaia.
Surely he would groan aloud, Peleus, the aged horseman,          125
the great man of counsel among the Myrmidons, and their speaker.
Once, as he questioned me in his house, he was filled with great joy
as he heard the generation and blood of all of the Argives.
Now if he were to hear how all cringe away before Hektor,
many a time he would lift up his very hands to the immortals,          130
and the life breath from his limbs would go down into the house of Hades.
If only, O father Zeus, Athene, Apollo,
I were in my youth as when the Pylians assembled

and the spear-fighting Arkadians battled by swirling Keladon,
135 by the streams of Iardanos and before the ramparts of Pheia.
Their champion stood forth, Ereuthalion, a man godlike,
wearing upon his shoulders the armor of lord Areïthoös,
Areïthoös the brilliant, given by the men of that time
and the fair-girdled women the name club-fighter, because he
140 went into battle armed neither with the bow nor the long spear,
but with a great bar clubbed of iron broke the battalions.
Lykourgos killed this man by craft, not strength, for he met him
in the narrow pass of the way, where the iron club served not to parry
destruction, for Lykourgos, too quick with a stab beneath it,
145 pinned him through the middle with the spear, so he went down backward
to the ground; and he stripped the armor brazen Ares had given him
and wore the armor thereafter himself through the grind of battle.
But when Lykourgos was grown an old man in his halls, he gave it
to his beloved henchman, Ereuthalion, to carry.
150 Wearing this armor he called forth all the bravest to fight him,
but they were all afraid and trembling: none had the courage,
only I, for my hard-enduring heart in its daring
drove me to fight him. I in age was the youngest of all of them.
And I fought with him, and Pallas Athene gave me the glory.
155 Of all the men I have killed this was the tallest and strongest.
For he sprawled in his great bulk this way and that way. If only
I were young now, as then, and the strength still steady within me;
Hektor of the glancing helm would soon find his battle.
But you, now, who are the bravest of all the Achaians,
160 are not minded with a good will to go against Hektor."

So the old man scolded them, and nine in all stood forth.
Far the first to rise up was the lord of men, Agamemnon,
and rose after him the son of Tydeus, strong Diomedes,
and next the two Aiantes rose, their fierce strength upon them,
165 and after these Idomeneus, and Idomeneus' companion,
Meriones, a match for the murderous Lord of Battles,
and after these Eurypylos, the glorious son of Euaimon,
and Thoas rose up, Andraimon's son, and brilliant Odysseus.
All of these were willing to fight against brilliant Hektor.
170 Now before them again spoke the Gerenian horseman, Nestor:

"Let the lot be shaken for all of you, to see who wins it.
He shall be the one to gladden the strong-greaved Achaians,
and to be glad within his own heart, if he can come off
whole again from the hateful battle and bitter combat."
So he spoke, and each of them marked a lot as his own one lot.     175
They threw them in the helmet of Atreus' son, Agamemnon,
and the people, holding up their hands to the gods, prayed to them.
Then would murmur any man, gazing into the wide sky:
"Father Zeus, let Aias win the lot, or else Diomedes,
Tydeus' son, or the king himself of golden Mykenai."     180
So they spoke, and Nestor the Gerenian horseman shook the lots,
and a lot leapt from the helmet, that one that they all had wished for,
the lot of Aias; and a herald carrying it all through the great throng
showed it from left to right to the great men of the Achaians,
all of them. Each man knew not the mark, and denied it,     185
but as carrying it all through the great throng he showed it to that one
who had marked it as his, and thrown it in the helmet, glorious Aias,
he held forth his hand, and the herald stood by him, and put the lot in it,
and he saw his mark on the lot, and knew it, and his heart was gladdened.
He threw it down on the ground beside his foot, and spoke to them:     190
"See, friends, the lot is mine, and I myself am made happy
in my heart, since I think I can win over brilliant Hektor.
Do this, then: while I put on my armor of fighting,
all of you be praying to the lord Zeus, the son of Kronos,
in silence and each to himself, let none of the Trojans hear you;     195
or openly out loud, since we have nothing to be afraid of
at all, since no man by force will beat me backward unwilling
as he wills, nor by craft either, since I think that the man who was born
and raised in Salamis, myself, is not such a novice."
So he spoke, and they prayed to the lord Zeus, the son of Kronos.     200
And then would murmur any man, gazing into the wide sky:
"Father Zeus, watching over us from Ida, most high, most honored,
grant that Aias win the vaunt of renown and the victory;
but if truly you love Hektor and are careful for him,
give to both of them equal strength, make equal their honor."     205

So they spoke, and meanwhile Aias armed him in shining
bronze. Then when he had girt his body in all its armor,

he strode on his way, as Ares the war god walks gigantic
going into the fighting of men whom the son of Kronos
210 has driven to fight angrily in heart-perishing hatred.
Such was Aias as he strode gigantic, the wall of the Achaians,
smiling under his threatening brows, with his feet beneath him
taking huge strides forward, and shaking the spear far-shadowing.
And the Argives looking upon him were made glad, while the Trojans
215 were taken every man in the knees with trembling and terror,
and for Hektor himself the heart beat hard in his breast, but he could not
anymore find means to take flight and shrink back into
the throng of his men, since he in his pride had called him to battle.
Now Aias came near him, carrying like a wall his shield
220 of bronze and sevenfold ox-hide which Tychios wrought him with much
        toil;
Tychios, at home in Hyle, far the best of all workers in leather
who had made him the great gleaming shield of sevenfold ox-hide
from strong bulls, and hammered an eighth fold of bronze upon it.
Telamonian Aias, carrying this to cover
225 his chest, came near to Hektor and spoke to him in words of menace:
"Hektor, single man against single man you will learn now
for sure what the bravest men are like among the Danaäns
even after Achilleus the lion-hearted who breaks men in battle.
He lies now apart among his own beaked seafaring
230 ships, in anger at Agamemnon, the shepherd of the people.
But here are we; and we are such men as can stand up against you;
there are plenty of us; so now begin your fight and your combat."

        Tall Hektor of the glancing helm answered him: "Aias,
son of Telamon, seed of Zeus, O lord of the people,
235 do not be testing me as if I were some ineffectual
boy, or a woman, who knows nothing of the works of warfare.
I know well myself how to fight and kill men in battle;
I know how to turn to the right, how to turn to the left the ox-hide
tanned into a shield which is my protection in battle;
240 I know how to storm my way into the struggle of flying horses;
I know how to tread my measures on the grim floor of the war god.
Yet great as you are I would not strike you by stealth, watching
for my chance, but openly, so, if perhaps I might hit you."

So he spoke, and balanced the spear far-shadowed, and threw it,
and struck the sevenfold-ox-hide terrible shield of Aias                    245
in the uttermost bronze, which was the eighth layer upon it,
and the unwearying bronze spearhead shore its way through six folds
but was stopped in the seventh ox-hide. Then after him Aias
the illustrious in turn cast with his spear far-shadowing
and struck the shield of Priam's son on its perfect circle.                 250
All the way through the glittering shield went the heavy spearhead,
and crashed its way through the intricately worked corselet;
straight ahead by the flank the spearhead shore through his tunic,
yet he bent away to one side and avoided the dark death.
Both now gripping in their hands the long spears pulled them              255
out, and went at each other like lions who live on raw meat,
or wild boars, whose strength is no light thing. The son of
Priam stabbed then with his spear into the shield's center,
nor did the bronze point break its way through, but the spearhead bent back.
Now Aias plunging upon him thrust at the shield, and the spearhead        260
passed clean through, and pounded Hektor back in his fury,
and tore at his neck passing so that the dark blood broke. Yet
even so Hektor of the shining helmet did not stop fighting,
but gave back and in his heavy hand caught up a stone that
lay in the plain, black and rugged and huge. With this                    265
he struck the sevenfold-ox-hide terrible shield of Aias
in the knob of the center so that the bronze clashed loud about it.
After him Aias in turn lifting a stone far greater
whirled it and threw, leaning into the cast his strength beyond measure,
and the shield broke inward under the stroke of the rock like a millstone,  270
and Hektor's very knees gave, so that he sprawled backward,
shield beaten upon him, but at once Apollo lifted him upright.
And now they would have been stabbing with their swords at close quarters,
had not the heralds, messengers of Zeus and of mortals,
come up, one for the bronze-armored Achaians, one for the Trojans,        275
Idaios and Talthybios, both men of good counsel.
They held their staves between the two men, and the herald Idaios
out of his knowledge of prudent advices spoke a word to them:
"Stop the fight, dear children, nor go on with this battle.
To Zeus who gathers the clouds both of you are beloved,                   280

and both of you are fighters; this thing all of us know surely.
Night darkens now. It is a good thing to give way to the night-time."
    Aias the son of Telamon spoke to him in answer:
"Bid Hektor answer this, Idaios, since it was he who
285    in his pride called forth all our bravest to fight him.
Let him speak first; and I for my part shall do as he urges."
    Tall Hektor of the glancing helm answered him: "Aias,
seeing that God has given you strength, stature and wisdom
also, and with the spear you surpass the other Achaians,
290    let us now give over this fighting and hostility
for today; we shall fight again, until the divinity
chooses between us, and gives victory to one or the other.
Night darkens now. It is a good thing to give way to the night-time.
Thus you may bring joy to all the Achaians beside their
295    ships, and above all to those who are your own kindred and company;
and I in the great city of lord Priam will gladden
the Trojans, and the women of Troy with their trailing robes, who
will go before the divine assembly in thanksgiving for my sake.
Come then, let us give each other glorious presents,
300    so that any of the Achaians or Trojans may say of us:
'These two fought each other in heart-consuming hate, then
joined with each other in close friendship, before they were parted.'"
    So he spoke, and bringing a sword with nails of silver
gave it to him, together with the sheath and the well-cut sword belt,
305    and Aias gave a war belt colored shining with purple.
So separating, Aias went among the Achaian people,
and Hektor went back to the thronging Trojans, who were made happy
when they saw him coming alive and unwounded out of the combat,
escaping the strength and the unconquerable hands of Aias,
310    and they, who had not hoped to see him alive, escorted him
back to the town. On the other side the strong-greaved Achaians
led Aias, happy in his victory, to great Agamemnon.

    When these had come to the shelters of the son of Atreus,
Agamemnon the lord of men dedicated an ox among them,
315    a five-year-old male, to Zeus, all-powerful son of Kronos.
They skinned the victim and put it in order, and butchered the carcass,
and cut up the meat expertly into small pieces, and spitted them,

and roasted all carefully, and took off the pieces.
Then after they had finished the work and got the feast ready,
they feasted, nor was any man's hunger denied a fair portion;                    320
and Atreus' son, the hero wide-ruling Agamemnon,
gave to Aias in honor the long cuts of the chine's portion.
But when they had put away their desire for eating and drinking,
the aged man began to weave his counsel before them
first, Nestor, whose advice had shown best before this.                          325
He in kind intention toward all stood forth and addressed them:
"Son of Atreus, and you other great men of all the Achaians:
seeing that many flowing-haired Achaians have died here,
whose dark blood has been scattered beside the fair waters of Skamandros
by the fierce war god, while their souls went down into the house of Hades;      330
therefore with the dawn we should set a pause to the fighting
of Achaians, and assembling them wheel back the bodies
with mules and oxen; then must we burn them a little apart from
the ships, so that each whose duty it is may carry the bones back
to a man's children, when we go home to the land of our fathers.                 335
And let us gather and pile one single mound on the corpse-pyre
indiscriminately from the plain, and build fast upon it
towered ramparts, to be a defense of ourselves and our vessels.
And let us build into these walls gates strongly fitted
that there may be a way through them for the driving of horses;                  340
and on the outer side, and close, we must dig a deep ditch
circling it, so as to keep off their people and horses,
that we may not be crushed under the attack of these proud Trojans."
    So he spoke, and all the kings gave him their approval.
Now there was an assembly of Trojans high on the city of Ilion                   345
fiercely shaken to tumult before the doors of Priam,
and among these Antenor the thoughtful began to address them:
"Trojans and Dardanians and companions in arms: hear me
while I speak forth what the heart within my breast urges.
Come then: let us give back Helen of Argos and all her possessions              350
to the sons of Atreus to take away, seeing now we fight with
our true pledges made into lies; and I see no good thing's
accomplishment for us in the end, unless we do this."
    He spoke thus and sat down again, and among them rose up
brilliant Alexandros, the lord of lovely-haired Helen,                          355

who spoke to him in answer and addressed them in winged words:
"Antenor, these things that you argue please me no longer.
Your mind knows how to contrive a saying better than this one.
But if in all seriousness this is your true argument; then
360 it is the very gods who ruined the brain within you.
I will speak out before the Trojans, breakers of horses.
I refuse, straight out. I will not give back the woman.
But of the possessions I carried away to our house from Argos
I am willing to give all back, and to add to these from my own goods."
365   He spoke thus and sat down again, and among them rose up
Priam, son of Dardanos, equal of the gods in counsel,
who in kind intention toward all stood forth and addressed them:
"Trojans and Dardanians and companions in arms: hear me
while I speak forth what the heart within my breast urges.
370 Take now your supper about the city, as you did before this,
and remember your duty of the watch, and be each man wakeful;
and at dawn let Idaios go to the hollow ships, and speak with
the sons of Atreus, Menelaos and Agamemnon, giving
the word of Alexandros, for whose sake this strife has arisen,
375 and to add this solid message, and ask them if they are willing
to stop the sorrowful fighting until we can burn the bodies
of our dead. We shall fight again until the divinity
chooses between us, and gives victory to one or the other."

    So he spoke, and they listened to him with care, and obeyed him;
380 and so took their supper, watch succeeding watch, through the army.
Then at dawn Idaios went down to the hollow ships, where
he found the Danaäns, henchmen of the war god, in assembly
beside the stern of Agamemnon's ship; the herald
with the great voice took his stand in their midst, and spoke to them:
385 "Son of Atreus, and you other great men of all the Achaians,
Priam and the rest of the haughty Trojans have bidden me
give you, if this message be found to your pleasure and liking,
the word of Alexandros, for whose sake this strife has arisen.
All those possessions that Alexandros carried in his hollow
390 ships to Troy, and I wish that he had perished before then,
he is willing to give all back, and to add to these from his own goods.
But the very wedded wife of glorious Menelaos

he says that he will not give, though the Trojans would have him do it.
They told me to give you this message also, if you are willing;
to stop the sorrowful fighting until we can burn the bodies                    395
of our dead. We shall fight again afterward, until the divinity
chooses between us, and gives victory to one or the other."
    So he spoke, and all of them stayed quiet in silence;
but now at long last Diomedes of the great war cry addressed them:
"Now let none accept the possessions of Alexandros,                            400
nor take back Helen; one who is very simple can see it,
that by this time the terms of death hang over the Trojans."
    So he spoke, and all sons of the Achaians shouted
acclaim for the word of Diomedes, breaker of horses;
and now powerful Agamemnon spoke to Idaios:                                     405
"Idaios, you hear for yourself the word of the Achaians,
how they are answering you; and such is my pleasure also.
But about the burning of the dead bodies I do not begrudge you;
no, for there is no sparing time for the bodies of the perished,
once they have died, to give them swiftly the pity of burning.                 410
Let Zeus, high-thundering lord of Hera, witness our pledges."

    He spoke, and held up the scepter in the sight of all the gods. Then
Idaios made his way back once more to sacred Ilion.
The Trojans and Dardanians were in session of assembly,
all gathered in one place, awaiting Idaios when he might come                   415
back; and he returned to them and delivered his message
standing there in their midst, and they made their swift preparations,
for two things, some to gather the bodies, and the others firewood;
while the Argives on the other side from their strong-benched vessels
went forward, some to gather the bodies, and others firewood.                  420
    Now the sun of a new day struck on the ploughlands, rising
out of the quiet water and the deep stream of the ocean
to climb the sky. The Trojans assembled together. They found
it hard to recognize each individual dead man;
but with water they washed away the blood that was on them                     425
and as they wept warm tears they lifted them onto the wagons.
But great Priam would not let them cry out; and in silence
they piled the bodies upon the pyre, with their hearts in sorrow,
and burned them upon the fire, and went back to sacred Ilion.

430 In the same way on the other side the strong-greaved Achaians
piled their own slain upon the pyre, with their hearts in sorrow,
and burned them upon the fire, and went back to their hollow vessels.
But when the dawn was not yet, but still the pallor of night's edge,
a chosen body of the Achaians formed by the pyre;
435 and they gathered together and piled one single mound all above it
indiscriminately from the plain, and built a fort on it
with towered ramparts, to be a defense for themselves and their vessels;
and they built within these walls gates strongly fitted
that there might be a way through them for the driving of horses;
440 and on the outer side and against it they dug a deep ditch,
making it great and wide, and fixed the sharp stakes inside it.

So the flowing-haired Achaians labored, and meanwhile
the gods in session at the side of Zeus who handles the lightning
watched the huge endeavor of the bronze-armored Achaians;
445 and the god Poseidon who shakes the earth began speaking among them:
"Father Zeus, is there any mortal left on the wide earth
who will still declare to the immortals his mind and his purpose?
Do you not see how now these flowing-haired Achaians
have built a wall landward of their ships, and driven about it
450 a ditch, and not given to the gods any grand sacrifice?
Now the fame of this will last as long as dawnlight is scattered,
and men will forget that wall which I and Phoibos Apollo
built with our hard work for the hero Laomedon's city."
Deeply troubled, Zeus who gathers the clouds answered him:
455 "What a thing to have said, earth-shaker of the wide strength.
Some other one of the gods might fear such a thought, one who
is a god far weaker of his hands and in anger than you are;
but the fame of you shall last as long as dawnlight is scattered.
Come then! After once more the flowing-haired Achaians
460 are gone back with their ships to the beloved land of their fathers,
break their wall to pieces and scatter it into the salt sea
and pile again the beach deep under the sands and cover it;
so let the great wall of the Achaians go down to destruction."

As these two were talking thus together, the sun went
465 down, and the work of the Achaians was finished. They slaughtered

oxen then beside their shelters, and took their supper.
The ships came over to them from Lemnos bringing them wine, ships
sent over to them in numbers by the son of Jason, Euneos,
whom Hypsipyle had borne to the shepherd of the people, Jason.
Apart to the sons of Atreus, Agamemnon and Menelaos,                    470
Jason's son had given wine as a gift, a thousand
measures; and thence the rest of the flowing-haired Achaians
bought wine, some for bronze and others for shining iron,
some for skins and some for the whole oxen, while others
paid slaves taken in war; and they made their feasting abundant.        475
All night long thereafter the flowing-haired Achaians
feasted, and the Trojans and their companions in arms in the city;
but all night long Zeus of the counsels was threatening evil
upon them in the terrible thunderstroke. Green fear took hold of them.
They spilled the wine on the ground from their cups, and none was so hardy   480
as to drink, till he had poured to the all-powerful son of Kronos.
They lay down thereafter and took the blessing of slumber.

# BOOK EIGHT

Now Dawn the yellow-robed scattered over all the earth. Zeus
who joys in the thunder made an assembly of all the immortals
upon the highest peak of rugged Olympos. There he
spoke to them himself, and the other divinities listened:
5 "Hear me, all you gods and all you goddesses: hear me
while I speak forth what the heart within my breast urges.
Now let no female divinity, nor male god either,
presume to cut across the way of my word, but consent to it
all of you, so that I can make an end in speed of these matters.
10 And anyone I perceive against the gods' will attempting
to go among the Trojans and help them, or among the Danaäns,
he shall go whipped against his dignity back to Olympos;
or I shall take him and dash him down to the murk of Tartaros,
far below, where the uttermost depth of the pit lies under
15 earth, where there are gates of iron and a brazen doorstone,
as far beneath the house of Hades as from earth the sky lies.
Then he will see how far I am strongest of all the immortals.
Come, you gods, make this endeavor, that you all may learn this.
Let down out of the sky a cord of gold; lay hold of it
20 all you who are gods and all who are goddesses, yet not
even so can you drag down Zeus from the sky to the ground, not
Zeus the high lord of counsel, though you try until you grow weary.
Yet whenever I might strongly be minded to pull you,
I could drag you up, earth and all and sea and all with you,
25 then fetch the golden rope about the horn of Olympos

and make it fast, so that all once more should dangle in mid air.
So much stronger am I than the gods, and stronger than mortals."
So he spoke, and all of them stayed stricken to silence,
stunned at his word, for indeed he had spoken to them very strongly.
But now at long last the goddess gray-eyed Athene answered him:          30
"Son of Kronos, our father, O lordliest of the mighty,
we know already your strength and how none can stand up against it.
Yet even so we are sorrowful for the Danaän spearmen
who must fill out an unhappy destiny, and perish.
Still we shall keep out of the fighting, as you command us;              35
yet we will put good counsel in the Argives; if it may help them,
so that not all of them will die because of your anger."
Then Zeus the gatherer of the clouds smiled at her and answered:
"Tritogeneia, dear daughter, do not lose heart; for I say this
not in outright anger, and my meaning toward you is kindly."            40

He spoke, and under the chariot harnessed his bronze-shod horses,
flying-footed, with long manes streaming of gold; and he put on
clothing of gold about his own body, and took up the golden
lash, carefully compacted, and climbed up into his chariot,
and whipped them into a run, and they winged their way unreluctant     45
through the space between the earth and the starry heaven.
He came to Ida with all her springs, the mother of wild beasts,
to Gargaron, where was his holy ground and his smoking altar.
There the father of gods and of mortals halted his horses,
and slipped them from their harness, and drifted close mist about them,  50
and himself rejoicing in the pride of his strength sat down on the mountain
looking out over the city of Troy and the ships of the Achaians.

Now the flowing-haired Achaians had taken their dinner
lightly among their shelters, and they put on their armor thereafter;
and on the other side, in the city, the Trojans took up               55
their armor, fewer men, yet minded to stand the encounter
even so, caught in necessity, for their wives and their children.
And all the gates were made open, and the fighting men swept through
them,
the foot ranks and the horsemen, and the sound grew huge of their onset.

60    Now as these advancing came to one place and encountered,
      they dashed their shields together and their spears, and the strength of
      armored men in bronze, and the shields massive in the middle
      clashed against each other, and the sound grew huge of the fighting.
      There the screaming and the shouts of triumph rose up together
65    of men killing and men killed, and the ground ran blood.
        So long as it was early morning and the sacred daylight increasing,
      so long the thrown weapons of both took hold and men dropped under
          them.
      But when the sun god stood bestriding the middle heaven,
      then the father balanced his golden scales, and in them
70    he set two fateful portions of death, which lays men prostrate,
      for Trojans, breakers of horses, and bronze-armored Achaians,
      and balanced it by the middle. The Achaians' death-day was heaviest.
      There the fates of the Achaians settled down toward the bountiful
      earth, while those of the Trojans were lifted into the wide sky;
75    and he himself crashed a great stroke from Ida, and a kindling
      flash shot over the people of the Achaians; seeing it
      they were stunned, and pale terror took hold of all of them.

        Then Idomeneus dared not stand his ground, nor Agamemnon,
      nor did the two Aiantes stand, the henchmen of Ares,
80    only Gerenian Nestor stayed, the Achaians' watcher;
      not that he would, but his horse was failing, struck by an arrow
      from brilliant Alexandros, the lord of lovely-haired Helen;
      struck at the point of the head, where the utmost hairs of horses
      are grown along the skull, and which is a place most mortal.
85    He reared up in agony as the shaft went into the brain, then
      threw the team into confusion writhing upon the bronze point.
      Now as the old man hewed away the horse's trace-harness
      with a quick sword-cut, meanwhile the fast-running horses of Hektor
      came through the flux of the fighting and carried their daring driver,
90    Hektor; and now the old man would have lost his life there, had not
      Diomedes of the great war cry sharply perceived him.
      He cried out in a terrible voice to rally Odysseus:
      "Son of Laërtes and seed of Zeus, resourceful Odysseus,
      where are you running, turning your back in battle like a coward?
95    Do not let them strike the spear in your back as you run for it,

but stay, so that we can beat back this fierce man from the ancient."
    He spoke, but long-suffering great Odysseus gave no attention
as he swept by on his way to the hollow ships of the Achaians.
The son of Tydeus, alone as he was, went among the champions
and stood before the horses of the old man, the son of Neleus,                    100
and uttering his winged words he addressed him: "Old sir,
in very truth these young fighters are too much for you,
and all your strength is gone, and hard old age is upon you,
your henchman is a man of no worth, and your horses are heavy.
Come then, climb into my chariot, so that you may see                             105
what the Trojan horses are like, how they understand their
plain, and how to traverse it in rapid pursuit and withdrawal;
horses I took away from Aineias, who strikes men to terror.
Let the henchmen look after your horses now, while we two
steer these against the Trojans, breakers of horses, so Hektor                    110
even may know if my spear also rages in my hands' grip."
    He spoke, and Nestor the Gerenian horseman obeyed him.
Thereon the two strong henchmen, Sthenelos and the courtly
Eurymedon, looked after the horses of Nestor. The others
both together mounted the chariot of Diomedes.                                    115
Nestor in his hands took up the glittering reins, then
lashed the horses on, and soon they were close to Hektor,
and as he raged straight forward the son of Tydeus threw at him
and missed his man, but struck the charioteer, his henchman,
Eniopeus, the son of high-hearted Thebaios, striking him                          120
in the chest next to the nipple as he gripped the reins of his horses.
He fell out of the chariot, and the fast-footed horses
shied away. And there his life and his strength were scattered.
And bitter sorrow closed over Hektor's heart for his driver,
yet grieving as he did for his friend he left him to lie there,                   125
and went on after another bold charioteer; and it was not
long that the horses went lacking a driver, since soon he found one,
Archeptolemos, bold son of Iphitos, and gave into his hands
the reins, and mounted him behind the fast-running horses.

    And now there would have been fighting beyond control, and            130
        destruction,
now they would have been driven and penned like sheep against Ilion,

had not the father of gods and of men sharply perceived them.
He thundered horribly and let loose the shimmering lightning
and dashed it to the ground in front of the horses of Diomedes
135 and a ghastly blaze of flaming sulfur shot up, and the horses
terrified both cringed away against the chariot.
And the glittering reins escaped out of the hands of Nestor,
and he was afraid in his heart and called out to Diomedes:
"Son of Tydeus, steer now to flight your single-foot horses.
140 Can you not see that the power of Zeus no longer is with you?
For the time Zeus, son of Kronos, gives glory to this man;
for today; hereafter, if he will, he will give it
to us also; no man can beat back the purpose of Zeus, not
even one very strong, since Zeus is by far the greater."
145 Then in turn Diomedes of the great war cry answered:
"Yes, old sir, all this you have said is fair and orderly.
But this thought comes as a bitter sorrow to my heart and my spirit;
for some day Hektor will say openly before the Trojans:
'The son of Tydeus, running before me, fled to his vessels.'
150 So he will vaunt; and then let the wide earth open beneath me."
Nestor the Gerenian horseman spoke to him in answer:
"Ah me, son of brave Tydeus; what a thing to have spoken.
If Hektor calls you a coward and a man of no strength, then
the Trojans and Dardanians will never believe him,
155 nor will the wives of the high-hearted Trojan warriors,
they whose husbands you hurled in the dust in the pride of their manhood."

So he spoke, and turned to flight the single-foot horses
back again into the rout; and now the Trojans and Hektor
with unearthly clamor showered their baneful missiles upon them,
160 and tall Hektor of the shining helm called out in a great voice:
"Son of Tydeus, beyond others the fast-mounted Danaäns honored you
with pride of place, the choice meats and the filled wine-cups.
But now they will disgrace you, who are no better than a woman.
Down with you, you poor doll. You shall not storm our battlements
165 with me giving way before you, you shall not carry our women
home in your ships; before that comes I will give you your destiny."
He spoke, and the son of Tydeus pondered doubtfully, whether
to turn his horses about and match his strength against Hektor.

Three times in his heart and spirit he pondered turning,
and three times from the hills of Ida Zeus of the counsels                170
thundered, giving a sign to the Trojans that the battle was turning.
But Hektor called afar in a great voice to the Trojans:
"Trojans, Lykians and Dardanians who fight at close quarters,
be men now, dear friends, remember your furious valor.
I see that the son of Kronos has bowed his head and assented             175
to my high glory and success, but granted the Danaäns
disaster: fools, who designed with care these fortifications,
flimsy things, not worth a thought, which will not beat my strength
back, but lightly my horses will leap the ditch they have dug them.
But after I have come beside their hollow ships, let there              180
be some who will remember to bring me ravening fire,
so that I can set their ships on fire, and cut down
the very Argives mazed in the smoke at the side of their vessels."

    So he spoke, and called aloud to his horses, and spoke to them:
"Xanthos and you, Podargos, Aithon and Lampos the shining,             185
now repay me for all that loving care in abundance
Andromache the daughter of high-hearted Eëtion
gave you: the sweet-hearted wheat before all the others
and mixed wine with it for you to drink, when her heart inclined to it,
as for me, who am proud that I am her young husband.                    190
Follow close now and be rapid, so we may capture
the shield of Nestor, whose high fame goes up to the sky now,
how it is all of gold, the shield itself and the cross-rods;
and strip from the shoulders of Diomedes, breaker of horses,
that elaborate corselet that Hephaistos wrought with much toil.         195
Could we capture these two things, I might hope the Achaians
might embark this very night on their fast-running vessels."

    So he spoke, boasting, and the lady Hera was angry,
and started upon her throne, and tall Olympos was shaken,
and she spoke straight out to the great god Poseidon:                   200
"For shame, now, far-powerful shaker of the earth. In your breast
the heart takes no sorrow for the Danaäns who are dying,
they who at Helikē and at Aigai bring you offerings
numerous and delightful. Do you then plan that they conquer.

205 For if all of us who stand by the Danaäns only were willing
to hurl back the Trojans and hold off Zeus of the broad brows,
he would be desperate, there where he sits by himself on Ida."
    Deeply troubled, the powerful shaker of the earth answered her,
"Hera, reckless of word, what sort of thing have you spoken?
210 I would not be willing that all the rest of us fight with
Zeus, the son of Kronos, since he is so much the greater."

    Now as these two were talking thus to each other, meanwhile
for those others, all that space which the ditch of the wall held
off from the ships was filled with armored men and with horses
215 penned there; and he who penned them was a man like the rapid war god,
Hektor, Priam's son, since Zeus was giving him glory.
And now he might have kindled their balanced ships with the hot flame,
had not the lady Hera set it in Agamemnon's
heart to rush in with speed himself and stir the Achaians.
220 He went on his way beside the Achaians' ships and their shelters
holding up in his heavy hand the great colored mantle,
and stood beside the black huge-hollowed ship of Odysseus,
which lay in the midmost, so that he could call out to both sides,
either toward the shelters of Telamonian Aias,
225 or toward Achilleus, since these two had drawn their balanced ships up
at the utter ends, sure of the strength of their hands and their courage.
He lifted his voice and called in a piercing cry to the Danaäns:
"Shame, you Argives, poor nonentities splendid to look on.
Where are our high words gone, when we said that we were the bravest?
230 those words you spoke before all in hollow vaunting at Lemnos
when you were filled with abundant meat of the high-horned oxen
and drank from the great bowls filled to the brim with wine, how each man
could stand up against a hundred or even two hundred Trojans
in the fighting; now we together cannot match one of them,
235 Hektor, who must presently kindle our ships with the hot fire.
Father Zeus, is it one of our too strong kings you have stricken
in this disaster now, and stripped him of his high honor?
For I say that never did I pass by your fair-wrought altar
in my benched ships when I came here on this desperate journey;
240 but on all altars I burned the fat and the thighs of oxen
in my desire to sack the strong-walled city of the Trojans.

Still, Zeus, bring to pass at least this thing that I pray for.
Let our men at least get clear and escape, and let not
the Achaians be thus beaten down at the hands of the Trojans."

He spoke thus, and as he wept the father took pity upon him          245
and bent his head, that the people should stay alive, and not perish.
Straightway he sent down the most lordly of birds, an eagle,
with a fawn, the young of the running deer, caught in his talons,
who cast down the fawn beside Zeus' splendid altar
where the Achaians wrought their devotions to Zeus of the Voices.     250
They, when they saw the bird and knew it was Zeus who sent it,
remembered once again their warcraft, and turned on the Trojans.
    Then, many as the Danaäns were, there was no man among them
could claim he held his fast horses ahead of the son of Tydeus
to drive them once more across the ditch and fight at close quarters,  255
but he was far the first to kill a chief man of the Trojans,
Phradmon's son, Agelaos, as he turned his team to escape him.
For in his back even as he was turning the spear fixed
between the shoulders and was driven on through the chest beyond it.
He fell from the chariot, and his armor clattered upon him.           260
    After him came the Atreidai, Menelaos and Agamemnon,
and the two Aiantes gathering their fierce strength about them,
and with them Idomeneus and Idomeneus' companion
Meriones, a match for the murderous lord of battles,
and after these Eurypylos, the glorious son of Euaimon;               265
and ninth came Teukros, bending into position the curved bow,
and took his place in the shelter of Telamonian Aias'
shield, as Aias lifted the shield to take him. The hero
would watch, whenever in the throng he had struck some man with an arrow,
and as the man dropped and died where he was stricken, the archer     270
would run back again, like a child to the arms of his mother,
to Aias, who would hide him in the glittering shield's protection.

    Then which of the Trojans first did Teukros the blameless strike down?
Orsilochos first of all, and Ormenos, and Ophelestes,
Daitor and Chromios, and Lykophontes the godlike,                     275
and Amopaon, Polyaimon's son, and Melanippos.
All these he felled to the bountiful earth in close succession.

Agamemnon the lord of men was glad as he watched him
laying waste from the strong bow the Trojan battalions;
280 he went over and stood beside him and spoke a word to him:
"Telamonian Teukros, dear heart, O lord of your people,
strike so; thus you may be a light given to the Danaäns,
and to Telamon your father, who cherished you when you were little,
and, bastard as you were, looked after you in his own house.
285 Bring him into glory, though he is far away; and for my part,
I will tell you this, and it will be a thing accomplished:
if ever Zeus who holds the aegis and Athene grant me
to sack outright the strong-founded citadel of Ilion,
first after myself I will put into your hands some great gift
290 of honor; a tripod, or two horses and the chariot with them,
or else a woman, who will go up into the same bed with you."
     Then in answer to him again spoke Teukros the blameless:
"Son of Atreus, most lordly: must you then drive me, who am eager
myself, as it is? Never, so far as the strength is in me,
295 have I stopped, since we began driving the Trojans back upon Ilion;
since then I have been lurking here with my bow, to strike down
fighters. And by this I have shot eight long-flanged arrows,
and all of them were driven into the bodies of young men,
fighters; yet still I am not able to hit this mad dog."

300      He spoke, and let fly another shaft from the bowstring,
straight for Hektor, and all his heart was straining to hit him;
but missed his man, and struck down instead a strong son of Priam,
Gorgythion the blameless, hit in the chest by an arrow;
Gorgythion whose mother was lovely Kastianeira,
305 Priam's bride from Aisyme, with the form of a goddess.
He bent drooping his head to one side, as a garden poppy
bends beneath the weight of its yield and the rains of springtime;
so his head bent slack to one side beneath the helm's weight.
     But Teukros now let fly another shaft from the bowstring,
310 straight for Hektor, and all his heart was straining to hit him,
yet missed his man once again as Apollo faltered his arrow,
and struck Archeptolemos, bold charioteer of Hektor,
in the chest next to the nipple as he charged into the fighting.

He fell out of the chariot, and the fast-footed horses
shied away. And there his life and his strength were scattered.                    315
And bitter sorrow closed over Hektor's heart for his driver,
yet grieving as he did for his friend he left him to lie there,
and called to his brother Kebriones who stood near to take up
the reins of the horses, nor did he disobey him. But Hektor
himself vaulted down to the ground from the shining chariot                        320
crying a terrible cry and in his hand caught up a great stone,
and went straight for Teukros, heart urgent to hit him. Now Teukros
had drawn a bitter arrow out of his quiver, and laid it
along the bowstring, but as he drew the shaft by his shoulder,
there where between neck and chest the collar-bone interposes,                      325
and this is a spot most mortal; in this place shining-helmed Hektor
struck him in all his fury with the jagged boulder, smashing
the sinew, and all his arm at the wrist was deadened.
He dropped to one knee and stayed, and the bow fell from his hand. Aias
was not forgetful of his fallen brother, but running                               330
stood bestriding him and covered him under the great shield.
Thereon Mekisteus, son of Echios, and brilliant Alastor,
two staunch companions, stooping beneath it, caught up Teukros
and carried him, groaning heavily, to the hollow vessels.

   Now once again the Olympian filled the Trojans with fury                         335
and they piled the Achaians straight backward against the deep ditch,
as Hektor ranged in their foremost ranks in the pride of his great strength.
As when some hunting hound in the speed of his feet pursuing
a wild boar or a lion snaps from behind at his quarters
or flanks, but watches for the beast to turn upon him, so Hektor                    340
followed close on the heels of the flowing-haired Achaians,
killing ever the last of the men; and they fled in terror.
But after they had crossed back over the ditch and the sharp stakes
in flight, and many had gone down under the hands of the Trojans,
they reined in and stood fast again beside their ships, calling                     345
aloud upon each other, and to all of the gods uplifting
their hands each man of them cried out his prayers in a great voice,
while Hektor, wearing the stark eyes of a Gorgon, or murderous
Ares, wheeled about at the edge his bright-maned horses.

350     Now seeing them the goddess of the white arms, Hera, took pity
        and immediately she spoke to Pallas Athene her winged words:
        "For shame, daughter of Zeus who wears the aegis! No longer
        shall we care for the Danaäns in their uttermost hour of destruction?
        These must then fill out an evil destiny, and perish
355     in the wind of one man's fury where none can stand now against him,
        Hektor, Priam's son, who has wrought so much evil already."
            Then in turn the goddess gray-eyed Athene answered her:
        "Yet even this man would have his life and strength taken from him,
        dying under the hands of the Argives in his own country;
360     but it is my father who is so furious in his heart of evil.
        He is hard, and forever wicked; he crosses my high hopes,
        nor remembers at all those many times I rescued his own son,
        Herakles, when the tasks of Eurystheus were too much for his strength.
        And time and again he would cry out aloud to the heavens,
365     and Zeus would send me down in speed from the sky to help him.
        If in the wiliness of my heart I had had thoughts like his,
        when Herakles was sent down to Hades of the Gates, to hale back
        from the Kingdom of the Dark the hound of the grisly death god,
        never would he have got clear of the steep-dripping Stygian water.
370     Yet now Zeus hates me, and is bent to the wishes of Thetis
        who kissed his knees and stroked his chin in her hand, and entreated
        that he give honor to Achilleus, the sacker of cities.
        Yet time shall be when he calls me again his dear girl of the gray eyes.
        So then: do you put under their harness our single-foot horses
375     while I go back into the house of Zeus, the lord of the aegis,
        and arm me in my weapons of war. So shall I discover
        whether the son of Priam, Hektor of the shining helmet,
        will feel joy to see us apparent on the outworks of battle,
        or see if some Trojan give the dogs and the birds their desire
380     with fat and flesh, struck down beside the ships of the Achaians."

            She spoke, nor failed to persuade the goddess Hera of the white arms.
        And she, Hera, exalted goddess, daughter of Kronos
        the mighty, went away to harness the gold-bridled horses.
        Now in turn Athene, daughter of Zeus of the aegis,
385     beside the threshold of her father slipped off her elaborate
        dress which she herself had wrought with her hands' patience,

and now assuming the war tunic of Zeus who gathers
the clouds, she armed herself in her gear for the dismal fighting.
She set her feet in the blazing chariot, and took up a spear,
heavy, huge, thick, wherewith she beats down the battalions of fighting    390
men, against whom she of the mighty father is angered.
Hera laid the lash swiftly on the horses; and moving
of themselves groaned the gates of the sky that the Hours guarded,
those Hours to whose charge is given the huge sky and Olympos
to open up the dense darkness or again to close it.    395
Through the way between they held the speed of their goaded horses.
    But Zeus father, watching from Ida, was angered terribly
and stirred Iris of the golden wings to run with his message:
"Go forth, Iris the swift, turn them back again, let them not reach me,
since we would close in fighting thus that would be unseemly.    400
For I will say this straight out, and it will be a thing accomplished:
I will lame beneath the harness their fast-running horses,
and hurl the gods from the driver's place, and smash their chariot;
and not in the circle of ten returning years shall they be whole
of the wounds where the stroke of the lightning hits them; so that    405
the gray-eyed goddess may know when it is her father she fights with.
Yet with Hera I am not so angry, neither indignant,
since it is ever her way to cross the commands that I give her."
    He spoke, and Iris, storm-footed, rose with his message
and took her way from the peaks of Ida to tall Olympos,    410
and at the utmost gates of many-folded Olympos
met and stayed them, and spoke the word that Zeus had given her:
"Where so furious? How can your hearts so storm within you?
The son of Kronos will not let you stand by the Argives.
Since Zeus has uttered this threat and will make it a thing accomplished:    415
that he will lame beneath the harness your fast-running horses,
and hurl yourselves from the driver's place, and smash your chariot;
and not in the circle of ten returning years would you be whole
of the wounds where the stroke of the lightning hits you; so that
you may know, gray-eyed goddess, when it is your father you fight with.    420
Yes, you, bold brazen wench, are audacious indeed, if truly
you dare to lift up your gigantic spear in the face of your father.
Yet with Hera he is not so angry, neither indignant,
since it is ever her way to cross the commands he gives her."

425     So Iris the swift-footed spoke and went away from them,
        and now Hera spoke a word to Pallas Athene:
        "Alas, daughter of Zeus of the aegis: I can no longer
        let us fight in the face of Zeus for the sake of mortals.
        Let one of them perish then, let another live, as their fortune
430     wills; let him, as is his right and as his heart pleases,
        work out whatever decrees he will on Danaäns and Trojans."
            So she spoke, and turned back again her single-foot horses,
        and the Hours set free their flowing-maned horses from the harness,
        and tethered them at their mangers that were piled with ambrosia
435     and leaned the chariot against the shining inward wall. Meanwhile
        the goddesses themselves took their place on the golden couches
        among the other immortals, their hearts deep grieving within them.

            Now father Zeus steered back from Ida his strong-wheeled chariot
        and horses to Olympos, and came among the gods' sessions,
440     while for him the famed shaker of the earth set free his horses,
        and put the chariot on its stand, with a cloth spread over it.
        Then Zeus himself of the wide brows took his place on the golden
        throne, as underneath his feet tall Olympos was shaken.
        These two alone, Hera and Athene, stayed seated apart aside
445     from Zeus, and would not speak to him, nor ask him a question;
        but he knew the whole matter within his heart, and spoke to them.
        "Why then are you two sorrowful, Athene and Hera?
        Surely in the battle where men win glory you were not wearied
        out, destroying those Trojans on whom you have set your grim wrath.
450     In the whole account, such is my strength and my hand so invincible,
        not all the gods who are on Olympos could turn me backward,
        but before this the trembling took hold of your shining bodies,
        before you could look upon the fighting and war's work of sorrow;
        for I will say straight out, and it would now be a thing accomplished:
455     once hit in your car by the lightning stroke you could never
        have come back to Olympos, where is the place of the immortals."
            So he spoke; and Athene and Hera muttered, since they were
        sitting close to each other, devising evil for the Trojans.
        Still Athene stayed silent and said nothing, but only
460     sulked at Zeus her father, and savage anger took hold of her.
        But the heart of Hera could not contain her anger, and she spoke forth:

"Majesty, son of Kronos, what sort of thing have you spoken?
We know well already your strength, how it is no small thing.
Yet even so we are sorrowful for the Danaän spearmen
who must fill out an unhappy destiny, and perish.                             465
Still we shall keep out of the fighting, as you command us;
yet we will put good counsel in the Argives, if it may help them;
so that not all of them will die because of your anger."
    Zeus who gathers the clouds spoke to her again in answer:
"Tomorrow at the dawning, lady Hera of the ox eyes,                       470
you will see, if you have the heart, a still mightier son of Kronos
perishing the ranged numbers of Argive spearmen.
For Hektor the huge will not sooner be stayed from his fighting
until there stirs by the ships the swift-footed son of Peleus
on that day when they shall fight by the sterns of the beached ships       475
in the narrow place of necessity over fallen Patroklos.
This is the way it is fated to be; and for you and your anger
I care not; not if you stray apart to the undermost limits
of earth and sea, where Iapetos and Kronos seated
have no shining of the sun god Hyperion to delight them                    480
nor winds' delight, but Tartaros stands deeply about them;
not even if you reach that place in your wandering shall I
care for your sulks; since there is nothing more shameless than you are."

    So he spoke, and Hera of the white arms gave him no answer.
And now the shining light of the sun was dipped in the Ocean             485
trailing black night across the grain-giving land. For the Trojans
the daylight sank against their will, but for the Achaians
sweet and thrice-supplicated was the coming on of the dark night.

    Now glorious Hektor held an assembly of all the Trojans,
taking them aside from the ships, by a swirling river                      490
on clean ground, where there showed a space not cumbered with corpses.
They stepped to the ground from behind their horses and listened to Hektor
the loved of Zeus, and the words he spoke to them. He in his hand held
the eleven-cubit-long spear, whose shaft was tipped with a shining
bronze spearhead, and a ring of gold was hooped to hold it.               495
Leaning upon this spear he spoke his words to the Trojans:
"Trojans and Dardanians and companions in arms: hear me.

Now I had thought that, destroying the ships and all the Achaians,
we might take our way back once more to windy Ilion,
500  but the darkness came too soon, and this beyond all else rescued
the Argives and their vessels along the beach where the sea breaks.
But now let us give way to black night's persuasion; let us
make ready our evening meal, and as for your flowing-maned horses,
set them free from their harness, and cast down fodder before them.
505  And lead forth also out of the city oxen and fat sheep
in all speed, and convey out also the kindly sweet wine
with food out of our houses. And heap many piles of firewood,
so that all night long and until the young dawn appears
we may burn many fires, and the glare go up into heaven;
510  so that not in the night-time the flowing-haired Achaians
may set out to run for home over the sea's wide ridges.
No: not thus in their own good time must they take to their vessels,
but in such a way that a man of them at home will still nurse
his wound, the place where he has been hit with an arrow or sharp spear
515  springing to his ship; so that another may shrink hereafter
from bringing down fearful war on the Trojans, breakers of horses.
And let the heralds Zeus loves give orders about the city
for the boys who are in their first youth and the gray-browed elders
to take stations on the god-founded bastions that circle the city;
520  and as for the women, have our wives, each one in her own house,
kindle a great fire; let there be a watch kept steadily
lest a sudden attack get into the town when the fighters have left it.
Let it be thus, high-hearted men of Troy, as I tell you.
Let that word that has been spoken now be a strong one,
525  with that which I speak at dawn to the Trojans, breakers of horses.
For in good hope I pray to Zeus and the other immortals
that we may drive from our place these dogs swept into destruction
whom the spirits of death have carried here on their black ships.
Now for the night we shall keep watch on ourselves, and tomorrow
530  early, before dawn shows, shall arm ourselves in our weapons
and beside their hollow vessels waken the bitter war god;
and I shall know if the son of Tydeus, strong Diomedes,
will force me back from the ships against the wall, or whether I
shall cut him down with the bronze and take home the blooded war-spoils.
535  Tomorrow he will learn his own strength, if he can stand up to

my spear's advance; but sooner than this, I think, in the foremost
he will go down under the stroke, and many companions about him
as the sun goes up into tomorrow. Oh, if I only
could be as this in all my days immortal and ageless
and be held in honor as Athene and Apollo are honored                540
as surely as this oncoming day brings evil to the Argives."
      So Hektor spoke among them, and the Trojans shouted approval.
And they set free their sweating horses from under the harness
and tethered them by the reins, each one by his own chariot.
They led forth also out of the city oxen and fat sheep                545
in all speed, and conveyed out also the kindly sweet wine,
with food out of their houses, and heaped many piles of firewood.
They accomplished likewise full sacrifices before the immortals,
and the winds wafted the savor aloft from the plain to the heavens
in its fragrance; and yet the blessed gods took no part of it.        550
They would not; so hateful to them was sacred Ilion,
and Priam, and the city of Priam of the strong ash spear.


      So with hearts made high these sat night-long by the outworks
of battle, and their watchfires blazed numerous about them
As when in the sky the stars about the moon's shining                 555
are seen in all their glory, when the air has fallen to stillness,
and all the high places of the hills are clear, and the shoulders out-jutting,
and the deep ravines, as endless bright air spills from the heavens
and all the stars are seen, to make glad the heart of the shepherd;
such in their numbers blazed the watchfires the Trojans were burning  560
between the waters of Xanthos and the ships, before Ilion.
A thousand fires were burning there in the plain, and beside each
one sat fifty men in the flare of the blazing firelight.
And standing each beside his chariot, champing white barley
and oats, the horses waited for the dawn to mount to her high place.  565

# BOOK NINE

So the Trojans held their night watches. Meanwhile immortal
Panic, companion of cold Terror, gripped the Achaians
as all their best were stricken with grief that passes endurance.
As two winds rise to shake the sea where the fish swarm, Boreas
and Zephyros, north wind and west, that blow from Thraceward,
suddenly descending, and the darkened water is gathered
to crests, and far across the salt water scatters the seaweed,
so the heart in the breast of each Achaian was troubled.

And the son of Atreus, stricken at heart with the great sorrow,
went among his heralds the clear-spoken and told them
to summon calling by name each man into the assembly
but with no outcry, and he himself was at work with the foremost.
They took their seats in assembly, dispirited, and Agamemnon
stood up before them, shedding tears, like a spring dark-running
that down the face of a rock impassable drips its dim water.
So, groaning heavily, Agamemnon spoke to the Argives:
"Friends, who are leaders of the Argives and keep their counsel:
Zeus son of Kronos has caught me badly in bitter futility.
He is hard: who before this time promised me and consented
that I might sack strong-walled Ilion and sail homeward.
Now he has devised a vile deception and bids me go back
to Argos in dishonor having lost many of my people.
Such is the way it will be pleasing to Zeus, who is too strong,
who before now has broken the crests of many cities
and will break them again, since his power is beyond all others.

Come then, do as I say, let us all be won over; let us
run away with our ships to the beloved land of our fathers
since no longer now shall we capture Troy of the wide ways."
    So he spoke, and all of them stayed stricken to silence.
For some time the sons of the Achaians said nothing in sorrow;                30
but at long last Diomedes of the great war cry addressed them:
"Son of Atreus: I will be first to fight with your folly,
as is my right, lord, in this assembly; then do not be angered.
I was the first of the Danaäns whose valor you slighted
and said I was unwarlike and without courage. The young men                35
of the Argives know all these things, and the elders know it.
The son of devious-devising Kronos has given you
gifts in two ways: with the scepter he gave you honor beyond all,
but he did not give you a heart, and of all power this is the greatest.
Sir, sir, can you really believe the sons of the Achaians                40
are so unwarlike and so weak of their hearts as you call them?
But if in truth your own heart is so set upon going,
go. The way is there, and next to the water are standing
your ships that came—so many of them!—with you from Mykenai,
and yet the rest of the flowing-haired Achaians will stay here                45
until we have sacked the city of Troy; let even these also
run away with their ships to the beloved land of their fathers,
still we two, Sthenelos and I, will fight till we witness
the end of Ilion; for it was with God that we made our way hither."

    So he spoke, and all the sons of the Achaians shouted                50
acclaim for the word of Diomedes, breaker of horses.
And now Nestor the horseman stood forth among them and spoke to them:
"Son of Tydeus, beyond others you are strong in battle,
and in counsel also are noblest among all men of your own age.
Not one man of all the Achaians will belittle your words nor                55
speak against them. Yet you have not made complete your argument,
since you are a young man still and could even be my own son
and my youngest born of all; yet still you argue in wisdom
with the Argive kings, since all you have spoken was spoken fairly.
But let me speak, since I can call myself older than you are,                60
and go through the whole matter, since there is none who can dishonor
the thing I say, not even powerful Agamemnon.

Out of all brotherhood, outlawed, homeless shall be that man
who longs for all the horror of fighting among his own people.
65 But now let us give way to the darkness of night, and let us
make ready our evening meal; and let the guards severally
take their stations by the ditch we have dug outside the ramparts.
This I would enjoin upon our young men; but thereafter
do you, son of Atreus, take command, since you are our kingliest.
70 Divide a feast among the princes; it befits you, it is not
unbecoming. Our shelters are filled with wine that the Achaian
ships carry day by day from Thrace across the wide water.
All hospitality is for you; you are lord over many.
When many assemble together follow him who advises
75 the best counsel, for in truth there is need for all the Achaians
of good close counsel, since now close to our ships the enemy
burn their numerous fires. What man could be cheered to see this?
Here is the night that will break our army, or else will preserve it."

So he spoke, and they listened hard to him, and obeyed him,
80 and the sentries went forth rapidly in their armor, gathering
about Nestor's son Thrasymedes, shepherd of the people,
and about Askalaphos and Ialmenos, sons both of Ares,
about Meriones and Aphareus and Deïpyros
and about the son of Kreion, Lykomedes the brilliant.
85 There were seven leaders of the sentinels, and with each one a hundred
fighting men followed gripping in their hands the long spears.
They took position in the space between the ditch and the rampart,
and there they kindled their fires and each made ready his supper.

But the son of Atreus led the assembled lords of the Achaians
90 to his own shelter, and set before them the feast in abundance.
They put their hands to the good things that lay ready before them.
But when they had put away their desire for eating and drinking,
the aged man began to weave his counsel before them
first, Nestor, whose advice had shown best before this.
95 He in kind intention toward all stood forth and addressed them:
"Son of Atreus, most lordly and king of men, Agamemnon,
with you I will end, with you I will make my beginning, since you

are lord over many people, and Zeus has given into your hand
the scepter and rights of judgment, to be king over the people.
It is yours therefore to speak a word, yours also to listen,                    100
and grant the right to another also, when his spirit stirs him
to speak for our good. All shall be yours when you lead the way. Still
I will speak in the way it seems best to my mind, and no one
shall have in his mind any thought that is better than this one
that I have in my mind either now or long before now                           105
ever since that day, illustrious, when you went from the shelter
of angered Achilleus, taking by force the girl Briseis
against the will of the rest of us, since I for my part
urged you strongly not to, but you, giving way to your proud heart's
anger, dishonored a great man, one whom the immortals                          110
honor, since you have taken his prize and keep it. But let us
even now think how we can make this good and persuade him
with words of supplication and with the gifts of friendship."
      Then in turn the lord of men Agamemnon spoke to him:
"Aged sir, this was no lie when you spoke of my madness.                        115
I was mad, I myself will not deny it. Worth many
fighters is that man whom Zeus in his heart loves, as now
he has honored this man and beaten down the Achaian people.
But since I was mad, in the persuasion of my heart's evil,
I am willing to make all good, and give back gifts in abundance.               120
Before you all I will count off my gifts in their splendor:
seven unfired tripods; ten talents' weight of gold; twenty
shining cauldrons; and twelve horses, strong, race-competitors
who have won prizes in the speed of their feet. That man would not be
poor in possessions, to whom were given all these have won me,                 125
nor be unpossessed of dearly honored gold, were he given
all the prizes these single-foot horses have won for me.
I will give him seven women of Lesbos, the work of whose hands is
blameless, whom when he himself captured strong-founded Lesbos
I chose, and who in their beauty surpassed the races of women.                 130
I will give him these, and with them shall go the one I took from him,
the daughter of Briseus. And to all this I will swear a great oath
that I never entered into her bed and never lay with her
as is natural for human people, between men and women.

135  All these gifts shall be his at once; but again, if hereafter
the gods grant that we storm and sack the great city of Priam,
let him go to his ship and load it deep as he pleases
with gold and bronze, when we Achaians divide the war spoils,
and let him choose for himself twenty of the Trojan women
140  who are the loveliest of all after Helen of Argos.
And if we come back to Achaian Argos, pride of the tilled land,
he may be my son-in-law; I will honor him with Orestes
my growing son, who is brought up there in abundant luxury.
Since, as I have three daughters there in my strong-built castle,
145  Chrysothemis and Laodikē and Iphianassa,
let him lead away the one of these that he likes, with no bride-price,
to the house of Peleus, and with the girl I will grant him as dowry
many gifts, such as no man ever gave with his daughter.
I will grant to him seven citadels, strongly settled:
150  Kardamyle, and Enopē, and Hire of the grasses,
Pherai the sacrosanct, and Antheia deep in the meadows,
with Aipeia the lovely and Pedasos of the vineyards.
All these lie near the sea, at the bottom of sandy Pylos,
and men live among them rich in cattle and rich in sheepflocks,
155  who will honor him as if he were a god with gifts given
and fulfill his prospering decrees underneath his scepter.
All this I will bring to pass for him, if he changes from his anger.
Let him give way. For Hades gives not way, and is pitiless,
and therefore he among all the gods is most hateful to mortals.
160  And let him yield place to me, inasmuch as I am the kinglier
and inasmuch as I can call myself born the elder."
　　　Thereupon the Gerenian horseman Nestor answered him:
"Son of Atreus, most lordly and king of men, Agamemnon,
none could scorn any longer these gifts you offer to Achilleus
165  the king. Come, let us choose and send some men, who in all speed
will go to the shelter of Achilleus, the son of Peleus;
or come, the men on whom my eye falls, let these take the duty.
First of all let Phoinix, beloved of Zeus, be their leader,
and after him take Aias the great, and brilliant Odysseus,
170  and of the heralds let Odios and Eurybates go with them.
Bring also water for their hands, and bid them keep words of good omen,
so we may pray to Zeus, son of Kronos, if he will have pity."

So he spoke, and the word he spoke was pleasing to all of them.
And the heralds brought water at once, and poured it over
their hands, and the young men filled the mixing bowl with pure wine          175
and passed it to all, pouring first a libation in goblets.
Then when they had poured out wine, and drunk as much as their hearts
    wished,
they set out from the shelter of Atreus' son, Agamemnon.
And the Gerenian horseman Nestor gave them much instruction,
looking eagerly at each, and most of all at Odysseus,                        180
to try hard, so that they might win over the blameless Peleion.

So these two walked along the strand of the sea deep-thundering
with many prayers to the holder and shaker of the earth, that they
might readily persuade the great heart of Aiakides.
Now they came beside the shelters and ships of the Myrmidons                 185
and they found Achilleus delighting his heart in a lyre, clear-sounding,
splendid and carefully wrought, with a bridge of silver upon it,
which he won out of the spoils when he ruined Eëtion's city.
With this he was pleasuring his heart, and singing of men's fame,
as Patroklos was sitting over against him, alone, in silence,                190
watching Aiakides and the time he would leave off singing.
Now these two came forward, as brilliant Odysseus led them,
and stood in his presence. Achilleus rose to his feet in amazement
holding the lyre as it was, leaving the place where he was sitting.
In the same way Patroklos, when he saw the men come, stood up.              195
And in greeting Achilleus the swift of foot spoke to them:
"Welcome. You are my friends who have come, and greatly I need you,
who even to this my anger are dearest of all the Achaians."
    So brilliant Achilleus spoke, and guided them forward,
and caused them to sit down on couches with purple coverlets                 200
and at once called over to Patroklos who was not far from him:
"Son of Menoitios, set up a mixing bowl that is bigger,
and mix us stronger drink, and make ready a cup for each man,
since these who have come beneath my roof are the men that I love best."

    So he spoke, and Patroklos obeyed his beloved companion,                205
and tossed down a great chopping-block into the firelight,
and laid upon it the back of a sheep, and one of a fat goat,

with the chine of a fatted pig edged thick with lard, and for him
Automedon held the meats, and brilliant Achilleus carved them,
210    and cut it well into pieces and spitted them, as meanwhile
Menoitios' son, a man like a god, made the fire blaze greatly.
But when the fire had burned itself out, and the flames had died down,
he scattered the embers apart, and extended the spits across them
lifting them to the andirons, and sprinkled the meats with divine salt.
215    Then when he had roasted all, and spread the food on the platters,
Patroklos took the bread and set it out on a table
in fair baskets, while Achilleus served the meats. Thereafter
he himself sat over against the godlike Odysseus
against the further wall, and told his companion, Patroklos,
220    to sacrifice to the gods; and he threw the firstlings in the fire.
They put their hands to the good things that lay ready before them.
But when they had put aside their desire for eating and drinking,
Aias nodded to Phoinix, and brilliant Odysseus saw it,
and filled a cup with wine, and lifted it to Achilleus:
225    "Your health, Achilleus. You have no lack of your equal portion
either within the shelter of Atreus' son, Agamemnon,
nor here now in your own. We have good things in abundance
to feast on; here it is not the desirable feast we think of,
but a trouble all too great, beloved of Zeus, that we look on
230    and are afraid. There is doubt if we save our strong-benched vessels
or if they will be destroyed, unless you put on your war strength.
The Trojans in their pride, with their far-renowned companions,
have set up an encampment close by the ships and the rampart,
and lit many fires along their army, and think no longer
235    of being held, but rather to drive in upon the black ships.
And Zeus, son of Kronos, lightens upon their right hand, showing them
portents of good, while Hektor in the huge pride of his strength rages
irresistibly, reliant on Zeus, and gives way to no one,
neither god nor man, but the strong fury has descended upon him.
240    He prays now that the divine Dawn will show most quickly,
since he threatens to shear the uttermost horns from the ship-sterns,
to light the ships themselves with ravening fire, and to cut down
the Achaians themselves as they stir from the smoke beside them.
All this I fear terribly in my heart, lest immortals
245    accomplish all these threats, and lest for us it be destiny

to die here in Troy, far away from horse-pasturing Argos.
Up, then! if you are minded, late though it be, to rescue
the afflicted sons of the Achaians from the Trojan onslaught.
It will be an affliction to you hereafter, there will be no remedy
found to heal the evil thing when it has been done. No, beforehand          250
take thought to beat the evil day aside from the Danaäns.
Dear friend, surely thus your father Peleus advised you
that day when he sent you away to Agamemnon from Phthia:
'My child, for the matter of strength, Athene and Hera will give it
if it be their will, but be it yours to hold fast in your bosom             255
the anger of the proud heart, for consideration is better.
Keep from the bad complication of quarrel, and all the more for this
the Argives will honor you, both their younger men and their elders.'
So the old man advised, but you have forgotten. Yet even now
stop, and give way from the anger that hurts the heart. Agamemnon           260
offers you worthy recompense if you change from your anger.
Come then, if you will, listen to me, while I count off for you
all the gifts in his shelter that Agamemnon has promised:
Seven unfired tripods; ten talents' weight of gold; twenty
shining cauldrons; and twelve horses, strong, race-competitors             265
who have won prizes in the speed of their feet. That man would not be
poor in possessions, to whom were given all these have won him,
nor be unpossessed of dearly honored gold, were he given
all the prizes Agamemnon's horses won in their speed for him.
He will give you seven women of Lesbos, the work of whose hands            270
is blameless, whom when you yourself captured strong-founded Lesbos
he chose, and who in their beauty surpassed the races of women.
He will give you these, and with them shall go the one he took from you,
the daughter of Briseus. And to all this he will swear a great oath
that he never entered into her bed and never lay with her                  275
as is natural for human people, between men and women.
All these gifts shall be yours at once; but again, if hereafter
the gods grant that we storm and sack the great city of Priam,
you may go to your ship and load it deep as you please with
gold and bronze, when we Achaians divide the war spoils,                    280
and you may choose for yourself twenty of the Trojan women,
who are the loveliest of all after Helen of Argos.
And if we come back to Achaian Argos, pride of the tilled land,

you could be his son-in-law; he would honor you with Orestes,
285 his growing son, who is brought up there in abundant luxury.
Since, as he has three daughters there in his strong-built castle,
Chrysothemis and Laodikē and Iphianassa,
you may lead away the one of these that you like, with no bride-price,
to the house of Peleus; and with the girl he will grant you as dowry
290 many gifts, such as no man ever gave with his daughter.
He will grant you seven citadels, strongly settled:
Kardamyle and Enopē and Hire of the grasses,
Pherai the sacrosanct, and Antheia deep in the meadows,
with Aipeia the lovely, and Pedasos of the vineyards.
295 All these lie near the sea, at the bottom of sandy Pylos,
and men live among them rich in cattle and rich in sheepflocks,
who will honor you as if you were a god with gifts given
and fulfill your prospering decrees underneath your scepter.
All this he will bring to pass for you, if you change from your anger.
300 But if the son of Atreus is too much hated in your heart,
himself and his gifts, at least take pity on all the other
Achaians, who are afflicted along the host, and will honor you
as a god. You may win very great glory among them.
For now you might kill Hektor, since he would come very close to you
305 with the wicked fury upon him, since he thinks there is not his equal
among the rest of the Danaäns the ships carried hither."

Then in answer to him spoke Achilleus of the swift feet:
"Son of Laërtes and seed of Zeus, resourceful Odysseus:
without consideration for you I must make my answer,
310 the way I think, and the way it will be accomplished, that you may not
come one after another, and sit by me, and speak softly.
For as I detest the doorways of Death, I detest that man, who
hides one thing in the depths of his heart, and speaks forth another.
But I will speak to you the way it seems best to me: neither
315 do I think the son of Atreus, Agamemnon, will persuade me,
nor the rest of the Danaäns, since there was no gratitude given
for fighting incessantly forever against your enemies.
Fate is the same for the man who holds back, the same if he fights hard.
We are all held in a single honor, the brave with the weaklings.
320 A man dies still if he has done nothing, as one who has done much.

Nothing is won for me, now that my heart has gone through its afflictions
in forever setting my life on the hazard of battle.
For as to her unwinged young ones the mother bird brings back
morsels, wherever she can find them, but as for herself it is suffering,
such was I, as I lay through all the many nights unsleeping,                    325
such as I wore through the bloody days of the fighting,
striving with warriors for the sake of these men's women.
But I say that I have stormed from my ships twelve cities
of men, and by land eleven more through the generous Troad.
From all these we took forth treasures, goodly and numerous,                   330
and we would bring them back, and give them to Agamemnon,
Atreus' son; while he, waiting back beside the swift ships,
would take them, and distribute them little by little, and keep many.
All the other prizes of honor he gave the great men and the princes
are held fast by them, but from me alone of all the Achaians                    335
he has taken and keeps the bride of my heart. Let him lie beside her
and be happy. Yet why must the Argives fight with the Trojans?
And why was it the son of Atreus assembled and led here
these people? Was it not for the sake of lovely-haired Helen?
Are the sons of Atreus alone among mortal men the ones                          340
who love their wives? Since any who is a good man, and careful,
loves her who is his own and cares for her, even as I now
loved this one from my heart, though it was my spear that won her.
Now that he has deceived me and taken from my hands my prize of honor,
let him try me no more. I know him well. He will not persuade me.              345
Let him take counsel with you, Odysseus, and the rest of the princes
how to fight the ravening fire away from his vessels.
Indeed, there has been much hard work done even without me;
he has built himself a wall and driven a ditch about it,
making it great and wide, and fixed the sharp stakes inside it.                 350
Yet even so he cannot hold the strength of manslaughtering
Hektor; and yet when I was fighting among the Achaians
Hektor would not drive his attack beyond the wall's shelter
but would come forth only so far as the Skaian gates and the oak tree.
There once he endured me alone, and barely escaped my onslaught.               355
But, now I am unwilling to fight against brilliant Hektor;
tomorrow, when I have sacrificed to Zeus and to all gods,
and loaded well my ships, and rowed out onto the salt water,

you will see, if you have a mind to it and if it concerns you,
360 my ships in the dawn at sea on the Hellespont where the fish swarm
and my men manning them with good will to row. If the glorious
shaker of the earth should grant us a favoring passage
on the third day thereafter we might raise generous Phthia.
I have many possessions there that I left behind when I came here
365 on this desperate venture, and from here there is more gold, and red bronze,
and fair-girdled women, and gray iron I will take back;
all that was allotted to me. But my prize: he who gave it,
powerful Agamemnon, son of Atreus, has taken it back again
outrageously. Go back and proclaim to him all that I tell you,
370 openly, so other Achaians may turn against him in anger
if he hopes yet one more time to swindle some other Danaän,
wrapped as he is forever in shamelessness; yet he would not,
bold as a dog though he be, dare look in my face any longer.
I will join with him in no counsel, and in no action.
375 He cheated me and he did me hurt. Let him not beguile me
with words again. This is enough for him. Let him of his own will
be damned, since Zeus of the counsels has taken his wits away from him.
I hate his gifts. I hold him light as the strip of a splinter.
Not if he gave me ten times as much, and twenty times over
380 as he possesses now, not if more should come to him from elsewhere,
or gave all that is brought in to Orchomenos, all that is brought in
to Thebes of Egypt, where the greatest possessions lie up in the houses,
Thebes of the hundred gates, where through each of the gates two hundred
fighting men come forth to war with horses and chariots;
385 not if he gave me gifts as many as the sand or the dust is,
not even so would Agamemnon have his way with my spirit
until he had made good to me all this heartrending insolence.
Nor will I marry a daughter of Atreus' son, Agamemnon,
not if she challenged Aphrodite the golden for loveliness,
390 not if she matched the work of her hands with gray-eyed Athene;
not even so will I marry her; let him pick some other Achaian,
one who is to his liking and is kinglier than I am.
For if the gods will keep me alive, and I win homeward,
Peleus himself will presently arrange a wife for me.
395 There are many Achaian girls in the land of Hellas and Phthia,
daughters of great men who hold strong places in guard. And of these

any one that I please I might make my beloved lady.
And the great desire in my heart drives me rather in that place
to take a wedded wife in marriage, the bride of my fancy,
to enjoy with her the possessions won by aged Peleus. For not          400
worth the value of my life are all the possessions they fable
were won for Ilion, that strong-founded citadel, in the old days
when there was peace, before the coming of the sons of the Achaians;
not all that the stone doorsill of the Archer holds fast within it,
of Phoibos Apollo in Pytho of the rocks. Of possessions                405
cattle and fat sheep are things to be had for the lifting,
and tripods can be won, and the tawny high heads of horses,
but a man's life cannot come back again, it cannot be lifted
nor captured again by force, once it has crossed the teeth's barrier.
For my mother Thetis the goddess of the silver feet tells me           410
I carry two sorts of destiny toward the day of my death. Either,
if I stay here and fight beside the city of the Trojans,
my return home is gone, but my glory shall be everlasting;
but if I return home to the beloved land of my fathers,
the excellence of my glory is gone, but there will be a long life       415
left for me, and my end in death will not come to me quickly.
And this would be my counsel to others also, to sail back
home again, since no longer shall you find any term set
on the sheer city of Ilion, since Zeus of the wide brows has strongly
held his own hand over it, and its people are made bold.               420
    Do you go back therefore to the great men of the Achaians,
and take them this message, since such is the privilege of the princes:
that they think out in their minds some other scheme that is better,
which might rescue their ships, and the people of the Achaians
who man the hollow ships, since this plan will not work for them        425
which they thought of by reason of my anger. Let Phoinix
remain here with us and sleep here, so that tomorrow
he may come with us in our ships to the beloved land of our fathers,
if he will; but I will never use force to hold him."

    So he spoke, and all of them stayed stricken to silence            430
in amazement at his words. He had spoken to them very strongly.
But at long last Phoinix the aged horseman spoke out
in a stormburst of tears, and fearing for the ships of the Achaians:

"If it is going home, glorious Achilleus, you ponder
435   in your heart, and are utterly unwilling to drive the obliterating
fire from the fast ships, since anger has descended on your spirit,
how then shall I, dear child, be left in this place behind you
all alone? Peleus the aged horseman sent me forth with you
on that day when he sent you from Phthia to Agamemnon
440   a mere child, who knew nothing yet of the joining of battle
nor of debate where men are made pre-eminent. Therefore
he sent me along with you to teach you of all these matters,
to make you a speaker of words and one accomplished in action.
Therefore apart from you, dear child, I would not be willing
445   to be left behind, not were the god in person to promise
he would scale away my old age and make me a young man blossoming
as I was that time when I first left Hellas, the land of fair women,
running from the hatred of Ormenos' son Amyntor,
my father, who hated me for the sake of a fair-haired mistress.
450   For he made love to her himself, and dishonored his own wife,
my mother; who was forever taking my knees and entreating me
to lie with this mistress instead so that she would hate the old man.
I was persuaded and did it; and my father when he heard of it straightway
called down his curses, and invoked against me the dreaded furies
455   that I might never have any son born of my seed to dandle
on my knees; and the divinities, Zeus of the underworld
and Persephonē the honored goddess, accomplished his curses.
Then I took it into my mind to cut him down with the sharp bronze,
but some one of the immortals checked my anger, reminding me
460   of rumor among the people and men's maledictions repeated,
that I might not be called a parricide among the Achaians.
But now no more could the heart in my breast be ruled entirely
to range still among these halls when my father was angered.
Rather it was the many kinsmen and cousins about me
465   who held me closed in the house, with supplications repeated,
and slaughtered fat sheep in their numbers, and shambling horn-curved
cattle, and numerous swine with the fat abundant upon them
were singed and stretched out across the flame of Hephaistos,
and much wine was drunk that was stored in the jars of the old man.
470   Nine nights they slept nightlong in their places beside me,
and they kept up an interchange of watches, and the fire was never

put out; one below the gate of the strong-closed courtyard,
and one in the ante-chamber before the doors of the bedroom.
But when the tenth night had come to me in its darkness,
then I broke the close-compacted doors of the chamber                    475
and got away, and overleapt the fence of the courtyard
lightly, unnoticed by the guarding men and the women servants.
Then I fled far away through the wide spaces of Hellas
and came as far as generous Phthia, mother of sheepflocks,
and to lord Peleus, who accepted me with a good will                     480
and gave me his love, even as a father loves his own son
who is a single child brought up among many possessions.
He made me a rich man, and granted me many people,
and I lived, lord over the Dolopes, in remotest Phthia,
and, godlike Achilleus, I made you all that you are now,                 485
and loved you out of my heart, for you would not go with another
out to any feast, nor taste any food in your own halls
until I had set you on my knees, and cut little pieces
from the meat, and given you all you wished, and held the wine for you.
And many times you soaked the shirt that was on my body                  490
with wine you would spit up in the troublesomeness of your childhood.
So I have suffered much through you, and have had much trouble,
thinking always how the gods would not bring to birth any children
of my own; so that it was you, godlike Achilleus, I made
my own child, so that some day you might keep hard affliction from me.    495

  Then, Achilleus, beat down your great anger. It is not
yours to have a pitiless heart. The very immortals
can be moved; their virtue and honor and strength are greater than ours are
and yet with sacrifices and offerings for endearment,
with libations and with savor men turn back even the immortals           500
in supplication, when any man does wrong and transgresses.
For there are also the spirits of Prayer, the daughters of great Zeus,
and they are lame of their feet, and wrinkled, and cast their eyes sidelong,
who toil on their way left far behind by the spirit of Ruin:
but she, Ruin, is strong and sound on her feet, and therefore            505
far outruns all Prayers, and wins into every country
to force men astray; and the Prayers follow as healers after her.
If a man venerates these daughters of Zeus as they draw near,

such a man they bring great advantage, and hear his entreaty;
510 but if a man shall deny them, and stubbornly with a harsh word
refuse, they go to Zeus, son of Kronos, in supplication
that Ruin may overtake this man, that he be hurt, and punished.
So, Achilleus: grant, you also, that Zeus' daughters be given
their honor, which, lordly though they be, curbs the will of others.
515 Since, were he not bringing gifts and naming still more hereafter,
Atreus' son; were he to remain still swollen with rancor,
even I would not bid you throw your anger aside, nor
defend the Argives, though they needed you sorely. But see now,
he offers you much straightway, and has promised you more hereafter;
520 he has sent the best men to you to supplicate you, choosing them
out of the Achaian host, those who to yourself are the dearest
of all the Argives. Do not you make vain their argument
nor their footsteps, though before this one could not blame your anger.

Thus it was in the old days also, the deeds that we hear of
525 from the great men, when the swelling anger descended upon them.
The heroes would take gifts; they would listen, and be persuaded.
For I remember this action of old, it is not a new thing,
and how it went; you are all my friends, I will tell it among you.
The Kouretes and the steadfast Aitolians were fighting
530 and slaughtering one another about the city of Kalydon,
the Aitolians in lovely Kalydon's defense, the Kouretes
furious to storm and sack it in war. For Artemis,
she of the golden chair, had driven this evil upon them,
angered that Oineus had not given the pride of the orchards
535 to her, first fruits; the rest of the gods were given due sacrifice,
but alone to this daughter of great Zeus he had given nothing.
He had forgotten, or had not thought, in his hard delusion,
and in wrath at his whole mighty line the Lady of Arrows
sent upon them the fierce wild boar with the shining teeth, who
540 after the way of his kind did much evil to the orchards of Oineus.
For he ripped up whole tall trees from the ground and scattered them
      headlong
roots and all, even to the very flowers of the orchard.
The son of Oineus killed this boar, Meleagros, assembling

together many hunting men out of numerous cities
with their hounds; since the boar might not have been killed by a few men,     545
so huge was he, and had put many men on the sad fire for burning.
But the goddess again made a great stir of anger and crying
battle, over the head of the boar and the bristling boar's hide,
between Kouretes and the high-hearted Aitolians. So long
as Meleagros lover of battle stayed in the fighting     550
it went the worse for the Kouretes, and they could not even
hold their ground outside the wall, though they were so many.
But when the anger came upon Meleagros, such anger
as wells in the hearts of others also, though their minds are careful,
he, in the wrath of his heart against his own mother, Althaia,     555
lay apart with his wedded bride, Kleopatra the lovely,
daughter of sweet-stepping Marpessa, child of Euenos,
and Idas, who was the strongest of all men upon earth
in his time; for he even took up the bow to face the King's onset,
Phoibos Apollo, for the sake of the sweet-stepping maiden;     560
a girl her father and honored mother had named in their palace
Alkyone, sea-bird, as a by-name, since for her sake
her mother with the sorrow laden cry of a sea-bird
wept because far-reaching Phoibos Apollo had taken her;
with this Kleopatra he lay mulling his heart-sore anger,     565
raging by reason of his mother's curses, which she called down
from the gods upon him, in deep grief for the death of her brother,
and many times beating with her hands on the earth abundant
she called on Hades and on honored Persephonē, lying
at length along the ground, and the tears were wet on her bosom,     570
to give death to her son; and Erinys, the mist-walking,
she of the heart without pity, heard her out of the dark places.
Presently there was thunder about the gates, and the sound rose
of towers under assault, and the Aitolian elders
supplicated him, sending their noblest priests of the immortals,     575
to come forth and defend them; they offered him a great gift:
wherever might lie the richest ground in lovely Kalydon,
there they told him to choose out a piece of land, an entirely
good one, of fifty acres, the half of it to be vineyard
and the half of it unworked ploughland of the plain to be furrowed.     580

And the aged horseman Oineus again and again entreated him,
and took his place at the threshold of the high-vaulted chamber
and shook against the bolted doors, pleading with his own son.
And again and again his honored mother and his sisters
585  entreated him, but he only refused the more; then his own friends
who were the most honored and dearest of all entreated him;
but even so they could not persuade the heart within him
until, as the chamber was under close assault, the Kouretes
were mounting along the towers and set fire to the great city.
590  And then at last his wife, the fair-girdled bride, supplicated
Meleagros, in tears, and rehearsed in their numbers before him
all the sorrows that come to men when their city is taken:
they kill the men, and the fire leaves the city in ashes,
and strangers lead the children away and the deep-girdled women.
595  And the heart, as he listened to all this evil, was stirred within him,
and he rose, and went, and closed his body in shining armor.
So he gave way in his own heart, and drove back the day of evil
from the Aitolians; yet these no longer would make good
their many and gracious gifts; yet he drove back the evil from them.
600      Listen, then; do not have such a thought in your mind; let not
the spirit within you turn you that way, dear friend. It would be worse
to defend the ships after they are burning. No, with gifts promised
go forth. The Achaians will honor you as they would an immortal.
But if without gifts you go into the fighting where men perish,
605  your honor will no longer be as great, though you drive back the battle."

        Then in answer to him spoke Achilleus of the swift feet:
"Phoinix my father, aged, illustrious, such honor is a thing
I need not. I think I am honored already in Zeus' ordinance
which will hold me here beside my curved ships as long as life's wind
610  stays in my breast, as long as my knees have their spring beneath me.
And put away in your thoughts this other thing I tell you.
Stop confusing my heart with lamentation and sorrow
for the favor of great Atreides. It does not become you
to love this man, for fear you turn hateful to me, who love you.
615  It should be your pride with me to hurt whoever shall hurt me.
Be king equally with me; take half of my honor.

These men will carry back the message; you stay here and sleep here
in a soft bed, and we shall decide tomorrow, as dawn shows,
whether to go back home again or else to remain here."

He spoke, and, saying nothing, nodded with his brows to Patroklos      620
to make up a neat bed for Phoinix, so the others might presently
think of going home from his shelter. The son of Telamon,
Aias the godlike, saw it, and now spoke his word among them:
"Son of Laërtes and seed of Zeus, resourceful Odysseus:
let us go. I think that nothing will be accomplished                   625
by argument on this errand; it is best to go back quickly
and tell this story, though it is not good, to the Danaäns
who sit there waiting for us to come back, seeing that Achilleus
has made savage the proud-hearted spirit within his body.
He is hard, and does not remember that friends' affection              630
wherein we honored him by the ships, far beyond all others.
Pitiless. And yet a man takes from his brother's slayer
the blood price, or the price for a child who was killed, and the guilty
one, when he has largely repaid, stays still in the country,
and the injured man's heart is curbed, and his pride, and his anger    635
when he has taken the price; but the gods put in your breast a spirit
not to be placated, bad, for the sake of one single
girl. Yet now we offer you seven, surpassingly lovely,
and much beside these. Now make gracious the spirit within you.
Respect your own house; see, we are under the same roof with you,      640
from the multitude of the Danaäns, we who desire beyond all
others to have your honor and love, out of all the Achaians."
    Then in answer to him spoke Achilleus of the swift feet:
"Son of Telamon, seed of Zeus, Aias, lord of the people:
all that you have said seems spoken after my own mind.                 645
Yet still the heart in me swells up in anger, when I remember
the disgrace that he wrought upon me before the Argives,
the son of Atreus, as if I were some dishonored vagabond.
Do you then go back to him, and take him this message:
that I shall not think again of the bloody fighting                    650
until such time as the son of wise Priam, Hektor the brilliant,
comes all the way to the ships of the Myrmidons, and their shelters,

slaughtering the Argives, and shall darken with fire our vessels.
But around my own shelter, I think, and beside my black ship
655 Hektor will be held, though he be very hungry for battle."

He spoke, and they taking each a two-handled cup poured out
a libation, then went back to their ships, and Odysseus led them.
Now Patroklos gave the maids and his followers orders
to make up without delay a neat bed for Phoinix.
660 And these obeyed him and made up the bed as he had commanded,
laying fleeces on it, and a blanket, and a sheet of fine linen.
There the old man lay down and waited for the divine Dawn.
But Achilleus slept in the inward corner of the strong-built shelter,
and a woman lay beside him, one he had taken from Lesbos,
665 Phorbas' daughter, Diomede of the fair coloring.
In the other corner Patroklos went to bed; with him also
was a girl, Iphis the fair-girdled, whom brilliant Achilleus
gave him, when he took sheer Skyros, Enyeus' citadel.

Now when these had come back to the shelters of Agamemnon,
670 the sons of the Achaians greeted them with their gold cups
uplifted, one after another, standing, and asked them questions.
And the first to question them was the lord of men, Agamemnon:
"Tell me, honored Odysseus, great glory of the Achaians:
is he willing to fight the ravening fire away from our vessels,
675 or did he refuse, and does the anger still hold his proud heart?"
Then long-suffering great Odysseus spoke to him in answer:
"Son of Atreus, most lordly, king of men, Agamemnon.
That man will not quench his anger, but still more than ever
is filled with rage. He refuses you and refuses your presents.
680 He tells you yourself to take counsel among the Argives
how to save your ships, and the people of the Achaians.
And he himself has threatened that tomorrow as dawn shows
he will drag down his strong-benched, oarswept ships to the water.
He said it would be his counsel to others also, to sail back
685 home again, since no longer will you find any term set
on the sheer city of Ilion, since Zeus of the wide brows has strongly
held his own hand over it, and its people are made bold.
So he spoke. There are these to attest it who went there with me

also, Aias, and the two heralds, both men of good counsel.
But aged Phoinix stayed there for the night, as Achilleus urged him, 690
so he might go home in the ships to the beloved land of his fathers
if Phoinix will; but he will never use force to persuade him."

So he spoke, and all of them stayed stricken to silence
in amazement at his words. He had spoken to them very strongly.
For a long time the sons of the Achaians said nothing, in sorrow, 695
but at long last Diomedes of the great war cry spoke to them:
"Son of Atreus, most lordly and king of men, Agamemnon,
I wish you had not supplicated the blameless son of Peleus
with innumerable gifts offered. He is a proud man without this,
and now you have driven him far deeper into his pride. Rather 700
we shall pay him no more attention, whether he comes in with us
or stays away. He will fight again, whenever the time comes
that the heart in his body urges him to, and the god drives him.
Come then, do as I say, and let us all be won over.
Go to sleep, now that the inward heart is made happy 705
with food and drink, for these are the strength and courage within us.
But when the lovely dawn shows forth with rose fingers, Atreides,
rapidly form before our ships both people and horses
stirring them on, and yourself be ready to fight in the foremost."
So he spoke, and all the kings gave him their approval, 710
acclaiming the word of Diomedes, breaker of horses.
Then they poured a libation, and each man went to his shelter,
where they went to their beds and took the blessing of slumber.

# BOOK TEN

Now beside their ships the other great men of the Achaians
slept night long, with the soft bondage of slumber upon them;
but the son of Atreus, Agamemnon, shepherd of the people,
was held by no sweet sleep as he pondered deeply within him.
5 As when the lord of Hera the lovely-haired flashes his lightning
as he brings on a great rainstorm, or a hail incessant,
or a blizzard, at such time when the snowfall scatters on ploughlands,
or drives on somewhere on earth the huge edge of tearing battle,
such was Agamemnon, with the beating turmoil in his bosom
10 from the deep heart, and all his wits were shaken within him.
Now he would gaze across the plain to the Trojan camp, wondering
at the number of their fires that were burning in front of Ilion,
toward the high calls of their flutes and pipes, the murmur of people.
Now as he would look again to the ships and the Achaian
15 people, he would drag the hair by its roots from his head, looking
toward Zeus on high, and his proud heart was stricken with lamentation.
Now to his mind this thing appeared to be the best counsel,
first among men to seek out Nestor, the son of Neleus,
to see if Nestor with him could work out a plan that would not fail,
20 and one that might drive the evil away from all the Danaäns.
He stood upright, and slipped the tunic upon his body,
and underneath his shining feet he bound the fair sandals,
and thereafter slung across him the tawny hide of a lion
glowing and huge, that swung to his feet, and took up a spear.

So likewise trembling seized Menelaos, neither on his eyes          25
had sweet slumber descending settled, for fear that the Argives
might suffer some hurt, they who for his sake over much water
had come to Troy, bearing their bold attack to the Trojans.
First of all he mantled his broad back in a leopard's
spotted hide, then lifting the circle of a brazen helmet            30
placed it upon his head, and took up a spear in his big hand,
and went on his way to waken his brother, who was the great king
of all Argives, one honored in his own land as a god is.
He found him putting the splendid armor about his shoulders
beside the stern of his ship, and was welcomed as he came up to him.   35
It was Menelaos of the great war cry who spoke first:
"Why this arming, my brother? Is it some one of your companions
you are stirring to go and spy on the Trojans? Yet I fear sadly
there will not be any man to undertake this endeavor,
going against enemy fighters to spy on them, alone, through          40
the immortal night. Such a man will have to be very bold-hearted."
    Then in turn powerful Agamemnon answered him:
"You and I, illustrious, O Menelaos, have need now
of crafty counsel, if any man is to defend and rescue
the Argives and their ships, since the heart of Zeus is turned from us.   45
For the sacrifices of Hektor have stirred his heart more than ours have.
No, for I never saw nor heard from the lips of another
of a single man in a day imagining so much evil
as Hektor, beloved of Zeus, has wrought on the sons of the Achaians,
alone, being called true son neither of a god nor a goddess.         50
He has done things I think the Argives will remember with sorrow
long into the future, such harm has he devised the Achaians.
But go now, running lightly beside the ships, and call to us
Idomeneus and Aias, while I shall go after Nestor
the brilliant, and waken him to rise, if he might be willing         55
to approach the sacred duty of the guards, or give orders to them.
Above all, these would listen to him, seeing that his own son
commands the pickets, and with him the follower of Idomeneus,
Meriones. To these above all we entrusted the duty."
    Then in turn Menelaos of the great war cry answered him:         60
"How then do you intend this order that you have given me?

Shall I wait where I am, with them, and watch for your coming,
or run after you, when I have properly given the order?"
Then in turn the lord of men Agamemnon spoke to him:
65  "Better wait here, so there will be no way we can miss one another
as we come and go. There are many paths up and down the encampment.
Call out wherever you go, and waken each man to give him
your orders, naming him by descent with the name of his father.
Give each man due respect. Let not your spirit be haughty,
70  but let it be you and I ourselves who do the work, seeing
that Zeus cast on us as we were born this burden of evil."

So he spoke and with careful orders sent off his brother,
and he himself went in search of Nestor, shepherd of the people,
and came on him beside his own shelter and his own black ship
75  in a soft bed, and his bright gear was lying beside him,
the shield, and the two spears, and the glittering helmet, and by him
lay in all its shining the war belt, in which the old man
girt himself, when he armed for the fighting where men die, leading
his own people, since he gave no ground to sorrowful old age.
80  He straightened up and raised his head, leaning on one elbow,
and spoke to the son of Atreus, and asked him a question:
"Who are you, who walk alone through the ships and the army
and through the darkness of night when other mortals are sleeping?
Are you looking for one of your mules, or looking for some companion?
85  Speak, do not come upon me in silence. What would you of me?"
Then in turn the lord of men Agamemnon answered him:
"Nestor, son of Neleus, great glory of the Achaians,
you will know Atreus' son Agamemnon, whom beyond others
Zeus has involved in hard work forever, as long as life's wind
90  stays in my breast, as long as my knees have their spring beneath me.
I am driven thus, because the ease of sleep will not settle
on my eyes, but fighting and the cares of the Achaians perplex me.
Terribly I am in dread for the Danaäns, nor does my pulse beat
steadily, but I go distracted, and my heart is pounding
95  through my chest, and my shining limbs are shaken beneath me.
But if you are for action, since sleep comes neither upon you,
let us both go out to the pickets, so that we may see
if they might not have found weariness too much for them, and fallen

asleep, and altogether forgotten their duty, to keep watch.
There are men who hate us sitting nearby, nor do we know                 100
that they might not be pondering an attack on us in the darkness."
     Thereupon the Gerenian horseman Nestor answered him:
"Son of Atreus, most lordly and king of men, Agamemnon,
Zeus of the counsels, I think, will not accomplish for Hektor
all his designs and all he hopes for now; I think rather                 105
he will have still more hardships to wrestle, if ever Achilleus
turns again the heart within him from its wearisome anger.
Surely, I will go with you, and let us also awaken
others, the son of Tydeus the spear-famed, and Odysseus,
and Aias the swift-footed, and the powerful son of Phyleus.              110
But if one were to go also and call these others I speak of,
Aias the great, the godlike one, and the lord Idomeneus,
why, their ships lie farthest from us, and are not at all close.
But, beloved as he is and respected, I will still blame
Menelaos, even though you be angry, and I will not hide it,              115
for the way he sleeps and has given to you alone all the hard work.
For now he ought to be hard at work going to all the great men
in supplication. This need that has come is no more endurable."
     Then in turn the lord of men Agamemnon spoke to him:
"Aged sir, other times I also would tell you to blame him,               120
since often he hangs back and is not willing to work hard,
not that he shrinks from it and gives way, nor in the mind's dullness,
but because he looks to me, and waits till I make a beginning.
But this time he woke far before me, and came to rouse me,
and I sent him on to call those you ask after. Therefore                 125
let us go. We shall find those others there with the sentries
before the gates, where I told them to form and assemble."
     Thereupon the Gerenian horseman Nestor answered him:
"Thus no man of the Argives can disobey him nor find fault
with him, whenever he stirs up any of them and gives orders."            130


     With this speech, he slipped the tunic upon his body
and underneath his shining feet he bound the fair sandals,
and pinned about him a great vermilion mantle sweeping
in a double fold, with a thick fleece of wool upon it.
Then he caught up a powerful spear, edged with sharp bronze,             135

and went on his way down the ships of the bronze-armored Achaians.
First he came on Odysseus, the equal of Zeus in counsel,
and Nestor the Gerenian horseman wakened him from sleep,
speaking aloud, and the wave of the voice swept quick through his hearing
140    and he came forth from his shelter and called out his word to them:
"Why do you wander thus up and down the ships and the army
alone, through the immortal night? What need is upon you?"
     Thereupon the Gerenian horseman Nestor answered him:
"Son of Laërtes and seed of Zeus, resourceful Odysseus,
145    do not be angry; such grief has fallen upon the Achaians.
Come then with us to waken another, for whom it is becoming
to deliberate the question of running away or of fighting."
     He spoke, and resourceful Odysseus moving back into his shelter
put the bright-patterned shield on his shoulders, and went on with them.
150    They went to the son of Tydeus, Diomedes, and found him
with his gear outside the shelter, and his companions about him
slept with their shields underneath their heads, and their spears beside them
stood upright, the heels driven deep in the ground, and the bronze afar off
glared, like the lightning of Zeus father. The hero
155    slept, with the hide of a field-ranging ox laid beneath him,
but underneath his head was laid out a lustrous blanket.
Nestor the Gerenian horseman stood by to waken him
and roused him, stirring him with his heel, and scolded him to his face:
"Son of Tydeus, wake up! Why do you doze in slumber
160    nightlong? Do you not hear how the Trojans at the break of the flat land
are sitting close to our ships, and narrow ground holds them from us?"
     So he spoke, and the other rapidly stirred from his sleeping
and spoke winged words to him and addressed him thus: "Aged sir,
you are a hard man. You are never finished with working.
165    Now are there not other sons of the Achaians younger than you are
who could be going about everywhere to each of the princes
and waking them up? But you, aged sir, are too much for us."
     In turn Nestor the Gerenian horseman said to him:
"Yes, dear friend, all this that you said has been fairly spoken.
170    I myself have sons without blame, I have followers,
plenty of them, of whom any could go to summon the princes.
But this difficulty is very great that has come to the Achaians,
since for all of us the decision now stands on the edge of a razor

whether the Achaians shall have life or sorry destruction.
But go now to Aias the swift and the son of Phyleus                                     175
and waken them—you are younger than I—if truly you have pity."
     He spoke, and the other wrapped his shoulders in the hide of a lion
glowing and huge, that swung to his feet, and took up a spear.
The hero went, and waking the others brought them back with him.

     Now as these men mingled with the sentries assembling                           180
they found the leaders of the pickets by no means asleep
but all of them were wide awake, and sat by their weapons.
As dogs about the sheep in a yard are restless in watching
as they hear a wild beast boldly moving, who through the timber
goes among the mountains, and a clamor rises about him                              185
of men and of dogs, and all their sleep has been broken from them;
so for these the softness of sleep was broken from their eyes
as they held the bitter midwatch, since they were turning always
toward the plain, where they heard the Trojans coming and going.
The aged man was glad when he saw them, and with speech of good cheer   190
spoke winged words to them and addressed them thus: "Continue
to keep your watch this way, beloved children, and let not
sleep seize any, lest you become a delight to your enemies."

     So he spoke, and strode on through the ditch, and there followed with him
the kings of the Argives, all who had been called into conclave,                      195
and with them went Meriones and Nestor's glorious
son, since the kings themselves called these to take counsel with them.
After they had crossed the deep-dug ditch they settled
on clean ground, where there showed a space not cumbered with corpses
of the fallen, a place whence Hektor the huge had turned back                       200
from destroying the Argives, after the night had darkened about him.
There they seated themselves, and opened words to each other,
and the Gerenian horseman Nestor began speaking among them:
"O my friends, is there no man who, trusting in the daring
of his own heart, would go among the high-hearted Trojans?                           205
So he might catch some enemy, who straggled behind them,
or he might overhear some thing that the Trojans are saying,
what they deliberate among themselves, and whether they purpose
to stay where they are, close to the ships, or else to withdraw back

210 into their city, now that they have beaten the Achaians.
Could a man learn this, and then come back again to us
unhurt, why huge and heaven-high would rise up his glory
among all people, and an excellent gift would befall him;
for all those who hold by the ships high power as princes,
215 of all these each one of them will give him a black sheep,
female, with a lamb beneath; there shall be no gift like this one,
one that will be forever by at the feasts and festivals."

So he spoke, and all of them stayed stricken to silence;
but now Diomedes of the great war cry spoke forth among them:
220 "Nestor, my own heart and my own proud spirit arouse me
to go into the host of the hateful men who lie near us,
the Trojans; but if some other man would go along with me
there would be more comfort in it, and greater confidence.
When two go together, one of them at least looks forward
225 to see what is best; a man by himself, though he be careful,
still has less mind in him than two, and his wits have less weight."
He spoke, and many were willing to go with Diomedes.
The two Aiantes were willing, henchman of Ares, and likewise
Meriones, and Nestor's son altogether willing,
230 and Atreus' son was willing, Menelaos the spear-famed,
and patient Odysseus too was willing to enter the multitude
of Trojans, since forever the heart in his breast was daring.
Now it was the lord of men, Agamemnon, who spoke to them:
"Son of Tydeus, you who delight my heart, Diomedes,
235 pick your man to be your companion, whichever you wish,
the best of all who have shown, since many are eager to do it.
You must not, for the awe that you feel in your heart, pass over
the better man and take the worse, giving way to modesty
and looking to his degree—not even if he be kinglier."
240 So he spoke, and was frightened for Menelaos of the fair hair.
But now again Diomedes of the great war cry spoke forth:
"If indeed you tell me myself to pick my companion,
how then could I forget Odysseus the godlike, he whose
heart and whose proud spirit are beyond all others forward
245 in all hard endeavors, and Pallas Athene loves him.
Were he to go with me, both of us could come back from the blazing

of fire itself, since his mind is best at devices."
    Then in turn long-suffering brilliant Odysseus answered him:
"Son of Tydeus, do not praise me so, nor yet blame me.
These are the Argives, who know well all these matters you speak of.      250
But let us go: for the night draws far along, and the dawn nears,
the stars have gone far on their course, and the full of the night has passed by,
through two portions, and the third portion is that which is left us."

    So they spoke, and armed themselves in their weapons of terror,
and Thrasymedes the stubborn in battle gave the son of Tydeus           255
a two-edged sword (his own had been left behind by his vessel)
and a shield; and he put over his head a helmet
of bull's hide, with neither horn nor crest, which is known as
the skull cap, and guards the heads of strong men in battle;
while Meriones gave Odysseus a bow and a quiver                          260
and a sword; and he too put over his head a helmet
fashioned of leather; on the inside the cap was cross-strung firmly
with thongs of leather, and on the outer side the white teeth
of a tusk-shining boar were close sewn one after another
with craftsmanship and skill; and a felt was set in the center.         265
Autolykos, breaking into the close-built house, had stolen it
from Amyntor, the son of Ormenos, out of Eleon,
and gave it to Kytherian Amphidamas, at Skandeia;
Amphidamas gave it in turn to Molos, a gift of guest-friendship,
and Molos gave it to his son Meriones to carry.                         270
But at this time it was worn to cover the head of Odysseus.

    When these two had armed themselves in their weapons of terror
they went on their way, and left behind there all the princes,
and on the right near the way they were taking Pallas Athene
sent down a heron to them; indeed, their eyes could not see it          275
through the darkness of night, but they could hear it crying.
And Odysseus was glad at the bird-sign, and prayed to Athene:
"Hear me, daughter of Zeus of the aegis, you who forever
stand beside me in all hard tasks, nor am I forgotten
as I go my ways: now give me the best of your love, Athene,             280
and grant that we come back in glory to the strong-benched vessels
when we have done a great thing that will sadden the Trojans."

Diomedes of the great war cry spoke in prayer after him:
"Hear me also, Atrytone, daughter of great Zeus.
285 Come with me now as you went with my father, brilliant Tydeus,
into Thebes, when he went with a message before the Achaians,
and left the bronze-armored Achaians beside Asopos
while he carried a word of friendship to the Kadmeians
in that place; but on his way back he was minded to grim deeds
290 with your aid, divine goddess, since you stood in goodwill beside him.
So now again be willing to stand by me, and watch over me,
and I in turn will dedicate you a heifer, broad-browed,
one year old, unbroken, that no man ever led under
the yoke. I will drench her horns in gold and offer her to you."
295 So they spoke in prayer, and Pallas Athene heard them.
Then, after they had made their prayers to the daughter of great Zeus
they went on their way like two lions into the black night
through the carnage and through the corpses, war gear and dark blood.

Nor did Hektor either permit the high-hearted Trojans
300 to sleep, but had called together in a group all of their great men,
those who were the leaders of Troy and their men of deliberation.
Summoning these he compacted before them his close counsel:
"Who would take upon him this work and bring it to fulfillment
for a huge price? The reward will be one that will suffice him;
305 for I will give a chariot and two strong-necked horses
who are the finest of all beside the fast ships of the Achaians
to him who has the daring, winning honor for himself also,
to go close to the swift-running ships and find out for us
whether the swift ships are guarded, as they were before this,
310 or whether now the Achaians who are beaten under our hands
are planning flight among themselves, and no longer are willing
to guard them by night, now that stark weariness has broken them."
So he spoke, and all of them were stricken to silence.
But there was one among the Trojans, Dolon, Eumedes'
315 son, the sacred herald's, a man of much gold and much bronze.
He was an evil man to look on, but was swift-footed;
moreover he was a single son among five sisters.
This man now spoke his word before the Trojans and Hektor:
"Hektor, my own heart and my proud spirit arouse me

to go close to the swift-running ships and to learn about them.    320
Come then, hold up your scepter before me, and swear upon it
that you will give me the horses, and the chariot made bright
with bronze, that carry the blameless son of Peleus. I shall not
be a vain spy for you, nor less than your expectation,
for I shall go straight on through their army, until I come to    325
the ship of Agamemnon, where their greatest men must be gathered
to deliberate the question of running away or of fighting."
    He spoke, and Hektor took the staff in his hand, and swore to him:
"Let Zeus, loud-thundering lord of Hera, now be my witness
himself, that no other man of the Trojans shall mount these horses,    330
since I say they shall be utterly yours, and your glory."

    He spoke, and swore to an empty oath, and stirred the man onward.
And at once Dolon cast across his shoulders the bent bow.
He put on about him the pelt of a gray wolf, and on his head set
a cap of marten's hide, and took up a sharp throwing spear    335
and went on his way toward the ships from his own camp, nor was he ever
to come back again from the ships, and carry his word to Hektor.
Now when he had left behind the throng of men and of horses
he went on his way, eagerly, but illustrious Odysseus
was aware of him coming and spoke to Diomedes:    340
"This is some man, Diomedes, on his way from the army.
I do not know whether he comes to spy on our vessels
or to strip some one of the perished corpses, but we must let him
first go on past us a little way in the open
and afterward we will make a rush and fasten upon him    345
suddenly. But if in the speed of his feet he eludes us
then keep him crowded upon the ships, and away from the army
always, feinting with the spear, nor let him escape to the city."
    So they spoke, and bent aside from their way, through the corpses,
while he in the thoughtlessness of his heart ran swiftly by them.    350
But when he was gone from them as far as the range of a plough yoke
of mules, since these are better beasts than oxen for dragging
the wrought ploughshare through the depth of the harvest land, these two
ran after him, and he heard the thudding of their feet and stopped still.
He thought in his heart these would be friends from among the Trojans    355
to turn him back, and that Hektor had sped them to summon him again.

But when they got to a spear's throw from him, or less even,
he saw that these were enemy men, and moved his knees rapidly
to run away, and these set out in rapid chase of him.
360   And, as when two rip-fanged hounds have sighted a wild beast,
a young deer, or a hare, and go after it, eagerly always
through the spaces of the woods, and the chase runs crying before them,
so the son of Tydeus, and Odysseus, sacker of cities,
kept always hard on his heels and cut him off from his people.
365   But when he was on the point of reaching the Achaian pickets,
as he fled toward the vessels, then Athene put great power
in Tydeus' son, so that no other bronze-armored Achaian
might win the glory of striking him down, and he come in second.
Powerful Diomedes threatening with the spear spoke to him:
370   "Either wait, or my spear will catch you. I think that you will not
thus get clear from my hands for long, and sudden destruction."

He spoke, and let fly with his spear, but missed, on purpose,
his man, as the point of the polished spear went over his right shoulder
and stuck fast in the earth. And Dolon stood still in terror
375   gibbering, as through his mouth came the sound of his teeth's chatter
in green fear; and these two, breathing hard, came up to him
and caught him by the hands, and he broke into tears and spoke to them:
"Take me alive, and I will pay my ransom: in my house
there is bronze, and gold, and difficultly wrought iron,
380   and my father would make you glad with abundant ransom
were he to hear that I am alive by the ships of the Achaians."
Then resourceful Odysseus spoke in turn, and answered him:
"Do not fear, and let no thought of death be upon you.
But come, tell me this thing and recite it to me accurately:
385   where is it that you walk alone to the ships from the army
through the darkness of night when other mortals are sleeping?
Is it to strip some one of the perished corpses, or is it
that Hektor sent you out to spy with care upon each thing
beside our hollow ships? Or did your own spirit drive you?"
390   Then Dolon answered him, but his legs were shaking beneath him:
"Hektor has led my mind astray with many deceptions.
He promised me the single-foot horses of proud Achilleus,
Peleus' son, and the chariot bright with bronze, for my gift,

and gave me an order, to go through the running black night,
and get close to the enemy men, and find out for him                    395
whether the swift ships are guarded, as they were before this,
or whether now the Achaians who are broken under our hands
are planning flight among themselves, and no longer are willing
to guard them by night, now that stark weariness has broken them."
    Then Odysseus the resourceful smiled and spoke to him:             400
"Surely now, these were mighty gifts that your heart longed after,
the horses of valiant Aiakides. They are difficult horses
for mortal men to manage, or even to ride behind them
for all except Achilleus, who was born of an immortal mother.
But come, tell me this thing and recite it to me accurately.           405
Where did you leave Hektor, the people's shepherd, when you came here?
Where is his gear of war lying? Where are his horses?
How are the rest of the Trojans disposed, the guards and the sleepers?
What do they deliberate among themselves? Do they purpose
to stay where they are, close to the ships? Or else to withdraw back   410
into the city, now that they have beaten the Achaians?"
    Then in turn Dolon the son of Eumedes spoke to him:
"See, I will accurately recite all these things to you.
Hektor is now among those who are the men of counsel
and they hold their deliberations by the barrow of godlike Ilos        415
apart from the confusion. But those guards that you ask of, hero—
there is no detail that protects the army and guards it.
As for the watchfire hearths of the Trojans, those who must do it
keep awake by the fires and pass on the picket duty
to each other, but their far-assembled companions in battle           420
are sleeping, and pass on to the Trojans the duty of watching,
since their own children do not lie nearby, nor their women."
    Then resourceful Odysseus spoke in turn, and answered him:
"How, then, are these sleeping? And are they mixed with the Trojans,
breakers of horses, or apart? Tell me, so I may be clear."            425
    Then in turn Dolon the son of Eumedes answered him:
"See, I will accurately recite all these things to you.
Next the sea are the Karians, and Paionians with their curved bows,
the Leleges and Kaukonians and the brilliant Pelasgians.
By Thymbre are stationed the Lykians and the proud Mysians            430
with the Phrygians who fight from horses, and Maionians, lords of chariots.

But why do you question me on all this, each thing in detail?
For if you are minded to get among the mass of the Trojans,
here are the Thracians, new come, separate, beyond all others
435  in place, and among them Rhesos their king, the son of Eïoneus.
And his are the finest horses I ever saw, and the biggest;
they are whiter than snow, and their speed of foot is the winds' speed;
his chariot is fairly ornate with gold and with silver,
and the armor is golden and gigantic, a wonder to look on,
440  that he brought here with him. It is not like armor for mortal
men to carry, but for the immortal gods. And therefore
take me with you to some place by the fast-running vessels,
or else tie me fast here in a pitiless bond, and leave me,
until you can make your venture, and try out the truth of my story,
445  whether I have told you this fairly, or whether I have not."

     But powerful Diomedes looked darkly at him and spoke then:
"Do not, Dolon, have in your mind any thought of escape
now you have got in our hands, though you brought us an excellent message.
For if we let you get away now, or set you free, later
450  you will come back again to the fast ships of the Achaians
either to spy on us once more, or to fight strongly with us.
But if, beaten down under my hands, you lose your life now,
then you will nevermore be an affliction upon the Argives."
     He spoke, and the man was trying to reach his chin with his strong hand
455  and cling, and supplicate him, but he struck the middle of his neck
with a sweep of the sword, and slashed clean through both tendons,
and Dolon's head still speaking dropped in the dust. They took off
his cap of marten's hide from his head, and stripped off also
the wolf's pelt, and the back-strung bow, and the long spear.
460  Brilliant Odysseus held these up to Athene the Spoiler
high in his hand, and spoke a word, and prayed to Athene:
"Hail, goddess. These are yours. To you first of all the immortals
on Olympos we will give your due share. Only guide us
once again to where the Thracians sleep, and their horses."

465     So he spoke, and lifting the spoils high from him he placed them
upon a tamarisk bush, and piled a clear landmark beside them,
pulling reeds together and the long branches of tamarisk

that they might not miss them on their way back through the running
   black night.
These two went ahead on their way through war gear and dark blood
and came suddenly to the Thracians for whom they were looking.          470
These were asleep, worn out with weariness, and their armor
lay in splendor and good order on the ground beside them
in three rows, and beside each man stood his team of horses.
Rhesos slept in the center with his fast horses about him
tethered by the reins to the outer rail of the chariot. Odysseus        475
was the first to see him and pointed him out to Diomedes:
"Here is our man, see, Diomedes, and here are his horses,
those that Dolon, the man we killed, pointed out to us.
Come then, put forward your great strength. Here is no matter
for standing by idle in your weapons. Untie the horses;                 480
or else let me look after them, while you kill the people."
   He spoke, and gray-eyed Athene breathed strength into Diomedes
and he began to kill them one after another. Grim sounds rose
from there as they were stricken with the sword, and the ground
   reddened with blood.
As a lion advancing on the helpless herds unshepherded                  485
of sheep or goats pounces upon them with wicked intention,
so the son of Tydeus attacked the Thracian people
until he had killed twelve. Meanwhile resourceful Odysseus
as Tydeus' son stood over each man with the sword, and struck him,
would catch each dead man by the foot from behind, and drag him         490
away, with this thought in his mind, that the bright-maned horses
might pass easily through and not be shaken within them
at stepping on dead men. These horses were not yet used to them.
But when the son of Tydeus came to the king, and this was
the thirteenth man, he stripped the sweetness of life from him          495
as he lay heavily breathing—since a bad dream stood by his head
in the night—no dream, but Oineus' son, by device of Athene.
Meanwhile patient Odysseus was untying the single-foot horses,
and pulled them together with the reins, and drove them from the
   confusion
and whipped them with his bow, since he had not noticed nor taken       500
in his hands the glittering whip that was in the elaborate chariot.
He whistled to brilliant Diomedes as a signal to him.

But he waited, divided in his mind as to what he would best do,
whether to seize the chariot, wherein lay the bright armor,
505 and draw it away by the pole, or lift it and carry it off with him,
or strip the life from still more of the Thracians. Meanwhile
as he was pondering all this in his heart, Athene
came and stood beside him, and spoke to great Diomedes:
"Think now, son of great-hearted Tydeus, of getting back
510 to the hollow ships; else you might go back with men pursuing
if there should be some other god to waken the Trojans."
So she spoke, and he knew the voice of the goddess speaking
and lightly mounted behind the horses. Odysseus whipped them
with his bow, and they ran for the rapid ships of the Achaians.
515 Neither did Apollo of the silver bow keep blind watch,
since he saw Athene attending the son of Tydeus. Angered
with her he plunged into the great multitude of the Trojans
and roused a man of counsel among the Thracians, Hippokoön
the lordly cousin of Rhesos; and he, starting out of his sleep,
520 when he saw the place left empty where the fast horses had been standing
and his men in the shambles of slaughter gasping their lives out,
he groaned, and called aloud by name his beloved companion.
And a clamor rose up from the Trojans and a vast turmoil
as they swept together in confusion and stared at the ghastly work done
525 by these two men, before they went back to their hollow vessels.

But when these had come back to the place where they killed Hektor's
scout,
Odysseus beloved of Zeus reined in his running horses
while Tydeus' son leaping to the ground took the bloody war spoils
and handed them to Odysseus, and got up behind the horses.
530 Odysseus lashed them on, and they winged their way unreluctant
back to the hollow ships, since this was the way he desired it.
Nestor was the first to hear their thunder, and spoke forth:
"Friends, who are leaders of the Argives and keep their counsel,
shall I be wrong, or am I speaking the truth? My heart tells me.
535 The thunder is beating against my ears of fast-running horses.
Might this only be Odysseus and strong Diomedes
driving rapidly away from the Trojans their single-foot horses!

Yet terribly I fear in my heart that these bravest Achaians
might have suffered some disaster from the loud host of the Trojans."
    Yet he had not spoken all his words, and they came. The two men          540
dismounted to the ground, and their companions rejoicing
congratulated them with clasped hands and with words of welcome.
First to question them was the Gerenian horseman, Nestor:
"Come, tell me, honored Odysseus, great glory of the Achaians,
how did you win these horses? Did you go into the great company          545
of the Trojans, or did some god meet you and give them to you?
They shine, like the rays of the sun, terribly. Yet over and over
I encounter the Trojans, I say that I am not at all one
to hang back beside the ships, though I am an aged fighter.
Yet I have never seen horses like these, nor laid eyes upon them.          550
I think it must be some god who met you, and gave them to you.
Since both of you are beloved to Zeus who gathers the clouds, both
to the gray-eyed maiden of Zeus who wears the aegis, Athene."
    Then resourceful Odysseus spoke in turn and answered him:
"Son of Neleus, Nestor, great glory of the Achaians:          555
lightly a god, if he wished, could give us horses even better
than these, seeing that the gods are far stronger than we are.
These horses, aged sir, that you ask about are newcomers
from Thrace, and as for their master brave Diomedes killed him
and at his side killed twelve companions, all of them great men;          560
our thirteenth man killed was their scout, here by the vessels,
one whom Hektor and the rest of the haughty Trojans
had sent out between the lines to spy on our army."

    He spoke, and guided across the ditch the single-foot horses
laughing aloud, and the rest of the Achaians went with him          565
rejoicing. When they came to Diomedes' strong-fashioned shelter
there they tied up the horses by the carefully cut reins
by the horse trough where already the horses of Diomedes
were standing, rapid of foot, and eating their welcome provender.
And by the stern of the ship Odysseus laid down the bloody          570
battle spoils of Dolon, to dedicate to Athene.
And the men themselves waded into the sea and washed off
the dense sweat from shin and shoulder and thigh. Afterward

when the surf of the sea had rinsed the dense-running sweat away
575 from all their skin, and the inward heart had been cooled to refreshment,
they stepped into the bathtubs smooth-polished, and bathed there,
and after they had bathed and anointed themselves with olive oil
they sat down to dine, and from the full mixing bowl drawing
the sweet-hearted wine poured out an offering to Athene.

# BOOK ELEVEN

Now Dawn rose from her bed, where she lay by haughty Tithonos,
to carry her light to men and to immortals. Zeus sent down
in speed to the fast ships of the Achaians the wearisome goddess
of Hate, holding in her hands the portent of battle.
She took her place on the huge-hollowed black ship of Odysseus          5
which lay in the middle, so that she could cry out to both flanks,
either as far as the shelters of Telamonian Aias
or to those of Achilleus; since these had hauled their balanced ships up
at the ends, certain of their manhood and their hands' strength.
There the goddess took her place, and cried out a great cry             10
and terrible and loud, and put strength in all the Achaians'
hearts, to go on tirelessly with their fighting of battles.
And now battle became sweeter to them than to go back
in their hollow ships to the beloved land of their fathers.

And Atreus' son cried out aloud and drove the Achaians                  15
to gird them, while he himself put the shining bronze upon him.
First he placed along his legs the beautiful greaves linked
with silver fastenings to hold the greaves at the ankles.
Afterward he girt on about his chest the corselet
that Kinyras had given him once, to be a guest present.                 20
For the great fame and rumor of war had carried to Kypros
how the Achaians were to sail against Troy in their vessels.
Therefore he gave the king as a gift of grace this corselet.
Now there were ten circles of deep cobalt upon it,
and twelve of gold and twenty of tin. And toward the opening           25

at the throat there were rearing up three serpents of cobalt
on either side, like rainbows, which the son of Kronos
has marked upon the clouds, to be a portent to mortals.
Across his shoulders he slung the sword, and the nails upon it
30   were golden and glittered, and closing about it the scabbard
was silver, and gold was upon the swordstraps that held it.
And he took up the man-enclosing elaborate stark shield,
a thing of splendor. There were ten circles of bronze upon it,
and set about it were twenty knobs of tin, pale-shining,
35   and in the very center another knob of dark cobalt.
And circled in the midst of all was the blank-eyed face of the Gorgon
with her stare of horror, and Fear was inscribed upon it, and Terror.
The strap of the shield had silver upon it, and there also on it
was coiled a cobalt snake, and there were three heads upon him
40   twisted to look backward and grown from a single neck, all three.
Upon his head he set the helmet, two-horned, four-sheeted,
with the horse-hair crest, and the plumes nodded terribly above it.
Then he caught up two strong spears edged with sharp bronze
and the brazen heads flashed far from him deep into heaven.
45   And Hera and Athene caused a crash of thunder about him,
doing honor to the lord of deep-golden Mykenai.

Thereupon each man gave orders to his charioteer
to rein in the horses once again by the ditch, in good order,
while they themselves, dismounted and armed in their war gear, swept
      onward
50   to the ditch, and their incessant clamor rose up in the morning.
In battle array they came to the ditch well ahead of the horseman
and the horseman followed a little behind. And the son of Kronos
drove down the evil turmoil upon them, and from aloft cast
down dews dripping blood from the sky, since he was minded
55   to hurl down a multitude of strong heads to the house of Hades.
      On the other side of the ditch at the break of the plain the Trojans
gathered about tall Hektor and stately Poulydamas
and Aineias, honored by Trojans in their countryside as a god is,
and the three sons of Antenor, Polybos, and brilliant Agenor,
60   and Akamas, a young man still, in the likeness of the immortals.
And Hektor carried the perfect circle of his shield in the foremost,

as among the darkened clouds the bale star shows forth
in all shining, then merges again in the clouds and the darkness.
So Hektor would at one time be shining among the foremost,
and then once more urging on the last, and complete in bronze armor          65
glittered like the thunder-flash of Zeus of the aegis, our father.

And the men, like two lines of reapers who, facing each other,
drive their course all down the field of wheat or of barley
for a man blessed in substance, and the cut swathes drop showering,
so Trojans and Achaians driving in against one another          70
cut men down, nor did either side think of disastrous panic.
The pressure held their heads on a line, and they whirled and fought like
wolves, and Hate, the Lady of Sorrow, was gladdened to watch them.
She alone of all the immortals attended this action
but the other immortals were not there, but sat quietly          75
remote and apart in their palaces, where for each one of them
a house had been built in splendor along the folds of Olympos.
All were blaming the son of Kronos, Zeus of the dark mists,
because his will was to give glory to the Trojans. To these gods
the father gave no attention at all, but withdrawn from them          80
and rejoicing in the pride of his strength sat apart from the others
looking out over the city of Troy and the ships of the Achaians,
watching the flash of the bronze, and men killing and men killed.

So long as it was early morning and the sacred daylight increasing,
so long the thrown weapons of both took hold and men dropped under          85
     them.
But at that time when the woodcutter makes ready his supper
in the wooded glens of the mountains, when his arms and hands have
     grown weary
from cutting down the tall trees, and his heart has had enough of it,
and longing for food and for sweet wine takes hold of his senses;
at that time the Danaäns by their manhood broke the battalions          90
calling across the ranks to each other. First Agamemnon
drove on, and killed a man, Bienor, shepherd of the people,
himself, then his companion Oïleus, lasher of horses;
who, springing down from behind his horses, stood forth to face him,
but Agamemnon stabbed straight at his face as he came on in fury          95

with the sharp spear, nor did helm's bronze-heavy edge hold it,
but the spearhead passed through this and the bone, and the inward
brain was all spattered forth. So he beat him down in his fury,
and Agamemnon the lord of men left them lying there
100    and their white bodies showing, since he had stripped off their tunics.
Then he went on to kill and strip Isos and Antiphos,
two sons of Priam, bastard one and one lawful, both riding
in a single chariot. The bastard, Isos, was charioteer
and renowned Antiphos rode beside him. Before this Achilleus
105    had caught these two at the knees of Ida, and bound them in pliant
willows as they watched by their sheep, and released them for ransom.
This time the son of Atreus, wide-powerful Agamemnon,
struck Isos with the thrown spear in the chest above the nipple
and hit Antiphos by the ear with the sword and hurled him from his horses,
110    and in eager haste he stripped off from these their glorious armor
which he knew; he had seen these two before by the fast ships
when Achilleus of the swift feet had brought them in from Ida.
And as a lion seizes the innocent young of the running
deer, and easily crunches and breaks them caught in the strong teeth
115    when he has invaded their lair, and rips out the soft heart from them,
and even if the doe be very near, still she has no strength
to help, for the ghastly shivers of fear are upon her also
and suddenly she dashes away through the glades and the timber
sweating in her speed away from the pounce of the strong beast;
120    so there was no one of the Trojans who could save these two
from death, but they themselves were running in fear from the Argives.

Next he caught Peisandros and Hippolochos stubborn in battle,
sons of Antimachos the wise, who beyond all others
had taken the gold of Alexandros, glorious gifts, so that
125    he had opposed the return of Helen to fair-haired Menelaos.
Powerful Agamemnon caught his two sons riding
in one chariot, who together guided the running horses.
Now the glittering reins escaped from the hands of both of them
and they were stunned with fear, for against them rose like a lion
130    Atreus' son, and they supplicated him out of the chariot:
"Take us alive, son of Atreus, and take appropriate ransom.
In the house of Antimachos the treasures lie piled in abundance,

bronze is there, and gold, and difficultly wrought iron,
and our father would make you glad with abundant repayment
were he to hear we were alive by the ships of the Achaians."          135
    Thus these two cried out upon the king, lamenting
and in pitiful phrase, but they heard the voice that was without pity:
"If in truth you are the sons of wise Antimachos,
that man who once among the Trojans assembled advised them
that Menelaos, who came as envoy with godlike Odysseus,              140
should be murdered on the spot nor let go back to the Achaians,
so now your mutilation shall punish the shame of your father."
    He spoke, and spurned Peisandros to the ground from the chariot
with a spear-stroke in the chest, and he crashed on his back to the
        ground. Then
Hippolochos sprang away, but Atreides killed him dismounted,         145
cutting away his arms with a sword-stroke, free of the shoulder,
and sent him spinning like a log down the battle. Thereafter
he left them, and toward that place where the most battalions were shaken
drove, and beside him drove the rest of the strong-greaved Achaians,
and footmen killed footmen who fled under strong compulsion          150
and riders killed riders, and a storm of dust rose up under them
out of the plain uplifted by the thundering feet of their horses.
They killed with the bronze, and among them powerful Agamemnon
went onward always slaying and urged on the rest of the Argives.
As when obliterating fire comes down on the timbered forest          155
and the roll of the wind carries it everywhere, and bushes
leaning under the force of the fire's rush tumble uprooted,
so before Atreus' son Agamemnon went down the high heads
of the running Trojans, and in many places the strong-necked horses
rattled their empty chariots along the causeways of battle,          160
and longed for their haughty charioteers, who were lying
along the ground, to delight no longer their wives, but the vultures.

    But Zeus drew Hektor out from under the dust and the missiles,
out of the place where men were killed, the blood and confusion,
while Atreides followed urging the Danaäns forever onward.           165
The Trojans swept in their flight past the barrow of ancient Ilos
Dardanos' son, to the center of the level ground and the fig tree,
as they made for the city, and he followed them always, screaming,

Atreus' son, his invincible hands spattered with bloody filth.
170 But when they had made their way to the Skaian gates and the oak tree
the Trojans stood their ground, and each side endured the other,
while others still in the middle plain stampeded like cattle
when a lion, coming upon them in the dim night, has terrified
the whole herd, while for a single one sheer death is emerging.
175 First the lion breaks her neck caught fast in the strong teeth,
then gulps down the blood and all the guts that are inward;
so Atreus' son, powerful Agamemnon, went after them
killing ever the last of the men; and they fled in terror.
Many were hurled from behind their horses, face downward or sprawling
180 under the hands of Atreides who raged with his spear in the forefront.
But when he was on the point of making his way to the city
and the steep wall, the father of gods and of men descending
out of the sky took his place along the ridges of Ida
of the fountains, and held fast in his hands the thunderbolt.
185 He sent on her way Iris of the golden wings with a message:
"Go on your way, swift Iris, and carry my word to Hektor:
as long as he beholds Agamemnon, shepherd of the people,
raging among the champions and cutting down the ranged fighters,
so long let him hold back and urge on the rest of his people
190 to fight against the enemy through this strong encounter.
But when, either struck with a spear or hit by a flying arrow,
he springs up behind his horses, then I guarantee power to Hektor
to kill men, till he makes his way to the strong-benched vessels,
until the sun goes down and the blessed darkness comes over."

195    He spoke, and swift wind-footed Iris did not disobey him,
but went down along the hills of Ida to sacred Ilion,
and found the son of wise Priam, Hektor the brilliant,
standing among the compacted chariots and by the horses.
Iris the swift of foot came close beside and spoke to him:
200 "Hektor, O son of Priam and equal of Zeus in counsel,
Zeus my father has sent me down to tell you this message.
As long as you behold Agamemnon, shepherd of the people,
raging among the champions and cutting down the ranged fighters,
so long hold back from the fighting, but urge on the rest of your people
205 to fight against the enemy through this strong encounter.

But when, either struck with a spear or hit by a flying arrow,
he springs up behind his horses, then Zeus guarantees power to you
to kill men, till you make your way to the strong-benched vessels,
until the sun goes down and the blessed darkness comes over."
    Swift-foot Iris spoke to him thus and went away from him,             210
and Hektor in all his armor leapt to the ground from his chariot
and shaking two sharp spears in his hand ranged over the whole host
stirring them up to fight and waking the ghastly warfare.
So they whirled about and stood their ground against the Achaians,
and the Argives against them pulled together their battle lines.          215
So the fighting grew close and they faced each other, and foremost
Agamemnon drove on, trying to fight far ahead of all others.

    Tell me now, you Muses who have your homes on Olympos,
who was the first to come forth and stand against Agamemnon
of the very Trojans, or their renowned companions in battle.              220
    Iphidamas, Antenor's son, the huge and stalwart
who had been reared in generous Thrace, the mother of sheepflocks.
Kisseus had raised him in his own house when he was little,
his mother's father, whose child was Theano, the girl of the fair cheeks.
But when he had arrived at the stature of powerful manhood                225
Kisseus detained him there and gave him his daughter. Married
he went away from the bride chamber, looking for glory
from the Achaians, with twelve curved ships that followed with him.
These balanced vessels he had left behind in Perkote
and gone himself to fight on foot at Ilion; and there                     230
he came face to face with Atreus' son, Agamemnon.
Now when these in their advance were close to each other
the son of Atreus missed with his throw, and the spear was turned past him,
but Iphidamas stabbed to the belt underneath the corselet
and leaned in on the stroke in the confidence of his strong hand          235
but could not get clean through the bright war belt, far sooner
the spearpoint pushed against the silver bent back, like soft lead.
And in his hand wide-powerful Agamemnon catching it
dragged it against him, raging like a lion, and tore it
out of his hand, then struck the neck with his sword, and unstrung him.   240
So Iphidamas fell there and went into the brazen slumber,
unhappy, who came to help his own people, and left his young wife

a bride, and had known no delight from her yet, and given much for her.
First he had given a hundred oxen, then promised a thousand
245  head of goats and sheep, which were herded for him in abundance.
Now Agamemnon, son of Atreus, stripped him and went back
to the throng of the Achaians bearing the splendid armor.

When Koön, conspicuous among the fighters, perceived him,
he who was Antenor's eldest born, the strong sorrow
250  misted about his eyes for the sake of his fallen brother.
He came from the side and unobserved at great Agamemnon
and stabbed with his spear at the middle arm, underneath the elbow,
and the head of the glittering spear cut its way clean through.
Agamemnon the lord of men shuddered with fear then
255  but even so did not give up the attack or his fighting
but sprang at Koön, gripping a spear that struck with the wind's speed.
Now Koön was dragging his father's son, his brother Iphidamas,
by the foot back eagerly, and cried out on all the bravest,
but as he dragged him into the crowd, Agamemnon thrust at him
260  with the smoothed bronze spear underneath the knobbed shield, and
        unstrung him,
then came up and hewed off his head over Iphidamas.
There under the king, Atreus' son, the sons of Antenor
filled out their destiny and went down to the house of the death god.

But Agamemnon ranged the ranks of the other fighters
265  with spear and sword and with huge stones that he flung, for such time
as the blood was still running warm from the spear-wound.
But after the sore place was dry, and the flow of blood stopped,
the sharp pains began to break in on the strength of Atreides.
As the sharp sorrow of pain descends on a woman in labor,
270  the bitterness that the hard spirits of childbirth bring on,
Hera's daughters, who hold the power of the bitter birthpangs,
so the sharp pains began to break in on the strength of Atreides.
He sprang back into the car, and called to his charioteer
to drive him back to the hollow ships, since his heart was heavy.
275  He lifted his voice and called in a piercing cry to the Danaäns:
"Friends, O leaders and men of counsel among the Argives,
you must still continue to defend our seafaring vessels

from the wearying attack, since Zeus of the counsels would not
allow me to do battle daylong against the Trojans."
    He spoke, and the charioteer lashed on the bright-maned horses          280
back toward the hollow ships, and they winged their way unreluctant.
The foam ran down their chests, they were powdered with dust from
    beneath them
as they carried the stricken king away from the fighting.

    When Hektor was aware of Agamemnon withdrawing
he called out in a great voice to Trojans and Lykians:                      285
"Trojans, Lykians and Dardanians who fight at close quarters,
be men now, dear friends, remember your furious valor.
Their best man is gone, and Zeus, Kronos' son, has consented
to my great glory; but steer your single-foot horses straight on
at the powerful Danaäns, so win you the higher glory."                      290
    So he spoke, and stirred the spirit and strength in each man.
As when some huntsman drives to action his hounds with shining
teeth against some savage beast, wild boar or lion,
so against the Achaians Hektor the son of Priam,
a man like the murderous war god, lashed on the high-hearted Trojans.       295
And he himself with high thoughts strode out in the foremost
and hurled himself on the struggle of men like a high-blown storm-cloud
which swoops down from above to trouble the blue sea-water.

    Who then was the first, and who the last that he slaughtered,
Hektor, Priam's son, now that Zeus granted him glory?                       300
Asaios first, and then Autonoös and Opites,
and Dolops, Klytios' son, Opheltios and Agelaos,
and Aisymnos, and Oros, and Hipponoös stubborn in battle.
He killed these, who were lords of the Danaäns, and thereafter
the multitude, as when the west wind strikes in the deepening              305
whirlstorm to batter the clouds of the shining south wind,
so that the bulging big waves roll hard and the blown spume
scatters high before the force of the veering wind's blast.
So the massed high heads of the people were struck down by Hektor.
And now there might have been havoc and hopeless things done, now           310
the running Achaians might have tumbled back into their own ships
had not Odysseus cried out to Tydeus' son, Diomedes:

"Son of Tydeus, what has happened to us that we have forgotten
our fighting strength? Come here and stand with me, brother. There must be
315　shame on us, if Hektor of the glancing helm captures our vessels."
　　　Then in answer powerful Diomedes spoke to him:
"Yes, I will stand with you and take what I must, yet
we shall not have our way for long, since Zeus the cloud-gatherer
would wish to give the power to the Trojans rather than to us."
320　He spoke, and hurled down Thymbraios to the ground from his horses
with a stroke of the spear by the left nipple. Meanwhile Odysseus
killed this lord of battle's henchman, godlike Molion.
They left these to lie there, since they had ended their fighting,
then went into the ranks and wrought havoc, as when two wild boars
325　hurl themselves in their pride upon the hounds who pursue them.
So they whirled on the Trojans again and destroyed them. Meanwhile
the Achaians gladly drew breath again after their flight from great Hektor.
　　　There they took a chariot and two men, lords in their countryside,
sons both of Merops of Perkote, who beyond all men
330　knew the art of prophecy, and tried to prevent his two sons
from going into the battle where men die. Yet these would not
listen, for the spirits of dark death were driving them onward.
Tydeus' son, Diomedes of the renowned spear, stripped them
of life and spirit, and took away their glorious armor
335　while Odysseus killed Hypeirochos and Hippodamos.

　　　There the son of Kronos strained the battle even between them
as he looked down from Ida. They went on killing each other.
Now Tydeus' son stabbed with the spear Agastrophos, a chief
and son of Paion, striking at the hip joint. His horses
340　were not by for his escape, but he, strongly infatuate,
had a henchman holding them aside, while he, dismounted,
raged on among the champions until so he lost his dear life.
Hektor saw it sharply across the ranks and rose up against them
with a great cry, and behind him came on the Trojan battalions.
345　Diomedes of the great war cry shivered as he saw him
and suddenly he spoke to Odysseus as he came near:
"Here is this curse, Hektor the huge, wheeling down upon us.
Let us stand, and hold our ground against him, and beat him off from us."

So he spoke, and balanced the spear far-shadowed, and threw it
aiming at the head, and struck against his mark, nor missed it,                          350
at the high peak of the helm, but the bronze from the bronze was driven
back, nor reached his shining skin, the helmet guarded it,
three-ply and hollow-eyed, which Phoibos Apollo gave him.
But Hektor sprang far away back and merged among his own people,
and dropping to one knee stayed leaning on the ground with his heavy      355
hand, and a covering of black night came over both eyes.
But while the son of Tydeus was following his spear's cast
far through the front fighters where it fixed in the earth, meanwhile
Hektor got his wind again, and springing back into his chariot
drove back into the multitude and avoided the dark death.                         360
Then shaking his spear powerful Diomedes called to him:
"Once again now you escaped death, dog. And yet the evil
came near you, but now once more Phoibos Apollo has saved you,
he to whom you must pray when you go into the thunder of spears thrown.
Yet I may win you, if I encounter you ever hereafter,                                   365
if beside me also there is some god who will help me.
Now I must chase whoever I can overtake of the others."

He spoke, and set about stripping the spear-famed son of Paion.
But now Alexandros, the lord of lovely-haired Helen,
pulled his bow against Tydeus' son, the shepherd of the people,             370
leaning against the column, work of men's hand, on the gravemound
of Ilos, Dardanos' son, an elder of the folk in the old days.
Now Diomedes was stripping the corselet of strong Agastrophos
from about his chest, and the shining shield from his shoulders
and the heavy helm, as the other pulled his bow at the handgrip             375
and shot, and the arrow escaping his hand flew not vain
but struck the flat of the right foot, and the shaft driven clean through
stuck in the ground. Then Alexandros, laughing merrily,
sprang from his hiding-place and cried out his speech of triumph:
"You are hit, and my arrow flew not in vain. How I wish                          380
I had struck you in the depth of the belly and torn the life from you.
So the Trojans, who shudder before you as bleating goats do
before a lion, would have got their wind again after disaster."
Then not at all frightened strong Diomedes answered him:

385 "You archer, foul fighter, lovely in your locks, eyer of young girls.
     If you were to make trial of me in strong combat with weapons
     your bow would do you no good at all, nor your close-showered arrows.
     Now you have scratched the flat of my foot, and even boast of this.
     I care no more than if a witless child or a woman
390 had struck me; this is the blank weapon of a useless man, no fighter.
     But if one is struck by me only a little, that is far different,
     the stroke is a sharp thing and suddenly lays him lifeless,
     and that man's wife goes with cheeks torn in lamentation,
     and his children are fatherless, while he staining the soil with his red blood
395 rots away, and there are more birds than women swarming about him."
     He spoke, and Odysseus the spear-famed coming up from nearby
     stood in front; so he sat down behind him and pulled out
     the sharp arrow from his foot, and the hard pain came over his flesh.
     He sprang back into the car and called to his charioteer
400 to drive him back to the hollow ships, since his heart was heavy.

     Now Odysseus the spear-famed was left alone, nor did any
     of the Argives stay beside him, since fear had taken all of them.
     And troubled, he spoke then to his own great-hearted spirit:
     "Ah me, what will become of me? It will be a great evil
405 if I run, fearing their multitude, yet deadlier if I am caught
     alone; and Kronos' son drove to flight the rest of the Danaäns.
     Yet still, why does the heart within me debate on these things?
     Since I know that it is the cowards who walk out of the fighting,
     but if one is to win honor in battle, he must by all means
410 stand his ground strongly, whether he be struck or strike down another."
     While he was pondering these things in his heart and his spirit
     the ranks of the armored Trojans came on against him, and penned him
     in their midst, but made thereby a wound in their ranks, as when
     closing about a wild boar the hounds and the lusty young men
415 rush him, and he comes out of his lair in the deep of a thicket
     grinding to an edge the white fangs in the crook of the jawbones,
     and these sweep in all about him, and the vaunt of his teeth uprises
     as they await him, terrible though he is, without wavering;
     so closing on Odysseus beloved of Zeus the Trojans
420 rushed him. First he stabbed lordly Deïopites
     in the shoulder, lunging from above with a stroke of the sharp spear,

and after him he killed Thoön and Ennomos, and next
stabbed Chersidamas as he sprang down from behind his horses
in the navel with a spear's stroke underneath the massive
shield, and he dropping in the dust clawed the ground with his hand. These    425
he left lying, and stabbed with the spear the son of Hippasos,
Charops, full brother of Sokos, a man rich in substance. And Sokos
moved in, a man like a god, to stand over his fallen brother
and came and stood close by Odysseus and spoke a word to him:
"Honored Odysseus, insatiable of guile and endeavor,    430
today you will have two sons of Hippasos to vaunt over
for having killed two such men as we and stripping our armor,
or else, stricken underneath my spear, you might lose your own life."
He spoke, and stabbed Odysseus' shield in its perfect circle.
All the way through the glittering shield went the heavy spearhead    435
and crashed its way through the intricately wrought corselet,
and all the skin was torn away from his ribs, yet Pallas
Athene would not let the point penetrate the man's vitals.
Odysseus saw that the fatal end had not yet come to him,
and drew back and spoke a word to Sokos: "Ah, wretch,    440
surely now steep destruction is advancing upon you.
It is true, you have stopped my fighting against the Trojans,
but I declare that here and now dark death and slaughter
will come upon you this day, and that beaten down under my spear
you will give glory to me and your life to Hades of the horses."    445

He spoke, and Sokos turning from him was striding in flight
but in his back even as he was turning the spear fixed
between the shoulders and was driven on through the chest beyond it.
He fell, thunderously, and great Odysseus boasted over him:
"Sokos, son of wise Hippasos the breaker of horses,    450
death was too quick for you and ran you down; you could not
avoid it. Wretch, since now your father and your honored mother
will not be able to close your eyes in death, but the tearing
birds will get you, with their wings close-beating about you.
If I die, the brilliant Achaians will bury me in honor."    455
So he spoke, and dragged the heavy spear of wise Sokos
out of his flesh and out of the shield massive in the middle,
and as it was torn out the blood sprang and his heart was sickened.

But the great-hearted Trojans, when they saw the blood of Odysseus,
460    cried aloud through the close battle and all made a charge against him.
He gave back a little way and called out for his companions.
Three times he called, as much voice as a man's head could hold,
and three times Menelaos the warlike heard him shouting
and immediately spoke to Aias, who was nearby him:
465    "Son of Telamon, seed of Zeus, Aias, lord of the people,
the war cry of patient Odysseus is ringing about me
with a sound as if he had been cut off by himself, and the Trojans
were handling him violently in the strong encounter. Therefore
let us go to him through the battle. It is better to defend him against them.
470    I fear that, caught alone, he may be hurt by the Trojans
brave as he is, and so a great loss may befall the Danaäns."

He spoke, and led the way, and the other followed, a mortal
like a god. They found Odysseus beloved of Zeus, and around him
the Trojans crowded, as bloody scavengers in the mountains
475    crowd on a horned stag who is stricken, one whom a hunter
shot with an arrow from the string, and the stag has escaped him, running
with his feet, while the blood stayed warm, and his knees were springing
        beneath him.
But when the pain of the flying arrow has beaten him, then
the rending scavengers begin to feast on him in the mountains
480    and the shaded glen. But some spirit leads that way a dangerous
lion, and the scavengers run in terror, and the lion eats it;
so about wise much-devising Odysseus the Trojans
crowded now, valiant and numerous, but the hero
with rapid play of his spear beat off the pitiless death-day.
485    Now Aias came near him, carrying like a wall his shield,
and stood forth beside him, and the Trojans fled one way and another.
Then taking Odysseus by the hand warlike Menelaos
led him from the battle, while his henchman drove the horses close up.

But Aias leaping upon the Trojans struck down Doryklos,
490    Priam's son, but a bastard, and thereafter stabbed Pandokos,
and so also Lysandros and Pyrasos and Pylartes.
As when a swollen river hurls its water, big with rain,
down the mountains to the flat land following rain from the sky god,

and sweeps down with it numbers of dry oaks and of pine trees
numbers, until it hurls its huge driftwood into the salt sea;                    495
so now glittering Aias cumbered the plain as he chased them,
slaughtering men and horses alike, nor yet had Hektor
heard, since he was fighting at the left of the entire battle
by the banks of Skamandros river, where more than elsewhere
the high heads of men were dropping, and the tireless clamor        500
rising about tall Nestor and Idomeneus the warlike.
Now Hektor was encountering these and doing grim work
with spear and horsemanship, ruining the battalions of young men.
Yet even so the Achaians would not have given from his path
had not Alexandros, the lord of lovely-haired Helen,                    505
stayed from his bravery the shepherd of the people, Machaon,
hitting him with a three-barbed arrow in the right shoulder.
And the Achaians whose wind was fury were frightened for him,
that the enemy might catch him in the backturn of the fighting.
At once Idomeneus called out to brilliant Nestor:                      510
"Nestor, son of Neleus, great glory of the Achaians,
quick, get up on your chariot, let Machaon beside you
mount, and steer your single foot horses to the ships in all speed.
A healer is a man worth many men in his knowledge
of cutting out arrows and putting kindly medicines on wounds."        515
     He spoke, and the Gerenian horseman Nestor obeyed him.
Immediately he mounted the chariot, and Machaon,
son of the great healer Asklepios, mounted beside him.
He lashed on the horses, and they winged their way unreluctant
back toward the hollow ships, since this was the way they desired.    520

     Now Kebriones, who saw how the Trojans were being driven,
and who stood beside Hektor in the chariot, spoke a word to him:
"Hektor, you and I encounter the Danaäns at the utmost
edge of the sorrowful battle, but meanwhile the rest of the Trojans
are driven pell-mell upon each other, the men and their horses.       525
The Telamonian Aias drives them; I know him surely
for he carries the broad shield on his shoulders. So, let us also
steer our horses and chariot that way, since there the horsemen
and the foot-ranks more than elsewhere hurling the wicked war-hate
against each other, are destroying, and the ceaseless clamor has risen."  530

So he spoke, and lashed forward the bright-maned horses
with the singing whip, and they at the feel of the stroke lightly
carried the running chariot among Achaians and Trojans,
trampling down dead men and shields, and the axle under
535  the chariot was all splashed with blood and the rails which encircled
the chariot, struck by flying drops from the feet of the horses,
from the running rims of the wheels. So Hektor was straining to plunge in
the turmoil of men, and charge them and break them. He hurled the
      confusion
of disaster upon the Danaäns, and stayed from the spear's stroke
540  little, but with his spear and his sword and with huge stones flung
ranged about among the ranks of the rest of the fighters
yet kept clear still of the attack of Telamonian Aias.

But Zeus father who sits on high drove fear upon Aias.
He stood stunned, and swung the sevenfold ox-hide shield behind him
545  and drew back, throwing his eyes round the crowd of men, like a wild beast,
turning on his way, shifting knee past knee only a little;
as when the men who live in the wild and their dogs have driven
a tawny lion away from the mid-fenced ground of their oxen,
and will not let him tear out the fat of the oxen, watching
550  nightlong against him, and he in his hunger for meat closes in
but can get nothing of what he wants, for the raining javelins
thrown from the daring hands of the men beat ever against him,
and the flaming torches, and these he balks at for all of his fury
and with the daylight goes away, disappointed of desire;
555  so Aias, disappointed at heart, drew back from the Trojans
much unwilling, but feared for the ships of the Achaians. As when
a donkey, stubborn and hard to move, goes into a cornfield
in despite of boys, and many sticks have been broken upon him,
but he gets in and goes on eating the deep grain, and the children
560  beat him with sticks, but their strength is infantile; yet at last
by hard work they drive him out when he is glutted with eating;
so the high-hearted Trojans and companions in arms gathered
from far places kept after great Aias, the son of Telamon,
stabbing always with their spears at the center of the great shield.
565  And now Aias would remember again his furious valor
and turn upon them, and beat back the battalions of Trojans,

breakers of horses, and then again would turn and run from them.
He blocked them all from making their way on to the fast ships
and himself stood and fought on in the space between the Achaians
and Trojans, and of the spears thrown by the daring hands of the fighters          570
some that were driven forward stuck fast in the great shield, others
and many in the mid space before they had got to his white skin
stood fast in the ground, though they had been straining to reach his body.

     Now as Eurypylos the glorious son of Euaimon
saw how Aias was being overpowered by the dense spears,          575
he came and stood beside him and made a cast with his bright spear
and struck Apisaon, son of Phausias, shepherd of the people,
in the liver under the midriff, and at once took the strength from his knees.
Eurypylos springing forward stripped the armor from his shoulders
but godlike Alexandros watched him as he was stripping          580
the armor of Apisaon, and at once drew his bow, and shot
at Eurypylos, and hit him in the right thigh with the arrow,
and the reed shaft was broken off, and his thigh was heavy with pain.
To avoid death he shrank into the host of his own companions.
He lifted his voice and called in a piercing cry to the Danaäns:          585
"Friends, O leaders and men of counsel among the Argives,
turn again and stand and beat off the pitiless death-day
from Aias, who is being overpowered with spears thrown; and I think
he cannot escape out of this sorrowful battle. Therefore
stand fast and face them around great Aias, the son of Telamon."          590
     So spoke wounded Eurypylos, and the others about him
stood in their numbers and sloped their shields over his shoulders, holding
the spears away, and Aias came back to join them. He turned
and stood, when he had got back to the swarm of his own companions.

     So they fought on in the likeness of blazing fire. And meanwhile          595
the horses of Neleus sweating carried Nestor away from
the fighting, and carried also the shepherd of the people, Machaon.
Now swift-footed brilliant Achilleus saw him and watched him,
for he was standing on the stern of his huge-hollowed vessel
looking out over the sheer war work and the sorrowful onrush.          600
At once he spoke to his own companion in arms, Patroklos,
calling from the ship, and he heard it from inside the shelter, and came out

like the war god, and this was the beginning of his evil.
The strong son of Menoitios spoke first, and addressed him:
605 "What do you wish with me, Achilleus? Why do you call me?"
Then in answer again spoke Achilleus of the swift feet:
"Son of Menoitios, you who delight my heart, O great one,
now I think the Achaians will come to my knees and stay there
in supplication, for a need past endurance has come to them.
610 But go now, Patroklos beloved of Zeus, to Nestor
and ask him who is this wounded man he brings in from the fighting.
Indeed, seeing him from behind I thought he was like Machaon,
Asklepios' son, in all ways, but I got no sight of the man's face
since the horses were tearing forward and swept on by me."
615 So he spoke, and Patroklos obeyed his beloved companion
and went on the run along the shelters and ships of the Achaians.

Now when the others came to the shelter of the son of Neleus,
they themselves dismounted to the prospering earth, and the henchman
Eurymedon unharnessed the horses of the old man
620 from the chariot. The men wiped off the sweat on their tunics
and stood to the wind beside the beach of the sea, and thereafter
went inside the shelter and took their places on settles.
And lovely-haired Hekamede made them a potion, she whom
the old man won from Tenedos, when Achilleus stormed it.
625 She was the daughter of great-hearted Arsinoös. The Achaians
chose her out for Nestor, because he was best of them all in counsel.
First she pushed up the table in front of them, a lovely
table, polished and with feet of cobalt, and on it
she laid a bronze basket, with onion to go with the drinking,
630 and pale honey, and beside it bread, blessed pride of the barley,
and beside it a beautifully wrought cup which the old man brought with him
from home. It was set with golden nails, the eared handles upon it
were four, and on either side there were fashioned two doves
of gold, feeding, and there were double bases beneath it.
635 Another man with great effort could lift it full from the table,
but Nestor, aged as he was, lifted it without strain.
In this the woman like the immortals mixed them a potion
with Pramneian wine, and grated goat's-milk cheese into it
with a bronze grater, and scattered with her hand white barley into it.

When she had got the potion ready, she told them to drink it,                640
and both when they had drunk it were rid of their thirst's parching
and began to take pleasure in conversation, talking with each other,
and Patroklos came and stood, a godlike man, in the doorway.
Seeing him the old man started up from his shining
chair, and took him by the hand, led him in and told him to sit down,        645
but Patroklos from the other side declined, and spoke to him:
"No chair, aged sir beloved of Zeus. You will not persuade me.
Honored, and quick to blame, is the man who sent me to find out
who was this wounded man you were bringing. Now I myself
know, and I see it is Machaon, the shepherd of the people.                   650
Now I go back as messenger to Achilleus, to tell him.
You know yourself, aged sir beloved of Zeus, how *he* is;
a dangerous man; he might even be angry with one who is guiltless."

    Then in turn the Gerenian horseman Nestor answered him:
"Now why is Achilleus being so sorry for the sons of the Achaians            655
who have been wounded with spears thrown, he who knows nothing
of the sorrow that has risen along the host, since the bravest
are lying up among the ships with arrow or spear wounds?
The son of Tydeus, strong Diomedes, was hit by an arrow,
and Odysseus has a pike wound, and Agamemnon the spear-famed,               660
and Eurypylos has been wounded in the thigh with an arrow. And even now
I have brought this other one, Machaon, out of the fighting
hit by an arrow from the bowstring. Meanwhile Achilleus
brave as he is cares nothing for the Danaäns nor pities them.
Is he going to wait then till the running ships by the water                 665
are burned with consuming fire for all the Argives can do, till
we ourselves are killed one after another? Since there is not
any longer in my gnarled limbs the strength that there once was.
If only I were young now, and the strength still steady within me,
as that time when a quarrel was made between us and the Eleians             670
over a driving of cattle, when I myself killed Itymoneus,
the brave son of Hypeirochos who made his home in Elis.
I was driving cattle in reprisal, and he, as he was defending
his oxen, was struck among the foremost by a spear thrown from my hand
and fell, and his people who live in the wild fled in terror about him.     675
And we got and drove off together much spoil from this pastureland:

fifty herds of oxen, as many sheepflocks, as many
droves of pigs, and again as many wide-ranging goatflocks,
and a hundred and fifty brown horses, mares all of them
680 and many with foals following underneath. And all there
we drove inside the keep of Neleian Pylos, making
our way nightwise to the town. And Neleus was glad in his heart
that so much had come my way, who was young to go to the fighting.
And next day as dawn showed the heralds lifted their clear cry
685 for all to come who had anything owed them in shining Elis.
And the men who were chiefs among the Pylians assembling
divided the spoil. There were many to whom the Epeians owed something
since we in Pylos were few and we had been having the worst of it.
For Herakles had come in his strength against us and beaten us
690 in the years before, and all the bravest among us had been killed.
For we who were sons of lordly Neleus had been twelve, and now
I alone was left of these, and all the others had perished,
and grown haughty over this the bronze-armored Epeians
despised and outraged us, and devised wicked actions against us.
695 Now the old man took for himself a herd of cattle and a big flock
of sheep, choosing out three hundred of them along with the shepherds;
for indeed a great debt was owing to him in shining Elis.
It was four horses, race-competitors with their own chariot,
who were on their way to a race and were to run for a tripod,
700 but Augeias the lord of men took these, and kept them
and sent away their driver who was vexed for the sake of the horses.
Now aged Neleus, angry over things said and things done,
took a vast amount for himself, and gave the rest to the people
to divide among them, so none might go away without a just share.

705 So we administered all this spoil, and all through the city
wrought sacrifices to the gods; and on the third day the Epeians
came all against us, numbers of men and single-foot horses
in full haste, and among them were armored the two Moliones,
boys still, not yet altogether skilled in furious fighting.
710 There is a city, Thryoessa, a headlong hill town
far away by the Alpheios at the bottom of sandy Pylos.
They had thrown their encampment about that place, furious to smash it.
But when they had swept the entire plain, Athene came running

to us, a messenger from Olympos by night, and warned us
to arm. It was no hesitant host she assembled in Pylos                            715
but people straining hard toward the battle. Now Neleus would not
let me be armed among them, and had hidden away my horses
because he thought I was not yet skilled in the work of warfare.
Even so I was pre-eminent among our own horsemen
though I went on foot; since thus Athene guided the battle.                       720
There is a river, Minyeïos, which empties its water
in the sea beside Arene. There we waited for the divine Dawn,
we horsemen among the Pylians, and the hordes of the streaming foot-
    soldiers,
and from there having armed in all speed and formed in our armor
we came by broad daylight to the sacred stream of Alpheios.                       725
There we wrought fine sacrifices to Zeus in his great strength
and sacrificed a bull to Alpheios, a bull to Poseidon,
but to Athene of the gray eyes a cow from the herds. Then
we took our dinner along the host in divided watches
and went to sleep, each man in his own armor, by the current                      730
of the river, and meanwhile the high-hearted Epeians
had taken their places around the city, furious to smash it.
But sooner than this there was shown forth a great work of the war god,
for when the sun in his shining lifted above the earth, then
we joined our battle together, with prayers to Zeus and Athene.                   735

    Now when the battle came on between Pylians and Epeians,
I was first to kill a man, and I won his single-foot horses.
It was Moulios the spearman who was son-in-law to Augeias
and had as wife his eldest daughter, fair-haired Agamede
who knew of all the medicines that are grown in the broad earth.                  740
As he came on I threw and hit him with the bronze-headed spear
and he dropped in the dust, whereupon I springing into his chariot
took my place among the champions, as the high-hearted Epeians
fled one way and another in terror when they saw the man fall
who was leader of their horsemen and the best of them all in fighting.            745
Then I charged upon them like a black whirlwind, and overtook
fifty chariots, and for each of the chariots two men
caught the dirt in their teeth beaten down under my spear.
And now I would have killed the young Moliones, scions

750 of Aktor, had not their father who shakes the earth in his wide strength
caught them out of the battle, shrouding them in a thick mist.
Then Zeus gave huge power into the hands of the Pylians,
for we chased them on over the hollow plain, killing
the men themselves, and picking up their magnificent armor
755 until we brought our horses to Bouprasion of the wheatfields
and the Olenian rock, where there is a hill called the hill
of Alesios. There at last Athene turned back our people.
There I killed my last man and left him. There the Achaians
steered back from Bouprasion to Pylos their fast-running horses,
760 and all glorified Zeus among the gods, but among men Nestor.

That was I, among men, if it ever happened. But Achilleus
will enjoy his own valor in loneliness, though I think
he will weep much, too late, when his people are perished from him.
Dear child, surely this was what Menoitios told you
765 that day when he sent you out from Phthia to Agamemnon.
We two, brilliant Odysseus and I, were inside with you
and listened carefully to everything, all that he told you.
For we had come to the strong-established house of Peleus
assembling fighting men all through generous Achaia. We came
770 there, and found the hero Menoitios inside, and you,
Achilleus beside you, and Peleus the aged horseman was burning
the fat thigh pieces of an ox to Zeus who delights in the thunder
in the garth of the courtyard. He was holding a golden beaker
and pouring the bright wine over the burning dedications. You two
775 were over the meat of the ox attending to it, and we came
and stood in the forecourt, and Achilleus sprang up wondering
and took us by the hand and led us in, and told us to sit down,
and set hospitality properly before us, as is the stranger's
right. Now when we had taken our pleasure of eating and drinking
780 I began to talk, and invited you both to come with us,
and you were altogether willing, and your fathers spoke to you.
And Peleus the aged was telling his own son, Achilleus,
to be always best in battle and pre-eminent beyond all others,
but for you, Menoitios, Aktor's son, had this to say to you:
785 'My child, by right of blood Achilleus is higher than you are,
but you are the elder. Yet in strength he is far the greater.

You must speak solid words to him, and give him good counsel,
and point his way. If he listens to you it will be for his own good.'
This is what the old man told you, you have forgotten. Yet even
now you might speak to wise Achilleus, he might be persuaded.          790
Who knows if, with God helping, you might trouble his spirit
by entreaty, since the persuasion of a friend is a strong thing.
But if he is drawing back from some prophecy known in his own heart
and by Zeus' will his honored mother has told him of something,
let him send you out, at least, and the rest of the Myrmidon people    795
follow you, and you may be a light given to the Danaäns.
And let him give you his splendid armor to wear to the fighting,
if perhaps the Trojans might think you are he, and give way
from their attack, and the fighting sons of the Achaians get wind
again after hard work. There is little breathing space in the fighting. 800
You, unwearied, might with a mere cry pile men wearied
back upon their city, and away from the ships and the shelters."

    So he spoke, and stirred the feeling in the breast of Patroklos,
and he went on the run along the ships to the son of Aiakos,
Achilleus. But as Patroklos came in his running to the ships           805
of great Odysseus, where the Achaians had their assembly and dealt out
rights, and where were established their altars to the immortals,
there Eurypylos, who had been wounded in the thigh with an arrow,
met him, the illustrious son of Euaimon, limping
away from the battle, and the watery sweat was running                 810
down his shoulders and face, and from the sore wound dark blood
continued to drip, and yet the will stayed steady within him.
And the strong son of Menoitios looked on him in pity
and was sorrowful over him, and addressed him in winged words:
"Poor wretches, you leaders and men of counsel among the Danaäns,      815
was it your fate then, far from your friends and the land of your fathers,
to glut with your shining fat the running dogs here in Troy land?
But tell me this, my lord Eurypylos grown under God's hand:
will the Achaians somehow be able to hold huge Hektor
or must they now perish beaten down under his spear?"                  820
    Then Eurypylos who was wounded answered him in turn:
"No longer, illustrious Patroklos, can the Achaians
defend themselves, but they will be piled back into their black ships.

For all of these who were before the bravest in battle
825 are lying up among the ships with arrow or spear wounds
under the hands of the Trojans whose strength is forever on the uprise.
But help save me now at least, leading me away to my black ship,
and cut the arrow out of my thigh, wash the dark blood running
out of it with warm water, and put kind medicines on it,
830 good ones, which they say you have been told of by Achilleus,
since Cheiron, most righteous of the Centaurs, told him about them.
As for Machaon and Podaleirios, who are healers,
I think Machaon has got a wound, and is in the shelters
lying there, and himself is in need of a blameless healer,
835 while the other in the plain is standing the bitter attack of the Trojans."
        Then in turn the strong son of Menoitios spoke to him:
"But how shall this be, my lord Eurypylos, how shall we do it?
I am on my way carrying a message to wise Achilleus
given me by Gerenian Nestor, the Achaians' watcher.
840 But even so I will not leave you in your affliction."
        He spoke, and holding the shepherd of the host under the arms led him
to his shelter, and a henchman seeing them spread out some ox-hides,
and Patroklos laid him there and with a knife cut the sharp tearing
arrow out of his thigh, and washed the black blood running from it
845 with warm water, and, pounding it up in his hands, laid on
a bitter root to make pain disappear, one which stayed
all kinds of pain. And the wound dried, and the flow of blood stopped.

# BOOK TWELVE

So within the shelter the warlike son of Menoitios
tended stricken Eurypylos, and meanwhile the Argives
and Trojans fought on in massed battle, nor was the Danaäns'
ditch going to hold them back nor the wide wall above it
they had built for the sake of their ships, and driven a deep ditch          5
about it, and had not given to the gods grand sacrifices
so that it might guard their running ships and their masses
of spoil within it. It had been built in despite of the immortal
gods, and therefore it was not to stand firm for a long time.
So long as Hektor was still alive, and Achilleus was angry,          10
so long as the citadel of lord Priam was a city untaken,
for this time the great wall of the Achaians stood firm. But afterward
when all the bravest among the Trojans had died in the fighting,
and many of the Argives had been beaten down, and some left,
when in the tenth year the city of Priam was taken          15
and the Argives gone in their ships to the beloved land of their fathers,
then at last Poseidon and Apollo took counsel
to wreck the wall, letting loose the strength of rivers upon it,
all the rivers that run to the sea from the mountains of Ida,
Rhesos and Heptaporos, Karesos and Rhodios,          20
Grenikos and Aisepos, and immortal Skamandros,
and Simoeis, where much ox-hide armor and helmets were tumbled
in the river mud, and many of the race of the half-god mortals.
Phoibos Apollo turned the mouths of these waters together
and nine days long threw the flood against the wall, and Zeus rained          25

incessantly, to break the wall faster and wash it seaward.
And the shaker of the earth himself holding in his hands the trident
guided them, and hurled into the waves all the bastions' strengthening
of logs and stones the toiling Achaians had set in position
30   and made all smooth again by the hard-running passage of Helle
and once again piled the great beach under sand, having wrecked
the wall, and turned the rivers again to make their way down
the same channel where before they had run the bright stream of their
     water.

     Thus, afterward, Poseidon and Apollo were minded
35   to put things in place, but at this time battle and clamor were blazing
about the strong-founded wall and the bastion timbers were thundering
as they were struck, as the Argives broken under Zeus' lashing
were crowded back on their hollow ships, and struggled to get clear
in dread of Hektor, the strong one who drove men to thoughts of panic.
40   But Hektor, as he had before, fought on like a whirlwind.
As when among a pack of hounds and huntsmen assembled
a wild boar or lion turns at bay in the strength of his fury,
and the men, closing themselves into a wall about him,
stand up to face him, and cast at him with the volleying spears thrown
45   from their hands, and in spite of this the proud heart feels not
terror, nor turns to run, and it is his own courage that kills him;
and again and again he turns on them trying to break the massed men
and wherever he charges the masses of men break away in front of him;
such was Hektor as he went through the battle and rallied his companions
50   and drove them on to cross over the ditch, but now the fast-footed
horses balked at the edge of the lip, and dared not cross, whinnying
loud, since the ditch in its great width frightened them from it,
being not easy for them to overleap, nor to walk through,
since along the whole length the jut of the overhangs stood
55   on both sides, and the surface of the floor was thickset with pointed
palisades, which the sons of the Achaians had paled there
dense and huge, so as to hold off the rage of attackers.
And a horse straining at the strong-wheeled chariot might not easily
enter there, but the dismounted were strong in their effort.
60   And now Poulydamas stood beside bold Hektor, and spoke to him:
     "Hektor, and other lords of the Trojans and companions in battle,

we are senseless trying to drive our fast-footed horses over
this ditch. It is hard indeed to cross, and sharp stakes are planted
inside it, and across from these the wall of the Achaians.
There, there is no way to get down, no way again to do battle                    65
from horses, for the passage is narrow and I think they must be hurt there.
For now if Zeus who thunders on high in evil intention
toward these is destroying them utterly, sending aid to the Trojans,
this is the way I would wish it, may it happen immediately
that the Achaians be destroyed here forgotten and far from                       70
Argos; but if they turn again and a backrush comes on us
out of the ships, and we are driven against the deep ditch,
then I think no longer could one man to carry a message
get clear to the city, once the Achaians have turned back upon us.
Come then, do as I say, let us all be persuaded; let us                          75
tell our henchmen to check our horses here by the ditch, then
let ourselves, all of us dismounted and armed in our war gear,
follow Hektor in mass formation. As for the Achaians,
they will not hold, if the bonds of death are fastened upon them."

So spoke Poulydamas, and this counsel of safety pleased Hektor.                  80
And at once in all his armor he leapt to the ground from his chariot,
and the rest of the Trojans assembled, not mounted behind their horses,
but all sprang to the ground, when they saw brilliant Hektor had done it.
Then each man gave orders to his own charioteer
to check the horses in good order at the edge of the ditch,                      85
and the fighters formed apart into groups, then closing together
into five well-ordered battalions followed their leaders.

They who went with Hektor and Poulydamas the blameless,
these were most numerous, and bravest, and beyond others furious
to smash the wall and fight their way among the hollow ships,                    90
and Kebriones went with them as third man, while by the chariots
Hektor had left another man, not so good as Kebriones.
Paris led the next group with Alkathoös and Agenor,
and Helenos, with godlike Deïphobos, led the third group,
sons both of Priam, and Asios was with them as third man,                        95
Asios, son of Hyrtakos, whom his tall shining horses
had carried over from Arisbe and beside the river Selleëis.
The leader of the fourth group was the strong son of Anchises,

Aineias, and with him were the two sons of Antenor,
100 Archelochos and Akamas, both skilled in all fighting.
Sarpedon led the far-renowned companions in battle,
and had chosen to go with him Glaukos and warlike Asteropaios
since these seemed to him to be marked out as the bravest
of the rest, after himself, but among all he was pre-eminent.
105 Now when these had closed their wrought ox-hide shields together
they charged straight for the Danaäns, eagerly, with no thought longer
of being held, but rather to hurl themselves on the black ships.

Then the rest of the Trojans and renowned companions in battle
were willing to follow the order of blameless Poulydamas. Only
110 Asios, Hyrtakos' son, lord of men, was unwilling
to leave his horses there and a charioteer to attend them
but kept them with him, and so drove on at the fast-running vessels,
poor fool, who by the ships in the pride of his horses and chariot
was not destined to evade the evil spirits of destruction
115 nor ever to make his way back again to windy Ilion.
Before this the dark-named destiny had shrouded about him
through the spear of Idomeneus, proud son of Deukalion.
For he sent his horses to the left of the ships, where the Achaians
were streaming back from the level ground with horses and chariots,
120 and this way he drove his chariot and horses, and found there
the leaves not yet pushed home in the gates, nor the long door-bar,
but men were holding them wide apart, on the chance of rescuing
some one of their companions running for the ships from the battle.
Of a purpose he steered his horses straight there, and his men followed
125 screaming aloud, since they thought the Achaians no longer
would hold, but that they would be driven back on their dark ships.
Fools! since in the gates they found two men of the bravest,
high-hearted sons of the spear-fighting Lapithai, one
the son of Peirithoös, powerful Polypoites,
130 and one Leonteus, a man like the murderous god of battles.
Now these two, who had taken their place in front of the high gates,
stood there like two oaks who rear their crests in the mountains
and through day upon day stand up to the wind and the rainbeat
since their great roots reach far and are gripped in the ground. So
135 these two, in the confidence of their strength and their hands' work,

stood up to tall Asios advancing upon them, nor gave way.
But these, holding up high the tanned leather of their shields, moved
straight in on the strong-built wall with enormous clamor
around Asios their lord and Iamenos and Orestes,
and Asios' son Adamas, and Oinomaos and Thoön.                    140

      In this time the Lapithai still inside the wall were striving
to stir up the strong-greaved Achaians to defend the vessels,
but among the Danaäns, when they saw the Trojans sweeping
on against the wall, a clamor arose, and they gave way;
and the two bursting through the gates fought on in front of them.    145
They were in the likeness of two wild boars who in the mountains
await a rabble of men and dogs advancing upon them
and as they go tearing slantwise and rip the timber about them
to pieces at the stock, the grinding scream of their teeth sounds
high, until some man hits them with his throw and takes the life from them;   150
such was the grinding scream from the bright bronze covering their chests
struck hard on by spears, for they fought a very strong battle
in the confidence of their own strength and the people above them.
These flung about them with great stones torn from the strong founded
bastions, as they fought in defense of themselves, and the shelters,   155
and the fast-running vessels, so that the flung stones dropped to the ground
like snowflakes which the winds' blast whirling the shadowy clouds
drifts in their abundance along the prospering earth. So
the missiles flung from the hands of Achaians, and Trojans also,
went showering, and the helms and shields massive in the middle   160
crashed hollow underneath the impact of rocks like millstones.
And now Asios, Hyrtakos' son, groaned aloud and beat on
both thighs with his hands, and spoke aloud in his agony:
"Zeus father, now even you are made utterly a lover
of deception. For I never thought the fighting Achaians   165
would be able to hold our strength and our hands invincible.
But they, as wasps quick-bending in the middle, or as bees
will make their homes at the side of the rocky way, and will not
abandon the hollow house they have made, but stand up to
men who come to destroy them, and fight for the sake of their children,   170
so these, though they are only two, are unwilling to give back
from the gates, until they have killed their men, or are taken."

He spoke, but by such talk did not persuade the heart of Zeus
whose desire it was to extend the glory to Hektor.

175     And now at the various gates various men fought each other.
It were too much toil for me, as if I were a god, to tell all this,
for all about the stone wall the inhuman strength of the fire
was rising, and the Argives fought unhappily, yet they must fight
on, to defend their ships. And all the gods who were helpers
180  of the Danaäns in the fighting were dejected in spirit.

    But the Lapithai fought on and closed in the hateful fighting,
and there the son of Peirithoös, powerful Polypoites,
struck Damasos with the spear through the bronze-sided helmet,
and the brazen helmet could not hold, but the bronze spearhead
185  driven on through smashed the bone apart, and the inward
brain was all spattered forth. So he beat him down in his fury.
Then he went on to kill Pylon and Ormenos. Meanwhile
Leonteus, the scion of Ares, struck down Antimachos'
son, Hippomachos, with a spear cast into the war belt
190  and afterward drawing his sharp sword out of the scabbard
made a rush through the crowding men, and struck from close up
Antiphates first, so that he crashed on his back to the ground, then
beat down along the prospering earth Menon and Orestes
and Iamenos, all beaten down in rapid succession.

195     Now as these were stripping their men of the shining armor,
the fighting men following with Poulydamas and Hektor,
who were most numerous, and bravest, and beyond others furious
to smash the wall, and set fire to the vessels, these still
were divided in doubt as they stood there at the ditch's edge.
200  As they were urgent to cross a bird sign had appeared to them,
an eagle, flying high and holding to the left of the people
and carrying in its talons a gigantic snake, blood-colored,
alive still and breathing, it had not forgotten its warcraft
yet, for writhing back it struck the eagle that held it
205  by chest and neck, so that the eagle let it drop groundward
in pain of the bite, and dashed it down in the midst of the battle
and itself, screaming high, winged away down the wind's blast.

And the Trojans shivered with fear as they looked on the lithe snake
lying in their midst, a portent of Zeus of the aegis.
And now Poulydamas stood beside bold Hektor and spoke to him:          210
"Hektor, somehow in assembly you move ever against me
though I speak excellently, since indeed there is no good reason
for you, in your skill, to argue wrong, neither in the councils
nor in the fighting, and ever to be upholding your own cause.
Now once more I will speak out the way it seems best to me.             215
Let us not go on and fight the Danaäns by their ships. I think
it will end as the portent was accomplished, if the bird sign
that came to the Trojans as we were trying to cross was a true one,
an eagle, flying high and holding to the left of the people
and carrying in its talons a gigantic snake, blood-colored,             220
alive, but let it drop suddenly before winning his own home,
and could not finish carrying it back to give to his children.
So we, even though in our great strength we break in the gates
and the wall of the Achaians, and the Achaians give way before us,
we shall not take the same ways back from the ships in good order;      225
since we shall leave many Trojans behind us, whom the Achaians
will cut down with the bronze as they fight for themselves by their vessels.
So an interpreter of the gods would answer, one who knew
in his mind the truth of portents, and whom the people believed in."

        Looking darkly at him tall Hektor of the shining helm answered:  230
"Poulydamas, these things that you argue please me no longer.
Your mind knows how to contrive a saying better than this one.
But if in all seriousness this is your true argument, then
it is the very gods who ruined the brain within you,
you who are telling me to forget the counsels of thunderous             235
Zeus, in which he himself nodded his head to me and assented.
But you: you tell me to put my trust in birds, who spread
wide their wings. I care nothing for these, I think nothing of them,
nor whether they go by on our right against dawn and sunrise
or go by to the left against the glooming mist and the darkness.        240
No, let us put our trust in the counsel of great Zeus, he who
is lord over all mortal men and all the immortals.
One bird sign is best: to fight in defense of our country.
Why are you so afraid of war and hostility? Even

245 though all the rest of us were to be cut down around you
among the Argive ships, you would run no danger of dying
since your heart is not enduring in battle nor a fighter's.
But if you shrink away from the murderous work, or turn back
some other man from the fighting, beguiling him with your arguments,
250 at once beaten down under my spear you will lose your own life."

He spoke, and led the way, and the rest of them came on after him
with unearthly clamor, and over them Zeus who delights in the thunder
drove down from among the hills of Ida the blast of a windstorm
which swept the dust straight against the ships. He was mazing the minds
255 of the Achaians, and giving glory to the Trojans and Hektor,
and they in the confidence of the portents shown, and their own strength,
worked to break down the great wall of the Achaians. They tore
at the projections on the outworks, and broke down the battlements
and shook with levers the jut of the buttresses the Achaians
260 had stuck in the earth on the outer face to shore their defenses.
They tore at these, in hope of breaking down the Achaians'
wall, but now the Danaäns did not give way in front of them,
but they, fencing the battlements with the hides of oxen,
hurled from the wall at the enemy who came on beneath it.

265 The two Aiantes, walking up and down the length of the ramparts,
urged the men on, stirring up the warcraft of the Achaians,
and stung them along, using kind words to one, to another
hard ones, whenever they saw a man hang back from the fighting:
"Dear friends, you who are pre-eminent among the Argives, you who
270 are of middle estate, you who are of low account, since
all of us are not alike in battle, this is work for all now,
and you yourselves can see it. Now let no man let himself
be turned back upon the ships for the sound of their blustering
but keep forever forward calling out courage to each other.
275 So may Olympian Zeus who grips the thunderbolt grant us
a way to the city, when we beat off the attack of our enemies."

Such was their far cry, and they stirred the Achaians' war strength.
And they, as storms of snow descend to the ground incessant
on a winter day, when Zeus of the counsels, showing

before men what shafts he possesses, brings on a snowstorm                    280
and stills the winds asleep in the solid drift, enshrouding
the peaks that tower among the mountains and the shoulders out-jutting,
and the low lands with their grasses, and the prospering work of men's
      hands,
and the drift falls along the gray sea, the harbors and beaches,
and the surf that breaks against it is stilled, and all things elsewhere      285
it shrouds from above, with the burden of Zeus' rain heavy upon it;
so numerous and incessant were the stones volleyed from both sides,
some thrown on Trojans, others flung against the Achaians
by Trojans, so the whole length of the wall thundered beneath them.

    And not even then might the Trojans and glorious Hektor                   290
have broken in the gates of the rampart, and the long door-bar,
had not Zeus of the counsels driven his own son, Sarpedon,
upon the Argives, like a lion among horn-curved cattle.
Presently he held before him the perfect circle of his shield,
a lovely thing of beaten bronze, which the bronze-smith hammered             295
out for him, and on the inward side had stitched ox-hides
in close folds with golden staples clean round the circle.
Holding this shield in front of him, and shaking two spears,
he went onward like some hill-kept lion, who for a long time
has gone lacking meat, and the proud heart is urgent upon him                300
to get inside of a close steading and go for the sheepflocks.
And even though he finds herdsmen in that place, who are watching
about their sheepflocks, armed with spears, and with dogs, even so
he has no thought of being driven from the steading without some attack
      made,
and either makes his spring and seizes a sheep, or else                      305
himself is hit in the first attack by a spear from a swift hand
thrown. So now his spirit drove on godlike Sarpedon
to make a rush at the wall and break apart the battlements.
And now he spoke in address to Glaukos, son of Hippolochos:
"Glaukos, why is it you and I are honored before others                      310
with pride of place, the choice meats and the filled wine cups
in Lykia, and all men look on us as if we were immortals,
and we are appointed a great piece of land by the banks of Xanthos,
good land, orchard and vineyard, and ploughland for the planting of wheat?

315 Therefore it is our duty in the forefront of the Lykians
to take our stand, and bear our part of the blazing of battle,
so that a man of the close-armored Lykians may say of us:
'Indeed, these are no ignoble men who are lords of Lykia,
these kings of ours, who feed upon the fat sheep appointed
320 and drink the exquisite sweet wine, since indeed there is strength
of valor in them, since they fight in the forefront of the Lykians.'
Man, supposing you and I, escaping this battle,
would be able to live on forever, ageless, immortal,
so neither would I myself go on fighting in the foremost
325 nor would I urge you into the fighting where men win glory.
But now, seeing that the spirits of death stand close about us
in their thousands, no man can turn aside nor escape them,
let us go on and win glory for ourselves, or yield it to others."

He spoke, nor did Glaukos disobey him nor turn aside from him.
330 They, leading the great horde of the Lykians, advanced straight onward,
and the son of Peteos, Menestheus, shivered as he saw them
since they came against his bastion and carried disaster upon it.
He scanned the rampart of the Achaians in the hope of seeing
some great chief who could beat back the bane from his company,
335 and saw the two Aiantes, insatiate of battle, standing
on the wall, and Teukros even now coming up from the shelter,
and close by, but he was not able to cry out and make them
hear, so great was the clamor about him as the shouts hit skyward,
as shields were battered with missiles, and the helmets crested with horse-
hair,
340 and the gates, which all had been slammed shut, and the Trojans standing
against them were trying to break them down and force their way in.
At once he sent Thoötes off as a runner to Aias:
"Go on the run, brilliant Thoötes, and call Aias here,
or better, both Aiantes, since that would be far the best thing
345 that could happen, since here headlong destruction is building against us.
Such is the weight of the Lykian lords upon us, who even
before now have shown as deadly men in the strong encounters.
But if in their place also hard work and fury have arisen,
at least let powerful Telamonian Aias come by himself,
350 and let Teukros follow with him, with his craft in the bow's use."

He spoke, nor did the herald disobey when he heard him,
but went on the run along the wall of the bronze-armored Achaians
and came and stood by the two Aiantes, and spoke to them straight out:
"Aiantes, leaders of the bronze-armored Argives: Menestheus,
beloved son of Peteos engendered of Zeus, desires you                    355
to go where he is and meet the danger, if only for a little;
both of you for choice, since that would be far the best thing
that could happen, since there headlong destruction is building against
     him.
Such is the weight of the Lykian lords upon him, who even
before now have shown as deadly men in the strong encounters.            360
But if in this place also hard fighting and fury have arisen,
at least let powerful Telamonian Aias come by himself
and let Teukros follow with him, with his craft in the bow's use."
     He spoke, and huge Telamonian Aias did not disobey him,
but at once called out in winged words to Aias, the son of Oïleus:       365
"Aias, now you two, yourself and strong Lykomedes,
must stand your ground and urge on the Danaäns to fight strongly.
I am going over there to meet the attack, and afterward
I will come back soon, when I have beaten them back from the others."

     So speaking Telamonian Aias went away, and with him                 370
went Teukros, his brother by the same father, and following them
was Pandion, who carried the curved bow for Teukros.
They kept inside the wall as they went, till they came to the bastion
of high-hearted Menestheus, and found men who were hard pressed there,
for the strong lords and men of counsel among the Lykians               375
came on against the battlements like a darkening stormwind,
and they charged forward to fight with these, and the clamor rose high.

     First to kill his man was Telamonian Aias.
It was Sarpedon's companion in arms, high-hearted Epikles,
whom he struck with a great jagged stone, that lay at the inside         380
of the wall, huge, on top of the battlements. A man could not easily
hold it, not even if he were very strong, in both hands,
of men such as men are now, but he heaving it high threw it,
and smashed in the four-sheeted helm, and pounded to pieces
the bones of the head inside it, so that Epikles dropped                 385

like a diver from the high bastion, and the life left his bones.
And Teukros with an arrow struck the strong son of Hippolochos,
Glaukos, as he was swarming aloft the wall's high bastion,
where he saw the arm was bare of defense, and stayed his warcraft;
390  he sprang down from the wall, secretly, for fear some Achaian
might see that he had been hit and vaunt with high words over him.
Sarpedon, as soon as he was aware that Glaukos had gone back,
was downcast, nevertheless he did not forget his warcraft
but striking with his spear at Alkmaon, the son of Thestor,
395  stabbed him, then wrenched the spear out, and he following the spear fell
on his face, and the armor elaborate with bronze clashed about him.
And Sarpedon, grabbing in both ponderous hands the battlements,
pulled, and the whole thing came away in his hands, and the rampart
was stripped defenseless above. He had opened a pathway for many.
400      Aias and Teukros aimed at him together, and Teukros
hit him with an arrow in the shining belt that encircled
his chest to hold the man-covering shield, but Zeus brushed the death spirits
from his son, and would not let him be killed there beside the ships' sterns;
and Aias plunging upon him stabbed at the shield, but the spearhead
405  did not pass clean through. Still, he pounded him back in his fury
so that he gave back a little space from the battlement, and yet not
utterly gave way, since his heart was still hopeful of winning glory.
He whirled about and called aloud to the godlike Lykians:
"Lykians, why do you thus let go of your furious valor?
410  It is a hard thing for me, strong as I am, to break down
the wall, single-handed, and open a path to the vessels.
Come on with me then. This work is better if many do it."

So he spoke, and they, awed at the reproach of their leader,
put on the pressure of more weight around their lord of the counsels.
415  And on the other side the Argives stiffened their battalions
inside the wall, and a huge fight developed between the two sides.
For neither could the powerful Lykians break in the rampart
of the Danaäns, and so open a path through to the vessels,
nor had the Danaän spearmen strength to push back the Lykians
420  from the rampart, once they had won to a place close under it;
but as two men with measuring ropes in their hands fight bitterly
about a boundary line at the meeting place of two cornfields,

and the two of them fight in the strait place over the rights of division,
so the battlements held these armies apart, and across them
they hewed at each other, and at the ox-hide shields strong-circled          425
guarding men's chests, and at the fluttering straps of the guard-skins.
Many were torn in their white flesh by the bronze without pity
wherever one of the fighters turning aside laid bare
his back, and many were struck with the spear carried clean through the
    shield.
Everywhere the battlements and the bastions were awash               430
with men's blood shed from both sides, Achaian and Trojan.
But even so they could not drive panic among the Achaians,
but held evenly as the scales which a careful widow
holds, taking it by the balance beam, and weighs her wool evenly
at either end, working to win a pitiful wage for her children:          435
so the battles fought by both sides were pulled fast and even
until that time when Zeus gave the greater glory to Hektor,
Priam's son, who was first to break into the wall of the Achaians.
For he lifted his voice and called in a piercing cry to the Trojans:
"Rise up, Trojans, breakers of horses, and wreck the ramparts          440
of the Argives, and let loose the inhuman fire on their vessels."

    So he spoke, driving them on, and they all gave ear to him
and steered against the wall in a pack, and at once gripping
still their edged spears caught and swarmed up the wall's projections.
Meanwhile Hektor snatched up a stone that stood before the gates          445
and carried it along; it was blunt-massed at the base, but the upper
end was sharp; two men, the best in all a community,
could not easily hoist it up from the ground to a wagon,
of men such as men are now, but he alone lifted and shook it
as the son of devious-devising Kronos made it light for him.          450
As when a shepherd easily carries the fleece of a wether,
picking it up with one hand, and little is the burden weighting him,
so Hektor lifting the stone carried it straight for the door leaves
which filled the gateway ponderously close-fitted together.
These were high and twofold, and double door-bars on the inside          455
overlapping each other closed it, and a single pin-bolt secured them.
He came and stood very close and taking a strong wide stance threw
at the middle, leaning into the throw, that the cast might not lack

force, and smashed the hinges at either side, and the stone crashed
460 ponderously in, and the gates groaned deep, and the door-bars
could not hold, but the leaves were smashed to a wreckage of splinters
under the stone's impact. Then glorious Hektor burst in
with dark face like sudden night, but he shone with the ghastly
glitter of bronze that girded his skin, and carried two spears
465 in his hands. No one could have stood up against him, and stopped him,
except the gods, when he burst in the gates; and his eyes flashed fire.
Whirling, he called out across the battle to the Trojans
to climb over the wall, and they obeyed his urgency.
Immediately some swarmed over the wall, while others swept in
470 through the wrought gateways, and the Danaäns scattered in terror
among their hollow ships, and clamor incessant rose up.

# BOOK THIRTEEN

When Zeus had driven against the ships the Trojans and Hektor,
he left them beside these to endure the hard work and sorrow
of fighting without respite, and himself turned his eyes shining
far away, looking out over the land of the Thracian riders
and the Mysians who fight at close quarters, and the proud Hippomolgoi,   5
drinkers of milk, and the Abioi, most righteous of all men.
He did not at all now turn his shining eyes upon Troy land
for he had no idea in mind that any one of the immortals
would come down to stand by either Danaäns or Trojans.

Neither did the powerful shaker of the earth keep blind watch;                   10
for he sat and admired the fighting and the run of the battle,
aloft on top of the highest summit of timbered Samos,
the Thracian place; and from there all Ida appeared before him,
and the city of Priam was plain to see, and the ships of the Achaians.
There he came up out of the water, and sat, and pitied the Achaians             15
who were beaten by the Trojans, and blamed Zeus for it in bitterness.
So presently he came down from the craggy mountain, striding
on rapid feet, and the tall mountains trembled and the timber
under the immortal feet of Poseidon's progress.
He took three long strides forward, and in the fourth came to his goal,         20
Aigai, where his glorious house was built in the waters'
depth, glittering with gold, imperishable forever.
Going there he harnessed under his chariot his bronze-shod horses,
flying-footed, with long manes streaming of gold; and he put on
clothing of gold about his own body, and took up the golden                       25

lash, carefully compacted, and climbed up into his chariot
and drove it across the waves. And about him the sea beasts came up
from their deep places and played in his path, and acknowledged their
     master,
and the sea stood apart before him, rejoicing. The horses winged on
30 delicately, and the bronze axle beneath was not wetted.
The fast-running horses carried him to the ships of the Achaians.
     There is a cave, broad and deep down in the gloom of the water,
lying midway between Tenedos and Imbros of the high cliffs.
There Poseidon the shaker of the earth reined in his horses,
35 and slipped them from the yoke, and threw fodder immortal before them
so they could eat, and threw around their feet golden hobbles
not to be broken or slipped from, so they would wait there steadfast
for their lord gone. And Poseidon went to the ships of the Achaians.

     But the Trojans, gathered into a pack, like flame, like a stormcloud,
40 came on after Hektor the son of Priam, raging relentless,
roaring and crying as one, and their hopes ran high of capturing
the ships of the Achaians, and killing the best men beside them,
all of them. But Poseidon who circles the earth and shakes it
rose up out of the deep water to stir on the Argives,
45 likening himself in form and weariless voice to Kalchas.
First he spoke to the Aiantes, who were burning for battle already:
"Aiantes, you two, remembering the spirit of warcraft
and not that of shivering panic, must save the Achaian people.
Elsewhere in truth I do not fear the Trojans' invincible
50 hands, though in full force they have swarmed over our great wall;
since the strong-greaved Achaians will be able to hold the rest of them.
But I fear most terribly disaster to us in the one place
where that berserk flamelike leads them against us, Hektor,
who claims he must be son of Zeus of the high strength. May this
55 be the message some one of the gods gives your minds to carry,
that you stand fast strongly yourselves, urge the rest to stand also.
Thus, hard though he sweeps on, you might stay him beside the fast-running
ships, even though the very Olympian wakes him to battle."
     Poseidon who circles the earth and shakes it spoke, and striking
60 both of them with his staff filled them with powerful valor,
and he made their limbs light, and their feet, and their hands above them,

and burst into winged flight himself, like a hawk with quick wings
who from the huge height of an impassable rock lifting
leans to flight to pursue some other bird over the wide land;
so Poseidon shaker of the earth broke away from the Aiantes.                          65
And of the two swift Aias son of Oïleus was first
to know him, and spoke therewith to Aias the son of Telamon;
"Aias, since some one of the gods, whose hold is Olympos,
has likened himself to the seer, and told us to fight by our vessels,
this is not Kalchas, the bird interpreter of the gods, for I knew                      70
easily as he went away the form of his feet, the legs' form
from behind him. Gods, though gods, are conspicuous. Therefore
as for me, the spirit inside my inward breast drives me
all the harder to carry on the war and the fighting,
and my feet underneath me are eager and my hands above them."                          75
    Aias the son of Telamon spoke to him in answer:
"So for me also now the invincible hands on my spearshaft
are furious, my strength is rising, and both feet beneath me
are sweeping me onward, so that I long even for single combat
with Hektor, Priam's son, the forever avid of battle."                                80

    Now as these two were saying such things to each other, joyful
in the delight of battle the god had put into their spirits,
meanwhile the earth-encircler stirred up the Achaians behind them
who were cooling the heat of the inward heart back beside their vessels,
for their very limbs were broken with weariness of hard work, and also                 85
discouragement of the heart came over them, as they watched
the Trojans, and how in a mass they had overswarmed the great wall.
As they saw them the tears dripped from their eyes; they did not
think they could win clear of the evil, but the earth-shaker
lightly turning their battalions to strength drove them onward.                        90
He came first in encouragement to Teukros and Leïtos,
with the fighting Peneleos, and Deïpyros and Thoas,
to Meriones and Antilochos, both urgent for battle.
Calling out to these in winged words he rallied them onward:
"Shame, you Argives, young fighting men, since I for my part                           95
have confidence that by fighting you can save our ships from destruction;
but if you yourselves are to go slack from the sorrowful fighting
now is seen your day to be beaten down by the Trojans.

Oh for shame! Here is a great strange thing I see with my own eyes,
100 a terrible thing, and one that I thought never could happen,
that the Trojans could come against our ships, they who in time past
were like fugitive deer before us, who in the forests
are spoil for scavengers and wolves and leopards, who scatter
in absolute cowardice, there is no war spirit within them.
105 So before now the Trojans were unwilling to stand up
against the strength and hands of the Achaians, even for a little,
but now far from their city they fight by the hollow vessels
through the weakness of our leader, and the hanging back of our people
who have made their quarrel with him, and will not stand in defense
110 of the fast-running ships. Instead of this they are killed against them.
Yet even though it be utterly true that the son of Atreus
the hero wide-powerful Agamemnon is guilty
because he did dishonor to Peleus' son, the swift-footed,
still there is no way for us now to hang back from the fighting.
115 No, sooner let us heal it, for the hearts of great men can be healed.
But you can no longer in honor give way from your fighting valor
being all the best men along the host. Even I, for my part,
would not quarrel with any man who hung back from the fighting
because he was a weak thing, but with you my heart must be angry.
120 O friends, soon you will bring to pass some still greater evil
with this hanging back. Let every one of you plant in his heart's depth
discipline and shamefastness. A big battle rises against you.
For Hektor of the great war cry is fighting beside our vessels
in his power, and has broken our gates and the long door-bar."

125     So urging them on the earth-encircler stirred up the Achaians,
and their battalions formed in strength about the two Aiantes,
battalions the war god could not find fault with, coming among them,
nor Athene lady of storming armies, since there the bravest
formed apart and stood against the Trojans and brilliant Hektor
130 locking spear by spear, shield against shield at the base, so buckler
leaned on buckler, helmet on helmet, man against man,
and the horse-hair crests along the horns of their shining helmets
touched as they bent their heads, so dense were they formed on each other,
and the spears shaken from their daring hands made a jagged battle line.
135 Their thoughts were driving straight ahead in the fury of fighting.

The Trojans came down on them in a pack, and Hektor led them
raging straight forward, like a great rolling stone from a rock face
that a river swollen with winter rain has wrenched from its socket
and with immense washing broken the hold of the unwilling rock face;
the springing boulder flies on, and the forest thunders beneath it;          140
and the stone runs unwavering on a strong course, till it reaches
the flat land, then rolls no longer for all its onrush;
so Hektor for a while threatened lightly to break through
the shelters and ships of the Achaians and reach the water
cutting his way. But when he collided with the dense battalions          145
he was stopped, hard, beaten in on himself. The sons of the Achaians
against him stabbing at him with swords and leaf-headed spears
thrust him away from them so that he gave ground backward, staggering.
He lifted his voice and called in a piercing cry to the Trojans:
"Trojans, Lykians, Dardanians who fight at close quarters,          150
stand with me. The Achaians will not hold me back for a long time
for all they are building themselves into a bastion against me.
No, I think they will give back under my spear, if truly
I am driven by the greatest of gods, the thunderous lord of Hera."
    So he spoke, and stirred the spirit and strength in each man.          155
Among them Deïphobos in high purpose had come striding,
Priam's son, who held the perfect circle of his shield before him,
moving lightly on his feet as he walked in the shield's protection.
Meriones aimed at him with the shining spear, and threw it
nor missed his mark, but struck the shield on its perfect circle          160
of bull's hide, but the spear did not get through, but sooner
the long shaft was broken behind the head. Deïphobos
held the bull's-hide shield away from him, his heart frightened
by the spear of wise Meriones, but that hero drew back
into the host of his own companions, deeply angered          165
for two things, the broken spear and the loss of his battle,
and went away back to the shelters and ships of the Achaians
to bring back a long spear that was left behind in his shelter.

    But the rest fought on with clamor incessant rising about them.
Teukros, son of Telamon, was the first to kill his man, Imbrios          170
the spearfighter, son of Mentor of the many horses, one who
before the coming of the sons of the Achaians lived in Pedaios

and had married a bastard daughter of Priam, Medesikaste.
But when the oarswept ships of the Danaäns came, he went back
175   to Ilion, and was a great man among the Trojans, and lived
at Priam's side, who honored him as he did his own children.
Now the son of Telamon with the long spear stabbed him under
the ear, and wrenched the spear out again, and he dropped like an ash tree
which, on the crest of a mountain glittering far about, cut down
180   with the bronze axe scatters on the ground its delicate leafage;
so he dropped, and the armor elaborate with bronze clashed
about him, and Teukros ran up, eager to strip the armor.
As he came on Hektor threw at him with the shining javelin,
but Teukros with his eyes straight on him avoided the bronze spear
185   by a little, and Hektor struck Amphimachos, son of Aktorian
Kteatos, with a spear in his chest as he swept into battle.
He fell, thunderously, and his armor clattered upon him.
Then Hektor charged in to tear the helm of great-hearted Amphimachos
from his head where it fitted close on the brows, but Aias
190   thrust with the shining spear at Hektor as he came onward;
he could not manage to reach the skin, since this was all shrouded
in the ghastly bronze, but drove at the shield's mass in the middle
and beat him back in great strength so that Hektor gave ground backward
from both corpses. These the Achaians dragged out of the fighting.
195   Then Stichios and brilliant Menestheus, lords of the Athenians,
carried Amphimachos back among the Achaian people.
But the two Aiantes in the fury of their fierce war strength,
as two lions catch up a goat from the guard of rip-fanged
hounds, and carry it into the density of the underbrush,
200   holding it high from the ground in the crook of their jaws, so the lordly
two Aiantes lifted Imbrios high and stripped him
of his armor, and the son of Oïleus, in anger
for Amphimachos, hewed away his head from the soft neck
and threw it spinning like a ball through the throng of fighters
205   until it came to rest in the dust at the feet of Hektor.

Then Poseidon was angered about the heart at his grandson's
slaying in the bitter hostility, so the god went forth
on his way among the shelters and ships of the Achaians
and stirred the Danaäns, and worked disaster against the Trojans.

Idomeneus the spear-famed encountered him, on his way                    210
from a companion, who had just before come back from the fighting
wounded in the hollow behind the knee by the sharp bronze.
This man his companions carried away. Idomeneus had given
the healers instructions and gone on to his shelter, still burning
to face the battle, and now the strong earth-shaker spoke to him.        215
Poseidon likened his voice to Thoas, son of Andraimon,
lord of the Aitolians over all Pleuron, and headlong
Kalydon, who was honored in his countryside as a god is:
"Idomeneus, lord of the Kretans' councils, where are those threats you gave
now, that the sons of the Achaians uttered against the Trojans?"         220
    Then Idomeneus lord of the Kretans answered him in turn:
"Thoas, no man is responsible for this, so far as
my thought goes, since all of us understand how to wage war.
It is not that heartless fear holds anyone, that a man yielding
to dread emerges out of the evil fighting, but rather                    225
this way must be pleasurable to Kronos' son in his great strength,
that the Achaians must die here forgotten, and far from Argos.
Since you, Thoas, have been before this a man stubborn in battle
and stirred up another whenever you saw one hang back, so now
also do not give up, and urge on each man as you find him."              230
    Then in answer spoke the shaker of the earth, Poseidon:
"Idomeneus, may that man who this day willfully hangs back
from the fighting never win home again out of Troy land,
but stay here and be made dogs' delight for their feasting. Come then,
take up your armor and go with me. We must speed this action             235
together, since we, being two, might bring some advantage.
The warcraft even of sad fighters combined turns courage,
and you and I would have skill to fight even against good men."

    So he spoke and strode on, a god, through the mortals' struggle.
Idomeneus, when he came back to his strong-built shelter,                240
drew his splendid armor over his body, and caught up two spears,
and went on his way, as a thunderbolt, which the son of Kronos
catching up in his hand shakes from the shining edge of Olympos,
flashes as a portent to men and the bright glints shine from it.
Such was the glitter of bronze that girt his chest in his running.       245
Close to his shelter there encountered him his strong henchman,

Meriones, who was on his way to pick up a bronze spear
and bring it back. Idomeneus in his strength spoke to him:
"Meriones, son of Molos, swift-footed, dearest beloved
250   companion, why have you come back and left the battle and fighting?
Have you been hit somewhere? Does pain of a spear's head afflict you?
Have you come back with someone's message for me? For my part
my desire is to fight, not sit away in the shelters."
        Meriones, a thoughtful man, spoke to him in answer:
255   "Idomeneus, lord of the counsels of the bronze-armored Kretans,
I am on my way to bring back a spear, if you have any
left in your shelter. I broke just now the one I was carrying
with a throw made against the shield of haughty Deïphobos."
        Then Idomeneus lord of the Kretans answered him in turn:
260   "You will find one spear, and twenty spears, if you want them,
standing against the shining inward wall in my shelter,
Trojan spears I win from men that I kill, for my way
is not to fight my battles standing far away from my enemies.
Thereby I have spears there, and shields massive in the middle,
265   and helms and corselets are there in all the pride of their shining."
        Meriones, a thoughtful man, spoke to him in answer:
"For me also, beside my shelter and beside my black ship,
there are many spoils of the Trojans, but not near for me to get them.
For I tell you, neither am I one who has forgotten his war strength
270   but among the foremost, along the fighting where men win glory,
I take my stand, whenever the quarrel of battle arises.
Let my fighting be forgotten by some other bronze-armored
Achaian. You are the very one I think must know of it."
        Then Idomeneus lord of the Kretans answered him in turn:
275   "I know your valor and what you are. Why need you speak of it?
If now beside the ships all the best of us were to assemble
for a hidden position, and there man's courage is best decided,
where the man who is a coward and the brave man show themselves clearly:
the skin of the coward changes color one way and another,
280   and the heart inside him has no control to make him sit steady,
but he shifts his weight from one foot to another, then settles firmly
on both feet, and the heart inside his chest pounds violent
as he thinks of the death spirits, and his teeth chatter together:
but the brave man's skin will not change color, nor is he too much

frightened, once he has taken his place in the hidden position,                         285
but his prayer is to close as soon as may be in bitter division:
and there no man could make light of your battle strength or your hand's
    work.
Even were you to be wounded in your work with spearcast or spear-stroke,
the weapon would not strike behind your neck, nor in your back,
but would be driven straight against the chest or the belly                              290
as you made your way onward through the meeting of champions.
But come, let us no longer stand here talking of these things
like children, for fear some man may arrogantly scold us.
Go to my shelter and choose for yourself a heavy spear."

    So he spoke; Meriones, a match for the rapid war god,                               295
went into the shelter rapidly, and took up a bronze spear,
and with his mind deeply set on battle followed Idomeneus.
As manslaughtering Ares is when he strides into battle
and Terror goes on beside him, his beloved son, the powerful
and dauntless, who frightens even the patient-hearted warrior:                          300
these two come out of Thrace to encounter in arms the Ephyroi
or the great-hearted Phlegyes, but the two will not listen to prayers
from both sides, but give the glory to one side or the other:
such were Meriones and Idomeneus, leaders of armies,
as they went on into the fighting helmed in the bright bronze.                          305
First of the two, Meriones, spoke his word to Idomeneus:
"Deukalides, where are you minded to enter the battle?
Would it be on the right of the whole array, or in the center,
or to the left? Since I think that nowhere else in the fighting
are the flowing-haired Achaians overmatched so badly."                                  310
    Idomeneus lord of the Kretans answered him in turn:
"There are others beside us to defend the ships in the center,
the two Aiantes, and Teukros, best of all the Achaians
in archery, and a good man in the close of standing combat.
They can give Hektor, Priam's son, enough hard hitting,                                 315
even though he is very strong, and sweeps hard into battle.
Furious though he is for fighting, it will be very steep work
for him to win through their irresistible hands and their war strength
and fire the ships, unless the son of Kronos in person
should hurl the blazing firebrand into our fast-running vessels.                        320

Nor would huge Telamonian Aias give way to any man,
one who was mortal and ate bread, the yield of Demeter,
one who could be broken by the bronze and great stones flung at him.
He would not make way for Achilleus who breaks men in battle,
325 in close combat. For speed of feet none can strive with Achilleus.
Hold, as you say, for the left of the army, and thus soonest
shall we see whether we win glory or give it to others."

He spoke, and Meriones, a match for the running war god,
led the way, till they came to the place in the army he spoke for.

330 These, as they saw Idomeneus like a flame in his valor
himself and his henchman with him in their elaborate war gear,
they called out across the battle and gathered about him,
and an indiscriminate fight rose up by the sterns of the vessels.
And as when under the screaming winds the whirlstorms bluster
335 on that day when the dust lies deepest along the pathways
and the winds in the confusion of dust uplift a great cloud,
such was their indiscriminate battle, and their hearts were furious
to slaughter each other with the sharp bronze through the press of the
    fighting.

The battle where men perish shuddered now with the long
340 man-tearing spears they held in their hands, their eyes were blinded
in the dazzle of the bronze light from the glittering helmets,
from the burnished corselets and the shining shields as men came on
in confusion. That man would have to be very bold-hearted
who could be cheerful and not stricken looking on that struggle.
345 Two powerful sons of Kronos, hearts divided against each other,
were wreaking bitter agonies on the fighting warriors,
since Zeus willed the victory for the Trojans and Hektor,
glorifying swift-footed Achilleus, yet not utterly
did he wish the Achaian people to be destroyed before Ilion,
350 but only was giving glory to Thetis and her strong-spirited
son, while Poseidon emerging unseen from the gray salt water
went among the Argives and stirred them, since he was angered
that they were beaten by the Trojans and blamed Zeus for it bitterly.
Indeed, the two were of one generation and a single father,
355 but Zeus was the elder born and knew more. Therefore Poseidon

shrank from openly defending them, but secretly
in a man's likeness was forever stirring them up through the army.
So these two had looped over both sides a crossing
cable of strong discord and the closing of battle, not to be
slipped, not to be broken, which unstrung the knees of many.                360

There Idomeneus, graying though he was, called on the Danaäns
and charged in upon the Trojans and drove panic among them
for he killed Othryoneus, a man who had lived in Kabesos,
who was newly come in the wake of the rumor of war, and had asked
Priam for the hand of the loveliest of his daughters,                       365
Kassandra, without bride price, but had promised a great work for her,
to drive back the unwilling sons of the Achaians from Troy land,
and aged Priam had bent his head in assent, and promised
to give her, so Othryoneus fought in the faith of his promises.
Idomeneus aimed at him with the shining spear, and threw it,              370
and hit him as he came onward with high stride, and the corselet
of bronze he wore could not hold, the spear fixed in the middle belly.
He fell, thunderously, and Idomeneus vaunting cried out:
"Othryoneus, I congratulate you beyond all others
if it is here that you will bring to pass what you promised                  375
to Dardanian Priam, who in turn promised you his daughter.
See now, we also would make you a promise, and we would fulfill it;
we would give you the loveliest of Atreides' daughters,
and bring her here from Argos to be your wife, if you joined us
and helped us storm the strong-founded city of Ilion.                       380
Come then with me, so we can meet by our seafaring vessels
about a marriage; we here are not bad matchmakers for you."
The hero Idomeneus spoke and dragged him through the strong
    encounter
caught by the foot, but now Asios came to stand by him
dismounted, ahead of his horses whom his henchman held ever behind him   385
so that they breathed on his shoulders. He was striving in all his fury
to strike Idomeneus, but he, too quick with a spearcast,
struck him in the gorge underneath the chin, and drove the bronze clean
    through.
He fell, as when an oak goes down or a white poplar
or like a towering pine tree which in the mountains the carpenters          390

have hewn down with their whetted axes to make a ship timber.
So he lay there felled in front of his horses and chariot,
roaring, and clawed with his hands at the bloody dust. Meanwhile
the charioteer who was close behind him was stricken in the wits
395  and shrinking from the hands of the enemy did not have daring
to turn the horses about, but Antilochos stubborn in battle
pinned him through the middle with a spearstroke, and the corselet
of bronze he wore could not hold, the spear fixed in the middle belly,
so that he tumbled, gasping, out of the strong-wrought chariot.
400  But for the horses, Antilochos, son of great-hearted Nestor,
drove them away from the Trojans among the strong-greaved Achaians.

Deïphobos in sorrow for Asios now came close
in on Idomeneus, and with the bright spear made a cast at him,
but Idomeneus with his eyes straight on him avoided the bronze spear
405  since also he was hidden beneath his shield's perfect circle, that shield
he carried, hooped in circles of glaring bronze, and the skins
of oxen, fitted with double cross-stays. He was all gathered
together under this, and the brazen spear shot over him
and the shield gave out a hollow clash as the spear glanced from it.
410  Yet Deïphobos made no utterly vain cast from his strong hand,
but struck Hypsenor, son of Hippasos, shepherd of the people,
in the liver under the midriff, and at once took the strength from his knees.
And Deïphobos vaunted terribly over him, calling in a great voice:
"Asios lies not now all unavenged. I think rather
415  as he goes down to Hades of the Gates, the strong one,
he will be cheerful at heart, since I have sent him an escort."
He spoke, and sorrow came over the Argives at his vaunting,
and beyond others stirred the spirit in wise Antilochos,
yet sorrowful though he was he did not forget his companion
420  but running stood and bestrode him and covered him under the great
shield.
Thereon Mekisteus, son of Echios, and brilliant Alastor,
two staunch companions, stooping beneath it, caught up Hypsenor,
and carried him, groaning heavily, to the hollow vessels.

Idomeneus did not slacken his great fury, but always
425  was straining to shroud some one of the Trojans in dark night

or go down crashing himself as he fought the bane from the Achaians.
There was a man, loved son of illustrious Aisyetes,
the hero Alkathoös, who was son-in-law of Anchises,
and had married the eldest of his daughters, Hippodameia,
dear to the hearts of her father and the lady her mother                    430
in the great house, since she surpassed all the girls of her own age
for beauty and accomplishments and wit; for which reason
the man married her who was the best in the wide Troad.
But now Poseidon beat him down at the hands of Idomeneus,
for he bewitched his shining eyes, made moveless his bright limbs,          435
so that he could not run backward, neither evade him,
but stood like a statue or a tree with leaves towering
motionless, while fighting Idomeneus stabbed at the middle
of his chest with the spear, and broke the bronze armor about him
which in time before had guarded his body from destruction.                 440
He cried out then, a great cry, broken, the spear in him,
and fell, thunderously, and the spear in his heart was stuck fast
but the heart was panting still and beating to shake the butt end
of the spear. Then and there Ares the huge took his life away from him.
Idomeneus vaunted terribly over him, calling in a great voice:             445
"Deïphobos, are we then to call this a worthy bargain,
three men killed for one? It was you yourself were so boastful.
Strange man. Do you rather come yourself and stand up against me
so you can see what I am like, Zeus' seed, come here to face you.
Since Zeus first got by Krete Minos, who cared for his people,              450
and to Minos in turn was born a blameless son, Deukalion,
and Deukalion sired me to be lord over many people
in wide Krete, and now my ships have brought me to this place
to be an evil for you and your father and the rest of the Trojans."
    So he spoke, and the heart in Deïphobos was divided,                   455
pondering whether to draw back and find some other high-hearted
Trojan to be his companion, or whether to attempt him singly.
And in the division of his heart this way seemed best to him,
to go for Aineias. He found him at the uttermost edge of the battle
standing, since he was forever angry with brilliant Priam                   460
because great as he was he did him no honor among his people.
Deïphobos came and stood close to him and addressed him in winged
    words:

"Aineias, lord of the Trojans' counsels, now there is need of you
to stand by your brother-in-law, if this bond of kinship touches you.
465 Come then, stand by Alkathoös, who was your sister's husband
and in time past nursed you in his house when you were still little.
But now Idomeneus the spear-famed has killed him in battle."

So he spoke, and stirred the anger in the breast of Aineias.
He went against Idomeneus, strongly eager for battle,
470 yet no fear gripped Idomeneus as if he were a stripling,
but he stood his ground like a mountain wild boar who in the confidence
of his strength stands up to a great rabble of men advancing
upon him in some deserted place, and bristles his back up,
and both his eyes are shining with fire; he grinds his teeth
475 in his fury to fight off the dogs and the men. So
spear-famed Idomeneus held his ground, and would not give way
to Aineias coming against him, but bellowed to his companions,
looking to Askalaphos, and Aphareus, and Deïpyros,
at Meriones and Antilochos, both urgent for battle,
480 and stirring all these forward called out to them in winged words:
"This way, friends, stand by me, I am alone, and terribly
I fear the attack of swift-footed Aineias advancing upon me,
powerful as he is for the slaying of men in battle.
Likewise the flower of youth is his, where man's strength is highest,
485 since were we two of the same age, and in this same spirit,
soon he would win me in a great battle, or I would win him."
So he spoke, and all these, a single spirit within them,
came and stood in their numbers and sloped their shields over his shoulders,
and Aineias on the other side called to his own companions,
490 looking to Deïphobos, and Paris, and brilliant Agenor
who were lords of the Trojans along with him, and the people after them
followed on, as when the sheep follow the lead-ram
as they leave the pasture to drink, and make proud the heart of the shepherd,
and thus also the heart of Aineias was gladdened within him
495 as he saw the swarm of the host following his own leadership.

These then drove on in close combat about Alkathoös
with long spears, and the bronze girding the chests of the fighters
clashed horribly to the spears they threw in the press at each other,

and two men, for warcraft pre-eminent beyond the others,
Aineias and Idomeneus, both men like the war god,                          500
were straining with the pitiless bronze to tear at each other.
Aineias was first with a spear cast at Idomeneus,
but he, keeping his eyes straight on him, avoided the bronze spear,
so that the vibrant shaft of Aineias was driven groundward
since it had been thrown in a vain cast from his big hand.                   505
But Idomeneus hit Oinomaos in the middle belly
and broke the hollow of the corselet, so that the entrails spurted
from the bronze, and he fell clawing the dust in his fingers.
Idomeneus wrenched out the far-shadowing spear from his body
but had no power to strip the rest of his splendid armor                     510
away from his shoulders, since he was beaten back by their missiles,
and no longer in an outrush could his limbs stay steady beneath him
either to dash in after his spear, or to get clear again.
So in close-standing fight he beat off the pitiless death-day
as his feet no longer quick to run took him out of the fighting.            515
As he backed slowly Deïphobos made a cast with the shining
spear, since he held a fixed hatred forever against him,
but missed him yet once again and struck down with the spear the war god's
son Askalaphos, so that the powerful spear was driven
through his shoulder, and he dropping in the dust clawed the ground in        520
      his fingers.
But Ares the huge and bellowing had yet heard nothing
of how his son had fallen there in the strong encounter
but he, sheltered under the golden clouds on utmost Olympos,
was sitting, held fast by command of Zeus, where the rest also
of the immortal gods were sitting still, in restraint from the battle.       525

      But the men drove on in close combat about Askalaphos.
Deïphobos tore from Askalaphos the shining helmet;
but now Meriones, a match for the running war god,
plunging upon him stabbed his arm with the spear, and the hollow-eyed
helmet dropped from his hand and fell to the ground clashing.               530
Meriones in yet another swoop like a vulture
plucked out the heavy spear from the arm's base at the shoulder,
then shrank into the host of his own companions. Polites,
Deïphobos' brother, caught him about the waist with both arms

535 and got him out of the sorrowful fighting, and reached his fast-footed
horses, where they stood to the rear of the fighting and the battle
holding their charioteer and the elaborate chariot,
and these carried him, groaning heavily, back to the city
in pain, since the blood was running from his arm's fresh wound.

540     But the rest fought on with clamor incessant rising about them.
There Aineias lunging at Aphareus, the son of Kaletor,
struck him with the sharp spear in the throat where it was turned toward
        him.
His head bent over to one side, and his shield tumbled,
and the helm, and death breaking the spirit drifted about him.
545 Antilochos, watching Thoön as he turned about, dashed in on him
and slashed at him, and shore away the entire vein
which runs all the way up the back till it reaches the neck. This
he shore away entire, so he sprawled in the dust backward,
reaching out both hands to his beloved companions.
550 Antilochos rushed on him, trying to strip the armor
from his shoulders, but watchful, as the Trojans gathered about him
from all sides, and beat at the shining broad shield, but could not
get within it and tear with the pitiless bronze Antilochos'
tender flesh, for about him the earth-shaker Poseidon
555 guarded the son of Nestor even in the swarm of missiles.
Since he was not making his way back clear of the enemy,
but would turn to face them nor held motionless his spear, always
it was shaken or driven forward, the desire in his heart forever
to strike someone with a spearcast or drive at him in close combat.
560     Adamas, Asios' son, was not blind to how he kept aiming
with his spear in the battle, and charging close stabbed with the sharp
        bronze
at the shield's middle, but Poseidon the dark-haired made void
his spear's stroke, nor would let him win the life of Antilochos,
and half of the spear was stuck fast like a stake fire-hardened
565 in Antilochos' shield, and the other half lay on the ground.
To avoid death he shrank into the host of his own companions;
but as he went back Meriones dogging him threw with the spear
and struck between navel and genitals where beyond all places
death in battle comes painfully to pitiful mortals.

There the spear stuck fast driven and he, writhing about it,                     570
gasped as an ox does when among the mountains the herdsmen
have bound him strongly in twisted ropes and drag him unwilling.
So he, stricken, gasped for a little while, but not long,
until fighting Meriones came close and wrenched the spear out
from his body, and a mist of darkness closed over both eyes.                     575

   But Helenos closing struck Deïpyros on the temple
with a huge Thracian sword, and broke the helmet to pieces
so that it was knocked off and fell to the ground. An Achaian
picked it up where it rolled among the feet of the fighters;
but the darkness of night misted over the eyes of Deïpyros.                      580
   Then sorrow caught Atreus' son Menelaos of the great war cry,
and he came on menacing and shaking his sharp spear at Helenos
the lord and fighter, who pulled against him the bow at the handgrip,
and both let fly at each other together, one with a sharp spear
in a javelin cast, and one with the arrow from the bowstring.                    585
The son of Priam hit him then on the chest with an arrow
in the hollow of the corselet, but the bitter arrow sprang far back.
As along a great threshing floor from the broad blade
of a shovel the black-skinned beans and the chickpeas bounce high
under the whistling blast and the sweep of the winnowing fan, so               590
back from the corselet of glorious Menelaos the bitter
arrow rebounded far away, being driven hard back.
But Atreus' son Menelaos of the great war cry struck him
in the hand where he held the polished bow, and the bronze spear
was driven clean on through the bow and the hand beyond it.                      595
To avoid death he shrank into the host of his own companions,
dangling his wounded hand and dragging the ash spear with it.
But great-hearted Agenor drew from his hand the spear
and bound up his hand with a careful twist of wool fleece
in a sling the henchman held for the shepherd of the people.                     600

   Peisandros now came on straight against Menelaos
the glorious, but an evil destiny led him toward death's end,
to be beaten down by you, Menelaos, in the stark encounter.
Now when these in their advance were close to each other
the son of Atreus missed with his throw, and the spear was turned past him,   605

but Peisandros stabbed with the spear at the shield of glorious
Menelaos, but could not drive the bronze all the way through it
for the wide shield held against it and the spearshaft was broken
behind the head, yet he was light-hearted and hopeful of victory.
610   Drawing his sword with the silver nails, the son of Atreus
sprang at Peisandros, who underneath his shield's cover gripped
his beautiful axe with strong bronze blade upon a long polished
axe-handle of olive wood. They made their strokes at the same time
and Peisandros chopped at the horn of the helmet crested with
      horse-hair
615   at the very peak. Menelaos struck him as he came onward
in the forehead over the base of the nose, and smashed the bones, so that
both eyes dropped, bloody, and lay in the dust at his feet before him.
He fell, curling, and Menelaos, setting his heel on
his chest, stripped off his armor and spoke exulting over him:
620   "So, I think, shall you leave the ships of the fast-mounted Danaäns,
you haughty Trojans, never to be glutted with the grim war noises,
nor go short of all that other shame and defilement
wherewith you defiled me, wretched dogs, and your hearts knew no fear
at all of the hard anger of Zeus loud-thundering,
625   the guest's god, who some day will utterly sack your steep city.
You who in vanity went away taking with you my wedded
wife, and many possessions, when she had received you in kindness.
And now once more you rage among our seafaring vessels
to throw deadly fire on them and kill the fighting Achaians.
630   But you will be held somewhere, though you be so headlong for battle.
Father Zeus, they say your wisdom passes all others',
of men and gods, and yet from you all this is accomplished
the way you give these outrageous people your grace, these Trojans
whose fighting strength is a thing of blind fury, nor can they ever
635   be glutted full of the close encounters of deadly warfare.
Since there is satiety in all things, in sleep, and lovemaking,
in the loveliness of singing and the innocent dance. In all these
things a man will strive sooner to win satisfaction
than in war; but in this the Trojans cannot be glutted."
640        So Menelaos the blameless spoke, and stripping the bloody
armor away from his body gave it to his companions,
and turned back himself to merge in the ranks of the champions.

Now there sprang forth against him the son of King Pylaimenes,
Harpalion, who had followed his father into the fighting
at Troy, and did not come home again to the land of his fathers.          645
He from close up stabbed with his spear at the shield of Atreides
in the middle, but could not drive the bronze all the way through it.
To avoid death he shrank into the host of his own companions,
looking all about him, for fear somebody might wound him with the
      bronze;
but as he went back Meriones let fly at him with a bronze-shod          650
arrow, and hit him beside the right buttock, so that the arrow
was driven on through under the bone to fix in the bladder.
There, sitting among the arms of his beloved companions,
he gasped out his life, then lay like a worm extended
along the ground, and his dark blood drenched the ground in its running.   655
And the great-hearted Paphlagonians busied about him,
lifted him into a chariot and brought him to sacred Ilion
in sorrow, and his father, weeping tears, walked beside them,
and no man-price came his way for his son's slaying.

But Paris was deeply angered at heart for this man's slaying,          660
since he was his guest friend among many Paphlagonians,
and in anger for him he also let fly a bronze-shod arrow.
There was a man, Euchenor, son of the seer Polyidos,
a rich man and good, who lived in his house at Korinth,
who knew well that it was his death when he went on shipboard,          665
since many times the good old man Polyidos had told him
that he must die in his own house of a painful sickness
or go with the ships of the Achaians and be killed by the Trojans.
He therefore chose to avoid the troublesome price the Achaians
would ask, and the hateful sickness so his heart might not be afflicted.   670
Paris struck him by jaw and ear, and at once the life spirit
fled from his limbs, and the hateful darkness closed in about him.

So they fought on in the likeness of blazing fire. But meanwhile
Hektor beloved of Zeus had not heard of this, and knew nothing
of how to the left of the ships his people were being slaughtered          675
by the Argives, and glory for the Achaians might even have been
accomplished, such was Poseidon who circles the earth and shakes it
as he stirred on the Argives and fought for them and his own strength.

But Hektor held where first he had broken a way through the rampart
680 and the gates, and shattered the close ranks of the armored Danaäns,
where lay the ships of Aias and the ships of Protesilaos
hauled up along the beach of the gray sea; and above these
the wall they had built lay lowest, and there beyond other places
dangerous was the onslaught of the Trojans and of their horses.

685     There the Boiotians, and Ionians with their trailing tunics,
the Lokrians and the Phthians, with the shining Epeians
tried to hold him as he swept hard for the ships, but they could not
avail to beat brilliant flame-like Hektor back from them.
There also were the chosen Athenian men, and among them
690 Peteos' son Menestheus was lord, and there followed with him
Pheidas and Stichios and strong Bias; but the Epeians
were led by Meges, Phyleus' son, Amphion and Drakios,
and before the Phthians were Medon and battle-stubborn Podarkes.
Now of these one, Medon, was bastard son of Oïleus
695 the godlike, and brother of Aias, yet he was living away from
the land of his fathers, in Phylakē, since he had killed a man,
the brother of Eriopis, his stepmother and wife of Oïleus;
but the other was son of Iphiklos, the son of Phylakos.
And these in arms at the forefront of the great-hearted Phthians
700 fought beside the Boiotians in defense of their vessels.
    But swift Aias the son of Oïleus would not at all now
take his stand apart from Telamonian Aias,
not even a little; but as two wine-colored oxen straining
with even force drag the compacted plough through the fallow land,
705 and for both of them at the base of the horns the dense sweat gushes;
only the width of the polished yoke keeps a space between them
as they toil down the furrow till the share cuts the edge of the ploughland;
so these took their stand in battle, close to each other.
Now with the son of Telamon many people and brave ones
710 followed as companions, and took over the great shield from him
whenever the sweat and the weariness came over his body.
But no Lokrians went with the great-hearted son of Oïleus.
The heart was not in them to endure close-standing combat,
for they did not have the brazen helmets crested with horse-hair,

they did not have the strong-circled shields and the ash spears,                               715
but rather these had followed to Ilion with all their confidence
in their bows and slings strong-twisted of wool; and with these
they shot their close volleys and broke the Trojan battalions.
So now these others fought in front in elaborate war gear
against the Trojans and Hektor the brazen-helmed, and the Lokrians    720
unseen volleyed from behind, so the Trojans remembered
nothing of the joy of battle, since the shafts struck them to confusion.

    Now pitifully the Trojans might have gone back from the shelters
and the ships, to windy Ilion, had not Poulydamas
come and stood beside bold Hektor and spoken a word to him:            725
"Hektor, you are too intractable to listen to reason.
Because the god has granted you the actions of warfare
therefore you wish in counsel also to be wise beyond others.
But you cannot choose to have all gifts given to you together.
To one man the god has granted the actions of warfare,                  730
to one to be a dancer, to another the lyre and the singing,
and in the breast of another Zeus of the wide brows establishes
wisdom, a lordly thing, and many take profit beside him
and he saves many, but the man's own thought surpasses all others.
Now I will tell you the way that it seems best to my mind.            735
For you, everywhere the fighting burns in a circle around you,
but of the great-hearted Trojans since they crossed over the rampart
some are standing back in their war gear, others are fighting
fewer men against many, being scattered among the vessels.
Draw back now, and call to this place all of our bravest,              740
and then we might work out together our general counsel,
whether we can fall upon their benched ships, if the god might
be willing to give such power to us, or whether thereafter
we can win away from the ships unhurt; since I fear
the Achaians might wreak on us requital for yesterday;                 745
since beside their ships lurks a man insatiate of fighting
and I think we can no longer utterly hold him from the fighting."
    So spoke Poulydamas, and this counsel of safety pleased Hektor,
and at once in all his armor he leapt to the ground from his chariot
and spoke to him and addressed him in winged words: "Poulydamas,     750

do you rather call back to their place all of our bravest.
I am going over there to meet the attack, and afterward
I will come back soon, when I have properly given my orders."

So he spoke, and went on his way like a snowy mountain,
755 calling aloud, and swept through the Trojans and their companions.
But the rest of them rallied quickly around the son of Panthoös,
courtly Poulydamas, each as they heard the command of Hektor.
But Hektor ranged the ranks of the foremost fighters, searching
for Deïphobos, and the strength of Helenos the prince, and for Asios'
760 son Adamas, and Asios, Hyrtakos' son, if he might
find them; but found them no longer utterly unwounded or living,
but some were lying along the sterns of Achaian vessels,
they who had lost their lives at the hands of the Argives, and others
were lying away inside the city with arrow or spear wounds.
765 But he found one man away to the left of the sorrowful battle,
brilliant Alexandros, the lord of lovely-haired Helen,
encouraging his companions and urging them on into battle.
Hektor came and stood near, and in words of shame he rebuked him:
"Evil Paris, beautiful, woman-crazy, cajoling:
770 where is Deïphobos gone, and the strength of the prince Helenos,
Adamas, Asios' son, and Asios, son of Hyrtakos?
Where is Othryoneus? Now all steep Ilion is lost
utterly; now your own headlong destruction is certain."
Then in turn Alexandros the godlike answered him:
775 "Hektor, since it is your pleasure to blame me when I am blameless,
it would be better some other time to withdraw from the fighting
than now. My mother bore me not utterly lacking in warcraft.
For since that time when by the ships you wakened the battle
of our companions, we have stayed here and fought the Danaäns
780 without end. And our companions are killed you ask for.
Only Deïphobos and the strength of the prince Helenos
have gone away, wounded each in the hand by strokes
of the long spears, but the son of Kronos fended death from them.
Now lead on, wherever your heart and spirit command you,
785 and we shall follow you eagerly; I think that we shall not
come short in warcraft, in so far as the strength stays with us.
But beyond his strength no man can fight, although he be eager."

So the hero spoke, and persuaded the heart of his brother.
They went on, to where the clamor and fighting were greatest,
about Kebriones, and Poulydamas the blameless,                        790
about Phalkes, and Orthaios, and godlike Polyphetes,
Palmys, with Askanios and Morys, sons of Hippotion,
who had come over in their turn from fertile Askania
on the dawn before, and now Zeus stirred them into the fighting.
They went on, as out of the racking winds the stormblast               795
that underneath the thunderstroke of Zeus father drives downward
and with gigantic clamor hits the sea, and the numerous
boiling waves along the length of the roaring water
bend and whiten to foam in ranks, one upon another;
so the Trojans closing in ranks, some leading and others               800
after them, in the glare of bronze armor followed their leaders.
And Hektor led them, Priam's son, a man like the murderous
war god, and held the perfect circle of his shield before him
fenced deep in skins, with a great fold of bronze beaten upon it,
and about his temples was shaken as he went the glittering helmet.     805
He would step forward, to probe the Achaian battalions at all points,
if they might give way where he stalked on under his shield's cover,
but could not so confuse the heart in the breasts of the Achaians.
Aias was first to take long strides forward and challenge him:
"Man, you are mad. Come closer. Why try this way to terrify            810
the Argives? It is not that we are so unskilled in fighting,
but by the wicked whiplash of Zeus we Achaians are beaten.
I suppose, then, your heart is hopeful utterly to break up
our ships? We too have prompt hands among us strong to defend them.
Rather, far before this your own strong-founded citadel                815
must go down under our hands, stormed and utterly taken.
And for yourself I say that the time is close, when in flight
you will pray to Zeus father and the other immortals
that your bright-maned horses might be swifter than hawks are
as they carry you through the stirred dust of the plain to your city." 820

As he spoke so, an ominous bird winged by at his right hand,
a towering eagle, and the host of the Achaians, made brave
by the bird sign, shouted, but glorious Hektor answered him:
"Aias, you inarticulate ox, what is this you have spoken?

825 If I could only be called son to Zeus of the aegis
all the days of my life, and the lady Hera my mother,
and I be honored, as Apollo and Athene are honored,
so surely as this is a day that brings evil to the Argives,
all, and you will be killed with the rest of them, if you have daring
830 to stand up against my long spear, which will bite your delicate
body; yet then you will glut the dogs and birds of the Trojans
with fat and flesh, struck down beside the ships of the Achaians."

So he spoke and led the way, and the rest of them followed him
with unearthly clamor, and all the people shouted behind him.
835 But the Argives on the other side cried out, and would not
forget their warcraft, but stood the attack of the bravest Trojans,
and the clamor from both was driven high to Zeus' shining ether.

# BOOK FOURTEEN

Now Nestor failed not to hear their outcry, though he was drinking
his wine, but spoke in winged words to the son of Asklepios:
"Take thought how these things shall be done, brilliant Machaon.
Beside the ships the cry of the strong young men grows greater.
Now, do you sit here and go on drinking the bright wine,                    5
until Hekamede the lovely-haired makes ready a hot bath
for you, warming it, and washes away the filth of the bloodstains,
while I go out and make my way till I find some watchpoint."

So he spoke, and took up the wrought shield of his son
Thrasymedes, breaker of horses. It lay in the shelter                       10
all shining in bronze. Thrasymedes carried the shield of his father.
Then he caught up a powerful spear edged in sharp bronze
and stood outside the shelter, and at once saw a shameful action,
men driven to flight, and others harrying them in confusion,
the great-hearted Trojans, and the wall of the Achaians overthrown.         15
As when the open sea is deeply stirred to the ground-swell
but stays in one place and waits the rapid onset of tearing
gusts, nor rolls its surf onward in either direction
until from Zeus the wind is driven down to decide it;
so the aged man pondered, his mind caught between two courses,              20
whether to go among the throng of fast-mounted Danaäns
or in search of Atreus' son Agamemnon, shepherd of the people.
And in the division of his heart this way seemed best to him,
to go after the son of Atreus, while the rest went on with the murderous

25 battle, and the weariless bronze about their bodies was clashing
as the men were stabbing with swords and leaf-headed spears.

Now there came toward Nestor the kings under God's hand, they who
had been wounded by the bronze and came back along the ships, Tydeus'
son, and Odysseus, and Atreus' son Agamemnon. For there
30 were ships that had been hauled up far away from the fighting
along the beach of the gray sea. They had hauled up the first ones
on the plain, and by the sterns of these had built their defenses;
for, wide as it was, the seashore was not big enough to make room
for all the ships, and the people also were straitened; and therefore
35 they had hauled them up in depth, and filled up the long edge
of the whole sea-coast, all that the two capes compassed between them.
These lords walked in a group, each leaning on his spear, to look at
the clamorous battle, and for each the heart inside his body
was sorrowful; and Nestor the aged man who now met them
40 made still more cast down the spirit inside the Achaians.
Now powerful Agamemnon spoke aloud and addressed him:
"Nestor, son of Neleus, great glory of the Achaians,
why have you left the fighting where men die, and come back here?
I am afraid huge Hektor may accomplish that word against me
45 that he spoke, threatening, among the Trojans assembled,
that he would not make his way back from the ships toward Ilion
until he had set the ships on fire, and killed the men in them.
So he spoke then; now all these things are being accomplished.
Oh, shame, for I think that all the other strong-greaved Achaians
50 are storing anger against me in their hearts, as Achilleus
did, and no longer will fight for me by the grounded vessels."

Then answered him in turn the Gerenian horseman Nestor:
"All these things have been brought to fulfillment, nor in any other
way could even Zeus who thunders on high accomplish it.
55 For the wall has gone down in which we put our trust, that it
would be a protection for our ships and us, and could not be broken,
and our men beside the fast ships are fighting incessantly
without end, nor could you tell anymore, though you looked hard,
from which side the Achaians are broken into confusion,
60 so indiscriminately are they killed, and their crying goes skyward.

We then must take thought together how these things shall be done
if wit can do anything for us now. I think that we must not
enter the fight; a man cannot fight on when he is wounded."
    Then in turn the lord of men Agamemnon spoke to him:
"Nestor, since now they are fighting beside the grounded vessels          65
and the wall we built has done us no good, nor the ditch either
where the Danaäns endured so much, and their hearts were hopeful
it would be a protection to their ships and them, and could not be broken,
then such is the way it must be pleasing to Zeus, who is too strong,
that the Achaians must die here forgotten and far from Argos.              70
For I knew it, when with full heart he defended the Danaäns,
and I know it now, when he glorifies these people as if they
were blessed gods, and has hobbled our warcraft and our hands' strength.
Come then, do as I say, let us all be won over; let us
take all those ships that are beached near the sea in the first line       75
and haul them down, and row them out on the shining water,
and moor them at anchor stones out on the deep water, until
the immortal Night comes down, if the Trojans will give over fighting
for Night's sake; then we might haul down all the rest of our vessels.
There is no shame in running, even by night, from disaster.                80
The man does better who runs from disaster than he who is caught by it."

    Then looking darkly at him spoke resourceful Odysseus:
"Son of Atreus, what sort of word escaped your teeth's barrier?
Ruinous! I wish you directed some other unworthy
army, and were not lord over us, over us to whom Zeus                       85
has appointed the accomplishing of wars, from our youth
even into our old age until we are dead, each of us.
Are you really thus eager to abandon the wide-wayed city
of the Trojans, over which we have taken so many sorrows?
Do not say it; for fear some other Achaian might hear this                  90
word, which could never at all get past the lips of any man
who understood inside his heart how to speak soundly,
who was a sceptered king, and all the people obeyed him
in numbers like those of the Argives, whose lord you are.
Now I utterly despise your heart for the thing you have spoken;            95
you who in the very closing of clamorous battle
tell us to haul our strong-benched ships to the sea, so that even

more glory may befall the Trojans, who beat us already,
and headlong destruction swing our way, since the Achaians
100 will not hold their battle as the ships are being hauled seaward,
but will look about, and let go the exultation of fighting.
There, O leader of the people, your plan will be ruin."
    Then in turn the lord of men Agamemnon answered him:
"Odysseus, you have hit me somewhere deep in my feelings
105 with this hard word. But I am not telling the sons of the Achaians
against their will to drag their benched ships down to the water.
Now let someone speak who has better counsel than this was;
young man or old; and what he says will be to my liking."

    Now among them spoke Diomedes of the great war cry:
110 "That man is here, we shall not look far for him, if you are willing
to listen, and not be each astonished in anger against me
because by birth I am the youngest among you. I also
can boast that my generation is of an excellent father,
Tydeus, whom now the heaped earth covers over in Thebe.
115 For there were three blameless sons who were born to Portheus,
and their home was in Pleuron and headlong Kalydon. Agrios
was first, then Melas, and the third was Oineus the horseman,
the father of my father, and in valor beyond the others.
But Oineus stayed in the land, while my father was driven and settled
120 in Argos. Such was the will of Zeus and the other immortals.
He married one of the daughters of Adrestos, and established
a house rich in substance, and plenty of wheat-grown acres
were his, with many orchards of fruit trees circled about him,
and many herds were his. He surpassed all other Achaians
125 with the spear. If all this is true, you must have heard of it.
Therefore you could not, saying that I was base and unwarlike
by birth, dishonor any word that I speak, if I speak well.
Let us go back to the fighting wounded as we are. We have to.
Once there, we must hold ourselves out of the onfall, clear of
130 missiles, so that none will add to the wound he has got already,
but we shall be there to drive them on, since even before this
they have favored their anger, and stood far off, and will not fight for us."
    So he spoke, and they listened well to him, and obeyed him,
and went on their way. And the lord of men, Agamemnon, led them.

Neither did the glorious shaker of the earth keep blind watch,               135
but came among them now in the likeness of an old man,
and took hold of Agamemnon, Atreus' son, by the right hand,
and spoke to him and addressed him in winged words: "Son of Atreus,
I think that now that baleful heart in the breast of Achilleus
must be happy as he stares at the slaughter of the Achaians               140
and their defeat. There is no heart in him, not even a little.
Even so may the god strike him down, let him go to destruction.
But with you the blessed gods are not utterly angry.
There will still be a time when the lords of Troy and their counselors
shall send dust wide on the plain, and you yourself shall look on them      145
as they take flight for their city away from the ships and the shelters."
    So he spoke, and swept on over the plain, with a huge cry
like the yell nine thousand men send up, or ten thousand
in battle, as they close in the hateful strife of the war god.
So huge was the cry the powerful earth-shaker let go                 150
from his lungs, and in the heart of every Achaian implanted
great strength, to carry the battle on, and fight without flinching.

    Now Hera, she of the golden throne, standing on Olympos'
horn, looked out with her eyes, and saw at once how Poseidon,
who was her very brother and her lord's brother, was bustling            155
about the battle where men win glory, and her heart was happy.
Then she saw Zeus, sitting along the loftiest summit
on Ida of the springs, and in her eyes he was hateful.
And now the lady ox-eyed Hera was divided in purpose
as to how she could beguile the brain in Zeus of the aegis.             160
And to her mind this thing appeared to be the best counsel,
to array herself in loveliness, and go down to Ida,
and perhaps he might be taken with desire to lie in love with her
next her skin, and she might be able to drift an innocent
warm sleep across his eyelids, and seal his crafty perceptions.          165
She went into her chamber, which her beloved son Hephaistos
had built for her, and closed the leaves in the door-posts snugly
with a secret door-bar, and no other of the gods could open it.
There entering she drew shut the leaves of the shining door, then
first from her adorable body washed away all stains                   170
with ambrosia, and next anointed herself with ambrosial

sweet olive oil, which stood there in its fragrance beside her,
and from which, stirred in the house of Zeus by the golden pavement,
a fragrance was shaken forever forth, on earth and in heaven.
175 When with this she had anointed her delicate body
and combed her hair, next with her hands she arranged the shining
and lovely and ambrosial curls along her immortal
head, and dressed in an ambrosial robe that Athene
had made her carefully, smooth, and with many figures upon it,
180 and pinned it across her breast with a golden brooch, and circled
her waist about with a zone that floated a hundred tassels,
and in the lobes of her carefully pierced ears she put rings
with triple drops in mulberry clusters, radiant with beauty,
and, lovely among goddesses, she veiled her head downward
185 with a sweet fresh veil that glimmered pale like the sunlight.
Underneath her shining feet she bound on the fair sandals.
Now, when she had clothed her body in all this loveliness,
she went out from the chamber, and called aside Aphrodite
to come away from the rest of the gods, and spoke a word to her:
190 "Would you do something for me, dear child, if I were to ask you?
Or would you refuse it? Are you forever angered against me
because I defend the Danaäns, while you help the Trojans?"
    Then the daughter of Zeus, Aphrodite, answered her: "Hera,
honored goddess, daughter to mighty Kronos, speak forth
195 whatever is in your mind. My heart is urgent to do it
if I can, and if it is a thing that can be accomplished."
    Then, with false lying purpose the lady Hera answered her:
"Give me loveliness and desirability, graces
with which you overwhelm mortal men, and all the immortals.
200 Since I go now to the ends of the generous earth, on a visit
to Okeanos, whence the gods have risen, and Tethys our mother
who brought me up kindly in their own house, and cared for me
and took me from Rheia, at that time when Zeus of the wide brows
drove Kronos underneath the earth and the barren water.
205 I shall go to visit these, and resolve their division of discord,
since now for a long time they have stayed apart from each other
and from the bed of love, since rancor has entered their feelings.
Could I win over with persuasion the dear heart within them
and bring them back to their bed to be merged in love with each other

I shall be forever called honored by them, and beloved." 210
Then in turn Aphrodite the laughing answered her:
"I cannot, and I must not deny this thing that you ask for,
you, who lie in the arms of Zeus, since he is our greatest."

She spoke, and from her breasts unbound the elaborate, pattern-pierced
zone, and on it are figured all beguilements, and loveliness 215
is figured upon it, and passion of sex is there, and the whispered
endearment that steals the heart away even from the thoughtful.
She put this in Hera's hands, and called her by name and spoke to her:
"Take this zone, and hide it away in the fold of your bosom.
It is elaborate, all things are figured therein. And I think 220
whatever is your heart's desire shall not go unaccomplished."
So she spoke, and the ox-eyed lady Hera smiled on her
and smiling hid the zone away in the fold of her bosom.
So Aphrodite went back into the house, Zeus' daughter,
while Hera in a flash of speed left the horn of Olympos 225
and crossed over Piēria and Emathia the lovely
and overswept the snowy hills of the Thracian riders
and their uttermost pinnacles, nor touched the ground with her feet. Then
from Athos she crossed over the heaving main sea
and came to Lemnos, and to the city of godlike Thoas. 230
There she encountered Sleep, the brother of Death. She clung
fast to his hand and spoke a word and called him by name: "Sleep,
lord over all mortal men and all gods, if ever
before now you listened to word of mine, so now also
do as I ask; and all my days I shall know gratitude. 235
Put to sleep the shining eyes of Zeus under his brows
as soon as I have lain beside him in love. I will give you
gifts; a lovely throne, imperishable forever,
of gold. My own son, he of the strong arms, Hephaistos,
shall make it with careful skill and make for your feet a footstool 240
on which you can rest your shining feet when you take your pleasure."
Then Sleep the still and soft spoke to her in answer:
"Hera, honored goddess and daughter of mighty Kronos,
any other one of the gods, whose race is immortal,
I would lightly put to sleep, even the stream of that River 245
Okeanos, whence is risen the seed of all the immortals.

But I would not come too close to Zeus, the son of Kronos,
nor put him to sleep, unless when he himself were to tell me.
Before now, it was a favor to you that taught me wisdom,
250 on the day Herakles, the high-hearted son of Zeus, was sailing
from Ilion, when he had utterly sacked the city of the Trojans.
That time I laid to sleep the brain in Zeus of the aegis
and drifted upon him still and soft, but your mind was devising
evil, and you raised along the sea the blasts of the racking
255 winds, and on these swept him away to Kos, the strong-founded,
with all his friends lost, but Zeus awakened in anger
and beat the gods up and down his house, looking beyond all others
for me, and would have sunk me out of sight in the sea from the bright sky
had not Night who has power over gods and men rescued me.
260 I reached her in my flight, and Zeus let be, though he was angry
in awe of doing anything to swift Night's displeasure.
Now you ask me to do this other impossible thing for you."
      Then in turn the lady ox-eyed Hera answered him:
"Sleep, why do you ponder this in your heart, and hesitate?
265 Or do you think that Zeus of the wide brows, aiding the Trojans,
will be angry as he was angry for his son, Herakles?
Come now, do it, and I will give you one of the younger
Graces for you to marry, and she shall be called your lady;
Pasithea, since all your days you have loved her forever."

270      So she spoke, and Sleep was pleased and spoke to her in answer:
"Come then! Swear it to me on Styx' ineluctable water.
With one hand take hold of the prospering earth, with the other
take hold of the shining salt sea, so that all the undergods
who gather about Kronos may be witnesses to us.
275 Swear that you will give me one of the younger Graces,
Pasithea, the one whom all my days I have longed for."
      He spoke, nor failed to persuade the goddess Hera of the white arms,
and she swore as he commanded, and called by their names on all those
gods who live beneath the Pit, and who are called Titans.
280 Then when she had sworn this, and made her oath a complete thing,
the two went away from Lemnos, and the city of Imbros,
and mantled themselves in mist, and made their way very lightly
till they came to Ida with all her springs, the mother of wild beasts,

to Lekton, where first they left the water, and went on
over dry land, and with their feet the top of the forest was shaken.          285
There Sleep stayed, before the eyes of Zeus could light on him,
and went up aloft a towering pine tree, the one that grew tallest
at that time on Ida, and broke through the close air to the ether.
In this he sat, covered over and hidden by the pine branches,
in the likeness of a singing bird whom in the mountains                        290
the immortal gods call chalkis, but men call him kymindis.

But Hera light-footed made her way to the peak of Gargaros
on towering Ida. And Zeus who gathers the clouds saw her,
and when he saw her desire was a mist about his close heart
as much as on that time they first went to bed together                        295
and lay in love, and their dear parents knew nothing of it.
He stood before her and called her by name and spoke to her: "Hera,
what is your desire that you come down here from Olympos?
And your horses are not here, nor your chariot, which you would ride in."
Then with false lying purpose the lady Hera answered him:                      300
"I am going to the ends of the generous earth, on a visit
to Okeanos, whence the gods have risen, and Tethys our mother,
who brought me up kindly in their own house, and cared for me.
I shall go to visit these, and resolve their division of discord,
since now for a long time they have stayed apart from each other               305
and from the bed of love, since rancor has entered their feelings.
In the foothills by Ida of the waters are standing
my horses, who will carry me over hard land and water.
Only now I have come down here from Olympos for your sake
so you will not be angry with me afterward, if I                               310
have gone silently to the house of deep-running Okeanos."
Then in turn Zeus who gathers the clouds answered her:
"Hera, there will be a time afterward when you can go there
as well. But now let us go to bed and turn to lovemaking.
For never before has love for any goddess or woman                            315
so melted about the heart inside me, broken it to submission,
as now: not that time when I loved the wife of Ixion
who bore me Peirithoös, equal of the gods in counsel,
nor when I loved Akrisios' daughter, sweet-stepping Danaë,
who bore Perseus to me, pre-eminent among all men,                            320

nor when I loved the daughter of far-renowned Phoinix, Europa
who bore Minos to me, and Rhadamanthys the godlike;
not when I loved Semele, or Alkmene in Thebe,
when Alkmene bore me a son, Herakles the strong-hearted,
325    while Semele's son was Dionysos, the pleasure of mortals;
not when I loved the queen Demeter of the lovely tresses,
not when it was glorious Leto, nor yourself, so much
as now I love you, and the sweet passion has taken hold of me."
    Then with false lying purpose the lady Hera answered him:
330    "Most honored son of Kronos, what sort of thing have you spoken?
If now your great desire is to lie in love together
here on the peaks of Ida, everything can be seen. Then
what would happen if some one of the gods everlasting
saw us sleeping, and went and told all the other immortals
335    of it? I would not simply rise out of bed and go back
again, into your house, and such a thing would be shameful.
No, if this is your heart's desire, if this is your wish, then
there is my chamber, which my beloved son Hephaistos
has built for me, and closed the leaves in the door-posts snugly.
340    We can go back there and lie down, since bed is your pleasure."
    Then in turn Zeus who gathers the clouds answered her:
"Hera, do not fear that any mortal or any god
will see, so close shall be the golden cloud that I gather
about us. Not even Helios can look at us through it,
345    although beyond all others his light has the sharpest vision."

    So speaking, the son of Kronos caught his wife in his arms. There
underneath them the divine earth broke into young, fresh
grass, and into dewy clover, crocus and hyacinth
so thick and soft it held the hard ground deep away from them.
350    There they lay down together and drew about them a golden
wonderful cloud, and from it the glimmering dew descended.
    So the father slept unshaken on the peak of Gargaron
with his wife in his arms, when sleep and passion had stilled him;
but gently Sleep went on the run to the ships of the Achaians
355    with a message to tell him who circles the earth and shakes it,
Poseidon, and stood close to him and addressed him in winged words:
"Poseidon, now with all your heart defend the Danaäns

and give them glory, though only for a little, while Zeus still
sleeps; since I have mantled a soft slumber about him
and Hera beguiled him into sleeping in love beside her."                    360

He spoke so, and went away among the famed races
of men, and stirred Poseidon even more to defend the Danaäns.
He sprang among their foremost and urged them on in a great voice:
"Argives, now once more must we give the best of it to Hektor,
Priam's son, so he may take our ships and win glory from them?          365
Such is his thought and such is his prayer, because now Achilleus
in the anger of his heart stays still among the hollow ships.
But there will not be too much longing for him, if the others
of us can stir ourselves up to stand by each other.
Come; then, do as I say, let us all be won over; let us               370
take those shields which are best in all the army and biggest
and put them on, and cover our heads in the complete shining
of helmets, and take in our hands our spears that are longest
and go. I myself will lead the way, and I think that no longer
Hektor, Priam's son, can stand up to us, for all his fury.            375
Let the man stubborn in battle who wears a small shield on his shoulder
give it to a worse man, and put on the shield that is bigger."

So he spoke, and they listened hard to him, and obeyed him.
The kings in person marshaled these men, although they were wounded,
Tydeus' son, and Odysseus, and Atreus' son Agamemnon.                 380
They went among all, and made them exchange their armor of battle,
and the good fighter put on the good armor, and each gave the worse gear
to the worse. Then when in the shining bronze they had shrouded their
        bodies
they went forward, and Poseidon the shaker of the earth led them
holding in his heavy hand the stark sword with the thin edge          385
glittering, as glitters the thunderflash none may close with
by right in sorrowful division, but fear holds all men back.
On the other side glorious Hektor ordered the Trojans,
and now Poseidon of the dark hair and glorious Hektor
strained to its deadliest the division of battle, the one            390
bringing power to the Trojans, and the god to the Argives.
The breaking of the sea washed up to the ships and the shelters

of the Argives. The two sides closed together with a great war cry.
Not such is the roaring against dry land of the sea's surf
395   as it rolls in from the open under the hard blast of the north wind;
not such is the bellowing of fire in its blazing
in the deep places of the hills when it rises inflaming the forest,
nor such again the crying voice of the wind in the deep-haired
oaks, when it roars highest in its fury against them,
400   not so loud as now the noise of Achaians and Trojans
in voice of terror rose as they drove against one another.

    First glorious Hektor made a cast with his spear at Aias
since he had turned straight against him, nor missed with his throw
but struck, there where over his chest were crossed the two straps,
405   one for the sword with the silver nails, and one for the great shield.
These guarded the tenderness of his skin. And Hektor, in anger
because his weapon had been loosed from his hand in a vain cast,
to avoid death shrank into the host of his own companions.
But as he drew away huge Telamonian Aias
410   caught up a rock; there were many, holding-stones for the fast ships,
rolled among the feet of the fighters; he caught up one of these
and hit him in the chest next the throat over his shield rim,
and spun him around like a top with the stroke, so that he staggered
in a circle; as a great oak goes down root-torn under
415   Zeus father's stroke, and a horrible smell of sulfur uprises
from it, and there is no courage left in a man who stands by
and looks on, for the thunderstroke of great Zeus is a hard thing;
so Hektor in all his strength dropped suddenly in the dust, let
fall the spear from his hand, and his shield was beaten upon him,
420   and the helm, and his armor elaborate with bronze clashed over him.
Screaming aloud the sons of the Achaians ran forward
in hope to drag him away, and threw their volleying javelins
against him, yet no man could stab or cast at the shepherd
of the people; sooner the Trojans' bravest gathered about him,
425   Aineias, and Poulydamas, and brilliant Agenor,
Sarpedon, lord of the Lykians, and Glaukos the blameless;
and of the rest no man was heedless of him, but rather
sloped the strong circles of their shields over him, while his companions
caught him in their arms out of the fighting and reached his fast-footed

horses, where they stood to the rear of the fighting and the battle                    430
holding their charioteer and the elaborate chariot,
and these carried him, groaning heavily, back toward the city.

But when they came to the crossing place of the fair-running river,
of whirling Xanthos, whose father was Zeus the immortal,
they moved him from behind his horses to the ground, and splashed       435
water over him. He got his wind again, and his eyes cleared,
and he got up to lean on one knee and vomit a dark clot
of blood, then lay back on the ground again, while over both eyes
dark night misted. His strength was still broken by the stone's stroke.
But the Argives, when they saw Hektor withdrawing from them,              440
remembered once again their warcraft and turned on the Trojans.
There far before them all swift Aias son of Oïleus
made an outrush, and stabbed with the sharp spear Satnios,
Enops' son, whom the perfect naiad nymph had borne once
to Enops, as he tended his herds by Satnioeis river.                                     445
The spear-famed son of Oïleus, coming close to this man,
stabbed him in the flank so that he knocked him backward, and over him
Trojans and Danaäns closed together in strong encounter.
Poulydamas of the shaken spear came up to stand by him,
Panthoös' son, and struck in the right shoulder Prothoënor               450
son of Arcïlykos, and the powerful spear was driven
through the shoulder, and he dropping in the dust clawed the ground in
        his fingers.
Poulydamas vaunted terribly over him, calling in a great voice:
"I think this javelin leaping from the heavy hand of Panthoös'
high-hearted son was not thrown away in a vain cast. Rather              455
some Argive caught it in his skin. I think he has got it
for a stick to lean on as he trudges down into Death's house."

He spoke, and sorrow came over the Argives at his vaunting,
and beyond others he stirred the anger in wise Telamonian
Aias, for the man had fallen closest to him, and at once                   460
he made a cast with the shining spear at returning Poulydamas.
But Poulydamas himself avoided the dark death
with a quick spring to one side, and Archelochos son of Antenor
caught the spear, since the immortal gods had doomed his destruction.

465 He hit him at the joining place of head and neck, at the last
vertebra, and cut through both of the tendons, so that
the man's head and mouth and nose hit the ground far sooner
than did the front of his legs and knees as he fell. And Aias
spoke aloud in answer to unfaulted Poulydamas:
470 "Think over this, Poulydamas, and answer me truly.
Is not this man's death against Prothoënor's a worthwhile
exchange? I think he is no mean man, nor born of mean fathers,
but is some brother of Antenor, breaker of horses,
or his son; since he is close in blood by the look of him."
475      He spoke, knowing well what he said, and sorrow fastened on the Trojans.
There Akamas, bestriding his brother, stabbed the Boiotian
Promachos with the spear as he tried to drag off the body.
Akamas vaunted terribly over him, calling in a great voice:
"You Argives, arrow-fighters, insatiate of menace. I think
480 we shall not be the only ones to be given hard work
and sorrow, but you too must sometimes die, as this man did.
Think how Promachos sleeps among you, beaten down under
my spear, so that punishment for my brother may not go
long unpaid. Therefore a man prays he will leave behind him
485 one close to him in his halls to avenge his downfall in battle."
        He spoke, and sorrow came over the Argives at his vaunting,
and beyond others he stirred the anger in wise Peneleos.
He charged Akamas, who would not stand up against the onset
of lord Peneleos. He then stabbed with the spear Ilioneus
490 the son of Phorbas the rich in sheepflocks, whom beyond all men
of the Trojans Hermes loved, and gave him possessions.
Ilioneus was the only child his mother had borne him.
This man Peneleos caught underneath the brow, at the bases
of the eye, and pushed the eyeball out, and the spear went clean through
495 the eye-socket and tendon of the neck, so that he went down
backward, reaching out both hands, but Peneleos drawing
his sharp sword hewed at the neck in the middle, and so dashed downward
the head, with helm upon it, while still on the point of the big spear
the eyeball stuck. He, lifting it high like the head of a poppy,
500 displayed it to the Trojans and spoke vaunting over it:
"Trojans, tell haughty Ilioneus' beloved father
and mother, from me, that they can weep for him in their halls, since

neither shall the wife of Promachos, Alegenor's
son, take pride of delight in her dear lord's coming, on that day
when we sons of the Achaians come home from Troy in our vessels."     505
    So he spoke, and the shivers came over the limbs of all of them,
and each man looked about him for a way to escape the sheer death.

    Tell me now, you Muses who have your homes on Olympos,
who was first of the Achaians to win the bloody despoilment
of men, when the glorious shaker of the earth bent the way of the battle?     510
First Telamonian Aias cut down Hyrtios, he who
was son to Gyrtios, and lord over the strong-hearted Mysians.
Antilochos slaughtered Phalkes and Mermeros. Morys
and Hippotion were killed by Meriones. Teukros cut down
Periphetes and Prothoön. Next the son of Atreus,     515
Menelaos, stabbed Hyperenor, shepherd of the people,
in the flank, so the bronze head let gush out the entrails
through the torn side. His life came out through the wound of the spear-stab
in beating haste, and a mist of darkness closed over both eyes.
But Aias the fast-footed son of Oïleus caught and killed most,     520
since there was none like him in the speed of his feet to go after
men who ran, once Zeus had driven the terror upon them.

# BOOK FIFTEEN

But after they had crossed back over the ditch and the sharp stakes
in flight, and many had gone down under the hands of the Danaäns,
they checked about once more and stood their ground by the chariots,
green for fear and terrified. But now Zeus wakened
5  by Hera of the gold throne on the high places of Ida,
and stood suddenly upright, and saw the Achaians and Trojans,
these driven to flight, the others harrying them in confusion,
these last Argives, and saw among them the lord Poseidon.
He saw Hektor lying in the plain, his companions sitting
10  around him, he dazed at the heart and breathing painfully,
vomiting blood, since not the weakest Achaian had hit him.
Then the father of gods and men seeing Hektor pitied him
and looked scowling terribly at Hera, and spoke a word to her:
"Hopeless one, it was your evil design, your treachery, Hera,
15  that stayed brilliant Hektor from battle, terrified his people.
I do not know, perhaps for this contrivance of evil
and pain you will win first reward when I lash you with whip strokes.
Do you not remember that time you hung from high and on your feet
I slung two anvils, and about your hands drove a golden
20  chain, unbreakable. You among the clouds and the bright sky
hung, nor could the gods about tall Olympos endure it
and stood about, but could not set you free. If I caught one
I would seize and throw him from the threshold, until he landed
stunned on the earth, yet even so the weariless agony
25  for Herakles the godlike would not let go my spirit.
You with the north wind's aid winning over the stormwinds drove him

on across the desolate sea in evil intention
and then on these swept him away to Kos, the strong-founded.
I myself rescued him there and brought him back once more
to horse-pasturing Argos, when he had been through much hardship.                   30
I will remind you of all this, so you will give up
your deceptions, see if your lovemaking in bed will help you,
that way you lay with me apart from the gods, and deceived me."

He spoke, and the lady the ox-eyed goddess Hera was frightened
and she spoke to him and addressed him in winged words: "Now let          35
Earth be my witness in this, and the wide heaven above us,
and the dripping water of the Styx, which oath is the biggest
and most formidable oath among the blessed immortals.
The sanctity of your head be witness, and the bed of marriage
between us: a thing by which I at least could never swear vainly.                40
It is not through my will that the shaker of the earth Poseidon
afflicts the Trojans and Hektor and gives aid to the others,
but it is his own passion that urges him to it and drives him.
He saw the Achaians hard pressed beside their ships, and pitied them.
No, but I myself also would give him counsel                                              45
to go with you, O dark clouded, that way that you lead us."
She spoke, and now the father of gods and men smiled on her
and spoke again in answer to her, and addressed her in winged words:
"If even you, lady Hera of the ox eyes, hereafter
were to take your place among the immortals thinking as I do,                     50
then Poseidon, hard though he may wish it otherwise,
must at once turn his mind so it follows your heart, and my heart.
If now all this that you say is real, and you speak truthfully,
go now among the generations of the gods, and summon
Iris to come here to me, and Apollo the glorious archer,                              55
so that Iris may go among the bronze-armored people
of the Achaians, and give a message to lord Poseidon
to leave the fighting and come back to the home that is his. Also
let Phoibos Apollo stir Hektor back into battle,
breathe strength into him once more, and make him forget the agonies       60
that now are wearing out his senses. Let him drive strengthless
panic into the Achaians, and turn them back once more;
let them be driven in flight and tumble back on the benched ships

of Achilleus, Peleus' son. And he shall rouse up Patroklos
65   his companion. And glorious Hektor shall cut down Patroklos
with the spear before Ilion, after he has killed many others
of the young men, and among them my own son, shining Sarpedon.
In anger for him brilliant Achilleus shall then kill Hektor.
And from then on I would make the fighting surge back from the vessels
70   always and continuously, until the Achaians
capture headlong Ilion through the designs of Athene.
Before this I am not stopping my anger, and I will not let
any other of the immortals stand there by the Danaäns
until the thing asked by the son of Peleus has been accomplished
75   as I undertook at the first and bent my head in assent to it
on that day when embracing my knees immortal Thetis
supplicated honor for Achilleus, sacker of cities."

He spoke, and the goddess of the white arms Hera did not disobey him
but went back to tall Olympos from the mountains of Ida.
80   As the thought flashes in the mind of a man who, traversing
much territory, thinks of things in the mind's awareness,
"I wish I were this place, or this," and imagines many things;
so rapidly in her eagerness winged Hera, a goddess.
She came to sheer Olympos and entered among the assembled
85   immortal gods in the house of Zeus, and they seeing her
rose all to swarm about her and lifted their cups in greeting.
But Hera passed by the others and accepted a cup from Themis
of the fair cheeks, since she had first come running to greet her
and had spoken to her and addressed her in winged words: "Hera,
90   why have you come? You seem like one who has been terrified.
I know, it was the son of Kronos, your husband, frightened you."
In turn the goddess Hera of the white arms answered her:
"Ask me nothing of this, divine Themis. You yourself
know what his spirit is, how it is stubborn and arrogant.
95   Preside still over the gods in their house, the feast's fair division.
Yet so much may you hear, and with you all the immortals,
how Zeus discloses evil actions, and I do not think
the heart of all will be pleased alike, neither among mortals
nor gods either, although one now still feasts at his pleasure."
100      The lady Hera spoke so and sat down, and the gods

about the house of Zeus were troubled. Hera was smiling
with her lips, but above the dark brows her forehead
was not at peace. She spoke before them all in vexation:
"Fools, we who try to work against Zeus, thoughtlessly.
Still we are thinking in our anger to go near, and stop him          105
by argument or force. He sits apart and cares nothing
nor thinks of us, and says that among the other immortals
he is pre-eminently the greatest in power and strength. Therefore
each of you must take whatever evil he sends you.
Since I think already a sorrow has been wrought against Ares.          110
His son has been killed in the fighting, dearest of all men
to him, Askalaphos, whom stark Ares calls his own son."
     So she spoke. Then Ares struck against both his big thighs
with the flats of his hands, and spoke a word of anger and sorrow:
"Now, you who have your homes on Olympos, you must not blame me          115
for going among the ships of the Achaians, and avenging my son's
slaughter, even though it be my fate to be struck by Zeus'
thunderbolt, and sprawl in the blood and dust by the dead men."

     So he spoke, and ordered Fear and Terror to harness
his horses, and himself got into his shining armor.          120
And there might have been wrought another anger, and bitterness
from Zeus, still greater, more wearisome among the immortals,
had not Athene, in her fear for the sake of all gods,
sprung up and out through the forecourt, left her chair where she was sitting,
and taken the helmet off from his head, the shield from his shoulders,          125
and snatched out of his heavy hand the bronze spear, and fixed it
apart, and then in speech reasoned with violent Ares:
"Madman, mazed of your wits, this is ruin! Your ears can listen
still to reality, but your mind is gone and your discipline.
Do you not hear what the goddess Hera of the white arms tells us,          130
and she coming back even now from Zeus of Olympos?
Do you wish, after running the course of many misfortunes
yourself, still to come back to Olympos under compulsion
though reluctant, and plant seed of great sorrow among the rest of us?
Since he will at once leave the Achaians and the high-hearted          135
Trojans, and come back to batter us on Olympos
and will catch up as they come the guilty one and the guiltless.

Therefore I ask of you to give up your anger for your son.
By now some other, better of his strength and hands than your son was,
140   has been killed, or will soon be killed; and it is a hard thing
to rescue all the generation and seed of all mortals."
     So she spoke, and seated on a chair violent Ares.
But Hera called to come with her outside the house Apollo
and Iris, who is messenger among the immortal
145   gods, and spoke to them and addressed them in winged words: "Zeus wishes
both of you to go to him with all speed, at Ida;
but when you have come there and looked upon Zeus' countenance,
then you must do whatever he urges you, and his orders."
     So the lady Hera spoke, and once more returning
150   sat on her throne. They in a flash of speed winged their way onward.
They came to Ida with all her springs, the mother of wild beasts,
and found the wide-browed son of Kronos on the height of Gargaron,
sitting still, and fragrant cloud gathered in a circle about him.
These two came into the presence of Zeus the cloud-gatherer
155   and stood, nor was his heart angry when he looked upon them,
seeing they had promptly obeyed the message of his dear lady.
He spoke to Iris first of the two, and addressed her in winged words:
"Go on your way now, swift Iris, to the lord Poseidon,
and give him all this message nor be a false messenger. Tell him
160   that he must now quit the war and the fighting, and go back
among the generations of gods, or into the bright sea.
And if he will not obey my words, or thinks nothing of them,
then let him consider in his heart and his spirit
that he might not, strong though he is, be able to stand up
165   to my attack; since I say I am far greater than he is
in strength, and elder born; yet his inward heart shrinks not from calling
himself the equal of me, though others shudder before me."

     He spoke, and swift wind-footed Iris did not disobey him
but went down along the hills of Ida to sacred Ilion.
170   As those times when out of the clouds the snow or the hail whirls
cold beneath the blast of the north wind born in the bright air,
so rapidly in her eagerness winged Iris, the swift one,
and stood beside the famed shaker of the earth, and spoke to him:
"I have a certain message for you, dark-haired, earth-encircler,

and came here to bring it to you from Zeus of the aegis.                                   175
His order is that you quit the war and the fighting, and go back
among the generations of gods, or into the bright sea.
And if you will not obey his words, or think nothing of them,
his threat is that he himself will come to fight with you
here, strength against strength, but warns you to keep from under          180
his hands, since he says he is far greater than you are
in strength, and elder born. Yet your inward heart shrinks not from calling
yourself the equal of him, though others shudder before him."
     Then deeply vexed the famed shaker of the earth spoke to her:
"No, no. Great though he is, this that he has said is too much,                185
if he will force me against my will, me, who am his equal
in rank. Since we are three brothers born by Rheia to Kronos,
Zeus, and I, and the third is Hades, lord of the dead men.
All was divided among us three ways, each given his domain.
I when the lots were shaken drew the gray sea to live in                       190
forever; Hades drew the lot of the mists and the darkness,
and Zeus was allotted the wide sky, in the cloud and the bright air.
But earth and high Olympos are common to all three. Therefore
I am no part of the mind of Zeus. Let him in tranquility
and powerful as he is stay satisfied with his third share.                      195
And let him absolutely stop frightening me, as if I were
mean, with his hands. It were better to keep for the sons and the daughters
he got himself these blusterings and these threats of terror.
They will listen, because they must, to whatever he tells them."
     Then in turn swift wind-footed Iris answered him:                          200
"Am I then to carry, O dark-haired, earth-encircler,
this word, which is strong and steep, back to Zeus from you?
Or will you change a little? The hearts of the great can be changed.
You know the Furies, how they forever side with the elder."
     Then in turn the shaker of the earth Poseidon spoke to her:          205
"Now this, divine Iris, was a word quite properly spoken.
It is a fine thing when a messenger is conscious of justice.
But this thing comes as a bitter sorrow to my heart and my spirit,
when Zeus tries in words of anger to reprimand one who
is his equal in station, and endowed with destiny like his.                     210
Still, this time I will give way, for all my vexation.
But I will say this also, and make it a threat in my anger.

If ever, acting apart from me and Athene the spoiler,
apart from Hera and Hermes and the lord Hephaistos,
215    he shall spare headlong Ilion, and shall not be willing
to take it by storm, and bestow great victory on the Argives,
let him be sure, there will be no more healing of our anger."

The shaker of the earth spoke, and left the Achaian people,
and went, merging in the sea, and the fighting Achaians longed for him.
220    After this Zeus who gathers the clouds spoke to Apollo:
"Go now, beloved Phoibos, to the side of brazen-helmed Hektor,
since by this he who encircles the earth and shakes it
is gone into the bright sea and has avoided the anger
that would be ours. In truth, this would have been a fight those other
225    gods would have heard about, who gather to Kronos beneath us.
Now this way it was far better for me, and for himself
also, that, for all his vexation before, he gave way
to my hands. We would have sweated before this business was finished.
Now yourself take up in your hands the aegis with fluttering
230    tassels, and shake it hard to scare the Achaian fighters.
Then, striker from afar, let your own concern be glorious Hektor.
So long waken the huge strength in him, until the Achaians
run in flight, and come to the ships and the crossing of Helle.
From there on I myself shall think of the word and the action
235    to make the Achaians get wind once more, after their hard fighting."
He spoke so, and Apollo, not disregarding his father,
came down along the mountains of Ida in the likeness of a rapid
hawk, the dove's murderer and swiftest of all things flying.
He found brilliant Hektor, the son of wise Priam, sitting
240    now, no longer sprawled, as he gathered new strength back into him
and recognized his companions about him. The sweat and hard breathing
had begun to stop, once the will in Zeus of the aegis wakened him.
Apollo who works from afar stood beside him, and spoke to him:
"Hektor, son of Priam, why do you sit in such weakness
245    here apart from the others? Did some disaster befall you?"
In his weakness Hektor of the shining helm spoke to him:
"Who are you, who speak to me face to face, O noblest
of gods? Did you not know how by the Achaians' grounded
ships, Aias of the great war cry struck me in the chest with a boulder

as I slaughtered his companions, and stayed my furious valor?   250
Truly, I thought that on this day I would come to the corpses
and the house of the death god, once I had breathed the inward life from me."
  In turn the lord, the worker from afar, Apollo, spoke to him:
"Take heart; such an avenger am I whom the son of Kronos
sent down from Ida, to stand by your side and defend you,   255
Phoibos Apollo of the golden sword, who in time before this
also have stood to defend yourself and your sheer citadel.
So come now, and urge on your cavalry in their numbers
to drive on their horses against the hollow ships. Meanwhile
I shall move on before you and make all the way for the horses   260
smooth before them, and bend back the Achaian fighters."
  He spoke, and breathed huge strength into the shepherd of the people.
As when some stalled horse who has been corn-fed at the manger
breaking free of his rope gallops over the plain in thunder
to his accustomed bathing place in a sweet-running river   265
and in the pride of his strength holds high his head and the mane floats
over his shoulders; sure of his glorious strength, the quick knees
carry him to the loved places and the pasture of horses;
so Hektor moving rapidly his feet and his knees went
onward, stirring the horsemen when he heard the god's voice speak.   270
And as when men who live in the wilds and their dogs have driven
into flight a horned stag or a wild goat. Inaccessible
the rocky cliff or the shadowed forest has covered the quarry
so that the men know it was not their fortune to take him;
and now by their clamoring shows in the way a great bearded   275
lion, and bends them to sudden flight for all their eagerness;
so the Danaäns until that time kept always in close chase
assembled, stabbing at them with swords and leaf-headed spears,
but when they saw Hektor once more ranging the men's ranks
they were frightened, and by their feet collapsed all their bravery.   280

  Now Thoas spoke forth among them, the son of Andraimon,
far the best of the Aitolians, one skilled in the spear's throw
and brave in close fight. In assembly few of the Achaians
when the young men contended in debate could outdo him.
He in kind intention now spoke forth and addressed them:   285
"Can this be? Here is a strange thing I see with my own eyes,

how this Hektor has got to his feet once more, and eluded
the death spirits. I think in each of us the heart had high hope
he was killed under the hands of Telamonian Aias.

290 Now some one of the gods has come to his help and rescued
Hektor, who has unstrung the knees of so many Danaäns.
I think he will do it once more now. It is not without Zeus
the deep-thundering that he stands their champion in all this fury.
Come then, let us do as I say, let us all be persuaded.

295 Let us tell the multitude to make its way back toward the vessels
while we ourselves, who claim we are greatest in all the army,
stand, and see if we can face him first, and hold him off from them
with spears lifted against him, and I think for all of his fury
his heart will be afraid to plunge into our Danaän company."

300 So he spoke, and they listened to him with care, and obeyed him.
They who rallied about Aias, the lord Idomeneus,
Teukros, Meriones, and Meges, a man like the war god,
closed their order for hard impact, calling on the bravest
to face Hektor and the Trojans. Meanwhile behind them

305 the multitude made their way back toward the ships of the Achaians.
The Trojans came down on them in a pack, and Hektor led them
in long strides, and in front of him went Phoibos Apollo
wearing a mist about his shoulders, and held the tempestuous
terrible aegis, shaggy, conspicuous, that the bronze-smith

310 Hephaistos had given Zeus to wear to the terror of mortals.
Gripping this in both hands he led on the Trojan people.
But the Argives stood in close order against them, and the battle cry rose up
in a thin scream from either side, the arrows from the bowstrings
jumping, while from violent hands the numerous thrown spears

315 were driven, some deep in the bodies of quick-stirring young men,
while many in the space between before they had got to the white skin
stood fast in the ground, though they had been straining to reach the bodies.
So long as Phoibos Apollo held stilled in his hands the aegis,
so long the thrown weapons of both took hold, and men dropped under
      them.

320 But when he stared straight into the eyes of the fast-mounted Danaäns
and shook the aegis, and himself gave a great baying cry, the spirit
inside them was mazed to hear it, they forgot their furious valor.

And they, as when in the dim of the black night two wild beasts
stampede a herd of cattle or big flock of sheep, falling
suddenly upon them, when no herdsman is by, the Achaians                325
fled so in their weakness and terror, since Apollo drove
terror upon them, and gave the glory to the Trojans and Hektor.

There man killed man all along the scattered encounter.
Hektor first killed Stichios and Arkesilaos,
one the leader of the bronze-armored Boiotians, the other              330
trusted companion in arms of great-hearted Menestheus.
But Aineias slaughtered Medon and Iasos. Of these
Medon was a bastard son of godlike Oïleus
and therefore brother of Aias, but had made his home in Phylakē
away from the land of his fathers, having killed a man, a relation     335
of Eriopis, his stepmother, the wife of Oïleus.
Iasos was a leader appointed of the Athenians,
and was called the son of Sphelos, the son of Boukolos.
Poulydamas killed Mekisteus, and Polites Echios
in the first onfall, and brilliant Agenor cut down Klonios.            340
Paris struck Deïochos from behind at the shoulder's
base, as he ran away through the front ranks, and drove the bronze clean
    through.
While these stripped the armor from their men, meanwhile the Achaians
blundering about the deep-dug ditch and the sharp stakes
ran this way and that in terror, forced into their rampart.            345
But Hektor called aloud in a piercing cry to the Trojans:
"Make hard for the ships, let the bloody spoils be. That man
I see in the other direction apart from the vessels,
I will take care that he gets his death, and that man's relations
neither men nor women shall give his dead body the rite of burning.    350
In the space before our city the dogs shall tear him to pieces."
So speaking with a whipstroke from the shoulder he lashed on his horses
calling across the ranks to the Trojans, who along with him
all cried aloud as they steered the horses who pulled their chariots,
with inhuman clamor, and in front of them Phoibos Apollo               355
easily, kicking them with his feet, tumbled the banked edges
of the deep ditch into the pit between, and bridged over a pathway
both wide and long, about as long as the force of a spearcast

goes when a man has thrown it to try his strength. They streamed over
360   in massed formation, with Apollo in front of them holding
the tremendous aegis, and wrecked the bastions of the Achaians
easily, as when a little boy piles sand by the seashore
when in his innocent play he makes sand towers to amuse him
and then, still playing, with hands and feet ruins them and wrecks them.
365   So you, lord Apollo, piled in confusion much hard work
and painful done by the Argives and drove terror among them.
So they reined in and stood fast again beside their ships, calling
aloud upon each other, and to all of the gods, uplifting
their hands each man of them cried out his prayers in a great voice,
370   and beyond others Gerenian Nestor, the Achaians' watcher,
prayed, reaching out both arms to the starry heavens:
"Father Zeus, if ever in wheat-deep Argos one of us
burning before you the rich thigh pieces of sheep or ox prayed
he would come home again, and you nodded your head and assented,
375   remember this, Olympian, save us from the day without pity;
let not the Achaians be beaten down like this by the Trojans."
So he spoke in prayer, and Zeus of the counsels thundered
a great stroke, hearing the prayer of the old man, the son of Neleus.

But the Trojans, hearing the thunderstroke of Zeus of the aegis,
380   remembered even more their warcraft, and sprang on the Argives.
They, as when the big waves on the sea wide-wandering
wash across the walls of a ship underneath the leaning
force of the wind, which particularly piles up the big waves,
so the Trojans with huge clamor went over the rampart
385   and drove their horses to fight alongside the grounded vessels,
with leaf-headed spears, some at close quarters, others from their horses.
But the Achaians climbing high on their black ships fought from them
with long pikes that lay among the hulls for sea fighting,
shrouded about the heads in bronze that was soldered upon them.

390   Meanwhile Patroklos, all the time the Achaians and Trojans
were fighting on both sides of the wall, far away from the fast ships,
had sat all this time in the shelter of courtly Eurypylos
and had been entertaining him with words and applying
medicines that would mitigate the black pains to the sore wound.

But when he saw the Trojans were sweeping over the rampart          395
and the outcry and the noise of terror rose from the Danaäns
Patroklos groaned aloud then and struck himself on both thighs
with the flats of his hands and spoke a word of lamentation:
"Eurypylos, much though you need me I cannot stay here
longer with you. This is a big fight that has arisen.                400
Now it is for your henchman to look after you, while I
go in haste to Achilleus, to stir him into the fighting.
Who knows if, with God helping, I might trouble his spirit
by entreaty, since the persuasion of a friend is a strong thing."
    As he was speaking his feet carried him away. Meanwhile          405
the Achaians stood steady against the Trojan attack, but they could not
beat the enemy, fewer as they were, away from their vessels,
nor again had the Trojans strength to break the battalions
of the Danaäns, and force their way into the ships and the shelters.
But as a chalkline straightens the cutting of a ship's timber        410
in the hands of an expert carpenter, who by Athene's
inspiration is well versed in all his craft's subtlety,
so the battles fought by both sides were pulled fast and even.
Now by the ships others fought in their various places
but Hektor made straight for glorious Aias. These two                415
were fighting hard for a single ship, and neither was able,
Hektor to drive Aias off the ship, and set fire to it,
nor Aias to beat Hektor back, since the divinity
drove him. Shining Aias struck with the spear Kaletor,
Klytios' son, in the chest as he brought fire to the vessel.          420
He fell, thunderously, and the torch dropped from his hand. Then
Hektor, when his eyes were aware of his cousin fallen
in the dust in front of the black ship, uplifting
his voice in a great cry called to the Trojans and Lykians:
"Trojans, Lykians, Dardanians who fight at close quarters,            425
do not anywhere in this narrow place give way from the fighting
but stand by the son of Klytios, do not let the Achaians
strip the armor from him, fallen where the ships are assembled."

    So he spoke, and made a cast at Aias with the shining
spear, but missed him and struck the son of Mastor, Lykophron,        430
henchman of Aias from Kythera who had been living

with him; for he had killed a man in sacred Kythera.
Hektor struck him in the head above the ear with the sharp bronze
as he stood next to Aias, so that Lykophron sprawling
435 dropped from the ship's stern to the ground, and his strength was broken.
And Aias shuddered at the sight, and spoke to his brother:
"See, dear Teukros, our true companion, the son of Mastor,
is killed, who came to us from Kythera and in our household
was one we honored as we honored our beloved parents.
440 Now great-hearted Hektor has killed him. Where are your arrows
of sudden death, and the bow that Phoibos Apollo gave you?"
He spoke, and Teukros heard and came running to stand beside him
holding in his hand the backstrung bow and the quiver
to hold arrows, and let go his hard shots against the Trojans.
445 First he struck down Kleitos, the glorious son of Peisenor
and companion of Poulydamas, proud son of Panthoös.
Now Kleitos held the reins, and gave all his care to the horses,
driving them into that place where the most battalions were shaken,
for the favor of Hektor and the Trojans, but the sudden evil
450 came to him, and none for all their desire could defend him,
for the painful arrow was driven into his neck from behind him.
He fell out of the chariot, and the fast-footed horses
shied away, rattling the empty car; but Poulydamas
their master saw it at once, and ran first to the heads of the horses.
455 He gave them into the hands of Astynoös, Protiaon's
son, with many orders to be watchful and hold the horses
close; then himself went back into the ranks of the champions.
But Teukros picked up another arrow for bronze-helmed
Hektor, and would have stopped his fighting by the ships of the Achaians
460 had he hit him during his bravery and torn the life from him;
but he was not hidden from the close purpose of Zeus, who was guarding
Hektor, and denied that glory to Telamonian Teukros;
who broke in the unfaulted bow the close-twisted sinew
as Teukros drew it against him, so the bronze-weighted arrow
465 went, as the bow dropped out of his hands, driven crazily sidewise.
And Teukros shuddered at the sight, and spoke to his brother:
"See now, how hard the divinity cuts across the intention
in all our battle, who struck the bow out of my hand, who has broken
the fresh-twisted sinew of the bowstring I bound on

this morning, so it would stand the succession of springing arrows."          470
    Then in turn huge Telamonian Aias answered him:
"Dear brother, then let your bow and your showering arrows
lie, now that the god begrudging the Danaäns wrecked them.
But take a long spear in your hands, a shield on your shoulder,
and close with the Trojans, and drive on the rest of your people.          475
Let them not, though they have beaten us, easily capture
our strong-benched ships. We must remember the frenzy of fighting."
    He spoke, and Teukros put away the bow in his shelter
and threw across his shoulders the shield of the fourfold ox-hide.
Over his mighty head he set the well-fashioned helmet          480
with the horse-hair crest, and the plumes nodded terribly above it.
Then he caught up a powerful spear, edged with sharp bronze,
and went on his way, running fast, and stood beside Aias.

    But Hektor, when he saw how the arrows of Teukros were baffled,
lifted his voice in a great cry to the Trojans and Lykians:          485
"Trojans, Lykians, Dardanians who fight at close quarters,
be men now, dear friends, remember your furious valor
along the hollow ships, since I have seen with my own eyes
how by the hand of Zeus their bravest man's arrows were baffled.
Easily seen is the strength that is given from Zeus to mortals          490
either in those into whose hands he gives the surpassing
glory, or those he diminishes and will not defend them
as now he diminishes the strength of the Argives, and helps us.
Fight on then by the ships together. He who among you
finds by spear thrown or spear thrust his death and destiny,          495
let him die. He has no dishonor when he dies defending
his country, for then his wife shall be saved and his children afterward,
and his house and property shall not be damaged, if the Achaians
must go away with their ships to the beloved land of their fathers."
    So he spoke, and stirred the spirit and strength in each man.          500
But Aias on the other side called to his companions:
"Shame, you Argives; here is the time of decision, whether
we die, or live on still and beat back ruin from our vessels.
Do you expect, if our ships fall to helm-shining Hektor,
you will walk each of you back dryshod to the land of your fathers?          505
Do you not hear how Hektor is stirring up all his people,

how he is raging to set fire to our ships? He is not
inviting you to come to a dance. He invites you to battle.
For us there can be no design, no purpose, better than this one,
510   to close in and fight with the strength of our hands at close quarters.
Better to take in a single time our chances of dying
or living, than go on being squeezed in the stark encounter
right up against our ships, as now, by men worse than we are."
       So he spoke, and stirred the spirit and strength in each man.
515   There Hektor killed the son of Perimedes, Schedios,
lord of the men of Phokis; but Aias killed Laodamas,
leader of the foot-soldiers, and shining son of Antenor.
Then Poulydamas stripped Otos of Kyllene, companion
to Meges, Phyleus' son, and a lord among the great-hearted
520   Epeians. Meges seeing it lunged at him, but Poulydamas
bent down and away, so that Meges missed him. Apollo
would not let Panthoös' son go down among the front fighters,
but Meges stabbed with the spear the middle of the chest of Kroismos.
He fell, thunderously, and Meges was stripping the armor
525   from his shoulders, but meanwhile Dolops lunged at him, Lampos'
son, a man crafty with the spear and strongest of the sons born
to Lampos, Laomedon's son, one skilled in furious fighting.
He from close up stabbed with his spear at the shield of Phyleides
in the middle, but the corselet he wore defended him, solid
530   and built with curving plates of metal, which in days past Phyleus
had taken home from Ephyra and the river Selleëis.
A guest and friend had given him it, lord of men, Euphetes,
to carry into the fighting and beat off the attack of the enemy,
and now it guarded the body of his son from destruction.
535   But Meges stabbed with the sharp spear at the uttermost summit
of the brazen helmet thick with horse-hair, and tore off
the mane of horse-hair from the helmet, so that it toppled
groundward and lay in the dust in all its new shining of purple.
Yet Dolops stood his ground and fought on, in hope still of winning,
540   but meanwhile warlike Menelaos came to stand beside Meges,
and came from the side and unobserved with his spear, and from behind
threw at his shoulder, so the spear tore through his chest in its fury
to drive on, so that Dolops reeled and went down, face forward.
The two of them swept in to strip away from his shoulders

the bronze armor, but Hektor called aloud to his brothers,                    545
the whole lot, but first scolded the son of Hiketaon,
strong Melanippos. He in Perkote had tended his lumbering
cattle, in the days before when the enemy were still far off;
but when the oarswept ships of the Danaäns came, then
he returned to Ilion, and was a great man among the Trojans,    550
and lived with Priam, who honored him as he honored his children.
Now Hektor spoke a word and called him by name and scolded him:
"Shall we give way so, Melanippos? Does it mean nothing
even to you in the inward heart that your cousin is fallen?
Do you not see how they are busied over the armor of Dolops?    555
Come on, then; no longer can we stand far off and fight with
the Argives. Sooner we must kill them, or else sheer Ilion
be stormed utterly by them, and her citizens be killed."

He spoke, and led the way, and the other followed, a mortal
godlike. But huge Telamonian Aias stirred on the Argives:        560
"Dear friends, be men; let shame be in your hearts, and discipline,
and have consideration for each other in the strong encounters,
since more come through alive when men consider each other,
and there is no glory when they give way, nor warcraft either."
He spoke, and they likewise grew furious in their defense,       565
and put his word away in their hearts, and fenced in their vessels
in a circle of bronze, but Zeus against them wakened the Trojans.
Then Menelaos of the great war cry stirred on Antilochos:
"Antilochos, no other Achaian is younger than you are,
nor faster on his feet, nor strong as you are in fighting.       570
You could make an outrush and strike down some man of the Trojans."
So speaking, he hastened back but stirred Antilochos onward,
and he sprang forth from the champions and hefted the shining javelin,
glaring round about him, and the Trojans gave way in the face
of the man throwing with the spear. And he made no vain cast     575
but struck Hiketaon's son, Melanippos the high-hearted,
in the chest next to the nipple as he swept into the fighting.
He fell, thunderously, and darkness closed over both eyes.
Antilochos sprang forth against him, as a hound rushes
against a stricken fawn that as he broke from his covert         580
a hunter has shot at, and hit, and broken his limbs' strength.

So Antilochos stubborn in battle sprang, Melanippos,
at you, to strip your armor, but did not escape brilliant Hektor's
notice, who came on the run through the fighting against him.
585  Antilochos did not hold his ground, although a swift fighter,
but fled away like a wild beast who has done some bad thing,
one who has killed a hound or an ox-herd tending his cattle
and escapes, before a gang of men has assembled against him;
so Nestor's son ran away, and after him the Trojans and Hektor
590  with unearthly clamor showered their groaning weapons against him.
He turned and stood when he got into the swarm of his own companions.

But the Trojans in the likeness of ravening lions swept on
against the ships, and were bringing to accomplishment Zeus' orders,
who wakened always the huge strength in them, dazed the courage
595  of the Argives, and denied their glory, and stirred on the others.
Zeus' desire was to give glory to the son of Priam,
Hektor, that he might throw on the curved ships the inhuman
weariless strength of fire, and so make completely accomplished
the prayer of Thetis. Therefore Zeus of the counsels waited
600  the sight before his eyes of the flare, when a single ship burned.
From thereon he would make the attack of the Trojans
surge back again from the ships, and give the Danaäns glory.
With this in mind he drove on against the hollow ships Hektor,
Priam's son, though Hektor without the god was in fury
605  and raged, as when destructive fire or spear-shaking Ares
rages among the mountains and dense places of the deep forest.
A slaver came out around his mouth, and under the lowering
brows his eyes were glittering, the helm on his temples
was shaken and thundered horribly to the fighting of Hektor.
610  Out of the bright sky Zeus himself was working to help him
and among men so numerous he honored this one man
and glorified him, since Hektor was to have only a short life
and already the day of his death was being driven upon him
by Pallas Athene through the strength of Achilleus. And now
615  he was probing the ranks of men, and trying to smash them,
and made for where there were most men together, and the best armor.
But even so he could not break them, for all his fury,
for they closed into a wall and held him, like some towering

huge sea-cliff that lies close along the gray salt water
and stands up against the screaming winds and their sudden directions          620
and against the waves that grow to bigness and burst up against it.
So the Danaäns stood steady against the Trojans, nor gave way.
But he, lit about with flame on all sides, charged on their numbers
and descended upon them as descends on a fast ship the battering
wave storm-bred from beneath the clouds, and the ship goes utterly          625
hidden under the foam, and the dangerous blast of the hurricane
thunders against the sail, and the hearts of the seamen are shaken
with fear, as they are carried only a little way out of death's reach.
So the heart in the breast of each Achaian was troubled.
Hektor came on against them, as a murderous lion on cattle          630
who in the low-lying meadow of a great marsh pasture
by hundreds, and among them a herdsman who does not quite know
how to fight a wild beast off from killing a horn-curved
ox, and keeps pace with the first and the last of the cattle
always, but the lion making his spring at the middle          635
eats an ox as the rest stampede; so now the Achaians
fled in unearthly terror before father Zeus and Hektor,
all, but he got one only, Periphetes of Mykenai,
beloved son of Kopreus, who for the lord Eurystheus
had gone often with messages to powerful Herakles.          640
To him, a meaner father, was born a son who was better
for all talents, in the speed of his feet and in battle
and for intelligence counted among the first in Mykenai.
Thereby now higher was the glory he granted to Hektor.
For as he whirled about to get back, he fell over the out-rim          645
of the shield he carried, which reached to his feet to keep the spears from
     him.
Stumbling on this he went over on his back, and the helmet
that circled his temples clashed horribly as he went down.
Hektor saw it sharply, and ran up and stood beside him,
and stuck the spear into his chest and killed him before the eyes          650
of his dear friends, who for all their sorrowing could do nothing
to help their companion, being themselves afraid of great Hektor.

     Now they had got among the ships, and the ends were about them
of the ships hauled up in the first line, but the Trojans swarmed

655 on them. The Argives under force gave back from the first line
of their ships, but along the actual shelters they rallied
in a group, and did not scatter along the encampment. Shame held them
and fear. They kept up a continuous call to each other,
and beyond others Gerenian Nestor, the Achaians' watcher,
660 supplicated each man by the knees for the sake of his parents.
"Dear friends, be men; let shame be in your hearts and discipline
in the sight of other men, and each one of you remember
his children and his wife, his property and his parents,
whether a man's father and mother live or have died. Here now
665 I supplicate your knees for the sake of those who are absent
to stand strongly and not be turned to the terror of panic."
So he spoke, and stirred the spirit and heart in each man,
and from their eyes Athene pushed the darkness immortal
of mist, and the light came out hard against them on both sides
670 whether they looked from the ships or from the closing of battle.
They knew Hektor of the great war cry, they knew his companions
whether they stood away behind and out of the fighting
or whether alongside the fast ships they fought in the battle.
Nor did it still please great-hearted Aias to stand back
675 where the other sons of the Achaians had taken position;
but he went in huge strides up and down the decks of the vessels.
He wielded in his hands a great pike for sea fighting,
twenty-two cubits long and joined together by clinchers.
And as a man who is an expert rider of horses
680 who when he has chosen and coupled four horses out of many
makes his way over the plain galloping toward a great city
along the traveled road, and many turn to admire him,
men or women, while he steadily and never slipping
jumps and shifts his stance from one to another as they gallop;
685 so Aias ranged crossing from deck to deck of the fast ships
taking huge strides, and his voice went always up to the bright sky
as he kept up a terrible bellow and urged on the Danaäns
to defend their ships and their shelters, while on the other side Hektor
would not stay back among the mass of close-armored Trojans,
690 but as a flashing eagle makes his plunge upon other
flying birds as these feed in a swarm by a river,
whether these be geese or cranes or swans long-throated,

so Hektor steered the course of his outrush straight for a vessel
with dark prows, and from behind Zeus was pushing him onward
hard with his big hand, and stirred on his people beside him.                    695

   Now once again a grim battle was fought by the vessels;
you would say that they faced each other unbruised, unwearied
in the fighting, from the speed in which they went for each other.
This was the thought in each as they struggled on: the Achaians
thought they could not get clear of the evil, but must perish,                   700
while the heart inside each one of the Trojans was hopeful
to set fire to the ships and kill the fighting men of Achaia.
With such thoughts in mind they stood up to fight with each other.
Hektor caught hold of the stern of a grand, fast-running,
seafaring ship, that once had carried Protesilaos                                705
to Troy, and did not take him back to the land of his fathers.
It was around his ship that now Achaians and Trojans
cut each other down at close quarters, nor any longer
had patience for the volleys exchanged from bows and javelins
but stood up close against each other, matching their fury,                      710
and fought their battle with sharp hatchets and axes, with great
swords and with leaf-headed pikes, and many magnificent
swords were scattered along the ground, black-thonged, heavy-hilted,
sometimes dropping from the hands, some glancing from shoulders
of men as they fought, so the ground ran black with blood. Hektor             715
would not let go of the stern of a ship where he had caught hold of it
but gripped the sternpost in his hands and called to the Trojans:
"Bring fire, and give single voice to the clamor of battle.
Now Zeus has given us a day worth all the rest of them:
the ships' capture, the ships that came here in spite of the gods' will        720
and have visited much pain on us, by our counselors' cowardice
who would not let me fight by the grounded ships, though I wanted to,
but held me back in restraint, and curbed in our fighters.
But Zeus of the wide brows, though then he fouled our intentions,
comes now himself to urge us on and give us encouragement."                    725
   He spoke, and they thereby came on harder against the Argives.
Their volleys were too much for Aias, who could hold no longer
his place, but had to give back a little, expecting to die there,
back to the seven-foot midship, and gave up the high deck of the balanced

730  ship. There he stood and waited for them, and with his pike always
beat off any Trojan who carried persistent fire from the vessels.
He kept up a terrible bellowing, and urged on the Danaäns:
"Friends and fighting men of the Danaäns, henchmen of Ares,
be men now, dear friends, remember your furious valor.
735  Do we think there are others who stand behind us to help us?
Have we some stronger wall that can rescue men from perdition?
We have no city built strong with towers lying near us, within which
we could defend ourselves and hold off this host that matches us.
We hold position in this plain of the close-armored Trojans,
740  bent back against the sea, and far from the land of our fathers.
Salvation's light is in our hands' work, not the mercy of battle."
      He spoke, and came forward with his sharp spear, raging for battle.
And whenever some Trojan crashed against the hollow ships
with burning fire, who sought to wake the favor of Hektor,
745  Aias would wait for him and then stab with the long pike
and so from close up wounded twelve in front of the vessels.

# BOOK SIXTEEN

So they fought on both sides for the sake of the strong-benched vessel.
Meanwhile Patroklos came to the shepherd of the people, Achilleus,
and stood by him and wept warm tears, like a spring dark-running
that down the face of a rock impassable drips its dim water;
and swift-footed brilliant Achilleus looked on him in pity,                     5
and spoke to him aloud and addressed him in winged words: "Why then
are you crying like some poor little girl, Patroklos,
who runs after her mother and begs to be picked up and carried,
and clings to her dress, and holds her back when she tries to hurry,
and gazes tearfully into her face, until she is picked up?                      10
You are like such a one, Patroklos, dropping these soft tears.
Could you have some news to tell, for me or the Myrmidons?
Have you, and nobody else, received some message from Phthia?
Yet they tell me Aktor's son Menoitios lives still
and Aiakos' son Peleus lives still among the Myrmidons.                         15
If either of these died we should take it hard. Or is it
the Argives you are mourning over, and how they are dying
against the hollow ships by reason of their own arrogance?
Tell me, do not hide it in your mind, and so we shall both know."
        Then groaning heavily, Patroklos the rider, you answered:              20
"Son of Peleus, far greatest of the Achaians, Achilleus,
do not be angry; such grief has fallen upon the Achaians.
For all those who were before the bravest in battle
are lying up among the ships with arrow or spear wounds.
The son of Tydeus, strong Diomedes, was hit by an arrow,                        25

and Odysseus has a pike wound, and Agamemnon the spear-famed,
and Eurypylos has been wounded in the thigh with an arrow.
And over these the healers skilled in medicine are working
to cure their wounds. But you, Achilleus; who can do anything
30    with you? May no such anger take me as this that you cherish!
Cursed courage. What other man born hereafter shall be advantaged
unless you beat aside from the Argives this shameful destruction?
Pitiless: the rider Peleus was never your father
nor Thetis was your mother, but it was the gray sea that bore you
35    and the towering rocks, so sheer the heart in you is turned from us.
But if you are drawing back from some prophecy known in your own heart
and by Zeus' will your honored mother has told you of something,
then send me out at least, let the rest of the Myrmidon people
follow me, and I may be a light given to the Danaäns.
40    Give me your armor to wear on my shoulders into the fighting;
so perhaps the Trojans might think I am you, and give way
from their attack, and the fighting sons of the Achaians get wind
again after hard work. There is little breathing space in the fighting.
We unwearied might with a mere cry pile men wearied
45    back upon their city, and away from the ships and the shelters."

        So he spoke supplicating in his great innocence; this was
his own death and evil destruction he was entreating.
But now, deeply troubled, swift-footed Achilleus answered him:
"Ah, Patroklos, illustrious, what is this you are saying?
50    I have not any prophecy in mind that I know of;
there is no word from Zeus my honored mother has told me,
but this thought comes as a bitter sorrow to my heart and my spirit
when a man tries to foul one who is his equal, to take back
a prize of honor, because he goes in greater authority.
55    This is a bitter thought to me; my desire has been dealt with
roughly. The girl the sons of the Achaians chose out for my honor,
and I won her with my own spear, and stormed a strong-fenced city,
is taken back out of my hands by powerful Agamemnon,
the son of Atreus, as if I were some dishonored vagabond.
60    Still, we will let all this be a thing of the past; and it was not
in my heart to be angry forever; and yet I have said
I would not give over my anger until that time came

when the fighting with all its clamor came up to my own ships.
So do you draw my glorious armor about your shoulders;
lead the Myrmidons whose delight is battle into the fighting,                           65
if truly the black cloud of the Trojans has taken position
strongly about our ships, and the others, the Argives, are bent back
against the beach of the sea, holding only a narrow division
of land, and the whole city of the Trojans has descended upon them
boldly; because they do not see the face of my helmet                                    70
glaring close; or else they would run and cram full of dead men
the water-courses; if powerful Agamemnon treated me
kindly. Now the Argives fight for their very encampment.
For the spear rages not now in the hands of the son of Tydeus,
Diomedes, to beat destruction aside from the Danaäns,                                    75
nor have I heard the voice of the son of Atreus crying
from his hated head; no, but the voice of murderous Hektor
calling to the Trojans crashes about my ears; with their war cry
they hold the entire plain as they beat the Achaians in battle.
But even so, Patroklos, beat the bane aside from our ships; fall                         80
upon them with all your strength; let them not with fire's blazing
inflame our ships, and take away our desired homecoming.
But obey to the end this word I put upon your attention
so that you can win, for me, great honor and glory
in the sight of all the Danaäns, so they will bring back to me                           85
the lovely girl, and give me shining gifts in addition.
When you have driven them from the ships, come back; although later
the thunderous lord of Hera might grant you the winning of glory,
you must not set your mind on fighting the Trojans, whose delight
is in battle, without me. So you will diminish my honor.                                 90
You must not, in the pride and fury of fighting, go on
slaughtering the Trojans, and lead the way against Ilion,
for fear some one of the everlasting gods on Olympos
might crush you. Apollo who works from afar loves these people
dearly. You must turn back once you bring the light of salvation                         95
to the ships, and let the others go on fighting in the flat land.
Father Zeus, Athene and Apollo, if only
not one of all the Trojans could escape destruction, not one
of the Argives, but you and I could emerge from the slaughter
so that we two alone could break Troy's hallowed coronal."                               100

Now as these two were talking thus to each other, meanwhile
the volleys were too much for Aias, who could hold no longer
his place. The will of Zeus beat him back, and the proud Trojans
with their spears, and around his temples the shining helmet
105 clashed horribly under the shower of strokes; he was hit constantly
on the strong-wrought cheek-pieces, and his left shoulder was tiring
from always holding up the big glittering shield; yet they could not
beat him out of his place, though they piled their missiles upon him.
His breath came ever hard and painful, the sweat ran pouring
110 down his body from every limb, he could find no means
to catch his breath, but evil was piled on evil about him.

Tell me now, you Muses who have your homes on Olympos,
how fire was first thrown upon the ships of the Achaians.
Hektor stood up close to Aias and hacked at the ash spear
115 with his great sword, striking behind the socket of the spearhead,
and slashed it clean away, so that Telamonian Aias
shook there in his hand a lopped spear, while far away from him
the bronze spearhead fell echoing to the ground; and Aias
knew in his blameless heart, and shivered for knowing it, how this
120 was gods' work, how Zeus high-thundering cut across the intention
in all his battle, how he planned that the Trojans should conquer.
He drew away out of the missiles, and the Trojans threw weariless fire
on the fast ship, and suddenly the quenchless flame streamed over it.
So the fire was at work on the ship's stern; but Achilleus
125 struck his hands against both his thighs, and called to Patroklos:
"Rise up, illustrious Patroklos, rider of horses.
I see how the ravening fire goes roaring over our vessels.
They must not get our ships so we cannot run away in them.
Get on your armor; faster; I will muster our people."

130 He spoke, and Patroklos was helming himself in bronze that glittered.
First he placed along his legs the beautiful greaves, linked
with silver fastenings to hold the greaves at the ankles.
Afterward he girt on about his chest the corselet
starry and elaborate of swift-footed Aiakides.
135 Across his shoulders he slung the sword with the nails of silver,

a bronze sword, and above it the great shield, huge and heavy.
Over his mighty head he set the well-fashioned helmet
with the horse-hair crest, and the plumes nodded terribly above it.
He took up two powerful spears that fitted his hand's grip,
only he did not take the spear of blameless Aiakides,                   140
huge, heavy, thick, which no one else of all the Achaians
could handle, but Achilleus alone knew how to wield it;
the Pelian ash spear which Cheiron had brought to his father
from high on Pelion to be death for fighters. Patroklos
ordered Automedon rapidly to harness the horses,                       145
a man he honored most, after Achilleus breaker of battles,
who stood most staunchly by him against the fury of fighting.
For him Automedon led the fast-running horses under
the yoke, Xanthos and Balios, who tore with the winds' speed,
horses stormy Podarge once conceived of the west wind                  150
and bore, as she grazed in the meadow beside the swirl of the Ocean.
In the traces beside these he put unfaulted Pedasos
whom Achilleus brought back once when he stormed Eëtion's city.
He, mortal as he was, ran beside the immortal horses.

   But Achilleus went meanwhile to the Myrmidons, and arrayed them    155
all in their war gear along the shelters. And they, as wolves
who tear flesh raw, in whose hearts the battle fury is tireless,
who have brought down a great horned stag in the mountains, and then feed
on him, till the jowls of every wolf run blood, and then go
all in a pack to drink from a spring of dark-running water,            160
lapping with their lean tongues along the black edge of the surface
and belching up the clotted blood; in the heart of each one
is a spirit untremulous, but their bellies are full and groaning;
as such the lords of the Myrmidons and their men of counsel
around the brave henchman of swift-footed Aiakides                     165
swarmed, and among them was standing warlike Achilleus
and urged on the fighting men with their shields, and the horses.

   Fifty were the fast-running ships wherein Achilleus
beloved of Zeus had led his men to Troy, and in each one
were fifty men, his companions in arms, at the rowing benches.         170
He had made five leaders among them, and to these entrusted

the command, while he in his great power was lord over all of them.
One battalion was led by Menesthios of the shining
corselet, son of Spercheios, the river swelled from the bright sky,
175 born of the daughter of Peleus, Polydore the lovely,
to unremitting Spercheios, when a woman lay with an immortal;
but born in name to Perieres' son, Boros, who married
Polydore formally, and gave gifts beyond count to win her.
The next battalion was led by warlike Eudoros, a maiden's
180 child, born to one lovely in the dance, Polymele,
daughter of Phylas; whom strong Hermes Argeïphontes
loved, when he watched her with his eyes among the girls dancing
in the choir for clamorous Artemis of the golden distaff.
Presently Hermes the healer went up with her into her chamber
185 and lay secretly with her, and she bore him a son, the shining
Eudoros, a surpassing runner and a quick man in battle.
But after Eileithyia of the hard pains had brought out
the child into the light, and he looked on the sun's shining,
Aktor's son Echekles in the majesty of his great power
190 led her to his house, when he had given numberless gifts to win her,
and the old man Phylas took the child and brought him up kindly
and cared for him, in affection as if he had been his own son.
The leader of the third battalion was warlike Peisandros,
Maimalos' son, who outshone all the rest of the Myrmidons
195 in spear-fighting, next to Peleian Achilleus' henchman.
The fourth battalion was led by Phoinix, the aged horseman,
the fifth by Alkimedon, the blameless son of Laërkes.
But after Achilleus gave them their stations all in good order
beside their leaders, he laid his stern injunction upon them:
200 "Myrmidons: not one of you can forget those mutterings,
those threats that beside the running ships you made at the Trojans
in all the time of my anger, and it was I you were blaming,
as: 'Hard son of Peleus! Your mother nursed you on gall. You have no
pity, to keep your companions here by the ships unwilling.
205 We should go back home again, then, in our seafaring vessels
now that this wretched anger has befallen your spirit.'
Often you would gather in groups and so mutter against me,
and now is shown a great work of that fighting you longed for.
Then let each man take heart of strength to fight with the Trojans."

So he spoke, and stirred the spirit and strength in each man, 210
and their ranks, as they listened to the king, pulled closer together.
And as a man builds solid a wall with stones set close together
for the rampart of a high house keeping out the force of the winds, so
close together were the helms and shields massive in the middle.
For shield leaned on shield, helmet on helmet, man against man, 215
and the horse-hair crests along the horns of the shining helmets
touched as they bent their heads, so dense were they formed on each other.
And before them all were two men in their armor, Patroklos
and Automedon, both of them in one single fury
to fight in front of the Myrmidons. But meanwhile Achilleus 220
went off into his shelter, and lifted the lid from a lovely
elaborately wrought chest, which Thetis the silver-footed
had put in his ship to carry, and filled it fairly with tunics
and mantles to hold the wind from a man, and with fleecy blankets.
Inside this lay a wrought goblet, nor did any other 225
man drink the shining wine from it nor did Achilleus
pour from it to any other god, but only Zeus father.
He took this now out of the chest, and cleaned it with sulfur
first, and afterward washed it out in bright-running water,
and washed his own hands, and poured shining wine into the goblet 230
and stood in his middle forecourt and prayed, and poured the wine,
        looking
into the sky, not unseen by Zeus who delights in the thunder:
"High Zeus, lord of Dodona, Pelasgian, living afar off,
brooding over wintry Dodona, your prophets about you
living, the Selloi who sleep on the ground with feet unwashed. Hear me. 235
As one time before when I prayed to you, you listened
and did me honor, and smote strongly the host of the Achaians,
so one more time bring to pass the wish that I pray for.
For see, I myself am staying where the ships are assembled,
but I send out my companion and many Myrmidons with him 240
to fight. Let glory, Zeus of the wide brows, go forth with him.
Make brave the heart inside his breast, so that even Hektor
will find out whether our henchman knows how to fight his battles
by himself, or whether his hands rage invincible only
those times when I myself go into the grind of the war god. 245
But when he has beaten back from the ships their clamorous onset,

then let him come back to me and the running ships, unwounded,
with all his armor and with the companions who fight close beside him."

So he spoke in prayer, and Zeus of the counsels heard him.
250 The father granted him one prayer, and denied him the other.
That Patroklos should beat back the fighting assault on the vessels
he allowed, but refused to let him come back safe out of the fighting.
When Achilleus had poured the wine and prayed to Zeus father
he went back into the shelter, stowed the cup in the chest, and came out
255 to stand in front of the door, with the desire in his heart still
to watch the grim encounter of Achaians and Trojans.
     Now they who were armed in the company of great-hearted Patroklos
went onward, until in high confidence they charged on the Trojans.
The Myrmidons came streaming out like wasps at the wayside
260 when little boys have got into the habit of making them angry
by always teasing them as they live in their house by the roadside;
silly boys, they do something that hurts many people;
and if some man who travels on the road happens to pass them
and stirs them unintentionally, they in heart of fury
265 come swarming out each one from his place to fight for their children.
In heart and in fury like these the Myrmidons streaming
came out from their ships, with a tireless clamor arising,
and Patroklos called afar in a great voice to his companions:
"Myrmidons, companions of Peleus' son, Achilleus,
270 be men now, dear friends, remember your furious valor;
we must bring honor to Peleus' son, far the greatest of the Argives
by the ships, we, even the henchmen who fight beside him,
so Atreus' son wide-ruling Agamemnon may recognize
his madness, that he did no honor to the best of the Achaians."
275 So he spoke, and stirred the spirit and strength in each man.
They fell upon the Trojans in a pack, and about them
the ships echoed terribly to the roaring Achaians.
But the Trojans, when they saw the powerful son of Menoitios
himself and his henchman with him in the glare of their war gear,
280 the heart was stirred in all of them, the battalions were shaken
in the expectation that by the ships swift-footed Peleion
had thrown away his anger and chosen the way of friendship.
Then each man looked about him for a way to escape the sheer death.

Patroklos was the first man to make a cast with the shining
spear, straight through the middle fighting, where most men were stricken,     285
beside the stern on the ship of great-hearted Protesilaos,
and struck Pyraichmes, who had led the lords of Paionian
horses from Amydon and the wide waters of Axios.
He struck him in the right shoulder, so he dropped in the dust groaning,
on his back, and his Paionian companions about him                              290
scattered; for Patroklos drove the fear into all of them
when he cut down their leader, the best of them all in battle.
He drove them from the ships and put out the fire that was blazing,
and that ship was left half-burnt as it was, as the Trojans scattered
in terror and unearthly noise, and the Danaäns streamed back                    295
along the hollow ships, and clamor incessant rose up.
And as when from the towering height of a great mountain Zeus
who gathers the thunderflash stirs the cloud dense upon it,
and all the high places of the hills are clear and the shoulders out-jutting
and the deep ravines, as endless bright air spills from the heavens,            300
so when the Danaäns had beaten from their ships the ravening
fire, they got breath for a little, but there was no check in the fighting;
for the Trojans under the attack of the warlike Achaians
had not yet turned their faces to run away from the black ships.
They stood yet against them, but gave way from the ships under pressure.        305

There man killed man all along the scattered encounter
of the leaders, and first among them, the strong son of Menoitios,
threw and struck Areïlykos in the thigh, as he turned
back, with the sharp point of the spear, and drove the bronze clean through.
The spear smashed in the bone and he fell to the ground headlong               310
on his face. Meanwhile warlike Menelaos stabbed Thoas
in the chest where it was left bare by the shield, and unstrung his limbs'
    strength.
Meges, Phyleus' son, watched Amphiklos as he came on
and was too quick with a stab at the base of the leg, where the muscle
of a man grows thickest, so that on the spearhead the sinew                    315
was torn apart, and a mist of darkness closed over both eyes.
Of the sons of Nestor one, Antilochos, stabbed Atymnios
with the sharp spear, and drove the bronze head clean through his flank, so
that he fell forward; but Maris with the spear from close up

320 made a lunge at Antilochos in rage for his brother
standing in front of the corpse, but before him godlike Thrasymedes
was in with a thrust before he could stab, nor missed his quick stroke
into the shoulder, and the spearhead shore off the arm's base
clear away from the muscles and torn from the bone utterly.
325 He fell, thunderously, and darkness closed over both eyes.
So these two, beaten down under the hands of two brothers,
descended to the dark place, Sarpedon's noble companions
and spear-throwing sons of Amisodaros, the one who had nourished
the furious Chimaira to be an evil to many.
330 Aias, Oïleus' son, in an outrush caught Kleoboulos
alive, where he was fouled in the running confusion, and there
unstrung his strength, hewing with the hilted sword at the neck,
so all the sword was smoking with blood and over both eyes
closed the red death and the strong destiny. Then Peneleos
335 and Lykon ran up close together, since these with their spear-throws
had gone wide of each other, and each had made a cast vainly.
So now the two of them ran together with swords. There Lykon
hacked at the horn of the horse-hair crested helm, but the sword blade
broke at the socket; Peneleos cut at the neck underneath
340 the ear, and the sword sank clean inside, with only skin left
to hold it, and the head slumped aside, and the limbs were loosened.
Meriones on his light feet overtaking Akamas
stabbed him in the right shoulder as he climbed up behind his horses
and the darkness drifted over his eyes as he crashed from the chariot.
345 Idomeneus stabbed Erymas in the mouth with the pitiless
bronze, so that the brazen spearhead smashed its way clean through
below the brain in an upward stroke, and the white bones splintered,
and the teeth were shaken out with the stroke and both eyes filled up
with blood, and gaping he blew a spray of blood through the nostrils
350 and through his mouth, and death in a dark mist closed in about him.

So these lords of the Danaäns killed each his own man.
They as wolves make havoc among lambs or young goats in their fury,
catching them out of the flocks, when the sheep separate in the mountains
through the thoughtlessness of the shepherd, and the wolves seeing them
355 suddenly snatch them away, and they have no heart for fighting;
so the Danaäns ravaged the Trojans, and these remembered

the bitter sound of terror, and forgot their furious valor.

But the great Aias was trying forever to make a spearcast
at bronze-helmed Hektor, but he in his experience of fighting
with his broad shoulders huddled under the bull's-hide shield kept          360
watching always the whistle of arrows, the crash of spears thrown.
He knew well how the strength of the fighting shifted against him,
but even so stood his ground to save his steadfast companions.

As when a cloud goes deep into the sky from Olympos
through the bright upper air when Zeus brings on the hurricane,          365
so rose from beside the ships their outcry, the noise of their terror.
In no good order they went back, while his fast-running horses
carried Hektor away in his armor; he abandoned the people
of the Trojans, who were trapped by the deep-dug ditch unwilling,
and in the ditch many fast horses who pulled the chariots          370
left, broken short at the joining of the pole, their masters' chariots
while Patroklos was on them, calling hard and loud to the Danaäns
with evil intention for the Trojans, who, in clamorous terror,
choked all the ways where they were cut off; from under their feet stirred
the dust-storm scattered in clouds, their single-foot horses were straining          375
to get back to the city away from the ships and the shelters.
But Patroklos, where he saw the stirring of most people,
steered there, shouting, and men went down under the axles
headlong from chariots as the empty cars rattled onward.
Straight across the ditch overleapt those swift and immortal          380
horses the gods had given as shining gifts to Peleus,
hurtling onward, as Patroklos' rage stirred him against Hektor,
whom he tried to strike, but his fast horses carried him out of it.
As underneath the hurricane all the black earth is burdened
on an autumn day, when Zeus sends down the most violent waters          385
in deep rage against mortals after they stir him to anger
because in violent assembly they pass decrees that are crooked,
and drive righteousness from among them and care nothing for what the
     gods think,
and all the rivers of these men swell current to full spate
and in the ravines of their water-courses rip all the hillsides          390
and dash whirling in huge noise down to the blue sea, out of
the mountains headlong, so that the works of men are diminished;
so huge rose the noise from the horses of Troy in their running.

But Patroklos, when he had cut away their first battalions,
395 turned back to pin them against the ships, and would not allow them
to climb back into their city though they strained for it, but sweeping
through the space between the ships, the high wall, and the river,
made havoc and exacted from them the blood price for many.
There first of all he struck with the shining spear Pronoös
400 in the chest where it was left bare by the shield, and unstrung his limbs'
strength.
He fell, thunderously, and Patroklos in his next outrush
at Thestor, Enops' son, who huddled inside his chariot,
shrunk back, he had lost all his nerve, and from his hands the reins
slipped—Patroklos coming close up to him stabbed with a spear-thrust
405 at the right side of the jaw and drove it on through the teeth, then
hooked and dragged him with the spear over the rail, as a fisherman
who sits out on the jut of a rock with line and glittering
bronze hook drags a fish, who is thus doomed, out of the water.
So he hauled him, mouth open to the bright spear, out of the chariot,
410 and shoved him over on his face, and as he fell the life left him.
Next he struck Erylaos, as he swept in, with a great stone
in the middle of the head, and all the head broke into two pieces
inside the heavy helmet, and he in the dust face downward
dropped while death breaking the spirit drifted about him.
415 Afterward with Erymas, Amphoteros, and Epaltes,
Tlepolemos Damastor's son, Echios and Pyris,
Ipheus and Euippos, and Argeas' son Polymelos,
all these he felled to the bountiful earth in rapid succession.

But Sarpedon, when he saw his free-girt companions going
420 down underneath the hands of Menoitios' son Patroklos,
called aloud in entreaty upon the godlike Lykians:
"Shame, you Lykians, where are you running to? You must be fierce now,
for I myself will encounter this man, so I may find out
who this is who has so much strength and has done so much evil
425 to the Trojans, since many and brave are those whose knees he has unstrung."
He spoke, and sprang to the ground in all his arms from the chariot,
and on the other side Patroklos when he saw him leapt down
from his chariot. They as two hook-clawed beak-bent vultures
above a tall rock face, high-screaming, go for each other,

so now these two, crying aloud, encountered together.                               430
And watching them the son of devious-devising Kronos
was pitiful, and spoke to Hera, his wife and his sister:
"Ah me, that it is destined that the dearest of men, Sarpedon,
must go down under the hands of Menoitios' son Patroklos.
The heart in my breast is balanced between two ways as I ponder,     435
whether I should snatch him out of the sorrowful battle
and set him down still alive in the rich country of Lykia,
or beat him under at the hands of the son of Menoitios."
    In turn the lady Hera of the ox eyes answered him:
"Majesty, son of Kronos, what sort of thing have you spoken?           440
Do you wish to bring back a man who is mortal, one long since
doomed by his destiny, from ill-sounding death and release him?
Do it, then; but not all the rest of us gods shall approve you.
And put away in your thoughts this other thing I tell you;
if you bring Sarpedon back to his home, still living,                          445
think how then some other one of the gods might also
wish to carry his own son out of the strong encounter;
since around the great city of Priam are fighting many
sons of the immortals. You will waken grim resentment among them.
No, but if he is dear to you, and your heart mourns for him,            450
then let him be, and let him go down in the strong encounter
underneath the hands of Patroklos, the son of Menoitios;
but after the soul and the years of his life have left him, then send
Death to carry him away, and Sleep, who is painless,
until they come with him to the countryside of broad Lykia             455
where his brothers and countrymen shall give him due burial
with tomb and gravestone. Such is the privilege of those who have perished."
    She spoke, nor did the father of gods and men disobey her;
yet he wept tears of blood that fell to the ground, for the sake
of his beloved son, whom now Patroklos was presently                    460
to kill, by generous Troy and far from the land of his fathers.


    Now as these two advancing had come close to each other
there Patroklos threw first at glorious Thrasymelos
who was the strong henchman of lord Sarpedon, and struck him
in the depth of the lower belly, and unstrung his limbs' strength.    465
Sarpedon with the second throw then missed with the shining

spear, but the spear fixed in the right shoulder of Pedasos
the horse, who screamed as he blew his life away, and went down
in shrill noise into the dust, and the life spirit flittered from him.
470  The other horses shied apart, the yoke creaked, the guide reins
were fouled together as the trace horse lay in the dust beside them;
but at this spear-famed Automedon saw what he must do
and wrenching out the long-edged sword from beside his big thigh
in a flashing stroke and without faltering cut loose the trace horse
475  and the other horses were straightened out, and pulled in the guide reins,
and the two heroes came together in the heart-perishing battle.
    Once again Sarpedon threw wide with a cast of his shining
spear, so that the pointed head overshot the left shoulder
of Patroklos; and now Patroklos made the second cast with the brazen
480  spear, and the shaft escaping his hand was not flung vainly
but struck where the beating heart is closed in the arch of the muscles.
He fell, as when an oak goes down or a white poplar,
or like a towering pine tree which in the mountains the carpenters
have hewn down with their whetted axes to make a ship-timber.
485  So he lay there felled in front of his horses and chariots
roaring, and clawed with his hands at the bloody dust; or as
a blazing and haughty bull in a huddle of shambling cattle
when a lion has come among the herd and destroys him
dies bellowing under the hooked claws of the lion, so now
490  before Patroklos the lord of the shield-armored Lykians
died raging, and called aloud to his beloved companion:
"Dear Glaukos, you are a fighter among men. Now the need comes
hardest upon you to be a spearman and a bold warrior.
Now, if you are brave, let bitter warfare be dear to you.
495  First you must go among all men who are lords of the Lykians
everywhere, and stir them up to fight for Sarpedon,
and then you yourself also must fight for me with the bronze spear.
For I shall be a thing of shame and a reproach said of you
afterward, all your days forever, if the Achaians
500  strip my armor here where I fell by the ships assembled.
But hold strongly on and stir up all the rest of our people."
    He spoke, and as he spoke death's end closed over his nostrils
and eyes, and Patroklos stepping heel braced to chest dragged
the spear out of his body, and the midriff came away with it

so that he drew out with the spearhead the life of Sarpedon,                              505
and the Myrmidons close by held in the hard-breathing horses
as they tried to bolt away, once free of their master's chariot.

But when he heard the voice a hard sorrow came upon Glaukos,
and the heart was stirred within him, and he could not defend Sarpedon.
He took his arm in his hand and squeezed it, since the wound hurt him        510
where Teukros had hit him with an arrow shot as he swept in
on the high wall, and fended destruction from his companions.
He spoke in prayer to him who strikes from afar, Apollo:
"Hear me, my lord. You are somewhere in the rich Lykian countryside
or here in Troy, and wherever you are you can listen                              515
to a man in pain, as now this pain has descended upon me.
For see, I have this strong wound on me, and my arm on both sides
is driven with sharp pains about, my blood is not able
to dry and stop running, my shoulder is aching beneath it.
I cannot hold my spear up steady, I cannot go forward                              520
to fight against the enemy. And the best of men has perished,
Sarpedon, son of Zeus; who will not stand by his children.
No, but you at least, my lord, make well this strong wound;
and put the pains to sleep, give me strength, so that I may call out
to my companions, the Lykians, and stir them to fight on,                         525
and I myself do battle over the fallen body."
      So he spoke in prayer, and Phoibos Apollo heard him.
At once he made the pains stop, and dried away from the hard wound
the dark running of blood, and put strength into his spirit.
And Glaukos knew in his heart what was done, and was happy                       530
that the great god had listened to his prayer. And first of all
he roused toward battle all the men who were lords of the Lykians,
going everywhere among them, to fight for Sarpedon;
afterward he ranged in long strides among the Trojans,
by Poulydamas the son of Panthoös and brilliant Agenor,                         535
and went to Aineias and to Hektor of the brazen helmet
and stood near them and addressed them in winged words: "Hektor,
now you have utterly forgotten your armed companions
who for your sake, far from their friends and the land of their fathers,
are wearing their lives away, and you will do nothing to help them.          540
Sarpedon has fallen, the lord of the shield-armored Lykians,

who defended Lykia in his strength and the right of his justice.
Now brazen Ares has struck him down by the spear of Patroklos.
Then, friends, stand beside me, let the thought be shame in your spirit
545 that they might strip away his arms, and dishonor his body,
these Myrmidons, in anger for all the Danaäns perished,
those whom we Lykians have killed with the spear by the swift ships."
   He spoke, and the Trojans were taken head to heel with a sorrow
untakeable, not to be endured, since he was their city's
550 stay, always, though he was an outlander, and many people
came with him, but he was the best of them all in battle
always. They went straight for the Danaäns, raging, and Hektor
led them, in anger for Sarpedon. Meanwhile the Achaians
roused to the savage heart of Patroklos, the son of Menoitios.
555 First he spoke to the Aiantes, who were burning for battle already:
"Aiantes, now your desire must be to defend yourselves, and be
such as you were among men before, or even more valiant.
The man is fallen who first scaled the wall of the Achaians,
Sarpedon. If only we could win and dishonor his body
560 and strip the armor from his shoulders, and kill with the pitiless
bronze some one of his companions who fight to defend him."
   He spoke, and they likewise grew furious in their defense,
and when they on either side had made massive their battalions,
Trojans and Lykians, and Myrmidons and Achaians,
565 they clashed together in battle over the perished body
howling terribly, with a high crash of the men in their armor,
while Zeus swept ghastly night far over the strong encounter
that over his dear son might be deadly work in the fighting.

   First the Trojans shouldered back the glancing-eyed Achaians
570 when a man, and not the worst of the Myrmidons, was struck down,
son of high-hearted Agakles, Epeigeus the brilliant.
He was one who was lord before in strong-founded Boudeion,
but now, since he had happened to kill his high-born cousin,
had come suppliant to Peleus and to Thetis the silver-footed,
575 and these sent him to follow Achilleus, who broke men in battle,
to Ilion of the horses and the battle against the Trojans.
As he caught at a dead man glorious Hektor hit him
with a stone in the head, and all the head broke into two pieces

inside the heavy helmet, and he in the dust face downward
dropped, while death breaking the spirit drifted about him.                    580
And the sorrow took hold of Patroklos for his fallen companion.
He steered his way through the ranks of the front fighters, like a flying
hawk who scatters into flight the daws and the starlings.
So straight for the Lykians, O lord of horses, Patroklos,
you swept, and for the Trojans, heart angered for your companion.              585
Now he struck Sthenelaos, beloved son of Ithaimenes,
in the neck with a stone, and broke the tendons loose from about it.
The champions of Troy gave back then, and glorious Hektor.
As far as goes the driving cast of a slender javelin
which a man throws making trial of his strength, either in a contest          590
or else in battle, under the heart-breaking hostilities,
so far the Trojans gave way with the Achaians pushing them.
But Glaukos was first, lord of the shield-armored Lykians,
to turn again, and killed Bathykles the great-hearted, beloved
son of Chalkon, who had dwelled in his home in Hellas                         595
conspicuous for wealth and success among all the Myrmidons.
It was he whom Glaukos stabbed in the middle of the chest, turning
suddenly back with his spear as he overtook him. He fell,
thunderously, and the closing sorrow came over the Achaians
as the great man went down, but the Trojans were gladdened greatly           600
and came and stood in a pack about him, nor did the Achaians
let go of their fighting strength, but steered their fury straight at them.
And there Meriones cut down a chief man of the Trojans,
Laogonos, bold son of Onetor, who was Idaian,
Zeus' priest, and who was honored in his countryside as a god is.            605
Meriones struck him by jaw and ear, and at once the life spirit
fled from his limbs, and the hateful darkness closed in about him.
But Aineias threw his bronze spear at Meriones, hoping
to hit him as he came forward under his shield's covering,
but Meriones with his eyes straight on him avoided the bronze spear.         610
For he bent forward, and behind his back the long spearshaft
was driven into the ground so that the butt end was shaken
on the spear. Then and there Ares the huge took the force from it
[so that the vibrant shaft of Aineias was driven groundward
since it had been thrown in a vain cast from his big hand].                   615
But Aineias was angered in his spirit, and called out to him:

"Meriones, though you are a dancer my spear might have stopped you
now and for all time, if only I could have hit you."

Then in turn Meriones the spear-famed answered him:
620 "Aineias, strong fighter though you are, it would be hard for you
to quench the strength of every man who might come against you
and defend himself, since you also are made as a mortal.
But if I could throw and hit you with the sharp bronze in the middle,
then strong as you are and confident in your hands' work, you might
625 give the glory to me, and your soul to Hades of the horses."
He spoke, but the fighting son of Menoitios reprimanded him:
"Meriones, when you are a brave fighter, why say such things?—
See, dear friend, the Trojans will not give back from the body
for hard words spoken. Sooner the ground will cover them. Warfare's
630 finality lies in the work of hands, that of words in counsel.
It is not for us now to pile up talk, but to fight in battle."

He spoke, and led the way, and the other followed, a mortal
like a god. As the tumult goes up from men who are cutting
timber in the mountain valleys, and the sound is heard from far off,
635 such was the dull crashing that rose from earth of the wide ways,
from the bronze shields, the skins and the strong-covering ox-hides
as the swords and leaf-headed spears stabbed against them. No longer
could a man, even a knowing one, have made out the godlike
Sarpedon, since he was piled from head to ends of feet under
640 a mass of weapons, the blood and the dust, while others about him
kept forever swarming over his dead body, as flies
through a sheepfold thunder about the pails overspilling
milk, in the season of spring when the milk splashes in the buckets.
So they swarmed over the dead man, nor did Zeus ever
645 turn the glaring of his eyes from the strong encounter,
but kept gazing forever upon them, in spirit reflective,
and pondered hard over many ways for the death of Patroklos;
whether this was now the time, in this strong encounter,
when there over godlike Sarpedon glorious Hektor
650 should kill him with the bronze, and strip the armor away from his shoulders,
or whether to increase the steep work of fighting for more men.
In the division of his heart this way seemed best to him,

for the strong henchman of Achilleus, the son of Peleus,
once again to push the Trojans and bronze-helmed Hektor
back on their city, and tear the life from many. In Hektor          655
first of all he put a temper that was without strength.
He climbed to his chariot and turned to flight, and called to the other
Trojans to run, for he saw the way of Zeus' sacred balance.
Nor did the powerful Lykians stand now, but were all scattered
to flight, when they had seen their king with a spear in his heart, lying   660
under the pile of dead men, since many others had fallen
above him, once Zeus had strained fast the powerful conflict.
But the Achaians took from Sarpedon's shoulders the armor
glaring and brazen, and this the warlike son of Menoitios
gave to his companions to carry back to the hollow ships.           665
And now Zeus who gathers the clouds spoke a word to Apollo:
"Go if you will, beloved Phoibos, and rescue Sarpedon
from under the weapons, wash the dark suffusion of blood from him,
then carry him far away and wash him in a running river,
anoint him in ambrosia, put ambrosial clothing upon him;           670
then give him into the charge of swift messengers to carry him,
of Sleep and Death, who are twin brothers, and these two shall lay him
down presently within the rich countryside of broad Lykia
where his brothers and countrymen shall give him due burial
with tomb and gravestone. Such is the privilege of those who have perished."  675
    He spoke so, and Apollo, not disregarding his father,
went down along the mountains of Ida, into the grim fight,
and lifting brilliant Sarpedon out from under the weapons
carried him far away, and washed him in a running river,
and anointed him in ambrosia, put ambrosial clothing upon him,      680
then gave him into the charge of swift messengers to carry him,
of Sleep and Death, who are twin brothers, and these two presently
laid him down within the rich countryside of broad Lykia.


    But Patroklos, with a shout to Automedon and his horses,
went after Trojans and Lykians in a huge blind fury.               685
Besotted: had he only kept the command of Peleiades
he might have got clear away from the evil spirit of black death.
But always the mind of Zeus is a stronger thing than a man's mind.
He terrifies even the warlike man, he takes away victory

690　lightly, when he himself has driven a man into battle
　　　as now he drove on the fury in the heart of Patroklos.

　　　Then who was it you slaughtered first, who was the last one,
　　　Patroklos, as the gods called you to your death? Adrestos
　　　first, and after him Autonoös and Echeklos,
695　Perimos, son of Megas, and Epistor, and Melanippos,
　　　and after these Elasos, and Moulios, and Pylartes.
　　　These he killed, while each man of the rest was bent on escaping.

　　　There the sons of the Achaians might have taken gate-towering Ilion
　　　under the hands of Patroklos, who raged with the spear far before them,
700　had not Phoibos Apollo taken his stand on the strong-built
　　　tower, with thoughts of death for him, but help for the Trojans.
　　　Three times Patroklos tried to mount the angle of the towering
　　　wall, and three times Phoibos Apollo battered him backward
　　　with the immortal hands beating back the bright shield. As Patroklos
705　for the fourth time, like something more than a man, came at him
　　　he called aloud, and spoke winged words in the voice of danger:
　　　"Give way, illustrious Patroklos: it is not destined
　　　that the city of the proud Trojans shall fall before your spear
　　　nor even at the hand of Achilleus, who is far better than you are."
710　　He spoke, and Patroklos gave ground before him a great way,
　　　avoiding the anger of him who strikes from afar, Apollo.

　　　But Hektor inside the Skaian Gates held his single-foot horses,
　　　and wondered whether to drive back into the carnage, and fight there,
　　　or call aloud to his people to rally inside the wall. Thus
715　as he was pondering Phoibos Apollo came and stood by him,
　　　assuming the likeness of a man, a young and a strong one,
　　　Asios, who was uncle to Hektor, breaker of horses,
　　　since he was brother of Hekabē, and the son of Dymas,
　　　and had made his home in Phrygia by the stream of Sangarios.
720　In the likeness of this man Zeus' son Apollo spoke to him:
　　　"Hektor, why have you stopped fighting? You should not do it.
　　　If I were as much stronger than you as now I am weaker!
　　　So might you, in this evil way, hold back from the fighting.
　　　But come! Hold straight against Patroklos your strong-footed horses.

You might be able to kill him. Apollo might give you such glory." 725
    He spoke, and went once more, a divinity, into the mortals'
struggle, while glorious Hektor called to wise Kebriones
to lash their horses into the fighting. Meanwhile Apollo
went down into the battle, and launched a deadly confusion
upon the Argives, and gave glory to the Trojans and Hektor. 730
Now Hektor let the rest of the Danaäns be, and he would not
kill them, but drove his strong-footed horses straight for Patroklos.
On the other side Patroklos sprang to the ground from his chariot
holding his spear in his left hand. In the other he caught up
a stone, jagged and shining, in the hold of his hand, and threw it, 735
leaning into the throw, nor fell short of the man he aimed at
nor threw vainly, but hit the charioteer of Hektor,
Kebriones, a bastard son of glorious Priam,
as he held the reins on his horses. The sharp stone hit him in the forehead
and smashed both brows in on each other, nor could the bone hold 740
the rock, but his eyes fell out into the dust before him
there at his feet, so that he vaulted to earth like a diver
from the carefully wrought chariot, and the life left his bones. Now
you spoke in bitter mockery over him, rider Patroklos:
"See now, what a light man this is, how agile an acrobat. 745
If only he were somewhere on the sea, where the fish swarm,
he could fill the hunger of many men, by diving for oysters;
he could go overboard from a boat even in rough weather
the way he somersaults so light to the ground from his chariot
now. So, to be sure, in Troy also they have their acrobats." 750
    He spoke so, and strode against the hero Kebriones
with the spring of a lion, who as he ravages the pastures
has been hit in the chest, and his own courage destroys him.
So in your fury you pounced, Patroklos, above Kebriones.
On the other side Hektor sprang to the ground from his chariot, 755
and the two fought it out over Kebriones, like lions
who in the high places of a mountain, both in huge courage
and both hungry, fight together over a killed deer.
So above Kebriones these two, urgent for battle,
Patroklos, son of Menoitios, and glorious Hektor, 760
were straining with the pitiless bronze to tear at each other;
since Hektor had caught him by the head, and would not let go of him,

and Patroklos had his foot on the other side, while the other
Trojans and Danaäns drove together the strength of their onset.

765    As east wind and south wind fight it out with each other
in the valleys of the mountains to shake the deep forest timber,
oak tree and ash and the cornel with the delicate bark; these
whip their wide-reaching branches against one another
in inhuman noise, and the crash goes up from the splintering timber;
770    so Trojans and Achaians springing against one another
cut men down, nor did either side think of disastrous panic,
and many sharp spears were driven home about Kebriones
and many feathered arrows sprung from the bowstrings, many
great throwing stones pounded against the shields, as they fought on
775    hard over his body, as he in the turning dust lay
mightily in his might, his horsemanship all forgotten.
      So long as the sun was climbing still to the middle heaven,
so long the thrown weapons of both took hold, and men dropped under
        them;
but when the sun had gone to the time for unyoking of cattle,
780    then beyond their very destiny the Achaians were stronger
and dragged the hero Kebriones from under the weapons
and the clamor of the Trojans, and stripped the armor from his shoulders.
And Patroklos charged with evil intention in on the Trojans.
Three times he charged in with the force of the running war god,
785    screaming a terrible cry, and three times he cut down nine men;
but as for the fourth time he swept in, like something greater
than human, there, Patroklos, the end of your life was shown forth,
since Phoibos came against you there in the strong encounter
dangerously, nor did Patroklos see him as he moved through
790    the battle, and shrouded in a deep mist came in against him
and stood behind him, and struck his back and his broad shoulders
with a flat stroke of the hand so that his eyes spun. Phoibos
Apollo now struck away from his head the helmet
four-horned and hollow-eyed, and under the feet of the horses
795    it rolled clattering, and the plumes above it were defiled
by blood and dust. Before this time it had not been permitted
to defile in the dust this great helmet crested in horse-hair;
rather it guarded the head and the gracious brow of a godlike

man, Achilleus; but now Zeus gave it over to Hektor
to wear on his head, Hektor whose own death was close to him.                 800
And in his hands was splintered all the huge, great, heavy,
iron-shod, far-shadowing spear, and away from his shoulders
dropped to the ground the shield with its shield sling and its tassels.
The lord Apollo, son of Zeus, broke the corselet upon him.
Disaster caught his wits, and his shining body went nerveless.                 805
He stood stupidly, and from close behind his back a Dardanian
man hit him between the shoulders with a sharp javelin:
Euphorbos, son of Panthoös, who surpassed all men of his own age
with the throwing spear, and in horsemanship and the speed of his feet. He
had already brought down twenty men from their horses                          810
since first coming, with his chariot and his learning in warfare.
He first hit you with a thrown spear, O rider Patroklos,
nor broke you, but ran away again, snatching out the ash spear
from your body, and lost himself in the crowd, not enduring
to face Patroklos, naked as he was, in close combat.                           815

   Now Patroklos, broken by the spear and the god's blow, tried
to shun death and shrink back into the swarm of his own companions.
But Hektor, when he saw high-hearted Patroklos trying
to get away, saw how he was wounded with the sharp javelin,
came close against him across the ranks, and with the spear stabbed him        820
in the depth of the belly and drove the bronze clean through. He fell,
thunderously, to the horror of all the Achaian people.
As a lion overpowers a weariless boar in wild combat
as the two fight in their pride on the high places of a mountain
over a little spring of water, both wanting to drink there,                    825
and the lion beats him down by force as he fights for his breath, so
Hektor, Priam's son, with a close spear-stroke stripped the life
from the fighting son of Menoitios, who had killed so many,
and stood above him, and spoke aloud the winged words of triumph:
"Patroklos, you thought perhaps of devastating our city,                       830
of stripping from the Trojan women the day of their liberty
and dragging them off in ships to the beloved land of your fathers.
Fool! when in front of them the running horses of Hektor
strained with their swift feet into the fighting, and I with my own spear
am conspicuous among the fighting Trojans, I who beat from them                835

the day of necessity. For you, here the vultures shall eat you.
Wretch! Achilleus, great as he was, could do nothing to help you.
When he stayed behind, and you went, he must have said much to you:
'Patroklos, lord of horses, see that you do not come back to me
840 and the hollow ships, until you have torn in blood the tunic
of manslaughtering Hektor about his chest.' In some such
manner he spoke to you, and persuaded the fool's heart in you."
     And now, dying, you answered him, O rider Patroklos:
"Now is your time for big words, Hektor. Yours is the victory
845 given by Kronos' son, Zeus, and Apollo, who have subdued me
easily, since they themselves stripped the arms from my shoulders.
Even though twenty such as you had come in against me,
they would all have been broken beneath my spear, and have perished.
No, deadly destiny, with the son of Leto, has killed me,
850 and of men it was Euphorbos; you are only my third slayer.
And put away in your heart this other thing that I tell you.
You yourself are not one who shall live long, but now already
death and powerful destiny are standing beside you,
to go down under the hands of Aiakos' great son, Achilleus."

855      He spoke, and as he spoke the end of death closed in upon him,
and the soul fluttering free of his limbs went down into Death's house
mourning her destiny, leaving youth and manhood behind her.
Now though he was a dead man glorious Hektor spoke to him:
"Patroklos, what is this prophecy of my headlong destruction?
860 Who knows if even Achilleus, son of lovely-haired Thetis,
might before this be struck by my spear, and his own life perish?"
     He spoke, and setting his heel upon him wrenched out the bronze spear
from the wound, then spurned him away on his back from the spear.
     Thereafter
armed with the spear he went on, aiming a cast at Automedon,
865 the godlike henchman for the swift-footed son of Aiakos,
with the spear as he was carried away by those swift and immortal
horses the gods had given as shining gifts to Peleus.

# BOOK SEVENTEEN

As Patroklos went down before the Trojans in the hard fighting
he was not unseen by Atreus' son, warlike Menelaos,
who stalked through the ranks of the champions, helmed in the bright
    bronze,
and bestrode the body, as over a first-born calf the mother
cow stands lowing, she who has known no children before this.          5
So Menelaos of the fair hair stood over Patroklos
and held the spear and the perfect circle of his shield before him,
raging to cut down any man who might come forth against him.
Nor did the fall of blameless Patroklos pass unattended
by Panthoös' son of the strong ash spear, Euphorbos, who standing     10
close to face him spoke a word to warlike Menelaos:
"Son of Atreus, Menelaos, illustrious, leader of armies:
give way, let the bloody spoils be, get back from this body,
since before me no one of the Trojans, or renowned companions,
struck Patroklos down with the spear in the strong encounter.          15
Thereby let me win this great glory among the Trojans
before I hit you and strip the sweetness of life away from you."
    Deeply stirred, Menelaos of the fair hair answered him:
"Father Zeus, it is not well for the proud man to glory.
Neither the fury of the leopard is such, not such is the lion's,       20
nor the fury of the devastating wild boar, within whose breast
the spirit is biggest and vaunts in the pride of his strength, is so great
as goes the pride in these sons of Panthoös of the strong ash spear.
Yet even the strength of Hyperenor, breaker of horses,
had no joy of his youth when he stood against me and taunted me        25

and said that among all the Danaäns I was the weakest
in battle. Yet I think that his feet shall no more carry him
back, to pleasure his beloved wife and his honored parents.
So I think I can break your strength as well, if you only
30    stand against me. No, but I myself tell you to get back
into the multitude, not stand to face me, before you
take some harm. Once a thing has been done, the fool sees it."
    He spoke so, but did not persuade Euphorbos, who answered:
"Then, lordly Menelaos, you must now pay the penalty
35    for my brother, whom you killed, and boast that you did it,
and made his wife a widow in the depth of a young bride chamber
and left to his parents the curse of lamentation and sorrow.
Yet I might stop the mourning of these unhappy people
if I could carry back to them your head, and your armor,
40    and toss them into Panthoös' hands, and to Phrontis the lovely.
No, this struggle shall not go long untested between us
nor yet unfought, whether it prove our strength or our terror."
    He spoke, and stabbed Menelaos' shield in its perfect circle,
nor did the bronze break its way through, but the spearhead bent back
45    in the strong shield. And after him Atreus' son, Menelaos,
made his prayer to father Zeus and lunged with the bronze spear
and as he was drawing back caught him in the pit of the gullet
and leaned in on the stroke in the confidence of his strong hand,
and clean through the soft part of the neck the spearpoint was driven.
50    He fell, thunderously, and his armor clattered upon him,
and his hair, lovely as the Graces, was splattered with blood, those
braided locks caught waspwise in gold and silver. As some
slip of an olive tree strong-growing that a man raises
in a lonely place, and drenched it with generous water, so that
55    it blossoms into beauty, and the blasts of winds from all quarters
tremble it, and it bursts into pale blossoming. But then
a wind suddenly in a great tempest descending upon it
wrenches it out of its stand and lays it at length on the ground; such
was Euphorbos of the strong ash spear, the son of Panthoös,
60    whom Menelaos Atreides killed, and was stripping his armor.

    As when in the confidence of his strength some lion
hill-reared snatches the finest cow in a herd as it pastures;

first the lion breaks her neck caught fast in the strong teeth,
then gulps down the blood and all the guts that are inward
savagely, as the dogs and the herdsmen raise a commotion 65
loudly about him, but from a distance, and are not willing
to go in and face him, since the hard green fear has hold of them;
so no heart in the breast of any Trojan had courage
to go in and face glorious Menelaos. Then easily
the son of Atreus might have taken the glorious armor 70
from Panthoös' son, only Phoibos Apollo begrudged him
and stirred up Hektor, a match for the running war god, against him
in semblance of a man, the leader of the Kikones,
Mentes, and spoke aloud to him, and addressed him in winged words:
"While you, Hektor, run after what can never be captured, 75
the horses of valiant Aiakides; they are difficult horses
for mortal man to manage, or even to ride behind them
for all except Achilleus, who was born of an immortal mother;
meanwhile Menelaos, the warlike son of Atreus,
stands over Patroklos and has killed the best man of the Trojans, 80
Euphorbos, Panthoös' son, and stopped his furious valor."

So he spoke, and went back, a god, to the mortals' struggle.
But bitter sorrow closed over Hektor's heart in its darkness.
He looked about then across the ranks, and at once was aware
of the two men, one stripping the glorious armor, the other 85
sprawled on the ground, and blood running from the gash of the spear-
thrust.
He stalked through the ranks of the champions helmed in the bright bronze
with a shrill scream, and looking like the flame of Hephaistos,
weariless. Nor did Atreus' son fail to hear the sharp cry.
Deeply troubled, he spoke to his own great-hearted spirit: 90
"Ah me; if I abandon here the magnificent armor,
and Patroklos, who has fallen here for the sake of my honor,
shall not some one of the Danaäns, seeing it, hold it against me?
Yet if I fight, alone as I am, the Trojans and Hektor
for shame, shall they not close in, many against one, about me? 95
Hektor of the shining helm leads all of the Trojans
here. Then why does my own heart within me debate this?
When a man, in the face of divinity, would fight with another

whom some god honors, the big disaster rolls sudden upon him.
100 Therefore, let no Danaän seeing it hold it against me
if I give way before Hektor, who fights from God. Yet if somewhere
I could only get some word of Aias of the great war cry,
we two might somehow go, and keep our spirit of battle
even in the face of divinity, if we might win the body
105 for Peleïd Achilleus. It would be our best among evils."

Now as he was pondering this in his heart and his spirit
meanwhile the ranks of the Trojans came on, and Hektor led them;
and Menelaos backed away from them and left the dead man,
but kept turning on his way like some great bearded lion
110 when dogs and men drive him off from a steading with weapons
and shouts, and in the breast of the lion the strong heart of valor
freezes, and he goes reluctant away from the fenced ground.
So fair-haired Menelaos moved from Patroklos, but turning
stood fast when he had got back to the swarm of his own companions,
115 and looked all about for huge Aias, the son of Telamon,
and saw soon where he was, at the left of the entire battle
encouraging his companions and urging them into the fighting,
since Phoibos Apollo had smitten them all with unearthly terror.
He went on the run, and presently stood beside him and spoke to him:
120 "This way, Aias, we must make for fallen Patroklos
to try if we can carry back to Achilleus the body
which is naked; Hektor of the shining helm has taken his armor."
So he spoke, and stirred the spirit in valiant Aias
who strode among the champions, fair-haired Menelaos with him.
125 But Hektor, when he had stripped from Patroklos the glorious armor,
dragged at him, meaning to cut his head from his shoulders with the
    sharp bronze,
to haul off the body and give it to the dogs of Troy; but meanwhile
Aias came near him, carrying like a wall his shield,
and Hektor drew back to the company of his own companions
130 and sprang to his chariot, but handed over the beautiful armor
to the Trojans, to take back to the city and to be his great glory.
Now Aias covering the son of Menoitios under his broad shield
stood fast, like a lion over his young, when the lion
is leading his little ones along, and men who are hunting

come upon them in the forest. He stands in the pride of his great strength   135
hooding his eyes under the cover of down-drawn eyelids.
Such was Aias as he bestrode the hero Patroklos,
while on the other side Atreus' son, warlike Menelaos,
stood fast, feeding still bigger the great sorrow within him.

But Glaukos, lord of the Lykian men, the son of Hippolochos,   140
looked at Hektor, scowling, and laid a harsh word upon him:
"Hektor, splendid to look at, you come far short in your fighting.
That fame of yours, high as it is, belongs to a runner.
Take thought now how to hold fast your town, your citadel
by yourself, with those your people who were born in Ilion;   145
since no Lykian will go forth now to fight with the Danaäns
for the sake of your city, since after all we got no gratitude
for our everlasting hard struggle against your enemies.
How then, O hard-hearted, shall you save a worse man in all your
company, when you have abandoned Sarpedon, your guest-friend   150
and own companion, to be the spoil and prey of the Argives,
who was of so much use to you, yourself and your city
while he lived? Now you have not the spirit to keep the dogs from him.
Therefore now, if any of the Lykian men will obey me,
we are going home, and the headlong destruction of Troy shall be manifest.   155
For if the Trojans had any fighting strength that were daring
and unshaken, such as comes on men who, for the sake of their country,
have made the hard hateful work come between them and their enemies,
we could quickly get the body of Patroklos inside Ilion.
If, dead man though he be, he could be brought into the great city   160
of lord Priam, if we could tear him out of the fighting,
the Argives must at once give up the beautiful armor
of Sarpedon, and we could carry his body inside Ilion.
Such is the man whose henchman is killed. He is far the greatest
of the Argives by the ships, and his men fight hard at close quarters.   165
No, but you could not bring yourself to stand up against Aias
of the great heart, nor to look at his eyes in the clamor of fighting
men, nor attack him direct, since he is far better than you are."
Looking darkly at him tall Hektor of the shining helm answered:
"Glaukos, why did a man like you speak this word of annoyance?   170
I am surprised. I thought that for wits you surpassed all others

of those who dwell in Lykia where the soil is generous; and yet
now I utterly despise your heart for the thing you have spoken
when you said I cannot stand in the face of gigantic Aias.
175 I am not one who shudders at attack and the thunder of horses.
But always the mind of Zeus is a stronger thing than a man's mind.
He terrifies even the warlike man, he takes away victory
lightly, when he himself has driven a man into battle.
Come here, friend, and watch me at work; learn, standing beside me,
180 whether I shall be a coward all day, as you proclaim me,
or whether I stop some Danaän, for all of his fury,
from his fighting strength and from the defense of fallen Patroklos."
  So speaking he called afar in a great voice to the Trojans:
"Trojans, Lykians, Dardanians who fight at close quarters,
185 be men now, dear friends, remember your furious valor
while I am putting on the beautiful armor of blameless
Achilleus, which I stripped from Patroklos the strong when I killed him."

  So spoke Hektor of the shining helm, and departed
from the hateful battle, and running caught up with his companions
190 very soon, since he went on quick feet, and they had not gone far
carrying the glorious armor of Peleus' son toward the city.
He stood apart from the sorrowful fighting, and changed his armor,
and gave what he had worn to the fighting Trojans to carry
to sacred Ilion, and himself put on that armor immortal
195 of Peleïd Achilleus, which the Uranian gods had given
to his loved father; and he in turn grown old had given it
to his son; but a son who never grew old in his father's armor.
  When Zeus who gathers the clouds saw him, apart from the others
arming himself in the battle gear of godlike Peleïdes,
200 he stirred his head and spoke to his own spirit: "Ah, poor wretch!
There is no thought of death in your mind now, and yet death stands
close beside you as you put on the immortal armor
of a surpassing man. There are others who tremble before him.
Now you have killed this man's dear friend, who was strong and gentle,
205 and taken the armor, as you should not have done, from his shoulders
and head. Still for the present I will invest you with great strength
to make up for it that you will not come home out of the fighting,
nor Andromachē take from your hands the glorious arms of Achilleus."

He spoke, the son of Kronos, and nodded his head with the dark brows.
The armor was fitted to Hektor's skin, and Ares the dangerous                     210
war god entered him, so that the inward body was packed full
of force and fighting strength. He went onward calling in a great voice
to his renowned companions in arms, and figured before them
flaming in the battle gear of great-hearted Peleion.
He ranged their ranks, and spoke a word to encourage each captain,               215
to Mesthles and Glaukos, to Thersilochos and Medon,
Deisenor and Hippothoös and Asteropaios,
to Phorkys and Chromios and the bird interpreter Ennomos,
and stirring all of these forward called to them in winged words:
"Hear me, you numberless hordes of companions who live at our borders.          220
It was not for any desire nor need of a multitude
that man by man I gathered you to come here from your cities,
but so that you might have good will to defend the innocent
children of the Trojans, and their wives, from the fighting Achaians.
With such a purpose I wear out my own people for presents                          225
and food, wherewith I make strong the spirit within each one of you.
Therefore a man must now turn his face straight forward, and perish
or survive. This is the sweet invitation of battle.
That man of you who drags Patroklos, dead as he is, back
among Trojans, breakers of horses, and Aias gives way before him,                230
I will give him half the spoils for his portion, and keep half
for myself, and his glory shall be as great as mine is."

     So he spoke, and they lifted their spears and went straight for the Danaäns
who felt their weight, and inside each man the spirit was hopeful
to get the body away from Telamonian Aias.                                         235
Fools! since over the dead man he tore the life out of many.
Then Aias himself spoke to Menelaos of the great war cry:
"Illustrious Menelaos, dear friend, I no longer have hope
that even you and I can win back out of the fighting.
My fear is not so much for the dead body of Patroklos                             240
who presently must glut the dogs and the birds of Troy, so much
as I fear for my own head, my life, and what may befall it,
and for yours, since this cloud of war is darkened on all things,
this Hektor, while for you and me sheer death is emerging.
Come then, call the great men of the Danaäns, if one might hear you."            245

He spoke, and Menelaos of the great war cry obeyed him.
He lifted his voice and called in a piercing cry to the Danaäns:
"Friends, O leaders and men of counsel among the Argives,
you that beside Agamemnon and Menelaos, the two sons
250  of Atreus, drink the community's wine and give, each man, his orders
to the people; and from Zeus the respect and honor attend you.
It is hard for me to discriminate among you each man
who is a leader, so big is the bitter fight that has blazed up.
Then let a man come of his own accord, think it shameful
255  that Patroklos be given to the dogs of Troy to delight them."
He spoke, and swift Aias son of Oïleus was sharp to hear him
and was first to come running along the battle, and join him,
and after him Idomeneus, and Idomeneus' companion
Meriones, a match for the murderous lord of battles.
260  But what man could tell forth from his heart the names of the others,
all who after these waked the war strength of the Achaians?

The Trojans came down on them in a pack, and Hektor led them.
As when at the outpouring place of a rain-glutted river
the huge surf of the sea roars against the current, out-jutting
265  beaches thunder aloud to the backwash of the salt water,
with such a bellow the Trojans came on, but now the Achaians
stood fast about the son of Menoitios, in a single courage
and fenced beneath their bronze-armored shields, while the son of Kronos
drifted across the glitter of their helmets a deepening
270  mist; since before this time he had not hated Menoitios'
son, while he lived yet and was Achilleus' companion,
and loathed now that he should become the spoil of the hated
Trojans' dogs, and stirred his companions on to defend him.
First the Trojans shouldered back the glancing-eyed Achaians,
275  who abandoned the body and ran for terror, nor did the high-hearted
Trojans take any with their spears, for all of their striving,
but dragged at the dead man, only the Achaians were not long destined
to fail him, since they were pulled around in sudden speed
by Aias, who for his beauty and the work of his hands surpassed
280  all other Danaäns, after the blameless son of Peleus.
He steered through the front fighters in pride of strength like a savage

wild boar, who among the mountains easily scatters
the dogs and strong young men when he turns at bay in the valley.
So now the son of haughty Telamon, glorious Aias,
turned to charge and easily scatter the Trojan battalions,                    285
who had taken their stand bestriding Patroklos, in high hope
of dragging him off to their own city, and so winning honor.
    Indeed, Hippothoös, glorious son of Pelasgian Lethos,
was trying to drag him by the foot through the strong encounter
by fastening the sling of his shield round the ankle tendons           290
for the favor of Hektor and the Trojans, but the sudden evil
came to him, and none for all their desire could defend him.
The son of Telamon, sweeping in through the mass of the fighters,
struck him at close quarters through the brazen cheeks of his helmet
and the helm crested with horse-hair was riven about the spearhead       295
to the impact of the huge spear and the weight of the hand behind it
and the brain ran from the wound along the spear by the eye-hole,
bleeding. There his strength was washed away, and from his hands
he let fall to the ground the foot of great-hearted Patroklos
to lie there, and himself collapsed prone over the dead man              300
far away from generous Larissa, and he could not
render again the care of his dear parents; he was short-lived,
beaten down beneath the spear of high-hearted Aias.
    Again Hektor threw at Aias with the shining javelin,
but Aias with his eyes straight on him avoided the bronze spear          305
by a little, and Hektor struck Schedios, the son of high-hearted
Iphitos and far the best of the Phokians, one who lived
in his home in famous Panopeus and was lord over many people.
He struck him fair beneath the collar-bone, and the pointed
bronze head tore clean through and came out by the base of the shoulder.  310
He fell, thunderously, and his armor clattered upon him.
    But Aias in turn cut at Phorkys, the wise son of Phainops,
in the middle of the belly as he stood over fallen Hippothoös,
and broke the hollow of the corselet, so that the entrails spurted
from the bronze, and he went down clawing the dust in his fingers.        315
The champions of Troy gave back then, and glorious Hektor,
and the Argives gave a great cry and dragged back the bodies
of Hippothoös and Phorkys, and eased the armor from their shoulders.

Then, once more, might the Trojans have climbed back into Ilion's
320 wall, subdued by terror before the warlike Achaians,
and the Argives, even beyond Zeus' destiny, might have won glory
by their own force and strength, had not Apollo in person
stirred on Aineias; he had assumed the form of the herald
Periphas, Epytos' son, growing old in his herald's office
325 by Aineias' aged father, and a man whose thoughts were of kindness.
In the likeness of this man Zeus' son Apollo spoke to him:
"Aineias, how could you be the man to defend sheer Ilion
even against a god's will, as I have seen other men do it
in the confidence of their own force and strength, their own manhood
330 and their own numbers, though they had too few people for it?
But now Zeus wishes the victory far rather for our side
than the Danaäns', only yourselves keep blenching and will not fight them."

So he spoke, but Aineias knew far-striking Apollo
as he looked him straight in the face, and called in a great voice to Hektor:
335 "Hektor, and you other lords of the Trojans and their companions,
here is a shameful thing! We are climbing back into Ilion's
wall, subdued by terror before the warlike Achaians.
Yet see, some one of the gods is standing beside me, and tells me
that Zeus the supreme counselor lends his weight to our fighting.
340 Therefore we must go straight for the Danaäns, so that they may not
carry thus easily back to their ships the fallen Patroklos."

He spoke, and with a long leap stood far before the front fighters,
and the Trojans turned and held their ground against the Achaians.
And now Aineias killed Leiokritos, with a spear-thrust,
345 the son of Arisbas and noble companion of Lykomedes;
but as he fell the warrior Lykomedes pitied him,
and stood close in, and made a cast with the shining javelin
and struck Apisaon, son of Hippasos, shepherd of the people,
in the liver under the midriff, and the strength of his knees was broken.
350 He was one who had come from Paionia of the rich soil
and was best of her men in fighting next to Asteropaios.

As this man fell, warlike Asteropaios pitied him
and he in turn drove forward eager to fight with the Danaäns,
but was not able to do it, for they, standing about Patroklos,
355 fenced him behind their shields on all sides, and held their spears out-thrust.
For Aias ranged their whole extent with his numerous orders,

and would not let any man give back from the body, nor let one
go out and fight by himself far in front of the other Achaians,
but made them stand hard and fast about him and fight at close quarters.
Such were the orders of gigantic Aias. The ground ran                           360
with red blood, the dead men dropped one after another
from the ranks alike of Trojans and their mighty companions
and Danaäns also, since these fought not without bloodletting,
but far fewer of them went down, since they ever remembered
always to stand massed and beat sudden death from each other.                   365

So they fought on in the likeness of fire, nor would you have thought
the sun was still secure in his place in the sky, nor the moon, since
the mist was closed over all that part of the fight where the bravest
stood about Patroklos, the fallen son of Menoitios.
Now elsewhere the rest of the Trojans and strong-greaved Achaians              370
fought naturally in the bright air, with the sun's sharp glitter
everywhere about them, no cloud was showing anywhere
on earth nor on the mountains. They fought their battle by intervals
standing each well off at a distance, avoiding the painful
shots from the other side; but they in the middle were suffering              375
distress in the mist and the fighting, with the cruel bronze wearing them.
These men were the bravest, but there were two men of glory,
Thrasymedes and Antilochos, who had not yet heard
how Patroklos the blameless had been killed, but still thought
he was alive and fighting in the first shock with the Trojans.                380
But these two, watching against death or flight in their company,
fought their separate battle, since such was their order from Nestor
as he was urging them forth from the black ships into the fighting.
So for these daylong the hard bitterness of the wearing
battle rose. With the ever-relentless sweat and the weariness                 385
knees, legs, and feet that supported from underneath each fighter,
their hands and eyes also were running wet as they fought on
over the brave henchman of swift-footed Aiakides.
As when a man gives the hide of a great ox, a bullock,
drenched first deep in fat, to all his people to stretch out;                 390
the people take it from him and stand in a circle about it
and pull, and presently the moisture goes and the fat sinks
in, with so many pulling, and the bull's hide is stretched out level;

so the men of both sides in a cramped space tugged at the body
395    in both directions; and the hearts of the Trojans were hopeful
to drag him away to Ilion, those of the Achaians
to get him back to the hollow ships. And about him a savage
struggle arose. Not Ares who rallies men, not Athene,
watching this fight could have scorned it, not even in some strong anger,
400    such was the wicked work of battle for men and for horses
Zeus strained tight above Patroklos that day. But the brilliant
Achilleus did not yet know at all that Patroklos had fallen.
Since now the men were fighting far away from the fast ships
under the Trojan wall, and Achilleus had no expectation
405    that Patroklos was dead, but thought he was alive and close under
the gates, and would come back. He had not thought that Patroklos
would storm the city without himself, nor with himself either;
for often he had word from his mother, not known to mortals;
she was ever telling him what was the will of great Zeus; but this time
410    his mother did not tell Achilleus of all the evil
that had been done, nor how his dearest companion had perished.

So they about the body gripping their headed spears kept
inexorably close together, and slaughtered on both sides.
And such would be the saying of some bronze-armored Achaian:
415    "Friends, there is no glory for us if we go back again
to our hollow ships, but here and now let the black earth open
gaping for all; this would soon be far better for us
if we give up this man to the Trojans, breakers of horses,
to take away to their own city and win glory from him."
420    And such in turn would be the cry of some high-hearted Trojan:
"O friends, though it be destined for all of us to be killed here
over this man, still none of us must give ground from the fighting."

Thus a man would speak, and stir the spirit in each one
of his fellowship. So they fought on, and the iron tumult
425    went up into the brazen sky through the barren bright air.
But the horses of Aiakides standing apart from the battle
wept, as they had done since they heard how their charioteer
had fallen in the dust at the hands of murderous Hektor.
In truth Automedon, the powerful son of Diores,

hit them over and over again with the stroke of the flying          430
lash, or talked to them, sometimes entreating them, sometimes threatening.
They were unwilling to go back to the wide passage of Helle
and the ships, or back into the fighting after the Achaians,
but still as stands a grave monument which is set over
the mounded tomb of a dead man or lady, they stood there          435
holding motionless in its place the fair-wrought chariot,
leaning their heads along the ground, and warm tears were running
earthward from underneath the lids of the mourning horses
who longed for their charioteer, while their bright manes were made dirty
as they streamed down either side of the yoke from under the yoke pad.   440
     As he watched the mourning horses the son of Kronos pitied them,
and stirred his head and spoke to his own spirit: "Poor wretches,
why then did we ever give you to the lord Peleus,
a mortal man, and you yourselves are immortal and ageless?
Only so that among unhappy men you also might be grieved?          445
Since among all creatures that breathe on earth and crawl on it
there is not anywhere a thing more dismal than man is.
At least the son of Priam, Hektor, shall not mount behind you
in the carefully wrought chariot. I will not let him. Is it not
enough for him that he has the armor and glories in wearing it?          450
But now I will put vigor into your knees and your spirits
so that you bring back Automedon out of the fighting
safe to the hollow ships; since I shall still give the Trojans
the glory of killing, until they win to the strong-benched vessels,
until the sun goes down and the blessed darkness comes over."          455
     So spoke Zeus, and breathed great vigor into the horses,
and they shaking the dust from their manes to the ground lightly
carried the running chariot among the Achaians and Trojans.
Automedon fought from them, though grieving for his companion.
He would dash in, like a vulture among geese, with his horses,          460
and lightly get away out of the Trojans' confusion
and lightly charge in again in pursuit of a great multitude,
and yet could kill no men when he swept in in chase of them.
He had no way while he was alone in a separate chariot
to lunge with the spear and still keep in hand his fast-running horses.   465
But at last there was one of his companions who laid eyes upon him:
Alkimedon, the son of Laërkes, descended from Haimon.

He stood behind the chariot and called to Automedon:
"Automedon, what god put this unprofitable purpose
470 into your heart, and has taken away the better wits, so that
you are trying to fight the Trojans in the first shock of encounter
by yourself, since your companion has been killed, and Hektor
glories in wearing Aiakides' armor on his own shoulders?"
In turn Automedon answered him, the son of Diores:
475 "Alkimedon, which other of the Achaians could handle
the management and the strength of immortal horses as you can,
were it not Patroklos, the equal of the immortals in counsel,
while he lived? Now death and fate have closed in upon him.
Therefore take over from me the whip and the glittering guide reins
480 while I dismount from behind the horses, so I may do battle."

He spoke, and Alkimedon vaulted up to the charging chariot
and quickly gathered up the reins and the lash in his hands, while
Automedon sprang down. But glorious Hektor saw them
and immediately spoke to Aineias, who stood close beside him:
485 "Aineias, lord of the counsels of the bronze-armored Trojans,
I see before us the horses of swift-footed Aiakides
who appear now in the fighting with weak charioteers. Therefore
I could be hopeful of their capture, if you were willing
in heart to go with me. If we two went forth against them
490 they would not dare to stand their ground and do battle against us."

He spoke, and the strong son of Anchises did not disobey him.
The two went strongly forward, hooding their shoulders in well-tanned
and stubborn hides of oxen with deep bronze beaten upon them.
Along with these went Chromios and godlike Aretos
495 both together, and the spirit within each had high hopes
of killing the men and driving away the strong-necked horses;
poor fools, who were not going to come back from Automedon
without the shedding of blood; and he with a prayer to Zeus father
was filled about the darkening heart with war-strength and courage,
500 and spoke now to Alkimedon his trusted companion:
"Alkimedon, no longer check the horses back from me
but keep them breathing right against my back. I have no thought
that I can stand up to the strength of Hektor the son of Priam.
Sooner, I think, he will kill us and mount behind the mane-floating
505 horses of Achilleus, and scatter the ranks of the Argive

fighting men; or else himself go down in the first rush."
      He spoke, and called to the two Aiantes and Menelaos:
"Aiantes, lords of the Argives, and Menelaos, we call you
to leave the dead man in the care of those who are fittest
to stand bestriding him and fend off the ranks of the Trojans          510
while you beat back the day without pity from us who are living.
For Hektor and Aineias, the greatest men of the Trojans,
are leaning the weight of their charge this way through the sorrowful battle.
Yet all these are things that are lying upon the gods' knees.
I myself will cast; and Zeus will look after the issue."                515

      So he spoke, and balanced the spear far-shadowed, and threw it,
and struck the shield of Aretos on its perfect circle,
nor could the shield hold off the spear, but the bronze smashed clean through
and was driven on through the belt to the deep of the belly.
As when a strong-grown man with sharp axe in his hands chops          520
at an ox, ranger of the fields, behind the horns, cutting
all the way through the sinew, and the ox springing forward topples,
so Aretos sprang forward, then toppled back, and sharp-driven
into the depth of his belly the quivering spear unstrung him.
Then Hektor made a cast with the shining spear at Automedon,          525
but he, keeping his eyes straight on him, avoided the bronze spear.
For he bent forward, and behind his back the long spearshaft
was driven into the ground so that the butt end was shaken
on the spear. Then and there Ares the huge took the force from it.
And now they would have gone for each other with swords at close quarters,   530
had not the two Aiantes driven strongly between them,
who came on through the battle at the call of their companion,
and in fear before them Hektor and Aineias and godlike
Chromios gave ground back and away once more, leaving
Aretos lying there where he was with a wound in his vitals.          535
Then Automedon, a match for the running god of battles,
stripped the armor, and spoke a word of boasting above him:
"Now I have put a little sorrow from my heart for Patroklos'
death, although the man I killed was not great as he was."
      So he spoke, and took up the bloody war spoils and laid them     540
inside the chariot, and himself mounted it, the blood running
from hands and feet, as on some lion who has eaten a bullock.

Once again over Patroklos was close drawn a strong battle
weary and sorrowful, and Athene from the sky descending
545 waked the bitter fighting, since Zeus of the wide brows sent her
down to stir the Danaäns, for now his purpose had shifted.
As when in the sky Zeus strings for mortals the shimmering
rainbow, to be a portent and sign of war, or of wintry
storm, when heat perishes, such storm as stops mortals'
550 work upon the face of the earth, and afflicts their cattle,
so Athene shrouded in the shimmering cloud about her
merged among the swarming Achaians, and wakened each man.
And first she spoke, stirring him on, to the son of Atreus,
strong Menelaos, since he was the one who was standing close to her.
555 She likened herself in form and weariless voice to Phoinix:
"Menelaos, this will be a thing of shame, a reproach said
of you, if under the wall of the Trojans the dogs in their fury
can mutilate the staunch companion of haughty Achilleus.
But hold strongly on, and stir up all the rest of your people."
560 Then in turn Menelaos of the great war cry answered her:
"Phoinix, my father, aged and honored, if only Athene
would give me such strength, and hold the volleying missiles off from me!
So for my part I would be willing to stand by Patroklos
and defend him, since in his death he hurt my heart greatly.
565 Yet Hektor holds still the awful strength of a fire, nor falters
in raging with the bronze spear, since Zeus is giving him glory."

So he spoke, and the goddess gray-eyed Athene was happy
that first among all the divinities his prayer had bespoken her.
She put strength into the man's shoulders and knees, inspiring
570 in his breast the persistent daring of that mosquito
who though it is driven hard away from a man's skin, even
so, for the taste of human blood, persists in biting him.
With such daring she darkened to fullness the heart inside him.
He stood over Patroklos, and made a cast with the shining
575 spear. There was one among the Trojans, Podes, Eëtion's
son, a rich man and good, whom Hektor prized above others
in the countryside, since he was his friend and ate at his table.
Now fair-haired Menelaos struck this man, at the war belt
as he swept away in flight, and drove the bronze spear clean through it.

He fell, thunderously, and Atreus' son Menelaos                           580
dragged the body away from the Trojans among his companions.
But now Apollo came and stood beside Hektor, and stirred him,
assuming the shape of Phainops, Asios' son, who among all
guest friends was dearest to Hektor, and lived at home in Abydos.
In the likeness of this man far-striking Apollo spoke to him:              585
"Hektor, what other Achaian now shall be frightened before you?
See, you have shrunk before Menelaos, who in times before this
was a soft spearfighter; and now he has gone taking off single-handed
a body from among the Trojans. He has killed your trusted companion,
valiant among the champions, Podes, the son of Eëtion."                    590
   He spoke, and the dark cloud of sorrow closed over Hektor.
He took his way among the champions helmed in the shining
bronze. And now the son of Kronos caught up the betasseled
glaring aegis, and shrouded Ida in mists. He let go
a lightning flash and a loud thunderstroke, shaking the mountain,          595
gave victory to the Trojans, and terrified the Achaians.

   First to begin the flight was Peneleos the Boiotian.
For he, turning always toward the attack, was hit in the shoulder's
end, a slight wound, but the spear of Poulydamas, who had thrown it
from a stance very close to him, had grated the bone's edge.               600
Then Hektor wounded in the hand by the wrist Leïtos,
the son of great-hearted Alektryon, and halted his warcraft,
and he drew back staring about him since his spirit had hope no longer
of holding a spear steady in his hand to fight with the Trojans.
Now as Hektor made a rush for Leïtos, Idomeneus                            605
struck him on the corselet over the chest by the nipple,
but the long shaft was broken behind the head, and the Trojans
shouted. Now Hektor made a cast at Deukalian Idomeneus
as he stood in his chariot, and missed him by only a little,
but struck the follower and charioteer of Meriones,                       610
Koiranos, who had come with him from strong-founded Lyktos.
Now Idomeneus at the first had come on foot, leaving the oarswept
ships, and now would have given the Trojans a mighty triumph,
had not Koiranos swiftly come up with the fast-running horses;
came as light to the other and beat from him the day without pity,        615
but himself lost his life at the hands of manslaughtering Hektor,

who hit him under the jaw by the ear, and the spearshaft pushed out
his teeth by the roots from the base, and split the tongue through the middle.
He toppled from the chariot, with the reins on the ground scattered,
620    but Meriones leaning down caught these up in his own hands
from the surface of the plain, and called aloud to Idomeneus:
"Lash them now, until you can get back to our fast ships.
You see yourself there is no more strength left in the Achaians."
So he spoke, and Idomeneus whipped the mane-floating horses
625    back to the hollow ships, with fear fallen upon his spirit.

Nor was it unseen by great-hearted Aias how Zeus shifted
the strength of the fighting toward the Trojans, nor by Menelaos.
First of the two to speak was huge Telamonian Aias:
"Shame on it! By now even one with a child's innocence
630    could see how father Zeus himself is helping the Trojans.
The weapons of each of these take hold, no matter who throws them,
good fighter or bad, since Zeus is straightening all of them equally,
while ours fall to the ground and are utterly useless. Therefore
let us deliberate with ourselves upon the best counsel,
635    how at the same time to rescue the dead body, and also
win back ourselves, and bring joy to our beloved companions
who look our way and sorrow for us, and believe no longer
that the fury of manslaughtering Hektor, his hands irresistible,
can be held, but must be driven on to the black ships.
640    But there should be some companion who could carry the message
quickly to Peleus' son, since I think he has not yet heard
the ghastly news, how his beloved companion has fallen.
Yet I cannot make out such a man among the Achaians,
since they are held in the mist alike, the men and their horses.
645    Father Zeus, draw free from the mist the sons of the Achaians,
make bright the air, and give sight back to our eyes; in shining
daylight destroy us, if to destroy us be now your pleasure."

He spoke thus, and as he wept the father took pity upon him,
and forthwith scattered the mist and pushed the darkness back from them,
650    and the sun blazed out, and all the battle was plain before them.
Now Aias spoke to him of the great war cry, Menelaos:
"Look hard, illustrious Menelaos, if you can discover

Antilochos still living, the son of great-hearted Nestor,
and send him out to run with a message to wise Achilleus
how one who was far the dearest of his companions has fallen."    655
    He spoke, and Menelaos of the great war cry obeyed him,
and went on his way, as from a mid-fenced ground some lion
who has been harrying dogs and men, but his strength is worn out;
they will not let him tear out the fat of the oxen, watching
nightlong against him, and he in his hunger for meat closes in    660
but can get nothing of what he wants, for the raining javelins
thrown from the daring hands of the men beat ever against him,
and the flaming torches, and these he balks at for all of his fury,
and with the daylight goes away, disappointed of desire;
so Menelaos of the great war cry went from Patroklos    665
much unwilling, and was afraid for him, lest the Achaians
under pressure of fear might leave him as spoil for the enemy,
and had much to urge on Meriones and the Aiantes:
"Aiantes, O lords of the Argives, and you, Meriones,
now let each one of you remember unhappy Patroklos    670
who was gentle, and understood how to be kindly toward all men
while he lived. Now death and fate have closed in upon him."
    So spoke fair-haired Menelaos, and went away from them
peering about on all sides, like an eagle, who, as men say,
sees most sharply of all winged creatures under the heaven,    675
and lofty though he hover the cowering hare, the swift-footed,
escapes not his sight as he crouches in the shaggy bush, but the eagle
plunges suddenly to grab him and tear the life from him.
So now in you, Menelaos, illustrious, the eyes shining
circled everywhere your swarming hordes of companions,    680
if the man might see anywhere Nestor's son, still living,
and saw soon where he was, at the left of the entire battle,
encouraging his companions and urging them into the fighting.
Menelaos the fair-haired stood beside him and spoke to him:
"Antilochos, turn this way, illustrious, and hear from me    685
the ghastly message of a thing I wish never had happened.
You can see for yourself, I think, already, from watching,
how the god is wheeling disaster against the Danaäns
and how the Trojans are winning. The best of the Achaians has fallen,
Patroklos, and a huge loss is inflicted upon the Danaäns.    690

Run then quickly to Achilleus, by the ships of the Achaians,
and tell him. He might in speed win back to his ship the dead body
which is naked. Hektor of the shining helm has taken his armor."
      So he spoke, and Antilochos hated his word as he listened.
695 He stayed for a long time without a word, speechless, and his eyes
filled with tears, the springing voice was held still within him,
yet even so he neglected not Menelaos' order
but went on the run, handing his war gear to a blameless companion,
Laodokos, who had turned nearby his single-foot horses.

700      Now as his feet carried him, weeping, out of the battle,
with his message of evil for the son of Peleus, Achilleus,
so now, Menelaos, the spirit in you, illustrious,
wished not to defend his stricken companions, after Antilochos
was gone from them, and his loss wrought greatly upon the Pylians;
705 rather he sent Thrasymedes the brilliant over to help them,
while he himself went back again to the hero Patroklos
running, and took his place beside the Aiantes, and spoke to them:
"Now I have sent the man you spoke of back to the fast ships
on his way to swift-footed Achilleus, yet think not even
710 he can come now, for all his great anger with Hektor the brilliant.
There is no way he could fight bare of armor against the Trojans.
We by ourselves must deliberate upon the best counsel
how at the same time to rescue the dead body, and also
ourselves escape death and destiny from the clamoring Trojans."
715      Then in turn huge Telamonian Aias answered him:
"All you have said, renowned Menelaos, is fair and orderly.
But come: you and Meriones stoop and shoulder the body
at once, and carry it out of the hard fighting. Behind you
we two shall fight off the Trojans and glorious Hektor,
720 we, who have the same name, the same spirit, and who in times past
have stood fast beside each other in the face of the bitter war god."
      He spoke, and they caught the body from the ground in their arms, lifting
him high with a great heave, and the Trojan people behind them
shouted aloud as they saw the Achaians lifting the dead man,
725 and made a rush against them like dogs, who sweep in rapidly
on a wounded wild boar, ahead of the young men who hunt him,
and for the moment race in raging to tear him to pieces

until in the confidence of his strength he turns on them, at bay,
and they give ground and scatter for fear one way and another;
so the Trojans until that time kept always in close chase                    730
assembled, stabbing at them with swords and leaf-headed spears,
but every time the two Aiantes would swing round to face them
and stand fast, the color of their skin changed, and no longer
could any endure to sweep in further and fight for the body.
    So these, straining, carried the dead man out of the battle             735
and back to the hollow ships, and the fight that was drawn fast between
    them
was wild as fire which, risen suddenly, storming a city
of men sets it ablaze, and houses diminish before it
in the high glare, and the force of the wind on it roars it to thunder;
so, as the Danaäns made their way back, the weariless roaring             740
of horses, chariots, and spearmen was ever upon them.
But they, as mules who have put the on-drive of strength upon them
drag down from the high ground along a steep stony trail either
a beam or some big timber for a ship, and the heart in them
wearies under the hard work and sweat of their urgent endeavor;           745
so these, straining, carried the dead man away, and behind them
the two Aiantes held them off, as a timbered rock ridge
holds off water, one that is placed to divide an entire plain,
which, though flood-currents of strong rivers drive sorely against it,
holds them off and beats back the waters of them all to be scattered      750
over the plain, and all the strength of their streams cannot break it;
so behind the Achaians the Aiantes held off forever
the Trojan attack. But these stayed close, and two beyond others,
Aineias, who was son of Anchises, and glorious Hektor.
But before these, as goes a cloud of daws or of starlings                  755
screaming terror when they have seen coming forth against them
the hawk, whose coming is murder for the little birds, so now
before Aineias and Hektor the young Achaian warriors
went, screaming terror, all the delight of battle forgotten.
Many fine pieces of armor littered the ground on both sides              760
of the ditch, as the Danaäns fled. There was no check in the fighting.

# BOOK EIGHTEEN

So these fought on in the likeness of blazing fire. Meanwhile,
Antilochos came, a swift-footed messenger, to Achilleus,
and found him sitting in front of the steep-horned ships, thinking
over in his heart of things which had now been accomplished.
5 Disturbed, Achilleus spoke to the spirit in his own great heart:
"Ah me, how is it that once again the flowing-haired Achaians
are driven out of the plain on their ships in fear and confusion?
May the gods not accomplish vile sorrows upon the heart in me
in the way my mother once made it clear to me, when she told me
10 how while I yet lived the bravest of all the Myrmidons
must leave the light of the sun beneath the hands of the Trojans.
Surely, then, the strong son of Menoitios has perished.
Unhappy! and yet I told him, once he had beaten the fierce fire
off, to come back to the ships, not fight in strength against Hektor."

15 Now as he was pondering this in his heart and his spirit,
meanwhile the son of stately Nestor was drawing near him
and wept warm tears, and gave Achilleus his sorrowful message:
"Ah me, son of valiant Peleus; you must hear from me
the ghastly message of a thing I wish never had happened.
20 Patroklos has fallen, and now they are fighting over his body
which is naked. Hektor of the shining helm has taken his armor."
He spoke, and the black cloud of sorrow closed on Achilleus.
In both hands he caught up the grimy dust, and poured it
over his head and face, and fouled his handsome countenance,

and the black ashes were scattered over his immortal tunic.                                    25
And he himself, mightily in his might, in the dust lay
at length, and took and tore at his hair with his hands, and defiled it.
And the handmaidens Achilleus and Patroklos had taken
captive, stricken at heart cried out aloud, and came running
out of doors about valiant Achilleus, and all of them                                           30
beat their breasts with their hands, and the limbs went slack in each of them.
On the other side Antilochos mourned with him, letting the tears fall,
and held the hands of Achilleus as he grieved in his proud heart,
fearing Achilleus might cut his throat with the iron. He cried out
terribly, aloud, and the lady his mother heard him                                              35
as she sat in the depths of the sea at the side of her aged father,
and she cried shrill in turn, and the goddesses gathered about her,
all who along the depth of the sea were daughters of Nereus.
For Glauke was there, Kymodokē and Thaleia,
Nesaie and Speio and Thoë, and ox-eyed Halia;                                                   40
Kymothoë was there, Aktaia and Limnoreia,
Melitē and Iaira, Amphithoë and Agauë,
Doto and Proto, Dynamenē and Pherousa,
Dexamenē and Amphinomē and Kallianeira;
Doris and Panopē and glorious Galateia,                                                         45
Nemertes and Apseudes and Kallianassa;
Klymenē was there, Ianeira and Ianassa,
Maira and Oreithyia and lovely-haired Amatheia,
and the rest who along the depth of the sea were daughters of Nereus.
The silvery cave was filled with these, and together all of them                                50
beat their breasts, and among them Thetis led out the threnody:
"Hear me, Nereïds, my sisters; so you may all know
well all the sorrows that are in my heart, when you hear of them from me.
Ah me, my sorrow, the bitterness in this best of child-bearing,
since I gave birth to a son who was without fault and powerful,                                 55
conspicuous among heroes; and he shot up like a young tree,
and I nurtured him, like a tree grown in the pride of the orchard.
I sent him away with the curved ships into the land of Ilion
to fight with the Trojans; but I shall never again receive him
won home again to his country and into the house of Peleus.                                     60
Yet while I see him live and he looks on the sunlight, he has

sorrows, and though I go to him I can do nothing to help him.
Yet I shall go, to look on my dear son, and to listen
to the sorrow that has come to him as he stays back from the fighting."

65     So she spoke, and left the cave, and the others together
went with her in tears, and about them the wave of the water
was broken. Now these, when they came to the generous Troad,
followed each other out on the seashore, where close together
the ships of the Myrmidons were hauled up about swift Achilleus.
70     There as he sighed heavily the lady his mother stood by him
and cried out shrill and aloud, and took her son's head in her arms, then
sorrowing for him she spoke to him in winged words: "Why then,
child, do you lament? What sorrow has come to your heart now?
Speak out, do not hide it. These things are brought to accomplishment
75     through Zeus: in the way that you lifted your hands and prayed for,
that all the sons of the Achaians be pinned on their grounded vessels
by reason of your loss, and suffer things that are shameful."
       Then sighing heavily Achilleus of the swift feet answered her:
"My mother, all these things the Olympian brought to accomplishment.
80     But what pleasure is this to me, since my dear companion has perished,
Patroklos, whom I loved beyond all other companions,
as well as my own life. I have lost him, and Hektor, who killed him,
has stripped away that gigantic armor, a wonder to look on
and splendid, which the gods gave Peleus, a glorious present,
85     on that day they drove you to the marriage bed of a mortal.
I wish you had gone on living then with the other goddesses
of the sea, and that Peleus had married some mortal woman.
As it is, there must be on your heart a numberless sorrow
for your son's death, since you can never again receive him
90     won home again to his country; since the spirit within does not drive me
to go on living and be among men, except on condition
that Hektor first be beaten down under my spear, lose his life
and pay the price for stripping Patroklos, the son of Menoitios."
       Then in turn Thetis spoke to him, letting the tears fall:
95     "Then I must lose you soon, my child, by what you are saying,
since it is decreed your death must come soon after Hektor's."
       Then deeply disturbed Achilleus of the swift feet answered her:

"I must die soon, then; since I was not to stand by my companion
when he was killed. And now, far away from the land of his fathers,
he has perished, and lacked my fighting strength to defend him.                100
Now, since I am not going back to the beloved land of my fathers,
since I was no light of safety to Patroklos, nor to my other
companions, who in their numbers went down before glorious Hektor,
but sit here beside my ships, a useless weight on the good land,
I, who am such as no other of the bronze-armored Achaians                      105
in battle, though there are others also better in council—
why, I wish that strife would vanish away from among gods and mortals,
and gall, which makes a man grow angry for all his great mind,
that gall of anger that swarms like smoke inside of a man's heart
and becomes a thing sweeter to him by far than the dripping of honey.          110
So it was here that the lord of men Agamemnon angered me.
Still, we will let all this be a thing of the past, and for all our
sorrow beat down by force the anger deeply within us.
Now I shall go, to overtake that killer of a dear life,
Hektor; then I will accept my own death, at whatever                           115
time Zeus wishes to bring it about, and the other immortals.
For not even the strength of Herakles fled away from destruction,
although he was dearest of all to lord Zeus, son of Kronos,
but his fate beat him under, and the wearisome anger of Hera.
So I likewise, if such is the fate which has been wrought for me,              120
shall lie still, when I am dead. Now I must win excellent glory,
and drive some one of the women of Troy, or some deep-girdled
Dardanian woman, lifting up to her soft cheeks both hands
to wipe away the close bursts of tears in her lamentation,
and learn that I stayed too long out of the fighting. Do not                   125
hold me back from the fight, though you love me. You will not persuade me."
     In turn the goddess Thetis of the silver feet answered him:
"Yes, it is true, my child, this is no cowardly action,
to beat aside sudden death from your afflicted companions.
Yet, see now, your splendid armor, glaring and brazen,                        130
is held among the Trojans, and Hektor of the shining helmet
wears it on his own shoulders, and glories in it. Yet I think
he will not glory for long, since his death stands very close to him.
Therefore do not yet go into the grind of the war god,

135   not before with your own eyes you see me come back to you.
     For I am coming to you at dawn and as the sun rises
     bringing splendid armor to you from the lord Hephaistos."

     So she spoke, and turned, and went away from her son,
     and turning now to her sisters of the sea she spoke to them:
140   "Do you now go back into the wide fold of the water
     to visit the ancient of the sea and the house of our father,
     and tell him everything. I am going to tall Olympos
     and to Hephaistos, the glorious smith, if he might be willing
     to give me for my son renowned and radiant armor."
145   She spoke, and they plunged back beneath the wave of the water,
     while she the goddess Thetis of the silver feet went onward
     to Olympos, to bring back to her son the glorious armor.

     So her feet carried her to Olympos; meanwhile the Achaians
     with inhuman clamor before the attack of manslaughtering Hektor
150   fled until they were making for their own ships and the Hellespont;
     nor could the strong-greaved Achaians have dragged the body
     of Patroklos, henchman of Achilleus, from under the missiles,
     for once again the men and the horses came over upon him,
     and Hektor, Priam's son, who fought like a flame in his fury.
155   Three times from behind glorious Hektor caught him
     by the feet, trying to drag him, and called aloud on the Trojans.
     Three times the two Aiantes with their battle-fury upon them
     beat him from the corpse, but he, steady in the confidence of his great
        strength,
     kept making, now a rush into the crowd, or again at another time
160   stood fast, with his great cry, but gave not a bit of ground backward.
     And as herdsmen who dwell in the fields are not able to frighten
     a tawny lion in his great hunger away from a carcass,
     so the two Aiantes, marshals of men, were not able
     to scare Hektor, Priam's son, away from the body.
165   And now he would have dragged it away and won glory forever
     had not swift wind-footed Iris come running from Olympos
     with a message for Peleus' son to arm. She came secretly
     from Zeus and the other gods, since it was Hera who sent her.
     She came and stood close to him and addressed him in winged words:

"Rise up, son of Peleus, most terrifying of all men.                    170
Defend Patroklos, for whose sake the terrible fighting
stands now in front of the ships. They are destroying each other;
the Achaians fight in defense over the fallen body
while the others, the Trojans, are rushing to drag the corpse off
to windy Ilion, and beyond all glorious Hektor                          175
rages to haul it away, since the anger within him is urgent
to cut the head from the soft neck and set it on sharp stakes.
Up, then, lie here no longer; let shame come into your heart, lest
Patroklos become sport for the dogs of Troy to worry,
your shame, if the body goes from here with defilement upon it."        180
     Then in turn Achilleus of the swift feet answered her:
"Divine Iris, what god sent you to me with a message?"
     Then in turn swift wind-footed Iris spoke to him:
"Hera sent me, the honored wife of Zeus; but the son of
Kronos, who sits on high, does not know this, nor any other             185
immortal, of all those who dwell by the snows of Olympos."
     Then in answer to her spoke Achilleus of the swift feet:
"How shall I go into the fighting? They have my armor.
And my beloved mother told me I must not be armored,
not before with my own eyes I see her come back to me.                  190
She promised she would bring magnificent arms from Hephaistos.
Nor do I know of another whose glorious armor I could wear
unless it were the great shield of Telamonian Aias.
But he himself wears it, I think, and goes in the foremost
of the spear-fight over the body of fallen Patroklos."                  195
     Then in turn swift wind-footed Iris spoke to him:
"Yes, we also know well how they hold your glorious armor.
But go to the ditch, and show yourself as you are to the Trojans,
if perhaps the Trojans might be frightened, and give way
from their attack, and the fighting sons of the Achaians get wind       200
again after hard work. There is little breathing space in the fighting."

     So speaking Iris of the swift feet went away from him;
but Achilleus, the beloved of Zeus, rose up, and Athene
swept about his powerful shoulders the fluttering aegis;
and she, the divine among goddesses, about his head circled            205
a golden cloud, and kindled from it a flame far-shining.

As when a flare goes up into the high air from a city
from an island far away, with enemies fighting about it
who all day long are in the hateful division of Ares
210 fighting from their own city, but as the sun goes down signal
fires blaze out one after another, so that the glare goes
pulsing high for men of the neighboring islands to see it,
in case they might come over in ships to beat off the enemy;
so from the head of Achilleus the blaze shot into the bright air.
215 He went from the wall and stood by the ditch, nor mixed with the other
Achaians, since he followed the close command of his mother.
There he stood, and shouted, and from her place Pallas Athene
gave cry, and drove an endless terror upon the Trojans.
As loud as comes the voice that is screamed out by a trumpet
220 by murderous attackers who beleaguer a city,
so then high and clear went up the voice of Aiakides.
But the Trojans, when they heard the brazen voice of Aiakides,
the heart was shaken in all, and the very floating-maned horses
turned their chariots about, since their hearts saw the coming afflictions.
225 The charioteers were dumbfounded as they saw the unwearied dangerous
fire that played above the head of great-hearted Peleion
blazing, and kindled by the goddess gray-eyed Athene.
Three times across the ditch brilliant Achilleus gave his great cry,
and three times the Trojans and their renowned companions were routed.
230 There at that time twelve of the best men among them perished
upon their own chariots and spears. Meanwhile the Achaians
gladly pulled Patroklos out from under the missiles
and set him upon a litter, and his own companions about him
stood mourning, and along with them swift-footed Achilleus
235 went, letting fall warm tears as he saw his steadfast companion
lying there on a carried litter and torn with the sharp bronze,
the man he had sent off before with horses and chariot
into the fighting; who never again came home to be welcomed.

Now the lady Hera of the ox eyes drove the unwilling
240 weariless sun god to sink in the depth of the Ocean,
and the sun went down, and the brilliant Achaians gave over
their strong fighting, and the doubtful collision of battle.

The Trojans on the other side moved from the strong encounter
in their turn, and unyoked their running horses from under the chariots,
and gathered into assembly before taking thought for their supper.           245
They stood on their feet in assembly, nor did any man have the patience
to sit down, but the terror was on them all, seeing that Achilleus
had appeared, after he had stayed so long from the difficult fighting.
First to speak among them was the careful Poulydamas,
Panthoös' son, who alone of them looked before and behind him.               250
He was companion to Hektor, and born on the same night with him,
but he was better in words, the other with the spear far better.
He in kind intention toward all stood forth and addressed them:
"Now take careful thought, dear friends; for I myself urge you
to go back into the city and not wait for the divine dawn                    255
in the plain beside the ships. We are too far from the wall now.
While this man was still angry with great Agamemnon,
for all that time the Achaians were easier men to fight with.
For I also used then to be one who was glad to sleep out
near their ships, and I hoped to capture the oarswept vessels.               260
But now I terribly dread the swift-footed son of Peleus.
So violent is the valor in him, he will not be willing
to stay here in the plain, where now Achaians and Trojans
from either side sunder between them the wrath of the war god.
With him, the fight will be for the sake of our city and women.              265
Let us go into the town; believe me; thus it will happen.
For this present, immortal night has stopped the swift-footed
son of Peleus, but if he catches us still in this place
tomorrow, and drives upon us in arms, a man will be well
aware of him, be glad to get back into sacred Ilion,                         270
the man who escapes; there will be many Trojans the vultures
and dogs will feed on. But let such a word be out of my hearing!
If all of us will do as I say, though it hurts us to do it,
this night we will hold our strength in the market place, and the great walls
and the gateways, and the long, smooth-planed, close-joined gate timbers     275
that close to fit them shall defend our city. Then, early
in the morning, under dawn, we shall arm ourselves in our war gear
and take stations along the walls. The worse for him, if he endeavors
to come away from the ships and fight us here for our city.

280   Back he must go to his ships again, when he wears out the strong necks
      of his horses, driving them at a gallop everywhere by the city.
      His valor will not give him leave to burst in upon us
      nor sack our town. Sooner the circling dogs will feed on him."

         Then looking darkly at him Hektor of the shining helm spoke:
285   "Poulydamas, these things that you argue please me no longer
      when you tell us to go back again and be cooped in our city.
      Have you not all had your glut of being fenced in our outworks?
      There was a time when mortal men would speak of the city
      of Priam as a place with much gold and much bronze. But now
290   the lovely treasures that lay away in our houses have vanished,
      and many possessions have been sold and gone into Phrygia
      and into Maionia the lovely, when great Zeus was angry.
      But now, when the son of devious-devising Kronos has given
      me the winning of glory by the ships, to pin the Achaians
295   on the sea, why, fool, no longer show these thoughts to our people.
      Not one of the Trojans will obey you. I shall not allow it.
      Come, then, do as I say and let us all be persuaded.
      Now, take your supper by positions along the encampment,
      and do not forget your watch, and let every man be wakeful.
300   And if any Trojan is strongly concerned about his possessions,
      let him gather them and give them to the people, to use them in common.
      It is better for one of us to enjoy them than for the Achaians.
      In the morning, under dawn, we shall arm ourselves in our war gear
      and waken the bitter god of war by the hollow vessels.
305   If it is true that brilliant Achilleus is risen beside their
      ships, then the worse for him if he tries it, since I for my part
      will not run from him out of the sorrowful battle, but rather
      stand fast, to see if he wins the great glory, or if I can win it.
      The war god is impartial. Before now he has killed the killer."

310      So spoke Hektor, and the Trojans thundered to hear him;
      fools, since Pallas Athene had taken away the wits from them.
      They gave their applause to Hektor in his counsel of evil,
      but none to Poulydamas, who had spoken good sense before them.
      They took their supper along the encampment. Meanwhile the Achaians

mourned all night in lamentation over Patroklos.                                    315
Peleus' son led the thronging chant of their lamentation,
and laid his manslaughtering hands over the chest of his dear friend
with outbursts of incessant grief. As some great bearded lion
when some man, a deer hunter, has stolen his cubs away from him
out of the close wood; the lion comes back too late, and is anguished,        320
and turns into many valleys quartering after the man's trail
on the chance of finding him, and taken with bitter anger;
so he, groaning heavily, spoke out to the Myrmidons:
"Ah me. It was an empty word I cast forth on that day
when in his halls I tried to comfort the hero Menoitios.                      325
I told him I would bring back his son in glory to Opous
with Ilion sacked, and bringing his share of war spoils allotted.
But Zeus does not bring to accomplishment all thoughts in men's minds.
Thus it is destiny for us both to stain the same soil
here in Troy; since I shall never come home, and my father,                   330
Peleus the aged rider, will not welcome me in his great house,
nor Thetis my mother, but in this place the earth will receive me.
But seeing that it is I, Patroklos, who follow you underground,
I will not bury you till I bring to this place the armor
and the head of Hektor, since he was your great-hearted murderer.            335
Before your burning pyre I shall behead twelve glorious
children of the Trojans, for my anger over your slaying.
Until then, you shall lie where you are in front of my curved ships
and beside you women of Troy and deep-girdled Dardanian women
shall sorrow for you night and day and shed tears for you, those whom        340
you and I worked hard to capture by force and the long spear
in days when we were storming the rich cities of mortals."

    So speaking brilliant Achilleus gave orders to his companions
to set a great cauldron across the fire, so that with all speed
they could wash away the clotted blood from Patroklos.                       345
They set up over the blaze of the fire a bath-water cauldron
and poured water into it and put logs underneath and kindled them.
The fire worked on the swell of the cauldron, and the water heated.
But when the water had come to a boil in the shining bronze, then
they washed the body and anointed it softly with olive oil                   350

and stopped the gashes in his body with stored-up unguents
and laid him on a bed, and shrouded him in a thin sheet
from head to foot, and covered that over with a white mantle.

Then all night long, gathered about Achilleus of the swift feet,
355   the Myrmidons mourned for Patroklos and lamented over him.
But Zeus spoke to Hera, who was his wife and his sister:
"So you have acted, then, lady Hera of the ox eyes.
You have roused up Achilleus of the swift feet. It must be then
that the flowing-haired Achaians are born of your own generation."
360   Then the goddess the ox-eyed lady Hera answered him:
"Majesty, son of Kronos, what sort of thing have you spoken?
Even one who is mortal will try to accomplish his purpose
for another, though he be a man and knows not such wisdom as we do.
As for me then, who claim I am highest of all the goddesses,
365   both ways, since I am eldest born and am called your consort,
yours, and you in turn are lord over all the immortals,
how could I not weave sorrows for the men of Troy, when I hate them?"

Now as these two were saying things like this to each other,
Thetis of the silver feet came to the house of Hephaistos,
370   imperishable, starry, and shining among the immortals,
built in bronze for himself by the god of the dragging footsteps.
She found him sweating as he turned here and there to his bellows
busily, since he was working on twenty tripods
which were to stand against the wall of his strong-founded dwelling.
375   And he had set golden wheels underneath the base of each one
so that of their own motion they could wheel into the immortal
gathering, and return to his house: a wonder to look at.
These were so far finished, but the elaborate ear handles
were not yet on. He was forging these, and beating the chains out.
380   As he was at work on this in his craftsmanship and his cunning
meanwhile the goddess Thetis the silver-footed drew near him.
Charis of the shining veil saw her as she came forward,
she, the lovely goddess the renowned strong-armed one had married.
She came, and caught her hand and called her by name and spoke to her:
385   "Why is it, Thetis of the light robes, you have come to our house now?
We honor you and love you; but you have not come much before this.

But come in with me, so I may put entertainment before you."
She spoke, and, shining among divinities, led the way forward
and made Thetis sit down in a chair that was wrought elaborately
and splendid with silver nails, and under it was a footstool.                       390
She called to Hephaistos the renowned smith and spoke a word to him:
"Hephaistos, come this way; here is Thetis, who has need of you."
    Hearing her the renowned smith of the strong arms answered her:
"Then there is a goddess we honor and respect in our house.
She saved me when I suffered much at the time of my great fall              395
through the will of my own brazen-faced mother, who wanted
to hide me, for being lame. Then my soul would have taken much suffering
had not Eurynomē and Thetis caught me and held me,
Eurynomē, daughter of Ocean, whose stream bends back in a circle.
With them I worked nine years as a smith, and wrought many intricate      400
things; pins that bend back, curved clasps, cups, necklaces, working
there in the hollow of the cave, and the stream of Ocean around us
went on forever with its foam and its murmur. No other
among the gods or among mortal men knew about us
except Eurynomē and Thetis. They knew, since they saved me.              405
Now she has come into our house; so I must by all means
do everything to give recompense to lovely-haired Thetis
for my life. Therefore set out before her fair entertainment
while I am putting away my bellows and all my instruments."

    He spoke, and took the huge blower off from the block of the anvil       410
limping; and yet his shrunken legs moved lightly beneath him.
He set the bellows away from the fire, and gathered and put away
all the tools with which he worked in a silver strongbox.
Then with a sponge he wiped clean his forehead, and both hands,
and his massive neck and hairy chest, and put on a tunic,                      415
and took up a heavy stick in his hand, and went to the doorway
limping. And in support of their master moved his attendants.
These are golden, and in appearance like living young women.
There is intelligence in their hearts, and there is speech in them
and strength, and from the immortal gods they have learned how to do       420
    things.
These stirred nimbly in support of their master, and moving
near to where Thetis sat in her shining chair, Hephaistos

caught her by the hand and called her by name and spoke a word to her:
"Why is it, Thetis of the light robes, you have come to our house now?
425 We honor you and love you; but you have not come much before this.
Speak forth what is in your mind. My heart is urgent to do it
if I can, and if it is a thing that can be accomplished."
　　Then in turn Thetis answered him, letting the tears fall:
"Hephaistos, is there among all the goddesses on Olympos
430 one who in her heart has endured so many grim sorrows
as the griefs Zeus, son of Kronos, has given me beyond others?
Of all the other sisters of the sea he gave me to a mortal,
to Peleus, Aiakos' son, and I had to endure mortal marriage
though much against my will. And now he, broken by mournful
435 old age, lies away in his halls. Yet I have other troubles.
For since he has given me a son to bear and to raise up
conspicuous among heroes, and he shot up like a young tree,
I nurtured him, like a tree grown in the pride of the orchard.
I sent him away in the curved ships to the land of Ilion
440 to fight with the Trojans; but I shall never again receive him
won home again to his country and into the house of Peleus.
Yet while I see him live and he looks on the sunlight, he has
sorrows, and though I go to him I can do nothing to help him.
And the girl the sons of the Achaians chose out for his honor
445 powerful Agamemnon took her away again out of his hands.
For her his heart has been wasting in sorrow; but meanwhile the Trojans
pinned the Achaians against their grounded ships, and would not
let them win outside, and the elders of the Argives entreated
my son, and named the many glorious gifts they would give him.
450 But at that time he refused himself to fight the death from them;
nevertheless he put his own armor upon Patroklos
and sent him into the fighting, and gave many men to go with him.
All day they fought about the Skaian Gates, and on that day
they would have stormed the city, if only Phoibos Apollo
455 had not killed the fighting son of Menoitios there in the first ranks
after he had wrought much damage, and given the glory to Hektor.
Therefore now I come to your knees; so might you be willing
to give me for my short-lived son a shield and a helmet
and two beautiful greaves fitted with clasps for the ankles
460 and a corselet. What he had was lost with his steadfast companion

when the Trojans killed him. Now my son lies on the ground, heart
    sorrowing."
    Hearing her the renowned smith of the strong arms answered her:
"Do not fear. Let not these things be a thought in your mind.
And I wish that I could hide him away from death and its sorrow
at that time when his hard fate comes upon him, as surely        465
as there shall be fine armor for him, such as another
man out of many men shall wonder at, when he looks on it."

    So he spoke, and left her there, and went to his bellows.
He turned these toward the fire and gave them their orders for working.
And the bellows, all twenty of them, blew on the crucibles,        470
from all directions blasting forth wind to blow the flames high
now as he hurried to be at this place and now at another,
wherever Hephaistos might wish them to blow, and the work went forward.
He cast on the fire bronze which is weariless, and tin with it
and valuable gold, and silver, and thereafter set forth        475
upon its standard the great anvil, and gripped in one hand
the ponderous hammer, while in the other he grasped the pincers.

    First of all he forged a shield that was huge and heavy,
elaborating it about, and threw around it a shining
triple rim that glittered, and the shield strap was cast of silver.        480
There were five folds composing the shield itself, and upon it
he elaborated many things in his skill and craftsmanship.
    He made the earth upon it, and the sky, and the sea's water,
and the tireless sun, and the moon waxing into her fullness,
and on it all the constellations that festoon the heavens,        485
the Pleiades and the Hyadēs and the strength of Orion
and the Bear, whom men give also the name of the Wagon,
who turns about in a fixed place and looks at Orion
and she alone is never plunged in the wash of the Ocean.

    On it he wrought in all their beauty two cities of mortal        490
men. And there were marriages in one, and festivals.
They were leading the brides along the city from their maiden chambers
under the flaring of torches, and the loud bride song was arising.
The young men followed the circles of the dance, and among them

495    the flutes and lyres kept up their clamor as in the meantime
the women standing each at the door of her court admired them.
The people were assembled in the market place, where a quarrel
had arisen, and two men were disputing over the blood price
for a man who had been killed. One man promised full restitution
500    in a public statement, but the other refused and would accept nothing.
Both then made for an arbitrator, to have a decision;
and people were speaking up on either side, to help both men.
But the heralds kept the people in hand, as meanwhile the elders
were in session on benches of polished stone in the sacred circle
505    and held in their hands the staves of the heralds who lift their voices.
The two men rushed before these, and took turns speaking their cases,
and between them lay on the ground two talents of gold, to be given
to that judge who in this case spoke the straightest opinion.

But around the other city were lying two forces of armed men
510    shining in their war gear. For one side counsel was divided
whether to storm and sack, or share between both sides the property
and all the possessions the lovely citadel held hard within it.
But the city's people were not giving way, and armed for an ambush.
Their beloved wives and their little children stood on the rampart
515    to hold it, and with them the men with age upon them, but meanwhile
the others went out. And Ares led them, and Pallas Athene.
These were gold, both, and golden raiment upon them, and they were
beautiful and huge in their armor, being divinities,
and conspicuous from afar, but the people around them were smaller.
520    These, when they were come to the place that was set for their ambush,
in a river, where there was a watering place for all animals,
there they sat down in place shrouding themselves in the bright bronze.
But apart from these were sitting two men to watch for the rest of them
and waiting until they could see the sheep and the shambling cattle,
525    who appeared presently, and two herdsmen went along with them
playing happily on pipes, and took no thought of the treachery.
Those others saw them, and made a rush, and quickly thereafter
cut off on both sides the herds of cattle and the beautiful
flocks of shining sheep, and killed the shepherds upon them.
530    But the other army, as soon as they heard the uproar arising
from the cattle, as they sat in their councils, suddenly mounted

behind their light-foot horses, and went after, and soon overtook them.
These stood their ground and fought a battle by the banks of the river,
and they were making casts at each other with their spears bronze-headed;
and Hate was there with Confusion among them, and Death the destructive;   535
she was holding a live man with a new wound, and another
one unhurt, and dragged a dead man by the feet through the carnage.
The clothing upon her shoulders showed strong red with the men's blood.
All closed together like living men and fought with each other
and dragged away from each other the corpses of those who had fallen.   540

   He made upon it a soft field, the pride of the tilled land,
wide and triple-ploughed, with many ploughmen upon it
who wheeled their teams at the turn and drove them in either direction.
And as these making their turn would reach the end-strip of the field,
a man would come up to them at this point and hand them a flagon   545
of honey-sweet wine, and they would turn again to the furrows
in their haste to come again to the end-strip of the deep field.
The earth darkened behind them and looked like earth that has been
      ploughed
though it was gold. Such was the wonder of the shield's forging.

   He made on it the precinct of a king, where the laborers   550
were reaping, with the sharp reaping hooks in their hands. Of the cut swathes
some fell along the lines of reaping, one after another,
while the sheaf-binders caught up others and tied them with bind-ropes.
There were three sheaf-binders who stood by, and behind them
were children picking up the cut swathes, and filled their arms with them   555
and carried and gave them always; and by them the king in silence
and holding his staff stood near the line of the reapers, happily.
And apart and under a tree the heralds made a feast ready
and trimmed a great ox they had slaughtered. Meanwhile the women
scattered, for the workmen to eat, abundant white barley.   560
   He made on it a great vineyard heavy with clusters,
lovely and in gold, but the grapes upon it were darkened
and the vines themselves stood out through poles of silver. About them
he made a field-ditch of dark metal, and drove all around this
a fence of tin; and there was only one path to the vineyard,   565
and along it ran the grape-bearers for the vineyard's stripping.

Young girls and young men, in all their light-hearted innocence,
carried the kind, sweet fruit away in their woven baskets,
and in their midst a youth with a singing lyre played charmingly
570  upon it for them, and sang the beautiful song for Linos
in a light voice, and they followed him, and with singing and whistling
and light dance-steps of their feet kept time to the music.
    He made upon it a herd of horn-straight oxen. The cattle
were wrought of gold and of tin, and thronged in speed and with lowing
575  out of the dung of the farmyard to a pasturing place by a sounding
river, and beside the moving field of a reed bed.
The herdsmen were of gold who went along with the cattle,
four of them, and nine dogs shifting their feet followed them.
But among the foremost of the cattle two formidable lions
580  had caught hold of a bellowing bull, and he with loud lowings
was dragged away, as the dogs and the young men went in pursuit of him.
But the two lions, breaking open the hide of the great ox,
gulped the black blood and the inward guts, as meanwhile the herdsmen
were in the act of setting and urging the quick dogs on them.
585  But they, before they could get their teeth in, turned back from the lions,
but would come and take their stand very close, and bayed, and kept clear.
    And the renowned smith of the strong arms made on it a meadow
large and in a lovely valley for the glimmering sheepflocks,
with dwelling places upon it, and covered shelters, and sheepfolds.
590    And the renowned smith of the strong arms made elaborate on it
a dancing floor, like that which once in the wide spaces of Knosos
Daidalos built for Ariadne of the lovely tresses.
And there were young men on it and young girls, sought for their beauty
with gifts of oxen, dancing, and holding hands at the wrist. These
595  wore, the maidens long light robes, but the men wore tunics
of finespun work and shining softly, touched with olive oil.
And the girls wore fair garlands on their heads, while the young men
carried golden knives that hung from sword-belts of silver.
At whiles on their understanding feet they would run very lightly,
600  as when a potter crouching makes trial of his wheel, holding
it close in his hands, to see if it will run smooth. At another
time they would form rows, and run, rows crossing each other.
And around the lovely chorus of dancers stood a great multitude
happily watching, while among the dancers two acrobats

led the measures of song and dance revolving among them.                                 605
     He made on it the great strength of the Ocean River
which ran around the uttermost rim of the shield's strong structure.

     Then after he had wrought this shield, which was huge and heavy,
he wrought for him a corselet brighter than fire in its shining,
and wrought him a helmet, massive and fitting close to his temples,        610
lovely and intricate work, and laid a gold top-ridge along it,
and out of pliable tin wrought him leg-armor. Thereafter
when the renowned smith of the strong arms had finished the armor
he lifted it and laid it before the mother of Achilleus.
And she like a hawk came sweeping down from the snows of Olympos        615
and carried with her the shining armor, the gift of Hephaistos.

# BOOK NINETEEN

Now Dawn the yellow-robed arose from the river of Ocean
to carry her light to men and to immortals. And Thetis
came to the ships and carried with her the gifts of Hephaistos.
She found her beloved son lying in the arms of Patroklos
5   crying shrill, and his companions in their numbers about him
mourned. She, shining among divinities, stood there beside them.
She clung to her son's hand and called him by name and spoke to him:
"My child, now, though we grieve for him, we must let this man lie
dead, in the way he first was killed through the gods' designing.
10  Accept rather from me the glorious arms of Hephaistos,
so splendid, and such as no man has ever worn on his shoulders."

The goddess spoke so, and set down the armor on the ground
before Achilleus, and all its elaboration clashed loudly.
Trembling took hold of all the Myrmidons. None had the courage
15  to look straight at it. They were afraid of it. Only Achilleus
looked, and as he looked the anger came harder upon him
and his eyes glittered terribly under his lids, like sunflare.
He was glad, holding in his hands the shining gifts of Hephaistos.
But when he had satisfied his heart with looking at the intricate
20  armor, he spoke to his mother and addressed her in winged words:
"My mother, the god has given me these weapons; they are such
as are the work of immortals. No mortal man could have made them.
Therefore now I shall arm myself in them. Yet I am sadly
afraid, during this time, for the warlike son of Menoitios
25  that flies might get into the wounds beaten by bronze in his body
and breed worms in them, and these make foul the body, seeing

that the life is killed in him, and that all his flesh may be rotted."
    In turn the goddess Thetis the silver-footed answered him:
"My child, no longer let these things be a care in your mind.
I shall endeavor to drive from him the swarming and fierce things,          30
those flies, which feed upon the bodies of men who have perished;
and although he lie here till a year has gone to fulfillment,
still his body shall be as it was, or firmer than ever.
Go then and summon into assembly the fighting Achaians,
and unsay your anger against Agamemnon, shepherd of the people,             35
and arm at once for the fighting, and put your war strength upon you."
    She spoke so, and drove the strength of great courage into him;
and meanwhile through the nostrils of Patroklos she distilled
ambrosia and red nectar, so that his flesh might not spoil.


    But he, brilliant Achilleus, walked along by the seashore                40
crying his terrible cry, and stirred up the fighting Achaians.
And even those who before had stayed where the ships were assembled,
they who were helmsmen of the ships and handled the steering oar,
they who were stewards among the ships and dispensers of rations,
even these came then to assembly, since now Achilleus                       45
had appeared, after staying so long from the sorrowful battle.
And there were two who came limping among them, henchmen of Ares
both, Tydeus' son the staunch in battle, and brilliant Odysseus,
leaning on spears, since they had the pain of their wounds yet upon them,
and came and took their seats in the front rank of those assembled.         50
And last of them came in the lord of men Agamemnon
with a wound on him, seeing that Koön, the son of Antenor,
had stabbed him with the bronze edge of the spear in the strong encounter.
But now, when all the Achaians were in one body together,
Achilleus of the swift feet stood up before them and spoke to them:         55
"Son of Atreus, was this after all the better way for
both, for you and me, that we, for all our hearts' sorrow,
quarreled together for the sake of a girl in soul-perishing hatred?
I wish Artemis had killed her beside the ships with an arrow
on that day when I destroyed Lyrnessos and took her.                        60
For thus not all these too many Achaians would have bitten
the dust, by enemy hands, when I was away in my anger.
This way was better for the Trojans and Hektor; yet I think

the Achaians will too long remember this quarrel between us.
65 Still, we will let all this be a thing of the past, though it hurts us,
and beat down by constraint the anger that rises inside us.
Now I am making an end of my anger. It does not become me
unrelentingly to rage on. Come, then! The more quickly
drive on the flowing-haired Achaians into the fighting,
70 so that I may go up against the Trojans, and find out
if they still wish to sleep out beside the ships. I think rather
they will be glad to rest where they are, whoever among them
gets away with his life from the fury of our spears' onset."

He spoke, and the strong-greaved Achaians were pleasured to hear him
75 and how the great-hearted son of Peleus unsaid his anger.
Now among them spoke forth the lord of men Agamemnon
from the place where he was sitting, and did not stand up among them:
"Fighting men and friends, O Danaäns, henchmen of Ares:
it is well to listen to the speaker, it is not becoming
80 to break in on him. This will be hard for him, though he be able.
How among the great murmur of people shall anyone listen
or speak either? A man, though he speak very clearly, is baffled.
I shall address the son of Peleus; yet all you other
Argives listen also, and give my word careful attention.
85 This is the word the Achaians have spoken often against me
and found fault with me in it, yet I am not responsible
but Zeus is, and Destiny, and Erinys the mist-walking
who in assembly caught my heart in the savage delusion
on that day I myself stripped from him the prize of Achilleus.
90 Yet what could I do? It is the god who accomplishes all things.
Delusion is the elder daughter of Zeus, the accursed
who deludes all; her feet are delicate and they step not
on the firm earth, but she walks the air above men's heads
and leads them astray. She has entangled others before me.
95 Yes, for once Zeus even was deluded, though men say
he is the highest one of gods and mortals. Yet Hera
who is female deluded even Zeus in her craftiness
on that day when in strong wall-circled Thebe Alkmene
was at her time to bring forth the strength of Herakles. Therefore
100 Zeus spoke forth and made a vow before all the immortals:

'Hear me, all you gods and all you goddesses: hear me
while I speak forth what the heart within my breast urges.
This day Eileithyia of women's child-pains shall bring forth
a man to the light who, among the men sprung of the generation
of my blood, shall be lord over all those dwelling about him.'          105
Then in guileful intention the lady Hera said to him:
'You will be a liar, not put fulfillment on what you have spoken.
Come, then, lord of Olympos, and swear before me a strong oath
that he shall be lord over all those dwelling about him
who this day shall fall between the feet of a woman,                   110
that man who is born of the blood of your generation.' So Hera
spoke. And Zeus was entirely unaware of her falsehood,
but swore a great oath, and therein lay all his deception.
But Hera in a flash of speed left the horn of Olympos
and rapidly came to Argos of Achaia, where she knew                    115
was the mighty wife of Sthenelos, descended of Perseus.
And she was carrying a son, and this was the seventh month for her,
but she brought him sooner into the light, and made him premature,
and stayed the childbirth of Alkmene, and held back the birth pangs.
She went herself and spoke the message to Zeus, son of Kronos:          120
'Father Zeus of the shining bolt, I will tell you a message
for your heart. A great man is born, who will be lord over the Argives,
Eurystheus, son of Sthenelos, of the seed of Perseus,
your generation. It is not unfit that he should rule over
the Argives.' She spoke, and the sharp sorrow struck at his deep heart.  125
He caught by the shining hair of her head the goddess Delusion
in the anger of his heart, and swore a strong oath, that never
after this might Delusion, who deludes all, come back
to Olympos and the starry sky. So speaking, he whirled her
about in his hand and slung her out of the starry heaven,               130
and presently she came to men's establishments. But Zeus
would forever grieve over her each time that he saw his dear son
doing some shameful work of the tasks that Eurystheus set him.
So I in my time, when tall Hektor of the shining helm
was forever destroying the Argives against the sterns of their vessels,  135
could not forget Delusion, the way I was first deluded.
But since I was deluded and Zeus took my wits away from me,
I am willing to make all good and give back gifts in abundance.

Rise up, then, to the fighting and rouse the rest of the people.
140  Here am I, to give you all those gifts, as many
as brilliant Odysseus yesterday went to your shelter and promised.
Or if you will, hold back, though you lean hard into the battle,
while my followers take the gifts from my ship and bring them
to you, so you may see what I give to comfort your spirit."

145      Then in answer to him spoke Achilleus of the swift feet:
"Son of Atreus, most lordly and king of men, Agamemnon,
the gifts are yours to give if you wish, and as it is proper,
or to keep with yourself. But now let us remember our joy in warcraft,
immediately, for it is not fitting to stay here and waste time
150  nor delay, since there is still a big work to be done.
So can a man see once more Achilleus among the front fighters
with the bronze spear wrecking the Trojan battalions. Therefore
let each of you remember this and fight his antagonist."
       Then in answer to him spoke resourceful Odysseus:
155 "Not that way, good fighter that you are, godlike Achilleus.
Do not drive the sons of the Achaians on Ilion when they are hungry,
to fight against the Trojans, since not short will be the time
of battle, once the massed formations of men have encountered
together, with the god inspiring fury in both sides.
160  Rather tell the men of Achaia here by their swift ships,
to take food and wine, since these make fighting fury and warcraft.
For a man will not have strength to fight his way forward all day
long until the sun goes down if he is starved for food. Even
though in his heart he be very passionate for the battle,
165  yet without his knowing it his limbs will go heavy, and hunger
and thirst will catch up with him and cumber his knees as he moves on.
But when a man has been well filled with wine and with eating
and then does battle all day long against the enemy,
why, then the heart inside him is full of cheer, nor do his limbs
170  get weary, until all are ready to give over the fighting.
Come then, tell your men to scatter and bid them get ready
a meal; and as for the gifts, let the lord of men Agamemnon
bring them to the middle of our assembly so all the Achaians
can see them before their eyes, so your own heart may be pleasured.
175  And let him stand up before the Argives and swear an oath to you

that he never entered into her bed and never lay with her
as is natural for people, my lord, between men and women.
And by this let the spirit in your own heart be made gracious.
After that in his own shelter let him appease you
with a generous meal, so you will lack nothing of what is due you.          180
And you, son of Atreus, after this be more righteous to another
man. For there is no fault when even one who is a king
appeases a man, when the king was the first one to be angry."
    Then in turn the lord of men Agamemnon answered him:
"Hearing what you have said, son of Laërtes, I am pleased with you.          185
Fairly have you gone through everything and explained it.
And all this I am willing to swear to, and my heart urges me,
and I will not be foresworn before the gods. Let Achilleus
stay here the while, though he lean very hard toward the work of the war god,
and remain the rest of you all here assembled, until the gifts come          190
back from my shelter and while we cut our oaths of fidelity.
And for you yourself, Odysseus, I give you this errand, this order,
that you choose out excellent young men of all the Achaians
and bring the gifts back here from my ship, all that you promised
yesterday to Achilleus, and bring the women back also.                       195
And in the wide host of the Achaians let Talthybios make ready
a boar for me, and dedicate it to Zeus and Helios."
    Then in answer to him spoke Achilleus of the swift feet:
"Son of Atreus, most lordly and king of men, Agamemnon,
at some other time rather you should busy yourself about these things,       200
when there is some stopping point in the fighting, at some time
when there is not so much fury inside of my heart. But now
as things are they lie there torn whom the son of Priam
Hektor has beaten down, since Zeus was giving him glory,
and then you urge a man to eating. No, but I would now                       205
drive forward the sons of the Achaians into the fighting
starving and unfed, and afterward when the sun sets
make ready a great dinner, when we have paid off our defilement.
But before this, for me at least, neither drink nor food shall
go down my very throat, since my companion has perished                      210
and lies inside my shelter torn about with the cutting
bronze, and turned against the forecourt while my companions
mourn about him. Food and drink mean nothing to my heart

but blood does, and slaughter, and the groaning of men in the hard work."

215 Then in answer to him spoke resourceful Odysseus:
"Son of Peleus, Achilleus, far greatest of the Achaians,
you are stronger than I am and greater by not a little
with the spear, yet I in turn might overpass you in wisdom
by far, since I was born before you and have learned more things.

220 Therefore let your heart endure to listen to my words.
When there is battle men have suddenly their fill of it
when the bronze scatters on the ground the straw in most numbers
and the harvest is most thin, when Zeus has poised his balance,
Zeus, who is administrator to men in their fighting.

225 There is no way the Achaians can mourn a dead man by denying
the belly. Too many fall day by day, one upon another,
and how could anyone find breathing space from his labor?
No, but we must harden our hearts and bury the man who
dies, when we have wept over him on the day, and all those

230 who are left about from the hateful work of war must remember
food and drink, so that afterward all the more strongly
we may fight on forever relentless against our enemies
with the weariless bronze put on about our bodies. Let one not
wait longing for any other summons to stir on the people.

235 This summons now shall be an evil on anyone left behind
by the ships of the Argives. Therefore let us drive on together
and wake the bitter war god on the Trojans, breakers of horses."

He spoke, and went away with the sons of glorious Nestor,
with Meges, the son of Phyleus, and Meriones, and Thoas,

240 and Lykomedes, the son of Kreion, and Melanippos. These went
on their way to the shelter of Atreus' son Agamemnon.
No sooner was the order given than the thing had been done.
They brought back seven tripods from the shelter, those Agamemnon
had promised, and twenty shining cauldrons, twelve horses. They
brought back

245 immediately the seven women the work of whose hands was
blameless, and the eighth of them was Briseis of the fair cheeks.
Odysseus weighed out ten full talents of gold and led them
back, and the young men of the Achaians carried the other gifts.
They brought these into the midst of assembly, and Agamemnon

stood up, and Talthybios in voice like an immortal                                    250
stood beside the shepherd of the people with the boar in his hands.
Atreus' son laid hands upon his work-knife, and drew it
from where it hung ever beside the great sheath of his war sword,
and cut first hairs away from the boar, and lifting his hands up
to Zeus, prayed, while all the Argives stayed fast at their places         255
in silence and in order of station, and listened to their king.
He spoke before them in prayer gazing into the wide sky:
"Let Zeus first be my witness, highest of the gods and greatest,
and Earth, and Helios the Sun, and Furies, who underground
avenge dead men, when any man has sworn to a falsehood,                  260
that I have never laid a hand on the girl Briseis
on pretext to go to bed with her, or for any other
reason, but she remained, not singled out, in my shelter.
If any of this is falsely sworn, may the gods give me many
griefs, all that they inflict on those who swear falsely before them."   265
    So he spoke, and with pitiless bronze he cut the boar's throat.
Talthybios whirled the body about, and threw it in the great reach
of the gray sea, to feed the fishes. Meanwhile Achilleus
stood up among the battle-fond Achaians, and spoke to them:
"Father Zeus, great are the delusions with which you visit men.          270
Without you, the son of Atreus could never have stirred so
the heart inside my breast, nor taken the girl away from me
against my will, and be in helplessness. No, but Zeus somehow
wished that death should befall great numbers of the Achaians.
Go now and take your dinner, so we may draw on the battle."              275

    So he spoke, and suddenly broke up the assembly.
Now these scattered away each man to his own ship. Meanwhile
the great-hearted Myrmidons disposed of the presents.
They went on their way carrying them to the ship of godlike Achilleus,
and stowed the gifts in the shelters, and let the women be settled,      280
while proud henchmen drove the horses into Achilleus' horse-herd.
    And now, in the likeness of golden Aphrodite, Briseis
when she saw Patroklos lying torn with sharp bronze, folding
him in her arms cried shrilly above him and with her hands tore
at her breasts and her soft throat and her beautiful forehead.           285
The woman like the immortals mourning for him spoke to him:

"Patroklos, far most pleasing to my heart in its sorrows,
I left you here alive when I went away from the shelter,
but now I come back, lord of the people, to find you have fallen.
290  So evil in my life takes over from evil forever.
The husband on whom my father and honored mother bestowed me
I saw before my city lying torn with the sharp bronze,
and my three brothers, whom a single mother bore with me
and who were close to me, all went on one day to destruction.
295  And yet you would not let me, when swift Achilleus had cut down
my husband, and sacked the city of godlike Mynes, you would not
let me sorrow, but said you would make me godlike Achilleus'
wedded lawful wife, that you would take me back in the ships
to Phthia, and formalize my marriage among the Myrmidons.
300  Therefore I weep your death without ceasing. You were kind always."
So she spoke, lamenting, and the women sorrowed around her
grieving openly for Patroklos, but for her own sorrows
each. But the lords of Achaia were gathered about Achilleus
beseeching him to eat, but he with a groan denied them:
305  "I beg of you, if any dear companion will listen
to me, stop urging me to satisfy the heart in me
with food and drink, since this strong sorrow has come upon me.
I will hold out till the sun goes down and endure, though it be hard."

So he spoke, and caused the rest of the kings to scatter;
310  but the two sons of Atreus stayed with him, and brilliant Odysseus,
and Nestor, and Idomeneus, and the aged charioteer, Phoinix,
comforting him close in his sorrow, yet his heart would not
be comforted, till he went into the jaws of the bleeding battle.
Remembering Patroklos he sighed much for him, and spoke aloud:
315  "There was a time, ill fated, O dearest of all my companions,
when you yourself would set the desirable dinner before me
quickly and expertly, at the time the Achaians were urgent
to carry sorrowful war on the Trojans, breakers of horses.
But now you lie here torn before me, and my heart goes starved
320  for meat and drink, though they are here beside me, by reason
of longing for you. There is nothing worse than this I could suffer,
not even if I were to hear of the death of my father
who now, I think, in Phthia somewhere lets fall a soft tear

for bereavement of such a son, for me, who now in a strange land
make war upon the Trojans for the sake of accursed Helen;                    325
or the death of my dear son, who is raised for my sake in Skyros
now, if godlike Neoptolemos is still one of the living.
Before now the spirit inside my breast was hopeful
that I alone should die far away from horse-pasturing Argos
here in Troy; I hoped you would win back again to Phthia                      330
so that in a fast black ship you could take my son back
from Skyros to Phthia, and show him all my possessions,
my property, my serving men, my great high-roofed house.
For by this time I think that Peleus must altogether
have perished, or still keeps a little scant life in sorrow                   335
for the hatefulness of old age and because he waits ever from me
the evil message, for the day he hears I have been killed."

So he spoke, mourning, and the elders lamented around him
remembering each those he had left behind in his own halls.
The son of Kronos took pity on them as he watched them mourning             340
and immediately spoke in winged words to Athene:
"My child, have you utterly abandoned the man of your choice?
Is there no longer deep concern in your heart for Achilleus?
Now he has sat down before the steep horned ships and is mourning
for his own beloved companion, while all the others                          345
have gone to take their dinner, but he is fasting and unfed.
Go then to him and distil nectar inside his chest, and delicate
ambrosia, so the weakness of hunger will not come upon him."
Speaking so, he stirred Athene, who was eager before this,
and she in the likeness of a wide-winged, thin-crying                        350
hawk plummeted from the sky through the bright air. Now the Achaians
were arming at once along the encampment. She dropped the delicate
ambrosia and the nectar inside the breast of Achilleus
softly, so no sad weakness of hunger would come on his knees,
and she herself went back to the close house of her powerful                 355
father, while they were scattering out away from the fast ships.
As when in their thickness the snowflakes of Zeus come fluttering
cold beneath the blast of the north wind born in the bright sky,
so now in their thickness the pride of the helms bright shining
were carried out from the ships, and shields massive in the middle           360

and the corselets strongly hollowed and the ash spears were worn forth.
The shining swept to the sky and all earth was laughing about them
under the glitter of bronze and beneath their feet stirred the thunder
of men, within whose midst brilliant Achilleus helmed him.
365 A clash went from the grinding of his teeth, and his eyes glowed
as if they were the stare of a fire, and the heart inside him
was entered with sorrow beyond endurance. Raging at the Trojans
he put on the gifts of the god, that Hephaistos wrought him with much toil.

First he placed along his legs the fair greaves linked with
370 silver fastenings to hold the greaves at the ankles.
Afterward he girt on about his chest the corselet,
and across his shoulders slung the sword with the nails of silver,
a bronze sword, and caught up the great shield, huge and heavy
next, and from it the light glimmered far, as from the moon.
375 And as when from across water a light shines to mariners
from a blazing fire, when the fire is burning high in the mountains
in a desolate steading, as the mariners are carried unwilling
by storm winds over the fish-swarming sea, far away from their loved ones;
so the light from the fair elaborate shield of Achilleus
380 shot into the high air. And lifting the helm he set it
massive upon his head, and the helmet crested with horse-hair
shone like a star, the golden fringes were shaken about it
which Hephaistos had driven close along the horn of the helmet.
And brilliant Achilleus tried himself in his armor, to see
385 if it fitted close, and how his glorious limbs ran within it,
and the armor became as wings and upheld the shepherd of the people.
Next he pulled out from its standing place the spear of his father,
huge, heavy, thick, which no one else of all the Achaians
could handle, but Achilleus alone knew how to wield it,
390 the Pelian ash spear which Cheiron had brought to his father
from high on Pelion, to be death for fighters in battle.
Automedon and Alkimos, in charge of the horses,
yoked them, and put the fair breast straps about them, and forced the bits
        home
between their jaws, and pulled the reins back against the compacted
395 chariot seat, and one, Automedon, took up the shining
whip caught close in his hand and vaulted up to the chariot,

while behind him Achilleus helmed for battle took his stance
shining in all his armor like the sun when he crosses above us,
and cried in a terrible voice on the horses of his father:
"Xanthos, Balios, Bay and Dapple, famed sons of Podarge,        400
take care to bring in another way your charioteer back
to the company of the Danaäns, when we give over fighting,
not leave him to lie fallen there, as you did to Patroklos."

    Then from beneath the yoke the gleam-footed horse answered him,
Xanthos, and as he spoke bowed his head, so that all the mane     405
fell away from the pad and swept the ground by the cross-yoke;
the goddess of the white arms, Hera, had put a voice in him:
"We shall still keep you safe for this time, O hard Achilleus.
And yet the day of your death is near, but it is not we
who are to blame, but a great god and powerful Destiny.       410
For it was not because we were slow, because we were careless,
that the Trojans have taken the armor from the shoulders of Patroklos,
but it was that high god, the child of lovely-haired Leto,
who killed him among the champions and gave the glory to Hektor.
But for us, we two could run with the blast of the west wind      415
who they say is the lightest of all things; yet still for you
there is destiny to be killed in force by a god and a mortal."
    When he had spoken so the Furies stopped the voice in him,
but deeply disturbed, Achilleus of the swift feet answered him:
"Xanthos, why do you prophesy my death? This is not for you.     420
I myself know well it is destined for me to die here
far from my beloved father and mother. But for all that
I will not stop till the Trojans have had enough of my fighting."
    He spoke, and shouting held on in the foremost his single-foot horses.

# BOOK TWENTY

So these now, the Achaians, beside the curved ships were arming
around you, son of Peleus, insatiate of battle,
while on the other side at the break of the plain the Trojans
armed. But Zeus, from the many-folded peak of Olympos,
5    told Themis to summon all the gods into assembly. She went
everywhere, and told them to make their way to Zeus' house.
There was no river who was not there, except only Ocean,
there was not any one of the nymphs who live in the lovely
groves, and the springs of rivers and grass of the meadows, who came not.
10   These all assembling into the house of Zeus cloud gathering
took places among the smooth-stone cloister walks which Hephaistos
had built for Zeus the father by his craftsmanship and contrivance.
So they were assembled within Zeus' house; and the shaker
of the earth did not fail to hear the goddess, but came up among them
15   from the sea, and sat in the midst of them, and asked Zeus of his counsel:
"Why, lord of the shining bolt, have you called the gods to assembly
once more? Are you deliberating Achaians and Trojans?
For the onset of battle is almost broken to flame between them."
In turn Zeus who gathers the clouds spoke to him in answer:
20   "You have seen, shaker of the earth, the counsel within me,
and why I gathered you. I think of these men though they are dying.
Even so, I shall stay here upon the fold of Olympos
sitting still, watching, to pleasure my heart. Meanwhile all you others
go down, wherever you may go among the Achaians and Trojans
25   and give help to either side, as your own pleasure directs you.
For if we leave Achilleus alone to fight with the Trojans
they will not even for a little hold off swift-footed Peleion.

For even before now they would tremble whenever they saw him,
and now, when his heart is grieved and angered for his companion's
death, I fear against destiny he may storm their fortress."                        30
    So spoke the son of Kronos and woke the incessant battle,
and the gods went down to enter the fighting, with purposes opposed.
Hera went to the assembled ships with Pallas Athene
and with Poseidon who embraces the earth, and with generous
Hermes, who within the heart is armed with astute thoughts.                        35
Hephaistos went the way of these in the pride of his great strength
limping, and yet his shrunken legs moved lightly beneath him.
But Ares of the shining helm went over to the Trojans,
and with him Phoibos of the unshorn hair, and the lady of arrows
Artemis, and smiling Aphrodite, Leto, and Xanthos.                                 40
    Now in the time when the gods were still distant from the mortals,
so long the Achaians were winning great glory, since now Achilleus
showed among them, who had stayed too long from the sorrowful
    fighting.
But the Trojans were taken every man in the knees with trembling
and terror, as they looked on the swift-footed son of Peleus                        45
shining in all his armor, a man like the murderous war god.
But after the Olympians merged in the men's company
strong Hatred, defender of peoples, burst out, and Athene bellowed
standing now beside the ditch dug at the wall's outside
and now again at the thundering sea's edge gave out her great cry,                  50
while on the other side Ares in the likeness of a dark stormcloud
bellowed, now from the peak of the citadel urging the Trojans
sharply on, now running beside the sweet banks of Simoeis.
    So the blessed gods stirring on the opponents drove them
together, and broke out among themselves the weight of their quarrel.              55
From high above the father of gods and men made thunder
terribly, while Poseidon from deep under them shuddered
all the illimitable earth, the sheer heads of the mountains.
And all the feet of Ida with her many waters were shaken
and all her crests, and the city of Troy, the ships of the Achaians.               60
Aïdoneus, lord of the dead below, was in terror
and sprang from his throne and screamed aloud, for fear that above him
he who circles the land, Poseidon, might break the earth open
and the houses of the dead lie open to men and immortals,
ghastly and moldering, so the very gods shudder before them;                       65

such was the crash that sounded as the gods came driving together
in wrath. For now over against the lord Poseidon
Phoibos Apollo took his stand with his feathered arrows,
and against Enyalios the goddess gray-eyed Athene.
70  Against Hera stood the lady of clamor, of the golden distaff,
of the showering arrows, Artemis, sister of the far striker.
Opposite Leto stood the strong one, generous Hermes,
and against Hephaistos stood the great deep-eddying river
who is called Xanthos by the gods, but by mortals Skamandros.

75     Thus gods went on to encounter gods; and meanwhile Achilleus
was straining to plunge into the combat opposite Hektor
Priam's son, since beyond all others his anger was driving him
to glut with his blood Ares the god who fights under the shield's guard.
But it was Aineias whom Apollo defender of people
80  drove straight against Peleion, and inspired vast power within him.
Zeus' son Apollo made his voice like that of Lykaon
Priam's son, and assumed his appearance, and spoke to Aineias:
"Aineias, lord of the Trojans' counsels. Where are those threats gone
which as you drank your wine you made before Troy's kings, solemnly,
85  that you would match your battle strength with Peleian Achilleus?"
      In turn Aineias spoke to him in answer: "Lykaon
son of Priam, why do you urge me on against my will
to fight in the face of Peleus' son and his too great fury?
Since this will not be the first time I stand up against swift-footed
90  Achilleus, but another time before now he drove me
with the spear from Ida, when he came there after our cattle
the time he sacked Lyrnessos and Pedasos. But Zeus rescued me
when he put strength inside me and made my knees quick. Otherwise
I should have gone down at Achilleus' hands, and those of Athene
95  who goes before him and makes light before him, who then was urging
him on with the brazen spear to destroy Leleges and Trojans.
Thereby it is not for any man to fight with Achilleus.
There is always some one of the gods with him to beat death from him.
Without this, even, his spear wings straight to its mark, nor gives out
100  until it has gone through a man's body. But if the god only
would pull out even the issue of war, he would not so easily
win, not even though he claims to be made all of bronze."

In turn the lord the son of Zeus Apollo spoke to him:
"Hero, then make your prayer, you also, to the everlasting
gods, since they say that you yourself are born of Zeus' daughter          105
Aphrodite, but Achilleus was born of a lesser goddess,
Aphrodite being daughter of Zeus, Thetis of the sea's ancient.
Carry your weariless bronze straight against him, let him by no means
turn you back by blustering words and his threats of terror."
      So speaking, he inspired enormous strength in the shepherd of the      110
            people,
who strode on his way among the champions helmed in the bright bronze,
nor did Hera of the white arms fail to see the son of Anchises
as he went through the thronging men to face the son of Peleus,
and drew the other immortals about her and spoke to them, saying:
"Poseidon and Athene, now take counsel between you                          115
and within your hearts as to how these matters shall be accomplished.
Here is Aineias gone helmed in the shining bronze against
Peleus' son, and it was Phoibos Apollo who sent him.
Come then, we must even go down ourselves and turn him
back from here, or else one of us must stand by Achilleus                   120
and put enormous strength upon him, and let him not come short
in courage, but let him know that they love him who are the highest
of the immortals, but those who before now fended the fury
of war, as now, from the Trojans are as wind and nothing.
For all of us have come down from Olympos to take our part                  125
in this battle, so nothing may be done to him by the Trojans
on this day. Afterward he shall suffer such things as Destiny
wove with the strand of his birth that day he was born to his mother.
But if Achilleus does not hear all this from gods' voices
he will be afraid, when a god puts out his strength against him             130
in the fighting. It is hard for gods to be shown in their true shape."
      In turn Poseidon the shaker of the earth answered her:
"Hera, do not be angry without purpose. It does not
become you, since I at least would not have the rest of us gods
encounter in battle, since indeed we are far too strong for them.          135
Let us then go away and sit down together off the path
at a viewing place, and let the men take care of their fighting.
Only if Ares begins to fight, or Phoibos Apollo,
or if they hold Achilleus back and will not let him fight,

140     then at once they will have a quarrel with us on their hands
in open battle. But soon, I think, when they have fought with us
they will get back to Olympos and the throng of the other gods
beaten back by the overmastering strength of our hands."

    So he spoke, Poseidon of the dark hair, and led the way
145 to the stronghold of godlike Herakles, earth-piled on both sides,
a high place, which the Trojans and Pallas Athene had built him
as a place of escape where he could get away from the Sea Beast
when the charging monster drove him away to the plain from the seashore.
There Poseidon and the gods who were with him sat down
150 and gathered a breakless wall of cloud to darken their shoulders;
while they of the other side sat down on the brows of the sweet bluffs
around you, lord Apollo, and Ares sacker of cities.
    So they on either side took their places, deliberating
counsels, reluctant on both sides to open the sorrowful
155 attack. But Zeus sitting on high above urged them on.

    But all the plain was filled and shining with bronze of the mortals,
their men and horses, and underneath their feet the earth staggered
as they swept together. Two men far greater than all the others
were coming to encounter, furious to fight with each other,
160 Aineias, the son of Anchises, and brilliant Achilleus.
First of the two Aineias had strode forth in menace, tossing
his head beneath the heavy helm, and he held the stark shield
in front of his chest, and shook the brazen spear. From the other
side the son of Peleus rose like a lion against him,
165 the baleful beast, when men have been straining to kill him, the county
all in the hunt, and he at the first pays them no attention
but goes his way, only when some one of the impetuous young men
has hit him with the spear he whirls, jaws open, over his teeth foam
breaks out, and in the depth of his chest the powerful heart groans;
170 he lashes his own ribs with his tail and the flanks on both sides
as he rouses himself to fury for the fight, eyes glaring,
and hurls himself straight onward on the chance of killing some one
of the men, or else being killed himself in the first onrush.
So the proud heart and fighting fury stirred on Achilleus
175 to go forward in the face of great-hearted Aineias.

Now as these in their advance had come close to each other
first of the two to speak was swift-footed brilliant Achilleus:
"Aineias, why have you stood so far forth from the multitude
against me? Does the desire in your heart drive you to combat
in hope you will be lord of the Trojans, breakers of horses, 180
and of Priam's honor? And yet even if you were to kill me
Priam would not because of that rest such honor on your hand.
He has sons, and he himself is sound, not weakened.
Or have the men of Troy promised you a piece of land, surpassing
all others, fine ploughland and orchard for you to administer 185
if you kill me? But I think that killing will not be easy.
Another time before this, I tell you, you ran from my spear.
Or do you not remember when, apart from your cattle, I caught you
alone, and chased you in the speed of your feet down the hills of Ida
headlong, and that time as you ran you did not turn to look back. 190
Then you got away into Lyrnessos, but I went after you
and stormed that place, with the help of Athene and of Zeus father,
and took the day of liberty away from their women
and led them as spoil, but Zeus and the other gods saved you.
I think they will not save you now, as your expectation 195
tells you they will. No, but I myself urge you to get back
into the multitude, not stand to face me, before you
take some harm. Once a thing has been done, the fool sees it."
    Then in turn Aineias spoke to him and made his answer:
"Son of Peleus, never hope by words to frighten me 200
as if I were a baby. I myself understand well enough
how to speak in vituperation and how to make insults.
You and I know each other's birth, we both know our parents
since we have heard the lines of their fame from mortal men; only
I have never with my eyes seen your parents, nor have you seen mine. 205
For you, they say you are the issue of blameless Peleus
and that your mother was Thetis of the lovely hair, the sea's lady;
I in turn claim I am the son of great-hearted Anchises
but that my mother was Aphrodite; and that of these parents
one group or the other will have a dear son to mourn for 210
this day. Since I believe we will not in mere words, like children,
meet, and separate and go home again out of the fighting.
Even so, if you wish to learn all this and be certain

of my genealogy: there are plenty of men who know it.

215 First of all Zeus who gathers the clouds had a son, Dardanos
who founded Dardania, since there was yet no sacred Ilion
made a city in the plain to be a center of peoples,
but they lived yet in the underhills of Ida with all her waters.
Dardanos in turn had a son, the king, Erichthonios,

220 who became the richest of mortal men, and in his possession
were three thousand horses who pastured along the low grasslands,
mares in their pride with their young colts; and with these the North Wind
fell in love as they pastured there, and took on upon him
the likeness of a dark-maned stallion, and coupled with them,

225 and the mares conceiving of him bore to him twelve young horses.
Those, when they would play along the grain-giving tilled land
would pass along the tassels of corn and not break the divine yield,
but again, when they played across the sea's wide ridges
they would run the edge of the wave where it breaks on the gray salt water.

230 Erichthonios had a son, Tros, who was lord of the Trojans,
and to Tros in turn there were born three sons unfaulted,
Ilos and Assarakos and godlike Ganymedes
who was the loveliest born of the race of mortals, and therefore
the gods caught him away to themselves, to be Zeus' wine-pourer,

235 for the sake of his beauty, so he might be among the immortals.
Ilos in turn was given a son, the blameless Laomedon,
and Laomedon had sons in turn, Tithonos and Priam,
Lampos, Klytios and Hiketaon, scion of Ares;
but Assarakos had Kapys, and Kapys' son was Anchises,

240 and I am Anchises' son, and Priam's is Hektor the brilliant.
Such is the generation and blood I claim to be born from.
Zeus builds up and Zeus diminishes the strength in men,
the way he pleases, since his power is beyond all others'.
But come, let us no longer stand here talking of these things

245 like children, here in the space between the advancing armies.
For there are harsh things enough that could be spoken against us
both, a ship of a hundred locks could not carry the burden.
The tongue of man is a twisty thing, there are plenty of words there
of every kind, the range of words is wide, and their variance.

250 The sort of thing you say is the thing that will be said to you.
But what have you and I to do with the need for squabbling

and hurling insults at each other, as if we were two wives
who when they have fallen upon a heart-perishing quarrel
go out in the street and say abusive things to each other,
much true, and much that is not, and it is their rage that drives them.      255
You will not by talking turn me back from the strain of my warcraft,
not till you have fought to my face with the bronze. Come on then
and let us try each other's strength with the bronze of our spearheads."

He spoke, and on the terrible grim shield drove the ponderous
pike, so that the great shield moaned as it took the spearhead.      260
The son of Peleus with his heavy hand held the shield away
from him, in fright, since he thought the far-shadowing spear
of great-hearted Aineias would lightly be driven through it.
Fool, and the heart and spirit in him could not understand
how the glorious gifts of the gods are not easily broken      265
by mortal men, how such gifts will not give way before them.
Nor this time could the ponderous spear of war-wise Aineias
smash the shield, since the gold stayed it, the god's gift. Indeed
he did drive the spear through two folds, but there were three left
still, since the god of the dragging feet had made five folds on it,      270
two of bronze on the outside and on the inside two of tin
and between them the single gold, and in this the ash spear was held fast.
After him Achilleus let go his spear far shadowing
and struck the shield of Aineias along its perfect circle
at the utter rim where the circle of bronze ran thinnest about it      275
and the oxhide was laid thinnest there. The Pelian ash spear
crashed clean through it there, and the shield cried out as it went through.
Aineias shrank down and held the shield away and above him
in fright, and the spear went over his back and crashed its way
to the ground, and fixed there, after tearing apart two circles      280
of the man-covering shield. But Aineias, free of the long spear,
stood still, and around his eyes gathered the enormous emotion
and fear, that the weapon had fixed so close to him. Now Achilleus
drew his tearing sword and swept in fury upon him
crying a terrible cry, but Aineias now in his hand caught      285
up a stone, a huge thing which no two men could carry
such as men are now, but by himself he lightly hefted it.
And there Aineias would have hit him with the stone as he swept in,

on helm or shield, which would have fended the bitter death from him,
290  and Peleus' son would have closed with the sword and stripped the life
        from him,
     had not the shaker of the earth Poseidon sharply perceived all
     and immediately spoken his word out among the immortals:
     "Ah me; I am full of sorrow for great-hearted Aineias
     who must presently go down to death, overpowered by Achilleus,
295  because he believed the words of Apollo, the far ranging;
     poor fool, since Apollo will do nothing to keep grim death from him.
     But why does this man, who is guiltless, suffer his sorrows
     for no reason, for the sake of others' unhappiness, and always
     he gives gifts that please them to the gods who hold the wide heaven.
300  But come, let us ourselves get him away from death, for fear
     the son of Kronos may be angered if now Achilleus
     kills this man. It is destined that he shall be the survivor,
     that the generation of Dardanos shall not die, without seed
     obliterated, since Dardanos was dearest to Kronides
305  of all his sons that have been born to him from mortal women.
     For Kronos' son has cursed the generation of Priam,
     and now the might of Aineias shall be lord over the Trojans,
     and his sons' sons, and those who are born of their seed hereafter."
     In turn the lady of the ox eyes, Hera, answered him:
310  "Shaker of the earth, you yourself must decide in your own heart
     about Aineias, whether to rescue him or to let him
     go down, for all his strength, before Peleus' son, Achilleus.
     For we two, Pallas Athene and I, have taken
     numerous oaths and sworn them in the sight of all the immortals
315  never to drive the day of evil away from the Trojans,
     not even when all the city of Troy is burned in the ravening
     fire, on that day when the warlike sons of the Achaians burn it."

     When he had heard this, the shaker of the earth Poseidon
     went on his way through the confusion of spears and the fighting,
320  and came to where Aineias was, and renowned Achilleus.
     There quickly he drifted a mist across the eyes of one fighter,
     Achilleus, Peleus' son, and from the shield of Aineias
     of the great heart pulled loose the strong bronze-headed ash spear
     and laid it down again before the feet of Achilleus;

but Aineias he lifted high from the ground, and slung him through the air    325
so that many ranks of fighting men, many ranks of horses,
were overvaulted by Aineias, hurled by the god's hand.
He landed at the uttermost edge of the tossing battle
where the Kaukonians were arming them for the order of fighting.
And Poseidon, shaker of the earth, came and stood very near him    330
and spoke to him and addressed him in winged words: "Aineias,
which one of the gods is it who urges you to such madness
that you fight in the face of Peleus' son, against his high courage
though he is both stronger than you and dearer to the immortals?
Give back rather, whenever you find yourself thrown against him,    335
lest beyond your fate you go down into the house of the death god.
But once Achilleus has fulfilled his death and his destiny,
then take courage, and go on, and fight with their foremost,
since there shall be no other Achaian able to kill you."

He spoke, and left him there, when he had told him all this,    340
and at once scattered the mist away from the eyes of Achilleus
that the gods had sent, and now he looked with his eyes, and saw largely,
and in disgust spoke then to his own great-hearted spirit:
"Can this be? Here is a strange thing I see with my own eyes.
Here is my spear lying on the ground, but I can no longer    345
see the man, whom I was charging in fury to kill him.
Aineias was then one beloved of the immortal
gods. I thought what he said was ineffectual boasting.
Let him go. He will not again have daring to try me
in battle, since even now he was glad to escape my onset.    350
Come! I must urge on the Danaäns whose delight is in battle
and go on to face the rest of the Trojans, and see what they can do."

He spoke, and leapt back into the ranks, and urged each man on:
"No longer stand away from the Trojans, O great Achaians,
but let each one go to face his man, furious to fight him.    355
It is a hard thing for me, for all my great strength, to harry
the flight of men in such numbers or to fight with all of them.
Not Ares, who is a god immortal, not even Athene
could take the edge of such masses of men and fight a way through them.
But what I can do with hands and feet and strength I tell you    360
I will do, and I shall not hang back even a little
but go straight on through their formation, and I think that no man

of the Trojans will be glad when he comes within my spear's range."
He spoke, urging them on, but glorious Hektor called out
365  in a great voice to the Trojans, and was minded to face Achilleus:
"Do not be afraid of Peleion, O high-hearted Trojans.
I myself could fight in words against the immortals,
but with the spear it were hard, since they are far stronger than we are.
Even Achilleus will not win achievement of everything
370  he says. Part he will accomplish, but part shall be baulked halfway done.
I am going to stand against him now, though his hands are like flame,
though his hands are like flame, and his heart like the shining of iron."

He spoke, urging the Trojans, and they lifted their spears to face them.
Their fury gathered into bulk and their battle cry rose up.
375  But now Phoibos Apollo stood by Hektor and spoke to him:
"Hektor, do not go out all alone to fight with Achilleus,
but wait for him in the multitude and out of the carnage
lest he hit you with the spear or the stroke of the sword from close in."
He spoke, and Hektor plunged back into the swarm of the fighting
380  men, in fear, when he heard the voice of the god speaking.
But Achilleus, gathering the fury upon him, sprang on the Trojans
with a ghastly cry, and the first of them he killed was Iphition
the great son of Otrynteus and a lord over numbers of people,
born of a naiad nymph to Otrynteus, sacker of cities,
385  under the snows of Tmolos in the rich countryside of Hydē.
Great Achilleus struck him with the spear as he came in fury,
in the middle of the head, and all the head broke into two pieces.
He fell, thunderously. Great Achilleus vaunted above him:
"Lie there, Otrynteus' son, most terrifying of all men.
390  Here is your death, but your generation was by the lake waters
of Gyge, where is the allotted land of your fathers
by fish-swarming Hyllos and the whirling waters of Hermos."
He spoke, vaunting, but darkness shrouded the eyes of the other,
and the running-rims of Achaian chariots cut him to pieces
395  in the van of the onrush. Next, after him, facing Demoleon
lord defender of battle and son of Antenor, Achilleus
stabbed him in the temple through the brazen sides of the helmet,
and the brazen helmet could not hold, but the bronze spearhead
driven on through smashed the bone apart, and the inward

brain was all spattered forth. So he beat him down in his fury.           400
Next he stabbed with a spear-stroke in the back Hippodamas
as he fled away before him and sprang from behind his horses.
He blew his life away, bellowing, as when a bull
bellows as he is dragged for Poseidon, lord of Helikē,
and the young men drag him. In such bulls the earth shaker glories.        405
Such was his bellowing as the proud spirit flitted from his bones.
Next he went with the spear after godlike Polydoros,
Priam's son, whom his father would not let go into battle
because he was youngest born of all his sons to him, and also
the most beloved, and in speed of his feet outpassed all the others.       410
But now, in his young thoughtlessness and display of his running
he swept among the champions until thus he destroyed his dear life.
For as he shot by swift-footed brilliant Achilleus hit him
with a spear thrown in the middle of the back where the clasps of the war belt
were golden and came together at the joining halves of the corselet.       415
The spearhead held its way straight on and came out by the navel,
and he dropped, moaning, on one knee as the dark mist gathered
about him, and sagged, and caught with his hands at his bowels in front
    of him.


But now when Hektor saw Polydoros, his own brother,
going limp to the ground and catching his bowels in his hands,             420
the mist closed about his eyes also, he could stand no longer
to turn there at a distance, but went out to face Achilleus
hefting his sharp spear, like a flame. Seeing him Achilleus
balanced his spear in turn, and called out to him, and challenged him:
"Here is the man who beyond all others has troubled my anger,              425
who slaughtered my beloved companion. Let us no longer
shrink away from each other along the edgeworks of battle."
    He spoke, and looking darkly at brilliant Hektor spoke to him:
"Come nearer, so that sooner you may reach your appointed destruction."
    But with no fear Hektor of the shining helm answered him:              430
"Son of Peleus, never hope by words to frighten me
as if I were a baby. I myself understand well enough
how to speak in vituperation and how to make insults.
I know that you are great and that I am far weaker than you are.
Still, all this lies upon the knees of the gods; and it may be             435

that weaker as I am I might still strip the life from you
with a cast of the spear, since my weapon too has been sharp before this."
    He spoke, and balanced the spear and let it fly. But Athene
blew against it and turned it back from renowned Achilleus
440  with an easy blast. It came back again to glorious Hektor
and dropped to the ground in front of his feet. Meanwhile Achilleus
made a furious charge against him, raging to kill him
with a terrible cry, but Phoibos Apollo caught up Hektor
easily, since he was a god, and wrapped him in thick mist.
445  Three times swift-footed brilliant Achilleus swept in against him
with the brazen spear. Three times his stroke went into the deep mist.
But as a fourth time, like something more than a man, he charged in,
Achilleus with a terrible cry called in winged words after him:
"Once again now you escaped death, dog. And yet the evil
450  came near you, but now once more Phoibos Apollo has saved you,
he to whom you must pray when you go into the thunder of spears thrown.
Yet I may win you, if I encounter you ever hereafter,
if beside me also there is some god who will help me.
Now I must chase whoever I can overtake of the others."

455      He spoke, and with the spear full in the neck stabbed Dryops
so that he dropped in front of his feet. He left him to lie there
and with a spear thrown against the knee stopped the charge of
        Demouchos,
Philetor's son, a huge man and powerful. After the spearcast
with an inward plunge of the great sword he took the life from him.
460  Then Achilleus swooping on Dardanos and Laogonos, sons both
of Bias, dashed them to the ground from behind their horses,
one with a spearcast, one with a stroke of the sword from close up.
Now Tros, Alastor's son: he had come up against Achilleus'
knees, to catch them and be spared and his life given to him
465  if Achilleus might take pity upon his youth and not kill him;
fool, and did not see there would be no way to persuade him,
since this was a man with no sweetness in his heart, and not kindly
but in a strong fury; now Tros with his hands was reaching
for the knees, bent on supplication, but he stabbed with his sword at the
        liver
470  so that the liver was torn from its place, and from it the black blood

drenched the fold of his tunic and his eyes were shrouded in darkness
as the life went. Next from close in he thrust at Moulios
with the pike at the ear, so the bronze spearhead pushed through and
    came out
at the other ear. Now he hit Echeklos the son of Agenor
with the hilted sword, hewing against his head in the middle                    475
so all the sword was smoking with blood, and over both eyes
closed the red death and the strong destiny. Now Deukalion
was struck in the arm, at a place in the elbow where the tendons
come together. There through the arm Achilleus transfixed him
with the bronze spearhead, and he, arm hanging heavy, waited            480
and looked his death in the face. Achilleus struck with the sword's edge
at his neck, and swept the helmed head far away, and the marrow
gushed from the neckbone, and he went down to the ground at full length.
Now he went on after the blameless son of Peires,
Rhigmos, who had come over from Thrace where the soil is rich. This man    485
he stabbed in the middle with the spear, and the spear stuck fast in his belly.
He dropped from the chariot, but as Areïthoös his henchman
turned the horses away Achilleus stabbed him with the sharp spear
in the back, and thrust him from the chariot. And the horses bolted.

As inhuman fire sweeps on in fury through the deep angles                490
of a drywood mountain and sets ablaze the depth of the timber
and the blustering wind lashes the flame along, so Achilleus
swept everywhere with his spear like something more than a mortal
harrying them as they died, and the black earth ran blood.
Or as when a man yokes male broad-foreheaded oxen                          495
to crush white barley on a strong-laid threshing floor, and rapidly
the barley is stripped beneath the feet of the bellowing oxen,
so before great-hearted Achilleus the single-foot horses
trampled alike dead men and shields, and the axle under
the chariot was all splashed with blood and the rails which encircled      500
the chariot, struck by flying drops from the feet of the horses,
from the running rims of the wheels. The son of Peleus was straining
to win glory, his invincible hands spattered with bloody filth.

# BOOK TWENTY-ONE

But when they came to the crossing place of the fair-running river
of whirling Xanthos, a stream whose father was Zeus the immortal,
there Achilleus split them and chased some back over the flat land
toward the city, where the Achaians themselves had stampeded in terror
5    on the day before, when glorious Hektor was still in his fury.
Along this ground they were streaming in flight; but Hera let fall
a deep mist before them to stay them. Meanwhile the other half
were crowded into the silvery whirls of the deep-running river
and tumbled into it in huge clamor, and the steep-running water
10   sounded, and the banks echoed hugely about them, as they out-crying
tried to swim this way and that, spun about in the eddies.
As before the blast of a fire the locusts escaping
into a river swarm in air, and the fire unwearied
blazes from a sudden start, and the locusts huddle in water;
15   so before Achilleus the murmuring waters of Xanthos
the deep-whirling were filled with confusion of men and of horses.
But heaven-descended Achilleus left his spear there on the bank
leaning against the tamarisks, and leapt in like some immortal,
with only his sword, but his heart was bent upon evil actions,
20   and he struck in a circle around him. The shameful sound of their groaning
rose as they were struck with the sword, and the water was reddened
with blood. As before a huge-gaping dolphin the other fishes
escaping cram the corners of a deepwater harbor
in fear, for he avidly eats up any he can catch;
25   so the Trojans along the course of the terrible river
shrank under the bluffs. He, when his hands grew weary with killing,

chose out and took twelve young men alive from the river
to be vengeance for the death of Patroklos, the son of Menoitios.
These, bewildered with fear like fawns, he led out of the water
and bound their hands behind them with thongs well cut out of leather,    30
with the very belts they themselves wore on their ingirt tunics,
and gave them to his companions to lead away to the hollow ships,
then himself whirled back, still in a fury to kill men.

    And there he came upon a son of Dardanian Priam
as he escaped from the river, Lykaon, one whom he himself    35
had taken before and led him unwilling from his father's gardens
on a night foray. He with the sharp bronze was cutting young branches
from a fig tree, so that they could make him rails for a chariot,
when an unlooked-for evil thing came upon him, the brilliant
Achilleus, who that time sold him as slave in strong-founded Lemnos    40
carrying him there by ship, and the son of Jason paid for him;
from there a guest and friend who paid a great price redeemed him,
Eëtion of Imbros, and sent him to shining Arisbe;
and from there he fled away and came to the house of his father.
For eleven days he pleasured his heart with friends and family    45
after he got back from Lemnos, but on the twelfth day once again
the god cast him into the hands of Achilleus, who this time
was to send him down unwilling on his way to the death god.
Now as brilliant swift-footed Achilleus saw him and knew him
naked and without helm or shield, and he had no spear left    50
but had thrown all these things on the ground, being weary and sweating
with the escape from the river, and his knees were beaten with weariness,
disturbed, Achilleus spoke to his own great-hearted spirit:
"Can this be? Here is a strange thing that my eyes look on.
Now the great-hearted Trojans, even those I have killed already,    55
will stand and rise up again out of the gloom and the darkness
as this man has come back and escaped the day without pity
though he was sold into sacred Lemnos; but the main of the gray sea
could not hold him, though it holds back many who are unwilling.
But come now, he must be given a taste of our spearhead    60
so that I may know inside my heart and make certain
whether he will come back even from there, or the prospering
earth will hold him, she who holds back even the strong man."

So he pondered, waiting, and the other in terror came near him
65   in an agony to catch at his knees, and the wish in his heart was
to get away from the evil death and the dark fate. By this
brilliant Achilleus held the long spear uplifted above him
straining to stab, but he under-ran the stroke and caught him
by the knees, bending, and the spear went over his back and stood fast
70   in the ground, for all its desire to tear a man's flesh. Lykaon
with one hand had taken him by the knees in supplication
and with the other held and would not let go of the edged spear
and spoke aloud to him and addressed him in winged words: "Achilleus,
I am at your knees. Respect my position, have mercy upon me.
75   I am in the place, illustrious, of a suppliant who must be honored,
for you were the first beside whom I tasted the yield of Demeter
on that day you captured me in the strong-laid garden
and took me away from my father and those near me, and sold me
away into sacred Lemnos, and a hundred oxen I fetched you.
80   My release was ransom three times as great; and this is
the twelfth dawn since I came back to Ilion, after
much suffering. Now again cursed destiny has put me
in your hands; and I think I must be hated by Zeus the father
who has given me once more to you, and my mother bore me
85   to a short life, Laothoë, daughter of aged Altes,
Altes, lord of the Leleges, whose delight is in battle,
and holds headlong Pedasos on the river Satnioeis.
His daughter was given to Priam, who had many wives beside her.
We are two who were born to her. You will have cut the throats
90   of both, since one you beat down in the forefront of the foot-fighters,
Polydoros the godlike, with a cast of the sharp spear. This time
the evil shall be mine in this place, since I do not think
I shall escape your hands, since divinity drove me against them.
Still, put away in your heart this other thing I say to you.
95   Do not kill me. I am not from the same womb as Hektor,
he who killed your powerful and kindly companion."

So the glorious son of Priam addressed him, speaking
in supplication, but heard in turn the voice without pity:
"Poor fool, no longer speak to me of ransom, nor argue it.
100   In the time before Patroklos came to the day of his destiny
then it was the way of my heart's choice to be sparing

of the Trojans, and many I took alive and disposed of them.
Now there is not one who can escape death, if the gods send
him against my hands in front of Ilion, not one
of all the Trojans and beyond others the children of Priam.                105
So, friend, you die also. Why all this clamor about it?
Patroklos also is dead, who was better by far than you are.
Do you not see what a man I am, how huge, how splendid
and born of a great father, and the mother who bore me immortal?
Yet even I have also my death and my strong destiny,                       110
and there shall be a dawn or an afternoon or a noontime
when some man in the fighting will take the life from me also
either with a spearcast or an arrow flown from the bowstring."
    So he spoke, and in the other the knees and the inward
heart went slack. He let go of the spear and sat back, spreading           115
wide both hands; but Achilleus drawing his sharp sword struck him
beside the neck at the collar-bone, and the double-edged sword
plunged full length inside. He dropped to the ground, face downward,
and lay at length, and the black blood flowed, and the ground was soaked
        with it.
Achilleus caught him by the foot and slung him into the river              120
to drift, and spoke winged words of vaunting derision over him:
"Lie there now among the fish, who will lick the blood away
from your wound, and care nothing for you, nor will your mother
lay you on the death-bed and mourn over you, but Skamandros
will carry you spinning down to the wide bend of the salt water.           125
And a fish will break a ripple shuddering dark on the water
as he rises to feed upon the shining fat of Lykaon.
Die on, all; till we come to the city of sacred Ilion,
you in flight and I killing you from behind; and there will not
be any rescue for you from your silvery-whirled strong-running             130
river, for all the numbers of bulls you dedicate to it
and drown single-foot horses alive in its eddies. And yet
even so, die all an evil death, till all of you
pay for the death of Patroklos and the slaughter of the Achaians
whom you killed beside the running ships, when I was not with them."       135

    He spoke, but the anger was rising now in the heart of the river
and he pondered in his heart as to how he could stop the labor

of brilliant Achilleus, and fend destruction away from the Trojans.
And now with the spear far shadowing in his hands Peleus' son
140 was springing, furious to kill him, on Asteropaios
the son of Pelegon; who in turn was born of the wide-running river
Axios, and of Periboia, eldest of the daughters
of Akessamenos, for she lay in love with the deep-whirling river.
Against this man Achilleus rose up, and he came out to face him
145 from the river, holding two spears, for Xanthos had inspired valor
into his heart, in anger for the slaughter of the young men
whom Achilleus had slain beside his waters and taken no pity.
Now as these two in their advance encountered together
first of the two to speak was swift-footed brilliant Achilleus:
150 "What man are you, and whence, who dare stand up to my onset?
Since unhappy are those whose sons match warcraft against me."
  Then in turn the glorious son of Pelegon answered him:
"High-hearted son of Peleus, why ask of my generation?
I am from Paionia far away, where the soil is generous,
155 and lead the men of Paionia with long spears; and this for me
is the eleventh day since I arrived in Ilion.
For my generation, it is from the broad waters of Axios,
Axios, who floods the land with the loveliest waters.
His son was Pelegon the spear-famed; but men say I am Pelegon's
160 son; now, glorious Achilleus, we shall fight together."
  So he spoke, challenging, and brilliant Achilleus uplifted
the Pelian ash spear, but the warrior Asteropaios
threw with both spears at the same time, being ambidextrous.
With the one spear he hit the shield but could not altogether
165 break through the shield, since the gold stayed it that the god had given.
With the other spear he struck Achilleus on the right forearm
and grazed it so that the blood gushed out in a dark cloud, and the spear
overpassed him and fixed in the ground, straining to reach his body.
Throwing second Achilleus let fly at Asteropaios
170 with the straight-flying ash spear in a fury to kill him,
but missed his man and hit the high bank, so that the ash spear
was driven half its length and stuck in the bank of the river.
But the son of Peleus, drawing from beside his thigh the sharp sword,
sprang upon him in fury; and Asteropaios could not
175 with his heavy hand wrench Achilleus' ash spear free of the river-bank.

Three times he struggled straining to wrench it clear, and three times
gave over the effort, and now for the fourth time he was bending
over the ash spear of Aiakides, trying to break it,
but before this Achilleus took his life with the sword from close up
for he struck him in the belly next the navel, and all his guts poured     180
out on the ground, and a mist of darkness closed over both eyes
as he gasped life out, and springing upon his chest Achilleus
stripped his armor away and spoke in triumph above him:
"Lie so: it is hard even for those sprung of a river
to fight against the children of Kronos, whose strength is almighty.     185
You said you were of the generation of the wide-running river,
but I claim that I am of the generation of great Zeus.
The man is my father who is lord over many Myrmidons,
Peleus, Aiakos' son, but Zeus was the father of Aiakos.
And as Zeus is stronger than rivers that run to the sea, so     190
the generation of Zeus is made stronger than that of a river.
For here is a great river beside you, if he were able
to help; but it is not possible to fight Zeus, son of Kronos.
Not powerful Acheloios matches his strength against Zeus,
not the enormous strength of Ocean with his deep running waters,     195
Ocean, from whom all rivers are and the entire sea
and all springs and all deep wells have their waters of him, yet
even Ocean is afraid of the lightning of great Zeus
and the dangerous thunderbolt when it breaks from the sky crashing."

    So he spoke, and pulled the bronze spear free of the river bluff     200
and left him there, when he had torn the heart of life from him,
sprawled in the sands and drenched in the dark water. And about
Asteropaios the eels and the other fish were busy
tearing him and nibbling the fat that lay by his kidneys.
But Achilleus went on after the Paionians crested with horse-hair     205
who had scattered in fear along the banks of the eddying river
when they had seen their greatest man in the strong encounter
gone down by force under the sword and the hands of Peleïdes.
There he killed Thersilochos and Astypylos and Mydon,
Mnesos and Thrasios, and Ainios and Ophelestes.     210
Now swift Achilleus would have killed even more Paionians
except that the deep-whirling river spoke to him in anger

and in mortal likeness, and the voice rose from the depth of the eddies:
"O Achilleus, your strength is greater, your acts more violent
215 than all men's; since always the very gods are guarding you.
If the son of Kronos has given all Trojans to your destruction,
drive them at least out of me to the plain, and there work your havoc.
For the loveliness of my waters is crammed with corpses, I cannot
find a channel to cast my waters into the bright sea
220 since I am congested with the dead men you kill so brutally.
Let me alone, then; lord of the people, I am confounded."
  Then in answer to him spoke Achilleus of the swift feet:
"All this, illustrious Skamandros, shall be as you order.
But I will not leave off my killing of the proud Trojans
225 until I have penned them inside their city, and attempted Hektor
strength against strength, until he has killed me or I have killed him."

  He spoke, and like something more than mortal swept down on the
   Trojans.
And now the deep-whirling river called aloud to Apollo:
"Shame, lord of the silver bow, Zeus' son; you have not kept
230 the counsels of Kronion, who very strongly ordered you
to stand by the Trojans and defend them, until the sun setting
at last goes down and darkens all the generous ploughland."
  He spoke: and spear-famed Achilleus leapt into the middle water
with a spring from the bluff, but the river in a boiling surge was upon him
235 and rose making turbulent all his waters, and pushed off
the many dead men whom Achilleus had killed piled in abundance
in the stream; these, bellowing like a bull, he shoved out
on the dry land, but saved the living in the sweet waters
hiding them under the huge depths of the whirling current.
240 And about Achilleus in his confusion a dangerous wave rose
up, and beat against his shield and pushed it. He could not
brace himself with his feet, but caught with his hands at an elm tree
tall and strong grown, but this uptorn by the roots and tumbling
ripped away the whole cliff and with its dense tangle of roots stopped
245 the run of the lovely current and fallen full length in the water
dammed the very stream. Achilleus uprising out of the whirlpool
made a dash to get to the plain in the speed of his quick feet
in fear, but the great god would not let him be, but rose on him

in a darkening edge of water, minded to stop the labor
of brilliant Achilleus and fend destruction away from the Trojans.          250
The son of Peleus sprang away the length of a spearcast
running with the speed of the black eagle, the marauder
who is at once the strongest of flying things and the swiftest.
In the likeness of this he sped away, on his chest the bronze armor
clashed terribly, and bending away to escape from the river          255
he fled, but the river came streaming after him in huge noise.
And as a man running a channel from a spring of dark water
guides the run of the water among his plants and his gardens
with a mattock in his hand and knocks down the blocks in the channel;
in the rush of the water all the pebbles beneath are torn loose          260
from place, and the water that has been dripping suddenly jets on
in a steep place and goes too fast even for the man who guides it;
so always the crest of the river was overtaking Achilleus
for all his speed of foot, since gods are stronger than mortals.
And every time swift-footed brilliant Achilleus would begin          265
to turn and stand and fight the river, and try to discover
if all the gods who hold the wide heaven were after him, every
time again the enormous wave of the sky-fed river
would strike his shoulders from above. He tried, in his desperation,
to keep a high spring with his feet, but the river was wearing his knees out   270
as it ran fiercely beneath him and cut the ground from under
his feet. Peleïdes groaned aloud, gazing into the wide sky:
"Father Zeus, no god could endure to save me from the river
who am so pitiful. And what then shall become of me?
It is not so much any other Uranian god who has done this          275
but my own mother who beguiled me with falsehoods, who told me
that underneath the battlements of the armored Trojans
I should be destroyed by the flying shafts of Apollo.
I wish now Hektor had killed me, the greatest man grown in this place.
A brave man would have been the slayer, as the slain was a brave man.          280
But now this is a dismal death I am doomed to be caught in,
trapped in a big river as if I were a boy and a swineherd
swept away by a torrent when he tries to cross in a rainstorm."

    So he spoke, and Poseidon and Athene swiftly came near him
and stood beside him with their shapes in the likeness of mortals          285

and caught him hand by hand and spoke to him in assurance.
First of them to speak was the shaker of the earth, Poseidon.
"Do not be afraid, son of Peleus, nor be so anxious,
such are we two of the gods who stand beside you to help you,
290   by the consent of Zeus, myself and Pallas Athene.
Thereby it is not your destiny to be killed by the river,
but he shall be presently stopped, and you yourself shall behold it.
   "But we also have close counsel to give you, if you will believe us.
Do not let stay your hands from the collision of battle
295   until you have penned the people of Troy, those who escape you,
inside the famed wall of Ilion. Then when you have taken Hektor's life
go back again to the ships. We grant you the winning of glory."

   So speaking the two went back again among the immortals,
but Achilleus went on, and the urgency of the gods strongly stirred him,
300   into the plain. But the river filled with an outrush of water
and masses of splendid armor from the young men who had perished
floated there, and their bodies, but against the hard drive of the river
straight on he kept a high spring with his feet, and the river wide
      running
could not stop him now, since he was given great strength by Athene.
305   But Skamandros did not either abate his fury, but all the more
raged at Peleion, and high uplifting the wave of his waters
gathered it to a crest, and called aloud upon Simoeis:
"Beloved brother, let even the two of us join to hold back
the strength of a man, since presently he will storm the great city
310   of lord Priam. The Trojans cannot stand up to him in battle.
But help me beat him off with all speed, and make full your currents
with water from your springs, and rouse up all of your torrents
and make a big wave rear up and wake the heavy confusion
and sound of timbers and stones, so we can stop this savage man
315   who is now in his strength and rages in fury like the immortals.
For I say that his strength will not be enough for him nor his beauty
nor his arms in their splendor, which somewhere deep down under the
      waters
shall lie folded under the mud; and I will whelm his own body
deep, and pile it over with abundance of sands and rubble
320   numberless, nor shall the Achaians know where to look for

his bones to gather them, such ruin will I pile over him.
And there shall his monument be made, and he will have no need
of any funeral mound to be buried in by the Achaians."

He spoke, and rose against Achilleus, turbulent, boiling
to a crest, muttering in foam and blood and dead bodies                         325
until the purple wave of the river fed from the bright sky
lifted high and caught in its waters the son of Peleus.
But Hera, greatly fearing for Achilleus, cried in a loud voice
lest he be swept away in the huge deep-eddying river,
and at once thereafter appealed to her own dear son, Hephaistos:               330
"Rise up, god of the dragging feet, my child; for we believe
that whirling Xanthos would be fit antagonist for you in battle.
Go now quickly to the help of Achilleus, make shine a great flame
while I raise up and bring in out of the sea a troublesome
storm of the west wind and the whitening south wind, a storm                   335
that will burn the heads of the Trojans and burn their armor
carrying the evil flame, while you by the banks of Xanthos
set fire to the trees and throw fire on the river himself, and do not
by any means let him turn you with winning words or revilements.
Do not let your fury be stopped until such time as                             340
I lift my voice and cry to you. Then stay your weariless burning."

Hera spoke, and Hephaistos set on them an inhuman fire.
First he kindled a fire in the plain and burned the numerous
corpses that lay there in abundance, slain by Achilleus,
and all the plain was parched and the shining water was straitened.            345
As when the north wind of autumn suddenly makes dry
a garden freshly watered and makes glad the man who is tending it,
so the entire flat land was dried up with Hephaistos burning
the dead bodies. Then he turned his flame in its shining
into the river. The elms burned, the willows and tamarisks,                    350
the clover burned and the rushes and the galingale, all those
plants that grew in abundance by the lovely stream of the river.
The eels were suffering and the fish in the whirl of the water
who leaped out along the lovely waters in every direction
in affliction under the hot blast of resourceful Hephaistos.                   355
The strength of the river was burning away; he gave voice and called out

by name: "Hephaistos, not one of the gods could stand up against you.
I for one could not fight the flame of a fire like this one.
Leave your attack. Brilliant Achilleus can capture the city
360  of the Trojans, now, for me. What have I to do with this quarrel?"

He spoke, blazing with fire, and his lovely waters were seething.
And as a cauldron that is propped over a great fire boils up
dancing on its whole circle with dry sticks burning beneath it
as it melts down the fat of swine made tender, so Xanthos'
365  lovely streams were burned with the fire, and the water was boiling
and would not flow along but was stopped under stress of the hot blast
strongly blown by resourceful Hephaistos. And now the river
cried out to Hera in the winged words of strong supplication:
"Hera, why did your son assault me to trouble my waters
370  beyond others'? It is not so much I who have done anything against you
as all the rest of the gods who stand by to help the Trojans.
Now indeed I will leave off, if such is your order,
but let him leave off too, I will swear you a promise
not ever to drive the day of evil away from the Trojans,
375  not even when all the city of Troy is burned in the ravening
fire, on that day when the warlike sons of the Achaians burn it."

Now when the goddess of the white arms, Hera, had heard this
immediately she spoke to her own dear son, Hephaistos:
"Hephaistos, hold, my glorious child, since it is not fitting
380  to batter thus an immortal god for the sake of mortals."
So she spoke, and Hephaistos quenched his inhuman fire. Now
the lovely waters ran their ripples back in the channel.
But when the strength of Xanthos had been beaten, these two gods
rested, since Hera, for all she was still angry, restrained them.
385  But upon the other gods descended the wearisome burden
of hatred, and the wind of their fury blew from division,
and they collided with a grand crash, the broad earth echoing
and the huge sky sounded as with trumpets. Zeus heard it
from where he sat on Olympos, and was amused in his deep heart
390  for pleasure, as he watched the gods' collision in conflict.
Thereafter they stood not long apart from each other, for Ares
began it, the shield-stabber, and rose up against Athene

with the brazen spear in his hand, and spoke a word of revilement:
"Why once more, you dogfly, have you stirred up trouble among the gods
with the blast of your blown fury, and the pride of your heart driving you?    395
Do you not remember how you set on Diomedes, Tydeus'
son, to spear me, and yourself laying hold of the far-seen pike
pushed it straight into me and tore my skin in its beauty.
So now I am minded to pay you back for all you have done me."
    He spoke, and stabbed against the ghastly aegis with fluttering        400
straps, which gives way not even before the bolt of Zeus' lightning.
There blood-dripping Ares made his stab with the long spear,
but Athene giving back caught up in her heavy hand a stone
that lay in the plain, black and rugged and huge, one which men
of a former time had set there as boundary mark of the cornfield.        405
With this she hit furious Ares in the neck, and unstrung him.
He spread over seven acres in his fall, and his hair dragged
in the dust, and his armor clashed. But Pallas Athene laughing
stood above him and spoke to him in the winged words of triumph:
"You child; you did not think even this time how much stronger        410
I can claim I am than you, when you match your fury against me.
Therefore you are paying atonement to your mother's furies
since she is angry and wishes you ill, because you abandoned
the Achaians, and have given your aid to the insolent Trojans."

    She spoke, and turned the shining of her eyes away. But taking        415
Ares by the hand the daughter of Zeus, Aphrodite,
led him away, groaning always, his strength scarce gathered back into him.
But now, as the goddess of the white arms, Hera, noticed her
immediately she spoke to Pallas Athene her winged words:
"For shame now, Atrytone, daughter of Zeus of the aegis.        420
Here again is this dogfly leading murderous Ares
out of the fighting and through the confusion. Quick, go after her!"
    She spoke, and Athene swept in pursuit, heart full of gladness,
and caught up with her and drove a blow at her breasts with her ponderous
hand, so that her knees went slack and the heart inside her.        425
Those two both lay sprawled on the generous earth. But Athene
stood above them and spoke to them in the winged words of triumph:
"Now may all who bring their aid to the Trojans be in
such case as these, when they do battle with the armored Argives,

430     as daring and as unfortunate, as now Aphrodite
      came companion in arms to Ares, and faced my fury.
      So we should long ago have rested after our fighting
      once having utterly stormed the strong-founded city of Ilion."
          She spoke, and the goddess of the white arms, Hera, smiled on her.
435     But now the powerful shaker of the earth spoke to Apollo:
      "Phoibos, why do you and I stand yet apart. It does not suit
      when the others have begun, and it were too shameful if without fighting
      we go back to the brazen house of Zeus on Olympos.
      Begin, you; you are younger born than I; it is not well
440     for me to, since I am elder born than you, and know more.
      Young fool, what a mindless heart you have. Can you not even
      now remember all the evils we endured here by Ilion,
      you and I alone of the gods, when to proud Laomedon
      we came down from Zeus and for a year were his servants
445     for a stated hire, and he told us what to do, and to do it?
      Then I built a wall for the Trojans about their city,
      wide, and very splendid, so none could break into their city,
      but you, Phoibos, herded his shambling horn-curved cattle
      along the spurs of Ida with all her folds and her forests.
450     But when the changing seasons brought on the time for our labor
      to be paid, then headstrong Laomedon violated and made void
      all our hire, and sent us away, and sent threats after us.
      For he threatened to hobble our feet and to bind our arms,
      to carry us away for slaves in the far-lying islands.
455     He was even going to strip with bronze the ears from both of us.
      Then you and I took our way back with hearts full of anger
      and wrath for our hire which he promised us and would not accomplish it.
      Yet to his people you give now your grace, and you will not
      try with us to bring destruction on the insolent Trojans
460     evil and complete, with their honored wives and their children."
          In turn the lord who strikes from afar, Apollo, answered him:
      "Shaker of the earth, you would have me be as one without prudence
      if I am to fight even you for the sake of insignificant
      mortals, who are as leaves are, and now flourish and grow warm
465     with life, and feed on what the ground gives, but then again
      fade away and are dead. Therefore let us with all speed
      give up this quarrel and let the mortals fight their own battles."

He spoke so and turned away, for he was too modest
to close and fight in strength of hand with his father's brother.
But his sister, Artemis of the wild, the lady of wild beasts,                    470
scolded him bitterly and spoke a word of revilement:
"You run from him, striker from afar. You have yielded Poseidon
the victory entire. He can brag, where nothing has happened.
Fool, then why do you wear that bow, which is wind and nothing.
Let me not hear you in the halls of my father boasting                           475
ever again, as you did before among the immortals,
that you could match your strength in combat against Poseidon."
    So she spoke, but Apollo who strikes from afar said nothing
to her; but the august consort of Zeus, full of anger,
scolded the lady of showering arrows in words of revilement:                     480
"How have you had the daring, you shameless hussy, to stand up
and face me? It will be hard for you to match your strength with mine
even if you wear a bow, since Zeus has made you a lion
among women, and given you leave to kill any at your pleasure.
Better for you to hunt down the ravening beasts in the mountains                 485
and deer of the wilds, than try to fight in strength with your betters.
But if you would learn what fighting is, come on. You will find out
how much stronger I am when you try to match strength against me."
    She spoke, and caught both of her arms at the wrists in her left hand
and with her right hand stripped away the bow from her shoulders,                490
then with her own bow, smiling, boxed her ears as Artemis
tried to twist away, and the flying arrows were scattered.
She got under and free and fled in tears, as a pigeon
in flight from a hawk wings her way into some rock-hollow
and a cave, since it was not destiny for the hawk to catch her.                  495
So she left her archery on the ground, and fled weeping.
Meanwhile the Guide, Argeïphontes, addressed him to Leto:
"Leto, I will not fight with you; since it is a hard thing
to come to blows with the brides of Zeus who gathers the clouds. No,
sooner you may freely speak among the immortal                                   500
gods, and claim that you were stronger than I, and beat me."
    So he spoke, but Leto picked up the curved bow and the arrows
which had fallen in the turn of the dust one way and another.
When she had taken up the bow she went back to her daughter.
But the maiden came to the bronze-founded house on Olympos                       505

of Zeus, and took her place kneeling at the knees of her father
and the ambrosial veil trembled about her. Her father
Kronides caught her against him, and laughed softly, and questioned her:
"Who now of the Uranian gods, dear child, has done such
510  things to you, rashly, as if you were caught doing something wicked?"
     Artemis sweet-garlanded lady of clamors answered him:
"It was your wife, Hera of the white arms, who hit me,
father, since hatred and fighting have fastened upon the immortals."

     Now as these two were talking thus to each other, meanwhile
515  Phoibos Apollo went into the sacred city of Ilion,
since he was concerned for the wall of the strong-founded city
lest the Danaäns storm it on that day, before they were fated.
The rest of the gods who live forever went back to Olympos,
some in anger and others glorying greatly, and sat down
520  at the side of their father the dark-misted. Meanwhile Achilleus
was destroying alike the Trojans themselves and their single-foot horses;
and as when smoke ascending goes up into the wide sky
from a burning city, with the anger of the gods let loose upon it
which inflicted labor upon them all, and sorrow on many,
525  so Achilleus inflicted labor and sorrow upon the Trojans.
     The aged Priam had taken his place on the god-built bastion,
and looked out and saw gigantic Achilleus, where before him
the Trojans fled in the speed of their confusion, no war strength
left them. He groaned and descended to the ground from the bastion
530  and beside the wall set in motion the glorious guards of the gateway;
"Hold the gates wide open in your hands, so that our people
in their flight can get inside the city, for here is Achilleus
close by, stampeding them, and I think there will be disaster.
But once they are crowded inside the city and get wind again,
535  shut once more the door-leaves closely fitted together.
I am afraid this ruinous man may spring into our stronghold."
     He spoke, and they spread open the gates and shoved back the door bars
and the gates opening let in daylight. Meanwhile Apollo
sprang out to meet them, so that he could fend off destruction
540  from the Trojans, who, straight for the city and the lift of the rampart
dusty from the plain and throats rugged with thirst, fled

away, and Achilleus followed fiercely with the spear, strong madness
forever holding his heart and violent after his glory.

There the sons of the Achaians might have taken gate-towering Ilion
had not Phoibos Apollo sent on them brilliant Agenor,                          545
a man who was the son of Antenor, blameless and powerful.
He drove courage into his heart, and stood there beside him
in person, so as to beat the dragging death spirits from him,
and leaned there on an oak tree with close mist huddled about him.
When Agenor was aware of Achilleus, sacker of cities,                          550
he stood fast, but the heart was a storm in him as he waited,
and deeply disturbed he spoke to his own great-hearted spirit:
"Ah me! If I run away before the strength of Achilleus
in the way that others are stampeded in terror before him,
he will catch me even so and cut my throat like a coward's.                    555
But if I leave these men to be driven in flight by Achilleus,
Peleus' son, and run on my feet in another direction
away from the wall to the plain of Ilion, until I come to
the spurs of Ida, and take cover there within the undergrowth,
then in the evening, when I have bathed in the river, and washed off           560
the sweat, I could make my way back again to Ilion.
Yet still, why does the heart within me debate on these things?
This way, he might see me as I started to the plain from the city,
and go in pursuit, and in the speed of his feet overtake me.
Then there will be no way to escape death and the death spirits.               565
He is too strong, his strength is beyond all others'. But then if
I go out in front of the city and stand fast against him,
I think even his body might be torn by the sharp bronze.
There is only one life in him, and people say he is mortal.
It is only that Zeus, the son of Kronos, is granting him glory."               570
He spoke, and gathered himself to await Achilleus, and in him
the fighting heart was urgent for the encounter of battle.
But as a leopard emerges out of her timbered cover
to face the man who is hunting her, and takes no terror
in her heart nor thought of flight when she hears them baying against her;     575
and even though one be too quick for her with spear thrust or spear thrown
stuck with the shaft though she be she will not give up her fighting

fury, till she has closed with one of them or is overthrown;
so the son of proud Antenor, brilliant Agenor,
580  was unwilling to run away until he had tested Achilleus,
but held the perfect circle of his shield in front of him,
and with the spear aimed at him and cried out in a great voice:
"You must have hoped within your heart, O shining Achilleus,
on this day to storm the city of the proud Trojans.
585  You fool! There is much hard suffering to be done for its winning,
since there are many of us inside, and men who are fighters,
who will stand before our beloved parents, our wives and our children,
to defend Ilion; but in this place you will find your destiny,
for all you are so headlong and so bold a warrior."
590    He spoke, and from his heavy hand let fly with the sharp spear
and struck him in the leg below the knee, nor entirely
missed him, and taking the spear the greave of new-wrought tin clattered
horribly, and back from the struck greave the bronze rebounded
without getting through, but the gift of the god defended Achilleus.
595  After him Peleus' son made his spring at godlike Agenor,
but Apollo would no further grant him the winning of glory
but caught Agenor away closing him in a dense mist
and sent him to make his way quietly out of the battle.
Then by deception he kept Peleion away from the people.
600  The striker from afar likened himself in all ways to Agenor
and stood there before his feet, and Achilleus sprang in chase of him
in the speed of his feet; for the time he chased him across the wheat-bearing
plain, turning him toward the deep whirls of the river Skamandros
as he ran a little in front; with the trick Apollo beguiled him
605  so that he hoped ever by running to catch up with him;
all this time the rest of the Trojans fled in a body
gladly into the town, and the city was filled with their swarming.
They dared no longer outside the wall and outside the city
to wait for each other and find out which one had got away
610  and who had died in the battle, so hastily were they streaming
into the city, each man as his knees and feet could rescue him.

# BOOK TWENTY-TWO

So along the city the Trojans, who had run like fawns, dried
the sweat off from their bodies and drank and slaked their thirst, leaning
along the magnificent battlements. Meanwhile the Achaians
sloping their shields across their shoulders came close to the rampart.
But his deadly fate held Hektor shackled, so that he stood fast          5
in front of Ilion and the Skaian gates. Now Phoibos
Apollo spoke aloud to Peleion: "Why, son of Peleus,
do you keep after me in the speed of your feet, being mortal
while I am an immortal god? Even yet you have not
seen that I am a god, but strain after me in your fury.          10
Now hard fighting with the Trojans whom you stampeded means
        nothing
to you. They are crowded in the city, but you bent away here.
You will never kill me. I am not one who is fated."
    Deeply vexed Achilleus of the swift feet spoke to him:
"You have balked me, striker from afar, most malignant of all gods,          15
when you turned me here away from the rampart, else many Trojans
would have caught the soil in their teeth before they got back into Ilion.
Now you have robbed me of great glory, and rescued these people
lightly, since you have no retribution to fear hereafter.
Else I would punish you, if only the strength were in me."          20
    He spoke, and stalked away against the city, with high thoughts
in mind, and in tearing speed, like a racehorse with his chariot
who runs lightly as he pulls the chariot over the flat land.
Such was the action of Achilleus in feet and quick knees.

25       The aged Priam was the first of all whose eyes saw him
      as he swept across the flat land in full shining, like that star
      which comes on in the autumn and whose conspicuous brightness
      far outshines the stars that are numbered in the night's darkening,
      the star they give the name of Orion's Dog, which is brightest
30       among the stars, and yet is wrought as a sign of evil
      and brings on the great fever for unfortunate mortals.
      Such was the flare of the bronze that girt his chest in his running.
      The old man groaned aloud and with both hands high uplifted
      beat his head, and groaned amain, and spoke supplicating
35       his beloved son, who there still in front of the gateway
      stood fast in determined fury to fight with Achilleus.
      The old man stretching his hands out called pitifully to him:
      "Hektor, beloved child, do not wait the attack of this man
      alone, away from the others. You might encounter your destiny
40       beaten down by Peleion, since he is far stronger than you are.
      A hard man: I wish he were as beloved of the immortal
      as loved by me. Soon he would lie dead, and the dogs and the vultures
      would eat him, and bitter sorrow so be taken from my heart.
      He has made me desolate of my sons, who were brave and many.
45       He killed them, or sold them away among the far-lying islands.
      Even now there are two sons, Lykaon and Polydoros,
      whom I cannot see among the Trojans pent up in the city,
      sons Laothoë a princess among women bore to me.
      But if these are alive somewhere in the army, then I can
50       set them free for bronze and gold; it is there inside, since
      Altes the aged and renowned gave much with his daughter.
      But if they are dead already and gone down to the house of Hades,
      it is sorrow to our hearts, who bore them, myself and their mother,
      but to the rest of the people a sorrow that will be fleeting
55       beside their sorrow for you, if you go down before Achilleus.
      Come then inside the wall, my child, so that you can rescue
      the Trojans and the women of Troy, neither win the high glory
      for Peleus' son, and yourself be robbed of your very life. Oh, take
      pity on me, the unfortunate still alive, still sentient
60       but ill-starred, whom the father, Kronos' son, on the threshold of old age
      will blast with hard fate, after I have looked upon evils
      and seen my sons destroyed and my daughters dragged away captive

and the chambers of marriage wrecked and the innocent children taken
and dashed to the ground in the hatefulness of war, and the wives
of my sons dragged off by the accursed hands of the Achaians.                    65
And myself last of all, my dogs in front of my doorway
will rip me raw, after some man with stroke of the sharp bronze
spear, or with spearcast, has torn the life out of my body;
those dogs I raised in my halls to be at my table, to guard my
gates, who will lap my blood in the savagery of their anger                     70
and then lie down in my courts. For a young man all is decorous
when he is cut down in battle and torn with the sharp bronze, and lies there
dead, and though dead still all that shows about him is beautiful;
but when an old man is dead and down, and the dogs mutilate
the gray head and the gray beard and the parts that are secret,                  75
this, for all sad mortality, is the sight most pitiful."

    So the old man spoke, and in his hands seizing the gray hairs
tore them from his head, but could not move the spirit in Hektor.
And side by side with him his mother in tears was mourning
and laid the fold of her bosom bare and with one hand held out               80
a breast, and wept her tears for him and called to him in winged words:
"Hektor, my child, look upon these and obey, and take pity
on me, if ever I gave you the breast to quiet your sorrow.
Remember all these things, dear child, and from inside the wall
beat off this grim man. Do not go out as champion against him,                85
O hard one; for if he kills you I can no longer
mourn you on the death-bed, sweet branch, O child of my bearing,
nor can your generous wife mourn you, but a big way from us
beside the ships of the Argives the running dogs will feed on you."

    So these two in tears and with much supplication called out              90
to their dear son, but could not move the spirit in Hektor,
but he awaited Achilleus as he came on, gigantic.
But as a snake waits for a man by his hole, in the mountains,
glutted with evil poisons, and the fell venom has got inside him,
and coiled about the hole he stares malignant, so Hektor                      95
would not give ground but kept unquenched the fury within him
and sloped his shining shield against the jut of the bastion.
Deeply troubled he spoke to his own great-hearted spirit:

"Ah me! If I go now inside the wall and the gateway,
100 Poulydamas will be first to put a reproach upon me,
since he tried to make me lead the Trojans inside the city
on that accursed night when brilliant Achilleus rose up,
and I would not obey him, but that would have been far better.
Now, since by my own recklessness I have ruined my people,
105 I feel shame before the Trojans and the Trojan women with trailing
robes, that someone who is less of a man than I will say of me:
'Hektor believed in his own strength and ruined his people.'
Thus they will speak; and as for me, it would be much better
at that time, to go against Achilleus, and slay him, and come back,
110 or else be killed by him in glory in front of the city.
Or if again I set down my shield massive in the middle
and my ponderous helm, and lean my spear up against the rampart
and go out as I am to meet Achilleus the blameless
and promise to give back Helen, and with her all her possessions,
115 all those things that once in the hollow ships Alexandros
brought back to Troy, and these were the beginning of the quarrel;
to give these to Atreus' sons to take away, and for the Achaians
also to divide up all that is hidden within the city,
and take an oath thereafter for the Trojans in conclave
120 not to hide anything away, but distribute all of it,
as much as the lovely citadel keeps guarded within it;
yet still, why does the heart within me debate on these things?
I might go up to him, and he take no pity upon me
nor respect my position, but kill me naked so, as if I were
125 a woman, once I stripped my armor from me. There is no
way anymore from a tree or a rock to talk to him gently
whispering like a young man and a young girl, in the way
a young man and a young maiden whisper together.
Better to bring on the fight with him as soon as it may be.
130 We shall see to which one the Olympian grants the glory."

So he pondered, waiting, but Achilleus was closing upon him
in the likeness of the lord of battles, the helm-shining warrior,
and shaking from above his shoulder the dangerous Pelian
ash spear, while the bronze that closed about him was shining
135 like the flare of blazing fire or the sun in its rising.

And the shivers took hold of Hektor when he saw him, and he could no
    longer
stand his ground there, but left the gates behind, and fled, frightened,
and Peleus' son went after him in the confidence of his quick feet.
As when a hawk in the mountains who moves lightest of things flying
makes his effortless swoop for a trembling dove, but she slips away        140
from beneath and flies and he shrill screaming close after her
plunges for her again and again, heart furious to take her;
so Achilleus went straight for him in fury, but Hektor
fled away under the Trojan wall and moved his knees rapidly.
They raced along by the watching point and the windy fig tree             145
always away from under the wall and along the wagon-way
and came to the two sweet-running well springs. There, there are double
springs of water that jet up, the springs of whirling Skamandros.
One of these runs hot water and the steam on all sides
of it rises as if from a fire that was burning inside it.                  150
But the other in the summer-time runs water that is like hail
or chill snow or ice that forms from water. Beside these
in this place, and close to them, are the washing-hollows
of stone, and magnificent, where the wives of the Trojans and their lovely
daughters washed the clothes to shining, in the old days                  155
when there was peace, before the coming of the sons of the Achaians.
They ran beside these, one escaping, the other after him.
It was a great man who fled, but far better he who pursued him
rapidly, since here was no festal beast, no ox-hide
they strove for, for these are prizes that are given men for their running. 160
No, they ran for the life of Hektor, breaker of horses.
As when about the turnposts racing single-foot horses
run at full speed, when a great prize is laid up for their winning,
a tripod or a woman, in games for a man's funeral,
so these two swept whirling about the city of Priam                        165
in the speed of their feet, while all the gods were looking upon them.
First to speak among them was the father of gods and mortals:
"Ah me, this is a man beloved whom now my eyes watch
being chased around the wall; my heart is mourning for Hektor
who has burned in my honor many thigh pieces of oxen                       170
on the peaks of Ida with all her folds, or again on the uttermost
part of the citadel, but now the brilliant Achilleus

drives him in speed of his feet around the city of Priam.
Come then, you immortals, take thought and take counsel, whether
175 to rescue this man or whether to make him, for all his valor,
go down under the hands of Achilleus, the son of Peleus."
Then in answer the goddess gray-eyed Athene spoke to him:
"Father of the shining bolt, dark misted, what is this you said?
Do you wish to bring back a man who is mortal, one long since
180 doomed by his destiny, from ill-sounding death and release him?
Do it, then; but not all the rest of us gods shall approve you."
Then Zeus the gatherer of the clouds spoke to her in answer:
"Tritogeneia, dear daughter, do not lose heart; for I say this
not in outright anger, and my meaning toward you is kindly.
185 Act as your purpose would have you do, and hold back no longer."
So he spoke, and stirred on Athene, who was eager before this,
and she went in a flash of speed down the pinnacles of Olympos.

But swift Achilleus kept unremittingly after Hektor,
chasing him, as a dog in the mountains who has flushed from his covert
190 a deer's fawn follows him through the folding ways and the valleys,
and though the fawn crouched down under a bush and be hidden
he keeps running and noses him out until he comes on him;
so Hektor could not lose himself from swift-footed Peleion.
If ever he made a dash right on for the gates of Dardanos
195 to get quickly under the strong-built bastions, endeavoring
that they from above with missiles thrown might somehow defend him,
each time Achilleus would get in front and force him to turn back
into the plain, and himself kept his flying course next the city.
As in a dream a man is not able to follow one who runs
200 from him, nor can the runner escape, nor the other pursue him,
so he could not run him down in his speed, nor the other get clear.
How then could Hektor have escaped the death spirits, had not
Apollo, for this last and uttermost time, stood by him
close, and driven strength into him, and made his knees light?
205 But brilliant Achilleus kept shaking his head at his own people
and would not let them throw their bitter projectiles at Hektor
for fear the thrower might win the glory, and himself come second.
But when for the fourth time they had come around to the well springs
then the Father balanced his golden scales, and in them

he set two fateful portions of death, which lays men prostrate,          210
one for Achilleus, and one for Hektor, breaker of horses,
and balanced it by the middle; and Hektor's death-day was heavier
and dragged downward toward death, and Phoibos Apollo forsook him.
But the goddess gray-eyed Athene came now to Peleion
and stood close beside him and addressed him in winged words: "Beloved   215
of Zeus, shining Achilleus, I am hopeful now that you and I
will take back great glory to the ships of the Achaians, after
we have killed Hektor, for all his slakeless fury for battle.
Now there is no way for him to get clear away from us,
not though Apollo who strikes from afar should be willing to undergo      220
much, and wallow before our father Zeus of the aegis.
Stand you here then and get your wind again, while I go
to this man and persuade him to stand up to you in combat."

    So spoke Athene, and he was glad at heart, and obeyed her,
and stopped, and stood leaning on his bronze-barbed ash spear. Meanwhile  225
Athene left him there, and caught up with brilliant Hektor,
and likened herself in form and weariless voice to Deïphobos.
She came now and stood close to him and addressed him in winged words:
"Dear brother, indeed swift-footed Achilleus is using you roughly
and chasing you on swift feet around the city of Priam.                   230
Come on, then; let us stand fast against him and beat him back from us."
    Then tall Hektor of the shining helm answered her: "Deïphobos,
before now you were dearest to me by far of my brothers,
of all those who were sons of Priam and Hekabē, and now
I am minded all the more within my heart to honor you,                    235
you who dared for my sake, when your eyes saw me, to come forth
from the fortifications, while the others stand fast inside them."
    Then in turn the goddess gray-eyed Athene answered him:
"My brother, it is true our father and the lady our mother, taking
my knees in turn, and my companions about me, entreated                   240
that I stay within, such was the terror upon all of them.
But the heart within me was worn away by hard sorrow for you.
But now let us go straight on and fight hard, let there be no sparing
of our spears, so that we can find out whether Achilleus
will kill us both and carry our bloody war spoils back                    245
to the hollow ships, or will himself go down under your spear."

So Athene spoke and led him on by beguilement.
Now as the two in their advance were come close together,
first of the two to speak was tall helm-glittering Hektor:
250 "Son of Peleus, I will no longer run from you, as before this
I fled three times around the great city of Priam, and dared not
stand to your onfall. But now my spirit in turn has driven me
to stand and face you. I must take you now, or I must be taken.
Come then, shall we swear before the gods? For these are the highest
255 who shall be witnesses and watch over our agreements.
Brutal as you are I will not defile you, if Zeus grants
to me that I can wear you out, and take the life from you.
But after I have stripped your glorious armor, Achilleus,
I will give your corpse back to the Achaians. Do you do likewise."

260     Then looking darkly at him swift-footed Achilleus answered:
"Hektor, argue me no agreements. I cannot forgive you.
As there are no trustworthy oaths between men and lions,
nor wolves and lambs have spirit that can be brought to agreement
but forever these hold feelings of hate for each other,
265 so there can be no love between you and me, nor shall there be
oaths between us, but one or the other must fall before then
to glut with his blood Ares the god who fights under the shield's guard.
Remember every valor of yours, for now the need comes
hardest upon you to be a spearman and a bold warrior.
270 There shall be no more escape for you, but Pallas Athene
will kill you soon by my spear. You will pay in a lump for all those
sorrows of my companions you killed in your spear's fury."
    So he spoke, and balanced the spear far shadowed, and threw it;
but glorious Hektor kept his eyes on him, and avoided it,
275 for he dropped, watchful, to his knee, and the bronze spear flew over his
        shoulder
and stuck in the ground, but Pallas Athene snatched it, and gave it
back to Achilleus, unseen by Hektor shepherd of the people.
But now Hektor spoke out to the blameless son of Peleus:
"You missed; and it was not, O Achilleus like the immortals,
280 from Zeus that you knew my destiny; but you thought so; or rather
you are someone clever in speech and spoke to swindle me,
to make me afraid of you and forget my valor and war strength.

You will not stick your spear in my back as I run away from you
but drive it into my chest as I storm straight in against you;
if the god gives you that; and now look out for my brazen                        285
spear. I wish it might be taken full length in your body.
And indeed the war would be a lighter thing for the Trojans
if you were dead, seeing that you are their greatest affliction."
    So he spoke, and balanced the spear far shadowed, and threw it,
and struck the middle of Peleïdes' shield, nor missed it,                        290
but the spear was driven far back from the shield, and Hektor was angered
because his swift weapon had been loosed from his hand in a vain cast.
He stood discouraged, and had no other ash spear; but lifting
his voice he called aloud on Deïphobos of the pale shield,
and asked him for a long spear, but Deïphobos was not near him.                  295
And Hektor knew the truth inside his heart, and spoke aloud:
"No use. Here at last the gods have summoned me deathward.
I thought Deïphobos the hero was here close beside me,
but he is behind the wall and it was Athene cheating me,
and now evil death is close to me, and no longer far away,                       300
and there is no way out. So it must long since have been pleasing
to Zeus, and Zeus' son who strikes from afar, this way, though before this
they defended me gladly. But now my death is upon me.
Let me at least not die without a struggle, inglorious,
but do some big thing first, that men to come shall know of it."                 305
    So he spoke, and pulling out the sharp sword that was slung
at the hollow of his side, huge and heavy, and gathering
himself together, he made his swoop, like a high-flown eagle
who launches himself out of the murk of the clouds on the flat land
to catch away a tender lamb or a shivering hare; so                             310
Hektor made his swoop, swinging his sharp sword, and Achilleus
charged, the heart within him loaded with savage fury.
In front of his chest the beautiful elaborate great shield
covered him, and with the glittering helm with four horns
he nodded; the lovely golden fringes were shaken about it                        315
which Hephaistos had driven close along the horn of the helmet.
And as a star moves among stars in the night's darkening,
Hesper, who is the fairest star who stands in the sky, such
was the shining from the pointed spear Achilleus was shaking
in his right hand with evil intention toward brilliant Hektor.                   320

He was eyeing Hektor's splendid body, to see where it might best
give way, but all the rest of the skin was held in the armor,
brazen and splendid, he stripped when he cut down the strength of
    Patroklos;
yet showed where the collar-bones hold the neck from the shoulders,
325  the throat, where death of the soul comes most swiftly; in this place
brilliant Achilleus drove the spear as he came on in fury,
and clean through the soft part of the neck the spearpoint was driven.
Yet the ash spear heavy with bronze did not sever the windpipe,
so that Hektor could still make exchange of words spoken.
330  But he dropped in the dust, and brilliant Achilleus vaunted above him:
"Hektor, surely you thought as you killed Patroklos you would be
safe, and since I was far away you thought nothing of me,
O fool, for an avenger was left, far greater than he was,
behind him and away by the hollow ships. And it was I;
335  and I have broken your strength; on you the dogs and the vultures
shall feed and foully rip you; the Achaians will bury Patroklos."
    In his weakness Hektor of the shining helm spoke to him:
"I entreat you, by your life, by your knees, by your parents,
do not let the dogs feed on me by the ships of the Achaians,
340  but take yourself the bronze and gold that are there in abundance,
those gifts that my father and the lady my mother will give you,
and give my body to be taken home again, so that the Trojans
and the wives of the Trojans may give me in death my rite of burning."
    But looking darkly at him swift-footed Achilleus answered:
345  "No more entreating of me, you dog, by knees or parents.
I wish only that my spirit and fury would drive me
to hack your meat away and eat it raw for the things that
you have done to me. So there is no one who can hold the dogs off
from your head, not if they bring here and set before me ten times
350  and twenty times the ransom, and promise more in addition,
not if Priam son of Dardanos should offer to weigh out
your bulk in gold; not even so shall the lady your mother
who herself bore you lay you on the death-bed and mourn you:
no, but the dogs and the birds will have you all for their feasting."
355    Then, dying, Hektor of the shining helmet spoke to him:
"I know you well as I look upon you; I know that I could not
persuade you, since indeed in your breast is a heart of iron.

Be careful now; for I might be made into the gods' curse
upon you, on that day when Paris and Phoibos Apollo
destroy you in the Skaian gates, for all your valor."          360

He spoke, and as he spoke the end of death closed in upon him,
and the soul fluttering free of the limbs went down into Death's house
mourning her destiny, leaving youth and manhood behind her.
Now though he was a dead man brilliant Achilleus spoke to him:
"Die: and I will take my own death at whatever time          365
Zeus and the rest of the immortals choose to accomplish it."
He spoke, and pulled the brazen spear from the body, and laid it
on one side, and stripped away from the shoulders the bloody
armor. And the other sons of the Achaians came running about him,
and gazed upon the stature and on the imposing beauty          370
of Hektor; and none stood beside him who did not stab him;
and thus they would speak one to another, each looking at his neighbor:
"See now, Hektor is much softer to handle than he was
when he set the ships ablaze with the burning firebrand."
So as they stood beside him they would speak, and stab him.          375
But now, when he had despoiled the body, swift-footed brilliant
Achilleus stood among the Achaians and addressed them in winged words:
"Friends, who are leaders of the Argives and keep their counsel:
since the gods have granted me the killing of this man
who has done us much damage, such as not all the others together          380
have done, come, let us go in armor about the city
to see if we can find out what purpose is in the Trojans,
whether they will abandon their high city, now that this man
has fallen, or are minded to stay, though Hektor lives no longer.
Yet still, why does the heart within me debate on these things?          385
There is a dead man who lies by the ships, unwept, unburied:
Patroklos: and I will not forget him, never so long as
I remain among the living and my knees have their spring beneath me.
And though the dead forget the dead in the house of Hades,
even there I shall still remember my beloved companion.          390
But now, you young men of the Achaians, let us go back, singing
a victory song, to our hollow ships; and take this with us.
We have won ourselves enormous fame; we have killed the great Hektor
whom the Trojans glorified as if he were a god in their city."

395 He spoke, and now thought of shameful treatment for glorious Hektor.
In both of his feet at the back he made holes by the tendons
in the space between ankle and heel, and drew thongs of ox-hide through
them,
and fastened them to the chariot so as to let the head drag,
and mounted the chariot, and lifted the glorious armor inside it,
400 then whipped the horses to a run, and they winged their way unreluctant.
A cloud of dust rose where Hektor was dragged, his dark hair was falling
about him, and all that head that was once so handsome was tumbled
in the dust; since by this time Zeus had given him over
to his enemies, to be defiled in the land of his fathers.
405 So all his head was dragged in the dust; and now his mother
tore out her hair, and threw the shining veil far from her
and raised a great wail as she looked upon her son; and his father
beloved groaned pitifully, and all his people about him
were taken with wailing and lamentation all through the city.
410 It was most like what would have happened, if all lowering
Ilion had been burning top to bottom in fire.
His people could scarcely keep the old man in his impatience
from storming out of the Dardanian gates; he implored them
all, and wallowed in the muck before them calling on each man
415 and naming him by his name: "Give way, dear friends,
and let me alone though you care for me, leave me to go out
from the city and make my way to the ships of the Achaians.
I must be suppliant to this man, who is harsh and violent,
and he might have respect for my age and take pity upon it
420 since I am old, and his father also is old, as I am,
Peleus, who begot and reared him to be an affliction
on the Trojans. He has given us most sorrow, beyond all others,
such is the number of my flowering sons he has cut down.
But for all of these I mourn not so much, in spite of my sorrow,
425 as for one, Hektor, and the sharp grief for him will carry me downward
into Death's house. I wish he had died in my arms, for that way
we two, I myself and his mother who bore him unhappy,
might so have glutted ourselves with weeping for him and mourning."
So he spoke, in tears, and beside him mourned the citizens.
430 But for the women of Troy Hekabē led out the thronging
chant of sorrow: "Child, I am wretched. What shall my life be

in my sorrows, now you are dead, who by day and in the night
were my glory in the town, and to all of the Trojans
and the women of Troy a blessing throughout their city. They adored you
as if you were a god, since in truth you were their high honor          435
while you lived. Now death and fate have closed in upon you."

So she spoke in tears but the wife of Hektor had not yet
heard: for no sure messenger had come to her and told her
how her husband had held his ground there outside the gates;
but she was weaving a web in the inner room of the high house,          440
a red folding robe, and inworking elaborate figures.
She called out through the house to her lovely-haired handmaidens
to set a great cauldron over the fire, so that there would be
hot water for Hektor's bath as he came back out of the fighting;
poor innocent, nor knew how, far from waters for bathing,              445
Pallas Athene had cut him down at the hands of Achilleus.
She heard from the great bastion the noise of mourning and sorrow.
Her limbs spun, and the shuttle dropped from her hand to the ground.
    Then
she called aloud to her lovely-haired handmaidens: "Come here.
Two of you come with me, so I can see what has happened.               450
I heard the voice of Hektor's honored mother; within me
my own heart rising beats in my mouth, my limbs under me
are frozen. Surely some evil is near for the children of Priam.
May what I say come never close to my ear; yet dreadfully
I fear that great Achilleus might have cut off bold Hektor            455
alone, away from the city, and be driving him into the flat land,
might put an end to that bitter pride of courage, that always
was on him, since he would never stay back where the men were in numbers
but break far out in front, and give way in his fury to no man."
    So she spoke, and ran out of the house like a raving woman        460
with pulsing heart, and her two handmaidens went along with her.
But when she came to the bastion and where the men were gathered
she stopped, staring, on the wall; and she saw him
being dragged in front of the city, and the running horses
dragged him at random toward the hollow ships of the Achaians.        465
The darkness of night misted over the eyes of Andromachē.
She fell backward, and gasped the life breath from her, and far off

threw from her head the shining gear that ordered her headdress,
the diadem and the cap, and the holding-band woven together,
470 and the circlet, which Aphrodite the golden once had given her
on that day when Hektor of the shining helmet led her forth
from the house of Eëtion, and gave numberless gifts to win her.
And about her stood thronging her husband's sisters and the wives of his
     brothers
and these, in her despair for death, held her up among them.
475 But she, when she breathed again and the life was gathered back into her,
lifted her voice among the women of Troy in mourning:
"Hektor, I grieve for you. You and I were born to a single
destiny, you in Troy in the house of Priam, and I
in Thebe, underneath the timbered mountain of Plakos
480 in the house of Eëtion, who cared for me when I was little,
ill-fated he, I ill-starred. I wish he had never begotten me.
Now you go down to the house of Death in the secret places
of the earth, and left me here behind in the sorrow of mourning,
a widow in your house, and the boy is only a baby
485 who was born to you and me, the unfortunate. You cannot help him,
Hektor, anymore, since you are dead. Nor can he help you.
Though he escape the attack of the Achaians with all its sorrows,
yet all his days for your sake there will be hard work for him
and sorrows, for others will take his lands away from him. The day
490 of bereavement leaves a child with no agemates to befriend him.
He bows his head before every man, his cheeks are bewept, he
goes, needy, a boy among his father's companions,
and tugs at this man by the mantle, that man by the tunic,
and they pity him, and one gives him a tiny drink from a goblet,
495 enough to moisten his lips, not enough to moisten his palate.
But one whose parents are living beats him out of the banquet
hitting him with his fists and in words also abuses him:
'Get out, you! Your father is not dining among us.'
And the boy goes away in tears to his widowed mother,
500 Astyanax, who in days before on the knees of his father
would eat only the marrow or the flesh of sheep that was fattest.
And when sleep would come upon him and he was done with his playing,
he would go to sleep in a bed, in the arms of his nurse, in a soft
bed, with his heart given all its fill of luxury.

Now, with his dear father gone, he has much to suffer:  505
he, whom the Trojans have called Astyanax, lord of the city,
since it was you alone who defended the gates and the long walls.
But now, beside the curving ships, far away from your parents,
the writhing worms will feed, when the dogs have had enough of you,
on your naked corpse, though in your house there is clothing laid up  510
that is fine-textured and pleasant, wrought by the hands of women.
But all of these I will burn up in the fire's blazing,
no use to you, since you will never be laid away in them;
but in your honor, from the men of Troy and the Trojan women."
    So she spoke, in tears; and the women joined in her mourning.  515

# BOOK TWENTY-THREE

So they were mourning through the city. Meanwhile, the Achaians,
after they had made their way back to their ships and the Hellespont,
scattered, the rest of them, each man to his own ship. Except
Achilleus would not allow the Myrmidons to be scattered,
5   but called out to his companions whose delight was in battle:
"Myrmidons, you of the fast horses, my steadfast companions,
we must not yet slip free of the chariots our single-foot horses,
but with these very horses and chariots we must drive close up
to Patroklos and mourn him, since such is the privilege of the perished.
10   Then, when we have taken full satisfaction from the sorrowful
dirge, we shall set our horses free, and all of us eat here."
     He spoke, and all of them assembled moaned, and Achilleus led them.
Three times, mourning, they drove their horses with flowing manes about
the body, and among them Thetis stirred the passion for weeping.
15   The sands were wet, and the armor of men was wet with their tears. Such
was their longing after Patroklos, who drove men to thoughts of terror.
Peleus' son led the thronging chant of their lamentation,
and laid his manslaughtering hands over the chest of his dear friend:
"Good-bye, Patroklos. I hail you even in the house of the death god.
20   All that I promised you in time past I am accomplishing,
that I would drag Hektor here and give him to the dogs to feed on
raw, and before your burning pyre to behead twelve glorious
children of the Trojans for my anger over your slaying."
     He spoke, and thought of shameful treatment for glorious Hektor.
25   He laid him on his face in the dust by the bier of Menoitios'
son. Meanwhile the others took off each man his glittering

brazen armor, and all unyoked their proud neighing horses
and sat down in their thousands beside the ship of swift-footed
Aiakides, who set the funeral feast in abundance
before them; and many shining oxen were slaughtered with the stroke 30
of the iron, and many sheep and bleating goats and numerous
swine with shining teeth and the fat abundant upon them
were singed and stretched out across the flame of Hephaistos.
The blood ran and was caught in cups all around the dead man.

But now the kings of the Achaians brought the swift-footed 35
lord, the son of Peleus, to great Agamemnon, hardly
persuading him, since his heart was still angered for his companion.
When these had made their way to the shelter of Agamemnon
straightway they gave orders to the heralds, the clear crying,
to set a great cauldron over the fire, if so they might persuade 40
the son of Peleus to wash away the filth of the bloodstains,
but he denied them stubbornly and swore an oath on it:
"No, before Zeus, who is greatest of gods and the highest,
there is no right in letting water come near my head, until
I have laid Patroklos on the burning pyre, and heaped the mound over 45
    him,
and cut my hair for him, since there will come no second sorrow
like this to my heart again while I am still one of the living.
Then let us now give way to the gloomy feast; and with the dawn
cause your people to rise, O lord of men Agamemnon,
and bring in timber and lay it by, with all that is fitting 50
for the dead man to have when he goes down under the gloom and the
    darkness,
so that with the more speed the unwearying fire may burn him
away from our eyes, and the people turn back to that which they must do."
So he spoke, and they listened well to him and obeyed him,
and in speed and haste they got the dinner ready, and each man 55
feasted, nor was any man's hunger denied a fair portion.
But when they had put aside their desire for eating and drinking,
they went away to sleep, each man into his own shelter,
but along the beach of the thunderous sea the son of Peleus
lay down, groaning heavily, among the Myrmidon numbers 60
in a clear place where the waves washed over the beach; and at that time

sleep caught him and was drifted sweetly about him, washing
the sorrows out of his mind, for his shining limbs were grown weary
indeed, from running in chase of Hektor toward windy Ilion;
65  and there appeared to him the ghost of unhappy Patroklos
all in his likeness for stature, and the lovely eyes, and voice,
and wore such clothing as Patroklos had worn on his body.
The ghost came and stood over his head and spoke a word to him:
"You sleep, Achilleus; you have forgotten me; but you were not
70  careless of me when I lived, but only in death. Bury me
as quickly as may be, let me pass through the gates of Hades.
The souls, the images of dead men, hold me at a distance,
and will not let me cross the river and mingle among them,
but I wander as I am by Hades' house of the wide gates.
75  And I call upon you in sorrow, give me your hand; no longer
shall I come back from death, once you give me my rite of burning.
No longer shall you and I, alive, sit apart from our other
beloved companions and make our plans, since the bitter destiny
that was given me when I was born has opened its jaws to take me.
80  And you, Achilleus like the gods, have your own destiny;
to be killed under the wall of the prospering Trojans. There is one
more thing I will say, and ask of you, if you will obey me:
do not have my bones laid apart from yours, Achilleus,
but with them, just as we grew up together in your house,
85  when Menoitios brought me there from Opous, when I was little,
and into your house, by reason of a baneful manslaying,
on that day when I killed the son of Amphidamas. I was
a child only, nor intended it, but was angered over a dice game.
There the rider Peleus took me into his own house,
90  and brought me carefully up, and named me to be your henchman.
Therefore, let one single vessel, the golden two-handled
urn the lady your mother gave you, hold both our ashes."
        Then in answer to him spoke swift-footed Achilleus:
    "How is it, O hallowed head of my brother, you have come back to me
95  here, and tell me all these several things? Yet surely
I am accomplishing all, and I shall do as you tell me.
But stand closer to me, and let us, if only for a little,
embrace, and take full satisfaction from the dirge of sorrow."

So he spoke, and with his own arms reached for him, but could not
take him, but the spirit went underground, like vapor,                          100
with a thin cry, and Achilleus started awake, staring,
and drove his hands together, and spoke, and his words were sorrowful:
"Oh, wonder! Even in the house of Hades there is left something,
a soul and an image, but there is no real heart of life in it.
For all night long the phantom of unhappy Patroklos                            105
stood over me in lamentation and mourning, and the likeness
to him was wonderful, and it told me each thing I should do."
    So he spoke, and stirred in all of them the passion of mourning,
and Dawn of the rose fingers showed on them as still they mourned
about the forlorn body. Now powerful Agamemnon                                 110
gave order for men and mules to assemble from all the shelters
and bring in timber, and a great man led them in motion,
Meriones, the henchman of courtly Idomeneus. These then
went out and in their hands carried axes to cut wood
and ropes firmly woven, and their mules went on ahead of them.                115
They went many ways, uphill, downhill, sidehill and slantwise;
but when they came to the spurs of Ida with all her well springs,
they set to hewing with the thin edge of bronze and leaning
their weight to the strokes on towering-leafed oak trees that toppled
with huge crashing; then the Achaians splitting the timbers                    120
fastened them to the mules and these with their feet tore up
the ground as they pulled through the dense undergrowth to the flat land.
All the woodcutters carried logs themselves; such was the order
of Meriones, the henchman of courtly Idomeneus. These then
threw down their burdens in order along the beach, where Achilleus            125
had chosen place for a huge grave mound, for himself and Patroklos.
    Then when on all sides they had thrown down abundance of timber,
they sat down where they were, assembled. And now Achilleus
gave order at once to the Myrmidons, whose delight was in battle,
to belt themselves in bronze and each man to yoke his horses                   130
to the chariot. And they rose up and got into their armor
and stepped up, charioteer and sideman, into the chariots
with the horsemen in front, and behind them came on a cloud of foot-
        soldiers
by thousands; and in the midst his companions carried Patroklos.

135    They covered all the corpse under the locks of their hair, which they cut off
and dropped on him, and behind them brilliant Achilleus held the head
sorrowing, for this was his true friend he escorted toward Hades.

When these had come to the place Achilleus had spoken of to them
they laid him down, and quickly piled up abundant timber.
140    And now brilliant swift-footed Achilleus remembered one more thing.
He stood apart from the pyre and cut off a lock of fair hair
which he had grown long to give to the river Spercheios, and gazing
in deep distress out over the wine-blue water, he spoke forth:
"Spercheios, it was in vain that Peleus my father vowed to you
145    that there, when I had won home to the beloved land of my fathers,
I would cut my hair for you and make you a grand and holy
sacrifice of fifty rams consecrate to the waters
of your springs, where is your holy ground and your smoking altar.
So the old man vowed, but you did not accomplish his purpose.
150    Now, since I do not return to the beloved land of my fathers,
I would give my hair into the keeping of the hero Patroklos."
He spoke, and laid his hair in the hands of his beloved
companion, and stirred in all of them the passion of mourning.
And now the light of the sun would have set on their lamentation
155    had not Achilleus soon stood by Agamemnon and spoken:
"Son of Atreus, beyond others the people of the Achaians
will obey your words. There can be enough, even in mourning.
Now cause them to scatter from the fire and bid them make ready
their dinner; and we, who are most nearly concerned with the dead man,
160    shall do this work; except only let the leaders stay near us."
Then the lord of men, Agamemnon, when he had heard this,
at once caused the people to disperse among the balanced ships,
but the close mourners stayed by the place and piled up the timber,
and built a pyre a hundred feet long this way and that way,
165    and on the peak of the pyre they laid the body, sorrowful
at heart; and in front of it skinned and set in order numbers
of fat sheep and shambling horn-curved cattle; and from all
great-hearted Achilleus took the fat and wrapped the corpse in it
from head to foot, and piled up the skinned bodies about it.
170    Then he set beside him two-handled jars of oil and honey
leaning them against the bier, and drove four horses with strong necks

swiftly aloft the pyre with loud lamentation. And there were
nine dogs of the table that had belonged to the lord Patroklos.
Of these he cut the throats of two, and set them on the pyre;
and so also killed twelve noble sons of the great-hearted Trojans          175
with the stroke of bronze, and evil were the thoughts in his heart against
    them,
and let loose the iron fury of the fire to feed on them.
Then he groaned, and called by name on his beloved companion:
"Good-bye, Patroklos. I hail you even in the house of the death god
for all that I promised you in time past I am accomplishing.          180
Here are twelve noble sons of the great-hearted Trojans
whom the fire feeds on, all, as it feeds on you. But I will not
give Hektor, Priam's son, to the fire, but the dogs, to feast on."

So he spoke his threat. But the dogs did not deal with Hektor,
for Aphrodite, daughter of Zeus, drove the dogs back from him          185
by day and night, and anointed him with rosy immortal
oil, so Achilleus, when he dragged him about, might not tear him.
And Phoibos Apollo brought down a darkening mist about him
from the sky to the plain, and covered with it all the space that was taken
by the dead man, to keep the force of the sun from coming          190
first, and wither his body away by limbs and sinews.
But the pyre of dead Patroklos would not light. Then swift-footed
brilliant Achilleus thought of one more thing that he must do.
He stood apart from the pyre and made his prayer to the two winds
Boreas and Zephyros, north wind and west, and promised them splendid          195
offerings, and much outpouring from a golden goblet entreated them
to come, so that the bodies might with best speed burn in the fire
and the timber burst into flame. And Iris, hearing his prayer,
went swiftly as messenger to the winds for him. Now the winds
assembled within the house of storm-blowing Zephyros          200
were taking part in a feast, and Iris paused in her running
and stood on the stone doorsill; but they, when their eyes saw her,
sprang to their feet, and each one asked her to sit beside him.
But she refused to be seated and spoke her word to them: "I must not
sit down. I am going back to the running waters of Ocean          205
and the Aithiopians' land, where they are making grand sacrifice
to the immortals; there I, too, shall partake of the sacraments.

But Achilleus' prayer is that Boreas and blustering Zephyros
may come to him, and he promises them splendid offerings,
210   so that you may set ablaze the funeral pyre, whereon lies
Patroklos, with all Achaians mourning about him."
    She spoke so, and went away, and they with immortal
clamor rose up, and swept the clouds in confusion before them.
They came with a sudden blast upon the sea, and the waves rose
215   under the whistling wind. They came to the generous Troad
and hit the pyre, and a huge inhuman blaze rose, roaring.
Nightlong they piled the flames on the funeral pyre together
and blew with a screaming blast, and nightlong swift-footed Achilleus
from a golden mixing bowl, with a two-handled goblet in his hand,
220   drew the wine and poured it on the ground and drenched the ground with it,
and called upon the soul of unhappy Patroklos. And as
a father mourns as he burns the bones of a son, who was married
only now, and died to grieve his unhappy parents,
so Achilleus was mourning as he burned his companion's
225   bones, and dragged himself by the fire in close lamentation.

    At that time when the dawn star passes across earth, harbinger
of light, and after him dawn of the saffron mantle is scattered
across the sea, the fire died down and the flames were over.
The winds took their way back toward home again, crossing
230   the Thracian water, and it boiled with a moaning swell as they crossed it.
The son of Peleus turned aside and away from the burning
and lay down exhausted, and sweet sleep rose upon him. But now
they who were with the son of Atreus assembled together
and the sound and murmur of their oncoming wakened Achilleus,
235   who straightened himself and sat upright and spoke a word to him:
"Son of Atreus, and you other greatest of all the Achaians,
first put out with gleaming wine the pyre that is burning,
all that still has on it the fury of fire; and afterward
we shall gather up the bones of Patroklos, the son of Menoitios,
240   which we shall easily tell apart, since they are conspicuous
where he lay in the middle of the pyre and the others far from him
at the edge burned, the men indiscriminately with the horses.
And let us lay his bones in a golden jar and a double
fold of fat, until I myself enfold him in Hades.

And I would have you build a grave mound which is not very great       245
but such as will be fitting, for now; afterward, the Achaians
can make it broad and high—such of you Achaians as may be
left to survive me here by the benched ships, after I am gone."

So he spoke, and they did as swift-footed Peleion told them.
First with gleaming wine they put out the pyre that was burning,       250
as much as was still aflame, and the ashes dropped deep from it.
Then they gathered up the white bones of their gentle companion,
weeping, and put them into a golden jar with a double
fold of fat, and laid it away in his shelter, and covered it
with a thin veil; then laid out the tomb and cast down the holding walls   255
around the funeral pyre, then heaped the loose earth over them
and piled the tomb, and turned to go away. But Achilleus
held the people there, and made them sit down in a wide assembly,
and brought prizes for games out of his ships, cauldrons and tripods,
and horses and mules and the powerful high heads of cattle       260
and fair-girdled women and gray iron. First of all
he set forth the glorious prizes for speed of foot for the horsemen:
a woman faultless in the work of her hands to lead away
and a tripod with ears and holding twenty-two measures
for the first prize; and for the second he set forth a six-year-old       265
unbroken mare who carried a mule foal within her.
Then for the third prize he set forth a splendid unfired
cauldron, which held four measures, with its natural gloss still upon it.
For the fourth place he set out two talents' weight of gold, and for
the fifth place set forth an unfired jar with two handles.       270
He stood upright and spoke his word out among the Argives:
"Son of Atreus and all you other strong-greaved Achaians,
these prizes are in the place of games and wait for the horsemen.
Now if we Achaians were contending for the sake of some other
hero, I myself should take the first prize away to my shelter.       275
You know how much my horses surpass in their speed all others;
yes, for they are immortal horses, and Poseidon gave them
to Peleus my father, who in turn gave them into my hands.
But I stay here at the side, and my single-foot horses stay with me;
such is the high glory of the charioteer they have lost,       280
the gentle one, who so many times anointed their manes with

soft olive oil, after he had washed them in shining water.
Therefore these two horses stand here and grieve, and their manes
are swept along the ground as they stand with hearts full of sorrow.
285 But take, the rest of you, places in the field, whichever Achaian
has confidence in his horses and his compacted chariot."

So spoke the son of Peleus, and the swift riders gathered.
Far the first to rise up was the lord of men Eumelos,
own son of Admetos, who surpassed in horsemanship. After
290 him rose up the son of Tydeus, strong Diomedes,
and led under the yoke the Trojan horses whom he had taken
by force from Aineias, but Aineias himself was saved by Apollo.
After him rose the son of Atreus, fair-haired Menelaos
the sky-descended, and led beneath the yoke the swift horses,
295 Aithe, Agamemnon's mare, and his own Podargos.
Echepolos, son of Anchises, gave her to Agamemnon
as a gift, so as not to have to go with him to windy Ilion
but stay where he was and enjoy himself, since Zeus had given him
great wealth, and he made his home in the wide spaces of Sikyon.
300 This mare, who was straining hard for the race, Menelaos harnessed.
Fourth to order his horses with flowing manes was Antilochos,
the glorious son of Nestor, Neleus' son, the high-hearted
lord, and fast-running horses out of the breed of Pylos
pulled his chariot, and his father standing close beside him
305 gave well-intentioned advice to his own good understanding:
"Antilochos, you are young indeed, but Zeus and Poseidon
have loved you and taught you horsemanship in all of its aspects.
Therefore there is no great need to instruct you; you yourself
know well how to double the turning-post. Yet in this race your horse
310 should run slowest. Therefore I think your work will be heavy.
The horses of these men are faster, but they themselves do not
understand anymore than you of the science of racing.
Remember then, dear son, to have your mind full of every
resource of skill, so that the prizes may not elude you.
315 The woodcutter is far better for skill than he is for brute strength.
It is by skill that the sea captain holds his rapid ship
on its course, though torn by winds, over the wine-blue water.
By skill charioteer outpasses charioteer. He

who has put all his confidence in his horses and chariot
and recklessly makes a turn that is loose one way or another          320
finds his horses drifting out of the course and does not control them.
But the man, though he drive the slower horses, who takes his advantage,
keeps his eye always on the post and turns tight, ever watchful,
pulled with the ox-hide reins on the course, as in the beginning,
and holds his horses steady in hand, and watches the leader.          325
I will give you a clear mark and you cannot fail to notice it.
There is a dry stump standing up from the ground about six feet,
oak, it may be, or pine, and not rotted away by rain-water,
and two white stones are leaned against it, one on either side,
at the joining place of the ways, and there is smooth driving around it.   330
Either it is the grave-mark of someone who died long ago,
or was set as a racing goal by men who lived before our time.
Now swift-footed brilliant Achilleus has made it the turning-post.
You must drive your chariot and horses so as to hug this,
and yourself, in the strong-fabricated chariot, lean over          335
a little to the left of the course, and as for your right horse, whip him
and urge him along, slackening your hands to give him his full rein,
but make your left hand horse keep hard against the turning-post
so that the hub's edge of your fashioned wheel will seem to be
touching it, yet take care not really to brush against it,          340
for, if so, you might damage your horses and break your chariot,
and that will be a thing of joy for the others, and a failure
for you. So, dear son, drive thoughtfully and be watchful.
For if you follow the others but get first by the turning-post,
there is none who could sprint to make it up, nor close you, nor pass you,   345
not if the man behind you were driving the great Arion,
the swift horse of Adrestos, whose birth is from the immortals,
or Laomedon's horses, who were the pride of those raised in this country."
   So spoke Nestor the son of Neleus, and turned back to his place
and sat down, having talked to his son of each stage in the contest.          350
Fifth to order his horses with flowing manes was Meriones.
They climbed to the chariots and deposited the lots. Achilleus
shook them, and the first to fall out was that of Antilochos,
Nestor's son, and strong Eumelos drew next after him,
and after him the son of Atreus, Menelaos the spear-famed.          355
Meriones drew the next lane to drive, and the last for the driving

of horses was drawn by far the best of them all, Diomedes.
They stood in line for the start, and Achilleus showed them the turn-post
far away on the level plain, and beside it he stationed
360  a judge, Phoinix the godlike, the follower of his father,
to mark and remember the running and bring back a true story.

Then all held their whips high-lifted above their horses,
then struck with the whip thongs and in words urged their horses onward
into speed. Rapidly they made their way over the flat land
365  and presently were far away from the ships. The dust lifting
clung beneath the horses' chests like cloud or a stormwhirl.
Their manes streamed along the blast of the wind, the chariots
rocking now would dip to the earth who fosters so many
and now again would spring up clear of the ground, and the drivers
370  stood in the chariots, with the spirit beating in each man
with the strain to win, and each was calling aloud upon his own
horses, and the horses flew through the dust of the flat land.
But as the rapid horses were running the last of the race-course
back, and toward the gray sea, then the mettle of each began to
375  show itself, and the field of horses strung out, and before long
out in front was the swift-stepping team of the son of Pheres,
Eumelos, and after him the stallions of Diomedes,
the Trojan horses, not far behind at all, but close on him,
for they seemed forever on the point of climbing his chariot
380  and the wind of them was hot on the back and on the broad shoulders
of Eumelos. They lowered their heads and flew close after him.
And now he might have passed him or run to a doubtful decision,
had not Phoibos Apollo been angry with Diomedes,
Tydeus' son, and dashed the shining whip from his hands, so
385  that the tears began to stream from his eyes, for his anger
as he watched how the mares of Eumelos drew far ahead of him
while his own horses ran without the whip and were slowed. Yet
Athene did not fail to see the foul play of Apollo
on Tydeus' son. She swept in speed to the shepherd of the people
390  and gave him back his whip, and inspired strength into his horses.
Then in her wrath she went on after the son of Admetos
and she, a goddess, smashed his chariot yoke, and his horses
ran on either side of the way, the pole dragged, and Eumelos

himself was sent spinning out beside the wheel of the chariot
so that his elbows were all torn, and his mouth, and his nostrils,          395
and his forehead was lacerated about the brows, and his eyes
filled with tears, and the springing voice was held fast within him.
Then the son of Tydeus, turning his single-foot horses to pass him,
went far out in front of the others, seeing that Athene
had inspired strength in his horses and to himself gave the glory.          400
After him came the son of Atreus, fair-haired Menelaos.
But Antilochos cried out aloud to his father's horses:
"Come on, you two. Pull, as fast as you can! I am not
trying to make you match your speed with the speed of those others,
the horses of Tydeus' valiant son, to whom now Athene                       405
has granted speed and to their rider has given the glory.
But make your burst to catch the horses of the son of Atreus
nor let them leave you behind, for fear Aithe who is female
may shower you in mockery. Are you falling back, my brave horses?
For I will tell you this, and it will be a thing accomplished.              410
There will be no more care for you from the shepherd of the people,
Nestor, but he will slaughter you out of hand with the edge
of bronze, if we win the meaner prize because you are unwilling.
Keep on close after him and make all the speed you are able.
I myself shall know what to do and contrive it, so that                     415
we get by in the narrow place of the way. He will not escape me."
    So he spoke, and they fearing the angry voice of their master
ran harder for a little while, and presently after this
battle-stubborn Antilochos saw where the hollow way narrowed.
There was a break in the ground where winter water had gathered            420
and broken out of the road, and made a sunken place all about.
Menelaos shrinking from a collision of chariots steered there,
but Antilochos also turned out his single-foot horses
from the road, and bore a little way aside, and went after him;
and the son of Atreus was frightened and called out aloud to Antilochos:    425
"Antilochos, this is reckless horsemanship. Hold in your horses.
The way is narrow here, it will soon be wider for passing.
Be careful not to crash your chariot and wreck both of us."
    So he spoke, but Antilochos drove on all the harder
with a whiplash for greater speed, as if he had never heard him.           430
As far as is the range of a discus swung from the shoulder

and thrown by a stripling who tries out the strength of his young manhood,
so far they ran even, but then the mares of Atreides gave way
and fell back, for he of his own will slackened his driving
435 for fear that in the road the single-foot horses might crash
and overturn the strong-fabricated chariots, and the men
themselves go down in the dust through their hard striving for victory.
But Menelaos of the fair hair called to him in anger:
"Antilochos, there is no other man more cursed than you are.
440 Damn you. We Achaians lied when we said you had good sense.
Even so, you will not get this prize without having to take oath."
He spoke, and lifted his voice and called aloud to his horses:
"Never hold back now, never stop, for all your hearts are
sorrowful. The feet of these and their knees will weary
445 before yours do, seeing that the youth is gone from those horses."
So he spoke, and they fearing the angry voice of their master
ran the harder, and soon were close up behind the others.

Now the Argives who sat in their assembly were watching
the horses, and the horses flew through the dust of the flat land.
450 Idomeneus, lord of the Kretans, was first to make out the horses,
for he sat apart from the others assembled, and higher up, where
he could see all ways, and from far off he heard Diomedes
calling, and knew him, and made out one horse ahead of the others
who was conspicuous, all red, except on his forehead
455 there was a white mark, round, like the full moon. Idomeneus
rose to his feet upright and spoke his word out to the Argives:
"Friends, who are leaders of the Argives and keep their counsel:
am I the only one who can see the horses, or can you
also? It seems to me there are other horses leading
460 and I make out another charioteer. The mares of Eumelos
must have come to grief somewhere in the plain, who led on the way out,
for those I saw running out in front as they made the turn-post
I can see no longer anywhere, though I watch and though my eyes
look everywhere about the plain of Troy. But it must be
465 that the reins got away from the charioteer, or he could not hold them
well in hand at the goal and failed to double the turn-post.
There I think he must have been thrown out and his chariot broken,
and the mares bolted away with the wildness upon their spirit.

But you also stand up and look for yourselves; I cannot
well make out, but it seems to me the man who is leading                    470
is an Aitolian by birth, but lord of the Argives,
the son of Tydeus, breaker of horses, strong Diomedes."
    Swift Aias, son of Oïleus, spoke shamefully to him in anger:
"Idomeneus, what was all this windy talk? The light-footed
horses are still far where they sweep over the great plain.                 475
You are not by so much the youngest among the Argives,
nor do the eyes in your head see so much sharper than others.
But forever you are windy with your words, and you should not
be a windy speaker. There are others here better than you are.
The horses who are in front are the same as before, and they are            480
those of Eumelos, and he stands holding the reins behind them."
    The lord of the Kretans answered him to his face in anger:
"Aias, surpassing in abuse, yet stupid, in all else
you are worst of the Argives with that stubborn mind of yours. Come then,
let us put up a wager of a tripod or cauldron                               485
and make Agamemnon, son of Atreus, witness between us
as to which horses lead. And when you pay, you will find out."
    So he spoke, and swift Aias, son of Oïleus, was rising
up, angry in turn, to trade hard words with him. And now
the quarrel between the two of them would have gone still further,         490
had not Achilleus himself risen up and spoken between them:
"No longer now, Aias and Idomeneus, continue
to exchange this bitter and evil talk. It is not becoming.
If another acted so, you yourselves would be angry.
Rather sit down again among those assembled and watch for                   495
the horses, and they in their strain for victory will before long
be here. Then you each can see for himself, and learn which
of the Argives' horses have run first and which have run second."

    He spoke, and now Tydeus' son in his rapid course was close on them
and he lashed them always with the whipstroke from the shoulder. His        500
    horses
still lifted their feet light and high as they made their swift passage.
Dust flying splashed always the charioteer, and the chariot
that was overlaid with gold and tin still rolled hard after
the flying feet of the horses, and in their wake there was not much

505 trace from the running rims of the wheels left in the thin dust.
The horses came in running hard. Diomedes stopped them
in the middle of where the men were assembled, with the dense sweat starting
and dripping to the ground from neck and chest of his horses.
He himself vaulted down to the ground from his shining chariot
510 and leaned his whip against the yoke. Nor did strong Sthenelos
delay, but made haste to take up the prizes, and gave the woman
to his high-hearted companions to lead away and the tripod
with ears to carry, while Diomedes set free the horses.

    After him Neleian Antilochos drove in his horses,
515 having passed Menelaos, not by speed but by taking advantage.
But even so Menelaos held his fast horses close on him.
As far as from the wheel stands the horse who is straining
to pull his master with the chariot over the flat land;
the extreme hairs in the tail of the horse brush against the running
520 rim of the wheel, and he courses very close, there is not much
space between as he runs a great way over the flat land;
by so much Menelaos was left behind by Antilochos
the blameless. At first he was left behind the length of a discus
thrown, but was overhauling him fast, with Aithe
525 of the fair mane, Agamemnon's mare, putting on a strong burst.
If both of them had had to run the course any further,
Menelaos would have passed him, and there could have been no argument.
But Meriones, strong henchman of Idomeneus, was left
a spearcast's length behind by glorious Menelaos.
530 For his horses with splendid manes were slowest of all, and likewise
he himself was of least account for the racing of chariots.
Last and behind them all came in the son of Admetos
dragging his fine chariot and driving his horses before him,
and seeing this, brilliant swift-footed Achilleus took pity upon him
535 and stood forth among the Argives and spoke to them all in winged words:
"The best man is driving his single-foot horses in last.
Come then, we must give some kind of prize, and well he deserves it;
second prize; let first place go to the son of Tydeus."

    So he spoke, and all gave approval to what he was urging,
540 and he would have given him the horse, since all the Achaians
approved, had not Antilochos, son of great-hearted Nestor,

stood up to answer Peleid Achilleus, and argue:
"Achilleus, I shall be very angry with you if you accomplish
what you have said. You mean to take my prize away from me,
with the thought in mind that his chariot fouled and his running horses    545
but he himself is great. He should have prayed to the immortal
gods. That is why he came in last of all in the running.
But if you are sorry for him and he is dear to your liking,
there is abundant gold in your shelter, and there is bronze there
and animals, and there are handmaidens and single-foot horses.    550
You can take from these, and give him afterward a prize still greater
than mine, or now at once, and have the Achaians applaud you.
But the mare I will not give up, and the man who wants her
must fight me for her with his hands before he can take her."
     So he spoke, but brilliant swift-footed Achilleus, favoring    555
Antilochos, smiled, since he was his beloved companion,
and answered him and addressed him in winged words: "Antilochos,
if you would have me bring some other thing out of my dwelling
as special gift for Eumelos, then for your sake I will do it.
I will give him that corselet I stripped from Asteropaios;    560
it is bronze, but there is an overlay circled about it
in shining tin. It will be a gift that will mean much to him."
     He spoke, and told Automedon, his beloved companion,
to bring it out of the shelter, and he went away, and brought it back,
and put it in Eumelos' hands. And he accepted it joyfully.    565
     But now Menelaos, heart full of bitterness, stood up among them
in relentless anger against Antilochos, and the herald
put the staff into his hand and gave the call for the Argives
to be silent. And he stood forth, a man like a god, and spoke to them:
"Antilochos, you had good sense once. See what you have done.    570
You have defiled my horsemanship, you have fouled my horses
by throwing your horses in their way, though yours were far slower.
Come then, O leaders of the Argives and their men of counsel:
judge between the two of us now; and without favor;
so that no man of the bronze-armored Achaians shall say of us:    575
'Menelaos using lies and force against Antilochos
went off with the mare he won, for his horses were far slower
but he himself was greater in power and degree.' Or rather
come, I myself will give the judgment, and I think no other

580　man of the Danaäns can call it in question, for it will be right.
Antilochos, beloved of Zeus, come here. This is justice.
Stand in front of your horses and chariot, and in your hand take
up the narrow whip with which you drove them before, then
lay your hand on the horses and swear by him who encircles
585　the earth and shakes it you used no guile to baffle my chariot."
　　　Then in turn Antilochos of the good counsel answered him:
"Enough now. For I, my lord Menelaos, am younger
by far than you, and you are the greater and go before me.
You know how greedy transgressions flower in a young man, seeing
590　that his mind is the more active but his judgment is lightweight. Therefore
I would have your heart be patient with me. I myself will give you
the mare I won, and if there were something still greater you asked for
out of my house, I should still be willing at once to give it
to you, beloved of Zeus, rather than all my days
595　fall from your favor and be in the wrong before the divinities."

　　　He spoke, the son of Nestor the great-hearted, and leading
the mare up gave her to Menelaos' hands. But his anger
was softened, as with dew the ears of corn are softened
in the standing corn growth of a shuddering field. For you also
600　the heart, O Menelaos, was thus softened within you.
He spoke to him aloud and addressed him in winged words: "Antilochos,
I myself, who was angry, now will give way before you,
since you were not formerly loose-minded or vain. It is only
that this time your youth got the better of your intelligence.
605　Beware another time of playing tricks on your betters.
Any other man of the Achaians might not have appeased me.
But you have suffered much for me, and done much hard work,
and your noble father, too, and your brother for my sake. Therefore
I will be ruled by your supplication. I will even give you
610　the mare, though she is mine, so that these men too may be witnesses
that the heart is never arrogant nor stubborn within me."
　　　He spoke, and gave Antilochos' companion, Noëmon,
the mare to lead away, and himself took the glittering cauldron.
Fourth, in the order he had driven, Meriones took up
615　the two talents' weight of gold. But the fifth prize, the two-handled
jar, was left. Achilleus carried it through the assembly

of the Argives, and gave it to Nestor, and stood by and spoke to him:
"This, aged sir, is yours to lay away as a treasure
in memory of the burial of Patroklos; since never
again will you see him among the Argives. I give you this prize                620
for the giving; since never again will you fight with your fists nor wrestle,
nor enter again the field for the spear-throwing, nor race
on your feet; since now the hardship of old age is upon you."
     He spoke, and put it in the hands of Nestor, who took it
joyfully and spoke in answer and addressed him in winged words:                625
"Yes, child: all this you said to me was true as you said it.
My limbs are no longer steady, dear friend; not my feet, neither
do my arms, as once they did, swing light from my shoulders.
I wish I were young again and the strength still unshaken within me
as once, when great Amaryngkeus was buried by the Epeians                630
at Bouprasion, and his sons gave games for a king's funeral.
There, there was no man like me, not among the Epeians
nor yet of the Pylians themselves or great-hearted Aitolians.
At boxing I won against Klytomedes, the son of Enops,
at wrestling against Angkaios of Pleuron, who stood up against me.                635
In the foot-race, for all his speed, I outran Iphiklos,
and with the spear I out-threw Polydoros and Phyleus.
It was only in the chariot-race that the sons of Aktor
defeated me, crossing me in the crowd, so intent on winning
were they, for the biggest prizes had been left for the horse-race.                640
Now these sons of Aktor were twins; one held the reins at his leisure,
held the reins at his leisure while the other lashed on the horses.
This was I, once. Now it is for the young men to encounter
in such actions, and for me to give way to the persuasion
of gloomy old age. But once I shone among the young heroes.                645
Go now, and honor the death of your companion with contests.
I accept this from you gratefully, and my heart is happy
that you have remembered me and my kindness, that I am not forgotten
for the honor that should be my honor among the Achaians.
May the gods, for what you have done for me, give you great happiness."                650

     He spoke, and Peleides went back among the great numbers
of Achaians assembled, when he had listened to all the praise spoken
by Neleus' son, and set forth the prizes for the painful boxing.

He led out into the field and tethered there a hard-working
655 six-year-old unbroken jenny, the kind that is hardest
to break; and for the loser set out a two-handled goblet.
He stood upright and spoke his word out among the Argives:
"Son of Atreus, and all you other strong-greaved Achaians,
we invite two men, the best among you, to contend for these prizes
660 with their hands up for the blows of boxing. He whom Apollo
grants to outlast the other, and all the Achaians witness it,
let him lead away the hard-working jenny to his own shelter.
The beaten man shall take away the two-handled goblet."
He spoke, and a man huge and powerful, well skilled in boxing,
665 rose up among them; the son of Panopeus, Epeios.
He laid his hand on the hard-working jenny, and spoke out:
"Let the man come up who will carry off the two-handled goblet.
I say no other of the Achaians will beat me at boxing
and lead off the jenny. I claim I am the champion. Is it not
670 enough that I fall short in battle? Since it could not be
ever, that a man could be a master in every endeavor.
For I tell you this straight out, and it will be a thing accomplished.
I will smash his skin apart and break his bones on each other.
Let those who care for him wait nearby in a huddle about him
675 to carry him out, after my fists have beaten him under."
So he spoke, and all of them stayed stricken to silence.
Alone Euryalos stood up to face him, a godlike
man, son of lord Mekisteus of the seed of Talaos;
of him who came once to Thebes and the tomb of Oidipous after
680 his downfall, and there in boxing defeated all the Kadmeians.
The spear-famed son of Tydeus was his second, and talked to him
in encouragement, and much desired the victory for him.
First he pulled on the boxing belt about his waist, and then
gave him the thongs carefully cut from the hide of a ranging
685 ox. The two men, girt up, strode into the midst of the circle
and faced each other, and put up their ponderous hands at the same time
and closed, so that their heavy arms were crossing each other,
and there was a fierce grinding of teeth, the sweat began to run
everywhere from their bodies. Great Epeios came in, and hit him
690 as he peered out from his guard, on the cheek, and he could no longer
keep his feet, but where he stood the glorious limbs gave.

As in the water roughened by the north wind a fish jumps
in the weeds of the beach-break, then the dark water closes above him,
so Euryalos left the ground from the blow, but great-hearted Epeios
took him in his arms and set him upright, and his true companions          695
stood about him, and led him out of the circle, feet dragging
as he spat up the thick blood and rolled his head over on one side.
He was dizzy when they brought him back and set him among them.
But they themselves went and carried off the two-handled goblet.

    Now Peleides set forth the prizes for the third contest,          700
for the painful wrestling, at once, and displayed them before the Danaäns.
There was a great tripod, to set over fire, for the winner.
The Achaians among themselves valued it at the worth of twelve oxen.
But for the beaten man he set in their midst a woman
skilled in much work of her hands, and they rated her at four oxen.          705
He stood upright and spoke his word out among the Argives:
"Rise up, two who would endeavor this prize." So he spoke
and presently there rose up huge Telamonian Aias,
and resourceful Odysseus rose, who was versed in every advantage.
The two men, girt up, strode out into the midst of the circle,          710
and grappled each other in the hook of their heavy arms, as when
rafters lock, when a renowned architect has fitted them
in the roof of a high house to keep out the force of the winds' spite.
Their backs creaked under stress of violent hands that tugged them
stubbornly, and the running sweat broke out, and raw places          715
frequent all along their ribs and their shoulders broke out
bright red with blood, as both of them kept up their hard efforts
for success and the prize of the wrought tripod. Neither Odysseus
was able to bring Aias down or throw him to the ground, nor
could Aias, but the great strength of Odysseus held out against him.          720
But now as they made the strong-greaved Achaians begin to be restless,
at last great Telamonian Aias said to the other:
"Son of Laërtes and seed of Zeus, resourceful Odysseus:
lift me, or I will lift you. All success shall be as Zeus gives it."
    He spoke, and heaved; but not forgetting his craft Odysseus          725
caught him with a stroke behind the hollow of the knee, and unnerved
the tendons, and threw him over backward, so that Odysseus
fell on his chest as the people gazed upon them and wondered.

Next, brilliant much-enduring Odysseus endeavored to lift him
730  and budged him a little from the ground, but still could not raise him
clear, then hooked a knee behind, so that both of them went down
together to the ground, and lay close, and were soiled in the dust. Then
they would have sprung to their feet once more and wrestled a third fall,
had not Achilleus himself stood up and spoken to stop them:
735  "Wrestle no more now; do not wear yourselves out and get hurt.
You have both won. Therefore take the prizes in equal division
and retire, so the rest of the Achaians can have their contests."
     So he spoke, and they listened close to him and obeyed him
and wiped the dust away from their bodies, and put on their tunics.

740      At once the son of Peleus set out prizes for the foot-race:
a mixing bowl of silver, a work of art, which held only
six measures, but for its loveliness it surpassed all others
on earth by far, since skilled Sidonian craftsmen had wrought it
well, and Phoenicians carried it over the misty face of the water
745  and set it in the harbor, and gave it for a present to Thoas.
Euneos, son of Jason, gave it to the hero Patroklos
to buy Lykaon, Priam's son, out of slavery, and now
Achilleus made it a prize in memory of his companion,
for that man who should prove in the speed of his feet to run lightest.
750  For second place he set out a great ox with fat deep upon him,
and for the last runner half a talent's weight of gold. He stood
upright then and spoke his word out among the Argives:
"Rise up, you who would endeavor this prize." So he spoke
and presently there rose up swift Aias, the son of Oïleus,
755  and Odysseus the resourceful rose up, and after him Nestor's
son, Antilochos, the best runner among all the young men.
They stood in line for the start, and Achilleus showed them the turn-post.
The field was strung out from the scratch, and not long afterward
Oïleus' son was out in front, but brilliant Odysseus
760  overhauled him close, as near as to the breast of a woman
fair-girdled is the rod she pulls in her hands carefully
as she draws the spool out and along the warp, and holds it
close to her chest. So Odysseus ran close up, but behind him,
and his feet were hitting the other's tracks before the dust settled.
765  Great Odysseus was breathing on the back of the head of Aias

as he ran and held his speed, and all the Achaians were shouting
for his effort to win, and hallooed him hard along in his running.
But as they were running the last part of the race, then Odysseus
said a prayer inside his own mind to gray-eyed Athene:
"Hear me, goddess; be kind; and come with strength for my footsteps."     770
    So he spoke in prayer, and Pallas Athene heard him.
She made his limbs light, both his feet and the hands above them.
Now as they were for making their final sprint for the trophy,
there Aias slipped in his running, for Athene unbalanced him,
where dung was scattered on the ground from the bellowing oxen     775
    slaughtered
by swift-footed Achilleus, those he slew to honor Patroklos;
and his mouth and nose were filled with the cow dung, so that Odysseus
the great and much enduring took off the mixing bowl, seeing
he had passed him and come in first, and the ox went to glorious Aias.
He stood there holding in his hands the horn of the field-ox,     780
spitting the dung from his mouth, and spoke his word to the Argives:
"Ah, now! That goddess made me slip on my feet, who has always
stood over Odysseus like a mother, and taken good care of him."
    He spoke, and all the rest of them laughed happily at him.
In turn Antilochos took up prize for last place, and carried it     785
off, and grinning spoke his word out among the Argives:
"Friends, you all know well what I tell you, that still the immortals
continue to favor the elder men. For see now, Aias
is elder than I, if only by a little, but this man
is out of another age than ours and one of the ancients.     790
But his, they say, is a green old age. It would be a hard thing
for any Achaian to match his speed. Except for Achilleus."
    So he spoke, and glorified the swift-footed Peleion.
And Achilleus gave him an answer for what he said, and spoke to him:
"Antilochos, your good word for me shall not have been spoken     795
in vain. I shall give you another half-talent of gold in addition."

    He spoke, and put it in Antilochos' hands, who received it joyfully.
Then the son of Peleus carried into the circle and set down
a far-shadowing spear, and set down beside it a shield and a helmet:
the armor of Sarpedon, that Patroklos stripped from his body.     800
He stood upright and spoke his word out among the Argives:

"We invite two men, the best among you, to contend for these prizes.
Let them draw their armor upon them and take up the rending bronze spears
and stand up to each other in the trial of close combat. The fighter
805   who is first of the two to get in a stroke at the other's fair body,
to get through armor and dark blood and reach to the vitals,
to that man I will give this magnificent silver-nailed
sword of Thrace I stripped from the body of Asteropaios.
But let both men carry off this armor and have it in common;
810   and we shall set out a brave dinner before them both in our shelters."
       So he spoke, and there rose up huge Telamonian Aias,
and next the son of Tydeus rose up, strong Diomedes.
When these were in their armor on either side of the assembly,
they came together in the middle space, furious for the combat,
815   with dangerous looks, and wonder settled on all the Achaians.
Then as, moving forward, the two were closing in on each other,
there were three charges, three times they swept in close. Then Aias
stabbed at Diomedes' shield on its perfect circle
but did not get through to the skin, for the corselet inside it guarded him.
820   The son of Tydeus, over the top of the huge shield, was always
menacing the neck of Aias with the point of the shining
spear, but when the Achaians saw it in fear for Aias
they called for them to stop and divide the prizes evenly.
But the hero Achilleus carried the great sword, with its scabbard
825   and carefully cut sword belt, and gave it to Diomedes.

       Now the son of Peleus set in place a lump of pig-iron,
which had once been the throwing-weight of Eëtion in his great strength;
but now swift-footed brilliant Achilleus had slain him and taken
the weight away in the ships along with the other possessions.
830   He stood upright and spoke his word out among the Argives:
"Rise up, you who would endeavor to win this prize also.
For although the rich demesnes of him who wins it lie far off
indeed, yet for the succession of five years he will have it
to use; for his shepherd for want of iron will not have to go in
835   to the city for it, nor his ploughman either. This will supply them."
       So he spoke, and up stood Polypoites the stubborn in battle,
and Leonteus in his great strength, a godlike man, and there rose up
Aias, the son of Telamon, and brilliant Epeios.

They stood in order to throw, and great Epeios took up the weight
and whirled and threw it, and all the Achaians laughed when they saw him.  840
Second to throw in turn was Leonteus, scion of Ares,
and third in turn huge Telamonian Aias threw it
from his ponderous hand, and overpassed the marks of all others.
But when Polypoites stubborn in battle caught up the iron,
he overthrew the entire field by as far as an ox-herd  845
can cast with his throwing stick which spins through the air and comes down
where the cattle graze in their herds, and all the Achaians applauded,
and the companions of powerful Polypoites uprising
carried the prize of the king away to the hollow vessels.

But Achilleus set gloomy iron forth once more, for the archers.  850
He set ten double-bladed axes forth, ten with single
blades, and planted far away on the sands the mast pole
of a dark-prowed ship, and tethered a tremulous wild pigeon to it
by a thin string attached to her foot, then challenged the archers
to shoot at her: "Now let the man who hits the wild pigeon  855
take up and carry away home with him all the full axes.
But if one should miss the bird and still hit the string, that man,
seeing that he is the loser, still shall have the half-axes."
So he spoke, and there rose up in his strength the lord Teukros,
and Meriones rose up, Idomeneus' powerful henchman.  860
They chose their lots, and shook them up in a brazen helmet,
and Teukros was allotted first place to shoot. He let fly
a strong-shot arrow, but did not promise the lord of archery
that he would accomplish for him a grand sacrifice of lambs first born.
He missed the bird, for Apollo begrudged him that, but he did hit  865
the string beside the foot where the bird was tied, and the tearing
arrow went straight through and cut the string, and the pigeon
soared swift up toward the sky, while the string dropped and dangled
toward the ground. But still the Achaians thundered approval.
Meriones in a fury of haste caught the bow from his hand,  870
but had had out an arrow before, while Teukros was aiming,
and forthwith promised to the one who strikes from afar, Apollo,
that he would accomplish for him a grand sacrifice of lambs first born.
Way up under the clouds he saw the tremulous wild dove
and as she circled struck her under the wing in the body  875

and the shaft passed clean through and out of her, so that it dropped back
and stuck in the ground beside the foot of Meriones, but the bird
dropped and fell on top of the mast of the dark-prowed vessel
and drooped her neck and the beating wings went slack, and the spirit
880  of life fled swift away from her limbs. Far down from the mast peak
she dropped to earth. And the people gazed upon it and wondered.
Then Meriones gathered up all ten double axes,
but Teukros carried the half-axes back to the hollow ships.

Then the son of Peleus carried into the circle and set down
885  a far-shadowing spear and an unfired cauldron with patterns
of flowers on it, the worth of an ox. And the spear-throwers rose up.
The son of Atreus rose, wide-powerful Agamemnon,
and Meriones rose up, Idomeneus' powerful henchman.
But now among them spoke swift-footed brilliant Achilleus:
890  "Son of Atreus, for we know how much you surpass all others,
by how much you are greatest for strength among the spear-throwers,
therefore take this prize and keep it and go back to your hollow
ships; but let us give the spear to the hero Meriones;
if your own heart would have it this way, for so I invite you."
895  He spoke, nor did Agamemnon lord of men disobey him.
The hero gave the bronze spear to Meriones, and thereafter
handed his prize, surpassingly lovely, to the herald Talthybios.

# BOOK TWENTY-FOUR

And the games broke up, and the people scattered to go away, each man
to his fast-running ship, and the rest of them took thought of their dinner
and of sweet sleep and its enjoyment; only Achilleus
wept still as he remembered his beloved companion, nor did sleep
who subdues all come over him, but he tossed from one side to the other      5
in longing for Patroklos, for his manhood and his great strength
and all the actions he had seen to the end with him, and the hardships
he had suffered; the wars of men; hard crossing of the big waters.
Remembering all these things he let fall the swelling tears, lying
sometimes along his side, sometimes on his back, and now again            10
prone on his face; then he would stand upright, and pace turning
in distraction along the beach of the sea, nor did dawn rising
escape him as she brightened across the sea and the beaches.
Then, when he had yoked running horses under the chariot
he would fasten Hektor behind the chariot, so as to drag him,            15
and draw him three times around the tomb of Menoitios' fallen
son, then rest again in his shelter, and throw down the dead man
and leave him to lie sprawled on his face in the dust. But Apollo
had pity on him, though he was only a dead man, and guarded
the body from all ugliness, and hid all of it under the golden            20
aegis, so that it might not be torn when Achilleus dragged it.

So Achilleus in his standing fury outraged great Hektor.
The blessed gods as they looked upon him were filled with compassion
and kept urging clear-sighted Argeïphontes to steal the body.
There this was pleasing to all the others, but never to Hera            25
nor Poseidon, nor the girl of the gray eyes, who kept still

their hatred for sacred Ilion as in the beginning,
and for Priam and his people, because of the delusion of Paris
who insulted the goddesses when they came to him in his courtyard
and favored her who supplied the lust that led to disaster.
But now, as it was the twelfth dawn after the death of Hektor,
Phoibos Apollo spoke his word out among the immortals:
"You are hard, you gods, and destructive. Now did not Hektor
burn thigh pieces of oxen and unblemished goats in your honor?
Now you cannot bring yourselves to save him, though he is only
a corpse, for his wife to look upon, his child and his mother
and Priam his father, and his people, who presently thereafter
would burn his body in the fire and give him his rites of burial.
No, you gods; your desire is to help this cursed Achilleus
within whose breast there are no feelings of justice, nor can
his mind be bent, but his purposes are fierce, like a lion
who when he has given way to his own great strength and his haughty
spirit, goes among the flocks of men, to devour them.
So Achilleus has destroyed pity, and there is not in him
any shame; which does much harm to men but profits them also.
For a man must some day lose one who was even closer
than this; a brother from the same womb, or a son. And yet
he weeps for him, and sorrows for him, and then it is over,
for the Destinies put in mortal men the heart of endurance.
But this man, now he has torn the heart of life from great Hektor,
ties him to his horses and drags him around his beloved companion's
tomb; and nothing is gained thereby for his good, or his honor.
Great as he is, let him take care not to make us angry;
for see, he does dishonor to the dumb earth in his fury."
Then bitterly Hera of the white arms answered him, saying:
"What you have said could be true, lord of the silver bow, only
if you give Hektor such pride of place as you give to Achilleus.
But Hektor was mortal, and suckled at the breast of a woman,
while Achilleus is the child of a goddess, one whom I myself
nourished and brought up and gave her as bride to her husband
Peleus, one dear to the hearts of the immortals, for you all
went, you gods, to the wedding; and you too feasted among them
and held your lyre, O friend of the evil, faithless forever."
In turn Zeus who gathers the clouds spoke to her in answer:

"Hera, be not utterly angry with the gods, for there shall not          65
be the same pride of place given both. Yet Hektor also
was loved by the gods, best of all the mortals in Ilion.
I loved him too. He never failed of gifts to my liking.
Never yet has my altar gone without fair sacrifice,
the smoke and the savor of it, since that is our portion of honor.          70
The stealing of him we will dismiss, for it is not possible
to take bold Hektor secretly from Achilleus, since always
his mother is near him night and day; but it would be better
if one of the gods would summon Thetis here to my presence
so that I can say a close word to her, and see that Achilleus          75
is given gifts by Priam and gives back the body of Hektor."

He spoke, and Iris storm-footed sprang away with the message,
and at a point between Samos and Imbros of the high cliffs
plunged in the dark water, and the sea crashed moaning about her.
She plummeted to the sea floor like a lead weight which, mounted          80
along the horn of an ox who ranges the fields, goes downward
and takes death with it to the raw-ravening fish. She found Thetis
inside the hollow of her cave, and gathered about her
sat the rest of the sea goddesses, and she in their midst
was mourning the death of her blameless son, who so soon was destined          85
to die in Troy of the rich soil, far from the land of his fathers.
Iris the swift-foot came close beside her and spoke to her:
"Rise, Thetis. Zeus whose purposes are infinite calls you."
In turn Thetis the goddess, the silver-footed, answered her:
"What does he, the great god, want with me? I feel shamefast          90
to mingle with the immortals, and my heart is confused with sorrows.
But I will go. No word shall be in vain, if he says it."
So she spoke, and shining among the divinities took up
her black veil, and there is no darker garment. She went
on her way, and in front of her rapid wind-footed Iris          95
guided her, and the wave of the water opened about them.
They stepped out on the dry land and swept to the sky. There they found
the son of Kronos of the wide brows, and gathered about him
sat all the rest of the gods, the blessed, who live forever.
She sat down beside Zeus father, and Athene made a place for her.          100
Hera put into her hand a beautiful golden goblet

and spoke to her to comfort her, and Thetis accepting drank from it.
The father of gods and men began the discourse among them:
"You have come to Olympos, divine Thetis, for all your sorrow,
with an unforgotten grief in your heart. I myself know this.
But even so I will tell you why I summoned you hither.
For nine days there has risen a quarrel among the immortals
over the body of Hektor, and Achilleus, stormer of cities.
They keep urging clear-sighted Argeïphontes to steal the body,
but I still put upon Achilleus the honor that he has, guarding
your reverence and your love for me into time afterward. Go then
in all speed to the encampment and give to your son this message:
tell him that the gods frown upon him, that beyond all other
immortals I myself am angered that in his heart's madness
he holds Hektor beside the curved ships and did not give him
back. Perhaps in fear of me he will give back Hektor.
Then I will send Iris to Priam of the great heart, with an order
to ransom his dear son, going down to the ships of the Achaians
and bringing gifts to Achilleus which might soften his anger."

He spoke and the goddess silver-foot Thetis did not disobey him
but descended in a flash of speed from the peaks of Olympos
and made her way to the shelter of her son, and there found him
in close lamentation, and his beloved companions about him
were busy at their work and made ready the morning meal, and there
stood a great fleecy sheep being sacrificed in the shelter.
His honored mother came close to him and sat down beside him,
and stroked him with her hand and called him by name and spoke to him:
"My child, how long will you go on eating your heart out in sorrow
and lamentation, and remember neither your food nor going
to bed? It is a good thing even to lie with a woman
in love. For you will not be with me long, but already
death and powerful destiny stand closely above you.
But listen hard to me, for I come from Zeus with a message.
He says that the gods frown upon you, that beyond all other
immortals he himself is angered that in your heart's madness
you hold Hektor beside the curved ships and did not redeem him.
Come, then, give him up and accept ransom for the body."
Then in turn Achilleus of the swift feet answered her:

"So be it. He can bring the ransom and take off the body,
if the Olympian himself so urgently bids it."                                    140

    So, where the ships were drawn together, the son and his mother
conversed at long length in winged words. But the son of Kronos
stirred Iris to go down to sacred Ilion, saying:
"Go forth, Iris the swift, leaving your place on Olympos,
and go to Priam of the great heart within Ilion, tell him               145
to ransom his dear son, going down to the ships of the Achaians
and bringing gifts to Achilleus which might soften his anger:
alone, let no other man of the Trojans go with him, but only
let one elder herald attend him, one who can manage
the mules and the easily running wagon, so he can carry               150
the dead man, whom great Achilleus slew, back to the city.
Let death not be a thought in his heart, let him have no fear;
such an escort shall I send to guide him, Argeïphontes
who shall lead him until he brings him to Achilleus. And after
he has brought him inside the shelter of Achilleus, neither            155
will the man himself kill him, but will hold back all the others,
for he is no witless man nor unwatchful, nor is he wicked,
but will in all kindness spare one who comes to him as a suppliant."
    He spoke, and storm-footed Iris swept away with the message
and came to the house of Priam. There she found outcry and mourning.   160
The sons sitting around their father inside the courtyard
made their clothes sodden with their tears, and among them the old man
sat veiled, beaten into his mantle. Dung lay thick
on the head and neck of the aged man, for he had been rolling
in it, he had gathered and smeared it on with his hands. And his daughters   165
all up and down the house and the wives of his sons were mourning
as they remembered all those men in their numbers and valor
who lay dead, their lives perished at the hands of the Argives.
The messenger of Zeus stood beside Priam and spoke to him
in a small voice, and yet the shivers took hold of his body:          170
"Take heart, Priam, son of Dardanos, do not be frightened.
I come to you not eyeing you with evil intention
but with the purpose of good toward you. I am a messenger
of Zeus, who far away cares much for you and is pitiful.
The Olympian orders you to ransom Hektor the brilliant,               175

to bring gifts to Achilleus which may soften his anger:
alone, let no other man of the Trojans go with you, but only
let one elder herald attend you, one who can manage
the mules and the easily running wagon, so he can carry
180  the dead man, whom great Achilleus slew, back to the city.
Let death not be a thought in your heart, you need have no fear,
such an escort shall go with you to guide you, Argeïphontes
who will lead you till he brings you to Achilleus. And after
he has brought you inside the shelter of Achilleus, neither
185  will the man himself kill you but will hold back all the others;
for he is no witless man nor unwatchful, nor is he wicked
but will in all kindness spare one who comes to him as a suppliant."

So Iris the swift-footed spoke and went away from him.
Thereupon he ordered his sons to make ready the easily rolling
190  mule wagon, and to fasten upon it the carrying basket.
He himself went into the storeroom, which was fragrant
and of cedar, and high-ceilinged, with many bright treasures inside it.
He called out to Hekabē his wife, and said to her:
"Dear wife, a messenger came to me from Zeus on Olympos,
195  that I must go to the ships of the Achaians and ransom my dear son,
bringing gifts to Achilleus which may soften his anger.
Come then, tell me. What does it seem best to your own mind
for me to do? My heart, my strength are terribly urgent
that I go there to the ships within the wide army of the Achaians."
200  So he spoke, and his wife cried out aloud, and answered him:
"Ah me, where has that wisdom gone for which you were famous
in time before, among outlanders and those you rule over?
How can you wish to go alone to the ships of the Achaians
before the eyes of a man who has slaughtered in such numbers
205  such brave sons of yours? The heart in you is iron. For if
he has you within his grasp and lays eyes upon you, that man
who is savage and not to be trusted will not take pity upon you
nor have respect for your rights. Let us sit apart in our palace
now, and weep for Hektor, and the way at the first strong Destiny
210  spun with his life line when he was born, when I gave birth to him,
that the dogs with their shifting feet should feed on him, far from his
parents,

gone down before a stronger man; I wish I could set teeth
in the middle of his liver and eat it. That would be vengeance
for what he did to my son; for he slew him when he was no coward
but standing before the men of Troy and the deep-girdled women           215
of Troy, with no thought in his mind of flight or withdrawal."
    In turn the aged Priam, the godlike, answered her saying:
"Do not hold me back when I would be going, neither yourself be
a bird of bad omen in my palace. You will not persuade me.
If it had been some other who ordered me, one of the mortals,            220
one of those who are soothsayers, or priests, or diviners,
I might have called it a lie and we might rather have rejected it.
But now, for I myself heard the god and looked straight upon her,
I am going, and this word shall not be in vain. If it is my destiny
to die there by the ships of the bronze-armored Achaians,                225
then I wish that. Achilleus can slay me at once, with my own son
caught in my arms, once I have my fill of mourning above him."

    He spoke, and lifted back the fair covering of his clothes-chest
and from inside took out twelve robes surpassingly lovely
and twelve mantles to be worn single, as many blankets,                  230
as many great white cloaks, also the same number of tunics.
He weighed and carried out ten full talents of gold, and brought forth
two shining tripods, and four cauldrons, and brought out a goblet
of surpassing loveliness that the men of Thrace had given him
when he went to them with a message, but now the old man spared not      235
even this in his halls, so much was it his heart's desire
to ransom back his beloved son. But he drove off the Trojans
all from his cloister walks, scolding them with words of revilement:
"Get out, you failures, you disgraces. Have you not also
mourning of your own at home that you come to me with your sorrows?      240
Is it not enough that Zeus, son of Kronos, has given me sorrow
in losing the best of my sons? You also shall be aware of this
since you will be all the easier for the Achaians to slaughter
now he is dead. But, for myself, before my eyes look
upon this city as it is destroyed and its people are slaughtered,        245
my wish is to go sooner down to the house of the death god."
    He spoke, and went after the men with a stick, and they fled outside
before the fury of the old man. He was scolding his children

and cursing Helenos, and Paris, Agathon the brilliant,
250 Pammon and Antiphonos, Polites of the great war cry,
Deïphobos and Hippothoös and proud Dios. There were nine
sons to whom now the old man gave orders and spoke to them roughly:
"Make haste, wicked children, my disgraces. I wish all of you
had been killed beside the running ships in the place of Hektor.
255 Ah me, for my evil destiny. I have had the noblest
of sons in Troy, but I say not one of them is left to me,
Mestor like a god and Troilos whose delight was in horses,
and Hektor, who was a god among men, for he did not seem like
one who was child of a mortal man, but of a god. All these
260 Ares has killed, and all that are left me are the disgraces,
the liars and the dancers, champions of the chorus, the plunderers
of their own people in their land of lambs and kids. Well then,
will you not get my wagon ready and be quick about it,
and put all these things on it, so we can get on with our journey?"
265     So he spoke, and they in terror at the old man's scolding
hauled out the easily running wagon for mules, a fine thing
new-fabricated, and fastened the carrying basket upon it.
They took away from its peg the mule yoke made of boxwood
with its massive knob, well fitted with guiding rings, and brought forth
270 the yoke lashing (together with the yoke itself) of nine cubits
and snugged it well into place upon the smooth-polished wagon-pole
at the foot of the beam, then slipped the ring over the peg, and lashed it
with three turns on either side to the knob, and afterward
fastened it all in order and secured it under a hooked guard.
275 Then they carried out and piled into the smooth-polished mule wagon
all the unnumbered spoils to be given for the head of Hektor,
then yoked the powerful-footed mules who pulled in the harness
and whom the Mysians gave once as glorious presents to Priam;
but for Priam they led under the yoke those horses the old man
280 himself had kept, and cared for them at his polished manger.

Now in the high house the yoking was done for the herald
and Priam, men both with close counsels in their minds. And now came
Hekabē with sorrowful heart and stood close beside them
carrying in her right hand the kind, sweet wine in a golden
285 goblet, so that before they went they might pour a drink-offering.

She stood in front of the horses, called Priam by name and spoke to him:
"Here, pour a libation to Zeus father, and pray you may come back
home again from those who hate you, since it seems the spirit
within you drives you upon the ships, though I would not have it.
Make your prayer then to the dark-misted, the son of Kronos                    290
on Ida, who looks out on all the Troad, and ask him
for a bird of omen, a rapid messenger, which to his own mind
is dearest of all birds and his strength is the biggest, one seen
on the right, so that once your eyes have rested upon him
you can trust in him and go to the ships of the fast-mounted Danaäns.          295
But if Zeus of the wide brows will not grant you his own messenger,
then I, for one, would never urge you on nor advise you
to go to the Argive ships, for all your passion to do it."
    Then in answer to her again spoke Priam the godlike:
"My lady, I will not disregard this wherein you urge me.                        300
It is well to lift hands to Zeus and ask if he will have mercy."
    The old man spoke, and told the housekeeper who attended them
to pour unstained water over his hands. She standing beside them
and serving them held the washing-bowl in her hands, and a pitcher.
He washed his hands and took the cup from his wife. He stood up                305
in the middle of the enclosure, and prayed, and poured the wine out
looking up into the sky, and gave utterance and spoke, saying:
"Father Zeus, watching over us from Ida, most high, most honored:
grant that I come to Achilleus for love and pity; but send me
a bird of omen, a rapid messenger which to your own mind                       310
is dearest of all birds and his strength is biggest, one seen
on the right, so that once my eyes have rested upon him
I may trust in him and go to the ships of the fast-mounted Danaäns."

    So he spoke in prayer, and Zeus of the counsels heard him.
Straightway he sent down the most lordly of birds, an eagle,                   315
the dark one, the marauder, called as well the black eagle.
And as big as is the build of the door to a towering chamber
in the house of a rich man, strongly fitted with bars, of such size
was the spread of his wings on either side. He swept through the city
appearing on the right hand, and the people looking upon him                   320
were uplifted and the hearts made glad in the breasts of all of them.
    Now in urgent haste the old man mounted into his chariot

and drove out through the forecourt and the thundering close. Before him
the mules hauled the wagon on its four wheels, Idaios
325 the sober-minded driving them, and behind him the horses
came on as the old man laid the lash upon them and urged them
rapidly through the town, and all his kinsmen were following
much lamenting, as if he went to his death. When the two men
had gone down through the city, and out, and come to the flat land,
330 the rest of them turned back to go to Ilion, the sons
and the sons-in-law. And Zeus of the wide brows failed not to notice
the two as they showed in the plain. He saw the old man and took pity
upon him, and spoke directly to his beloved son, Hermes:
"Hermes, for to you beyond all other gods it is dearest
335 to be man's companion, and you listen to whom you will, go now
on your way, and so guide Priam inside the hollow ships
of the Achaians, that no man shall see him, none be aware of him,
of the other Danaäns, till he has come to the son of Peleus."

He spoke, nor disobeyed him the courier, Argeïphontes.
340 Immediately he bound upon his feet the fair sandals
golden and immortal, that carried him over the water
as over the dry land of the main abreast of the wind's blast.
He caught up the staff, with which he mazes the eyes of those mortals
whose eyes he would maze, or wakes again the sleepers. Holding
345 this in his hands, strong Argeïphontes winged his way onward
until he came suddenly to Troy and the Hellespont, and there
walked on, and there took the likeness of a young man, a noble,
with beard new grown, which is the most graceful time of young manhood.

Now when the two had driven past the great tomb of Ilos
350 they stayed their mules and horses to water them in the river,
for by this time darkness had descended on the land; and the herald
made out Hermes, who was coming toward them at a short distance.
He lifted his voice and spoke aloud to Priam: "Take thought,
son of Dardanos. Here is work for a mind that is careful.
355 I see a man; I think he will presently tear us to pieces.
Come then, let us run away with our horses, or if not, then
clasp his knees and entreat him to have mercy upon us."

So he spoke, and the old man's mind was confused, he was badly
frightened, and the hairs stood up all over his gnarled body

and he stood staring, but the kindly god himself coming closer                    360
took the old man's hand, and spoke to him and asked him a question:
"Where, my father, are you thus guiding your mules and horses
through the immortal night while other mortals are sleeping?
Have you no fear of the Achaians whose wind is fury,
who hate you, who are your enemies, and are near? For if one                      365
of these were to see you, how you are conveying so many
treasures through the swift black night, what then could you think of?
You are not young yourself, and he who attends you is aged
for beating off any man who might pick a quarrel with you.
But I will do you no harm myself, I will even keep off                            370
another who would. You seem to me like a beloved father."
     In answer to him again spoke aged Priam the godlike:
"Yes, in truth, dear child, all this is much as you tell me;
yet still there is some god who has held his hand above me,
who sent such a wayfarer as you to meet me, an omen                               375
of good, for such you are by your form, your admired beauty
and the wisdom in your mind. Your parents are fortunate in you."
     Then in turn answered him the courier Argeïphontes:
"Yes, old sir, all this that you said is fair and orderly.
But come, tell me this thing and recite it to me accurately.                      380
Can it be you convey these treasures in all their numbers and beauty
to outland men, so that they can be still kept safe for you?
Or are all of you by now abandoning sacred Ilion
in fear, such a one was he who died, the best man among you,
your son; who was never wanting when you fought against the Achaians."            385
     In answer to him again spoke aged Priam the godlike:
"But who are you, O best of men, and who are your parents?
Since you spoke of my ill-starred son's death, and with honor."
     Then in turn answered him the courier Argeïphontes:
"You try me out, aged sir. You ask me of glorious Hektor                          390
whom many a time my eyes have seen in the fighting where men win
glory, as also on that time when he drove back the Argives
on their ships and kept killing them with the stroke of the sharp bronze,
and we stood by and wondered at him; for then Achilleus
would not let us fight by reason of his anger at Agamemnon.                       395
For I am Achilleus' henchman, and the same strong-wrought vessel
brought us here; and I am a Myrmidon, and my father

is Polyktor; a man of substance, but aged, as you are.
He has six sons beside, and I am the seventh, and I shook
400 lots with the others, and it was my lot to come on this venture.
But now I have come to the plain away from the ships, for at daybreak
the glancing-eyed Achaians will do battle around the city.
They chafe from sitting here too long, nor have the Achaians'
kings the strength to hold them back as they break for the fighting."
405     In answer to him again spoke aged Priam the godlike:
"If then you are henchman to Peleïd Achilleus,
come, tell me the entire truth, and whether my son lies
still beside the ships, or whether by now he has been hewn
limb from limb and thrown before the dogs by Achilleus."
410     Then in turn answered him the courier Argeïphontes:
"Aged sir, neither have any dogs eaten him, nor have
the birds, but he lies yet beside the ship of Achilleus
at the shelters, and as he was; now here is the twelfth dawn
he has lain there, nor does his flesh decay, nor do worms feed
415 on him, they who devour men who have fallen in battle.
It is true, Achilleus drags him at random around his beloved
companion's tomb, as dawn on dawn appears, yet he cannot
mutilate him; you yourself can see when you go there
how fresh with dew he lies, and the blood is all washed from him,
420 nor is there any corruption, and all the wounds have been closed up
where he was struck, since many drove the bronze in his body.
So it is that the blessed immortals care for your son, though
he is nothing but a dead man; because in their hearts they loved him."
He spoke, and the old man was made joyful and answered him, saying:
425 "My child, surely it is good to give the immortals
their due gifts; because my own son, if ever I had one,
never forgot in his halls the gods who live on Olympos.
Therefore they remembered him even in death's stage. Come, then,
accept at my hands this beautiful drinking-cup, and give me
430 protection for my body, and with the gods' grace be my escort
until I make my way to the shelter of the son of Peleus."
In turn answered him the courier Argeïphontes:
"You try me out, aged sir, for I am young, but you will not
persuade me, telling me to accept your gifts when Achilleus
435 does not know. I fear him at heart and have too much reverence

to rob him. Such a thing might be to my sorrow hereafter.
But I would be your escort and take good care of you, even
till I came to glorious Argos in a fast ship or following
on foot, and none would fight you because he despised your escort."

The kind god spoke, and sprang up behind the horses and into          440
the chariot, and rapidly caught in his hands the lash and the guide reins,
and breathed great strength into the mules and horses. Now after
they had got to the fortifications about the ships, and the ditch, there
were sentries, who had just begun to make ready their dinner,
but about these the courier Argeïphontes drifted                       445
sleep, on all, and quickly opened the gate, and shoved back
the door-bars, and brought in Priam and the glorious gifts on the wagon.
But when they had got to the shelter of Peleus' son: a towering
shelter the Myrmidons had built for their king, hewing
the timbers of pine, and they made a roof of thatch above it           450
shaggy with grass that they had gathered out of the meadows;
and around it made a great courtyard for their king, with hedgepoles
set close together; the gate was secured by a single door-piece
of pine, and three Achaians could ram it home in its socket
and three could pull back and open the huge door-bar; three other      455
Achaians, that is, but Achilleus all by himself could close it.
At this time Hermes, the kind god, opened the gate for the old man
and brought in the glorious gifts for Peleus' son, the swift-footed,
and dismounted to the ground from behind the horses, and spoke forth:
"Aged sir, I who came to you am a god immortal,                        460
Hermes. My father sent me down to guide and go with you.
But now I am going back again, and I will not go in
before the eyes of Achilleus, for it would make others angry
for an immortal god so to face mortal men with favor.
But go you in yourself and clasp the knees of Peleion                  465
and entreat him in the name of his father, the name of his mother
of the lovely hair, and his child, and so move the spirit within him."
So Hermes spoke, and went away to the height of Olympos,
but Priam vaulted down to the ground from behind the horses
and left Idaios where he was, for he stayed behind, holding            470
in hand the horses and mules. The old man made straight for the dwelling
where Achilleus the beloved of Zeus was sitting. He found him

inside, and his companions were sitting apart, as two only,
Automedon the hero and Alkimos, scion of Ares,
475 were busy beside him. He had just now got through with his dinner,
with eating and drinking, and the table still stood by. Tall Priam
came in unseen by the other men and stood close beside him
and caught the knees of Achilleus in his arms, and kissed the hands
that were dangerous and manslaughtering and had killed so many
480 of his sons. As when dense disaster closes on one who has murdered
a man in his own land, and he comes to the country of others,
to a man of substance, and wonder seizes on those who behold him,
so Achilleus wondered as he looked on Priam, a godlike
man, and the rest of them wondered also, and looked at each other.
485 But now Priam spoke to him in the words of a suppliant:
"Achilleus like the gods, remember your father, one who
is of years like mine, and on the door-sill of sorrowful old age.
And they who dwell nearby encompass him and afflict him,
nor is there any to defend him against the wrath, the destruction.
490 Yet surely he, when he hears of you and that you are still living,
is gladdened within his heart and all his days he is hopeful
that he will see his beloved son come home from the Troad.
But for me, my destiny was evil. I have had the noblest
of sons in Troy, but I say not one of them is left to me.
495 Fifty were my sons, when the sons of the Achaians came here.
Nineteen were born to me from the womb of a single mother,
and other women bore the rest in my palace; and of these
violent Ares broke the strength in the knees of most of them,
but one was left me who guarded my city and people, that one
500 you killed a few days since as he fought in defense of his country,
Hektor; for whose sake I come now to the ships of the Achaians
to win him back from you, and I bring you gifts beyond number.
Honor then the gods, Achilleus, and take pity upon me
remembering your father, yet I am still more pitiful;
505 I have gone through what no other mortal on earth has gone through;
I put my lips to the hands of the man who has killed my children."

So he spoke, and stirred in the other a passion of grieving
for his own father. He took the old man's hand and pushed him
gently away, and the two remembered, as Priam sat huddled
510 at the feet of Achilleus and wept close for manslaughtering Hektor

and Achilleus wept now for his own father, now again
for Patroklos. The sound of their mourning moved in the house. Then
when great Achilleus had taken full satisfaction in sorrow
and the passion for it had gone from his mind and body, thereafter
he rose from his chair, and took the old man by the hand, and set him          515
on his feet again, in pity for the gray head and the gray beard,
and spoke to him and addressed him in winged words: "Ah, unlucky,
surely you have had much evil to endure in your spirit.
How could you dare to come alone to the ships of the Achaians
and before my eyes, when I am one who have killed in such numbers          520
such brave sons of yours? The heart in you is iron. Come, then,
and sit down upon this chair, and you and I will even let
our sorrows lie still in the heart for all our grieving. There is not
any advantage to be won from grim lamentation.
Such is the way the gods spun life for unfortunate mortals,          525
that we live in unhappiness, but the gods themselves have no sorrows.
There are two urns that stand on the door-sill of Zeus. They are unlike
for the gifts they bestow: an urn of evils, an urn of blessings.
If Zeus who delights in thunder mingles these and bestows them
on man, he shifts, and moves now in evil, again in good fortune.          530
But when Zeus bestows from the urn of sorrows, he makes a failure
of man, and the evil hunger drives him over the shining
earth, and he wanders respected neither of gods nor mortals.
Such were the shining gifts given by the gods to Peleus
from his birth, who outshone all men beside for his riches          535
and pride of possession, and was lord over the Myrmidons. Thereto
the gods bestowed an immortal wife on him, who was mortal.
But even on him the god piled evil also. There was not
any generation of strong sons born to him in his great house
but a single all-untimely child he had, and I give him          540
no care as he grows old, since far from the land of my fathers
I sit here in Troy, and bring nothing but sorrow to you and your children.
And you, old sir, we are told you prospered once; for as much
as Lesbos, Makar's hold, confines to the north above it
and Phrygia from the north confines, and enormous Hellespont,          545
of these, old sir, you were lord once in your wealth and your children.
But now the Uranian gods brought us, an affliction upon you,
forever there is fighting about your city, and men killed.

But bear up, nor mourn endlessly in your heart, for there is not
550   anything to be gained from grief for your son; you will never
bring him back; sooner you must go through yet another sorrow."
        In answer to him again spoke aged Priam the godlike:
"Do not, beloved of Zeus, make me sit on a chair while Hektor
lies yet forlorn among the shelters; rather with all speed
555   give him back, so my eyes may behold him, and accept the ransom
we bring you, which is great. You may have joy of it, and go back
to the land of your own fathers, since once you have permitted me
to go on living myself and continue to look on the sunlight."
        Then looking darkly at him spoke swift-footed Achilleus:
560   "No longer stir me up, old sir. I myself am minded
to give Hektor back to you. A messenger came to me from Zeus,
my mother, she who bore me, the daughter of the sea's ancient.
I know you, Priam, in my heart, and it does not escape me
that some god led you to the running ships of the Achaians.
565   For no mortal would dare come to our encampment, not even
one strong in youth. He could not get by the pickets, he could not
lightly unbar the bolt that secures our gateway. Therefore
you must not further make my spirit move in my sorrows,
for fear, old sir, I might not let you alone in my shelter,
570   suppliant as you are; and be guilty before the god's orders."

        He spoke, and the old man was frightened and did as he told him.
The son of Peleus bounded to the door of the house like a lion,
nor went alone, but the two henchmen followed attending,
the hero Automedon and Alkimos, those whom Achilleus
575   honored beyond all companions after Patroklos dead. These two
now set free from under the yoke the mules and the horses,
and led inside the herald, the old king's crier, and gave him
a chair to sit in, then from the smooth-polished mule wagon
lifted out the innumerable spoils for the head of Hektor,
580   but left inside it two great cloaks and a finespun tunic
to shroud the corpse in when they carried him home. Then Achilleus
called out to his serving-maids to wash the body and anoint it
all over; but take it first aside, since otherwise Priam
might see his son and in the heart's sorrow not hold in his anger

at the sight, and the deep heart in Achilleus be shaken to anger;                585
that he might not kill Priam and be guilty before the god's orders.
Then when the serving-maids had washed the corpse and anointed it
with olive oil, they threw a fair great cloak and a tunic
about him, and Achilleus himself lifted him and laid him
on a litter, and his friends helped him lift it to the smooth-polished             590
mule wagon. He groaned then, and called by name on his beloved
        companion:
"Be not angry with me, Patroklos, if you discover,
though you be in the house of Hades, that I gave back great Hektor
to his loved father, for the ransom he gave me was not unworthy.
I will give you your share of the spoils, as much as is fitting."                   595
        So spoke great Achilleus and went back into the shelter
and sat down on the elaborate couch from which he had risen,
against the inward wall, and now spoke his word to Priam:
"Your son is given back to you, aged sir, as you asked it.
He lies on a bier. When dawn shows you yourself shall see him                       600
as you take him away. Now you and I must remember our supper.
For even Niobē, she of the lovely tresses, remembered
to eat, whose twelve children were destroyed in her palace,
six daughters, and six sons in the pride of their youth, whom Apollo
killed with arrows from his silver bow, being angered                              605
with Niobē, and shaft-showering Artemis killed the daughters;
because Niobē likened herself to Leto of the fair coloring
and said Leto had borne only two, she herself had borne many;
but the two, though they were only two, destroyed all those others.
Nine days long they lay in their blood, nor was there anyone                        610
to bury them, for the son of Kronos made stones out of
the people; but on the tenth day the Uranian gods buried them.
But she remembered to eat when she was worn out with weeping.
And now somewhere among the rocks, in the lonely mountains,
in Sipylos, where they say is the resting place of the goddesses                    615
who are nymphs, and dance beside the waters of Acheloios,
there, stone still, she broods on the sorrows that the gods gave her.
Come then, we also, aged magnificent sir, must remember
to eat, and afterward you may take your beloved son back
to Ilion, and mourn for him; and he will be much lamented."                         620

So spoke fleet Achilleus and sprang to his feet and slaughtered
a gleaming sheep, and his friends skinned it and butchered it fairly,
and cut up the meat expertly into small pieces, and spitted them,
and roasted all carefully and took off the pieces.
625  Automedon took the bread and set it out on the table
in fair baskets, while Achilleus served the meats. And thereon
they put their hands to the good things that lay ready before them.
But when they had put aside their desire for eating and drinking,
Priam, son of Dardanos, gazed upon Achilleus, wondering
630  at his size and beauty, for he seemed like an outright vision
of gods. Achilleus in turn gazed on Dardanian Priam
and wondered, as he saw his brave looks and listened to him talking.
But when they had taken their fill of gazing one on the other,
first of the two to speak was the aged man, Priam the godlike:
635  "Give me, beloved of Zeus, a place to sleep presently, so that
we may even go to bed and take the pleasure of sweet sleep.
For my eyes have not closed underneath my lids since that time
when my son lost his life beneath your hands, but always
I have been grieving and brooding over my numberless sorrows
640  and wallowed in the muck about my courtyard's enclosure.
Now I have tasted food again and have let the gleaming
wine go down my throat. Before, I had tasted nothing."
    He spoke, and Achilleus ordered his serving-maids and companions
to make a bed in the porch's shelter and to lay upon it
645  fine underbedding of purple, and spread blankets above it
and fleecy robes to be an over-all covering. The maid-servants
went forth from the main house, and in their hands held torches,
and set to work, and presently had two beds made. Achilleus
of the swift feet now looked at Priam and said, sarcastic:
650  "Sleep outside, aged sir and good friend, for fear some Achaian
might come in here on a matter of counsel, since they keep coming
and sitting by me and making plans; as they are supposed to.
But if one of these come through the fleeting black night should notice you,
he would go straight and tell Agamemnon, shepherd of the people,
655  and there would be delay in the ransoming of the body.
But come, tell me this and count off for me exactly
how many days you intend for the burial of great Hektor.
Tell me, so I myself shall stay still and hold back the people."

In answer to him again spoke aged Priam the godlike:
"If you are willing that we accomplish a complete funeral     660
for great Hektor, this, Achilleus, is what you could do and give
me pleasure. For you know surely how we are penned in our city,
and wood is far to bring in from the hills, and the Trojans are frightened
badly. Nine days we would keep him in our palace and mourn him,
and bury him on the tenth day, and the people feast by him,     665
and on the eleventh day we would make the grave-barrow for him,
and on the twelfth day fight again; if so we must do."
Then in turn swift-footed brilliant Achilleus answered him:
"Then all this, aged Priam, shall be done as you ask it.
I will hold off our attack for as much time as you bid me."     670
So he spoke, and took the aged king by the right hand
at the wrist, so that his heart might have no fear. Then these two,
Priam and the herald who were both men of close counsel,
slept in the place outside the house, in the porch's shelter;
but Achilleus slept in the inward corner of the strong-built shelter,     675
and at his side lay Briseis of the fair coloring.

Now the rest of the gods and men who were lords of chariots
slept nightlong, with the easy bondage of slumber upon them,
only sleep had not caught Hermes the kind god, who pondered
now in his heart the problem of how to escort King Priam     680
from the ships and not be seen by the devoted gate-wardens.
He stood above his head and spoke a word to him, saying:
"Aged sir, you can have no thought of evil from the way
you sleep still among your enemies now Achilleus has left you
unharmed. You have ransomed now your dear son and given much for him.     685
But the sons you left behind would give three times as much ransom
for you, who are alive, were Atreus' son Agamemnon
to recognize you, and all the other Achaians learn of you."
He spoke, and the old man was afraid, and wakened his herald,
and lightly Hermes harnessed for them the mules and the horses     690
and himself drove them through the encampment. And no man knew of
     them.
But when they came to the crossing-place of the fair-running river,
of whirling Xanthos, a stream whose father was Zeus the immortal,
there Hermes left them and went away to the height of Olympos,

695  and dawn, she of the yellow robe, scattered over all earth,
and they drove their horses on to the city with lamentation
and clamor, while the mules drew the body. Nor was any other
aware of them at the first, no man, no fair-girdled woman,
only Kassandra, a girl like Aphrodite the golden,
700  who had gone up to the height of the Pergamos. She saw
her dear father standing in the chariot, his herald and crier
with him. She saw Hektor drawn by the mules on a litter.
She cried out then in sorrow and spoke to the entire city:
"Come, men of Troy and Trojan women; look upon Hektor
705  if ever before you were joyful when you saw him come back living
from battle; for he was a great joy to his city, and all his people."

She spoke, and there was no man left there in all the city
nor woman, but all were held in sorrow passing endurance.
They met Priam beside the gates as he brought the dead in.
710  First among them were Hektor's wife and his honored mother
who tore their hair, and ran up beside the smooth-rolling wagon,
and touched his head. And the multitude, wailing, stood there about them.
And now and there in front of the gates they would have lamented
all day till the sun went down and let fall their tears for Hektor,
715  except that the old man spoke from the chariot to his people:
"Give me way to get through with my mules; then afterward
you may sate yourselves with mourning, when I have him inside the palace."

So he spoke, and they stood apart and made way for the wagon.
And when they had brought him inside the renowned house, they laid him
720  then on a carved bed, and seated beside him the singers
who were to lead the melody in the dirge, and the singers
chanted the song of sorrow, and the women were mourning beside them.
Andromachē of the white arms led the lamentation
of the women, and held in her arms the head of manslaughtering Hektor:
725  "My husband, you were lost young from life, and have left me
a widow in your house, and the boy is only a baby
who was born to you and me, the unhappy. I think he will never
come of age, for before then head to heel this city
will be sacked, for you, its defender, are gone, you who guarded
730  the city, and the grave wives, and the innocent children,
wives who before long must go away in the hollow ships,

and among them I shall also go, and you, my child, follow
where I go, and there do much hard work that is unworthy
of you, drudgery for a hard master; or else some Achaian
will take you by hand and hurl you from the tower into horrible          735
death, in anger because Hektor once killed his brother,
or his father, or his son; there were so many Achaians
whose teeth bit the vast earth, beaten down by the hands of Hektor.
Your father was no merciful man in the horror of battle.
Therefore your people are grieving for you all through their city,       740
Hektor, and you left for your parents mourning and sorrow
beyond words, but for me passing all others is left the bitterness
and the pain, for you did not die in bed, and stretch your arms to me,
nor tell me some last intimate word that I could remember
always, all the nights and days of my weeping for you."                  745

    So she spoke in tears, and the women were mourning about her.
Now Hekabē led out the thronging chant of their sorrow:
"Hektor, of all my sons the dearest by far to my spirit;
while you still lived for me you were dear to the gods, and even
in the stage of death they cared about you still. There were others     750
of my sons whom at times swift-footed Achilleus captured,
and he would sell them as slaves far across the unresting salt water
into Samos, and Imbros, and Lemnos in the gloom of the mists. You,
when he had taken your life with the thin edge of the bronze sword,
he dragged again and again around his beloved companion's              755
tomb, Patroklos', whom you killed, but even so did not
bring him back to life. Now you lie in the palace, handsome
and fresh with dew, in the likeness of one whom he of the silver
bow, Apollo, has attacked and killed with his gentle arrows."

    So she spoke, in tears, and wakened the endless mourning.            760
Third and last Helen led the song of sorrow among them:
"Hektor, of all my lord's brothers dearest by far to my spirit:
my husband is Alexandros, like an immortal, who brought me
here to Troy; and I should have died before I came with him;
and here now is the twentieth year upon me since I came                 765
from the place where I was, forsaking the land of my fathers. In this time
I have never heard a harsh saying from you, nor an insult.

No, but when another, one of my lord's brothers or sisters, a fair-robed
wife of some brother, would say a harsh word to me in the palace,
770   or my lord's mother—but his father was gentle always, a father
indeed—then you would speak and put them off and restrain them
by your own gentleness of heart and your gentle words. Therefore
I mourn for you in sorrow of heart and mourn myself also
and my ill luck. There was no other in all the wide Troad
775   who was kind to me, and my friend; all others shrank when they saw me."
So she spoke in tears, and the vast populace grieved with her.
Now Priam the aged king spoke forth his word to his people:
"Now, men of Troy, bring timber into the city, and let not
your hearts fear a close ambush of the Argives. Achilleus
780   promised me, as he sent me on my way from the black ships,
that none should do us injury until the twelfth dawn comes."
He spoke, and they harnessed to the wagons their mules and their oxen
and presently were gathered in front of the city. Nine days
they spent bringing in an endless supply of timber. But when
785   the tenth dawn had shone forth with her light upon mortals,
they carried out bold Hektor, weeping, and set the body
aloft a towering pyre for burning. And set fire to it.

But when the young dawn showed again with her rosy fingers,
the people gathered around the pyre of illustrious Hektor.
790   But when all were gathered to one place and assembled together,
first with gleaming wine they put out the pyre that was burning,
all where the fury of the fire still was in force, and thereafter
the brothers and companions of Hektor gathered the white bones
up, mourning, as the tears swelled and ran down their cheeks. Then
795   they laid what they had gathered up in a golden casket
and wrapped this about with soft robes of purple, and presently
put it away in the hollow of the grave, and over it
piled huge stones laid close together. Lightly and quickly
they piled up the grave-barrow, and on all sides were set watchmen
800   for fear the strong-greaved Achaians might too soon set upon them.
They piled up the grave-barrow and went away, and thereafter
assembled in a fair gathering and held a glorious
feast within the house of Priam, king under God's hand.
Such was their burial of Hektor, breaker of horses.

# Notes to the *Iliad*

These notes, while not comprehensive, seek to illuminate points of mythology, social structure, material culture, and poetic convention that might lead readers to a fuller appreciation of the epic. The style and design of the poem as a whole have always been kept in mind. Thus, some passages that might have been clear enough without further annotation serve as prompts to the discussion of broader compositional trends. Brief identifications of many persons and places have been left to the glossary reprinted from the original edition. The line numbers match Lattimore's, which in almost all cases exactly correspond to the numbering of verses in the Oxford Classical Text of D. B. Monro and T. W. Allen (3rd edition, 1919).

The notes (as in the introduction) draw on the latest Homeric scholarship, to which the bibliography records my debt. I have relied heavily on the most recent full English commentary (Kirk et al., *The Iliad: A Commentary* [1985]), and to a lesser extent on the older notes by Leaf in *A Companion to the Iliad for English Readers* (1892), and in his *The Iliad* (1900). While making a conscious effort to avoid overlap with the existing companions by Willcock (*A Companion to the Iliad* [1976]), Postlethwaite (*Homer's Iliad* [2000]), and Jones (*Homer's "Iliad"* [2003]), and the notes by the late Bernard Knox to the Fagles translation (*Homer: The Iliad* [1990]), I have inevitably commented on many of the same passages, in what I hope is a complementary fashion. On several points, the ongoing German commentary by Latacz and others has been a help, as have commentaries on individual books (especially Macleod (*Homer: Iliad, Book XXIV* [1982]) and Chantraine and Goube (*Iliade: Chant XXIII* [1964]).

Numbers pinpoint the starting line of the scene to be elucidated. Citations of more distant *Iliad* passages are by book and line number only; those to book and lines of the *Odyssey* are headed "*Od.*"

## BOOK ONE

1    The opening word of the *Iliad*, "anger" (*mênis*), announces the theme of the poem. The word designates not just ordinary anger but the particularly destructive wrath possessed by a god: Achilleus is the only mortal whose emotion is so described.

The Muse is asked to "sing" the story, a reminder both that long poems could be accompanied by music, and that the Muses (daughters of Memory) are the ultimate preservers of traditional lore and wisdom. Poets are their mouthpieces. This type of invocation became standard for epics and hymns to gods in ancient Greek and in later literary imitations.

4   Heroes. Any warrior in Homeric epic can be designated with this word, not just outstanding protagonists of a story, since all are thought to be far beyond average in their abilities.

5   Will of Zeus. Two possible references: before the events of the *Iliad*, Zeus had promised Earth (Gaia) to relieve the oppressive weight of people on her surface, and allowed the Trojan War to lessen the population (as the now lost epic *Cypria* narrated). Within the time frame of the *Iliad*, the fulfillment of Zeus' will can refer to the carrying out of his plan (at Thetis' request) to honor Achilleus by letting his comrades suffer in his absence.

14   Heralds, suppliants, and kings all carry the *skêptron* ("scepter" or "staff") as a token of their special status. The fillets, or ribbons, were pieces of wool attached as a further marker of protection by the god: participants in sacrifice or ritual meals also wore them.

17   Greaves are shin protectors. The consistent use of the epithet "strong-greaved" for Greek warriors may refer to a distinctive form of armor they possessed, although in general both sides in the war appear similarly equipped.

26   A first glimpse of Agamemnon's character: harsh, arrogant, and selfish. Throughout the poem, character is developed largely through the speeches made by various figures.

44   The typical scene (a mortal prays and a god answers) is made distinctive by the extended description of the god's arrival, "as night comes down," combining sound (the clanging of his arrows on his quiver) and sight (the blackness of night's descent parallel to Apollo's coming down from Olympos, the gods' mountain home).

53   A common pattern: nine days or years represent an unmarked stretch of time that is then contrasted with and fulfilled by a significant tenth day or year. The ten years of the war itself fit this template.

59   In contrast to Agamemnon, Achilleus' first words are reasonable and calm, seeking an explanation for events. Significantly, he is the first among the warriors and their leaders to question the status quo and seek to improve conditions.

62   The division of work among religious specialists is noteworthy. Priests were closely associated with sacrifice (but not absolutely needed for carrying it out, since chieftains like Nestor and Agamemnon can do so on their own). Dream interpreters are less commonly mentioned, although we know of their existence throughout antiquity. Seers (like Kalchas in the *Iliad*) provide useful advice on everything from religious obligations to navigation and morality (cf. Theoklymenos in *Odyssey* 17). It is another deft touch of characterization that Achilleus instantly recognizes that any one of these specialists might be called for.

81   The faulty king is literally dyspeptic, unable to "swallow down" his anger. Later Greek literature characterizes hubristic transgressors as those unable to

"keep down" prosperity (Pindar, Solon), as if physical and ethical systems are interconnected.

91 "Greatest of all the Achaians" is a formulaic phrase that properly designates Achilleus, but is applied to various other Greeks while he is out of the battle. Its employment for Agamemnon sounds ironic in Achilleus' speech.

106 The failure of Kalchas to ever foretell good may allude to the sacrifice of Agamemnon's daughter Iphigeneia, which, according to other sources, the seer is said to have advised as the will of Artemis.

118 Another ironic touch of characterization. No sooner does Agamemnon express his desire to keep the troops safe than he makes a move to grab another's prize of honor: precisely the action that will lead to the destruction of his warriors.

125 Achilleus mentions carrying out twenty-three earlier raids (9.328–29). Andromachē tells Hektor about one of these, in which Achilleus killed her father (6.414–16); the same raid yielded the war prize Chryseis (1.365–69).

138 The three singled out—Aias, Odysseus, Achilleus—are those whose ships, drawn up onshore, mark the extreme ends and middle of the Greek camp (11.5–9).

154 A list of the most common causes for counterraiding: theft of cattle or horses, and destruction of crops. Military action to recover a wife appears less glorious and less common. The epithet Achilleus hurls at Agamemnon (dog-faced) is the same that Helen applies to herself (3.180), perhaps significantly as the topic here is her husband and brother-in-law.

186 The core of the dispute—might versus authority—is put by Agamemnon with two comparative adjectives: Achilleus may be *karteros* ("mightier") but that is almost accidental, the gift of an unnamed god (1.177), whereas he himself is more powerful (*pherteros*), which, he implies, results from being honored by Zeus (1.175). Angered by Achilleus' implication that a single warrior should profit as much as the expedition's leader, Agamemnon seizes the opportunity to make good on his earlier threat (1.137–39) and thus scare off other potential competitors for power.

188 A type-scene of decision making. Cf. the same phrase used to describe Diomedes hesitating about continuing the assault at 8.167. In Homeric psychology heroic action involves such internal contests; poetically, such moments foreshadow a course of action while holding out the possibility of alternative plots.

203 The Greek word translated by "outrageousness" is *hubris*, an arrogant abuse of power stemming from excessive pride and self-centeredness, often in defiance of divine will.

234 Achilleus' description of the royal scepter as dead wood contrasted with its original flourishing state is clearly a negative characterization of Agamemnon's regime. He identifies himself as "best of the Achaians" at 244 (contrast 1.91).

247 Nestor's long speeches are evidence of his honeyed, fluent rhetoric, not an old man's talkativeness. His advice is taken seriously at all times (although Agamemnon begins to resist it here). The reminiscences of the ancient warrior of Pylos (a place famous in Mykenaian times) provide a glimpse into the world of a generation or two before the Trojan War. The battle recalled here was between the Lapiths, a tribe of men in Thessaly, and their neighbors the Centaurs, half men, half horses living around Mount Pelion. Theseus, king of Athens, intervened to aid his friend

Peirithoös, whose wedding to Hippodameia was overrun by these lascivious beast-men. The couple's son Polypoites is a chieftain of the Lapiths at Troy (2.738–44).

307 Patroklos, companion of Achilleus, will play a major role in the unfolding drama.

313 The purification is to remove the pollution (*miasma*) caused by angering Apollo in dishonoring his priest Chryses. The subsequent "hecatomb" (literally, a sacrifice of one hundred cows—though here it comprises goats and bulls) is meant to make amends with the god.

331 Achilleus as head of his Myrmidon troops can be called "king," like Agamemnon, but the latter functions as an overlord, a first among equals for the Greek leaders, each of whom possesses a sort of localized royalty.

349 It was not unmanly for heroes to weep under pressures of grief and loss. The poet does not prolong the scene of departing with a depiction of emotional states, other than to say that Briseis went unwillingly. Achilleus restrains his tears until he finds solitude at the shore.

352 Achilleus seems to think that a connection with divinity (through his goddess mother) should ensure being honored by Zeus (the sort of honor Agamemnon claims at 1.175). If emphasis is placed on the adjective "with a short life," his logic is different: since he is fated to die young, he should have god-given honor. In the latter case, he alludes to the prophecy once given him by Thetis and referred to explicitly only at 9.410–16 (that he can choose a short life with glory or a long life without it).

395 Just as mortals ask return favors from a god by recalling the sacrifices they have made (compare Chryses' prayer at 1.40–42), so Thetis can request aid for her son (Achilleus imagines) because she once helped Zeus in a dispute with his fellow Olympian gods. The hundred-handed Briareus is a primeval creature, son of Earth (Gaia) and Sky (Ouranos), who in Hesiod's *Theogony* is said to have aided Zeus in his struggles against an older divine generation, the Titans. Other sources make him a son-in-law of Poseidon or son of the sea, perhaps to explain his association with the sea nymph Thetis.

407 Clasping the knees is the regular gesture made by one supplicating a person in a more powerful position.

472 Poetry and song have a ritual function: the *paian*, a group song dedicated to Apollo, and performed usually in thanksgiving or supplication, is depicted as pleasing the god as though he were an audience member, much as a sacrifice does.

516 Thetis brings up the topic of honor that has marked the quarrel between her son and Agamemnon, subtly implying that she has the status and power to cause similar strife if her wishes are not satisfied.

541 The poet depicts a vividly real divine family by such touches, giving the impression of long-standing personal relations among the gods.

565 Although gods cannot die, the threat of violent treatment keeps them under control. In structure and language, the scene mirrors Agamemnon's threats against Chryses at the opening of this book. In addition, the mediation attempted by Hephaistos recalls Nestor's advice during the quarrel between Agamemnon and Achilleus (1.248–84). This squabble at a divine feast makes a deliberate ironic contrast with the mortal struggles earlier, as does the calm ending of the episode.

586 Several times characters in the *Iliad* encourage others by reference to previous events that have a mythical status (e.g., 5.381–404; 9.524–99; 24.602–20). Hephaistos makes his own experiences into this kind of paradigmatic myth. Lemnos, a volcanic island in the northeastern Aegean not far from Troy, was associated with fire and the forges of the smith-god (although it has never possessed an active volcano, unlike other spots where Hephaistos was worshiped). The Sintians are an otherwise unattested people whose name derives from the verb "to harm." Hephaistos tells a quite different story at 18.395–405, where it is Hera herself who threw him out of Olympos, ashamed of his lameness. Thetis at that time rescued and for nine years sheltered him—perhaps a cause for Hera's apparent antagonism toward the nymph now.

BOOK TWO

6 "Evil" Dream. The adjective literally means "causing destruction," related to a verb just used ("destroy") in lines above. Like Sleep and Death, Dream is a half-personified abstraction, and along with them is one of the many children of Night, including Nemesis, Old Age, Strife, Deception, and the Fates, according to Hesiod's *Theogony* (211–25).

33 Dream relates the message of Zeus verbatim, but cannot resist adding his own touch, telling Agamemnon not to forget what he has just heard. The poet elsewhere plays with such minor variations on repeated speeches (as in Odysseus' speech to Achilleus in book 9).

38 Foreshadowing by the poet about facts someone in the story does not yet know is frequently accompanied by the remark that the character is a "fool" (*nêpios*).

48 Dawn (Êôs) is a goddess living at the edge of the world (where myths relate that she keeps her mortal lover Tithonos). The rare and beautiful expression "message of light" draws a contrast with the loud noise of the camp as heralds summon the troops.

53 The council of elders always meets to discuss important matters before they are announced to the general assembly of fighting men, a system that is echoed in the later Athenian democratic institutions of small executive council (*boulê*—the same word used here) and legislative assembly (*ekklêsia*).

70 Agamemnon produces his own twist on the message of Dream, omitting the final advice to not forget (clearly he has not). He also adds to the command to arm the troops a quite odd verbal "testing," which he claims is "customary" (*themis*), in which he will suggest the opposite of what he really wants: that everyone take ship for home. As if already unsure whether this test will backfire (as it eventually does) Agamemnon advises his fellow commanders to stand at the ready with encouraging words.

80 Nestor's seconding of the advice is ironic, since Dream took none other than his form (as Agamemnon's most trusted advisor)—something Agamemnon has explicitly revealed (58). The old warrior takes the opportunity to flatter Agamemnon as "best of the Achaians" while tacitly affirming his own great worth.

86 A vivid, cinematic depiction of mass movement and loud noise. The complex simile echoes sound and scenery, while also bearing thematic overtones: the Greeks first resemble swarming bees (hence dangerous, but numerous, organized, and acting communally).

101 Although the other kings have just been described as all "sceptered," the poet singles out the ancestral scepter of the leader Agamemnon for genealogical digression that increases his stature and ties him to divinity (since the gods made it). The history of the scepter hints at a darker side through the mention of Agamemnon's family. His father Atreus won the kingship of Mykenai after a dispute with his brother Thyestes; after learning that Thyestes had seduced his wife, Atreus killed, cooked, and served to Thyestes his own children. The son of Thyestes, Aigisthos, will kill Agamemnon (with the aid of Agamemnon's wife Klytaimestra) on his arrival home. Although none of this sad history is narrated, an audience aware of the myths might think the scepter's description ironic. Since Agamemnon can lean on the implement (109), it must be long, like a staff or shepherd's crook: appropriately Atreus has just been named with the formula "shepherd of the people" (105), and Thyestes is called "of the rich flocks" (106).

111 In his speech pretending to give up, Agamemnon does not hesitate to accuse the chief god of deception and of willing his destruction (*atê*).

122 Agamemnon's excuse is that the Greeks could easily outnumber the inhabitants of the citadel of Troy, but cannot make headway against the many allies who have been summoned. The claim (albeit used only in a false speech) protects the commander against complaints that the Greeks badly overestimated their troop strength.

155 The technique of relating what would have happened if a more immediate cause had not intervened is often used to heighten dramatic effect, and also lets an audience imagine counterplots. The intervention of Hera and Athene, based on their favoring the Greek side, goes back to their resentment at being rejected in the judgment of Paris, although it is put in the language of fairness and the efforts of the Achaians.

169 As the *Odyssey* demonstrates, this hero is Athene's favorite among mortals. While he is "the equal of Zeus" in cunning intelligence (*mêtis*), she is the daughter of the goddess who embodies this trait. Zeus swallowed Mêtis, one of his consorts, out of fear that a son greater than himself would come from her; Athene subsequently emerged from his head.

197 Honor from Zeus. Odysseus defends the authority of Agamemnon using the same terms that Nestor had used at 1.278–79 and Agamemnon himself used at 1.175.

198 One of few passages where the presence of nonaristocrats in the ranks at Troy is acknowledged. The rhetorical abuse uttered by Odysseus makes them sound useless; his support of "one king" draws attention to his own continuing role in propping up the authority of Agamemnon, while his employment of the scepter to beat objectors ironically contrasts with his exalted claims for the scepter-bearing king.

212 Thersites, with his store of abusive words, seems to be a forerunner of the satirist. Mocking poetry, called *iambos*, is attested as early as the seventh century in

Greece. His ugliness parallels the quality of his discourse. That his usual targets were the best fighter and best planner in the army, the protagonists respectively of the *Iliad* and the *Odyssey*, suggests an old tradition of antiheroic rhetoric shadowing aristocratic epic traditions. Thersites repeats and amplifies the complaints of Achilleus in book 1 concerning Agamemnon's rapacity and injustice. The audience may know the story of Thersites' eventual death (narrated in the *Aithiopis*, an archaic continuation of the *Iliad* narrative): he will be slain by Achilleus for mocking him about his alleged love for the Amazon woman and Trojan ally Penthesileia.

271 Recording the reaction by anonymous members of the crowd creates a sense of immediacy and closeness to the action, as well as producing an apparent majority opinion. That Odysseus' threats and assault please so many among the fighters deepens the time dimension, helping the audience imagine the previous duration of Thersites' annoying behavior.

286 Odysseus' rhetorical technique is to induce guilt in the Greeks by blaming them for not keeping their own promises (rather than by doubting Zeus). After showing his sympathy for the sufferings of his audience (292), he vividly evokes the portent interpreted by Kalchas and rouses the troops with his conclusion that the prophesied time has come.

349 Nestor's complementary advice centers on an intellectual aspect of the struggle, as if the whole war is an experiment: only by staying will the Greeks learn about Zeus' trustworthiness or their own capacities (367). His counsel regarding the order of battle seems more suited to the fighters of an established city-state: Athenian life was organized along lines of clan (*phrêtrai*: literally "brotherhood") and tribe (*phula*). The old warrior's commonsensical words about organization chillingly mark his encouragement as well (355) that the victorious army commit mass rape.

405 The list of seven counselors is a good guide to those who will be prominent in the coming battle. The chief commander's role as chief sacrificer and provider of meat and wine undergirds his power, especially as it must involve awarding portions according to his view of his warriors' prowess.

445 The grandeur of the coming battle is highlighted by Athene's magical intervention, a chain of six similes, and a fresh, extended invocation to the Muses. The aegis of Athene is a shield-like goatskin that in the hands of Zeus or the goddess can stun and terrify enemies (although here it seems to inspire). The similes stress the ways in which the clash resembles powerful aspects of nature: forest fire (the armor's gleam); migrating birds, insects, and plant life (multitudes of fighters); herds of goats (separate army divisions of men); and an ox (Agamemnon). The Muses are asked to provided detailed information about the chief men and the strength to recite it. The subsequent Catalogue of Ships must have been a tour de force in recitation. The contrast between hearing (a secondary form of knowing) and autopsy (available occasionally to humans but always to the Muses, as they are eternal) persists in later Greek literature, especially the historical writings of Herodotus and Thucydides.

494 Debates still surround the origins, accuracy, date, and poetics of the so-called Catalogue of Ships. A few manuscripts and at least one papyrus copy of the *Iliad* omit this section altogether, but the majority transmit it. Twenty-nine Greek

contingents, totaling 1,186 ships (and carrying an estimated 100,000 troops) are listed, with the description spiraling outward from Boeotia in central Greece, in a clockwise direction around the mainland, out to the islands of Crete and Rhodes, then back to northern Greece. The style resembles that of the poetry attributed to Hesiod, especially the (now fragmentary) *Catalogue of Women*, and parts of the *Works and Days* and *Theogony*, but this need not mean that this long passage was composed by someone outside the Homeric tradition: it is simply a different sub-genre of poetry. Historians and archaeologists recognize that some of the information must date back to Mykenaian times—perhaps even to accurate memories of an actual Trojan expedition in the twelfth century. Eutresis, for example, seems to have been abandoned after the end of the Bronze Age and not resettled until the sixth century BC. Appropriately, the Ionian Greek cities are omitted, as these were known to be post–Trojan War foundations. (The Cycladic Islands, however, even though they do contain Mykenaian remains, are also missing.) At the same time, the alignments of ethnicities, cities, and political connections seem mainly to re-flect later Iron Age conditions. Even if it may not equal a modern census-taker's work, the Catalogue nevertheless offers a significant mapping of on-the-ground social relations of archaic Greece.

NB: In the following notes, Only those names of persons and places will be mentioned for which there is information of interest beyond simple identification of locale; for the rest, the glossary on page 573 and the maps on pages 70 and 71 should be consulted. For further details see T. W. Allen, *The Homeric Catalogue of Ships* (Oxford, 1921); R. Hope Simpson and J. F. Lazenby, *The Catalogue of the Ships in Homer's Iliad* (Oxford, 1970); and (in German) E. Visser, *Homers Katalog der Schiffe* (Stuttgart, 1997).

494 Boiotian fighters, puzzlingly, do not play a major role in the *Iliad* (even though evidence now suggests it was a powerful region in Mykenaian times). But the Cata-logue may take this starting point because it includes Aulis, the gathering spot for the expedition and site of the sacrifice of Iphigeneia, daughter of Agamemnon, to appease Artemis and obtain favoring winds.

505 "Lower Thebes" is all that remained after the sack of the upper city, so this detail fits the myth of a pre–Trojan War attack carried out by Diomedes and other sons of the Seven against Thebes.

513 The genealogical detail is in the style of the Hesiodic *Catalogue of Women*, which arranges large segments of tradition according to which mythical women bore what offspring. A smaller selection in this style occurs in Odysseus' account of women he met in the underworld (*Odyssey*, book 11).

530 This is the only example in Homer in which "Hellenes" means *all* Greeks (as do the synonymous Danaäns, Argives, and Achaians), rather than the inhabitants of a smaller region named Hellas, corresponding to the area near Phthia (Achilleus' territory: see 683–84 below). The term became the Classical (and modern) desig-nation for the Greeks.

536 The Abantes are distinguished from other Greeks, regularly "long-haired" in Homer, by having their hair shaved in the front (to prevent being grabbed by en-emies), while left long in back.

546 Erechtheus was born directly from the earth (and is thus "autochthonous"—as later Athenians, like a number of Native American tribes, claimed to be), although Athene is his patron and in some versions foster mother. His establishment in her temple reflects the representation of a hero cult, as do the annual sacrifices—perhaps a reminiscence of something like the annual Panathenaic festival.

557 From an early period of Homeric criticism, this line has been suspected as an Athenian interpolation (attributed either to Solon or Peisistratos in the sixth century BC) intended to make a political claim for Salamis in the face of competition from Megara.

595 Thamyris comes from Thrace, like the mythical bard Orpheus, and like him, suffers for his art. The Muses in other cases blind a singer but give the art of song in compensation (e.g., *Od.* 8.63 concerning Demodocus). By contrast, Thamyris is stripped of his ability because he challenged the Muses (e.g., the story of Marsyas who challenged Apollo and was flayed). There may be professional jealousy among epic singers beneath the otherwise gratuitous reference: Oichalia, from which presumably Thamyris would be bringing the latest news, was associated with another strata of saga, connected with Herakles, a hero who is otherwise continuously put in the shade in the *Iliad*.

670 The shower of wealth on Rhodes was literal: Zeus is reputed to have poured down gold like snow on the island.

671 Nireus, from the insignificant island, is never heard of again in the *Iliad*. The mention of his beauty, however, allows the poet to slip in a reminder of the otherwise absent Achilleus, to foreground the theme of the relative distribution of gods' gifts (beauty but not power), and to continue to create the overarching sense that the entire world of Greeks and Trojans came to this war.

721 Philoktetes, abandoned on Lemnos because his pained groans and stinking wound disturbed Greek rites, will be remembered after the death of Achilleus, when the Greeks obtain a prophecy that the bow of Herakles—in the possession of Philoktetes—is needed to take Troy. Sophocles' *Philoktetes* dramatizes the machinations by which Odysseus tries to get it.

731 Asklepios, son of Apollo, was a hero and healer; Trikke had an early healing cult (although the later Epidauros complex, with its theater and hospital, became more famous).

743 The "hairy beast men" are Centaurs, humans with the lower bodies of horses, who dwelled in the woods of Mount Pelion. Cheiron, the wisest of them, was tutor to many heroes, including Achilleus, but his brethren were lawless and uncontrolled, especially when exposed to wine. The battle of the Lapiths with the Centaurs is alluded to at 1.262–68.

751 Titaressos contains waters of the Styx, the underworld river by which oaths are taken. Two other rivers associated with the underworld are also connected, above ground, with the Pindos mountain region of northwestern Greece (Akheron and Kokutos).

793 The barrow of Aisyetes is one of several tombs mentioned as being on the Trojan plain (e.g., Myrina at 2.814 and Ilos at 10.415). The topography is accurate, as the plain is studded even today with ancient mounds.

867 The "outland" (literally "barbarous sounding") speech of the Karians seems to be an archaizing touch, as Greek-speakers inhabited the place from Mykenaian times onward. But there is evidence Karian did survive alongside the newcomers' tongue even through the Classical period. Nastes, "like a girl," is a grace note to the Catalogue of Trojan Allies, an elegiac touch that contrasts the pomp and beauty of war with its darker realities of death. He is never mentioned again.

## BOOK THREE

2 The Trojans often are associated with noise or confused languages (e.g., 2.810), while the Greeks move in silence (4.429). A war between cranes and pygmies may stem from an Egyptian folktale in oral tradition. Greeks of the Classical period knew of pygmies in Africa; the earliest depiction of a conflict with cranes is on the François vase in Florence, from 570 BC by the black-figure artist Kleitias.

15 The initial picture of Paris (also called Alexandros) is not flattering. His unusual leopard skin may mark him as overly concerned about appearances. Nor does the pairing of similes (Menelaos as a hungry lion, Paris as a scared hiker) present him favorably.

54 Hektor's torrent of abuse includes reference to the combination of erotic and musical attractions his brother has. That he does not exaggerate will be established at 394 and 442. Paris himself (65) confirms the characterization but shifts responsibility to the gods.

70 The terms of the agreement make clear that it was not simply the abduction (or elopement) of Helen, but also the taking of possessions from the palace of Menelaos that provided the rationale for war.

103 The black lamb is for Earth, the white for Sun, in accordance with Greek ideas of offerings appropriate for chthonic (earthbound) versus Olympian deities. Zeus fits as the expected additional recipient, since he was overseer of offenses related to hospitality (such as the behavior of Paris).

125 Helen's web is analogous to the poem itself as a record of the struggle at Troy. She is thus imagined as having some agency in representing her own story (and one would like to have seen the result). The audience may be reminded of the weaving of Penelope, a very different heroine, also a cause of contention.

144 Aithre was the mother of the Athenian hero Theseus, who does not figure in the Trojan War epic. (In other versions, his son recovers her at the end of the conflict.) Theseus helped his friend Peirithoös abduct Helen as a child, and Helen's brothers in return captured Aithre, according to some myths. The line has been seen as an Athenian interpolation (as has Nestor's earlier mention of Theseus: 1.265).

156 Helen, for all her beauty, is never physically described in the poem, except for these side comments. As her appearance and presence can only be traced to the action of the divine, the old men of Troy (and Priam) cannot hold her responsible.

173 Helen's tone is most often regretful and she has a habit of reviling herself (180; 6.344). Her description of Agamemnon, meanwhile, seems at odds with what the audience has sensed of his leadership qualities in book 1.

189 The Amazons, women warriors of the east, were in an unspecified past enemies of Troy and its allies (6.186). Yet the Cyclic epic sequel to the *Iliad*, the *Aithiopis*, opens with their arrival at Troy as reinforcements.

205 A fascinating contrast of heroes based on their rhetorical abilities. Menelaos, from Sparta, is laconic (the word derives from the proverbially terse speech of Laconia, the surrounding region). Odysseus typically disguises his real character, acting dumb but speaking with almost overwhelming fluency. The mission to which Antenor refers nevertheless failed, with the embassy barely escaping (11.140).

236 Helen cannot see her brothers Kastor and Polydeukes (twins known in Greek as Dioscuri, in Latin as Gemini) because they had been slain in a skirmish with rivals in Sparta. In most versions Polydeukes, who was the immortal brother, shares his deathlessness with Kastor, so that each can be alive part of the year.

287 Two familiar legal notions are already at work: precedent and punitive damages. The idea of a standard that will be set for all time parallels the very notion of heroic excellence as establishing a benchmark for future endeavors.

332 Paris is an archer, usually operating at a distance from the front line, and so does not possess his own corselet, designed to protect the wearer in close combat. His brother Lykaon will meet his death at the hands of Achilleus (21.35).

374 Menelaos seems about to prove that Zeus is in fact with him (despite his failure to wound with spear or sword), but the action of Paris' patron goddess foils him—one of the complications within polytheism richly explored throughout the poem.

396 The trickiness of Aphrodite is a continuing theme in Greek literature. Her disguise here seems almost intentionally incomplete, as a provocation to Helen who must recognize her power and submit to it (despite her initial feisty revolt: 399).

428 Helen's regret and nostalgia for her former life has been hinted at (139) and now breaks into sarcastic rejection of her current spouse. Paris' insouciant response (that next time he might win) hardly seems enough to defuse Helen's scorn, but once more the power of Aphrodite, transmitted via Paris, subdues her.

## BOOK FOUR

1 The gods in assembly, like the audience in a theater, gaze at the struggle around Troy while drinking nectar; Zeus uses the contrasting situations to needle his wife and daughter about being distanced from the battle, while their nemesis Aphrodite has intervened on the spot to help Paris.

19 Both Helen and Hera (8) are called "Argive." Hera had an important shrine (the Heraion) near the city of Argos, but Helen's association with the area stems from marriage to Menelaos, whose origin was in the ancient fortress city of Mykenai in the area near Argos (the "Argolid"). In the *Odyssey*, the couple resides in Helen's hometown, Sparta (along with Argos and Mykenai, one of Hera's three favored cities: 52). Local lore from antiquity and archaeological finds make it clear that Helen was worshiped as a goddess in the region around her birthplace. The application of the epithet "Argive" makes it more natural to view Helen's marriage as somewhat parallel to Hera's. The end of book 3 has shown her criticizing Paris in a manner not unlike that of Zeus' wife.

27 That the gods sweat and toil seems odd, but to make them more real the *Iliad* regularly presents divinities as undergoing nearly mortal suffering; they simply do not expire. Of Hera's personal efforts to gather armies against Troy, we know nothing further.

35 The desire to eat an enemy is expressed (under pressure of great grief) by Achilleus, before killing Hektor (22.347), and by Hekabē, mother of the dead hero (24.213). In similes, lions (e.g., 5.782) and wolves (16.156) devour prey raw. The bargain made here between gods is first in a series of such compromises in the poem, all of them fatal to mortals.

48 Zeus favors Troy for reasons of ritual correctness: he has never lacked offerings of meat and wine from the inhabitants. His concern for such perquisites is not unlike Agamemnon's; he uses the word *geras* (49: "prize; portion of honor") to describe sacrifices, the term with which the Greek commander characterized his war bride Chryseis (1.118, 120, etc.).

52 Hera's major mainland shrine the Heraion was halfway between Argos and Mykenai, both of which are important Bronze Age sites. In Sparta she had a hilltop temple (Pausanias 3.13.8).

75 The image, a blend of comet and meteor, provides a fine tracking shot from Olympos to the scene of the battle. Its ambiguous significance (war or peace?) gives the keynote for the next several books, as the audience awaits the turn of battle promised by Zeus.

91 The Aisepos flows from the foothills of Mount Ida (southeast of Troy) northward to the Propontis. (Map 1, p. 70.)

95 Pandaros' rewards typify the motivations for many Iliadic warriors: the thanks (*kharis*) of a community, which could lead to reciprocal favors in the future; glory (*kudos*); and immediate material payoff (*dôra*). In return for a successful shot, he must pledge an eventual sacrifice of one hundred lambs to Apollo.

130 An unusual sequence of slow-motion, close-up narrative, framed by two similes related to women (a mother swatting a fly; a woman crafting a horse's cheek piece), and with such attention to materials, color, and design that the actual wounding almost resembles an artwork. The combination of corselet, war belt, and skin guard (possibly a metallic piece to protect the lower abdomen) is unusual, and may owe more to poetic elaboration (or even misunderstanding) than actual defense wear.

163 Agamemnon, while not losing confidence that Troy is doomed, fears nevertheless that the death of Menelaos would discourage the troops and lead to his own humiliating return empty-handed. Imagining what someone might say in the future is a characteristic of Hektor's rhetoric, most often (see, e.g., 7.87–91).

200 Machaon ("Battler") is one of two doctors in the field, his brother Podaleirios being the other; both are sons of the healing hero Asklepios (2.731), a son of Apollo by Coronis.

241 The ensuing scene gives a good sense of the role of rhetoric in battle, a continuing feature of later Greek historical narratives (e.g., Xenophon's *Anabasis*). A combination of pep talk, flattery, and ritual insult, this series of short speeches includes regular reference to the feasts provided by the commander (260, 345), with hints that repayment is due from his fighters.

301 Nestor's advice to "drivers of horses" is for chariot drivers, as fighting from horse-back is unknown in Homer. Here and elsewhere the use of chariots in Bronze Age battle appears to be only vaguely understood by the Iron Age poet, who most often represents fighters as traveling in them to the front lines, then stepping down to fight.

354 A pun underlies Odysseus' mention of his son, Telemachos ("far-fighter"), since "champion" is literally "near-fighter" (*promakhos*).

372 Tydeus was one of the Seven against Thebes, allies sworn to restore Polyneikes to the throne of his late father Oedipus. The story of his valor is meant to inspire Diomedes, and so Agamemnon tactfully omits reference to its seamier side: Tydeus lost Athene's favor because, enraged, he ate the brain of a decapitated enemy, Melanippos.

405 The son of Kapaneus is Sthenelos, who with Diomedes and five others (known collectively as the Epigoni or "After-born"), razed Thebes to the ground a decade after their fathers had perished in the first assault on the city.

437 The disciplined silence of the Greeks is contrasted several times with Trojan noise (e.g., 3.1–10), which is here further related to the linguistic diversity of the Trojan side.

474 The flashback humanizes the victim, while the simile's image of a poplar laid low alongside water circles back to the circumstances of the birth and naming of Simoeisios, near the local river. That the poplar's wood is used to make a chariot wheel brings us forward into the world of battle.

507 Apollo, like a coach or spectator, keeps his distance while Athene actively enters the fray (515, 542) as had Ares (439). It is Apollo who mentions the equally distant Achilleus, the hero who is most like the god in other respects as well.

536 In such images as this (enemies lying next to one another in the dust) the poem draws attention to the common humanity and shared fate of the opposed sides.

BOOK FIVE

1 In this book, the first extended *aristeia* ("display of warrior's excellence") in the poem, Diomedes, the "best of the Achaians" next to Achilleus, takes the field with Athene's divine help. Her wish to make him conspicuous is visible in his armor's fiery blaze (like the dog-star Sirius). His success, even against intervening gods, will give the Greek side temporary hopes of victory.

10 The Trojans and their allies are consistently depicted as worshiping the same gods as the Greeks (see, e.g., 1.35–42, 6.297–310).

15 In the stylized convention of the *Iliad*, the first warrior to strike generally loses in any single-combat encounter. Complicating the action here is the recurrent motif of two warriors against one. Another frequent motif, the battle over a corpse, is repeated in vastly expanded form in the fight to retrieve the body of Patroklos (book 17).

23 The god to whom Idaios' father is devoted (10) intervenes at the crucial moment, with the emotional motivation foregrounded (Hephaistos did not want his priest

to suffer distress). A related motif is divine rescue of favorites: 3.380, 20.325, etc. (Contrast 5.53: Artemis fails to save her protégée.)

31　Athene mentions the potential destructive anger of Zeus (*mênis*) in her proposal that she and the war god defer to him and withdraw. Sensible as this is in light of Zeus' later threats to punish any intervention by the gods (8.5–27), it also at this point conveniently allows Diomedes, one of Athene's favorites, to rage in battle, unchecked by opposing divinities.

37　The highly cinematic scan beginning here pinpoints the leading Greek heroes, who will then in turn be contrasted with the most successful fighter, Diomedes. As in similar extended catalogues of slayings, the poet never exactly repeats details. The basic descriptive pattern (strike; location of wounded part; fall of victim) is expanded and varied with further elements (armor stripped; horses taken). Emotional peaks are crafted through brief "obituaries" (glimpses into the previous life or motives of the deceased), which make the audience sympathize even with the enemies of the Greeks.

95　Pandaros the son of Lykaon appears to make his bowshot into a test of Apollo's support for him, but does not remark on the religious import when he fails to subdue Diomedes. His opponent gets immediate reassurance, on the other hand, from his patroness Athene that she had indeed supported Tydeus his father (and will also help him). This is confirmed when she collaborates in his killing of Pandaros (290).

144　The "shepherd of the people," a common phrase, here picks up on the immediately preceding image (Diomedes as a lion grazed by a shepherd's throw) and recalls earlier comparisons of Trojans to sheep (e.g., 4.433).

149　The rapid execution of the sons (two apiece) of Eurydamas, Phainops, and Priam highlights the theme of severed father-son ties that is crucial to Diomedes' biography and will epitomize the isolation of Achilleus (esp. books 18 and 24).

171　Aineias appeals, in his mild rebuke, solely to the pride of Pandaros (contrast Athene's multiple motivations in 4.93) and recommends prayer to Zeus (not Apollo).

197　The theme of father-son relations once again surfaces, as Pandaros regrets his failure to heed paternal advice about taking his chariot to Troy. Along with touching detail (his concern about horse fodder), Pandaros' story contains motifs common to "obituary" descriptions (e.g., 205, about the ultimate uselessness of weapons).

260　Ganymede, on account of his surpassing beauty, was taken by the gods to serve on Olympos as Zeus' wine-pourer (as Aineias explains in 20.234). The divine horses given as compensation to the boy's father Tros were passed down to Tros' grandson Laomedon. Anchises, the father of Aineias, was the son of Laomedon's cousin.

303　Strength beyond that of current men is one of the few ways in which the poem marks its heroes as being of a different generation.

313　The audience anticipates the clash, as Athene has allowed Diomedes (130) to wound this goddess alone of immortals. Aphrodite's care for her son Aineias recalls the simile of maternal care in 4.130 (Athene protecting Menelaos).

339 The gods can be wounded, but they do not bleed like humans. Spilling blood implies death; gods are immortal; therefore they must have not blood, but another substance, *ikhôr*, in their veins. But blood is generated by human food and drink; the gods therefore do not eat food, but survive on nectar and ambrosia (literally "the immortal"). This idea avoids conflict with the notion that they appreciate sacrificial smoke and libations, as we do not hear of them directly consuming such nourishment.

349 Diomedes' remark probably alludes to Helen's ongoing subordination to the goddess: see 3.413.

370 Nowhere else in epic is Dione attested as mother of Aphrodite, whose origin from the genitals of Ouranos is vividly described in Hesiod's *Theogony* (188–206). The name is a feminine form of "Zeus"; the goddess was associated with him in the oracle cult of Dodona in northwestern Greece.

385 There is a slightly comic tinge to Dione's catalogue, since immortals will only be discomforted, not die. The gigantic sons of Aloeus are more famous for their attempt to pile Mount Pelion onto Mount Ossa to reach the sky and dislodge the gods. The son of Amphitryon is Herakles; the two woundings attributed to him are otherwise unattested. Pylos (397) could refer to the home of Nestor (which Herakles attacked: see 11.689), for which Hades may have been acting as protector. Related to *pylê*, "gate," the city seems to have been known as an entrance to the underworld.

401 Paiëon is in book 5 (and at *Od.* 4.232) a separate, minor divinity of healing. (The name is old, attested as *pajawone* on Linear B tablets from Knossos.) The name in Classical Greek becomes a title for Apollo; already in epic (1.473, e.g.) as a common noun, it denotes a song of thanksgiving (for healing?) dedicated to Apollo—the "paean."

438 Charging "like more than man" (literally "equal to a divinity," *daimoni isos*) signals either retreat or death for the mortal fighter. Patroklos is described thus once when yielding to Apollo (16.705) and again when he persists and is killed (16.786).

472 Tension between Hektor and the allies of the Trojans is a recurrent theme, and the Lykians (Sarpedon and Glaukos) the most frequent voices of rebuke (e.g., 16.536, 17.140), as having traveled farthest to aid Priam and his people. Sarpedon's observation that he risks no losses of his own at Troy (480–85) echoes Achilleus' dissenting words to Agamemnon (1.152–57).

522 The similes of cloud and wind (499) not only slow the narration of immediate action but also naturalize it, making war into an expected, necessary phenomenon like winnowing or weather.

604 Athene's gift of extra sight enables Diomedes to discern the presence of the god of war.

633 The scene is a reminder that both sides feature as champions descended from Zeus. The Lykian Sarpedon's maternal line goes back to the Greek trickster Sisyphos of Argos (see 6.154). Herakles sacked Troy after Laomedon reneged on a promised reward for defeating the sea monster that had menaced his daughter Hesione. The tale is more fully sketched at 20.145–48 and 21.451.

697 Of the four scenes of loss of consciousness in the *Iliad* (5.310; 14.438; 22.466), only here does wind revive a person. The north wind, Boreas, is a divinity with human form (23.195), whose life-giving capacity appears also in his generating divine horses (20.223).

785 The only Homeric mention of this loud character, whose name has become an English adjective (stentorian).

800 Athene's rebuke refers to the episode, from the Seven against Thebes saga, narrated in more detail by Agamemnon (4.385) in the course of a similar speech. Diomedes has not, in fact, held back beyond the limits set by Athene, who now changes the rules of engagement to let him attack Ares, with her help.

838 As heroes are stronger than men of the current day, so gods are weightier than heroes.

872 Ares bases his appeal to Zeus on a presumed sense of outrage on the part of the chief god, as had Hera and Athene at 757; Zeus' response to their earlier appeal is precisely what led to Ares' wounding. The rather adolescent tone, in a complaint about family favoritism, transposes into a comic key the theme of fathers and sons so prominent throughout this book.

BOOK SIX

6 Fighting throughout the poem presents an alternation of mass formations—the "battalion" (*phalanx*)—and looser, individual engagements against the foe. This may not be far from the reality of archaic warfare. Around 700–650 BC, Greek states began employing the fast-moving collision force of contingents of hoplites (heavily armed men) who maintained close formation. This tactic left little room or time for the display of heroic individualism. It may have been known to the poet of the *Iliad*, but is never unambiguously depicted in the poem.

16 The motif of friends or equipment being powerless to save one in battle punctuates the poem: cf. 2.873, 15.530.

21 Naiads are one of several nymph varieties, *oreads* (of mountains) and *dryads* (of trees) being the other main groups, along with sea nymphs called Okeanids or Nereids (daughters of Nereus, like Thetis). The naiad dwells in a lake, spring, or river. The flashback to a bucolic scene, as occurs in similes as well, makes for a jarring contrast with the ongoing battle.

45 Supplication scenes include the grasping of the would-be protector's knees (sometimes chin, too); mention of ransom; and, on occasion, biographical details that the suppliant imagines might evoke pity: see 11.131, and the most developed scene (Lykaon), 21.74. The contrasted reactions of the two brothers are a deft touch of characterization.

68 Nestor makes explicit the mixed motivations among the fighters throughout the battle, as the common goal of subduing the Trojans competes with individual desires for plundered armor.

75 Helenos later overhears the wishes of the gods (7.44), but here we do not learn his source for the advice to placate Athene in her shrine. The offering of a robe

resembles the presentation to Athene during the Panathenaic festival in Athens (memorably depicted on the frieze of the Parthenon). The focus on Diomedes as most dangerous of the Greek threats keeps the audience in mind of his raging attacks in the preceding book.

117 From the detail, we learn that Hektor carries an archaic Mykenaian-era full-body shield; other warriors have a smaller round shield of more recent type.

123 Diomedes' tough talk is intended to diminish his opponent, and therefore we can read his questioning (whether Glaukos has divine status) as highly ironic, rather than as contradicting his special temporary capacity to detect gods. The tale of Lykourgos is one of many such stories about misdirected rejections of Dionysos, the most famous of which underlies Euripides' *Bacchae*. In the current analogy, Diomedes professes fear of resembling Lykourgos, but his focus on Dionysos' flight seems like a taunt directed toward Glaukos.

146 The line offers the oldest surviving quotation from Homer, in a poem by Simonides who flourished circa 500 BC and attributes it to "the man of Chios." The image of leaves is used to make a different point by Apollo (21.464), that ephemeral humans should not disturb divine harmony.

153 Sisyphos tricked Death once, and another time Hades, in order to return to his life, but was finally tasked with constantly rolling an eternally returning boulder up a hill in the underworld.

158 The story of Bellerophontes combines the motifs of a young hero driven from his kingdom (Jason, Perseus) with the "Potiphar's wife" plot (Genesis 39:1–20; cf. the ancient Egyptian *Tale of Two Brothers*, from the thirteenth century BC).

168 The "murderous symbols" may be a vague recollection of an early form of writing (perhaps Linear B or a script of Asia Minor) by a poet whose audience does not know letters, or an archaizing touch, for a literate public, focalizing the imagined viewpoint of the Bronze Age hero. Folding writing tablets dating to the fourteenth century BC were recovered in the 1980s from the Uluburun shipwreck off the coast of Turkey, close to what was ancient Lykia.

179 The Chimaira ("she-goat") is one of the few monsters mentioned by Homer, a type more at home in the poetry of Hesiod, whose *Theogony* (325) refers also to the role of Pegasos, the famous winged horse of Bellerophontes, in the story of his conquest of the beast. The *Iliad* version omits Pegasos just as it avoids mention of the hero's unwise attempt to fly to Olympos, only vaguely referring to his unhappy end.

184 Herodotus (1.173) reports that the Solymoi, original inhabitants of Lykia, were driven out by invaders from Crete. The Amazons, a famous race of women warriors, fought against the Trojans in Priam's youth (3.189) and will reappear later in the saga, when Penthesileia, daughter of Ares, leads them to aid Troy (a story told in the Cyclic epic sequel to the *Iliad*, the *Aithiopis*).

216 The connection of Glaukos with a leading Greek clan is not what prompts the offer of friendship from Diomedes. Instead, it is the (alleged) guest-friendship (*xenia*) of their grandfathers. A cynic might read Diomedes' whole tale as a devious ploy to wrest gold armor from his innocent opponent. Most critics see the episode as a

sincere, humane interlude amid mutual slaughter. Either way, Diomedes has benefited from the iron-clad rules of exchange, which ignore asymmetry of gifts.

255 Hekabē is convincingly sketched as a doting mother, whose conjectures about Hektor's motives (that he was exhausted from the fighting, that he wanted to pray to Zeus) the audience already knows are wrong. Hektor's piety is embodied in the concern for ritual purity.

289 Sidon and Tyre were cities of Phoenicia. Herodotus (2.116) cites this passage with its mention of a Near Eastern detour as evidence that the Cyclic epic *Cypria* (according to which Paris and Helen reached Troy from mainland Greece in three days) could not have been composed by Homer.

321 A significant contrast is intended between weary, bloodstained Hektor, whose anxious wife awaits, and his brother Paris ensconced in domestic comfort with his paramour. Lattimore has Hektor and Paris argue whether "coldness" (326, 335) is the motive for Paris' withdrawal. The Greek at both places is *kholos* (anger, resentment), which has been seen as a narrative slip caused by the pressure of the more central theme, Achilleus' anger. A compromise interpretation could be that Paris nurses a sort of passive aggression because his fellow Trojans are by now themselves angry enough to let him be killed (3.454).

403 Possibly Hektor does not allow himself, for reasons of modesty or superstition, to apply the praise name Astyanax (deriving from his own role as protector) to his son, preferring the neutral Skamandrios (from the nearby river's name). For a similar application of father's status to son's name, compare Telemachos—the "far-fighter"—the son of Odysseus (who himself battles from afar, either by being an Ithacan at Troy or by his skill as an archer, who usually shoots from behind the front rank).

415 Ironically, this sack of Thebes led to the capture of Chryseis (1.369), whose return home has indirectly triggered Achilleus' angry withdrawal, which in turn will ultimately result in Hektor's death. Although one might expect Andromachē to press her husband to take vengeance for her family's extinction, she instead worries about preserving his life, as he is her last hope.

423 Tradition held that the Trojan wall was scalable in one vulnerable spot and would be breached by offspring of Aiakos (grandfather of both Achilleus and Telamonian Aias), who had assisted Poseidon and Apollo in building it (Pindar, *Olympian*, 8.30–45 [460 BC]). The fig tree (433; like the oak tree, 5.693) is one of several landscape features used to orient the action near Troy (see also 11.167, 22.145).

454 As often in the poem, Hektor easily articulates images and remarks set in the future. His fear for his wife's status as a Greek slave is exacerbated by the way he imagines it reflecting back on his own heroic status. This psychologically apt speech shifts through many tones: professions of shame and desire for glory, his affection for his wife even over his blood kin, his realization of Troy's impending doom. More than any words, the image of Hektor removing his helmet to calm his baby captures the pathos of his imminent death while defending his family.

21 Pergamos is the highest point of Troy. The oak tree, marking a spot near the Skaian gates of the city (6.237), is regularly associated with safety, while the fig tree gets mentioned at moments of danger (see note to 6.423).

44 The most reliable mode of communicating divine will in the poem is through what is heard, rather than through (often debatable) visual signs, perhaps a clue to the poem's own origins in oral tradition and the poet's reliance on the word of the Muse. Having Helenos overhear the gods enables the narrative to move more quickly, while varying the usual pattern of divine descent and intervention. The seer adds his own encouraging improvement on the message, telling Hektor it is not his time to die (52).

58 One of the few passages where gods take the actual form of birds (as opposed to moving *like* birds: e.g., 5.778). Sleep at 14.290 similarly perches in a tree. The gods' aesthetic pleasure in the sight of the troops is carried over into the perspective of the ensuing simile (63), which presents an aerial view of wind-stirred waters.

77 Hektor's instructions and promise foreshadow the major crisis of the end of the poem, the treatment of his corpse (an ongoing anxiety while he is alive: cf. 22.259 and 22.338). Characteristically, he adds a vivid example of what people will say in the future (cf. 6.460) when glorifying him as they view his foe's tomb.

104 The second-person address to Menelaos (as later with Patroklos) adds pathos and draws the audience to his point of view. His volunteering resembles a theatrical gesture, and is quickly deflected by Agamemnon and Nestor, who use the occasion to shame the other Greeks into accepting the challenge (124).

128 Nestor's biography lends authority. His role as the most skilled speaker and keeper of heroic genealogies resembles the poet's. His narrative style differs, however, by continually looping backward before circling around to the starting point: the mention of Ereuthalion's armor prompts recollection of Areïthoös and his nickname, then of Lykourgos, who stripped the armor and gave it eventually to Ereuthalion. The war of Pylians against Arkadians is further recalled at 11.669. Though the rivers cannot be located, Pheia appears to have been near modern Katakolo, a port on the Ionian sea, not far west of Olympia in the territory of Elis.

220 The special connection of Aias with the tower shield is reflected even in the name of his son, Eurysakes ("broad shield"). Its unusually thick construction with multiple layers makes suspenseful any spear-cast against it, as the audience waits to hear how deep the weapon will go.

237 Hektor compares his knowledge of fighting to dance: the "measures" which he treads with his shield are even reflected in the meter and phrasing of these lines. A war dance in armor (*pyrrhikê*), well known and practiced in Classical times, surely had predecessors, to which these lines may allude.

290 The end of the duel seems abrupt, with the heralds like umpires calling a game on account of nightfall. But it has made the point that the men are equally matched and fulfills the prayer of the Greeks (204) that, short of a win, Zeus grant the pair equal strength.

303 The gifts exchanged are linked in lore to the eventual deaths of each: Hektor's corpse is bound and dragged by the belt; Aias kills himself with the sword.

336 The mound is to be both tomb and defensive wall: if the latter function had been most important, constructing the wall now would be anachronistic (although seeming anachronisms in the poem, such as the elementary identification of warriors from the Trojan wall in book 3, are tolerated for drama's sake). If sepulchral commemoration is the goal, construction after this major slaughter makes more sense.

348 Another abrupt surprise: the proposal by Antenor to give back Helen sets up the forceful rejection by Paris, albeit with the concession that he is willing to return Menelaos' treasures along with punitive damages.

421 The moving scene of each army trying to recognize their dead, side by side, is given added emotional impact by the complete silence. The basic human sameness of Greek and Trojan is emphasized by the exact repetition of phrases to describe either side's actions.

445 Nestor's plan arouses the competitive instinct of the sea god. It is less the alleged impiety of failing to perform foundation sacrifices that annoys Poseidon than it is the threat that the new wall will outshine his and Apollo's building. The objection (like the Antenor-Paris exchange) appears to be a setup for Zeus' further promise that the Greek construction will be short-lived (confirmed at 12.15–30, viewed from a time after Troy's fall). The projection forward is a rarely used technique for setting the tragic action at Troy *sub specie aeternitatis*, making all human concerns look minuscule.

467 Lemnos (where the Greeks had left behind the commander Philoktetes with his festering snakebite: 2.725) lies fifty miles to the west of Troy. Jason visited it with his Argonauts, welcomed by the Lemnian women (who had killed their errant husbands). Euneos ("good ship") is his son by Hypsipyle, the Lemnian queen. There may be implied contrasts between Jason's expedition (in search of an emblem of kingship, the golden fleece; taking back a dangerous woman, Medea) and the current Trojan mission. A subtle touch of class distinction relevant to aristocratic gift-economy: the Atreidai get their wine free, while the ordinary troops must barter for it (even trading slaves).

### BOOK EIGHT

13 Tartaros is here distinct from Hades (both names can denote deities as well). Rather than a place of punishments for mortals, it is the furthest a god can be from divine society and so forms a holding place for Zeus' enemies (cf. 479–81; and Hesiod, *Theogony*, 865). The gold cord scenario (19) prompted much speculation by Neoplatonist philosophers who saw in it an allegorical expression of the relation of godhead to the material world (see Lamberton, *Homer the Theologian* [Berkeley, 1986], 271–72).

39 Tritogeneia was obscure even in antiquity as an epithet for Athene. It may mean "Triton-born" in relation to various bodies of water so named, although the god-

dess has nothing to do with Triton, son of Poseidon; more likely it means "genuine daughter" (literally "third-born").

48  Gargaron is the highest peak of Mount Ida, near Troy, and the site mentioned may be where Hektor used to make sacrificial offerings to Zeus (22.171).

69  The scales of Zeus may seem to contradict his recent assertion of total power, since he seems to hand over the fate of the armies to chance. But a balance is not a dice toss: it vividly makes concrete the decision he had already reached in agreeing with Thetis to honor Achilleus. The only other time Zeus employs it, Hektor's doom tips down: 22.209.

108  These are the immortal horses which Aineias' father got from the gift of the gods to Tros (5.265–73).

161  The honors mentioned—privileged seating at banquets and so on—are further expanded in the discussion of heroic rights between Glaukos and Sarpedon (at 12.310). The implicit contract (wine and food in exchange for fighting) is the background for the nearly comic rhetoric of Hektor to his horses (185) urging them to repay their upkeep.

200  Hektor's confidence that defeating Nestor and Diomedes will immediately make the Greeks flee prompt's Hera's appeal to Poseidon. Of the sea god's many shrines, Helikē (203) was in territory ruled by Agamemnon (2.575), while Aigai, featuring an undersea palace, may have been imagined as near Lesbos (13.21).

223  The configuration of ships mirrors the character of the leaders: Odysseus, the master of compromise, is midway between the powerful individualists with a taste for isolation, Aias and Achilleus.

230  The stopover at Lemnos probably happened when Philoktetes was abandoned there (2.722).

245  Prayer and pity in response trump the apparent power of Fate (expressed by Zeus' balance). The sending of a fawn recalls various substitute-sacrifice stories (e.g., Artemis, in one version, accepting a fawn in lieu of Agamemnon's daughter Iphigeneia). Symbolically, Zeus accepts the animal instead of the human slaughter, for the present.

271  The mother-child simile lends an unexpectedly tender coloration to the relations of fellow fighters. For a similar usage, see 16.7.

306  The lyric poignancy is increased by the implied contrast: unlike the flower after rain, the warrior will not lift his head.

348  Gorgons petrify opponents with their stare (most famously in the tale of Perseus and Medusa), so depictions were commonly used on shields (e.g., Agamemnon's at 11.36) or as devices to ward off evil from temples.

360  Athene uses of Zeus the same verb (*mainetai*, "rage, be furious") that Hera had used of Hektor's manic rush (355). As emerges now, Athene keeps track of the deeds for which she is owed thanks, especially her protection of Herakles (hero of the earlier generation, to be contrasted with Achilleus). There are hints of jealous competition between Athene and the sea nymph Thetis.

393  The Hours (*Horai*), which can also be translated "Seasons," are (in Hesiod, *Theogony*, 901) Eunomia (Good Order), Eirene (Peace), and Dikê (Justice), names more

indicative of their function as regulators of all sorts of rhythms, including (as here) the exits and entrances of the gods, which folklore may have connected with the changes of weather.

399 Iris, divine messenger, is (unlike the other go-between, Hermes) associated with the rainbow, whence she lends her name, in English, to the flower and the colored membrane of the eye.

421 Iris adds tags on her own insult to what she has been commanded to say. It is unclear whether the goddesses intend to attack Zeus himself, or this is just the chief god's anxiety. At any rate, Hera's judgment that saving humans is not worth causing divine conflict—a frequent theme—calms the rebellion.

470 As Zeus has a role in making the future, this is more a promise than a prediction. Iapetos was the father of Prometheus, the benefactor of mankind who challenged Zeus; Kronos was the violent father whom Zeus overthrew. (Both stories are narrated in Hesiod's *Theogony* and *Works and Days*.) Zeus seems to dismiss the possibility that an indignant Hera might successfully recruit his old enemies for her cause.

538 Hektor's certainty of killing Diomedes sounds hubristic and short-sighted when contrasted with what we have heard in Zeus' foreshadowing of events. Some critics have misconstrued his words to assert an equivalence with the gods; in fact, the "if only" wish is a rhetorical flourish highlighting the commander's confidence for the benefit of his troops.

555 The final simile comparing fires on the plain to stars shifts its focus to the all-revealing moonlight in a moving panoramic view. The contrast between the shepherd's joy and the tense prebattle expectation adds a personal viewpoint to the regular theme (war versus peace) of such comparisons.

BOOK NINE

14 The infrequent image of the dark-running water draws attention to another crisis point, when Patroklos seeks to enter the fray (16.3), a significant repetition if, as has been suggested, the poem was performed over the course of three days with books 9 and 16 each starting a new day's recitation.

30 Whereas Agamemnon's speech of despair in book 2 was staged (and backfired) his apparently sincere speech now is counteracted by the words of Diomedes, whose exploits are shown to have gained him confidence in speaking out as an equal. Ironically Diomedes treats the commander as dispensable, just as Agamemnon has treated Achilleus. Nestor's suggestion for a feast is intended to right the imbalance and restore Agamemnon's status as chief dispenser of rewards.

120 "Gifts in abundance" translates a more technical phrase (*apereisi' apoina*: "unbounded compensation") that is appropriate for ransom (cf. the same phrase in 1.13), but not to describe what should be punitive damages demanded by the aggrieved party and recognizing guilt on the part of the giver. (For the latter, *poinê* "expiation" is the proper term.) The crucial difference in attitude can explain Achilleus' refusal. See D. Wilson, *Ransom, Revenge, and Heroic Identity in the Iliad* (Cambridge, 2002).

149 Another indication of the surpassing wealth and power of Agamemnon is that his territories extend to Pylos. The seven towns mentioned differ from the nine listed as ruled by Nestor in the Catalogue of Ships (2.591–602), and may reflect a real Mykenaian-era political division between "near" and "far" Pylian territories.

182 The translation "these two" accurately reflects the Greek use of an archaic "dual" number (neither singular nor plural, used to denote pairs), here and five other times in this scene. But the embassy is either five (if one counts the two heralds) or three (Aias, Odysseus, Phoinix). The poet may be repurposing a more traditional scene involving a pair (cf. the heralds' dispatch at 1.320). Homerists have not yet proposed an entirely convincing solution.

186 The violent warrior is hinted at in the brief description of the lyre's origins (in the sack of the city that also yielded Agamemnon's war bride Chryseis: 1.369), while the scene that meets the embassy is one of harmony and companionship, perhaps a musical evening in which the warriors take turns singing heroic epics (about themselves?).

223 Odysseus interposes himself, although Aias had signaled to Phoinix, perhaps because he believes his skill is greater than the older man's; the resulting order of speeches nicely juxtaposes the clever compromiser and the defender of the extreme heroic ideal. A significant quarrel between Achilleus and Odysseus, at a sacrifice, is alluded to in *Od.* 8.75; throughout the *Iliad* one detects tension between the men.

252 Having tried appeals to comradeship and to self-interest, Odysseus finally adds a quotation, said to be from Achilleus' father, designed to shame the hero into giving up his anger.

300 Instead of repeating Agamemnon's words at this point (cf. 158–61), Odysseus diplomatically substitutes a plea that Achilleus have compassion for his companions, despite his ongoing hatred for Agamemnon. Achilleus, in turn, may be describing his preference for straight talk (312) by mentioning his detestation of the man who hides realities; he could also be indirectly blaming Odysseus himself, as if his concealment of Agamemnon's exact words had been obvious.

328 Achilleus alludes to the attacks he carried out in the area around Troy over the past nine years, such as the sack of Thebes.

381 Orchomenos reached its peak of wealth in the thirteenth century BC. Unless this is a very ancient reminiscence, Thebes of Egypt (modern Luxor) could not be so described until its revival in fortunes after 715 BC (and before its destruction by the Assyrians in 663 BC). Thus some scholars believe the line offers a clue to the dating of the *Iliad*.

405 Apollo's shrine at Delphi ("Pytho") contained vast wealth from dedications by Greeks and foreigners, and grew rapidly from the eighth century BC to become a Panhellenic sanctuary and international center. This crowning comparison by Achilleus gains ironic resonance when the audience knows that Achilleus' son Neoptolemos later attacked Delphi in revenge for Apollo's role in causing his father's death.

410 Only here do we learn of the prophecy, where it makes for the most powerful rhetorical effect. The phrase "glory shall be everlasting" (413) occurs only here, as

well, but an etymologically matching phrase occurring in the poetic hymns of the Sanskrit *Rig Veda* (circa 1000 BC) has led scholars to believe this may be a formulaic remnant of Indo-European praise traditions.

443 The most concise summary of heroic expectations in the *Iliad* balances words and deeds. Achilleus' speaking ability has just been shown, so Phoinix's teaching succeeded; his autobiographical account therefore gains credibility as well. In other sources, the centaur Cheiron is said to have tutored Achilleus, but the *Iliad* prefers realistic persons to fantasy creatures.

481 Just as Peleus acted as foster father to Phoinix, so the old tutor can claim to be a father figure to Achilleus, freely admitting that he treated him as the son he was cursed never to have.

502 The personified Prayers and Ruin are described in ways that match their behavior. The former are halting and wrinkled because they act slowly, while the latter (*Atê*, "ruinous blindness"), comes swiftly upon her victims. It is appropriate that the Prayers be old, since the aged Phoinix himself is embodying the Greek entreaty.

524 Phoinix's third mode of communicating, after allegory and autobiography, is, like the epic itself, a recollection of famous mortal feats. The Kalydonian boar hunt was among the most important joint heroic undertakings of an earlier generation. A war erupted over the division of spoils (note the Iliadic theme) between Kalydon and its neighbor Pleuron (the city of the Kouretes), both located near modern Messolonghi on the northwestern shore of the Corinthian Gulf. In most sources Althaia, the wife of Oineus, has concealed a brand which, at the suggestion of the Fates, she snatched from the fire when Meleagros was born. As long as it remains unburnt, her son will live. When he accidentally kills her brothers in the boar hunt, Althaia returns the wood to the fire and he dies. In the Homeric version, the motif of the hero being angry at his mother's curse prolongs the episode and makes it more closely match the details of Achilleus' situation.

571 The Erinys appears here for the second time in Phoinix's speech (cf. the furies at 454, his father's curse). The goddesses (most often pluralized) enacted vengeance for murder or other offences involving kin. Their most famous representation in Classical literature comes in the *Eumenides* ("Kindly Ones"), the third play of the *Oresteia* trilogy of Aeschylus (produced 458 BC).

590 Kleopatra, whose brief biography is given at 556, has a name that matches semantically "Patroklos," both meaning "ancestor glory." Her role as the closest person in Meleagros' affection and only successful pleader parallels that of the companion of Achilleus. It may be a convenient fiction on the part of Phoinix to make the hero heed his friend.

633 Aias' speech, meant to shame Achilleus for neglecting his comrades, is addressed to *them*, ostensibly. The analogy made is imperfect: while a victim's brother might accept *compensation* from a killer, Agamemnon has offered *gifts*, which (more like a bribe) put the recipient in his debt, do not acknowledge the grievance, and imply that the giver holds the superior position.

1 The "Doloneia" (book 10, centered on Dolon) was thought by some ancient critics to have been a separate composition added to the *Iliad* in the course of its textual fixation, perhaps in the sixth century BC. Many modern critics as well have stressed its un-Iliadic or un-Homeric aspects. While it is true that it bears no organic relation to the rest of the poem, and that its dictional choices, prolix development, archaizing touches, and subject matter (including fascination with armor and dress) are unusual (and more akin to the *Odyssey*), there is no reason to think the book was not a living part of the Homeric performance tradition. See C. Dué and M. Ebbott, *Iliad 10 and the Poetics of Ambush: A Multitext Edition with Essays and Commentary* (Washington, DC, 2010).

5 The opening simile brings together Zeus and Agamemnon to the disadvantage of the latter's image. The commander's uncontrollable symptoms of despair are likened to the chief god's masterfully executed and powerful weather effects.

91 Agamemnon's description of his symptoms displays more self-awareness than he has shown to this point, underlining his desperation now that Achilleus has spurned his entreaties. His keen analysis of his brother's psychology (121) shows another previously unnoticed dimension of his intelligence.

212 One mark of the difference in tone of book 10 is its radical reinterpretation of "glory" as something that can be gained by a sneak attack on a spying mission. The rest of the *Iliad* treats *kleos* (glory, especially as transmitted through poetry) as the result of conspicuous fighting ability in the midst of battle. The *Odyssey*, on the other hand, does associate its hero's *kleos* with mastery of deceptions, such as the Trojan Horse (*Od.* 9.20).

243 A sense of the *Odyssey*'s protagonist emerges from Diomedes' reference to his steadfastness, intelligence, relation to Athene, and ability to come back from any danger (noted here with the same verb that describes Odysseus' return in the tale of his voyages).

255 The formality and detail with which this giving of arms is described make it sound like a ritual. The importance is underlined by the antiquity of the objects described: the boar's-tooth helmet (dating to 1600–1200 BC) must have been a precious heirloom by the time of the poem's composition (if it was not simply a memory). The reference to Odysseus' thievish grandfather Autolykos reminds the audience of the hero's own shiftier side.

285 While Odysseus' prayer to Athene (278) looks forward to the themes of the *Odyssey*, Diomedes once more recalls the topic of sonship and his father Tydeus' role in another major epic event, the battle for Thebes (cf. 4.370).

303 Hektor stresses, first, material reward rather than fame and association with the elite (cf. 212–17), as if the Trojans have different motivating priorities. The insistence by Dolon ("Tricky") on an oath also bespeaks a more mercantile attitude.

415 The tomb of Ilos (the son of Tros and father of Laomedon), like the fig and oak trees, is one of the rare spatial markers in the poem's stylized picture of the Trojan plain. It has not been identified with any detectable archaeological feature.

429 The list of Trojan allies is a contracted and slightly varied form of that found in the catalogue at 2.840–77. This correspondence with the narrator's words has the effect of making Dolon's report ring true. The story of the slaughter is the subject of a tragedy attributed to Euripides, the *Rhesus*.

496 The bad dream, becoming reality (Diomedes), is a unique and unusually strong metaphor, unlike either the conventional simile technique or other dream appearances (e.g., 2.20, 23.68).

BOOK ELEVEN

1 The major battle of the *Iliad*, continuing through book 17, begins with the participation of the primary warriors, several of whom are soon put out of action.

15 Agamemnon's elaborate armor prompts description that highlights the geographic and even cosmic impact of the Trojan siege. The Cypriot king has acknowledged the commander's status, in hopes of getting a reciprocal gift, perhaps at Troy's fall—an event that would increase his island's political power. In drawing attention to the upcoming action, the extended arming scene functions like the description of Achilleus' shield (see book 18 and his preparation for battle at 19.369).

45 Usually it is Zeus' exclusive privilege to thunder, but Hera and Athene employ the encouraging noise here, while Zeus rains blood to mark the imminent slaughter (53). Hektor's appearance completes the meteorological effects—his armor gleams like lightning (66).

86 The simile of the woodcutter imaginatively transforms the chaos of battle into ordered, necessary labor, with its own life-sustaining rewards.

104 Achilleus' deeds are kept in the audience's mind through such narrative recollections, though he has been out of the fray since book 1 and has not been seen since the end of book 9. For an expansion of the motif of captured and released enemies see 21.34. Another vignette (9.138) similarly fills in the exposition of past events at Troy (explaining Agamemnon's present brutality).

218 A series of crescendo movements (Agamemnon's battle rage, Zeus' orders, Hektor's urging of the troops) culminates in a renewed invocation of the Muses (cf. 2.484), marking the onset of the height of Agamemnon's performance of glory (his *aristeia*).

223 That this son of Antenor is raised by a maternal grandfather seems to fit the pattern of aristocratic "fosterage" attested in other Indo-European cultures (especially Celtic), although marriage to an aunt is unusual. The geographic scope is again widened (as in 10.21) by the mention of Iphidamas coming from Thrace on the report of a Greek expedition.

269 In the midst of masculine combat, the strongest expression of pain is childbirth pangs. As it was at Menelaos' wounding (4.141), women's experience is recalled via simile.

292 As the action intensifies, the narration becomes more impressionistic, employing a kaleidoscopic series of similes within fifteen lines, with Hektor seen as a hunter (292), Ares (295), a storm cloud (297), and a whirlwind (306).

353 Apollo's gift protects Hektor, as the audience hears, but Diomedes is speculating when he assumes that his opponent regularly prays to the protector of Troy.

403 As often in the *Odyssey*, Odysseus addresses his spirit (*thumos*), giving the audience the impression that he is more self-aware than such heroes as Diomedes or Agamemnon. Unlike in the *Odyssey*, where such dramatic monologues conclude with his strategic withdrawal, here the warrior ends with a ringing affirmation of the value of engagement.

452 Odysseus' boast employs the language of laments by the kin of a slain warrior, especially the rhetorical focus on the absence of mourners (cf. 22.86). A similar speaking strategy marked Diomedes' threat (393).

512 The fighters realize that their fortunes will worsen if they lose the surgeon Machaon, son of Asklepios, who in turn learned healing from his father Apollo.

547 Retreat out of fear is unusual, especially for a warrior as prominent as Aias, so a double simile highlights his essential unwillingness: he is a lion beset by dogs and villagers, or a stubborn donkey beaten by boys.

603 The touch of foreshadowing will come to mind later in this book when Nestor advises Patroklos. Achilleus' call is set in the immediate context of companions aiding one another in battle (590), but Achilleus interprets the scene as prelude to a renewed supplication for his individual services.

631 Both beverage and cup are special. The cup resembles, down to the details of its golden birds, a chalice-shaped, two-handled example from about 1500 BC, found in a shaft grave at Mykenai, although Nestor's version is heroically weightier. The mixed drink (*kukeón*) has been compared to the concoction of the same name used in the mystery rituals of Demeter at Eleusis outside Athens.

670 Nestor's long, twisting tale centers on his initiation as warrior during an episode of cattle-raiding and reprisal. Its practical application as advice hinges on an inexact parallel, never made explicit, that would figure Patroklos as a younger warrior whose chance for glory has now come. In fact, Patroklos is older than Achilleus (as Nestor himself notes: 786).

690 Nestor starts, like an epic poet, in the middle of things, with his glorious return (685). We can reconstruct earlier events: Herakles devastated the house of Neleus in Pylos. The men of Elis (the Epeians) took advantage of this to raid the city. Then or later, they perpetrated other abuses, such as taking Neleus' racing chariot and team. Some time later, the Pylians conducted a cattle raid to recover damages and with the young Nestor successfully brought home many goods; three days thereafter the Epeians counterattacked, the Pylians mustered, and Nestor won glory in battle.

749 The Moliones were said by other ancient sources (Hesiod, fr. 18, MW) to be Siamese twins, but this is not clear from the Homeric description and, if known, may have been suppressed, as are other monstrous or fantastic elements.

763 Nestor makes the point of the story the contrast between his own fight for the Pylian community versus Achilleus' selfish isolation.

797 Ironically, in the parable, Nestor's father had not allowed him to wear armor; Nestor now by quoting Patroklos' father (785–86) lures the younger man into asking for Achilleus' armor—a fatal suggestion.

843 The picture of Patroklos tending expertly to the wound of Eurypylos anticipates his role as potential savior of the Greeks, healing and battle being conceived as in many ways analogous crafts. See R. P. Martin, *Healing, Sacrifice and Battle: Amechania and Related Concepts in Early Greek Poetry* (Innsbruck, 1983).

BOOK TWELVE

1 The already perilous situation, culminating in the wounding of Greek leaders in the previous book, becomes more ominous with the reminder that the Greeks constructed their wall irreverently. But the long-distance foreshadowing goes beyond the current setbacks in battle and even the fall of Troy, becoming instead a reminder of the fragility of all mortal things, from the gods' view. The distant scene, now looked back upon from the poet's day, recalls Greek and Near Eastern stories of a primeval flood that wiped out earlier periods of civilization.

145 With the sustained attack on its wall, the Greek camp comes to resemble a miniature Troy, a defensive site, enabling the audience to imagine the ineffectiveness of a Greek assault on the much sturdier and taller city ramparts.

167 Unusually, a character employs a full-scale Homeric simile in his own speech, during battle.

175 The basic scenario of simultaneous attack on multiple gates may owe something to the story of the Seven against Thebes, the gates of which were attacked by as many companies of warriors with their champions. Such a complex scene is intrinsically challenging for the omniscient narrator, as the poet goes on to say (176), but it may have provided a tour de force exhibition of compositional skill.

195 From the ill fate of the division under Asios—the most reckless ally in the attack— the focus moves to Hektor, usually the most sensible. The mood of near victory and its unbearable tension is encapsulated in Hektor's response to Poulydamas' counsel of caution. Favored as he thinks he is by Zeus, Hektor scorns omens. The striking line 243 ("One bird sign is best . . . ") was a favorite in antiquity: Pliny the Younger recalls (*Letter* 1.18.3) how as an eighteen-year-old apprentice Roman lawyer (in 80 AD), he plucked up his courage with this sentiment. Teachers of rhetoric in the fourth century AD were still urging pupils to make use of the maxim.

310 The most explicit expression in Homer of a heroic contract: Sarpedon reminds his cousin of the warrior's obligation to fight in the front line in exchange for community support and special treatment. The point of 323 seems to be that such regard continues *after* the fighter's death. The word *temenos* ("piece of land": 313) can designate a plot set aside as a gift, but also (and primarily, in post-Homeric Greek) a sacred precinct for a god or hero. The latter were worshiped in cults with dedications of wine and other liquids, and animal sacrifice (cf. 319, of the living). In addition to outlining the economy of heroism, Sarpedon implies that war itself is a non-zero-sum game in which one can get glory by slaying but also give it by being slain.

391 So powerful are words as a kind of ammunition in battle that enemies avoid even the appearance of weakness lest the other side boast. The word translated "glory"

at 328 means literally "a boast" (*eukhos*), and shares the root of the verb translated at 391 as "vaunt."

445 The exaggerated strength of heroes increases with the ferocity of the attack: at 380, Aias hefts a stone such as no man nowadays might grasp with two hands. Now Hektor pries one loose that would take two ordinary men (with a wagon) to lift. As if on second thought, the poet adds that Zeus made the rock lighter (450)—but leading ancient scholars rejected the additional line.

462 At the poem's midpoint, the darkest moment of the Greeks' situation is embodied in the ambiguous figure of Hektor, bursting through the defensive wall, like blazing fire but also swift night.

## BOOK THIRTEEN

4 Zeus turns aside to gaze at peoples to the north, who were to the Greeks distant and semibarbarous. Thracian territory overlaps the border between current Greece and Turkey; Mysians lived in today's Bulgaria (though the Catalogue of Trojan Allies knows of a another branch: 2.858); Hippomolgoi (the "horse milker") and the Abioi (whose name was interpreted as "without violence") were associated with lands the Classical Greeks knew as Scythia (now the Ukraine and southern Russia). The righteousness of these tribes accords with the mythical notion that peoples furthest removed in time or space from current civilization are least damaged by its problems.

13 "Thracian" Samos (later "Samothrace"), in the northern Aegean forty miles northwest of Troy, was so called to distinguish it from the Greek island Samos that lies to the south, off the coast near modern Kusadasi. The island was a center of the worship of the Great Mother of importance to sailors throughout antiquity. The mountain on which Poseidon sits, 5,250 feet tall, in fact offers a full view of the Trojan plain—evidence that this portion of the poem must be based on someone's personal observation of landscape.

54 Although the audience has not heard Hektor make this boast, his actions and words from book 7 onward could lead one to interpret his behavior as hubristic in this way.

71 A fleeting reference to the gods' slight differences in appearance: even when disguised they can be bigger, heavier (cf. 5.838), or more lovely (3.396), and even, as it seems here, have distinctive legs (or perhaps gait). The idea that gods are conspicuous goes against the sense of book 5, where Athene had to grant Diomedes special power to perceive them.

108 Poseidon/Kalchas interprets the quarrel from Achilleus' point of view, and the "weakness" refers to Agamemnon. But he still urges courage on the part of the troops. The "healing" of the rift between fighters (or of their slackness in battle—an ambiguity) foregrounds the theme that is associated with the saving action of Patroklos: see 11.843.

203 Decapitation is unusual and here shows the height of the Greeks' despair and grief. Achilleus, bereaved of Patroklos, vows to bring back Hektor's head (18.334). Ethnographers record that modern headhunters (e.g., among the Ilongot of the

Philippines) are often motivated by grief and anger at the deaths of friends: see R. Rosaldo, "Grief and a Headhunter's Rage," in *Violence in War and Peace*, ed. N. Scheper-Hughes and P. Bourgois, 150–56 (Malden, MA, 2004).

206 Poseidon's grandson is Amphimachos (185), son of Kteatos (whose mortal father was Aktor, but whose actual father was the sea god).

278 One of the clusters of details in the poem that convince an audience the composer has seen men in war.

301 Ares is associated with the half-wild land of Thrace. The Ephyroi and Phlegyes (named for Phlegyas, a son of Ares) are Greek tribes associated with Thessaly.

324 The rating of Aias as Achilleus' equal in a fight (though not in a race) coheres with the tradition that he was deserving of Achilleus' armor after the hero's death. The story of his defeat by Odysseus and subsequent suicide was part of the Cyclic *Little Iliad* and is dramatized in the *Ajax* of Sophocles.

374 Harsh sarcasm from Idomeneus comes as a surprise, but book 13 has already featured the roughest war-making. At the same time, it is interspersed with delicate and carefully observed arboreal similes (178, 389).

414 A triple phonic echo makes it sound as if Deïphobos is punning: *Asios* is not unavenged (*atitos*) as he goes to the house of Hades (*Aïdos*).

435 Poseidon's spell is unparalleled as a form of divine intervention in the battle thus far. The closest scene to this is 16.791 (Apollo strikes Patroklos), but only here is there the sense that the god puts his victim in a paralyzed trance by visual contact. The ensuing death ends with the equally bizarre image of Alkathoös' heartbeat causing the spear butt to pulsate (443).

450 The Cretan king Minos, a son of Zeus, was keeper, in the famous labyrinth, of the Minotaur, a bull-headed human-bodied monster that met its end at the hands of the Athenian hero Theseus.

460 The theme of heroic anger against a superior (like that of Achilleus) was suggested (perhaps inadvertently) in the case of another Trojan, Paris (6.326). Here it seems to involve an actual rivalry between branches of the royal house.

521 Gods are not omniscient but must learn, like mortals, over time. The pathos of late-learning about a family death recalls the narrator's observation (3.236) concerning Helen's ignorance of the fate of her brothers Kastor and Polydeukes.

603 Still not fully explained, the narrator's second-person address to Menelaos (thus treated seven times, compared to eight times for Patroklos) may depend on a perceived sympathy with the loser in the story of Helen's abduction. Menelaos refers to the offense explicitly (626) in his boast over the body of Peisandros (who is here subjected to one of the gorier deaths in the poem).

643 Harpalion, son of Pylaimenes the king, is followed by his father while carried wounded from the field. A minor mistake seems to have occurred, since an identically named man, also identified as king of the Paphlagonians, was slain by Menelaos at 5.576. The missing blood price (659) underscores the pathos of the situation: a son might avenge his father in war by killing, or by taking recompense in peace, but the aging father is unable to do so for his offspring.

665 A grimmer version of Achilleus' choice (9.410). Euchenor can have death by dis-

ease or by war; at least the latter relieves him of paying a fine (apparently levied on war dodgers: see 23.296 on Echepolos).

681 Protesilaos (see the Catalogue of Ships, 2.698) was first to be killed when the Greeks landed at Troy, having leapt from his ship to shore. His ship is thus located farthest up the beach, as it arrived earliest.

685 The "Ionians" sounds anachronistic, as Ionia (the west coast of Asia Minor as far north as Smyrna) was not settled by Greeks until some two centuries after the time of the Trojan war. But here they are identical to the Athenians, an accurate memory of the fact that many early colonists hailed from that city. The Phthians come from the broader region around the homeland of Achilleus, while his troops are specifically Myrmidons. These, by contrast, are led by Podarkes ("swift-footed"—a name that happens to be an epithet of the great hero).

730 The principle of diversity of divine gifts underlies the characterization of heroes on both sides. Achilleus has fighting power, but Patroklos has greater wisdom, a pairing like that of Hektor and Poulydamas. It is interesting that dance as a skill is kept separate from the playing and singing of music (treated together).

741 The imminent reentry of Achilleus is a real possibility for the audience as well, since we have heard him pledge to return when Trojan fire reaches his ships (9.651).

754 The comparison to a mountain does not suit rapid movement, but perhaps alludes to the towering presence of the warrior (cf. *Od.* 9.190), while the gleam of his armor matches the dazzling snow.

825 This exaggerated rhetorical expression, like that of 8.539, is not in itself impious but manages to associate Hektor with a high ambition bordering on the wish for deification.

## BOOK FOURTEEN

16 The simile is remarkable because the powerful image of sea and wind—usually describing the actual movement of armies—is here transferred to Nestor's mental and emotional turmoil as he decides on his direction.

83 The exchange encapsulates both Agamemnon's feckless decisions and Odysseus' capacity for enduring long pain (as he will over the next decade). The reference to their lifelong war careers underlines the exceptional nature of this siege: no amateurs, they have nevertheless spent nine years in an assault.

113 Diomedes' growth as warrior and speaker is given yet another nod. As usual, the theme of his father's exploits arises. We learn yet more detail: that Tydeus is buried at Thebes and had once moved from Aitolia to Argos.

132 The men who "favored their anger" are probably the Myrmidons. The subsequent swipe at Achilleus by the disguised Poseidon (141) is meant to keep in view the overarching problem that has brought the Greeks to this crisis.

170 Hera's anger leads her to use sex as a weapon. The extended scene of preparation is therefore the functional equivalent of a warrior's arming scene.

201 Tethys and Okeanos as foster parents of Hera are not known from the mainstream

Hesiodic version of early divine history, but as Hera's discourse in general here is deceptive, this detail, too, could be a purely mythical construction. Another possibility is that she refers to a creation story otherwise only hinted at in some Greek versions (cf. Plato, *Cratylus*, 402b) and possibly influenced by Babylonian myths that name gods of fresh and salt water as the primal elements.

250 On Herakles' sack of Troy in the previous generation, see 5.638–51. Zeus punished Hera by dangling her with anvils attached to her feet from Olympos (15.18–24), the incident mentioned by Hephaistos (1.590), who was punished in turn when he sought to rescue his mother.

271 On swearing an oath to confirm the promise of a prize, see 10.321. Hera's cosmic witnesses include the previous generation of divinities, now imagined as confined to Tartaros. The penalty for a god breaking an oath sworn by Styx is to lie in a death-like trance for one year and spend the next nine cut off from the company of the Olympians (*Theogony* 738).

291 The gods' term is transparent and poetic (*chalkis*, "the brazen bird"), while the human term is without obvious etymology. For similar alternative names, see Hektor's son Astyanax/Skamandrios (6.402) and the river Xanthos/Skamandros (20.74).

317 The Catalogue of Loves provides a humorous diversion for the audience but seems somewhat uncouth as love talk to one's wife and sister. It is perhaps another power play by Zeus to remind Hera of his supreme will. The daughter of Phoinix is Europa, abducted by Zeus in the form of a bull. Zeus omits the detail that Semele was incinerated when she persuaded him to appear in all his glory and Dionysos was rescued from her womb. Demeter was mother of Persephonē, Leto of the twins Artemis and Apollo.

346 The marvelous growth and dew underscore the cosmic fertility brought about by this sacred marriage ("hierogamy"), which can be paralleled in many myths worldwide.

392 Reality in the narrative (the encroaching sea) turns immediately into simile (the sound of battle is louder than the surf's roar).

473 Aias' knowledge of his enemy's identity and kin is authentic enough, in view of the nine-year struggle during which both sides had time to become intimately acquainted.

497 The goriness of this killing, culminating in a horrific exhibition and taunt, reinforces the feeling that all boundaries to the excesses of war have been removed. The ferocious cycle accelerates as men kill in order to avenge their comrades.

518 The life force (*psykhē*) escaping through a wound is an unusually specific anatomical detail within the poem's conventions for the representation of death.

### BOOK FIFTEEN

26 Hera was constantly opposed to Herakles (whose name ironically means "glory of Hera") out of jealousy that Zeus had produced such a champion with a mortal woman. The further story of how she made Herakles subordinate to his cousin Eurystheus is told in 19.96.

64   Zeus' commands to his fellow gods shift into a foretelling of the plot, covering the main points of books 16 through 22: Achilleus' dispatch of Patroklos; that hero's death soon after Sarpedon's; and the subsequent killing of Hektor. Even the fall of Troy is reaffirmed—a point beyond the *Iliad*.

112  Askalaphos was killed without Ares' knowledge (13.518). The gesture of smacking the thighs with the palms portends imminent death (e.g., 16.125; and see S. Lowenstam, *The Death of Patroklos: A Study in Typology* [Königstein/Ts., 1981]). The death of a god's son (cf. the similar scene of Sarpedon's killing in book 16) shows how the fear of dissent on Olympos is what determines mortals' fates.

165  The unwillingness of Zeus to brook a rival who would declare himself equal echoes Agamemnon's problem with Achilleus (1.186), while the reminder that he is stronger "in authority" (*pherteros*, which Lattimore translates "in strength") uses the same word that describes Agamemnon's claim to power.

189  The triple division of the cosmos is not stressed in Hesiod's *Theogony*, focused as it is on the story of Zeus' rise to power. The motif, however, is ancient, found in Near Eastern myths.

204  On the Erinys see 9.454.

214  This is the first indication of which side Hermes and Hephaistos favor in the conflict. Unlike Hera, Athene, Aphrodite, and Poseidon, they have limited participation.

229  The aegis, used by Zeus and Athene, is thought of as a tasseled goatskin, perhaps shield-shaped, with magical power to stun and terrify. Most likely an ancient sign of Zeus' sovereignty, it may be related to the word for "heartwood" (also *aigis* in Greek) and thus to the god's sacred oak, the goatskin explanation (from "goat," *aix*) being a later reinterpretation.

263  Two similes mark the crucial reentry of Hektor—he is like a liberated steed, then like a lion—with no sense of incongruity, the emotional association of each image overriding linear sense, and the viewpoint varying in line with his own subjective feeling versus the way he is perceived by the Greeks as an object of terror.

379  Ironically, the Trojans mistake Zeus' thunder, which was made in positive response to Nestor's prayer, as an indication that he is still supporting *their* attack.

461  Despite his encouragement after Nestor's prayer (370), Zeus still protects Hektor. Teukros and Aias, however, are unsure as to which god is inhibiting their fight by frustrating their bow shots. Hektor acknowledges this to be the work of Zeus (489).

582  The pairing of the youngest Greek (Antilochos) with the peaceful cowherd Melanippos, recently moved to Troy, is ripe for pathos. As with Menelaos and Patroklos, the poet addresses Melanippos in the second person at the emotional climax of his wounding. The prewar life of Melanippos is picked up by the ensuing simile comparing Antilochos to a wild beast that has slain a herdsman.

595  One effect of the foreshadowing is to increase suspense: although the audience is given the plot outcome in outline, they await the exact details of battle and Hektor's death with sustained interest.

641  Naming alone offers the sign that Periphetes is better than his father Kopreus ("Dung man"). He carries a shield of the archaic Mykenaian type, as tall as the body.

705  The choice of location, the ship of Protesilaos, who was first to land and killed instantly, must prompt some foreboding for the Greeks.

721  The first we hear of Hektor's blame directed toward his elders for excessive caution. At 6.431 it was his wife Andromachē who urged him to stay close to the city walls.

## BOOK SIXTEEN

7  The picture of a young girl begging to be taken up by her mother is not a peaceful vignette, but (as shown in K. L. Gaca, "Reinterpreting the Homeric Simile of *Iliad* 16.7–11," *American Journal of Philology* 129 [2008]: 145–71) a specific reference to the fate of families after the fall of cities, and thus an ominous image.

18  At first Achilleus lumps together all Greeks with Agamemnon in speaking of their general arrogance. Later, he restricts blame to the individual who has injured him (54).

100  The wish for exclusive glory, to be shared only with Patroklos, is somewhat broader than the self-absorbed desire for recognition that Achilleus has just expressed (84–90), but still remarkably harsh in dismissing Greek as well as Trojan suffering.

124  A good example of "double motivation," when the urges of gods and humans coincide. Zeus wants to drive back the Trojans once fire has touched the first ship (15.599). Simultaneously, Achilleus has decided to let Patroklos carry out Nestor's independent suggestion about entering battle.

143  Tradition held that Cheiron the half-man, half-horse tutor of heroes, presented the ash spear at the wedding of Peleus and Thetis. Although Patroklos has been entrusted with Cheiron's medical knowledge (via Achilleus: 11.830), he cannot master fully the martial arts of the Centaur.

154  Like Achilleus himself, his chariot team is a mixture of mortal and divine genealogy. Two of his Myrmidon comrades (Menesthios, 173, and Eudoros, 179) are similarly half divine.

225  The special character of Achilleus is highlighted by what appear to be private or family rituals. Their extraordinary nature is further underlined by the reference to Dodona, a cult site of Zeus far in the northwest Greek territory. "Pelasgian" designates a semimythical pre-Greek population. The mysterious Selloi (Helloi, in some manuscripts, a name perhaps related to "Hellenes") differ from the usual Greek priests. Their closeness to the earth might indicate earlier chthonic origins of the cult. The scene is unusual, finally, because elsewhere in the *Iliad* a god never grants only half a prayer.

328  The king, Amisodaros, was not named when the Chimaira was introduced in the story of Bellerophontes (6.179).

385  The flood tied to Zeus' punishment of wrongdoing resembles the biblical account (*Genesis* 6–9). Although missing from Hesiod's *Theogony*, the flood tale appears to be a regional commonplace, showing up in early Near Eastern literature, such as *Gilgamesh*.

423  Sarpedon's ignorance of the identity of the raging Patroklos seems inconsistent with the Trojans' belief (281) that Achilleus has returned to battle; perhaps

the Lykian contingent on the edges of the fight has not seen Patroklos' initial foray.

433 Although Zeus laments that it is fate (*moira*) for his son to die, he nevertheless considers saving him, thereby overriding the set course of events. Hera's response affirms that Zeus is able to go against fate, but he risks the anger and disapproval of the other gods, in a lost cause (since Sarpedon, a mortal, must die sometime).

482 Sarpedon's end, the first of three extended death scenes that climax the poem, is accompanied by two similes (the tree and bull), a death speech with last words (492–501), but no speech by the killer (unlike the subsequent examples). The presence of Glaukos here foregrounds the theme of intense comradeship embodied by Achilleus and Patroklos: one man's close companion has now slain another's.

584 The poet begins to increase the frequency of direct address to Patroklos, heightening the pathos and intensity of the episode and situating the audience on his side of the struggle.

614 These two lines may have been interpolated from 13.504–5.

682 This scene is reproduced on one of the finest, best-known Greek vases, a wine mixing bowl by Euphronios from about 515 BC, showing Sleep and Death with Hermes as they lift the wound-riddled body of Sarpedon. The prized piece was at the Metropolitan Museum of Art in New York until 2008, when it was repatriated to Italy (where it had been looted from a tomb in the early 1970s).

765 An extended simile that well shows how the poet introduces a purely natural, uninhabited landscape to parallel the action or look of human events. At the same time, we are made aware that nature—in this case a wood of mixed trees struck by contending winds—can be thought to have its own warlike processes. Struggle is inescapable even off the battlefield.

787 Apollo's attack is the most direct and brutal of any god's in the *Iliad*, as well as being deceptive. The gradual dissolution of Patroklos is like a prolonged slow-motion film sequence. Even the close-up of Achilleus' helmet, now covered by dust, is highly cinematic.

830 Hektor's taunt to the dying Patroklos gets details wrong, and an audience realizes the grim irony. Achilleus, for example, did not tell him to slay Hektor. It is interesting that Hektor begins with mention of the capture of Trojan women, as if his parting conversation with Andromachē (book 6) remains foremost in his thoughts.

853 The pervasive folk tradition that a dying person's last words are prophetic can be seen already at work here. Cf. Socrates' at his trial predicting punishment for the Athenians (Plato, *Apology*, 39c).

BOOK SEVENTEEN

4 As the struggle to claim Patroklos' corpse begins, the hero is once more compared to young offspring needing protection, here a calf (cf. 16.7, a young girl).

51 The poem humanely refuses to denigrate enemies. One of Patroklos' killers can still be described in terms of beauty, with hair like the Graces (daughters of Zeus who embody all elegance and joy), resembling a lovely tree.

92 Menelaos admits that it was his own quest to regain Helen that has led to the death of Patroklos. His defense of the corpse is motivated by shame as well as comradeship.

126 Neither side are headhunters, but the intensity of grief over slain comrades leads both increasingly to consider decapitation. Compare the threat uttered by Euphorbos that he will console his parents, for his brother's death, by taking home the head of Menelaos (38).

147 Glaukos, who has once before shamed Hektor into fighting, uses exactly the words of Achilleus against Agamemnon (9.316–17) to complain that he and his men are treated unfairly by the Trojan prince and to threaten to leave. He wants Patroklos' corpse as a bargaining chip to regain the armor of his friend Sarpedon—not as a prop for the glorification of Hektor.

194 In the poet's brief comment and Zeus' speech, the armor becomes a portentous symbol of the mortality of Achilleus and Hektor, a sign of their imminent deaths.

250 Like Hektor speaking to the Lykians (225), Menelaos baldly states the quid pro quo for his insisting on help: he and his brother have wined and dined their fellow commander; now is time for payback.

290 The recompense theme is kept going in a minor key as Hippothoös, in dying while doing a favor for Hektor (291), fails to return to his parents what he owes for his upbringing.

404 The tragedy of partial knowledge (similar to the partial fulfillment of Achilleus' prayer to Zeus at 16.250) corresponds to the hero's half-mortal nature, as if he can never achieve divine omniscience. Although Achilleus realizes he will not take Troy, he has not known that Patroklos will die.

434 The perfect relevance of this simile to the context is increased if the poet has in mind tombstones such as were made in Athens in the early sixth century BC. Scenes with sculpted or painted warriors and horses might have been familiar to the audiences for epic poetry; other *stêlai* depicted lamenting kinfolk. This image captures both aspects. Once more the tragic incompatibility of mortal and divine is stressed.

570 The courage of the mosquito may seem a backhanded compliment. The image recalls 4.130 when Athene warded off a deadly missile from Menelaos like a mother swatting away a fly. Here the hero is at the other end of the simile, as it were—the persistent attacker rather than the helpless victim.

631 The signs of lightning and thunder (595) must convince the Greeks that it is specifically Zeus rather than Apollo who is frustrating their shots at the Trojans. This does not prevent Aias from praying to Zeus to make clear the skies (645), and the prayer succeeds.

709 Although Menelaos has told Antilochos (692) that Achilleus might help recover Patroklos' corpse, he realizes that this is not possible, since Hektor now has the warrior's armor (pending the manufacture of a new set in book 18).

755 The image seems reversed: one would imagine the following crowd of Trojans to be noisy in pursuit. But the comparison hinges on the frantic movement of the fleeing Greek troops, and the cries, like those of small birds instead of raptors, emphasize their weak position.

10 As usual, we learn from Achilleus of Thetis' prophecies only in the face of a crisis or after the fact (cf. 9.410). The technique is more common in the *Odyssey* (e.g., *Od.* 9.507, 13.173).

26 The description of Achilleus stretched in the dust matches that of warriors who have been slain (e.g., 16.775), a foreshadowing of his own death once he is drawn back into war. The image of clustering women who lament reinforces the idea that soon he, too, will be an object of grief (as Thetis acknowledges: 96).

39 The names of the nymphs, daughters of Nereus, reflect their habitat. Most are epithets for the sea (Glauke, "Gray"; Kymothoë, "Wave-swift"), while some refer to the mythical character of their father as a wise old man of the sea (Nemertes, "Unerring"; Apseudes, "Without lie"). Thetis' words are a lament for Achilleus rather than for Patroklos, whom she does not mention.

72 The resemblance here to Thetis' interview with Achilleus by the shore in book 1 underscores the irony that her son has now achieved what he begged her for, with unforeseen consequences. He now realizes that glory is less important than his companion's life.

117 Herakles died after being accidentally poisoned through a mistake by his wife Deianeira, who sent him a cloak thinking that the potion with which she had smeared it was a love charm (rather than a mixture of Hydra's blood). The story is dramatized in Sophocles' *Trachiniae*. After his incineration on a pyre, Herakles ascended to Olympos, where he was reconciled with Hera and given Youth (Hebe) as bride.

206 The blaze that Athene makes rise from Achilleus begins a complex simile that is at once a foreshadowing of the fall of Troy (a city under siege) and a recollection of the hero's wrath, just described as rising like smoke (109). Within the terms of the simile, the flame is a call for help, while the actual fiery warrior is the answer to such a call. A similar duality occurs in the trumpet simile (219).

301 Hektor interprets Poulydamas' words as demagogic pleading and so calls his bluff by challenging one who cares about possessions (by implication, one who urged immediate concern for the city) to distribute goods to the *dêmos* before the Greeks acquire them.

373 The automatic tripods are almost allegories for the ease with which prestige goods, such as Hephaistos makes, take on a life of their own when circulating in a culture of gift-exchange through guest-friendship and inheritance. Their mobility is a striking contrast to their maker's lameness.

395 Another fall from Olympos, different from that described earlier (1.590), which was caused by Zeus, not Hera. Although they seem on good terms, Hera, according to her son, has tried to eliminate him.

417 The golden robot maidens are described in terms similar to those used for Pandora (Hesiod, *Works and Days*, 70–82), gifted by all the gods with adornment and endowments.

483 Archaeologists have not discovered anything as elaborate as this shield. The closest parallels are silver plates from Phoenicia and bronze shields from Crete

(possibly imports from Asia Minor), both types having several concentric illustrated bands. The basic aesthetic principles—that big is beautiful, that the cosmos can be imitated in one epic work—apply to the *Iliad* as a whole. The divine craftsman stands in for the poet himself. It is worth noting, however, that Zenodotus, an early Homeric critic in Alexandria (third century BC), rejected the entire description as non-Homeric.

497 The city at peace, along with its harmonies of music and marriage, also contains disputes, but has a legal framework to deal with them. The issue at law—whether to accept a blood price or demand a death in return—echoes the choice of Achilleus (to take compensation for being dishonored or let his companions die).

510 The city at war is, like Troy, under siege, with the attacking army undecided as to whether it should take a ransom (half the city's goods) or sack the entire place. Unlike Troy, the besieged have planned a foray outside in the form of an ambush, and unlike in the *Iliad*, Ares is on the same side as Athene (516).

570 The Linos song was a lament for one who died young, perhaps because he rivaled Apollo. The story has Near Eastern parallels in worship of, for instance, Adonis. In modern Greek folk custom, stylized laments are still used as work songs.

590 Pastoral and agricultural scenes are capped by the dance, itself modeled on what the ultimate mythical artificer, Daidalos, made at Knossos in Crete (home of Minos and the labyrinth). The intricate and rapid motions of the dance are described by yet another craft image.

### BOOK NINETEEN

38 Infusion of the divine food and drink, nectar and ambrosia, gives a sort of immortality to Patroklos' flesh. Ancient Egyptian embalming practice involved extractions and infusions through the nostrils (Herodotus, 2.86).

60 Lyrnessos, a city sacked by Achilleus during his frequent coastal raids, yielded the war bride Briseis (2.690).

77 It is unclear whether Agamemnon's wound prevents him from standing or he stays seated as a form of abasement, symbolically lowering himself in the presence of the man he insulted.

86 Agamemnon admits he made a mistake (not that he was guilty of an ethical breach), but at the same time saves face by blaming three divinities for leading him astray (Zeus, Destiny, Erinys). *Atê* (destructive blindness) is personified and then made into an instrument of the gods. Her power, even over her own father Zeus, is illustrated by the subsequent tale of Herakles' delayed birth, a tale made more plausible by what the audience has already heard of Hera's deceptiveness (book 14).

141 Actually, the offer was made two days before. At this point the gifts can no longer be taken as a bribe (which they resembled in book 9), so Achilleus feels free to accept, though it is not his priority.

155 Odysseus' remarks on diet and exercise appear out of place. But they fit well with the *Odyssey* version of this hero, deeply involved with food and drink (see Pietro Pucci, *The Song of the Sirens: Essays on Homer* [Lanham, MD, 1998]). A contrast is

also made with Achilleus' own words in book 24, persuading Priam to put aside mourning and eat.

197 Zeus and the Sun are regularly invoked in oath-taking (3.276), since both hold commanding positions in the sky allowing them to observe right and wrong actions.

210 A gulf of feeling opens between the grief-frenzied Achilleus and the defenders of institutional norms. The younger man makes revenge primary, an occasion for something like a ritual fast and vow, while his elders dwell on practicalities like breakfast (see further 305–8).

282 The dramatic arrival of Briseis brings together the cause of the quarrel and its result (Patroklos dead). For the first time, we hear her own story as widow, survivor, and trophy. Patroklos' gentle ways are recalled by reference to his consoling personal promise to her. The effect is amplified by the moving line (302) about public lament for private sorrows.

327 Neoptolemos will be summoned from his maternal home on the island Skyros to Troy after Achilleus' death to participate in the final attack (see section B above). Achilleus' speech accurately captures the psychology of grief, remembering trivial events (cf. 316, on meals) while confusing personal distress with the imagination of how others might feel.

353 As Thetis preserved Patroklos (38) so Athene nourishes Achilleus, making the pair of companions look identical in yet another aspect.

389 An extended wordplay: Achilleus knows how to wield (*pêlai*) the spear of Peleus (*Pêliada*) received on Mount Pelion (*Pêliou*).

409 Talking horses are not found elsewhere in Greek epic, although common in Central Asian sagas (such as the *Manas* epic of Kyrgyzstan). Xanthos' words resemble the account by Agamemnon, earlier in this book, in shifting responsibility to Destiny and a great god (Apollo), the latter now named as Patroklos' killer and, by implication, Achilleus'. The tragic outcome was known (18.95), but the details (death at the hands of a god and mortal) may be news to the hero.

BOOK TWENTY

5 Themis, goddess of law and social order, is the wife (and aunt) of Zeus, and daughter of Gaia and Ouranos (Earth and Heaven). Okeanos (Ocean: 7) is the cosmic river encircling the disc-shaped earth.

92 The raid on Lyrnessos has recently been mentioned (19.60) as the event that brought Briseis to be Achilleus' consort. The detail (perhaps merely imagined by Aineias) that Achilleus was accompanied by Athene there and at Pedasos (city of the Leleges) enables one to imagine him, like Diomedes in book 5, as protégé of the daughter of Zeus, and foreshadows the goddess' fatal intervention in the encounter with Hektor in book 22.

105 The *Iliad* depicts Aphrodite as daughter of Zeus, in contrast to the well-known version in Hesiod's *Theogony* (190–206) according to which she arose in the open sea from the cast-off genitals of his grandfather Ouranos, and is thus older than the Olympian cohort. The latter version would make her more like Thetis, connected

to open water. The story of how Aineias was fathered on Aphrodite by Anchises, Priam's cousin, is told in the *Homeric Hymn to Aphrodite*.

122 From Hera's speech, it is clear that the *theomakhia* (Battle of the Gods) has taken on a very human element of competition, to show which ones are highest of the immortals (*aristoi*).

127 Yet another view of mortality: Destiny (also translated as Fate: the Greek here has *aisa*, "portion," synonymous with *moira*, "share") is said to have spun a thread of a certain length corresponding to one's allotted span of life. In other sources, three *Moirai* (Klotho, Lachesis, and Atropos) are responsible, respectively, for spinning, measuring, and cutting off the lifethread.

145 The wall is distinct from the main defenses of Troy and appears to be an improvised shelter that Athene had used to protect another of her favorites. Poseidon (with Apollo, in some versions) built the original walls for Laomedon, but after being defrauded of payment, the sea god sent a monster to ravage the city. Herakles slew the monster (saving Laomedon's daughter from it) but was also defrauded, receiving mortal horses instead of the divine steeds that had been promised. Mention of this tale foreshadows Achilleus' upcoming struggle with a watery opponent, the river Skamandros.

180 Looking to rattle Aineias, his opponent cunningly selects plausible topics that hit at the weakest point—his exclusion from the ruling branch at Troy and his former flight from Achilleus. Despite saying in response (203) that they already know one another's genealogies, Aineias plunges into a detailed history of the Trojan royal house, perhaps playing for time.

303 The survival of Aineias is necessary in order to start another chain of saga, culminating ultimately in the foundation account of Rome (elaborated by the Latin authors Virgil [*Aeneid*] and Livy [*History of Rome*]). A tradition about this important lineage probably existed in Greek-speaking areas of Asia Minor, where some families might have claimed Aineias as ancestor even at the time of the *Iliad*'s shaping. The significance of Dardanos (304) as Zeus' favorite explains why Aineias is at pains to trace his ancestry back to him (215).

371 The immediate repetition of a half line (a figure of speech called *epanalepsis*) expresses tense emotion, as if the speaker is fascinated with one thought: cf. 22.127.

382 Achilleus seems to shares the narrator's wide knowledge (e.g., locating Iphition in the hills near Tmolos) and adds even more precise details of topography. Knowing the genealogy and origins of the foe lends authority to warriors' rhetoric on the battlefield and burnishes their own fame by highlighting the importance of the slain.

404 Helikē, on the Corinthian gulf in Agamemnon's territory, had a famous shrine of Poseidon (8.203), but the sea god was also worshiped as "Helikonian" in Ionia at Mykalē, a promontory opposite the island of Samos (Herodotus 1.148.1). Site of the Pan-Ionian festival, this has been suggested as a possible location for early performances of Homer, so that this brief allusion would refer to a relevant spot familiar to audiences: see H. T. Wade-Gery, *The Poet of the Iliad* (Cambridge, 1952).

26 The sacrifice of these twelve youths will fulfill the vow made by Achilleus to Patroklos (18.336). Only here in the battle are prisoners taken, although there have been several references to earlier instances of opportunistic capture and return for ransom (e.g., 11.105).

54 The return of Lykaon disconcerts Achilleus since it is as if Trojan opponents are mysteriously being recycled. The same impression arises from the frantic rush of killing at the end of book 20, and the similes comparing victims to masses of locusts and fish (12, 22).

87 Achilleus already sacked Pedasos (20.92), home of Lykaon's mother. The weird fate of the son emphasizes the shift in Achilleus' attitude. Sold off once, Lykaon now must die, like all whom the enraged hero encounters. The change is framed by Achilleus' consciousness of his own inevitable death (whatever its superficial circumstances will be: 111).

132 Horses (dedicated to Poseidon) were sacrificed to a spring at Argos (Pausanias 8.7.2), but such offerings are more often associated with more exotic nations— Persians and Scythians, for example (Herodotus 4.61, 7.113). Achilleus may be denigrating it as a "barbarian" Trojan custom.

145 Xanthos is angered by pitiless slaughter and the buildup of corpses in his stream, but the imminent death of yet another man, who happens to be the grandson of a different river, brings his resentment to a boil. Achilleus uses the fluvial affiliation to mock Asteropaios (184–99), whose backstory centers on the "recent arrival" motif already seen in the case of Lykaon.

199 The implied threat in this increasingly cosmic standoff is that Zeus can and will evaporate the world's waters (as nearly happened in his struggle with the monster Typhoeus: cf. Hesiod, *Theogony*, 844–49). The upcoming contest of Achilleus (great-grandson of Zeus) and the river Xanthos is like a replay of that primeval battle.

274 The first we hear from Achilleus hints of a crisis of faith. Until now he has been confident of the support of Thetis and Athene; in addition, he has learned that Hera and Hephaistos have given their support. The potential of death by water creates here the same dread that Odysseus feels in the *Odyssey*, that lack of burial would mean loss of fame (*Od.* 5.306–12).

390 For Zeus the battle of gods provides entertainment, since it is known that no one will die (and even their wounds heal easily). As it turns out, their fights do not even affect the central clash of the Greeks and Trojans.

436 On the service of Poseidon and Apollo, see further 20.145. In reminding Apollo, Poseidon appeals to his honor and self-interest; Apollo's reply (461) looks like an attempt to save face. For another employment of the image of humans as leaves, see 6.146.

483 A woman's death in illness or childbirth could be said to have been caused by arrows shot by Artemis. The usage may be connected with the goddess's imagined role in symbolic mock "killing" of girls during initiation rituals. The sacrifice of

Iphigeneia to Artemis, enabling the Greek expedition to set sail at Aulis (an event ignored by the *Iliad*), has been tied to such an initiatory motif.

600 Apollo's ruse to lure away Achilleus is a foretaste of the disguise taken by Athene to trick Hektor as his death approaches (22.227). With the mass of Trojans thus allowed to seek safety behind the city walls, it also clears the stage for the one-on-one encounter of the poem's primary antagonists.

## BOOK TWENTY-TWO

15 The book is structured around dual deceptions by gods, who arrive finally at stunned recognition (*anagnôrisis*, in later Greek literary analysis): Achilleus is tricked by Apollo, as Hektor is by Athene. The latter's realization is tragic in tone and outcome (296–305).

29 Orion's Dog is Sirius, the "Dog Star" thought to bring the burning heat and fevers of midsummer (its heliacal dawn rising being in mid-July).

46 To Priam's unawareness of the deaths of his sons, compare Helen's equally pathetic ignorance of the loss of her brothers (3.243), noted as she gazes, in similar manner, from the Trojan wall over the plain.

66 Priam's supplication of Hektor contains vivid scenes of the fate of Troy, should Hektor not choose to defend it from inside the wall. Now it shifts into a lament for Priam himself, who pictures the contrast between beautiful and ugly corpses. He will be killed (according to the Cyclic epic *Little Iliad*) by Neoptolemos at his own doorway.

105 As earlier (6.441), Hektor is trapped by his sense of shame and pride, always imagining (to the extent of quoting) what others will say. He briefly considers a pact involving the return of Helen and payment of punitive damages, but rejects it as possibly leading to a disgraceful death.

147 The hot and cold springs are not only expressive of the heroes who run past them (Achilleus, who has been compared to a blazing fire; Hektor, who feels chill fear). They also embody the open and peaceful existence of earlier Troy in contrast to its present pent-in terror.

159 The imagery of footraces anticipates an event at the funeral games for Patroklos (23.740). An ox at those games is second prize, the first being a silver mixing bowl.

255 Hektor apparently still believes Achilleus can be persuaded at least to a covenant covering burial procedures, despite his decision (123) that further negotiation with Achilleus is out of the question.

299 The realization that he has been tricked is all the more swift and grim, since moments earlier Hektor could seriously doubt that the gods were helping Achilleus (279), even though the audience knew better.

340 Hektor's repeated request for kind treatment of his corpse appears to be out of consideration for his family's feelings. It instead prompts an outburst that shows the depth of Achilleus' rage: his desire to have the strength to eat Hektor's flesh (347).

359 This is the most detailed prediction yet of the manner and causes of Achilleus' death. It follows the pattern of prophetic last words (e.g., 16.852).

392 "Victory song" translates *paiêon* (whence English "paean"), which can also designate a song of thanksgiving after healing, usually for Apollo, Hektor's protector. The following lines (393–94) can be read as the words of the actual song.

437 Pathos arises from the poet's momentary suspension of the tragic scene in order to show Andromachē awaiting her husband in domestic calm. While she has a warm bath prepared, the audience knows his corpse is being dragged to the Greek camp.

460 "Like a raving woman" translates *mainadi isê*. In Greek mythical imagination "maenads" or "maddened ones," enthused female followers of Dionysos, are associated with ecstatic dance and consumption of the god's substance, wine, in outdoor settings. They also can exhibit murderous loss of control (as in the episode dramatized in the *Bacchae* of Euripides).

484 The focus on the experiences of Hektor's son brings down to human scale the disaster about to befall the entire city. Knowledge that Astyanax will be killed by the victorious Greeks makes all the more pitiful Andromachē's words imagining her son's fatherless future.

BOOK TWENTY-THREE

13 Riding around the honored dead warrior on his pyre may be an ancient Indo-European custom: cf. the ceremony at *Beowulf* 3169–82.

72 It was a common belief that the spirit of an unburied or uncremated person could not enter the realm of Hades but wandered outside it on the far side of the underworld river Styx. In his state of suspension between worlds, Patroklos does not know that Achilleus has planned his funeral for the next day.

85 Only now for the first time do we learn of Patroklos' early misfortune, exiled from Opous for manslaughter. Epeigeus (16.571) was likewise received by Peleus at Phthia, after killing a cousin.

104 Achilleus understands the look and words of Patroklos to indicate that soul (*psykhê*) and image (*eidôlon*) survive death. That he draws the conclusion about the absence of the "heart of life" (*phrenes*, the seat of intelligence, in Homer) is not surprising, since Greeks connected thought and consciousness closely with physical organs. The *phrenes* were localized near the lungs.

135 Cutting of hair was an outward sign of grief and symbolic separation. The additional detail that the corpse was thereby covered expresses the sheer number of sorrowing companions. Achilleus had vowed to keep his long hair until, on his return, he would honor the river Spercheios with his locks (significantly, as the gesture often accompanies initiation rituals). Now his hair-cutting will be redirected into a mourning dedication.

171 Tombs at Lefkandi in Euboea (tenth century BC) and Salamis in Cyprus, among others, have yielded multiple skeletons of horses, sometimes with chariots, in what are clearly aristocratic burials. Evidence for human sacrifice at burial sites in Greece is rare but not unattested: the early site of Lefkandi seems to offer some.

245 The temporary mound will shelter the urn with Patroklos' bones until those of Achilleus can be added later and a more splendid tomb constructed. The urn will

repose in the hut, it seems (254), only until the smaller barrow is ready for it. The practice of wrapping bones or container in cloth, as here, has been confirmed archaeologically.

296 A minor but illuminating detail, revealing that at least one potential recruit could buy his way out of service at Troy with a gift to the commander.

311 Nestor's advice, on winning despite disadvantages, becomes a hymn to skill or "cunning intelligence" (*mêtis*), a practical mode of thinking that verges sometimes on guile. Odysseus in the *Odyssey* is master of this skill and therefore regularly named *polymêtis* ("very shrewd").

441 Antilochos will be pressured later to take an oath that he did not use illegal moves to win, but will decline to do so (582).

461 The remarks of Idomeneus enable the narrator to introduce a range of potential plot directions (crashes and other mishaps), while holding the audience in suspense. It has already heard the close-up racing sequence and therefore is ironically superior in knowledge to this distant observer.

485 The first instance of sports betting in Western literature is proposed to depend not on the outcome but on the jockeys' positions midrace.

536 The awarding of a consolation prize equal in value to that for a second-place finish ignites a dispute that, in a small way, resembles that between Achilleus and Agamemnon over the spoils of war. Here the impetuous Antilochos plays the role of disgruntled young hero. Achilleus smiles at him (555) in recognition of the kinship in temperament.

581 The oath procedure is presented as customary (*themis*, translated "justice" here), which argues for a long tradition of chariot racing and related customs. That it is made to Poseidon makes sense in view of his traditional ties to chariots and horses (and his cult epithet Hippios).

610 The elaborate exchanges of the prizes satisfy all parties: Eumelos, who would have won, had it not been for divine intervention, nominally gets the award and a substitution prize; Antilochos saves face by claiming the mare and immediately handing it to Menelaos, who finally gains the uppermost hand by displaying princely generosity in giving it back to his young rival ("though she is mine": 610).

641 Nestor nearly killed the same twins in a skirmish against the Epeians (11.749), where they are called the Moliones. Tradition held that they were Siamese twins (and thus two were allowed to race against Nestor on his own). The other possible hint of this odd situation is the obscure phrase translated "crossing me in the crowd" (639, *plêthei prosthe balontes*), if one interprets it (*pace* Lattimore) as "going ahead by reason of their greater number."

665 Epeios made the wooden horse, at the suggestion of Odysseus (a fact not mentioned in the *Iliad* but at *Od.* 8.493).

679 That funeral games for Oidipous were held at Thebes, his native place, goes against the fifth-century tragic dramas that depict him as dying in exile (at Athens, usually) after the discovery of his parricide and incest.

705 A modern audience finds it unconscionable that a serving woman fetches one-third the price of a tripod, but the ranking no doubt reflects low life expectancy for working women, along with a highly utilitarian outlook and market conditions.

725 The guile of Odysseus takes on added meaning for an audience aware of his later contest with Aias over the armor of Achilleus, which Odysseus was reputed to have finally gained by trick or bribe. (The aftermath is dramatized in Sophocles' *Ajax*.)

826 A lump of pig-iron, said to be useful for making farm implements, disrupts slightly the effort to recreate Bronze Age conditions on the part of the poet, who lets a detail of his own era intrude.

890 Achilleus' decision to award first prize to Agamemnon based on status and repute (even before a contest) pointedly demonstrates the change from his earlier attitude to a newfound geniality (as if material goods have ceased to matter). On any account, Meriones deserves an extra prize in further recognition of the spectacular display of shooting skill that won him ten axes (850).

BOOK TWENTY-FOUR

24 Hermes (here "Argeïphontes," one of his epithets) was patron of thieves and master of cunning intelligence (*mêtis*); he stole Apollo's cattle when only a newborn baby (as recounted in the *Homeric Hymn to Hermes*).

29 This is the only *Iliad* passage referring to the judgment of Paris. His choice of Aphrodite to receive the apple designated "for the fairest" was taken by the two other competing goddesses, Hera and Athene, as an insult. Aphrodite's reward for his choice (the favors of Helen) started the war.

59 Hera's close relationship with Thetis, not previously disclosed, gives further motivation for her favoring attitude here (though it was ignored in book 1). Apollo's betrayal of Achilleus, whose good fortune he had predicted at the wedding of Thetis and Peleus, was recalled bitterly in a speech by Thetis that survives from a lost drama of Aeschylus. If the prophecy motif is as old as Homer, the audience will hear even more point in Hera's denigration of the god as "faithless" here (63).

119 The solution by Zeus is intended to save Achilleus' honor by granting him Priam's treasures while taking into account the objections of Apollo (and Zeus' own respect for Hektor's regular sacrifices). Priam's journey is thus motivated on divine and human levels.

165 The befouling of head and neck symbolically expresses the wish for the living lamenter to be close to the corpse's condition.

248 The depiction is psychologically apt—a grief-maddened father recklessly turns on the living to take out his resentment.

291 Hekabē's pious insistence that Priam entreat Zeus for an omen contrasts with her son's attitude toward bird signs (12.237). Elsewhere, only in the *Odyssey* are signs elicited (e.g., *Od.* 20.100). Usually the gods send them unbidden.

334 Hermes the *psychopompos* ("soul-conductor") was credited with accompanying spirits to and from the realm of the dead, a role related to the knack of inducing sleep. Priam's journey resembles a trip to the underworld.

480 Interesting reversals mark the simile: Achilleus, whose manslaughtering hands were just mentioned, rather than being the suppliant killer is compared to the crowd who marvel at him. At the same time, the autobiography of Patroklos (23.85–90) is evoked by this mention of an outlaw exile.

486 Priam's plea that Achilleus remember his father makes psychological sense to the audience that has heard the hero recall him with increased frequency over the last days, at 16.15, 18.87, 18.331, and 23.144.

527 The parable of the jars, meant to console Priam, presents a bleak view of life's hardships, but one not unique in archaic Greek literature: compare the story of Pandora and her jar (Hesiod, *Works and Days*, 47–105). Rather than doling out good to one and evil to another, the best Zeus can offer humans is a mixture, while the worst comprises evil undiluted.

560 Achilleus' dangerously rapid change of mood is triggered by Priam's well-meaning wish that he return home, since the hero knows well that he is doomed never to go back to Phthia. He draws back, in reaction, from the human sympathy just witnessed to a divine framework, saying that only the gods' command makes him surrender the corpse. In taking care that the body be prepared out of sight, Achilleus shows acute sensitivity to the limits of his own self-control (584).

602 A second consolatory narrative selects an example from myth, the tale of Niobē's boast of superiority to the goddess Leto and its consequence. Achilleus does not draw a moral about hubris but points instead to the necessity for food even in extreme grief. Niobē's transformation to stone seems a reward for endurance, a natural memorial to her eternal mourning (since water must run down the rock face).

649 The sarcasm has as its object the sons of Atreus, as Achilleus knows they are of the sort to try to contravene his wishes even now.

699 Kassandra, fairest of Priam's daughters (13.366), in other sources is said to have spurned Apollo's love, and as punishment her warnings to the Trojans were never believed. At the fall of Troy, she is dragged away from her refuge at Athene's altar, although clasping the statue of the goddess, and raped by Aias the son of Oïleus.

720 The singers (male, as the Greek text makes clear) as professional lamenters lead the mourning ritual. The less formal lament by women is described in descending order of closeness (mother, wife, sister-in-law), but in ascending dramatic order, concluding with the woman whose fate started the war.

735 For the fist time, Andromachē envisions the possibility that her son Astyanax will be killed at Troy, as finally happens.

765 While Andromachē and Hekabē dwelt on the effect of Hektor's death and his appearance, respectively, only Helen captures the essence of his personality, his generosity and gentle protection. Furthermore, only Helen admits openly that she laments for herself as well (773). Her remark that it has been *twenty* years since coming to Troy is an odd slip, unless it is a rhetorical exaggeration, or the remnant of another version (traces of which are found later) according to which the Greeks took ten years after their initial expedition (which went astray, to Mysia) before regrouping and mounting a second.

782 The poem ends with a glimmer of hope: the doomed Achilleus relents long enough to allow the enemy to bury their champion. That the emotional climax should center not on Achilleus but his victim Hektor (shown to be every bit as heroic as the Greeks) speaks for the deep humanity of the whole composition.

# Bibliography

## EDITIONS AND COMMENTARIES

Chantraine, P., and H. Goube, eds. *Iliade: Chant XXIII*. Paris, 1964.

Griffin, J. *Homer: Iliad IX*. Oxford, 1995.

Kirk, G. S. et al., eds. *The Iliad: A Commentary*. 6 vols. Cambridge, 1985–93.

Leaf, W., ed. *The Iliad*. Edited with apparatus criticus, prolegomena, notes, and appendices. London, 1900–1902.

Macleod, C. W., ed. *Homer: Iliad, Book XXIV*. Cambridge, 1982.

## OTHER TRANSLATIONS AND CRITIQUES

Arnold, M. "On Translating Homer." In *Matthew Arnold: Selected Essays*, edited by Noel Annan. Oxford, 1964.

Chapman, G., trans. *Chapman's Homer: The Iliad*. Edited with introduction and glossary by A. Nicoll; with a new preface by Garry Wills. Princeton, 1998.

Fagles, R., trans. *Homer: The Iliad*. Introduction and notes by Bernard Knox. New York, 1990.

Fitzgerald, R., trans. *Homer: The Iliad*. New York, 1974.

———. "Heroic Poems in English." Review of *The Iliad of Homer*, translated by Richmond Lattimore. *Kenyon Review* 14 (1952): 698–706.

Logue, Christopher. *War Music: An Account of Books 16 to 19 of Homer's Iliad*. New York, 1987.

Lombardo, S., trans. *Homer: The Iliad*. Introduction by Sheila Murnaghan. Indianapolis, 1997.

Newman, F., trans. *The Iliad of Homer*. London, 1856.

Pope, A., trans. *The Iliad of Homer*. Edited by M. Mack. New Haven, 1967.

## COMPANIONS

Foley, J. M., ed. *A Companion to Ancient Epic*. Malden, MA, 2005.

Fowler, R., ed. *The Cambridge Companion to Homer*. Cambridge, 2004.

Jones, P. V. *Homer's Iliad: A Commentary on Three Translations*. Bristol, 2003.

Leaf, W. *A Companion to the Iliad for English Readers*. London, 1892.

Postlethwaite, N. *Homer's Iliad: A Commentary on the Translation of Richmond Lattimore*. Exeter, 2000.

Powell, B., and I. Morris, eds. *A New Companion to Homer*. Leiden, 1997.

Wace, A. J. B., and F. H. Stubbings, eds. *A Companion to Homer*. London, 1962.

Willcock, M. *A Companion to the Iliad: Based on the Translation by Richmond Lattimore*. Chicago, 1976.

ESSAY COLLECTIONS WITH FURTHER BIBLIOGRAPHY

Cairns, D. L., ed. *Oxford Readings in Homer's Iliad*. Oxford, 2001.

Emlyn-Jones, C., ed. *Homer: Readings and Images*. London, 1992.

Kirk, G. S., ed. *The Language and Background of Homer*. Cambridge, 1964.

McAuslan, I., and P. Walcot, eds. *Homer*. Greece and Rome Studies 4. Oxford, 1998.

Montanari, F., ed. *Omero tremila anni dopo*. Rome, 2002.

Myrsiades, K., ed. *Approaches to Homer's Iliad and Odyssey*. New York, 2010.

Rubino, C. A., and C. W. Shelmerdine, eds. *Approaches to Homer*. Austin, 1983.

Wright, G. M., and P. V. Jones, eds. *Homer: German Scholarship in Translation*. Oxford, 1997.

Wright, J., ed. *Essays on the Iliad*. Bloomington, IN, 1978.

THE EPIC CYCLE, HESIOD, GREEK MYTHOLOGY

Athanassakis, A. *Hesiod: Theogony; Works and Days; Shield*. Baltimore, 1983.

———. *The Homeric Hymns*. Baltimore, 1976.

Burgess, J. S. *The Tradition of the Trojan War in Homer and the Epic Cycle*. Baltimore, 2001.

Davies, M. *The Greek Epic Cycle*. Bristol, 1989.

Griffin, J. "The Epic Cycle and the Uniqueness of Homer." *Journal of Hellenic Studies* 97 (1977): 39–53.

Martin, R. P. *Myths of the Ancient Greeks*. New York, 2003.

Penglase, C. *Greek Myths and Mesopotamia*. London, 1994.

West, M. L. "*Iliad* and *Aethiopis*." *Classical Quarterly* 53 (2003): 1–14.

———. *Greek Epic Fragments*. Cambridge, MA, 2003.

HOMER AND HISTORY

Carter, J., and S. Morris. *The Ages of Homer: A Tribute to Emily Townsend Vermeule*. Austin, 1995.

Chadwick, J. *The Decipherment of Linear B*. Cambridge, 1958.

———. *Linear B and Related Scripts*. Berkeley, 1987.

Crielaard, J. P. "Homer, History and Archaeology: Some Remarks on the Date of the Homeric World." In *Homeric Questions: Essays in Philology, Ancient History and Archaeology*, ed. J. P. Crielaard, 201–88. Amsterdam, 1995.

Dalby, A. *Rediscovering Homer: Inside the Origins of the Epic*. New York, 2006.

Easton, D. "Has the Trojan War Been Found?" *Antiquity* 59 (1985): 188–95.

Erskine, A. *Troy between Greece and Rome: Local Tradition and Imperial Power.* New York, 2001.

Finley, M. *The World of Odysseus.* 2nd ed. Harmondsworth, 1979.

Foxhall, L., and J. K. Davies, eds. *The Trojan War: Its Historicity and Context.* Bristol, 1984.

Latacz, J. *Troy and Homer: Towards a Solution of an Old Mystery.* Translated by K. Windle and R. Ireland. Oxford, 2004.

Mellink, M. J., ed. *Troy and the Trojan War.* Bryn Mawr, 1986.

Morris, I. "The Use and Abuse of Homer." *Classical Antiquity* 5 (1986): 81–136.

Morris, S. P. "A Tale of Two Cities: The Miniature Frescoes from Thera and the Origins of Greek Poetry." *American Journal of Archaeology* 93 (1989): 511–35.

Nagy, G. *Plato's Rhapsody and Homer's Music: The Poetics of the Panathenaic Festival in Classical Athens.* Washington, DC, 2002.

Powell, B. *Homer and the Origin of the Greek Alphabet.* Cambridge, 1991.

Puhvel, J. "Homeric Questions and Hittite Answers." *American Journal of Philology* 104 (1983): 217–27.

Sherratt, E. S. "Reading the Texts: Archaeology and the Homeric Question." *Antiquity* 64 (1990): 807–24.

Van Wees, H. *Status Warriors: War, Violence, and Society in Homer and History.* Amsterdam, 1992.

Vermeule, E. T. *Greece in the Bronze Age.* 2nd ed. Chicago, 1972.

Wade-Gery, H. T. *The Poet of the Iliad.* Cambridge, 1952.

Wood, M. *In Search of the Trojan War.* London, 1985.

Wood, R. *An Essay on the Original Genius of Homer.* Hildesheim, 1976. Orig. 1769 and 1775.

## HOMERIC SOCIETY AND VALUES

Alexiou, M. *The Ritual Lament in Greek Tradition.* Cambridge, 1974.

Dodds, E. R. *The Greeks and the Irrational.* Berkeley, 1951.

Fisher, N. *Hybris: A Study in the Values of Honour and Shame in Ancient Greece.* Warminster, 1992.

Haubold, J. *Homer's People: Epic Poetry and Social Formation.* Cambridge, 2000.

Lloyd-Jones, H. *The Justice of Zeus.* 2nd ed. Berkeley, 1983.

Martin, R. P. *Healing, Sacrifice, and Battle: Amechania and Related Concepts in Early Greek Poetry.* Innsbruck, 1983.

Yamagata, N. *Homeric Morality.* Leiden, 1994.

## HOMER AND ANCIENT ART

Anderson, M. J. *The Fall of Troy in Early Greek Poetry and Art.* Oxford, 1997.

Carpenter, T. H. *Art and Myth in Ancient Greece: A Handbook.* London, 1991.

Hedreen, G. M. "Image, Text, and Story in the Recovery of Helen." *Classical Antiquity* 15 (1996): 152–84.

Johansen, K. F. *The Iliad in Early Greek Art.* Copenhagen, 1967.

Snodgrass, A. *Homer and the Artists.* Cambridge, 1998.

Woodford, S. *The Trojan War in Ancient Art.* London, 1993.


ORAL POETRY: INTERPRETATION AND IMPLICATIONS

Edwards, M. W. "Homer and Oral Tradition: The Type-Scene." *Oral Tradition* 7 (1992): 284–330.

Fenik, B., ed. *Homer: Tradition and Invention.* Leiden, 1978.

———. *Typical Battle Scenes in the Iliad.* Wiesbaden, 1968.

Foley, J. M. *Immanent Art: From Structure to Meaning in Traditional Oral Epic.* Bloomington, IN, 1991.

Hainsworth, J. B. "The Criticism of an Oral Homer." *Journal of Hellenic Studies* 90 (1970): 90–98.

Honko, L. *Textualising the Siri Epic.* Helsinki, 1998.

Janko, R. "The Homeric Poems as Oral Dictated Texts." *Classical Quarterly* 48 (1998): 1–13.

Jensen, M. S. *The Homeric Question and the Oral-Formulaic Theory.* Copenhagen, 1980.

Kim, J. *The Pity of Achilles: Oral Style and the Unity of the Iliad.* Lanham, MD, 2000.

Létoublon, F., ed. *Hommage à Milman Parry: Le Style formulaire de l'épopée homérique et la théorie de l'oralité poétique.* Amsterdam, 1997.

Lord, A. B. *Epic Singers and Oral Tradition.* Ithaca, NY, 1991.

———. *The Singer of Tales.* 2nd ed. With introduction by S. Mitchell and G. Nagy. Cambridge, MA, 2000. Orig. 1960.

Morrell, K. S. "Chaos Theory and the Oral Tradition: Nonlinearity and Bifurcation in the *Iliad.*" *Helios* 23 (1996): 107–34.

Nagy, G. *Homeric Questions.* Austin, 1996.

———. *Homeric Responses.* Austin, 2003.

———. *Poetry as Performance: Homer and Beyond.* Cambridge, 1996.

Nagler, M. *Spontaneity and Tradition: A Study in the Oral Art of Homer.* Berkeley, 1974.

Parry, M. *The Making of Homeric Verse: The Collected Papers of Milman Parry.* Edited by Adam Parry. Oxford, 1971.

Reece, S. *The Stranger's Welcome: Oral Theory and the Aesthetics of the Homeric Hospitality Scene.* Ann Arbor, MI, 1993.

Reynolds, D. *Heroic Poets, Poetic Heroes: The Ethnography of Performance in an Arabic Oral Epic Tradition.* Ithaca, NY, 1995.


RECEPTION

Clarke, H. *Homer's Readers: A Historical Introduction to the Iliad and the Odyssey.* Newark, 1981.

Graziosi, B. *Inventing Homer: The Early Reception of Epic.* Cambridge, 2002.

Graziosi, B., and E. Greenwood, eds. *Homer in the Twentieth Century: Between World Literature and the Western Canon.* New York, 2007.

Graziosi, B., and J. Haubold. *Homer: The Resonance of Epic.* London, 2005.

King, K. *Achilles: Paradigms of the War Hero from Homer through the Middle Ages.* Berkeley, 1987.

Lamberton, R. *Homer the Theologian.* Berkeley, 1986.

Lamberton, R., and J. Keaney. *Homer's Ancient Readers: The Hermeneutics of Greek Epic's Earliest Exegetes.* Princeton, NJ, 1992.

Michelakis, P. *Achilles in Greek Tragedy.* Cambridge, 2002.

Myres, J. L. *Homer and His Critics.* London, 1958.

Prins, Y. "Nineteenth-Century Homers and the Hexameter Mania." In *Nation/ Language and the Ethics of Translation.* Edited by S. Berman and M. Wood. Princeton, 2005.

Reid, J. D., ed. *The Oxford Guide to Classical Mythology in the Arts, 1300–1900s.* New York, 1993.

Schwartz, E. et al., eds. *The Legacy of Homer: Four Centuries of Art from the École nationale supérieure des beaux-arts, Paris.* New Haven, 2005.

Vandiver, E. *Stand in the Trench, Achilles: Classical Receptions in British Poetry of the Great War.* New York, 2010.

HOMERIC POETRY IN GENERAL

Crotty, K. *The Poetics of Supplication: Homer's Iliad and Odyssey.* Ithaca, NY, 1994.

Dalby, A. "The *Iliad,* the *Odyssey* and Their Audiences." *Classical Quarterly* 45 (1995): 269–79.

Ford, A. *Homer: The Poetry of the Past.* Ithaca, NY, 1992.

Frame, D. *Hippota Nestor.* Washington, DC, 2009.

———. *The Myth of Return in Early Greek Epic.* New Haven, 1978.

Griffin, J. *Homer on Life and Death.* Oxford, 1980.

Kirk, G. S. *The Songs of Homer.* Cambridge, 1962. Repr. 1977.

Minchin, E. *Homer and the Resources of Memory: Some Applications of Cognitive Theory to the Iliad and the Odyssey.* Oxford, 2001.

Moulton, C. *Similes in the Homeric Poems.* Göttingen, 1977.

Nagy, G. *Homer the Classic.* Washington, DC, 2009.

Pucci, P. *The Song of the Sirens: Essays on Homer.* Lanham, MD, 1998.

Scott, W. *The Oral Nature of the Homeric Simile.* Leiden, 1974.

Scully, S. *Homer and the Sacred City.* Ithaca, NY, 1990.

Seaford, R. *Reciprocity and Ritual: Homer and Tragedy in the Developing City-State.* Oxford, 1994.

Thalmann, W. G. *Conventions of Form and Thought in Early Greek Epic Poetry.* Baltimore, 1984.

Vivante, P. *The Homeric Imagination: A Study of Homer's Poetic Perception of Reality.* Bloomington, IN, 1970.

Whitman, C. H. *Homer and the Heroic Tradition.* Cambridge, MA, 1958.

Wolf, F. A. *Prolegomena to Homer.* Translated with introduction and notes by A. Grafton, G. W. Most, and J. E. G. Zetzel. Princeton, NJ, 1985. Orig. 1795.

Bouvier, D. *Le sceptre et la lyre: L'Iliade ou les héros de la mémoire.* Grenoble, 2002.

Bowra, C. M. *Tradition and Design in the Iliad.* Oxford, 1930.

Collins, L. *Studies in Characterization in the Iliad.* Frankfurt am Main, 1988.

De Jong, I. J. F. *Narrators and Focalizers: The Presentation of the Story in the Iliad.* Amsterdam, 1987.

Dué, C., and M. Ebbott. *Iliad 10 and the Poetics of Ambush: A Multitext Edition with Essays and Commentary.* Washington, DC, 2010.

Edwards, M. W. *Homer: Poet of the Iliad.* Baltimore, 1987.

Gaca, K. L. "Reinterpreting the Homeric Simile of *Iliad* 16.7–11: The Girl and Her Mother in Ancient Greek Warfare." *American Journal of Philology* 129 (2008): 145–71.

Hammer, D. C. *The Iliad as Politics: The Performance of Political Thought.* Norman, OK, 2002.

Holoka, J. P., ed. *Simone Weil's The Iliad, or The Poem of Force: A Critical Edition.* New York, 2003.

Lowenstam, S. *The Death of Patroklos: A Study in Typology.* Königstein im Taunus, 1981.

Lynn-George, M. *Epos: Word, Narrative, and the Iliad.* Atlantic Highlands, NJ, 1988.

Mackie, H. *Talking Trojan.* Lanham, MD, 1996.

Martin, R. *The Language of Heroes: Speech and Performance in the Iliad.* Ithaca, NY, 1989.

Morrison, J. V. *Homeric Misdirection: False Predictions in the Iliad.* Ann Arbor, 1992.

Mueller, M. *The Iliad.* London, 1984.

Muellner, L. *The Anger of Achilles: Mênis in Greek Epic.* Ithaca, NY, 1996.

Nagy, G. *The Best of the Achaeans.* Baltimore, 1979; 2nd ed., 1999.

Redfield, J. *Nature and Culture in the Iliad.* Chicago, 1975; 2nd ed., 1994.

Schein, S. *The Mortal Hero.* Berkeley, 1984.

Segal, C. *The Theme of the Mutilation of the Corpse in the Iliad.* Leiden, 1971.

Slatkin, L. M. *The Power of Thetis: Allusion and Interpretation in the Iliad.* Berkeley, 1991.

Stanley, K. *The Shield of Homer: Narrative Structures in the Iliad.* Princeton, 1993.

Taplin, O. *Homeric Soundings: The Shaping of the Iliad.* Oxford, 1992.

Thornton, A. *The Iliad: Its Composition and the Motif of Supplication.* Göttingen, 1984.

Visser, E. *Homers Katalog der Schiffe.* Stuttgart, 1997.

Wilson, D. *Ransom, Revenge, and Heroic Identity in the Iliad.* Cambridge, 2002.

Zecchin de Fasano, Graciela C. "Memoria y funeral: Priamo y Aquiles en *Iliada* XXIV.472–551." *Synthesis* 7 (2000): 57–68.

OTHER WORKS MENTIONED IN INTRODUCTION AND NOTES

Bridges, R. *Ibant Obscuri: An Experiment in the Classical Hexameter.* Oxford, 1916.

Cunliffe, R. J. *A Lexicon of the Homeric Dialect.* London, 1924. Repr. Norman, OK, 1963.

Cunningham, J. V. *The Exclusions of a Rhyme: Poems and Epigrams.* Denver, 1960.

Rosaldo, R. "Grief and a Headhunter's Rage." In *Violence in War and Peace,* edited by N. Scheper-Hughes and P. Bourgois, 150–56. Malden, MA, 2004.

Schmidt, C. E. *Parallel-Homer: Oder, Index aller homerischen Iterati in lexikalischer Anordnung zusammengestellt.* Göttingen, 1885. Repr. 1965.

Shay, J. *Achilles in Vietnam: Combat Trauma and the Undoing of Character.* New York, 1994.

Smith, W. B. and W. Miller. *The Iliad of Homer: A Line for Line Translation in Dactylic Hexameters.* New York, 1944.

# Glossary of Names

It is a frequent, though not universal, practice to Latinize Greek names, then Anglicize the Latin forms, at least in pronunciation. I have generally avoided this practice, but have followed it on some occasions. Names ending in *ees* have been made to end in *es*; some names end (falsely) in *an*, as *Danaän, Boiotian*. Some endings in *e* have been changed to *a*, as *Ida* (not *Ide*), *Hera* (not *Here*). Other Anglo-Latin forms are: Apollo, Argives, Athens, Centaurs, Egypt, Hades, Helen, Hermes, Jason, Myrmidons, Priam, Rhodes, Thrace and Thracian, Titans, Trojans, Troy.

This glossary is not meant to be a complete index, but gives at least one reference for each name in question (frequently there is only one) except in the case of major characters, for whom only a complete index would be useful. References are to book and line.

Aban'tes: The people of Euboia, 2.536.

Abar'bare: A nymph, 6.22.

A'bas: Trojan killed by Diomedes, 5.148.

A'bioi: Barbarians of the north, 13.6.

Able'ros: Trojan killed by Antilochos, 6.33.

Aby'dos: A city on the Hellespont, 2.836.

Achai'a: Greece.

Achai'ans: Greeks.

Acheloi'os: (1) A river in west-central Greece, 21.194. (2) A river in Phrygia, 24.616.

Achill'eus: Son of Peleus and Thetis, (Pelei'on, Pele'ides) leader of the Myrmidons, 1.7, etc.

A'damas: Trojan killed by Meriones, 13.560 sqq.

Adme'tos: King in Thessaly, husband of Alkestis, father of Eumelos, 2.713.

Adrestei'a: City near Troy, 2.828.

Adres'tos: (1) King of Sikyon, 2.572. (2) Warrior from Adresteia, 2.830; killed by Diomedes, 11.328 sqq. (3) Trojan killed by Agamemnon and Menelaos, 6.37 sqq. (4) Trojan killed by Patroklos, 16.693.

Ag'akles: Father of Epeigeus, 16.571.

Agame'de: Wife of Moulios, 11.740.

Agamem'non: Son of Atreus (therefore sometimes called Atreides), brother of Menelaos, king of Mykenai and chief leader of the Achaians, 1.24, etc.

Agape'nor: Leader of the Arkadians, 2.609.

Agas'thenes: Of Elis, father of Polyxeinos, 2.624.

Agas'trophos: Trojan killed by Diomedes, 11.338.

Agathon: Son of Priam, 24.249.

Agau'e: A Nereïd, 18.42.

Agela'os: (1) Trojan killed by Diomedes, 8.257. (2) Achaian killed by Hektor, 11.302.

Age'nor: Son of Antenor, one of the great captains and fighters of Troy. Fights Achilleus, 21.544 sqq.

Aglai'a: Mother of Nireus, 2.672.

A'grios: A prince of Kalydon, 14.116.

Aia'kides: Meaning "descendent of Aiakos," used of Achilleus.

Ai'akos: Son of Zeus, father of Peleus, 21.189.

Aian'tes: The two called Aias when spoken of together.

Ai'as: (1) Son of Telamon, "Telamonian" Aias, of Salamis, 2.557, etc. (2) Son of Oïleus, of Lokris, 2.527–30, etc.

Aïdo'neus: Another name for Hades.

Ai'gai: City in Achaia, 8.203.

Aigai'os: God of the sea, father of Briareos, 1.404.

Ai'geus: Father of Theseus, 1.265.

Aigialei'a: Wife of Diomedes, 5.412.

Aigi'alos: City in Paphlagonia, 2.855.

Ai'gilips: City or locality in the domain of Odysseus, 2.633.

Aigi'na: Island in the domain of Argos, 2.562.

Ai'gion: City in Achaia, 2.574.

Ainei'as: Son of Anchises and Aphrodite, leader of the Dardanians, 2.820, etc.

Ai'nios: Paionian killed by Achilleus, 21.210.

Ai'nos: City in Thrace, 4.520.

Ai'olos: Father of Sisyphos, 6.154.

Aipei'a: Town in Pylos, 9.152.

Ai'py: City near Pylos, 2.592.

Ai'pytos: Hero of Arkadia, 2.604.

Aise'pos: (1) River near Zeleia, 2.825. (2) Trojan killed by Euryalos, 6.21.

Aisye'tes: (1) Hero buried in the Trojan plain, 2.793. (2) Father of Alkathoös, 13.427.

Aisy'me: City in Thrace, 8.304.

Aisym'nos: Achaian killed by Hektor, 11.303.

Ai'the: Mare belonging to Agamemnon, 23.295.

Aithi'kes: A people of Thessaly, 2.744.

Ai'thon: One of Hektor's horses, 8.185.

Ai'thre: One of Helen's handmaidens, 3.144.

Aito'lians: People of Aitolia in western Greece, led by Thoas, 2.638–44, etc.

A'kamas: (1) Son of Antenor and companion of Aineias, killed by Meriones, 16.342.

(2) Thracian killed by Aias, 6.8.

Akessa'menos: A Thracian chief, 21.143.

Akri'sios: Father of Danaë, 14.319.

Aktai'e: A Nereïd, 18.41.

Ak'tor: (1) Father of Astyoche, 2.513. (2) Apparently, an ancestor of Kteatos and Eurytos, 2.621. (3) Father of Menoitios, so grandfather of Patroklos, 11.785. (4) Father of Echekles, 16.189.

Alas'tor: (1) Follower of Nestor, 4.295. (2) Lykian, killed by Odysseus, 5.677. (3) Father of Tros (2), 20.463.

Alege'nor: Father of Promachos, 14.504.

Alei'os: A plain in Asia, 6.201.

Alexan'dros: Another, and in the *Iliad* more usual, name for Paris, q.v.

Alkan'dros: Lykian killed by Odysseus, 5.678.

Alkath'oös: Brother-in-law of Aineias, killed by Idomeneus, 13.427–44.

Alkes'tis: Wife of Admetos, mother of Eumelos, 2.715.

Alkim'edon: A Myrmidon chief, 16.197.

Al'kimos: Follower of Achilleus, 19.392.

Alkma'on: Achaian killed by Sarpedon, 12.394.

Alkme'ne: Mother of Herakles, 14.323.

Alky'one: "Sea-bird," a byname for Marpessa, 9.562.

Alo'eus: Father of Ephialtes and Otos, 5.386.

Al'ope: Town in the domain of Achilleus, 2.682.

Al'os: Town in the domain of Achilleus, 2.682.

Alphei'os: A river in the western Peloponnese, 2.592, etc.

Al'tes: King of the Leleges, whose daughter, Laothoe, was one of Priam's wives, 21.85.

Althai'a: Mother of Meleagros, 9.555.

Al'ybē: The city of the Halizones, on the south shore of the Black Sea, 2.857.

Amaryng'keus: An Elean hero, father of Diores, 2.622.

Amathei'a: A Nereïd, 18.48.

A'mazons: A race of warrior women who invaded Asia Minor, 3.189, 6.186.

Amiso'daros: A lord of Lykia, father of Atymnios and Maris, 16.328.

Amopa'on: Trojan killed by Teukros, 8.276.

Amphi'damas: (1) A hero of Kythera, 10.268. (2) A hero of Opous, 23.87.

Amphigenei'a: City near Pylos, 2.593.

Amphi'klos: Trojan killed by Meges, 16.313.

Amphi'machos: (1) A leader of the Epeians, killed by Hektor, 13.185. (2) A leader of the Karians, 2.870.

Amphi'nomē: A Nereïd, 18.44.

Amphi'on: A leader of the Epeians, 13.692.

Amphi'os: (1) Trojan ally from Adresteia, son of Merops, 2.830; killed by Diomedes, 11.328. (2) Trojan ally, son of Selagos, killed by Aias, 5.612.

Amphi'thoë: A Nereïd, 18.42.

Amphi'tryon: Putative father of Herakles, 5.392.

Ampho'teros: Trojan killed by Patroklos, 16.415.

A'mydon: City of the Paionians, 2.849.

Amy'klai: City near Sparta, 2.584.

Amyn'tor: Father of Phoinix, 9.448.

Anchi'alos: Achaian killed by Hektor, 5.609.

Anchi'ses: Second cousin of Priam, lover of Aphrodite, father of Aineias, 5.268–73, 20.230–40.

Andrai'mon: Father of Thoas, 2.638.

Andro'machē: Daughter of Eëtion, wife of Hektor, 6.371.

Anemorei'a: City in Phokis, 2.521.

Angkai'os: (1) Father of Agapenor, 2.609. (2) Of Pleuron, a wrestler beaten by Nestor, 23.635.

Antei'a: Wife of Proitos, who tempted Bellerophontes, 6.160.

Ante'nor: An important counselor of Priam and the Trojans, father of numerous sons who figure in the *Iliad*, 3.148, 7.347, etc.

Anthe'don: Town in Boiotia, 2.508.

Anthei'a: Town near Pylos, 11.151.

Anthe'mion: Father of Simoeisios, 4.473.

Anti'lochos: Son of Nestor, close friend of Achilleus, a prominent warrior, 4.457, etc.

Anti'machos: Father of Peisandros (1) and Hippolochos (2), and of Hippomachos, 11.123, 12.188.

Anti'phates: Trojan killed by Leonteus, 12.192.

Anti'phonos: Son of Priam, 24.250.

An'tiphos: (1) A leader of the men from Kos and adjacent islands, 2.678. (2) A leader of the Maionians, 2.864. (3) Son of Priam, killed by Agamemnon, 11.101.

An'tron: City in Thessaly, in the domain of Protesilaos, 2.697.

Apai'sos: City in the Troad, 2.828.

A'phareus: Achaian killed by Aineias, 13.541.

Aphrodi'te: Daughter of Zeus and Dione, mother of Aineias, protectress of Helen, called also the Lady of Kypros, 3.374, etc.

Apisa'on: (1) Trojan killed by Eurypylos, 11.578. (2) Trojan killed by Lykomedes, 17.348.

Apollo: Son of Zeus and Leto, chief protector of the Trojans, 1.9, etc.

Apseu'des: A Nereïd, 18.46.

Araithyr'ea: City in the domain of Agamemnon, 2.571.

Arche'lochos: Son of Antenor, killed by Aias, 14.463.

Archepto'lemos: Charioteer of Hektor, killed by Teukros, 8.312.

Areï'lykos: (1) Father of Prothoënor, 14.451. (2) Trojan killed by Patroklos, 16.308.

Areï'thoös: (1) "The club-fighter," father of Menesthios, killed by Lykourgos (2), 7.8, 7.137. (2) Trojan killed by Achilleus, 20.487.

Are'ne: City near Pylos, 2.591.

A'res: Son of Zeus and Hera, fights on the side of the Trojans, 5.30, etc.

Areta'on: Trojan killed by Teukros, 6.31.

Are'tos: Trojan killed by Automedon, 17.517.

Ar'geas: Father of Polymelos, 16.417.

Argeïphon'tes: A name given to Hermes.

Argis'sa: City in Thessaly, in the domain of Polypoites, 2.738.

Ar'gives: The same as Achaians.

Ar'gos: (1) Place-name denoting sometimes a city (under the sway of Diomedes), sometimes a larger district in the northeast Peloponnese, and used also to mean simply "Greece." (2) Pelasgian Argos, the domain of Achilleus.

Ariad'ne: Daughter of Minos, 18.592.

Ar'imoi: A people of Kilikia, 2.783.

Ari'on: A famous racehorse, 23.346.

Aris'bas: Father of Leiokritos, 17.345.

Aris'be: City in the Troad, 2.836.

Ar'ne: City in Boiotia, 2.507.

Arsi'noös: Father of Hekamede, 11.626.

Ar'temis: Sister of Apollo, 5.51, etc.

Asai'os: Achaian killed by Hektor, 11.301.

A'sinē: City near Argos, 2.560.

A'sios: (1) Son of Hyrtakos, a Trojan ally, killed by Idomeneus, 13.389. (2) Brother of Hekabē and uncle of Hektor, 16.717.

Aska'laphos: Son of Ares, a chief of Orchomenos, 2.511; killed by Deïphobos, 13.519.

Aska'nia: City in Phrygia, 2.863.

Aska'nios: Leader from Askania, 13.792.

Askle'pios: The great healer, father of Machaon and Podaleirios, 2.731.

Aso'pos: River in Boiotia, 4.383.

Asple'don: City of the Minyai, near Orchomenos, 2.511.

Assar'akos: Son of Tros, brother of Ilos, great-grandfather of Aineias, 20.232.

Aster'ion: City in Thessaly, in the domain of Eurypylos, 2.735.

Asteropai'os: Leader of the Paionians, one of the greatest of the Trojan allies, 12.102; killed by Achilleus, 21.140–83.

Asty'alos: Trojan killed by Polypoites, 6.29.

Asty'anax: Hektor's infant son, 6.403.

Asty'noös: (1) Trojan killed by Diomedes, 5.144. (2) A Trojan charioteer, 15.455.

Asty'ochē: Mother, by Ares, of Askalaphos and Ialmenos, 2.513.

Astyochei'a: Mother of Tlepolemos, 2.658.

Asty'pylos: Paionian killed by Achilleus, 21.209.

Athe'ne: or Pallas Athene, also called Tritogeneia, daughter of Zeus, protectress of the Achaians, particularly Achilleus, Diomedes, and Odysseus, 1.194, etc.

Ath'ens: The city of Erechtheus, in east-central Greece, 2.546.

Ath'os: Mountain and promontory in the northern Aegean, 14.229.

Atrei'des: "Son of Atreus," used of Agamemnon, less often of Menelaos.

At'reus: Father of Agamemnon and Menelaos, 2.105.

Atryto'ne: Epithet of Athene, 1.157.

Atym'nios: (1) Father of Mydon, 5.581. (2) Trojan, brother of Maris, killed by Antilochos, 16.317.

Augei'ai: (1) City in Lokris, 2.532. (2) City in Lakedaimon, 2.583.

Augei'as: Lord of Elis, 11.701.

Au'lis: A city at the narrows between Euboia and the mainland, where the ships of the Achaians assembled for the expedition to Troy, 2.303.

Auto'lykos: Maternal grandfather of Odysseus, 10.266.

Auto'medon: Follower and charioteer of Achilleus and Patroklos, a considerable warrior in his own right, 16.145, 17.429.

Auto'noös: (1) Achaian killed by Hektor, 11.301. (2) Trojan killed by Patroklos, 16.694.

Auto'phonos: Father of Polyphontes, 4.395.

Ax'ios: A river, and river-god, in Paionia, 2.849.

Ax'ylos: Trojan ally from Arisbe, killed by Diomedes, 6.12.

A'zeus: Father, or ancestor, of Aktor (1), 2.513.


Bal'ios: One of the immortal horses of Achilleus, 16.149.

Bath'ykles: Myrmidon killed by Glaukos, 16.594.

Bellerophon'tes: Hero from Korinth, killer of the Chimaira, grandfather of Sarpedon and Glaukos (now usually called Bellerophon), 6.155–202.

Bes'sa: City in Lokris, 2.532.

Bias: (1) Leader under Nestor, 4.296. (2) Athenian, leader under Menestheus, 13.691. (3) Father of Dardanos (2) and Laogonos (2), 20.461.

Bie'nor: Trojan killed by Agamemnon, 11.92.

Boag'rios: River in Lokris, 2.533.

Boi'be: Thessalian city in the domain of Eumelos, 2.712.

Boibe'is: The lake by which Boibe was situated, 2.711.

Boio'tians: The people of Boiotia, in central Greece northwest of Attica, 2.494.

Bor'eas: The north (more accurately northeast) wind, 9.4.

Bo'ros: (1) Father of Phaistos, 5.44. (2) Husband of Polydore, 16.177.

Boudei'on: Town in the territory of the Myrmidons, 16.572.

Boukol'ion: Son of Laomedon, father of Aisepos (2) and Pedasos (1), 6.22.

Bou'kolos: Father of Sphelos, grandfather of Iasos, 15.338.

Boupra'sion: City in Elis, 2.615.

Briar'eos: A hundred-handed giant, 1.403.

Brise'is: The captive mistress of Achilleus, 1.184; her life story, 19.282–300.

Bri'seus: Father of Briseis, 1.392.

Brysei'ai: City in Lakedaimon, 2.583.


Cen'taurs: Creatures, part human and part beast, at home around Mount Pelion, 11.832.

Chal'kis: (1) City in Euboia, 2.537. (2) City in Aitolia, 2.640. (3) Name of a bird, 14.291.

Chalko'don: Father, or ancestor, of Elephenor, 2.541.

Charis: Goddess, wife of Hephaistos, 18.382–93.

Char'opos: Father of Nireus, 2.672.

Charops: Trojan killed by Odysseus, 11.427.

Chei'ron: "Most righteous of the Centaurs," friend and teacher of Asklepios, 4.219; of Achilleus, 11.832; of Peleus, 16.143.

Chersi'damas: Trojan killed by Odysseus, 11.423.

Chimai'ra: Lykian monster killed by Bellerophontes, 6.179.

Chro'mios: (1) Follower (in the *Odyssey*, 11.286, brother) of Nestor, 4.295. (2) Son of

Priam killed by Diomedes, 5.160. (3) Lykian killed by Odysseus, 5.677. (4) Trojan killed by Teukros, 8.275. (5) A Trojan captain, 17.218.

Chromis: Leader of the Mysians, killed by Achilleus, 2.858.

Chry'se: Town near Troy, the home of Chryses, 1.37.

Chryse'is: Daughter of Chryses, captive mistress of Agamemnon, released by him to her father (later Criseyde, Cressida), 1.111, etc.

Chryses: Priest of Apollo, father of Chryseis, 1.11.

Chryso'themis: Daughter of Agamemnon, 9.145.


Dai'dalos: Builder in Krete, 18.592.

Dai'tor: Trojan killed by Teukros, 8.275.

Dam'asos: Trojan killed by Polypoites, 12.183.

Damas'tor: Father of Tlepolemos (2), 16.416.

Dan'aäns: Achaians, Argives.

Dan'aë: Mother, by Zeus, of Perseus, 14.319.

Dardan'ia: The domain of Dardanos, 20.216.

Dardanian, Dardanians: Of Dardania, or descended from, or pertaining to, Dardanos. Used of the group of Trojans whose lord was Aineias, 2.819.

Dar'danos: (1) Son of Zeus, father of Erichthonios, ancestor of the Trojan kings, 20.215. (2) Son of Bias, killed by Achilleus, 20.460.

Dar'es: Priest of Hephaistos in Troy, father of Phegeus and Idaios (2), 5.9.

Dau'lis: City near Pytho, 2.520.

Deï'koön: Companion of Aineias, killed by Agamemnon, 5.534.

Deï'ochos: Achaian killed by Paris, 15.341.

Deïopi'tes: Trojan killed by Odysseus, 11.420.

Deï'phobos: Son of Priam, one of the more powerful Trojan fighters, 13.156, 13.402; impersonated by Athene in order to swindle Hektor, 22.227–95.

Deï'pylos: Companion of Sthenelos, 5.325.

Deï'pyros: Achaian killed by Helenos, 13.576.

Deise'nor: Trojan captain, 17.217.

Deme'ter: Sister of Zeus, goddess of the earth as giver of food, 5.500, etc.

Demo'koön: Bastard son of Priam, killed by Odysseus, 4.499.

Demo'leon: Son of Antenor, killed by Achilleus, 20.395.

Demou'chos: Trojan killed by Achilleus, 20.457.

Deuka'lion: (1) Hero of Krete, father of Idomeneus, 12.117, 13.451. (2) Trojan killed by Achilleus, 20.477.

Dexa'menē: A Nereïd, 18.44.

Dex'ios: Father of Iphinoös, 7.15.

Dio'kles: Father of Orsilochos (1) and Krethon, 5.542.

Diome'de: Captive mistress of Achilleus, 9.665.

Diome'des: Son of Tydeus, lord, with Sthenelos and Euryalos, of Argos proper, one of the greatest of the Achaian fighters, prominent in battle until wounded by Paris, 11.368–400.

Di'on: City in Euboia, 2.538.

Dio'ne: Mother of Aphrodite, 5.370–417.

Diony'sos: Son of Zeus and Semele, driven into the sea by Lykourgos, 6.132–37.

Dio'res: (1) A leader of the Epeians, 2.622; killed by Peiros, 4.517. (2) Father of Automedon, 17.429.

Di'os: Son of Priam, 24.251.

Dodo'na: Place in Epeiros in extreme northwest Greece, site of an oracle of Zeus, 2.750, 16.233.

Do'lon: Trojan scout, killed by Diomedes and Odysseus, 10.313–464.

Dol'opes: People "in remotest Phthia" ruled over by Phoinix, 9.484.

Dolopi'on: Priest of Skamandros in Troy, father of Hypsenor (1), 5.77.

Dol'ops: (1) Achaian killed by Hektor, 11.302. (2) Trojan killed by Menelaos, 15.525–43.

Doris: A Nereïd, 18.45.

Dory'klos: Son of Priam, killed by Aias, 11.489.

Doto: A Nereïd, 18.43.

Douli'chion: Island in the domain of Meges, 2.625.

Dra'kios: A leader of the Epeians, 13.692.

Dry'as: (1) Hero of the generation of Nestor, 1.263. (2) Father of Lykourgos (1), 6.130.

Dry'ops: Trojan killed by Achilleus, 20.455.

Dy'mas: Father of Hekabē and of Asios (2), 16.718.

Dyna'menē: A Nereïd, 18.43.


Eche'kles: Myrmidon, son of Aktor (4), husband of Polymele, 16.189.

Eche'klos: (1) Trojan killed by Patroklos, 16.694. (2) Trojan, son of Agenor, killed by Achilleus, 20.474.

Echem'mon: Son of Priam, killed by Diomedes, 5.160.

Echepo'los: (1) Trojan killed by Antilochos, 4.458. (2) Son of Anchises, 23.296.

Echi'nai: Islands in the domain of Meges, 2.625.

E'chios: (1) Father of Mekisteus, 8.332. (2) Achaian killed by Polites, 15.339. (3) Lykian killed by Patroklos, 16.416.

Eëriboi'a: Stepmother of Ephialtes and Otos, 5.389.

Eë'tion: (1) King of Thebe, father of Andromache, killed by Achilleus, 6.414–20. (2) Father of Podes, 17.575 (perhaps identical with the aforementioned). (3) A lord of Imbros, 21.43.

Eileithy'ia: Goddess of childbirth, 16.187.

Eile'sion: City in Boiotia, 2.499.

Eï'ones: City near Argos, 2.561.

Eï'oneus: (1) Achaian killed by Hektor, 7.11. (2) Father of Rhesos, 10.435.

El'asos: Trojan killed by Patroklos, 16.696.

El'atos: Trojan ally killed by Agamemnon, 6.33.

Elei'ans: The people of Elis, 11.673.

El'eon: City in Boiotia, 2.500.

Elephe'nor: Leader of the Abantes, 2.540; killed by Agenor, 4.463–69.

Elis: City and district of the western Peloponnese, adjoining the domain of Nestor, 2.615, etc.

Elo'ne: City in Thessaly, in the domain of Polypoites, 2.739.

Ema'thia: District to the northwest of the Aegean, later part of Macedonia, 14.226.

En'etoi: A Paphlagonian tribe, 2.852.

Enie'nes: People from the extreme northwest of Thessaly, 2.749.

Eni'opeus: Charioteer of Hektor, killed by Diomedes, 8.120.

Enis'pe: Town in Arkadia, 2.606.

En'nomos: (1) Leader of the Mysians and augur, killed by Achilleus, 2.858–61. (2) Trojan killed by Odysseus, 11.422.

En'opē: Town near Pylos, 9.150.

En'ops: (1) Father of Satnios, 14.444. (2) Father of Thestor, 16.402 (perhaps identical with the aforementioned). (3) Father of Klytomedes, 23.634.

Eny'eus: King of Skyros, 9.668.

Eny'o: War goddess, 5.333.

Epal'tes: Lykian killed by Patroklos, 16.415.

Epei'ans: People of Elis, 2.619.

Epei'geus: Myrmidon killed by Hektor, 16.570–80.

Epei'os: Achaian, a great boxer and winner of this event in the games for Patroklos, 23.664–99 (in the *Odyssey*, 8.493, builder of the Trojan Horse).

Ephial'tes: Giant who with his brother Otos imprisoned Ares, 5.385.

Eph'yra or Eph'yrē: (1) A place on the river Selleëis, exact location unknown, 2.659. (2) Homeric name for Korinth, 6.152.

Eph'yroi: A northern people visited by Ares, 13.301.

Epidau'ros: City in the domain of Diomedes, 2.561.

Epi'kles: Lykian killed by Aias, 12.379.

Epis'tor: Trojan killed by Patroklos, 16.695.

Epis'trophos: (1) Leader of the men of Phokis, 2.517. (2) Prince of Lyrnessos, killed by Achilleus, 2.692. (3) Leader of the Halizones, 2.856.

Ep'ytos: Father of Periphas, 17.324.

Erech'theus: Hero of Athens, 2.547.

Ereutha'lion: Arkadian hero killed by Nestor, 7.136.

Erichthon'ios: Son of Dardanos, ancestor of the kings of Troy, 20.219.

Erin'ys: Spirit of vengeance, 9.571.

Erio'pis: Wife of Oïleus (1) and stepmother of Medon (1), 13.697.

Eryla'os: Trojan killed by Patroklos, 16.411.

Er'ymas: (1) Trojan killed by Idomeneus, 16.345. (2) Trojan killed by Patroklos, 16.415.

Erythi'noi: Place in Paphlagonia, 2.855.

Ery'thrai: City in Boiotia, 2.499.

Eteo'kles: Son of Oidipous, defender of Thebes against the Argives, 4.386.

Eteo'nos: City in Boiotia, 2.497.

Euai'mon: Father of Eurypylos (1), 2.736.

Euboi'a: Island lying close off east-central Greece, 2.536.

Euche'nor: Achaian killed by Paris, 13.663–72.

Eudor'os: Son of Hermes and Polymele, a Myrmidon captain, 16.179.

Eue'nos: (1) Father of Epistrophos (2) and Mynes, 2.693. (2) Father of Marpessa, 9.557.

Euip'pos: Lykian killed by Patroklos, 16.417.

Eume'des: Herald in Troy, father of Dolon, 10.314.

Eume'los: Son of Admetos and Alkestis, lord of the Thessalians from Pherai, 2.713. Prominent in the chariot race in the games for Patroklos, 23.288–565.

Eune'os: Son of Jason and Hypsipyle, lord in Lemnos, 7.468.

Euphe'mos: Trojan ally, leader of the Kikonians, 2.846.

Euphe'tes: Lord of Ephyra (1), 15.532.

Euphor'bos: Dardanian, son of Panthoös, who struck down Patroklos, 16.806–15; killed by Menelaos, 17.43–60.

Euro'pa: Daughter of Phoinix, mother of Minos and Rhadamanthys, 14.321.

Eury'alos: Leader, with Diomedes and Sthenelos, of the men of Argos proper, 2.565.

Eury'bates: (1) Herald for Agamemnon, 1.320. (2) Herald for Odysseus, 2.184. (The two are probably the same person.)

Eury'damas: A dream-interpreter, father of Abas and Polyidos (1), 5.149.

Eury'medon: (1) Charioteer of Agamemnon, 4.228. (2) Charioteer of Nestor, 8.114.

Eury'nomē: Daughter of Ocean, 18.398.

Eury'pylos: (1) Son of Euaimon, lord of a district in Thessaly which has not been certainly located, 2.736; wounded and put out of action by Paris, 11.575–95, etc. (2) Hero of Kos, 2.677.

Eurys'theus: Taskmaster of Herakles, 8.363, 19.107–25.

Eu'rytos: (1) Hero of Oichalia, 2.596. (2) Father of Thalpios, brother of Kteatos, 2.621; he and his brother called Moliones, 11.709, 11.750.

Eusso'ros: Father of Akamas (2), 6.8.

Eutre'sis: City in Boiotia, 2.502.

Exa'dios: Hero of the generation of Nestor, 1.264.


Galatei'a: A Nereïd, 18.45.

Ganyme'des: Son of Tros (1), caught up among the gods and made immortal, 20.232–35.

Gar'garon or Gar'garos: The peak of Ida, 8.48.

Gere'nian: Epithet of Nestor, 2.336, etc.

Gla'phyrai: Thessalian city in the domain of Eumelos, 2.712.

Glau'ke: A Nereïd, 18.39.

Glau'kos: (1) Companion of Sarpedon, second in command of the Lykians, 2.876; wounded by Teukros, 12.387–89. (2) Father of Bellerophontes, great-grandfather of Glaukos (1), 6.154–55.

Glisas: City in Boiotia, 2.504.

Gonoës'sa: Achaian city in the domain of Agamemnon, 2.573.

Gor'gon: A staring monster, 5.741.

Gorgy'thion: Son of Priam and Kastianeira, killed by Teukros, 8.302–8.

Gor'tyna: City in Krete, 2.646.

Gou'neus: Lord of the peoples around Dodona, 2.748.

Grai'a: City in Boiotia, 2.498.

Greni'kos: River of the Troad, 12.21.

Gygai'an: Of a lake in Mysia, 2.865.

Gy'ge: The same lake, 20.391.

Gyr'tios: Father of Hyrtios, 14.512.

Gyrto'ne: Thessalian city in the domain of Polypoites, 2.738.


Ha'des: Properly Aï'des. Son of Kronos and Rhea, full brother of Zeus, Poseidon, Hera, and Demeter, 15.187–92. Lord over the dead, loc. cit.; 1.3, etc. (n.b. A person, not a place.)

Hai'mon: (1) Companion of Nestor, 4.296. (2) Father of Maion, 4.394. (3) Father of Laërkes, 17.467.

Ha'lia: A Nereïd, 18.40.

Haliar'tos: City in Boiotia, 2.503.

Ha'lios: Lykian killed by Odysseus, 5.678.

Halizo'nes: A tribe from the Black Sea district, led by Odios (1) and Epistrophos (3), 2.856.

Harma: City in Boiotia, 2.499.

Harmon'ides: Smith in Troy, father of Phereklos, 5.60.

Harpal'ion: Paphlagonian ally of Troy killed by Meriones, 13.643–59.

He'be: Or Youth, daughter of Zeus and Hera, ministrant to other Olympians, 4.2, 5.722, etc.

Hek'abē: Daughter of Dymas, Priam's queen, 6.251, 22.79, etc.

Hekame'de: Captive mistress of Nestor, 11.624.

Hektor: Son of Priam, field commander of the Trojans and their greatest fighter, killer of Patroklos, 16.816–42; killed by Achilleus, 22.273–363.

Helen: Wife of Menelaos who ran away with Paris, the cause of the war, 3.121, etc.

Hel'enos: (1) Achaian killed by Hektor, 5.707. (2) Son of Priam, augur and fighter, 6.76, 6.576, etc.

Helika'on: Son of Antenor, husband of Laodike, 3.123.

Hel'ikē: Place in the domain of Agamemnon, on the Corinthian Gulf, 2.575.

Hellas: The domain, or part of the domain, of Peleus, 2.683, etc.

Hellenes: The people of Hellas, 2.684.

Hel'lespont: Strait between the Troad and Thrace, now Dardanelles, 2.845, etc.

Helos: (1) City in Lakedaimon, 2.584. (2) City near Pylos, 2.594.

Hephais'tos: Son of Hera, 1.571; artificer, 1.607, etc.; fire god, 21.330–81, etc.

Hepta'poros: River in the Troad, 12.20.

Hera: Daughter of Kronos and Rhea, full sister and wife of Zeus, protector of the Achaians, 1.55, etc.

Her'akles: Son of Alkmene and Zeus, 14.324; father of Tlepolemos (1), 2.658; of Thessalos, 2.679.

Her'mes: Son of Zeus, called guide and Argeïphontes, 2.104, etc.

Hermi'onē: City in the domain of Diomedes, 2.560.

Hermos: River in Phrygia, 20.392.

Hesper: The evening star, 22.318.

Hiketa'on: Son of Laomedon, 20.238; father of Melanippos (2), 15.546.

Hippo'damas: Trojan killed by Achilleus, 20.401.

Hippodamei'a: (1) Wife of Peirithoös, mother of Polypoites, 2.472. (2) Daughter of Anchises, wife of Alkathoös, 13.429.

Hippo'damos: Trojan killed by Odysseus, 11.335.

Hippo'koön: Cousin of Rhesos, 10.518.

Hippo'lochos: (1) Father of Glaukos (1), 6.119. (2) Trojan killed by Agamemnon, 11.122–47.

Hippo'machos: Trojan killed by Leonteus, 12.189.

Hippomol'goi: A northern tribe, "horse-milkers," presumably nomads, 13.5.

Hippo'noös: Achaian killed by Hektor, 11.303.

Hippo'thoös: (1) Trojan ally, leader of the Pelasgians, 2.840; killed by Aias, 17.293. (2) Son of Priam, 24.251.

Hippo'tion: Chief from Askania, 13.793; killed by Meriones, 14.514.

Hi're: Town near Pylos, 9.150.

Histiai'a: City in Euboia, 2.537.

Hy'adēs: The stars still so called, 18.486.

Hyam'polis: City in Phokis, 2.521.

Hy'de: District around Mount Tmolos, 20.385.

Hy'le: City in Boiotia, 2.500.

Hyl'los: River in Mysia, 20.392.

Hypei'rochos: (1) Trojan killed by Odysseus, 11.335. (2) Father of Itymoneus, 11.673.

Hypei'ron: Trojan killed by Diomedes, 5.144.

Hyperei'a: A spring in the domain of Eurypylos, 2.734.

Hypere'nor: Son of Panthoös, killed by Menelaos, 14.516, 17.24.

Hypere'sia: Achaian city in the domain of Agamemnon, 2.573.

Hyper'ion: Epithet of Helios, the Sun, 8.480.

Hypse'nor: (1) Trojan killed by Eurypylos, 5.76–83. (2) Achaian killed by Deïphobos, 13.411.

Hypsi'pyle: Mother, by Jason, of Euneos, 7.469.

Hy'ria: City in Boiotia, 2.496.

Hyrmi'ne: City in Elis, 2.616.

Hyr'takos: Father of Asios (1), 2.837.

Hyr'tios: Mysian killed by Aias, 14.511.


Iai'ra: A Nereïd, 18.42.

Ial'menos: A leader of the Minyai from Orchomenos, 2.512.

Ialy'sos: City in Rhodes, 2.656.

Ia'menos: Trojan killed by Leonteus, 12.194.

Ianas'sa: A Nereïd, 18.47.

Ianei'ra: A Nereïd, 18.47.

Ia'petos: One of the Titans, 8.479.

Iar'danos: River apparently on the borders of Pylos and Arkadia, 7.135.

I'asos: Athenian killed by Aineias, 15.332–38.

Ida: Mountain and range in the Troad, 2.821, etc.

Idai'os: (1) Herald of Priam, 3.248, 7.381–97. (2) Trojan, son of Dares and brother of Phegeus, rescued from Diomedes by Hephaistos, 5.11–24.

Idas: Husband of Marpessa and father of Kleopatra, who contended against Apollo for the sake of Marpessa, 9.556–60.

Ido'meneus: Son of Deukalion, lord of Krete, one of the great princes and fighters of the Achaians, 2.645, etc.

Ika'ria: Island off the coast of Asia Minor, 2.145.

Ilion: Or Ilios; Troy, the city of Ilos.

Ili'oneus: Trojan killed by Peneleos, 14.489–99.

Ilos: Eldest son of Tros, father of Laomedon, grandfather of Priam, 20.232.

Im'brasos: Thracian, father of Peiros, 4.520.

Im'brios: Trojan ally from Pedaios, killed by Teukros, 13.170.

Im'bros: Island northwest of Troy, 13.33.

Iol'kos: Thessalian town in the domain of Eumelos, 2.712.

Io'nians: A people closely associated with, perhaps identified with, the Athenians, 13.685.

Iph'eus: Lykian killed by Patroklos, 16.417.

Iphianas'sa: Daughter of Agamemnon, 9.145.

Iphi'damas: Son of Antenor, killed by Agamemnon, 11.221–47.

Iphi'klos: Runner defeated by Nestor, 23.636.

Iphi'noös: Achaian killed by Glaukos, 7.14.

Iphis: Captive mistress of Patroklos, 9.667.

Iphi'tion: Lydian killed by Achilleus, 20.382.

Iph'itos: (1) Father of Schedios (1) and Epistrophos (1), 2.518. (2) Father of Archeptolemos, 8.128.

Iris: The messenger of the gods, 2.786, etc.

Isan'dros: Son of Bellerophontes, 6.197.

Isos: Son of Priam, killed by Agamemnon, 11.111–21.

Ithai'menes: Father of Sthenelaos, 16.586.

Ith'aka: Island off west-central Greece, the home of Odysseus, 2.632, etc.

Itho'me: Thessalian city in the domain of Podaleirios and Machaon, 2.729.

Iton: Thessalian city in the domain of Protesilaos, 2.696.

Ity'moneus: Eleian killed by Nestor in his youth, 11.672.

Ixi'on: Putative father of Peirithoös, 14.317.


Jason: The Argonaut, father of Euneos, 7.468.


Kabe'sos: City, location unknown, on the Trojan side, 13.363.

Kadmei'ans: Thebans, 4.388, etc.

Kai'neus: Hero of the generation of Nestor, 1.264.

Kal'chas: Augur for the Achaians, 1.68–100, 2.300–332. Impersonated by Poseidon, 13.45.

Kale'sios: Charioteer of Axylos, killed by Diomedes, 6.18.

Kale'tor: (1) Father of Aphareus, 13.541. (2) Trojan killed by Aias, 15.419.

Kallianas'sa: A Nereïd, 18.46.

Kallianei′ra: A Nereïd, 18.44.

Kalli′aros: City in Lokris, 2.531.

Kalyd′nai: Islands in the southeast Aegean, 2.677.

Kal′ydon: City of Aitolia, its men led by Thoas, 2.640. For a part of the Kalydonian Saga, see 9.529–99.

Kamei′ros: City of Rhodes, 2.656.

Kap′aneus: Father of Sthenelos, 2.564.

Kap′ys: Son of Assarakos, father of Anchises, so grandfather of Aineias, 20.239.

Karda′mylē: Town near Pylos, 9.150.

Kare′sos: River in the Troad, 12.20.

Kar′ians: People of Asia Minor who held the city of Miletos, 2.867.

Karys′tos: City of Euboia, 2.539.

Ka′sos: Island near Kos, 2.676.

Kassan′dra: Daughter of Priam, 13.366, 24.699.

Kastianei′ra: Mother, by Priam, of Gorgythion, 8.304.

Kastor: Brother of Helen, 3.327.

Kaukon′ians: People of Asia Minor allied to the Trojans, 10.429.

Kaÿst′rian: Of the river Kaÿstros in Asia Minor, 2.461.

Ke′as: Father of Troizenos, 2.847.

Kebri′ones: Brother of Hektor, 8.318; killed by Patroklos, 16.737–76.

Kel′adon: River apparently on the borders of Pylos and Arkadia, 7.134.

Kephalle′nia: Island off west-central Greece, in the domain of Odysseus, 2.631.

Kephisian mere: A lake, more commonly called Kopa′is, in Boiotia, 5.709.

Kephi′sos: River in Phokis (and Boiotia), 2.522.

Kerin′thos: City in Euboia, 2.538.

Kikonian: Of a Thracian people, also called Kiko′nes, 2.846.

Kili′kians: In Homer, only of the people in Asian Thebe, 6.397, 6.415.

Kil′la: Town in the Troad, 1.38.

Kin′yras: King of Cyprus who gave a corselet to Agamemnon, 11.20.

Kis′seus: Father of Theano, 11.223.

Klei′tos: Charioteer of Poulydamas, killed by Teukros, 15.445–53.

Kleobou′los: Trojan killed by Aias (2), 16.330–34.

Kleo′nai: City in the domain of Agamemnon, 2.570.

Kleopat′ra: Daughter of Idas and Marpessa, wife of Meleagros, 9.556.

Klo′nios: A leader of the Boiotians, 2.495; killed by Agenor, 15.340.

Kly′menē: (1) One of Helen's handmaidens, 3.144. (2) A Nereïd, 18.47.

Klytaimes′tra: Wife of Agamemnon, 1.113.

Kly′tios: (1) Son of Laomedon, brother of Priam, father of Kaletor, 3.147, 15.419, 20.238. (2) Father of Dolops (1), 11.302.

Klytome′des: Boxer defeated by Nestor in his youth, 23.634.

Kno′sos: City in Krete, 2.646.

Koi′ranos: (1) Lykian killed by Odysseus, 5.677. (2) Charioteer of Meriones, killed by Hektor, 17.610–19.

Ko′ön: Son of Antenor, killed by Agamemnon after wounding him, 11.248–63.

Ko′pai: City in Boiotia, 2.502.

Kop'reus: Herald of Eurystheus, father of Periphetes, 15.639.

Kor'inth: City in the domain of Agamemnon, 2.570.

Koronei'a: City in Boiotia, 2.503.

Koro'nos: Father of Leonteus, 2.746.

Kos: Island in the southeast Aegean, 2.677.

Koure'tes: A people at war with the Aitolians, 9.529–99.

Kran'aë: Island on the homeward route of Paris from Lakedaimon, 3.445.

Kra'pathos: Island in the southeast Aegean, 2.676.

Krei'on: Father of Lykomedes, 9.84.

Krete: Large island south of the Aegean, the domain of Idomeneus, 2.649.

Kre'thon: Achaian killed by Aineias, 5.541–60.

Krisa: City in Phokis, 2.519.

Krois'mos: Trojan killed by Meges, 15.523.

Krokylei'a: Place on or near Ithaka, 2.633.

Krom'na: City in Paphlagonia, 2.855.

Kronos: Father of Zeus, Hades, Poseidon, Hera, Demeter, 1.498, etc.; overthrown and in Tartaros, 8.479–81.

Kte'atos: Brother of Eurytos (2), q.v.; father of Amphimachos (1), 2.620–21.

Kylle'ne: Mountain bounding Arkadia to the north, 2.603.

Kymin'dis: Name for a bird, 14.291.

Kymo'dokē: A Nereïd, 18.39.

Kymo'thoë: A Nereïd, 18.41.

Kynos: City in Lokris, 2.531.

Kyparisse'eis: City near Pylos, 2.593.

Kyparis'sos: City in Phokis, 2.519.

Ky'phos: City of Gouneus, 2.748.

Kythe'ra: Island off the southern tip of Lakedaimon, 15.431.

Kyto'ros: City in Paphlagonia, 2.853.


La'as: City in Lakedaimon, 2.585.

Laër'kes: Myrmidon, father of Alkimedon, 16.197.

Laër'tes: Father of Odysseus, 2.173.

Lakedai'mon: The city, with its surrounding country, of Menelaos, in southeastern Greece, 2.581, etc.

Lampos: (1) Son of Laomedon, father of Dolops (2), 15.525–27. (2) One of Hektor's horses, 8.185.

Lao'damas: Trojan, son of Antenor, killed by Aias, 15.516.

Laodamei'a: Daughter of Bellerophontes, mother, by Zeus, of Sarpedon, 6.197–99.

Lao'dikē: (1) Daughter of Priam and wife of Helikaon, impersonated by Iris, 3.121–24. (2) Daughter of Agamemnon, 9.145.

Lao'dokos: (1) Son of Antenor, impersonated by Athene, 4.87. (2) Charioteer of Antilochos, 17.699.

Lao'gonos: (1) Trojan killed by Meriones, 16.603–7. (2) Trojan killed by Achilleus, 20.460.

Lao'medon: King of Troy, son of Ilos and father of Priam, Tithonos, Lampos (1), Klytios (1) and Hiketaon, 20.236–38; who earned the hatred of Poseidon by his treatment of him and Apollo, 21.443–60.

Lao'thoë: Daughter of Altes, mother, by Priam, of Lykaon (2) and Polydoros (1), 21.84–91.

La'pithai: Thessalian people led by Polypoites and Leonteus, 12.128–30.

Laris'sa: City, location unknown, allied to Troy, 2.841.

Leio'kritos: Achaian killed by Aineias, 17.344.

Le'itos: Leader, with Peneleos, of the Boiotians, 2.494; wounded and put out of action by Hektor, 17.601–4.

Lektos: Or Lekton, promontory of the Troad, 14.284.

Le'leges: People of Asia Minor allied to the Trojans, 10.429.

Lemnos: Island in the Aegean, west of Troy, 1.593, 2.722, etc.

Leon'teus: Leader, with Polypoites, of the Lapithai from Argissa, etc., 2.745.

Lesbos: Island and city close to the coast of Asia Minor south of Troy, 9.129, etc.

Lethos: Lord of Larissa, 2.843.

Leto: Mother (by Zeus) of Apollo and Artemis, 1.9, 21.498–504, 24.607–9.

Leu'kos: Companion of Odysseus, killed by Antiphos (3), 4.489–93.

Likym'nios: Uncle of Herakles, killed by Tlepolemos (1) who was his great-nephew, 2.663.

Lilai'a: City in Phokis, 2.523.

Limnorei'a: A Nereïd, 18.41.

Lindos: City in Rhodes, 2.656.

Lok'rians: People of Lokris, 2.535.

Lokris: District in east-central Greece, the domain of Aias the son of Oïleus, 2.527.

Lyka'on: (1) Father of Pandaros, 2.826, etc. (2) Son of Priam and Laothoë, killed by Achilleus, 21.34–135.

Lykas'tos: City in Krete, 2.647.

Ly'kia: (1) District on the southern coast of Asia Minor, the domain of Sarpedon and Glaukos (1), 2.877, etc. (2) Apparently the country around Zeleia, close to Troy, home of Pandaros, 5.105, 5.173.

Lykome'des: Achaian, killer of Apisaon (2), 17.345–49.

Lykon: Trojan killed by Peneleos, 16.334–41.

Lykophon'tes: Trojan killed by Teukros, 8.275.

Ly'kophron: Achaian from Kythera, friend of Aias, killed by Hektor, 15.429–35.

Lykour'gos: (1) Son of Dryas, who assaulted Dionysos and was punished by the gods, 6.130–40. (2) Hero who killed Areïthoös (1), 7.142–49.

Lyktos: City in Krete, 2.647.

Lyrnes'sos: City in the Troad, the home of Briseis, 2.690, etc.

Lysan'dros: Trojan killed by Aias, 11.491.


Macha'on: Son of Asklepios, fighter and healer, with his brother Podaleirios leader of the Thessalians from Trikka and Oichalia, 2.729–33; ministers to the wounded Menelaos, 4.192–218; wounded and put out of action by Paris, 11.504–20.

Magne'sians: People of Thessaly led by Prothoös, 2.756.

Maian'dros: River of Asia Minor emptying near Miletos (2), 2.869.

Mai'malos: Father of Peisandros (3), 16.194.

Mai'on: Kadmeian who led an ambuscade against Tydeus, 4.393–98.

Maio'nians: People from around the lake of Gyge, 2.864.

Mai'ra: A Nereïd, 18.48.

Makar: Lord of Lesbos, 24.544.

Mantinei'a: City in Arkadia, 2.607.

Maris: Lykian killed by Thrasymedes, 16.319–29.

Marpes'sa: Daughter of Euenos, wife of Idas, 9.557.

Ma'ses: City in the domain of Diomedes, 2.562.

Mastor: Father of Lykophron, 15.430.

Med'eon: City in Boiotia, 2.501.

Medesikas'te: Daughter of Priam, wife of Imbrios, 13.173.

Medon: (1) Bastard son of Oïleus (1), 13.694–97; killed by Aineias, 15.332. (2) A captain on the Trojan side, 17.216.

Megas: Father of Perimos, 16.695.

Me'ges: Leader of the men from Doulichion, son of Phyleus, 2.627; leader of the Epeians, 13.692.

Mekis'teus: (1) Father of Euryalos, 2.566 (and one of the Seven against Thebes); a great boxer in his youth, 23.678–80. (2) Achaian killed by Poulydamas, 15.339.

Melanip'pos: (1) Trojan killed by Teukros, 8.276. (2) Trojan, son of Hiketaon, killed by Antilochos, 15.576. (3) Trojan killed by Patroklos, 16.695. (4) A younger Achaian chief, 19.240.

Melan'thios: Trojan killed by Eurypylos, 6.36.

Melas: Son of Portheus, brother of Oineus, 14.117.

Melea'gros: Son of Oineus and prince of Kalydon, 9.529–99.

Meliboi'a: Thessalian city in the domain of Philoktetes, 2.717.

Mel'itē: A Nereïd, 18.42.

Menela'os: Son of Atreus, brother of Agamemnon, first husband of Helen, lord of Lakedaimon, 2.581–90, etc.

Menes'thes: Achaian killed by Hektor, 5.609.

Menes'theus: Leader of the Athenians, 2.552–56.

Menes'thios: (1) Achaian from Arne killed by Paris, 7.9. (2) Myrmidon leader under Achilleus, 16.173–78.

Menoi'tios: Son of Aktor (3) and father of Patroklos, 1.307, etc.

Menon: Trojan killed by Leonteus, 12.193.

Men'tes: Leader of the Kikones impersonated by Apollo, 17.73.

Mentor: Father of Imbrios, 13.171.

Meri'ones: Companion in arms of Idomeneus, one of the most prominent of the younger Achaian warriors, charioteer and archer, 2.651, 13.244–329, etc.

Mer'meros: Trojan killed by Antilochos, 14.513.

Merops: Augur in Perkote, father of Adrestos (2) and Amphios (1), 2.831.

Mes'se: City in Lakedaimon, 2.582.

Messe'is: Wellspring in Greece, exact location unknown, 6.457.

Mesth'les: Leader of the Maionians, 2.864.

Mestor: Son of Priam, 24.257.

Metho'ne: Thessalian city in the domain of Philoktetes, 2.716.

Midei'a: City in Boiotia, 2.507.

Mile'tos: (1) City in Krete, 2.647. (2) City of the Karians, 2.868.

Minos: Son of Zeus and Europa, father of Deukalion, king of Krete, 13.450–54, 14.321–22.

Min'yai: People of Orchomenos (1) led by Askalaphos and Ialmenos, 2.511.

Minyei'os: River on the border of Nestor's domain, 11.722.

Mnesos: Paionian killed by Achilleus, 21.210.

Moli'on: Follower of Thymbraios, killed by Odysseus, 11.322.

Moli'ones: Eurytos (2) and Kteatos (qq.v.), 11.709.

Molos: Father of Meriones, 10.270.

Morys: Trojan killed by Meriones, 14.513.

Mou'lios: (1) Epeian hero killed by Nestor in his youth, 11.739. (2) Trojan killed by Patroklos, 16.696. (3) Trojan killed by Achilleus, 20.472.

Mydon: (1) Charioteer of Pylaimenes, killed by Antilochos, 5.580. (2) Paionian killed by Achilleus, 21.209.

Mygdon: King of Phrygia, 3.186.

My'kalē: Promontory across the bay from Miletos (2), 2.869.

Mykales'sos: City in Boiotia, 2.498.

Myke'nai: Agamemnon's capital, a few miles north of the city of Argos, 2.569, etc.

My'nes: King of Lyrnessos, 19.296.

Myri'ne: Heroine after whom a hill before Troy was named, 2.814.

Myr'midons: The people of Phthia, subjects of Peleus and led by Achilleus, 2.684, etc.

Myr'sinos: City in Elis, 2.616.

My'sians: A people living to the east of Troy and allied to the Trojans, 2.858.


Nai'ad: A well-nymph, 6.21.

Nas'tes: Leader of the Karians, killed by Achilleus, 2.867–75.

Nau'bolos: Phokian hero, father of Iphitos, 2.518.

Ne'leus: King of Pylos, father of Nestor, 11.692, etc.

Nemer'tes: A Nereïd, 18.46.

Neopto'lemos: Son of Achilleus, 19.327.

Ne'reïds: The daughters of Nereus, nymphs of the sea, 18.36–49.

Ne'reus: Aged god of the sea, father of Thetis, 1.556; and of the other Nereïds, 18.36.

Ne'ritos or Ne'riton: Mountain on Ithaka, 2.632.

Nesai'e: A Nereïd, 18.40.

Nestor: Leader of the Pylians, once a great warrior and still active as a commander and counselor, 1.247–84, etc.; father of Antilochos, 5.565; of Thrasymedes, 9.81.

Ni'obē: Heroine of Asia, whose six daughters and six sons were killed by Apollo and Artemis, 24.602–17.

Ni'reus: Leader from Syme, handsomest (next to Achilleus) of the Achaians, 2.671.

Ni'sa: City in Boiotia, 2.508.

Nisy'ros: Island near Kos, 2.676.

Noë'mon: (1) Lykian killed by Odysseus, 5.678. (2) Henchman of Antilochos, 23.612.

Nomi'on: Father of Amphimachos (2) and Nastes, 2.871.

Nysei'an: Of a mountain sacred to Dionysos, 6.133.


Ocean or Oke'anos: The waters surrounding the world and the god of those waters, 1.423, 14.201, etc.

Oche'sios: Father of Periphas, 5.843.

Odys'seus: Son of Laërtes, lord of Ithaka and the neighboring islands, great fighter and counselor, close friend of Agamemnon, 2.631, etc.

Oicha'lia: Thessalian city of Eurytos (1) in the domain of Podaleirios and Machaon, 2.730.

Oid'ipous: Hero of Thebes (1), 23.679. (In Homer, strictly, Oidipodes.)

Oï'leus: (1) Lokrian hero, father of Aias (2), 2.527. (2) Trojan killed by Agamemnon, 11.93.

Oi'neus: Hero of Kalydon, son of Portheus, 14.117; father of Tydeus, 5.813; of Meleagros, 5.981.

Oino'maos: (1) Achaian killed by Hektor, 5.706. (2) Trojan killed by Idomeneus, 13.506.

Oi'nops: Father of Helenos (1), 5.707.

Oi'tylos: City in Lakedaimon, 2.585.

Okal'ea: City in Boiotia, 2.501.

Olen'ian Rock: Landmark on the borders of Elis, 2.617.

O'lenos: City in Aitolia, 2.639.

Oli'zon: Thessalian city in the domain of Philoktetes, 2.717.

Oloös'son: Thessalian city in the domain of Polypoites, 2.739.

Olym'pos: Mountain north of Thessaly, the home of the gods, 1.499, etc.

Onches'tos: City of Boiotia, 2.506.

One'tor: Father of Laogonos (1), 16.604.

Opheles'tes: (1) Trojan killed by Teukros, 8.274. (2) Paionian killed by Achilleus, 21.210.

Ophel'tios: (1) Trojan killed by Euryalos, 6.20. (2) Achaian killed by Hektor, 11.302.

Opi'tes: Achaian killed by Hektor, 11.301.

Op'oeis or O'pous: City in Lokris, 2.531.

Orcho'menos: (1) City of the Minyai, adjoining the territory of the Boiotians, 2.511. (2) City in Arkadia, 2.605.

Oreithy'ia: A Nereïd, 18.48.

Ores'bios: Boiotian killed by Hektor, 5.707–10.

Ores'tes: (1) Achaian killed by Hektor, 5.705. (2) Son of Agamemnon, 9.142. (3) Trojan killed by Leonteus, 12.193.

Ori'on: The constellation, 18.486.

Orme'nion: Thessalian city in the domain of Eurypylos, 2.734.

Or'menos: (1) Trojan killed by Teukros, 8.274. (2) Father of Amyntor, 9.448. (3) Trojan killed by Polypoites, 12.187.

Orne'ai: City in the domain of Agamemnon, 2.571.

Oros: Achaian killed by Hektor, 11.303.

Orsi'lochos: (1) Achaian killed by Aineias, 5.542–60. (2) Trojan killed by Teukros, 8.274.

Orthai'os: A Trojan captain, 13.791.

Or'the: Thessalian city in the domain of Polypoites, 2.739.

Orti'lochos: Father of Diokles, 5.546.

Othry'oneus: Suitor of Kassandra, killed by Idomeneus, 13.363–82.

Otos: (1) Giant who with his brother Ephialtes imprisoned Ares, 5.385. (2) Achaian from Kyllene, killed by Poulydamas, 15.518.

Ot'reus: Lord of Phrygia, 3.186.

Otryn'teus: Father of Iphition, 20.382–84.

Ouka'legon: An elder in Troy, 3.148.


Paië'on: The healing god, 5.899.

Paio'nia: A district, its people allied to the Trojans, in what was later Macedonia, 17.350.

Pai'sos: Apparently the same as Apaisos (q.v.), 5.612.

Pallas: Epithet of Athene, 1.200, etc.

Pal'mys: A Trojan captain, 13.792.

Pammon: Son of Priam, 24.250.

Pan'daros: Son of Lykaon (1), leader of the Trojans from Zeleia, 2.824–27; but spoken of as being from Lykia, 5.173; breaks the truce by treacherously wounding Menelaos, 4.85–140; wounds Diomedes, 5.95–105; killed by him, 5.280–96.

Pandi'on: Henchman of Teukros, 12.372.

Pan'dokos: Trojan killed by Aias, 11.490.

Pan'opē: A Nereïd, 18.45.

Pan'opeus: (1) City in Phokis, 2.520. (2) Father of Epeios, 23.665.

Pan'thoös: An elder of Troy, 3.147; father of Poulydamas, 13.756; of Euphorbos, 16.808; of Hyperenor, 17.19–35.

Paphla'gonēs: People of Paphlagonia on the southern shore of the Black Sea, allied to the Trojans, 2.851.

Paris: Son of Priam and Hekabē, who carried Helen from Lakedaimon, 3.15, etc. (in the *Iliad* more frequently called by his other name, Alexandros).

Parrha'sia: City in Arkadia, 2.608.

Parthe'nios: River in Paphlagonia, 2.854.

Pasi'thea: One of the Graces, 14.269.

Patro'klos: Son of Menoitios, henchman and close friend of Achilleus, killed by Hektor, 1.307, etc.

Pedai'on or Pedai'os: City in the Troad, 13.172.

Pedai'os: Trojan, son of Antenor, killed by Meges, 5.69–75.

Pe'dasos: (1) Trojan killed by Euryalos, 6.21. (2) City on the river Satnioeis, 6.35. (3) Town near Pylos, 9.152. (4) One of the horses of Achilleus, 16.152.

Peirai'os: Father of Ptolemaios, 4.228.

Pei'res: Father of Rhigmos, 20.484.

Peiri'thoös: Son of Zeus, father of Polypoites, 2.741.

Pei'ros: Thracian killed by Thoas, 4.517–38.

Peisan'dros: (1) Trojan killed by Agamemnon, 11.122–44. (2) Trojan killed by Menelaos, 13.601–19. (3) One of the leaders of the Myrmidons, 16.193.

Peise'nor: Father of Kleitos, 15.445.

Pel'agon: (1) Follower of Nestor, 4.295. (2) Follower of Sarpedon, 5.694.

Pelas'gian: A term of disputed and apparently variable significance. Applied to Argos (2), the home of Achilleus, 2.681; but the Pelasgians of Larissa are allied with the Trojans, 2.840–43.

Pel'egon: Father of Asteropaios, 21.141.

Pel'eus: Son of Aiakos, 21.189; father of Achilleus, 1.1, etc.; husband of Thetis, 18.85, etc.

Pel'ian: Of the spear of Achilleus, cut from Mount Pelion, 16.143.

Pel'ias: Father of Alkestis, 2.715.

Pelle'ne: Achaian city in the domain of Agamemnon, 2.574.

Pelops: Lord of Argos, father of Atreus, 2.104.

Penei'os: The chief river of Thessaly, 2.752.

Pene'leos: Leader, with Leïtos, of the Boiotians, 2.494.

Perei'a: Place where Apollo had bred the mares of Eumelos, 2.766.

Per'gamos or Per'gamon: The citadel of Troy, 4.508, etc.

Per'gasos: Father of Deïkoön, 5.535.

Periboi'a: Mother, by the river Axios, of Pelegon, 21.142.

Perie'res: Father of Boros, 16.177.

Perime'des: Father of Schedios (2), 15.515.

Per'imos: Trojan killed by Patroklos, 16.695.

Per'iphas: (1) Aitolian killed by Ares, 5.842. (2) Herald of Anchises, 17.324.

Periphe'tes: (1) Trojan killed by Teukros, 14.515. (2) Achaian from Mykenai, killed by Hektor, 15.638–52.

Perko'te: City in the Troad, 2.835.

Perrhai'bians: People from the region of Dodona, led by Gouneus, 2.749.

Perse'phonē: Wife of Hades and queen of the dead, 9.457.

Per'seus: Son of Zeus and Danaë, 14.320; grandfather of Eurystheus, 19.116.

Pe'teon: City in Boiotia, 2.500.

Pe'teos: Father of Menestheus, 2.552.

Phai'nops: (1) Father of Xanthos (2) and Thoön (1), 5.152. (2) Father of Phorkys, 17.312.

Phais'tos: (1) City in Krete, 2.648. (2) Maionian killed by Idomeneus, 5.43.

Phal'kes: Trojan killed by Antilochos, 14.513.

Pharis: City in Lakedaimon, 2.582.

Phau'sias: Father of Apisaon (1), 11.578.

Phe'geus: Trojan killed by Diomedes, 5.9–19.

Phe'ia: City on the borders of Pylos and Arkadia, 7.135.

Phei'das: Captain under Menestheus, 13.691.

Pheidip'pos: A leader of the men from Kos and the adjacent islands, 2.678.

Phe'neos: City in Arkadia, 2.605.

Phe'rai: (1) Thessalian city of Eumelos, 2.711. (2) City near Pylos, 5.543, 9.151.

Phere'klos: Builder in Troy, who made ships for Paris, killed by Meriones, 5.59–68.

Phe'res: Father of Admetos, grandfather of Eumelos, 2.763.

Pherou'sa: A Nereïd, 18.43.

Phile'tor: Father of Demouchos, 20.458.

Philokte'tes: Leader of the Thessalians from Methone and thereabouts, archer, during the action of the *Iliad* ill of an infection in Lemnos, 2.716–25.

Phleg'yes: A northern people visited by Ares, 13.302.

Phoenicians: A nation, well known as seafarers, living on the Syrian coast, 23.744.

Phoi'bos: Epithet of Apollo, 1.43, etc.

Phoi'nix: (1) Son of Amyntor, a refugee befriended by Peleus, companion and tutor of Achilleus; his story, 9.430–95. (2) Father of Europa, 14.321.

Phokis: District in central Greece, adjoining Boiotia, 2.517.

Phor'bas: (1) Man of Lesbos, father of Diomede, 9.665. (2) Father of Ilioneus, 14.490.

Phor'kys: Phrygian killed by Aias, 17.312.

Phrad'mon: Father of Agelaos (1), 8.257.

Phron'tis: Wife of Panthoös, 17.40.

Phry'gia: District east of the Troad, allied with Troy, 2.862, etc.

Phthi'a: The home of Achilleus, in southern Thessaly, 2.683, etc.

Phthi'ron: Mountain near Miletos (2), 2.868.

Phyl'akē: Thessalian city in the domain of Protesilaos, 2.695.

Phy'las: Father of Polymele, 16.181.

Phy'leus: Father of Meges, 2.628, etc.; defeated in spear-throwing by Nestor, 23.637.

Phylomedou'sa: Wife of Areïthoös (1), 7.10.

Pidy'tes: Trojan ally from Perkote, killed by Odysseus, 6.30.

Piē'ria: The region around Olympos, 14.226.

Pit'theus: Father of Aithre, 3.144.

Pityei'a: City on the Hellespont, 2.829.

Plak'os: Mountain dominating Thebe (2), 6.396.

Platai'a: City in Boiotia, 2.504.

Plei'ades: The constellation, 18.486.

Pleu'ron: City in Aitolia, 2.639.

Podalei'rios: Son of Asklepios, fighter and healer, with his brother Machaon leader of the men from Oichalia and thereabouts, 2.732.

Podar'ge: Harpy, mother by the West Wind of the horses of Achilleus, 16.150.

Podar'gos: (1) One of the horses of Hektor, 8.185. (2) One of the horses of Menelaos, 23.295.

Podar'kes: Brother of Protesilaos, succeeding him as leader of the men from Phylake, etc., 2.703–8.

Po'des: Son of Eëtion, friend (possibly brother-in-law) of Hektor, killed by Menelaos, 17.575–81.

Poli'tes: Son of Priam, 2.791, etc.

Polyai'mon: Father of Amopaon, 8.276.

Pol'ybos: Son of Antenor, 11.59.

Polydeu'kes: Brother of Helen, 3.237.

Polydo're: Daughter of Peleus, mother, by the river Spercheios, of Menesthios, 16.173–78.

Polydo'ros: (1) Youngest son of Priam, killed by Achilleus, 20.407–18. (2) Spear-thrower defeated by Nestor, 23.637.

Polyi'dos: (1) Trojan killed by Diomedes, 5.148–51. (2) Augur in Korinth, father of Euchenor, 13.663.

Polyk'tor: Named as his father by Hermes to Priam, 24.398.

Polyme'le: Mother, by Hermes, of Eudoros, 16.179–90.

Polyme'los: Lykian killed by Patroklos, 16.417.

Polynei'kes: Son of Oidipous, leader of the Seven against Thebes, 4.377.

Polyphe'mos: Hero of the generation of Nestor, 1.264.

Polyphe'tes: A Trojan captain, 13.791.

Polyphon'tes: Kadmeian killed by Tydeus, 4.395.

Polypoi'tes: Son of Peirithoös, leader of the Lapithai from Argissa, etc., 2.740, etc.

Polyxei'nos: A leader of the Epeians, 2.623.

Por'theus: Aitolian hero, father of Agrios, Melas, and Oineus, 14.115.

Posei'don: Son of Kronos and Rheia, so younger brother of Zeus, lord of the sea, 15.185–92; protector of the Achaians, 13.10–124, etc.

Pouly'damas: Son of Panthoös, fighter and careful counselor, frequently opposed to the reckless strategy of Hektor, 12.210–29, 18.249–83, etc.

Prak'tios: River in the Troad, 2.835.

Pramnei'an wine: A wine used medicinally, origin unknown, 11.639.

Priam: Son of Laomedon, king of Troy, father of Hektor, Paris, and many other children (fifty sons, 24.495), 3.161, etc.

Proi'tos: King of Ephyra, who designed against the life of Bellerophontes, 6.156–70.

Pro'machos: Boiotian killed by Akamas (1), 14.476.

Pro'noös: Trojan killed by Patroklos, 16.399.

Protesila'os: Leader of the men from Phylake, etc., first of the Achaians to land at Troy and first to be killed, 2.695–709.

Prothoë'nor: A Boiotian leader, 2.495; killed by Poulydamas, 14.450.

Pro'thoön: Trojan killed by Teukros, 14.515.

Pro'thoös: Leader of the Magnesians from Pelion, 2.756.

Protia'on: Father of Astynoös (2), 15.455.

Proto: A Nereïd, 18.43.

Pry'tanis: Lykian killed by Odysseus, 5.678.

Ptel'eos: (1) City in the domain of Nestor, 2.594. (2) City in the domain of Protesilaos, 2.697.

Ptolemai'os: Father of Eurymedon (1), 4.228.

Pygmai'ans: That small infantry warred on by cranes, 3.6.

Pylai'menes: Lord of the Paphlagonians, killed by Menelaos, 5.576–79.

Pylai'os: Leader, with his brother Hippothoös, of the Pelasgians from Larissa, 2.842.

Pylar'tes: (1) Trojan killed by Aias, 11.491. (2) Trojan killed by Patroklos, 16.696.

Pyle'ne: City in Aitolia, 2.639.

Py'lon: Trojan killed by Polypoites, 12.187.

Py'los: The city of Nestor, with the district surrounding it, on the western coast of the Peloponnese (south Greece: exact location disputed), 1.252, 2.591, etc.

Pyraich'mes: Paionian chief killed by Patroklos, 16.287.

Pyr'asos: (1) City in the domain of Protesilaos, 2.695. (2) Trojan killed by Aias, 11.491.

Py'ris: Trojan killed by Patroklos, 16.416.

Py'tho: Place in Phokis sacred to Apollo, later called Delphoi, 2.519, 9.404–5.

Rhadaman'thys: Son of Zeus and Europa, brother of Minos, 14.321–22.

Rhe'a, or Rhei'a: Mother, by Kronos, of Zeus, Poseidon, Hades, Hera, and Demeter, 15.187–88.

Rhe'ne: Mother, by Oïleus (1), of Medon (1), 2.728.

Rhe'sos: (1) King of the Thracians, killed by Diomedes, 10.432–502. (2) River of the Troad, 12.20.

Rhig'mos: Thracian killed by Achilleus, 20.484–89.

Rhi'pe: City in Arkadia, 2.606.

Rhodes: Island just southeast of the Aegean, its men led by Tlepolemos (1), 2.654.

Rho'dios: River of the Troad, 12.20.

Rhy'tion: City in Krete, 2.648.

Sal'amis: Island off the shore by Athens, home of Aias (1), 2.557.

Sa'mos: (1) Large island, later called Kephallenia, near Ithaka and part of the domain of Odysseus, 2.634. (2) Island, later called Samothrace, in the northern Aegean or Thracian Sea, 13.13, 24.78.

Sangar'ios: River in Phrygia, 3.187.

Sarpe'don: Son of Zeus and Laodameia, lord of the Lykians, 2.876, 6.198–99; one of the strongest fighters on the Trojan side, kills Tlepolemos, 5.629–62; killed by Patroklos, 16.462–507.

Satni'oeis: River of the Troad, 6.34, etc.

Sat'nios: Trojan killed by Aias (2), 14.443.

Sche'dios: (1) Son of Iphitos (1) and a leader of the Phokians, 2.517; killed by Hektor, 17.304–11. (2) Son of Perimedes, also leader of the Phokians and killed by Hektor, 15.515. (It is quite possible that there is confusion in the tradition here, and that the same man is meant.)

Schoi'nos: City in Boiotia, 2.497.

Sel'agos: Father of Amphios (2), 5.612.

Sele'pios: Father of Euenos, 2.693.

Selle'eis: (1) River of unknown location associated with Ephyra (1), 2.659, 15.531. (2) River of the Troad, 2.839.

Sel'loi: Prophets of Zeus at Dodona, 16.235.

Sem'elē: Mother, by Zeus, of Dionysos, 14.323–25.

Se'samos: City of the Paphlagones, 2.853.

Ses'tos: City on the European side of the Hellespont, its people allies of Troy, 2.836.

Sidon: City of the Phoenicians, 6.291.

Sik'yon: City once ruled by Adrestos (1) in the domain of Agamemnon, 2.572.

Sim'oeis: River by Troy, tributary of Skamandros, 5.774, etc.

Simoei'sios: Trojan named after the river, killed by Aias, 4.473–89.

Sin'tians: People of Lemnos, 1.594.

Sip'ylos: Mountain in Lydia, 24.615.

Sis'yphos: Hero of Ephyre (2), grandfather of Bellerophontes, 6.153.

Skai'an: Of one of the gates of Troy, 3.145, etc.

Skaman'drios: (1) Trojan huntsman and fighting man killed by Menelaos, 5.49–58. (2) Another name for Astyanax, 6.402.

Skaman'dros: Chief river of the Trojan plain, 2.465, etc.; as a god, fights and discomfits Achilleus, 21.211–382; called also, by the gods, Xanthos, 20.74.

Skandei'a: City on Kythera, 10.268.

Skar'phe: City in Lokris, 2.532.

Skolos: City in Boiotia, 2.497.

Sky'ros: Island off Euboia, 9.668, 19.332.

Smin'theus: Epithet of Apollo, 1.39.

Sokos: Trojan killed by Odysseus, but only after wounding and nearly killing him, 11.427–55.

Sol'ymoi: Tribe in Asia Minor; Bellerophontes fought against them, 6.184–85.

Spar'ta: The same as Lakedaimon (q.v.) except that the name Sparta applies only to the city, Lakedaimon to the district as well, 2.582, etc.

Spei'o: A Nereïd, 18.40.

Sperchel'os: River running through the domain of Peleus and Achilleus, 16.174, etc.

Sphe'los: Father of Iasos, 15.338.

Sten'tor: Achaian with a big voice, impersonated by Hera, 5.785.

Sthenela'os: Trojan killed by Patroklos, 16.586.

Sthen'elos: (1) Son of Kapaneus, leader, with Diomedes and Euryalos, of the men of Argos (1), 2.563–64; companion in arms and charioteer of Diomedes, 5.108, etc. (2) Father of Eurystheus, 19.116, 19.123.

Sti'chios: A leader of the Athenians, killed by Hektor, 15.329–31.

Stra'tia: City in Arkadia, 2.606.

Stro'phios: Father of Skamandrios (1), 5.50.

Stympha'los: City in Arkadia, 2.608.

Sty'ra: City of Euboia, 2.539.

Styx: The river (later, at least, a river of the dead, and see 8.369) by which the gods swear, 2.755, etc.

Sy'me: Island just north of Rhodes, its people led by Nireus, 2.671.


Talai'menes: Father of Mesthles and Antiphos (2), 2.865.

Tal'aos: Father of Mekisteus (1), 2.566.

Talthy'bios: Herald of Agamemnon, 1.320, etc.

Tar'ne: City of the Maionians, 5.44.

Tar'phe: City in Lokris, 2.533.

Tar'taros: The pit of perdition, 8.13–16, 8.478–81.

Te'gea: City in Arkadia, 2.607.

Tel'amon: Father of Aias (1) and Teukros, 2.528, 8.283, etc.

Tele'machos: Son of Odysseus, 2.260.

Ten'edos: Island off the coast of the Troad, 1.38.

Tenthre'don: Father of Prothoös, 2.756.

Terei'a: Hill near the Hellespont, 2.829.

Te'thys: Wife of Okeanos, 14.201.

Teukros: Bastard son of Telamon, so half brother of Aias (1), archer and spear-
fighter, 8.266–334, etc.

Teu'tamos: Father of Lethos, 2.843.

Teu'thras: (1) Achaian killed by Hektor, 5.705. (2) Father of Axylos, 6.13.

Thalei'a: A Nereïd, 18.39.

Thal'pios: Son of Eurytos (2), leader of the Epeians, 2.620.

Thaly'sias: Father of Echepolos (1), 4.458.

Tha'myris: Thracian singer ruined by the Muses, 2.594–600.

Thauma'kia: City in the domain of Philoktetes, 2.716.

Thea'no: Wife of Antenor, 5.70, etc.; priestess of Athene, 6.298–311.

Thebai'os: Father of Eniopeus, 8.120.

The'be or Thebes: (1) City of Eëtion near Troy, sacked by Achilleus, 1.366, etc.
   (2) City of the Kadmeians in Boiotia, attacked by Polyneikes and his companions,
   4.376–81; and taken by their sons, 4.404–9; only the lower city remaining at the
   time of the Trojan War, 2.505. (3) City of Egypt, 9.381–82.

The'mis: Olympian goddess of order and custom, 15.87, 20.5.

Thersi'lochos: Paionian killed by Achilleus, 21.209.

Thersi'tes: Achaian of indefinite social and military status, ugly and scurrilous and
   eloquent, squelched by Odysseus, 2.211–77.

The'seus: Hero of Athens, 1.265.

Thespei'a: City in Boiotia, 2.498.

Thes'salos: Son of Herakles, father of Antiphos (1) and Pheidippos, 2.679.

Thes'tor: (1) Father of Kalchas, 1.69. (2) Father of Alkmaon, 12.394. (3) Trojan killed
   by Patroklos, 16.402.

The'tis: Nereïd, given by the gods in marriage to the mortal Peleus, and by him
   mother of Achilleus, 1.351–457, 18.35–147, etc.

This'be: City in Boiotia, 2.502.

Tho'as: (1) Son of Andraimon, leader of the Aitolians, 2.638; one of the more im-
   portant younger chiefs, characterized, 15.281–84. (2) King in Lemnos, 14.230.
   (3) Trojan killed by Menelaos, 16.311.

Tho'ë: A Nereïd, 18.40.

Tho'ön: (1) Trojan killed by Diomedes, 5.152. (2) Trojan killed by Odysseus, 11.422.
   (3) Trojan killed by Antilochos, 13.545.

Thoö'tes: Henchman or herald of Menestheus, 12.342.

Thrace: The seaboard and inlying territory north of the Aegean, the inhabitants
   called Thracians, 9.5, 10.434, etc.

Thra'sios: Paionian killed by Achilleus, 21.210.

Thrasyme'des: Son of Nestor, 9.81, etc.

Thrasyme'los: Henchman of Sarpedon, killed by Patroklos, 16.463.

Thro'nion: Lokrian city, 2.533.

Thryoes'sa: Town in Pylos by the Alpheios, 11.711.

Thry'on: City in the domain of Nestor, on the Alpheios, probably identical with the
   foregoing, 2.592.

Thyes'tes: Son of Pelops and brother of Atreus, 2.106.

Thymbrai'os: Trojan killed by Diomedes, 11.320.

Thym'bre: Town or village near Troy, 10.430.

Thymoi'tes: Elder of Troy, 3.146.

Tir'yns: Argive city in the domain of Diomedes, 2.559.

Ti'tanos: A place in the domain of Eurypylos (1), 2.735.

Ti'tans: The elder gods in Tartaros, 14.279.

Titares'sos: Thessalian river, tributary of the Peneios, 2.751.

Titho'nos: Son of Laomedon and brother of Priam, 20.237; husband of the Dawn, 11.1.

Tlepo'lemos: (1) Son of Herakles and leader of the men from Rhodes, 2.653–70; killed, after severely wounding him, by Sarpedon, 5.628–69. (2) Lykian killed by Patroklos, 16.416.

Tmo'los: Mountain in Maionia, 2.866.

Tra'chis: City near the Spercheios in the domain of Peleus and Achilleus, 2.682.

Tre'chos: Aitolian killed by Hektor, 5.706.

Trik'ke: Thessalian city in the domain of Machaon, 2.729.

Tritogenei'a: Epithet of Athene, 4.515.

Tro'ad: Term used for the whole country of the Trojans, of which Troy was the capital, 6.315, etc.

Tro'ilos: Son of Priam, killed at some time before Hektor, 24.257.

Troi'zen: City on the Argive coast in the domain of Diomedes, 2.561.

Troize'nos: Father of Euphemos, 2.847.

Tros: (1) Son of Erichthonios, father of Ilos, Assarakos, and Ganymedes, thus ancestor of the kings and princes of Troy, 20.230–40. (2) Trojan killed by Achilleus, 20.463–71.

Troy: Ilion, the city of Tros and of the Trojans, 1.128, etc.

Ty'chios: Leatherworker of Hyle, who made the great shield of Aias, 7.220–24.

Ty'deus: Son of Oineus and father of Diomedes; his genealogy and history, 14.113–25.

Typho'eus: Giant (later called Typhon) put underground in the land of the Arimoi, 2.783.


Xan'thos: (1) River of Lykia, 2.877, etc. (2) River of the Troad, also called Skamandros (q.v.), 6.4, etc. (3) Trojan killed by Diomedes, 5.152. (4) One of Hektor's horses, 8.185. (5) One of the horses of Achilleus, 16.149, etc.


Zakyn'thos: Island off the western coast of Greece, part of the domain of Odysseus, 2.634.

Zelei'a: City of the Troad, its men led by Pandaros, 2.824–27.

Ze'phyros: The west wind, 9.5.

Zeus: Son of Kronos, brother and husband of Hera, most powerful of the gods, 1.5, etc.